By Anne Commire

Plays
Shay
Put Them All Together
The Melody Sisters
Starting Monday

Books (Editor); Publisher: Gale
Yesterday's Authors of Books for Children
World Leaders: People Who Shaped the World (with Rob Nagel)
Something About the Author
Historic World Leaders
Dictionary of Women Worldwide (with Deborah Klezmer)
Authors and Artists for Young Adults, Vol. 1, 2
Women in World History (with Deborah Klezmer) Yorkin
        Publications

Books
Breaking the Silence – Mariette Hartley & Anne Commire
Mooreville

Book Design: Marian Willmott, www.willmottstudios.com

Cover Photograph
George Moore (left) Town Marshall and barber, along with brother-in-law Peck LeBlanc (right) both leaning on their Flying Merkels as two of the first motorcycle policemen in Ecorse. Agnes and Murph are behind screen door at George's first barbershop, 4426 Jefferson Ave. Freda is on the motorcycle.

Mooreville

by Anne Commire

ONION
RIVER
PRESS

191 Bank Street
Burlington, Vermont 05401

Mooreville is the story of the Moore family in Ecorse, Michigan, as told to Anne by two generations of her relatives and neighbors. An award-winning playwright, Anne created dialogue and characterizations based on real people and events. Many of the photographs, including the cover, are taken from Agnes Moore's scrapbook.

The Moore Family			
			*
		Melvin (Murph)	1907
	*	Alfreda (Freda)	1910
George A. Moore	1884	Rowena (Rowe)	1913
Agnes (LeBlanc)	1884	Joyce	1916
Married 1904		Doris (Dia)	1918
		Shirley (Shay)	1921
		Marcia (Marce)	1924

Onion River Press
191 Bank Street
Burlington, VT 05401
Printed in the United States of America

Publisher's Cataloging-in-Publication data
Names: Commire, Anne, author.
Title: Mooreville / by Anne Commire
Description: Includes bibliographical references. | Burlington, VT: Onion River Press, 2018.
Identifiers: ISBN 978-0-9976458-5-9 | LCCN 2018935637
Subjects: LCSH Moore, George--Family. | Ecorse (Mich.)--History. | Ecorse (Mich.)--Biography. | Ecorse (Mich.)--Social life and customs. | Detroit River (Mich. and Ont.)--History. | Smuggling--Detroit River (Mich. and Ont.)--History--20th century. | Smuggling--Michigan--Detroit--History--20th century. | Smuggling--Ontario--Windsor--History--20th century. | Prohibition--United States--History--20th century. | BISAC HISTORY / United States / State & Local / Midwest (IA, IL, IN, KS, MI, MN, MO, ND, NE, OH, SD, WI) | HISTORY / United States / 20th Century | BIOGRAPHY & AUTOBIOGRAPHY / Historical
Classification: LCC F574.E35 .C66 2018 | DDC 977.4/33--dc23

for Shay

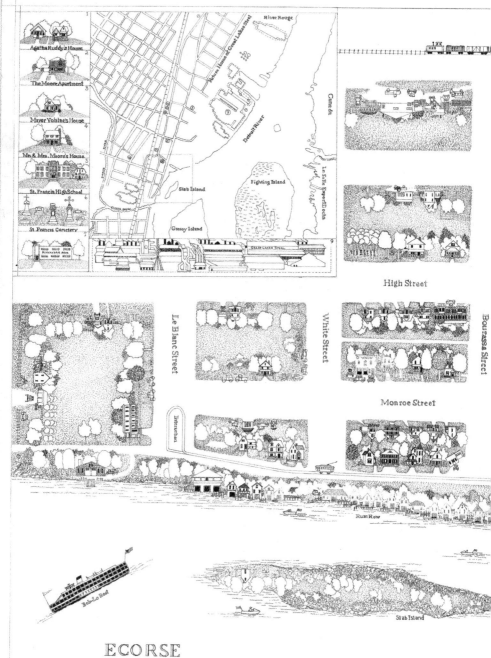

Agatha Ruddy's House

The Moore Apartment

Mayor Voisine's House

Mr. & Mrs. Moore's House

St. Francis High School

St. Francis Cemetery

River Rouge

Detroit River

Canada

Fighting Island

Slab Island

Grassy Island

High Street

Le Blanc Street

White Street

Bourassa Street

Monroe Street

Interurban

Rum Row

Bob-Lo Boat

Slab Island

ECORSE
1921–1938

Detroit River

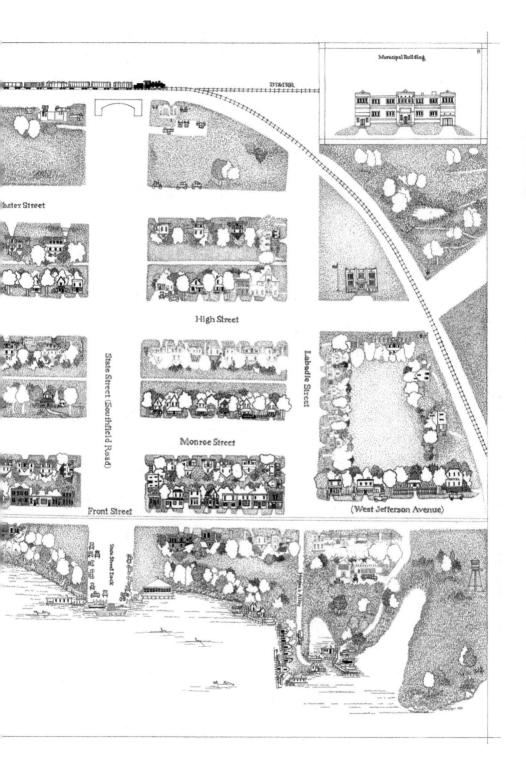

Drawn for the author by Patricia Coombs Fox

Early photo of George & Agnes Moore

Chapter 1

Monday, March 31, 1924, early morning

In the downstairs bedroom of the second house on Monroe Street, on the day Ben Montie died, George Moore awoke with the light, braced for the cold and plunged out of bed. His momentum stalled, however, with a glance out the window.

"Snow," he groaned. "End of March and more snow. Come see."

Flipping back the bedclothes, Agnes Moore rolled out of bed and joined him at the window. "Snow," she sighed. "Sure am glad I took down the storm windows."

But in a wide upstairs hallway, sleeping three abreast in a room with no door, Shirley Ann Moore, usually known as Shay, slid out of bed, tiptoed toward the landing and peeked over the windowsill.

"Snow," she crooned. "Oh, snow."

Everywhere she gazed the world was swaddled in white. White covered the Hothams' lot next door. White covered their garage, their evergreens, their grape trellis.

"Lookit, snow!" Shay yelled, whirling round to greet her stirring bedmates.

"Aw, tell it to the judge," grumped Dia, nearly 6, as she pulled a quilt over her head—the same quilt that had been covering her sister.

"Hey!" said Joyce with a jerk of the quilt. Then disentangling from a confusion of sheets, she danced on point across the cold wooden floor. "Shay's right," she said, surveying the stillness below. "Everything's white."

"How deep?"

"'Bout two inches."

"TWO INCHES!" Shay, just shy of three, was delirious, but her deliria turned to alarm as a seven-year-old troll trudged into view: Bunny Strassner was out. Peering through a Tartan scarf wound round his head, Bunny Strassner was out helping his brother, hauling the *Detroit News* in a pouch on his sled. And right behind him came runner marks, piercing the purity.

"Tell him stop!" wailed Shay.

"Who?" asked Dia.

"Bunny," said Joyce, who was seven and sensible. "He's messing up her snow."

"Tell him he's gonna roon-it!" cried Shay.

As if on cue, Bunny gave an ivory mound a kick, sending a mass of wet leaves aloft, pocking the pristine powder with blotches; he then plucked a rolled-up paper from his bag and with the flick of a wrist sailed it onto Mrs. Ostrander's porch.

Shay bolted across the frigid floor, threw open the door to the front bedroom that smelled of Noxzema, dashed past her two older sisters in their wide brass bed, and flung back the curtains.

"Hey! What's going on?" blurted ten-year-old Rowe, dawn light hitting her face. The other lump simulated sleep.

"Look, Rowe, snow!" shouted Shay.

"And heee's gon-na ROON-it!" sang Dia, barreling in, attaching herself Iago-like to Shay's left ear. "Oh my-my my-my-my, now he's shaking the snow off that poor little tree. Oh, my-my my-my-my."

"Tell him stop!" cried Shay.

"Will you kids get outta here! The alarm hasn't even gone off yet!"

"Oh, my-my my-my-my," sang Dia. With that, she threw up the sash. "Tell him to stay off our property."

"Hey, Bunny!" yelled Shay. My sister says stay off our probberdy. You're gonna mess it *all* up!"

Halting in his tainted tracks, Bunny craned his neck slowly upward until he locked eyeballs with Shirley Ann Moore as she leaned out the window, at-

(L to R) Dia, Shay and Joyce in front of the Moore house

tired in her one-piece sleeper with drop seat. Then Bunny sauntered diagonally, sled in tow, from the opposite side of the snowbound street, ambled up the sidewalk toward the Moore house in exaggerated, snow-defiling steps, took his mittened hand and wantonly ran it down the length of the snow-heaped privet hedge that lined the front. Cavities of dull brown, leafless branches stood out in bold relief.

Shay's voice became very small. "I ast you nice, Bunny."

Then Dia mumbled to Shay from behind the white-lace curtains, "Tell him …" But Dia had no nifty comeback. She just stood there, grinning, and her mole grinned with her, for Dia had a mole at the peak of her cheek, an animated dot that bounced along on a jovial course of its own.

"Tell him our pa's Justice of the Peace," said Rowe.

"Our pa's Justice of the Peace!" repeated Shay, though the word "justice" came out "juvtis."

"Ah, he's only a barber," sneered Bunny.

"He's bofe!"

"Big deal!"

"Could someone please tell me who invited the Lost Patrol in here?" The 13-year-old silent lump known as Freda had had enough. Sighing, she lumbered out of bed, strolled across the Arctic floor, perched her folded arms on the sill while calling down, "Hey, Bunny, wouldja go peddle your papers?" Then she shut the window and crawled back in bed. Rowe and Freda were older, so they had four walls.

"Geez, Freeds, what's wrong?" asked Joyce. Others might be grumpy in the morning, but not Freda.

"The Mother-Daughter Planning Committee got out late last night," replied Freda.

"So?"

"So, Miss Munn stayed over."

"Miss Munn!"

"Sh!" hissed Rowe, pointing to the door.

"Who's Miss Munn?" mouthed Dia.

"Freda's teacher at School One," whispered Joyce. "Freda's got her for sixth grade. She's real tall, wears neat clothes and lives in Detroit."

"Where's she sleeping?" asked Dia.

"Murph's room," replied Freda.

"Where's Murph?"

"At Clayt's."

"She wasn't there when we went to bed," said Joyce.

"She came in after," said Rowe. "She phoned over."

Joyce was appalled. "She saw us sleeping? She walked right past and saw us sleeping?"

"Yeah," said Rowe, "and your mouth was wide open and you had drool down your chin."

"But she's never stayed here," groaned Joyce. "Who told her we take boarders?"

"Teachers talk. Miss Zeno probably told her, or Miss Cappy," said Rowe, retrieving her wire-rimmed glasses from the nightstand. "Gotta admit she's pretty."

"I don't gotta admit nothin'," said Freda.

"Freda can't stand her," explained Joyce.

"Aw, she's not so bad," said Rowe.

"You ain't had her yet," snapped Freda. "Murph had her. He can't stand her, neither."

"How's come?"

Freda sat up, shoved her pillow behind her and smacked it into position.

"I always do everything for her," she said. "I dust her desk and all her books. Then on Thursdays, we have library day. I clean the library thinking she'll let me give the books out, but *no* she picks the brains, or the kids who come from snazzy houses.

"And what does Mumma call you?" asked Rowe.

"Sucker," admitted Freda. "Mumma calls me 'Sucker.'"

"You won't catch me dusting her desk," bragged Rowe.

"She's like a warden. She once took this kid and threw him clear down the aisle. They call her the One-Armed Bandit."

"How's come?" asked Dia.

"Miss Munn has a stump," explained Rowe. "Her right arm comes to a stump below the elbow."

"It's not a stump," said Joyce.

"What would you call it?" asked Rowe.

"I don't know, but it's not a stump." Joyce thought about it. "It's an infirmity and I feel sorry for her."

"What for?" said Freda, eyes rolling. "She can do anything with that arm. It don't hold her back."

"It's not nice to not like a cripple," said Joyce.

"I like the shoemaker and he's a cripple," said Freda. "Some cripples are nice, some ain't. You don't have to like every cripple." "Besides," said Freda, "Mumma can't stand her, either."

"She doesn't show it," said Joyce.

"Oh, yeah? Watch Mumma's mouth at PTA when Old Lady Munn talks to her. It twitches," said Freda. "When I stay home some Mondays to help Mumma with washday, Old Lady Munn don't like it. I think she knows I'm not sick. But Mumma don't give a hoot."

"Good thing," deadpanned Rowe. "'Cuz today's Monday."

"Oh, geez," said Freda. Then she threw back the covers. "Now, everybody out. We gotta get dressed. Mumma'll kill us if we let the furnace go out."

Privacy was in short supply in the outer chamber. The hallway shared by the younger girls led to Rowe and Freda's room, to the bathroom, to the stairs, to the linen closet and to Murph's room, where the door was still ominously shut. The younger girls dressed rapidly, wriggling into long johns, fumbling with buttons and sashes, aware that Miss Munn might intrude at any moment, while Shay still clung to the windowsill.

Two crows flapped their wings against the wakening sky, then soared on an updraft. Smoke curled from the Hotham chimney, while a leaf cartwheeled across the white expanse of their garden and the rising sun sprinkled diamonds across the frosty crust. It was a winter banquet—a dash of Currier, a pinch of Ives.

But before the day was out, there'd be blood all over Shay's snow.

———

"That car's still there in front of Ouellettes'," said Agnes as she washed the plate from her husband's breakfast and set it in the drainer. Then, bending over the sink, she peered out the window for the third time and muttered. "Wonder who it belongs to."

"Probably a bootlegger," said Freda.

"What car?" chimed in Dia.

"Never mind," said Freda.

"What car?"

Agnes lifted the coffee pot off the stove, poured herself a cup and sat down. A tiny woman, five feet even, her long brown hair swept up casually in a top knot, she had on a homemade housedress with rounded neck and ruffled hem, having selected it from a closet sparsely filled with dresses from the same round-ed-neck pattern, the same hem ruffle, in assorted prints.

"Any sign of life from Murph's room?" asked Agnes.

"Not a peep," said Joyce.

"Swell," said Agnes, her back to the stove. She seemed far away.

"Mumma," said Rowe. "Shouldn't we be using the company tablecloth?"

"What for?"

"Miss Munn."

"She's not company," snapped Freda.

"This is how we eat in the kitchen," said Agnes, placing her cup on page two of the *Ecorse Weekly Review*. "Why put on airs?"

"But we eat in the dining room for Miss Cappy," countered Rowe.

"Yeah, well, . . ." Agnes had a stubborn streak. "When you phone over at the last minute, you can't expect the Ritz. Besides, Cappy's a friend."

"Didn't you sleep good, Mumma?" asked Joyce.

"Not very."

"Something wrong?"

"I'm fine." Then Agnes leaned back, softening. "I can't seem to turn off my brain," she said, warming her palms with her coffee. "I lie there half the night with my eyes clenched."

"Whatcha thinking about?"

"Same thing I think about all day. What I'm gonna do next. When I'm washing the dishes, I think about the pile of ironing waiting for me. When I'm doing the ironing, I think about the curtains that have to be washed and stretched. When I'm stretching the curtains, I think about what I'm gonna have for dinner." Then, remembering the bouillon cubes for the soup, she placed her hands flat on the table with a sigh, pushed herself up and crossed to the cup-board, aware all eyes were on her. "And where's Shay?" she asked. "She's here one minute, gone the next."

"On the landing, digging through boots," said Joyce.

"He's gon-na ROON-it!" sang Dia.

"Ruin what?" asked Agnes.

"Bunny Strassner's ruining her snow."

Agnes unwrapped a bouillon cube and dropped it into the Dutch oven. "Shay!" she yelled.

"Comin'!" sang Shay.

"You sure you're okay, Mumma?" asked Freda.

"Ignore me," said Agnes. "It's just old age."

"Thirty-nine isn't old," said Rowe.

"Shay!" Agnes bellowed.

With one galosh on and one galosh not, Shay two-footed it up each step from the landing and stood steadfast in the kitchen, the left boot pointing north, the right sock pointing east. "Can I go out?"

"Later, Pavlova, it's washday," said Agnes, wanting to laugh.

"So?"

"So, I can't take you out."

"Can Freeds?"

"Freda has to go to school today." Then Agnes reached over and touched Freda's shoulder. "Right, kiddo? No time for a stand, eh Custer?"

"Right," replied Freda.

"That's not fair," whined Shay.

"What's fair? Life?" scoffed Agnes. Then sensing a quivering lip, she added hurriedly, "You can go out this afternoon. When Dia takes your father his sandwich. Now sit. Eat your cereal."

"Awww," whined Shay.

"Awww," whined Dia.

"Don't you start," said Agnes.

Shay climbed reluctantly onto her chair, boot and all, then, fisting her spoon, sank a bran flake.

"If your face gets any longer, we'll have to haul it in a hay wagon," said Agnes. "What's wrong with you?"

"Well, explained Joyce, "Shay wants the snow to stay the way it landed."

"It doesn't last," noted the ever-practical Rowe.

"Nothing lasts," muttered Agnes as she strolled to the doorway, hands in pockets, listening for sounds from above. "I wish she'd come down. Her breakfast is getting cold. Maybe I'd better make sure she's up," and drifted from the room. Freda quickly followed.

There was the mandatory delay while Dia checked the perimeter. Clearance confirmed, Joyce leaned in to the center of the table. Three heads leaned in to meet her. "You think Miss Munn needs help getting dressed?"

"Nah," whispered Rowe. "She does everything with that stump. I watched her make a peanut butter sandwich once for a school picnic. She just anchored the bread with her stump and spread the peanut butter with the knife in her left hand."

"It's not a stump," said Joyce.

"Okay, so she spreads peanut butter with her infirmity."

"She still keeps it covered, unless she's using it," confided Joyce. "She wears them long sleeves with little cuffs."

"Why don't you just hold a convocation on Miss Munn's bed?" said Agnes, returning with Freda and a box of bicarbonate of soda.

"Is she up?" asked Joyce.

"I hear movement." Agnes put some bicarb in a glass, put the box in the cupboard and closed the cupboard door. A little harder than intended. She was amazed by her own irritability that seemed to be perking on low flame of late, bubbling over at odd times.

Agnes was pregnant and feeling queasy. She had suspected it all week, now she was certain. She would be 40 by the time the baby arrived, a common occurrence for women of the papal persuasion. Alice Pilon, who lived two doors over and had 11 children, was also past 40, with one on the way. This would be Agnes's eighth pregnancy; her first-born, Amelia, named after Agnes's mother, had only lived a few hours.

"Let's use a tablecloth. Please, Mumma," begged Rowe. "I can put it on fast."

"It'll just get spilled on," said Freda.

"It's gon-na ROON-it!"

"Dang it, Dia, keep your voice down," said Rowe.

"Enough!" yelled Agnes.

Just then a voice said softly, "I'm sorry I'm late, Mrs. Moore," and there was Miss Munn standing in the archway with her coat and overnight case, while "Enough!" hovered in the air.

Agnes pointed to the head of the table, "Sit there, Miss Munn, your breakfast is ready."

"I can't be-lieve I slept in," said the teacher, setting down her bag, pulling out her chair. "But with school only a few yards away and that quilt so warm." She spoke in a melodious singsong, varying the sound with modest crescendos.

"Not at all," said Agnes, removing a plate of sausage and eggs from the oven.

Miss Munn was much taller than Agnes. And she was handsome and smartly attired. Her navy blue, store-bought dress was trimmed in white, with a white lace handkerchief peeking from her breast pocket. Somewhere hidden under the right cuff that buttoned at the wrist was the object of fascination for every child in School One.

"I wasn't sure I'd make it back to Detroit last night, what with the snow, so I packed a bag to be on the safe side. Miss Cappucelli told me to call. You come high-ly recommended, my dear."

"Glad to hear it," smiled Agnes, setting the plate in front of her. "Toast?"

"Please," said Miss Munn. "Good morning, girls."

"Good morning, Miss Munn," chirped the girls.

Agnes went to the sink and began cutting off a thick slice of bread. "Freda, pour Miss Munn some coffee."

"I can get it, dear," said Miss Munn, rising. She picked up her cup, walked to the stove, set the cup down, picked up the coffee pot with her left hand, poured, set the pot down, picked up the cup with her left hand, returned to the table and set the cup down, pulled out her chair, took her seat, then pinched the napkin with two fingers and draped it across her lap. The younger Moore girls all looked away to watch.

"The planning committee so *rare-ly* meets on Sunday night," she said, reaching across her plate for her spoon, "but with the Mother-Daughter Banquet a month away, we had little choice."

Agnes buttered the bread's soft interior. "What's the date?"

"Oddly enough, May 1st. My birthday." Then she inclined her head toward Dia on her left and said confidentially, "I'll be 29." Old Lady Munn was not nearly so old as reported. In fact, she was ten years younger than Agnes and certainly less tired. "Will you be attending this year, Mrs. Moore?"

"Wouldn't miss it."

"I wish all mothers were as conscientious," said Miss Munn, peppering her eggs. "I don't know *how* you find the time."

"I like to keep busy," smiled Agnes, setting the bread under the broiler. "Gives me something to complain about.

With the sisters sitting mute, on grammar alert, there was an awkward silence, filled only by the distant moan of a morning train, awkward to all but Miss Munn. "I love the way you wear your hair, my dear."

"Thank you," said Agnes. "Mr. Moore cuts it."

"I prefer the Theda Bara look," said Rowe, sitting directly opposite the teacher.

"The Theda Bara look does nothing for the Agnes Moore head," said Agnes.

"You must be so proud of Judge Moore."

Agnes didn't mean to laugh but she did. So did Freda. Miss Munn didn't. Miss Munn took her fork with her left hand and said, "I'm sure he works hard. He's such a fine, *fine* man," then delicately divided her sausage. "And what's your name, dear?" she said, tilting toward Shay.

In response, Shay inched the Post Toasties box directly between herself and Miss Munn, then furrowed her brow with Zen-like concentration and silently skimmed the hieroglyphics.

"Dear?" repeated Miss Munn.

Shay, eyes wide, looked to Joyce for a bailout. Ordinarily, Joyce would now do three minutes on how Bunny had corrupted her name to "Shay" because he couldn't say "Shirley," and another two on how the same incoherent Bunny had said "Dia" for "Doris." Shay just mumbled "shirley" into the Post's Toasties. That's all, just "shirley."

"Well, Shirley, that was some snowfall last night, wasn't it?" confided Miss Munn. "I'm sure Bunny had no *i-dea* he was ruining it."

Shay ate her fist.

"Rainstorms can be just as bad," said Rowe, rushing to the rescue. "Remember, Mumma? When we were living over Pa's barbershop."

"Oh, here we go," said Dia.

"This tree blew right through the front window upstairs. We were having dinner and all the lights went out and Mumma said, 'Everybody downstairs.' But Dia was tied into her highchair . . ."

"Tied to her chair?" inquired Miss Munn, affably.

"And Freda couldn't get the knots out," continued Rowe. "We had to carry the highchair with Dia in it all the way down the stairs. There was rain and leaves over everything. Wasn't there, Mumma?"

"It was a mess all right," said Agnes.

"Tied to her chair?" repeated Miss Munn, looking to her hostess for an explanation. Agnes picked up her coffee cup to avoid her gaze.

"Hey, Rowe. Tell Miss Munn about last winter when you got your eye cut out," said Joyce.

"Yep, here we go," said Dia.

"It was awful," said Rowe, needing little prompting. "Freda and I were getting ready to sled down that slope at School One—me on my stomach, Freda on top—and this kid broke the rule."

"Rule?" asked Miss Munn.

"The rule that everybody has to slide down the middle and walk up the side. Anyway, this kid walked up the middle and got me right in the eye.

Suddenly self-conscious, Rowe reached up and adjusted her glasses, then lifted the cork off the communal pitcher, poured herself some water and set it back down. "We don't always use a newspaper," she said. "And then only sometimes."

"Why, I think it's a *mar-vel-ous* idea," said Miss Munn. "Practicing little economies is the sign of a well-run house."

Agnes smiled, but Freeds was right. They all caught the twitch. The hint at poverty did not sit well with Agnes. Six kids cost money, sure, and boarders helped, but George was a respectable wage earner and reputable citizen. They lived on a good block.

"It's more about economy of effort," said Agnes as she retrieved the toast.

Miss Munn leaned in toward Agnes. Like many tall women of her day, she often bent forward while seated. "And how is Melvin?"

"Melvin?" blurted Dia, drinking from her water glass.

"Your brother, dodo," muttered Rowe.

"Melvin! You mean Murph?" Dia howled, so hastily her water backed straight up her nose, causing a piglet sound. Ordinarily, a snort of that magnitude would have elicited roars in the Moore kitchen, but on this particular occasion, Agnes had shot a collective don't-you-dare.

"He's doing quite well," she said. "He likes School Three."

"Murph's on the swimming and rowing teams," bragged Freda. "And track. Ain't he, Mumma?"

"Isn't," corrected Miss Munn, smiling.

"Have you seen his column in the *Ecorse Tribune*?" enthused Freda. "He writes the school notes for School One and Three."

"My, Freda, that's a pretty dress," purred Miss Munn. "Will we be seeing it at school today?"

The atmosphere in the kitchen shifted. Freda could barely look at her mother. "What do you mean?"

"Will you be coming to school?"

"Of course," mumbled Freda.

Agnes was stunned, stunned that Miss Munn would broach the subject in front of the girls. Despite Freda's bragging, Agnes, it seemed, gave a hoot.

Agnes Moore knew from past encounters that Miss Munn meant to be forthright, professional. But she had an unsteady grasp of the force behind what she said, of the impact a teacher had in a small town. So Agnes sat simmering, until she felt calm enough to ask, "Why wouldn't you see her?"

"Frankly, Mrs. Moore, Freda has a poor track record. So did Melvin. Although I'm glad to hear he's taking school more seriously."

"You may have had a run-in or two with my son, Miss Munn," said Agnes, her voice low, "but he always took school seriously."

"I thought he was a grade behind."

"He is. Because of illness."

"Like Freda?"

"Pardon me?"

"Like Freda?"

"Yes. Freda also missed a year because of illness. What's your point?"

"Mrs. Moore, I don't mean to sound harsh . . . but Freda still has far too many absences."

"Miss Munn, be fair. Freda missed seven days last semester. Granted, she may not earn a perfect attendance badge, but I don't think she deserves an on-going reprimand."

"On-going?"

"Well, you *do* keep bringing it up."

"Even so, it does seem strange," said Miss Munn, trailing off.

"What seems strange?"

Miss Munn lifted her cup, then set the cup down without a sip. "It's only fair to tell you, Mrs. Moore. There has been talk."

"Talk?"

"Well. Some find it odd that Freda's always sick on the same day of the week. Every other Monday to be precise."

"Is that a fact?"

The Moore girls sat erect, glued to their chair backs. But when Freda attempted to respond, her mother silenced her with a raised palm.

Agnes knew she was on shaky ground. It was true Murph repeated second grade and Freda repeated third, both because of illness. But Freda's semimonthly absenteeism was for another reason: she hated school and was happier staying home to help on alternate washdays, and Agnes had come to rely on her. Agnes would have preferred to take the high road, to say, "Look, Miss Munn, sometimes I need her help, especially now." Yet, Agnes instinctively knew that Miss Munn was not the kind to level with.

"Does she do her homework?" asked Agnes.

"Yes," said Miss Munn.

"Does she pass her tests?"

"Barely."

"Is she courteous?"

"Generally."

"Only generally?"

"Yes, she's courteous."

"That's all I ask."

"I'm sure you know best, Mrs. Moore, but. . . ." Miss Munn leaned in towards Agnes. "I wonder if Freda might not be better off, dear, if you raised your expectations a little?"

"Freda, Rowe, Joyce," said Agnes. "Are you finished with breakfast?"

"Yes, Mumma."

"Then why don't you go up and get your books, make your beds."

They stood up, excused themselves, and tripped over each other leaving the room.

Agnes was tired. "Freda's a good girl."

"Freda's a very good girl," echoed Miss Munn.

"Rowe likes school; so does Murph," said Agnes. "But Freda's never been much of a student."

"Perhaps you're selling her short."

"Perhaps," said Agnes, outwardly calm, inwardly quaking.

Worn down, possibly because of the pregnancy, possibly because of the prospect of dealing with Miss Munn until 1935, Agnes threw in the towel. "Look," she sighed, "this isn't worth it. From now on, except for typhus, Freda won't miss school again. Would you like some more sausage, Miss Munn?"

"That would be love-ly , my dear." Miss Munn glanced at her watch, then hastily returned to her breakfast. "These sausages are su-perb ," she said, smiling at her tablemates. "You're a lucky young lady," she said to Dia. "Your mother's a won-der-ful cook."

Dia, finally offered the floor, took full advantage. "I see they're still draggin' the river for that missing bootlegger, eh, Miss Munn?"

"Is that so?"

"Yeah. I think they oughtta look in that limestone quarry in Wyandotte. Pa says, 'If you fall in, there'll be nothing left but your teeth.' With that Dia lunged across the table to retrieve a hot cross bun and knocked over her glass. A stream of water cascaded across the kitchen table, bleeding into the newspaper, darkening Hudson's 43rd Anniversary Sale, soaking the missing bootlegger on direct course to Miss Munn's lap.

"Gracious," said Miss Munn, snatching the white-lace handkerchief from her breast pocket and dabbing at her dress. "You must not reach for things, dear. Can't you say, 'Please, pass the buns?'"

"I'm sorry, Miss Munn," said Agnes, throwing a towel at the headwaters of the on-rushing stream and pressing down. "Did it get you?"

Miss Munn rose and dabbed her dress with the napkin once more. "That was a *love-ly* breakfast, my dear. Just *love-ly*." Freda was right. At this point, Miss Munn looked capable of throwing a kid from the front of the class down the aisle. And in less time than it took to say the Confiteor, she had slipped on her boots, donned her coat, picked up her case and bid an effusive adieu.

"Coast is clear!" hollered Dia, though the coast had barely shut the back door. While Agnes removed the cereal bowls from the table, still glaring at Dia, Freda and Rowe tumbled downstairs, books in hand.

"Mumma," said Freda, inserting her fist into a coat sleeve. "Why didn't you just tell Miss Munn it was my idea. That I don't want to go to school?"

"Because she knows everything and what she doesn't know she knows."

"But she thinks you're keeping me from going," complained Freda. "And why didn't you tell her Dia was tied in her highchair 'cuz she was always falling out? She thinks you tied her up so you didn't have to watch her."

"She wants to think it. Let her think it," said Agnes, lifting Miss Munn's plate. An odd expression came over her face.

"Hey, a dime!" shouted Dia.

"That's not a dime," said Rowe. "It's a tip. Miss Munn left Mumma a tip."

Chapter 2

March 31, 1924, that afternoon

It was three in the afternoon; the Moore girls were drifting home from school. Agnes, outfitting Shay and Dia for their walk to the barbershop while warning them to stay off Front Street,[1] could barely be heard above the din.

Parting was relatively free from sorrow for a Moore. The word *goodbye* was seldom used. Instead, an inmate left home under a barrage of parting shots. Each child slunk down the street pelted by a salvo of warnings, "gotchalasts," rude remarks and stale punchlines. As Dia retrieved the sled from the garage, a chorus from the dining room beseeched her to "Get a horse." Shay, feeling the cold, adjusted her wool tam with elasticized headband to "Isn't that a snappy number."

The day was cold and gray with a snowy hush, except for the crunch from Dia's boots. Shay leaned in, stiff, as the American Racer lurched along. A door slammed. Freda, Rowe and Joyce barreled out of the house, galosh buckles chinging. Commandeering another sled, they took off in the opposite direction.

"Where they goin'?" asked Shay.

"Lookin' for Humo cigar boxes," said Dia, pitching forward as she trudged, chewing her Beech Nut with vigor.

"Where?"

"Behind blind pigs."

"Can we go?"

"Nah," said Dia. "We gotta get Pa his sandwich."

To their left, the Hothams' house and two-lot yard were all that separated the Moore house from a short street called Labadie that petered out at Front and to the north at the railroad tracks, just past High.

Facing the girls as they trekked mid-street were two double-story houses. The one on the left, a watered-down Gothic, belonged to the Gregorys. The one

---

[1] Over the years, the towns south of Detroit became known as "downriver" communities, connubially defined by Detroit and the Detroit River and linked by a common road, an old Indian trail. In the 1800s, it was known as Military Turnpike. By 1876, it was marked Ship Street on maps, or Monroe Road, since it was a direct route from Detroit to the town of Monroe. In Ecorse, it was River Road, then Front Street. By the 1920s, it was officially West Jefferson, though many in Ecorse continued to call it Front Street. For our purposes, because it would be correct for the era, Front Street it will be. West Jefferson Avenue runs out of Detroit along the river—past River Rouge, past Ecorse—managing to go for eleven miles until it enters fiercely independent Wyandotte. There it becomes Biddle Avenue until it exits and becomes West Jefferson again.

on the right, a large, sprawling house, belonged to the Ouellettes and separated the wayfarers from the back of their father's barbershop on Front Street, the town's main thoroughfare. From the Moore porch, they could glimpse the back of his shop half a block away in a green, two-story wood-frame building, with an outside staircase in the rear that led to the second floor where renters now lived, where the Moores had lived, where the tree had blown into the upstairs front window while Dia was tied to her chair.

Just then, Ouellette's front door shot open and out came Dempsey, giddy with freedom, doing the hula.

"Uh-oh," said Shay, gaping at the oversized, gyrating pup. The mutt raced down the steps, soared in the air, landed with a bellyflop, then rolled on his back, four legs churning. Dempsey was all paws. "Gonna be a big one," said Mrs. Strassner to Mrs. Pilon over the back fence. "Gonna be?" hooted Alice.

Shay glanced down at the paper bag cradled warmly in her lap, its ketchuppy fragrance rising. She knew that dogs and food were a volatile mix; she knew because she and Dempsey had recently shared a muffin. Bounding over to Shay, he planted a smack on her unprotected schnoz, sprang toward Dia, froze in his tracks, then bounded back to Shay.

"Go home," shouted Shay, as the large hound nuzzled his muzzle between her mittens and the flopping brown bag. "Shoo, Dempsey, shoo!" she said, fending him off with her elbow.

"Sit, Dempsey, sit!" tried Dia, but it was lost on the dancing pooch.

Now Dia knew that Dempsey chased squirrels. And even though there were no squirrels in sight, she pointed past the Moore house, past Strassners' and Pilons', deep into the ivory terrain that was Monroe, and seeing Valencourt's cat, Sandusky, Dia yelled, "Hey, Dempsey, get the squirrel!" That hound took off, and Sandusky, seeing what was bearing down on her, took off even faster.

Mission accomplished, Dia stopped in her tracks. In consequence, so did Shay. Because there, parked in front of the Ouellettes', was the car in question, the car that Agnes had made the mistake of mentioning in front of Old Big Ears that morning. Curiosity kindled, Dia abandoned Shay at the curb and stood in front of it, snapping her Beech Nut.

"Whatcha doin'?" asked Shay.

Dia answered with a swipe at the car's hood, revealing a radiator cap, a flat, uninspired ornament that left her guessing. But a swipe at the grillwork unearthed the script she was looking for. "Buick," she said proudly. "Could be Capone's. Could be the fed's."

"Whatcha doin'?" Shay asked again, then added with certainty, "Mumma won't like it."

Dia, inured to caveats of that nature, brushed off the passenger-side running board, climbed on and, while grasping the frigid handle on the car's middle door with her mittened left hand, cleared a patch on the large center window with her right. Dia was on the hunt. Stretching on tiptoe, she began to excavate in a flurry. "Sedan," she said. "Four door." Dia was precocious in the ways of private transport. When it came to an auto, she could toss out make, model and year with the best. "Bet there's a body in there," she said.

"Whatcha see?" asked Shay.

"Chiclets box, crummy plaid lap robe."

"Can I look?"

"There's jist junk."

"*Please.* "

"Okay," begrudged Dia, "but like I tol' ya. There's jist junk."

Grabbing Shay from behind, locked in a wobbly embrace, she hoisted her up the side of the Buick for a look.

A large hand tapped Dia on the shoulder.

"Whaddyas doin'?"

Time stood still. Shay, left unattended, slid slowly down the side of the sedan, then, following a sluggish landing, held her hand over her eyes and squinted upward.

Two men towered above them, hands deep in pockets. The shoulder-tapper, around 28 and on the short side, had a thin face, hawkish nose, and wore a brown fedora and brown tweed coat, collar up. The other, much younger, had a cigarette cemented to his lower lip which enhanced his sneer. Best of all, at least to Dia, a black patch covered his right eye, a black patch that would be featured on the front page of the *Detroit News* the following day.

"Hi," said Shay.

"Hi, yourself," said the man in tweed, pulling his brim lower to block his face.

"I said, Whaddyas doin'?" grumped the other.

"Cleaning your car," said Dia. "This your car?"

"What's it to you?"

"Just thought I'd clean it off for ya," she said, wiping the sidelamps to avoid his glare.

"Maybe we oughta let it go, Leo," mumbled the man in tweed, using his bare hands to clear the car of snow. Neither of them was dressed for snow. No boots, no gloves. Where they had come from was anyone's guess. Dia thought the barbershop, but there was no sign of talcum. Besides, they looked a little unkempt. Besides, they looked like crooks.

"Wanna use my gloves?" offered Dia.

"Doin' just fine," said the man in tweed, his hands raw. He stood on the running board, pulled his coat sleeve over his fist, and ran his arm across the top of the car; a blanket of snow avalanched down the side. Leo, whose right hand never left the pocket of his rumpled coat, jumped on the rear bumper, elbowed off the back window, then jumped down.

"Want a broom?" asked Dia.

"Don't need no broom, don't need no kids," snarled Leo, the cigarette bobbing with each consonant, "and don't need no damn dog." Dempsey was back.

"He ain't our dog," said Dia.

"Don't care whose dog he is. Get 'em outta here."

Leo tried shoving the dog away. But Dempsey pushed his nose between the front flaps of the rumpled coat. "Get the hell outta here!" yelled Leo, raising his arm to strike.

"Hey, Leo, might wanna think about that," offered the man in tweed, nervously.

"Might wanna shut your trap, Alva." With that, Leo gave the animal a swift kick in the rear. Dempsey yelped and took off running. "Dempsey hell," laughed Leo. "More like Firpo." Leo was acting pretty tough for a guy who'd soon be dead.

"Whatchas got there?" cut in Alva, pointing to the brown bag under Shay's arm.

"Pa's fried egg sandwich," said Shay.

"Give ya five bucks for it."

"But it's Pa's."

"So?"

"It's Pa's!"

"Got any grocery stores around here?" asked Leo.

"Two on Front Street," said Dia pointing south. "C.F. Smith's, half a block down. Pilon's on the next corner, across from the State Street dock."

"Any up that way?" said Alva, pointing north.

"Yeah, Kroger's." Dia leaned against the snowy car, as if she were having a cozy chat with a friendly moviegoer on dish night. "Where you from?" she asked. There was no answer, though Leo had a menacing slit for his only peeper. "How come you're wearin' a patch? Got a sty?"

"Look, kid, just go where you was goin', okay?" said Alva.

"Can't."

"Why?"

"We're already there." Dia's sweeping gesture included the side of the green building directly in front of them and the peppermint barber pole on the corner.

"Our pa's the barber," said Dia. "And the judge."

The men seemed to lose interest in vehicular snow removal. Leo, who had shown no sign of a cold, began to cough loudly. Alva began a casual sprint toward Front Street and Leo tore nonchalantly up Labadie toward High. But Dia wasn't at all perplexed; she was downright suspicious. And when Leo gave Alva the high sign and Alva crossed back over and joined him, her suspicions were confirmed. Intercepting questionable coughs, high signs and eye rolls was her specialty.

The two men walked north toward High Street, glancing back twice.

"Hey, the stores are that way!" yelled Dia, pointing south.

The men ignored her and kept on going.

"Hey, why you walkin'?" shouted Dia. "Why aren'tcha taking your car?"

Leo spun round and walked backwards. "Ain't our car. That your car?" he yelled, then singsonged, "Just thought we'd clean it off for ya." Then he laughed, until Alva reached over and gave him a yank and he turned once more. They arrived at the corner across from School One, halted briefly, then quickly veered right and vanished.

"Betcha they're bootleggers," Dia said, grabbing a twig, heading for the car. "Bet I can jimmy the door."

"But they'll come back!" cried Shay.

Shay majored in foreboding and dread, and for a child of three they were highly developed. She had an advanced uh-oh system. The uh-ohs generally announced the end of something, mostly the end of good times and the arrival of parents. If she'd been on the *Titanic* on embarkation day and heard even one person utter "Neither God nor man can sink this ship," pursers would have heard a tiny uh-oh coming from Cabin 5.

And Dia? Dia had no internal uh-oh system at all. Consequently, she was busy wiping the last of the snow off the back door of the Buick. "Bet they got hooch in the back," she said, standing on tiptoe on the running board to peer in the window for a better look. "Betcha he was packin' a gat."

"Whad'ya doin?" came an emphatic growl.

Turning slowly, Shay squinted upward and saw two men.

"Didn't ma tell ya to stay off Front Street?" sneered the taller of the two.

"We're not on Front Street," said Dia, jumping down from the car.

"You're heading for it," said 16-year-old Murph, standing next to his pal Clayton Riopelle. Both had schoolbooks tucked under their arms; both were dressed for Alaska.

"We're bringing Pa his sandwich," said Dia.

"Just stay off Front Street," said Murph.

"Rowe and Joyce are on Front Street."

"Doing what?"

"Hunting down Humo cigar boxes. The shoemaker gives 'em a nickel a box. Keeps his tacks in 'em," she said.

"Are they with Freda?"

"Yeah."

"Then that's okay."

Murph turned away, beckoning Clayt.

So Dia stood on the step, Shay by her side, their eyes on Murph and Clayt as they gingerly crossed Front, jumping to avoid the slush left by the tracks of the Interurban. She knew they were going into the alley, though God knew it wasn't just any alley. It was the infamous Hogan's Alley, a forbidding fist of land that poked out of the coastline of the Detroit River. To the right of its entrance stood a large Victorian house; to the left, Tank's Candy Store. And as predicted, Murph and Clayt took the cindered path in between that ambled down to the river and to a row of ramshackle shacks along the water's edge. From there, an elaborate webbing of stilts and docks offered moorings for boats and house-boats all the way to the State Street dock a block away. But peninsula was too grand a name for the alley; it was more like a coastal bulge, with a series of tinier bumps, surrounded by a navigable, dockable, concealable, smugglerable marsh.

Dia and Shay didn't know it, but Murph had plans for that day. Big plans. And they didn't include half-baked sisters.

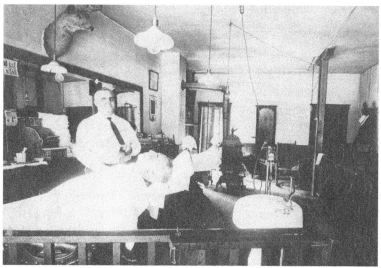

Left side of George's 2nd barbershop at 4410 W. Jefferson Ave. George is standing. Railing in the foreground leads to the courtroom on the right.

The barbershop had two large windows. One bragged **Williams Shaving Soap Used Here**; the other noted in script: *George Moore, Justice of the Peace.* Below the outside windows sat a backless bench, now three ridges of white. In the summer, chairs were added, allowing four or five idlers to watch the passing show. Alex Bourassa, the ex-constable, was usually in residence, along with his bushy mustache and ever-present constable cap. But on this wintry day no one was sitting on the bench outside to tell George Moore they'd just seen his son.

As Dia opened the door to the shop, the smell of witch hazel mingled with the sound of a tinkling bell and the roar of laughter.

"I heard of false gas tanks, I heard of inner tubes," someone was howling, "but a garden hose?"

"Yeah," erupted another, "the guy had a garden hose, a 50-foot garden hose coiled in the bottom of his boat; filled it with whiskey on the Canadian side."

"Hey, George, here come the kids. Hide the *Police Gazette*," said Constable Ben Montie, sitting under a sheet in the first chair of the three-chair shop. The barber, distinguished in white drill coat and dark tie, straightened up—scissors in one hand, comb in the other. "Well, if it isn't Tizzie Lish. And who's that tagging behind? Bessie Barriscale?"

Tizzie Lish cased the joint as she closed the door, cutting off the double-clang of the interurban. Bessie Barriscale grinned and ate her mitten. They were standing behind a low-slung, mahogany railing that separated them from the interior of the room. This spindled fence paralleled the windows, leaving a three-foot walkway across the front of the shop, then ran up the middle of the room, splitting it in half. The railing divided the barbershop on the left from the courtroom on the right and provided a handy rack for drying towels. On crowded days, George Moore's patrons spilled into the stiff-backed chairs in the court and vice versa. Patrons for a shave mingled with known malefactors.

In contrast to the cold without, the barbershop was a house of steam: steam welled from the potbellied stove and the gloves drying just above its surface; steam haloed the hot water heater, sizzed from the copper boiler and hissed from the hose in the sink; steam clouded the corners of the large front windows, encircled the framed mirror lining the side wall mirror in the back. The moist warmth was palpable, as was Ollie Raupp's eagerness to continue the conversation.

"How long's that guy been 'gardening?'" he asked, rocking, draped in his greatcoat from The Great War.

"Ever since the feds caught on to hot water bottles," said Ernie Boudreau, slumped against the back wall, reclining on a backless, armless black leather sofa. "Cripes, everyone was carrying around hot water bottles. Seavitt's couldn't keep 'em in stock."

"He's not kidding," said Frank Lafferty, neighborhood butcher occupying the second chair, his head lowered for a back trim since there was nothing to trim up front. "Last summer, Louie Seavitt leans over his lunch counter and says to me, 'Frank, what's going on around here with hot water bottles?' I says, 'Gosh, I don't know.'" More laughter. "Not that I tried it, Benny."

George Moore pointed his scissors at the bag in Shay's hand. "That for me, Tee?"

Tee was undone. In lieu of a response, Dia unpeeled Shay's fingers from her burden and handed it over the railing. The barber inspected the compressed sack quizzically.

"Whatcha got there, George?" asked Ben.

"Flattened fried egg sandwich," said George, proudly.

Sandwich delivered, Dia begged for a chance to stay a few minutes. George responded that the two might be "too young" to which Dia masterfully reminded him of the in-shop presence of one Milton Montie, age six, seated in a courtroom chair, waiting for his father.

"All right," grinned George. "Take your coats off and sit quietly over there while I finish Mr. Montie." He had a husky, soothing voice, like an amused cello. "Arthur," he said, as a man in a white jacket came from the back room and set a pile of clean towels near the cash register, "would you grab a couple of chairs for Hans and Fritz?" Hans and Fritz could barely contain themselves. "Then call Agnes and tell her the kids are staying for a while."

"Sure, Mr. Moore," replied Arthur, who was having a good day, his corduroy pockets lined with coin. Arthur was tall, rangy and self-contained, though if anyone in the room had been asked to describe him, bigoted and non-bigoted alike would have summed him up in one word: "colored." If Arthur had a last name, George was the only one in that shop who knew it. Arthur, who was close to 30 and would forever be known as the "shoeshine boy," leaned into the courtroom, plucked out two high-backs and placed them by the front window for the girls. Shay smiled shyly at him as he helped her doff her coat; he smiled back.

The barbershop was an Ecorse hub. Men like Ernie dropped in to get warm, read the *Gazette*, gossip and argue politics. With the advent of the shingle cut, women were also welcome: a man with five daughters often sees things differently. Civic-minded, George Moore had been Ecorse's first motorcycle cop, only police officer and village marshal. Now he was not only the barber but a justice of the peace. When Agnes cracked that George was busy holding court, he really was.

He was not a sleek man, though he was too well-liked to be thought fat; solid would have been the word of choice. Before marriage, he was dark-eyed and dashing, but six children, a bit of the grape and good home cooking had widened his horizons. Come July, he would turn 40, but his hair had grayed early, lending him salt-and-pepper authority. He had remarkable eyes: bright black, with an Irish melancholy slant so deeply set that they were ringed by dark shadows.

With the girls settled in, the men returned to their concerns. "I heard of people excavating watermelon," said Dominic Dalton, sitting next to Ernie, his legs stretched out before him, his hands tucked into his trouser pockets. "Then they pour booze inside, cork the bung hole and come through customs hole-side down. Not that I've tried it, Benny," the repetitive reference to the constable causing as much levity as the bung in the watermelon.

"I take it, if it's any kind of container, it's usable," said the second barber, turning the teeth of the comb outward with each snip. Bob White had only been there a few days—which was why George Moore's clientele were into serious boasting of local bootlegging lore.

"My all-time favorite's that guy that hired the hearse," said Peck LeBlanc, brother-in-law of George, brother of Agnes, who had been seemingly slumbering in the third barber chair. "Instead of high-tailing it to Chicago with feds in hot pursuit, here's this hearse filled with hooch moving slowly up Front Street, slowly up State, slowly up Outer Drive to US 112, slowly through Ypsi, Clinton, Niles."

"Cripes, by the time he gets slowly to Chicago we'll have repeal," said George.

"That road to Chicago's like a conga line, car after car after car," griped Ben. "The feds figure at least 50 loads a day leave Ecorse, Wyandotte and Detroit for Chicago. The whole thing's giving me a big fat headache. It's outta control."

"How'd all this get started?" asked White.

"You mean, who was the first?" asked Ernie. "I can tell you to the minute. January 1920. The Detroit River was froze solid. Two guys I know walked over to Canada on the ice with suitcases and brought 'em back filled with liquor."

"I heard it started off as a two-bottle carry on the Detroit-Windsor ferry," said Ollie.

But Frank Lafferty wanted ground rules. "Are we talking firsts when Michigan went dry in '18 and they brought in stuff from Ohio? Or are we talking firsts when the whole country went dry in '20 and they started bringing it in from Canada?"

"I think it should count from 1918," said Peck.

"Smuggling from Ohio was same old, same old," said Dom, lifting his galoshes as Arthur swept under them. "Smuggling from Canada's got more razzmatazz."

"Whaddya mean, same old?" said Ernie. "Them Michigan cops stopped any car coming from Toledo for inspection, anything coming up Dixie Highway—the old Avenue de Booze. They boarded buses, interurbans, trains. Cripes, they were boarding little red wagons pulled by five-year olds."

"Remember when they put up that inspection station on Dixie, then put another station a little farther on and rigged up that huge telephone pole?" said Ollie.

"What for?" asked White.

"When a car ran the first station, they'd lower the telephone pole at the next station to stop it."

"Lower?" said Peck. "That's not the word I heard."

"Yeah, they didn't have no time to lower it. It just came down, blam!" laughed Ernie. "One day it creamed a car and driver. There was this big hue and cry."

The consensus in the shop was that Ontario was, indeed, more fun, methods more ingenious—all those people crossing the ferry with telltale bulges. Honorable mentions went to the first guy who came across in a priest's cassock and the first with rubber tubing wound round his waist. Most agreed that Minnie Stinson was the first to put bottles in her spare tire; that Teargas Johnny was the first to use a modified gas tank: half gas, half booze; that Clarence DeWallot was the first to remove the seat springs and replace them with cases of liquor, but all admitted his car was no joy to ride in, since it was a little hard on the keister.

"Guy I know's grown partial to Canadian bread," said Ollie. "Twice a week, he crosses on the ferry and brings back a loaf or two. Goes to a special Canadian bakery where the main ingredients are yeast, flour, egg and an unopened bottle of Schenleys; they call the batter high-rising rye."

"Aw, baking whiskey bottles in bread's old news," said Ernie. "Some of these guys is now cementing bottles into bricks. They take a full bottle of whiskey, put it in a brick mold and pour concrete into the mold. After it sets, you got a brick with a twist cap sticking out its side."

"How do they get rid of their empties?"

"Throw 'em at feds," said Ernie.

As the men droned on for Bob White's benefit, Shay sat deep in her chair, dinky boots dangling, her eyes riveted on the snipping scissors, fascinated with all things tonsorial, while avoiding the eyes of the antlered deer head gazing blankly down on her from the wall above the counter mirror.

A placard for chewing tobacco was the only item on exhibit in the two large front windows, unless you counted the floral array. Someone had placed an antediluvian fern in each window, atop rickety plant stands. The two ferns, with their unruly green tresses and browning leaves, had been in the family longer than the family. Agnes called them a sight and begged George to get rid of them.

While Dia gazed out the window, Mrs. Salliotte hurried by, hunched against the cold. The wind had kicked up, flakes swirled in the air. A few seconds later, Al Jaeger, coming from the Municipal Building, lumbered up the shop steps.

To Shay, Mr. Jaeger was the father of Marie and Gen who lived directly behind the Moore house. To Dia, Mr. Jaeger was the man who had been shot while chasing robbers in a Lincoln Park cafe in the summer of '22, the bullet lodging a half-inch from his spine. To the men in the shop, Al Jaeger was both the fire chief and the police chief. Since the police station and fire station shared the same building, the two-hat position was workable. On this day, he was sporting his police cap.

"Morning, George."

"Morning, Al," said George, retrieving a serving plate from the back counter and extending it. "Lenten cookie?"

Al grinned. "Lenten cookie?"

"You know Agnes. Hits every holiday."

Al reached for the platter. "Anybody seen any suspicious characters hanging around Hogan's Alley or Rum Row?" They all laughed at that one. "You know what I mean," grumped Al, holding the dish, selecting a dainty vanilla heart smothered in red-and-white sprinkles.

"Why? What's up?" asked George.

"We think the guys that broke into B.L. Sims last week and took the safe could still be around," said Al, popping the sprinkled orb in his mouth. "We're gonna go on a fishing expedition."

"They took the safe?" Dom was incredulous. "No one saw them coming out the front door of Sims carrying a safe?"

"As far as I can see, they went in the back window and came out the front door," said Al, munching.

Dom shook his head in disbelief. "How on earth do you hide a hot safe?"

"Could put a doily on it. Call it an end table," said Ernie.

"How big was it," asked Dom, intrigued. "How much did it weigh?"

Al inspected the last four cookies, wolfed down a potted tulip, secured the plate on the lap of a startled Shay, "Hold this for a second, would ya," then pulled out a small notepad from his jacket pocket and began to read: "Diebold safe, 28 inches high, 18 wide, weighed 317½ pounds, and held 643 bucks."

"Oh, my sweet hernia," groaned Dom.

"Know who did it?" asked Bob White.

"We've got some ideas," said Al. "We hear Soxy Goodell's been bragging."

"Just look for guys wearing trusses," laughed Dom.

"Anyway, two Wayne County deputies are meeting me here in a few minutes," said Jaeger. "We're gonna check the Alley and some of the boathouses in Rum Row, especially Robbers' Roost."

"Say, why don't I take Milt home and catch up with you?" said Ben.

"But you just got off duty."

"Almost done, George?" asked Ben.

"Yep," said George, swiping Ben's neck with a brush, yanking the sheet off.

Ben stepped down from the chair, fished in his pocket for change and checked the mirror. He looked dapper in his navy uniform with its banded collar and shiny badge. Ben was also doing double duty; he drove the fire truck and was a deputy marshal. He handed a quarter to George, tossed in a tip, then walked to the coatrack.

Shay held the cookie platter with both hands, like a canonical offering. Three miniature confections remained: a roller skate, a pink umbrella, and a small, golden-brown bunny with a belly of white icing, a bow of purple sprinkles, and the tiniest hint of charring around its vanilla edges. But even if she could free a hand, she knew she could not take a cookie, for none had been offered. Dia, having no such qualms, reached over and snatched the umbrella.

Al returned the notepad to his pocket, retrieved the plate from Shay with a mechanical "thanks" and studied the contents. "Only two cookies left," he said. "Milty, want a cookie?"

"Yes, please," said one Milton Montie, who, looking over his options, asked for and received the roller skate.

"Who wants the other?" asked Al.

"I do!" piped Dia.

"You already had one, Blackie," said George.

"Anybody else?"

Shay hoisted a hesitant hand, but Al didn't notice.

"Going once, going twice . . ." Shay advanced her hand once more, but no one seemed to notice. Probably because the entire shop had caught on to the torment Al was inflicting on her.

"Why don'tcha pass the plate," said Peck.

"Good idea." Al leaned over the railing and handed the large platter with the wee cookie to Barrett, who thought about taking it, then shook his head and handed the plate to Ollie, who sniffed it, ummmmed appreciatively, then passed the plate to Dom. As the platter passed from man to man, each inspected the cream-bellied cookie, each praised it, but each ultimately declined what all agreed must surely be a savory morsel.

"Heck, if no one wants it, I'll take it," said Ben Montie. He reached over, cupped the bunny in his large fist and shoved it in his mouth, munching with gusto as he turned to get his hat.

All were taken aback, except Ben Montie, who must have been donning his overcoat when the winks and nudges went round. Without a doubt, every man in that room had been party to the hazing, except Ben Montie, who was whisking sprinkles off his blue front. The men shifted in their seats. Ben Montie, sucked a crumb from his right bicuspid, then positioned his officer's cap as he always did, at a rakish angle, still unaware of his blunder.

"Benny," muttered Peck, as he handed the empty plate to George. "Benny," repeated Peck, nodding his head toward Shay.

Ben glanced at Shay, then reared back. "Oh geez, I'm sorry. Did I eat your cookie?"

Shay looked to her father for guidance, but he was avoiding her eyes.

"Oh, geez," muttered Ben, turning to the others for support. I didn't know it was a gag. Ollie? Ernie?" Ernie smiled wanly but Ben stood alone. "Oh, geez, George," repeated Ben.

"She gets plenty of cookies at home," said George.

Ben turned to Al. But no one was more crimson than Al Jaeger, the instigator, who was viewing the arrival of the Wayne County deputies—Harold Truax and Archie Fraser—out front with great relief. "The guys are here, Benny. I gotta go." He opened the door and fled without waiting, leaving behind a resounding tinkle.

Ben just stood there. Then he sheepishly buttoned his topcoat, pulled on his gloves, signaled for his son, "C'mon, Milt, I'll drop you home first," and was halfway out the door before he twirled round and said to Shay with a grin, "Sure this isn't your cookie?" She stared at his open hand. Beaming up at her was a golden-brown bunny, with charred edges and a belly of white, sprinkles intact. He set the bunny in her hand, tipped his cap and left. The men roared with relief.

As George Moore waved Dom Dalton to the barber chair, Bob White managed to steer the discussion back to the topic at hand and the men were delighted to comply. Then the bell tinkled once more. The new arrival was Carlo Nebiolo, a fairly natty dresser for a gas station attendant. He stamped his boots, trudged to the coat rack, reaching for a hangar to hang his fur-lined overcoat, then reluctantly doffed his hat, revealing his balding head.

"You inna line?" he yelled over to young Barrett Lafferty, with a lingering trace of his Italian childhood.

"Yeah."

"How far back?"

"Third."

"Give you a buck for your place."

"Sure." Barrett reached over the rail and took the buck. As a "waiter" or "placeholder," he was now at the end of the line for the second time.

> *"All these big league bootleggers would come into George Moore's shop for haircuts," recalled Barrett. "The best night was Saturday. The big night for haircutting. So we kids would go in there and we'd hold the chair down and when they'd come in, they'd say, 'Hey, can I have your place for a buck?' We'd make five or six dollars every Saturday night. George didn't care; he didn't care who was there. So we always kept rotating. Finally, it'd get late and we'd go home. But we always went home with five or six bucks. You always had money in your jeans."* [2]

Carlo Nebiolo, having jumped the line, quickly divined the day's topic. He sat down, lit a stogie, fingered his pant crease and waded in. "Guy I know uses his daughter and a stroller," he said. "Has a fake bottom in it, you know, underneet, where the kid sits. Enough room for a row of bottles. Guy goes to Canada, loads up. Then when he gets off the Windsor ferry in Detroit, he gives his kid a box of Cracker Jacks. Gets to customs, grabs the Cracker Jacks, the kid howls. Customs guy, who's got enough headaches and don't need no wailing kid, flags him by. Guy gives his kid back the Cracker Jacks, and he's home free."

"I draw the line when it comes to kids," said Ollie Raupp.

"Yeah, not with the kids," said Ernie. "Too risky."

"What're they gonna do? Lock up a four-year-old?" protested Carlo. "Lotsa guys haul their family along to look innocent. Done alla time." He dug in, lamely. "Hey, George, can I rent your kids?"

George grew serious. "That's the trouble."

"What?"

"The kids."

"What about 'em?" asked Ernie.

George hesitated, scissors poised. "They're gonna get corrupted by this. I know it, you know it. They're learning to flout the law."

"Why not? Everybody's flouting it. It's *stupido*."

"Maybe. But how's a kid gonna know where to draw the line? Cripes, they're finding bottles in the marsh, then selling 'em from their news bags for huge bucks." George raised his hand to halt the retorts. "I know, I know, that's funny. Fishing for Canadian Club is funny. I laugh, too, but."

---

[2] This and subsequent indented excerpts are taken from transcripts of interviews by Anne over the course of many years. See "A Note from the Editor" at the end of the book.

"Oh, c'mon, George," scoffed Ernie. "If you was their age, wouldn't you be out searching for bottles in the marsh?"

"If I was their age," said George. "I'd be wearing waders to school." Laughter. "But what happens when they get tired of wading? Where do they go for their spending money? Have to admit, their allowance pales."

"So what're you sayin'?" asked Ollie.

"I'm saying, it's funny 'til it's not." He raised a clump of hair with his comb and snipped.

"You saying we should arrest them?" asked Carlo. "Sentence them?"

"And start a kid off with a felony? Not on your life. But how do we support this law with a straight face? Most everyone in here still drinks, including yours truly. Kids pick up on that. Right,?" He took another snip. "We're losing our credibility."

"I second that," said Ollie.

"Look, no matter how you slice it, this law makes hypocrites of us all. Police, judges, council members, journalists. Certainly fathers. Right?"

"Yep."

"So whadda we do?"

"Got me, Ernie." George Moore went back to cutting, seemingly absorbed, then added as an afterthought. "By the way, Carlo, I can rent Blackie out cheap; one look at her and they'll haul you in. Shay rents for about $5 a day. Look at that face. With that face you could get a trainload of Cincinnati Cream in from Windsor."

While that face ducked under the sleeve of its coat, Dia faced the window, her focus diverted once more. There was movement in Hogan's Alley. The three familiars of the local constabulary were walking behind their catch of the day: the infamous Diebold safe bandits. Al Jaeger and Deputy Fraser had their guns drawn; Deputy Truax was lugging a sagging wool overcoat. The two thieves were hatless, gloveless, coatless and seemed to be missing their arms. They were also dripping wet.. One of the crooks, Dia said later, looked like death eating crackers, he was shivering so badly. As the shackled thieves were marched past the shop on their way to the Municipal Building, Dia opened her mouth to announce the arrests but only got as far as "Hey, Pa."

"Not now, Blackie. Wait'll I finish this cut."

Dia's attention turned outward once more. The constabulary had returned, a slew of them. Though there was no sign of Truax and Fraser, Al Jaeger was now standing on the corner accompanied by Fred Bouchard, the village president, and two other Wayne County deputy sheriffs, George Frahm and Bill Albrecht. They all stopped for a minute and chatted. Then Ben Montie came running up to join the group as they crossed Front and headed toward the State Street dock.

"Hey, Pa," said Dia.

"Couple more minutes, Blackie."

Anxious to report, Dia's attention was riveted on her father. Had she looked out the window again, she would have seen a car drive by, a car containing two men—one in a tweed coat, one with a black patch. Leo was back and Alva was with him. If Dia had not been so absorbed, she would have wondered why they were driving a black Chevy coupe, not their Buick sedan. If Dia had been on her game, she would have followed the coupe with craned neck as it turned left onto the access lane that led to the boathouses and the State Street dock.

"Time to go, ladies," said George.

Chapter 3

Monday, March 31, 1924, later that afternoon

The girls emerged from the shop, bundled once more, with a little help from George. A March wind stung their cheeks and churned the settled snow. Dia retrieved the sled, positioned Shay for the journey home, then halted. On the next block, two doors up, Miss Munn came out of B.L. Sims' Dry Goods[1], head down, suitcase in hand, then fought for her hat as she entered Seavitt's[2], the corner drugstore. "Bet she's waiting for the Interurban to Detroit," said Dia. "Bet she's getting a cuppa joe."

"I wanna go home," complained Shay, eyes watering from the wind.

Dia snatched the rope and hauled the sled across Labadie, while Shay leaned deftly backward on the down curb and forward on the up. Instead of turning homeward, however, Dia inched the sled a few feet up Front and dawdled before Seavitt's window, seemingly entranced with the money-saving offers on display.

"Whatcha doin?" asked Shay, brushing a moist nose with the back of a mitten.

But Dia was engrossed in the store's interior. Curious, Shay knelt on the sled, grabbed hold of the window ledge and gazed deep into the shop. There was Miss Munn sitting at the lunch counter scissoring a cigarette—coat off, while Louie Seavitt set before her a steaming white mug of coffee, spoon handle protruding.

Suddenly shouts came from the State Street dock, followed by two short bursts from a police whistle and a pop, followed by another pop, followed by a series of pop, pop, pops. Then a black Chevy coupe came barreling up the access path from the State Street dock and careened onto Front, its back tires sliding in the slush. Giving chase on foot, guns blazing, were Al Jaeger and Deputies Frahm and Albrecht. Bullets were bouncing, zinging, pinging. Dia rammed Shay back down on the sled and hunched as the driver sped wildly toward them, weaving and dodging, his car riddled with holes, while the two deputies ran out into the street, dropped to their knees in the slush and emptied their guns. As he passed Seavitt's, close enough for the girls to see his face, the driver made a sharp turn, skidding onto Labadie, slush flying in all directions. It was Alva.

---

[1] B.L. Sims would later move to the corner of Josephine and West Jefferson and deal only in men's clothing.
[2] Seavitt's becomes Liggett's during the course of this narrative. It was Seavitt's, then Reno, then Liggett's, then Seavitte's. To save readers from tearing their hair out, I chose to keep one name.

"Duck!" yelled Albrecht as he ran up the middle of the street. "Get into Seavitt's!" But what Albrecht was yelling was unintelligible to Dia, who was already racing up Front, making a beeline for the corner, where they could scale the steps of the Ecorse State Bank onto a generous landing and huddle above the street.

Meanwhile, the remainder of the police and fire departments poured out of the Municipal Building on High Street, as Alva, facing a wall of men, shifted into reverse, narrowly missing his abandoned Buick, shifted into forward, barely dodging a bullet, lurched onto Monroe Street under a hail of gunfire, leapt out of his car with gun and satchel, and tore between the Moore house and Strassner's, heading for the alley. Agnes, having finished the wash, was on her knees upstairs scouring the tub when she heard the shots. Rising with effort to check the bathroom window, she nearly missed seeing a man in street shoes slip-sliding through her backyard and into the alley. Then two officers, guns drawn, entered that alley from Labadie, and Alva disappeared between two High Street houses, firing as he went. Agnes threw down her sponge and bolted for the front door.

Dia and Shay sped by Theisen's candy store, hearing shots coming from Monroe. They sped by Frank Lafferty's butcher shop; they sped by C.F. Smith's grocery store; they sped by Elmer Labadie's house. Then yanking Shay by the arm, Dia abandoned the sled and sped up the steps of the bank, Shay nearly airborne. But the summit had already been claimed. Standing on the broad fourth step, signaling frantically, were Freda, Rowe, Joyce, and a stack of Humo Cigar boxes.

All along Front, shoppers had darted into stores or remained huddled inside. Mrs. Strassner stood motionless in B.L. Sims, flowered chintz in one hand, scissors in another. Louie Seavitt, having shooed his customers to the back of the drugstore, crawled to a window to get a look, while the men of the barbershop peeked nervously through the fern.

George Moore was certain the children weren't on Front. Dia knew better than to go on Front Street alone and never had. But fearing they might have dallied, he threw on his coat and galoshes and sprinted out the door, making his way up Labadie.

"Are the kids at the shop?" yelled a coatless Agnes, high-stepping toward him through the snow, skimpy felt slippers on her feet.

"Yes!" he lied.

"Have you seen the others!"

"They're at Jaeger's!" he lied once more.

"How do you know?"

"Al told me. Now, get back in the house." Though Agnes protested, George held firm. "I'll get 'em. Get back in the house! No sense making them motherless." And despite his clunky boots and the rheumatism in his hip, George Moore took off for High Street faster than he had run in years.

From the steps of the bank, the girls had a fine view. They could see the river; they could see a freighter gliding downstream toward Wyandotte; they could see two boys, possibly Murph and Clayt, standing near a boatman at the dock; they could see Al Jaeger trudging back toward the river, then lost him as he veered to his right and approached the boathouse known as Robbers' Roost. At least most of the Moore girls saw all this; Rowe's glasses kept fogging up.

"Halt!" yelled Al, as a man with a gun in one hand, a handcuff dangling from the other, burst from the boathouse and darted onto the snow-covered path. Evading Al, he ran in the tire ruts, heading for Front, while Al plodded after him, warning he'd shoot, yelling "Halt!" again. When the man was halfway between the dock and Front, he looked frantically round with his lone available eye. It was Leo.

Al took careful aim and fired. Leo's head flew back; his shoulders stiffened. He did an about-face and lurched, bent over, toward the dock, possibly heading for a boat, possibly planning a cold swim to Canada.

Now it so happened that Murph and Clayt were indeed hanging out at the dock, there to help Mike Kinney gas up and shove off in an old lugger. Where Kinney was going in that weather, and whether Murph and Clayt were serving in more than an advisory capacity, would be a matter of conjecture to some and mirth to others.

As Leo staggered toward the dock, Al Jaeger yelled "Stop that guy!" before turning on his heels and running back to the shack called Robber's Roost. Clayt dove for Leo but missed. Murph briefly grasped him. Then Mike Kinney, about to cast off, firmed his grip on the frozen rope in his hand, swung it, and coldcocked the fleeing Leo, who reeled back, then hit the ground hard, face up, legs splayed.

The sound of gunfire ceased. In its place, a police car from River Rouge, siren wailing, screeched to a halt near the barbershop; two officers jumped out and began setting up a roadblock. Other sirens could be heard. Within seconds the cook at the Polar Bear Café on the northeast corner of the access path had raised a small kitchen window to get a better look. Thus, sirens mingled with the aroma of fried onions and hot licks from a clarinet, while a Jukebox Mama told her fella in spirited syncopation that he'd better see mama ev'ry night or he might not get a gander at all.

The barbershop soon emptied. Ollie Raupp was the first out the door, followed by Bob White, followed by a stream of men, young Barrett ahead of the pack, some heading for High, some heading toward the dock. Arthur, no fool he, remained inside, leery of guns where whites were involved.

George Moore, desperate to find his children, came running from High, running down State and rounded the corner onto Front. "Pa!" yelled Joyce from her perch. Hitting the brakes, George bent over to breathe, then took an anxious count of his daughters between gasps. "You owe me a new ticker," he grinned. But his smile evaporated as he glanced toward the river. A car coming from Robbers' Roost turned onto the path, Al Jaeger walking beside it, motioning the burgeoning crowd to stand back. The driver turned onto Front and accelerated in the direction of Wyandotte. The news spread like wildfire. Ben Montie had been shot. His cousin Sharkie Montie, another cop, was taking him to Wyandotte Emergency Hospital.

"Stay there! Don't move!" George told his daughters, before catching up with Al. And they hurried to the dock and the supine Leo.

Alva was nowhere to be seen. Since the police were unsure of his escape route, all cars coming out of Ecorse were being stopped and searched by armed River Rouge deputies. Police arriving from Lincoln Park used their patrol cars to block the entrance to the dock path and began herding onlookers to the opposite side of the street. Soon the Moore sisters were ringed by a crowd. The steps below them had quickly filled up. Ernie Boudreau and Ollie Raupp, heeding an officer, moved to the right of the bank steps.

"Think them's the guys that took the safe?" said Ernie.

"Haven't you heard?" said another onlooker. "They're the guys that robbed the Commonwealth Bank in Detroit."

"And they wonder why the town attracts bank robbers," groused Ralph Montrose, president of the local Anti-Saloon League, standing near, though apart. "They wouldn't have been in that boathouse if there was any law in this town."

"If there wasn't no law in this town, a cop wouldn't be shot," said Ernie. "For cripes sake, Ralph, why d'you think Ben was shot? He was in the alley looking for crooks."

"Certainly wasn't looking for bootleggers," said Ralph.

"No, he was looking for guys who stole the safe from Sims," challenged Ernie. "But to heck with burglars, swindlers and thieves, let's get them evil bootleggers."

Rowe laughed.

"Rowena." A voice purred from below.

Rowe squinted down through foggy lenses. "Yes, Miss Munn?"

"Does your mother know you're here? I can't be-lieve she allows you on Front Street."

"They're with me, Miss Munn," said Freda from the opposite side of the stoop, inwardly furious. "Mumma knows I'll take care of them."

Just then, Agnes rushed through the Lafferty cut-through from Monroe, hands and voice trembling. "Have you seen my girls?" she asked the crowd. "Where's George? Does he have them? Ollie, Ernie, have you seen the kids?"

"They're over here, Mrs. Moore," said Miss Munn, a slight edge to her voice, while Ollie Raupp and the multitude grinned and pointed up the steps.

Agnes's relief turned to fury. "Why'd you leave Jaeger's?" she shouted, pressing toward them through the crowd. They stared down at her quizzically.

As Ollie filled her in, Agnes spied Mrs. Pilon coming through the cut-through, shooing back a string of little Pilons. "Stay there, don't move," Agnes cautioned her daughters, then rushed toward Alice. Miss Munn was appalled. "Her children are wandering alone on Front, in the line of fire," she complained to her sisters that evening, "then she lets them take in that *grue-some* sight, while she chats with a neighbor." But Agnes Moore had done no such thing. Alice Pilon's sister Cora was married to Ben Montie. Agnes had gone over to break the news.

The crowd grew larger, spilling into the street.

"Roy, can you hunch down? I can't see a thing," groused Mrs. Livernois on the third step of the bank.

Mrs. L was not alone. Shay, who was staring at the back of Mr. Nebiolo's fur-lined coat, had no idea what was going on. Dia, better off but not by much, scanned the crowd for assistance. Hot dog! There was Tommy Ouellette standing on the curb, the news bag on his sled bulging with what looked like bottles. Good old Tommy had two things going for him, a recent growth spurt and his back pocket, where he kept a genuine leather telescope. For reasons known only to Tommy and every other boy in Ecorse, telescopes had replaced slingshots and sawed-off peashooters as standard equipment in the back pocket of their knickers.

"Hey, Tommy!" yelled Dia. "Got your telescope?"

Tommy Ouellette's shoulders went stiff as a plank. He did not look back. "What's it to you?"

"Boost me up and let me use it."

"Now why would I wanna do that?"

"So you can stand up here."

"Aw, she's such a pest," said Tommy, handing off the reins of his sled. Squeezing his way up the steps, he gave Dia the telescope, hoisted her up on his shoulders and anchored her boots with his gloves. "And keep your grimy mitts off the lens," he said, while Dia extended the scope to its full length.

The police had done their job. There was now a 50-foot buffer zone between the onlookers and the six or so men leaning over Leo. Through the scope, Dia found a sliver of daylight between her father and Al Jaeger, enough to see Fred Bouchard, village president, looking down at the crook, though each time her father moved, the curtain closed.

"What's happening now?" asked Ernie Boudreau.

"Mr. Bouchard just got down on his knees near Leo."

"Who's Leo?" asked Rowe.

"Now he's checking Leo's coat pockets. Now he's unbuttoning his coat. Now he's pulling something out. Wow!"

"Wow, what?" asked Joyce

"He's got his wallet."

"Now he's handing it to Mr. Jaeger; now Mr. Jaeger's lookin' through it." Dia clutched Tommy below his chin for a better sit and looked through the scope one-handed. "Now Mr. Bouchard's tryin' to search Leo's pants pocket, tryin' to get his hand in, now Mr. Bouchard's looking up. . . . Wow!"

"Wow what?"

"Some guy just opened a knife and handed it to Mr. Bouchard."

"Mike Kinney?" asked Ernie.

"I guess. . . . Wow! Mr. Bouchard's cutting Leo's pocket with it. Now he's pulling something out...Aw!" groaned Dia.

"What?"

"Pa moved."

"Awwww," groaned the crowd.

"Wait, wait!" Dia braced her heels firmly into Tommy's chest, adjusting the eyepiece once more. "Mr. Bouchard just took a wad of dough outta Leo's pocket and handed it to Pa.[3] Now he's cutting the other pocket. There's another wad! Aw!" groaned Dia.

"What?" groaned the crowd.

"Pa moved."

An Ecorse police car, coming from Wyandotte, turned onto the access path as the Lincoln Park police made way, then inched its way down the path and pulled up next to the men standing over Leo.

"What's happening now?" asked Ollie Raupp.

"A deputy just got out of the car," said Dia. "He's talking to Pa and Mr. Jaeger."

Another siren wailed; an ambulance was arriving from Wyandotte Emergency Hospital. As it turned onto the path, those standing over the gunman parted, offering Dia a better telescopic view. Leo was lying on a clean canvas of snow, his black patch askew, his arms and legs splayed out. The bullet had entered his right lung and heart. All along the access path, there was a string of dots, of dark red blotches; there was also a large, deep red puddle encircling his body. Leo was bleeding to death—all over Shay's snow.

---

[3] All told, $1,100 would be confirmed by a later tally.

Chapter 4

What Deputy Fraser was saying and no one heard was that Ben Montie was dead. He had died in the emergency room of Wyandotte Hospital, 15 minutes after his arrival, Father Champion at his side. Ben Montie was 34.

The following morning, Ecorse made the front page of two of Detroit's three dailies. This much was known: on Monday noon, the day of the Ecorse shooting, four men—Leo Corbett, Alva Meade[1], Gene Murray[2] and Bernard Maley[3]—had entered a branch of the Commonwealth Bank on West Fort Street and Military Avenue. While one thief stood guard at the door, another trained his gun on the bookkeeper and the branch manager, forcing them to lie down on the floor behind the cashier's cage. Then the assistant manager was conscripted to open cash drawers and vaults while the three men cleaned them out. Suddenly, noted the *Times*, there was "a rhythmic tapping of feet . . . at the front entrance." The fourth bandit on guard at the door was doing the jig. "You folks may as well have some entertainment," he was quoted as saying. "I'm being well paid for it." When George Moore read this narrative to the family the next afternoon, Dia was convinced the dancer was Alva, since he seemed the sort who would know how to tap.

"How would you know?" jeered Rowe.

"Well, it sure wasn't Leo," said Dia.

Whoever it was, the thief had reason to dance: all told, the robbers netted $17,480. They ran to a waiting car, driven by a fifth man,[4] and sped up Military Avenue. Presumably, they had planted two cars in Ecorse the day before, the Buick sedan on Labadie and the black Chevy coupe on Cicotte. The getaway man dropped them at Jim Ormond's boathouse to hole up while he continued on, probably to Cleveland, where an abandoned auto with Michigan plates would later be spotted by police.

Jim Ormond's shack was typical of the other boathouses along Rum Row. Though accessed by land, it jutted over the water on a foundation of pilings. Thus, as Leo and friends entered and sat down at a table to count their take, they were sitting directly above the boat well.

Later, bored and hungry, Leo and Alva went out to get some eats. That's

---

[1] Also seen as Elza Meade.
[2] Gene Murray, alias Tom Owen or Thomas Owens, also seen as Tim Murray or Jean Murray, age 23, of Ecorse.
[3] Also seen as Bernard Matley, Robert Maley or Malley.
[4] Charles Howes.

when they encountered Dia horsing around the Buick. Next they dawdled at a lunch counter before stopping at Kroger's, around the time that Chief Al Jaeger and the deputy sheriffs, Truax and Fraser, began checking the waterfront. After inspecting Hogan's Alley, Al walked the path along the river. Arriving at the State Street dock, he stopped abruptly when he saw a fellow open the front door of Ormond's shack and look out. As soon as the man glimpsed Jaeger, he did an about-face and rushed back in, slamming the door behind him. Al signaled the patrol party and raced for the shack.

Jaeger banged on the door - no answer - shouted for the man to open up - no answer - drew out his gun, kicked in the door and cautiously entered the outer room. The main room above looked empty, but the door leading to the boat well had been flung open, and he could see two men racing away. As Al gave chase, the men threw open the riverside door, ran out on the catwalk, and scrambled onto the ice along the shore.

As the crooks ran, money they had scooped up in their arms, crammed in their pockets, jammed in their coats, trailed behind them like confetti, wafting down with the help of that March breeze. Other bills, bound together in wrappers from the Commonwealth Bank, dropped with plop, plop, plops on the ice. The trail of legal tender on later count would amount to over $1,650 in $10 and $20 denominations. Greenbacks would be found floating around town for months. Mrs. Hotham would clear 60 bucks weeding her rhubarb patch come spring.

Back then, before icebreakers became a constant, the Detroit River froze clear across to Canada some years. Unfortunately for the hapless bandits, 1924 was not one of those years. While Al and his deputies followed along the bank, the crooks soon ran out of ice. Fedoras soaring and soon bobbing, they took flying leaps into the icy water and began to swim around the ice floes toward Canada. Al Jaeger knew it would only be a matter of minutes before the men turned around, because, as George told Ollie, that river was colder than Agnes when he'd been on a binge. Instead of swimming directly to Canada, where their arrival would have given new meaning to "frozen stiff," they turned toward Hogan's Alley, possibly hoping to escape through the frozen marshes.

Al and his deputies walked the path, patiently waiting, taunting them with "Had enough?" as the robbers turned back toward shore, eager to get out of the bitter-cold water, then greeted them with "Hands on your head" as the bandits scrambled over rocks. But these were not two-bit punks. While patting them down, Jaeger found two guns on Gene Murray, 23. Bernard Maley, 25, had thrown his into the river, just before coming ashore. Their pockets were weighted down with cartridges.

While Dia watched from the barbershop, Jaeger and the other officers escorted the bandits through Hogan's Alley, across Front, and down Labadie to the Municipal Building, where Al learned of the bank robbery by teletype and booked them. Then Fraser and Truax drove the prisoners to the Wayne County

jail. After Chief Jaeger advised Wayne County authorities of the catch and reported that they were returning to the shack to check for more evidence and
recoup the money, Wayne County Sheriff George Walters promised that he and
his men would be along soon.

That's when Ben Montie caught up to Chief Jaeger in front of the barbershop, and, along with Village President Fred Bouchard and Deputy Sheriffs
Frahm and Albrecht, walked over to Ormond's boathouse. As they entered the
shack, Al and Ben left Albrecht and Frahm to chase down bills in the outer
room, then clambered up the short staircase into the main room which, according to the next day's tabloid-style photo in the *Detroit News,*[5] was a dingy tall-
ceilinged affair, sparsely furnished, where the gang had idled away the hours.
In the middle of the room, below a high-hanging bulb, was a table strewn with
playing cards and a slew of empty whiskey bottles, while the only chairs—four
seatable beer kegs—lined one wall. What the photos did not reveal was the
amount of cash that had also been strewn around the room. Louie Seavitt said
he read in the *Times* that, all told, Jaeger and his men recovered Commonwealth
wrappers totaling $5,798. Ollie countered that the *News* said $3,750. "Depends
if they counted before or after the Wayne County deputies got there," laughed
Ernie. No matter. Either number was large for that era.

The police had only been in the boathouse a few minutes when Leo Corbett opened the front door and sauntered in, patch over eye, arms wrapped
around groceries, carton of Luckies protruding. It was hard to tell who was
more startled, Corbett or Bill Albrecht, the deputy nearest the door. But Leo was
cagey. He took one look at Albrecht's uniform and asked, "Where's Bob?" Asking for the nonexistent Bob warned Alva who was outside. Albrecht, ignoring
the inquiry for Bob, asked Leo who he was. Corbett sneered, "Who wants to
know?" Al Jaeger did. Chief Jaeger appeared at the archway of the main room
with pistol drawn and said "Stick up your hands," and came down the steps,
Ben Montie close behind. Corbett hesitated, moving as if to reach in his pockets
for a revolver, when Chief Jaeger grabbed his hands and called to Montie to slip
handcuffs on him." Albrecht took Corbett's gun from his coat pocket.

While Ben was handcuffing Corbett's left hand, Frahm shouted, "There
goes the other one!" Thinking Corbett secured, the entire squad, except for Ben,
ran outside to see Alva fleeing in the Chevy coupe. Albrecht and Frahm took off
after him, shooting at will. In the ensuing gunfire, no one heard the shot fired
by Corbett. He had broken loose from Ben's grasp and had shot the unarmed
officer through the heart. Jaeger later told George that Corbett must have had a
second pistol up his sleeve.

As Ben staggered to the door, gasping "I'm shot, Al, get him," Leo Corbett
rushed past and headed for Front Street. That's when Chief Jaeger warned him
to halt, then fired. Corbett died on the way to Wyandotte Hospital. Hearing the

[5] Detroit News, April 1, 1924.

shots from his house, Sharkie Montie drove over to the shack, arriving just in time to drive his dying cousin Ben to the hospital.

Alva escaped the net. Outrunning the deputies in the Monroe alley, he ran out onto State Street, flagged down a car, leapt in, and with gun in hand, forced the driver to keep on going toward Lincoln Park. Lincoln Park officers and state police joined in the chase, following him to the Wabash railroad tracks and firing at him as he leapt aboard a moving Chicago-bound freight train. It was thought he had a large share of the loot.

Word of Alva's escape was telegraphed along the train line. A deputy sheriff at the patrol booth at Belleville organized a posse of armed citizens, stopping the freight train at Romulus. They boarded and searched the cars for 45 minutes but came up empty. Months later, Alva Meade would be caught in Tucson, Arizona.[6]

Around seven that night, a large touring car pulled up in front of Robbers' Roost. Out stepped James Ormond, 25, and Rose Collins, 28, both of Detroit and both apparently oblivious of the day's commotion. On questioning, Ormond acknowledged he owned the shack. When apprised of the bank robbery, Ormond admitted he was a bootlegger, said he'd been a bootlegger since last September but didn't know nothing about no bank robbery. Rose, an ample woman with a Dutch-boy cut, may not have helped his cause when she defended her honey to reporters while in the County lockup, sounding a lot like Harlow: "Jim Ormond isn't a robber—he's a bootlegger, the biggest bootlegger in the country. I have been going with Jim since Christmas. I know he has had nothing to do with any robber gang. He didn't have to because he makes all the money he wants bootlegging. He brings more stuff across the river than any other man in Ecorse or Detroit." She said they planned a June wedding. "And I still think we will," she said, flashing a diamond boulder. "Have I ever been in jail before? Sure I have. But I'm not saying what it was for."[7]

Before the night was out, a pension fund was set up for Cora Thibeault Montie and her son Milton. Routinely, Milton had walked across the street to the Municipal Building after school. Then he and his father had walked home hand in hand for supper, sometimes stopping by the barbershop on the way. Reported the *Detroit News* : "Monday, just as usual, Montie and his son came home for supper, but the patrolman kissed his boy goodbye, waved his hand to his wife and said he'd be back in half an hour—he was going on a raid. He swung off down the street with Milton sitting on the front porch looking after him. That was the last they saw of him."[8]

In 1942, at age 24, Milton Montie would join the Ecorse Fire Department and serve for 35 years becoming Ecorse's fifth fire chief.

---

[6] Chief Jaeger arrested Soxy Goodell, 17, who lived five doors down from the Moores, and two others from Detroit for the theft of the B.L. Sims' safe. The safe was never found.
[7] "Rum Romance," Detroit News , April 2, 1924, p. 15.
[8] "Death's Tragedy at 6," in Detroit News, April 1, 1924, p 43.

Ecorse Riverfront (Virtual Motor City Collection, Walter P. Reuther Library, Wayne State University)

West Jefferson Street, Ecorse (Louis Pesha, photographer, 1868-1912)

Looking down Labadie St. (Louis Pesha, photographer, 1868-1912)

Chapter 5

Originally known as Grandport[1] when it was located in New France and governed by Quebec, Ecorse began as a cluster of stores and homes along the waterfront, at the intersection of Front and State.[2] For 115 years, it was a village within Ecorse Township until it broke away in 1942. Ecorse is now a city of Wayne County, seven miles below Detroit, covering an area close to 3.6 square miles. Two of those miles stretch along its eastern border, the Detroit River.

The river is a 28-mile funnel which gradually descends from Lake St. Clair down a six-foot grade into Lake Erie. The colonizing French named the strait, *le Détroit* —a lovely Gallic term pronounced "Daytwa." Ecorse's history is tightly linked to the waterway. Functioning as an international boundary line between the United States and Canada, the channel is so narrow in spots, sometimes less than half a mile wide, that it becomes a connector rather than a barrier.

By the first decade of the 20th century, Ecorse had become not only a home to the descendants of the first French families, but also a sleepy resort colony known as "The Little Venice of the West End" – a popular getaway for Detroit's middle class. While the wealthy summered in Grosse Pointe, strolling fine expanses of lawn, the middle class spent their limited leisure in the marshes of Ecorse with no lawn at all—just a passing show of Great Lakes vessels a pitcher's throw from their front porches.

A half mile of modest cottages was built along the banks of the river from Labadie Street to Ecorse Creek. Cottages of different hues and patterns could be rented for ten dollars a month: one story, two story, two windowed, four windowed, some with awnings, some with shutters, some shingled. Built on pilings driven into the marsh, their back doors leading to dry ground, they sat nestled shoulder to shoulder, connected by a crisscross of stilts and catwalks.

From the cottages or houseboats that moored along the banks, it was just a short walk across the narrow bricks of Front Street to Lafferty's General Store, Seavitt's Drugs, or George Moore's first barbershop. Ladies would lift their skirts and gingerly cross the rails of the Detroit United Railway line, known as the Interurban. They could buy fish from the local boaters, affectionately known as river rats, who kept their boats in a cindered alley—a small L-shaped peninsula dotted with boat shacks—at the foot of Labadie.

Renters who had business in Detroit could travel back and forth on the

---

[1] Also seen as Grand Port.
[2] Now Southfield Road.

Lake Shore trolley. In the evening, they could swim, boat, or dangle bait from their front porches and reel in herring, sturgeon, pike, bass, perch, muskellunge, panfish trout, and the venerable whitefish. They could watch the side-wheelers, day cruisers, excursion launches—ships that had been built just up the road—paddling down the river, flags flying, bands playing, and wave to the man in the derby on the upper deck or the woman fluttering her handkerchief from the deck below; or they could just sit and enjoy the cool of the river, gazing the half-mile across to the flatland of Canada, watching horse-drawn carts roll along the river road of Windsor, Ontario, where villagers under a different flag answered to kings named Edward VII or George V.

Sounds were distinct. The clipclop of a horse, the jangle of a bridle, the dingding of a trolley bell had not yet been fused into one loud urban whine. Early residents recall walking along its tree-lined streets enjoying the sounds emanating from the homes—of singing, of children practicing piano, of dishes clattering in a busy kitchen. And as the day softened and the workers headed for home, Father Champion would stand in the bell tower and exhort "Pull!" Then one of the Raupp boys and the priest would leap into the air, clutch the rope, and descend by way of gravity. With the downward yank, the great cast-iron bell—bearing the names of early settlers—would shoot straight up, its clapper slamming against its mouth, emitting a protest so loud that the reverberating gong could be heard across the fields and across the river. Every night at six o'clock, as regular as the sunset, the bell of St. Francis Xavier Church would ring out the Angelus. And the town's vacationers would fold their newspapers and rest their heads on the backs of their rattan rockers. They had it all. Water, sun, boats, rest, and God.[3]

There were winter people, of course, approximately 1,400 of them. With more houses and more businesses, the century-old riverfront settlement decided to incorporate as a village on December 4, 1902. The newly formed council met under the gavel of Moses Salliotte, brother of Joe, held a handwriting competition for village clerk, and went to work. Pay for Dan Lafferty of the volunteer fire department was set at $1.50 per fire. Barney Beaubien charged a buck to haul and set up the voting booth with his ice wagon.

That year, the community collected $907 in real and personal taxes. The biggest contributor was Tecumseh Salt Works which was assessed $84. (A vein of salt brine discovered along Ecorse Creek was pumped from the ground into large vats, reclaimed by evaporation, then placed in barrels for shipment to Chicago packing plants for use in meat processing.) Others who bore the tax brunt were the Salliotte & Raupp Sawmill and Barney Beaubien's Ice Company.

Street lights appeared in 1904 when the Wellsbach Street Lighting Company

---

[3] Freely adapted from "Antiques Bared by Excavation," March 7, 1973, source unknown, which included the bell-ringing memories of Russell Raupp, Leonard's son. But the Raupp boys, living so near the church, had been on call from the early years.

agreed to install 33 gas lamps, turn them on nightly and clean them. But the lamps didn't burn properly and became a source of considerable controversy. Nine years later, when the town installed electric lights, the squabbling ceased—as did the Wellsbach Street Lighting Company.

Mud was an issue. Streets of mud. During the rainy months, streets weren't crossed, they were forged. Bicycles sank to their fenders. In 1907, the firm of Julius Porath & Co. was given a contract to pave Front Street. Long after the original red bricks were covered with black top, the village was still paying off the bonds. Ten years later, side streets were ordered paved. In 1914, among other monies, the village took in $5,083 in levied taxes, $37 in dog taxes and $1,980 in liquor taxes, while it paid out, among other compensations, $30 to George Moore for serving as town marshal.

Then came Prohibition.

———————

In 1918, sixteen years after village incorporation, there was a new type of renter willing to pay ten times the monthly fee for a row house on the river with a view of Canada. Cottage interiors were gutted, connected, and transformed into gaudy cabarets, theme-park saloons, and chandeliered gambling casinos. Fancy cars were soon sitting beside the old fishing shacks of the cindered peninsula off Labadie Street now dubbed Hogan's Alley. Covered boat wells no longer housed pleasure boats; they housed high-powered speedboats and luggers.

Ecorse's sleepy half-mile of waterfront row houses would become Rum Row, described by the *Detroit News* as "the most notorious strip of bootlegging property of the Prohibition era." It was a Barbary Coast that grew rich as the chief port of entry for thousands of gallons of Canadian liquor worth millions.

By day, Ecorse remained a quiet community—residents still shopped at Lafferty's, passed their time over backyard fences or strolled the wooden aisles in Sims. By night, it was a changed world. As Rum Row blossomed with blinking neon, tinkling pianos and barrelhouse jazz, thousands would descend on that ten-block strip. "Ladies in evening dress from Grosse Pointe kicked up their respectable heels on Jefferson Avenue, or did the Varsity Drag in the joints that were high class enough for dancing,"[4] wrote Crellin. Tight-lipped gangsters in face-shading fedoras or snap-brimmed hats walked the same street where children had played hopscotch just before dusk. Residents with names like Flora and Sadie ran the shops by day while Gawky Al, Irish Jack and Old Overcoat worked the streets by night.

Opulent roadhouses were open around the clock. There was the White Tree Inn, Marty Kennedy's, the Riverview, the Manhattan Club and the Polar Bear. Charley Dollar had a place. So did Clarence DeWallot. So did Tim Regan, a for-

———————

[4] Charles Crellin, "Legend of Roaring Days of Ecorse Recalled," Detroit Times, August 3, 1956.

mer cop. The politicians preferred raising their mead at Johnny Boyd's. Defined by a newspaper reporter as "one of the most pretentious,"[5] it had a back porch on the river and a small game going on in front. The drys called it "a half mile of hell." The wets referred to it as "Sodom and Begorra," in honor of the Irish portion of the constabulary.

There would be great gambling salons with slot machines, roulette wheels, blackjack, and crap games. And the toastmaster general would be Lefty Clark. There would be numbers rackets, houses of ill repute. Minnie Stinson's was in a brick storefront that mingled with the shacks of Mill Street. Frenchie's was on Knox and High. Patsy Lowrie had a joint on 8th and Mill—the backroom was Western style with sawdust and a tinny nickelodeon. There was once even a brothel on Fighting Island—in the middle of the river.

Much of the action was invisible. Except for the roaring approach of a motor boat at midnight or a flashing signal across the water, the night shift moved in and out of the shadows. During the day, the only violence along the shore was mink against muskrat. But in the dark of night, the waterfront was an amalgam of shapes, shadows and cryptic sounds: the putt-putt of a hushed motor, the hiss of a whispered oath, the squeak of a dock board, the purr of an idling truck engine, the unhooking of a chain latch on the gate of an REO truck.

For most of America, Prohibition started on January 17, 1920, at 12:01 a.m., and ran to December 5, 1933—a month shy of 13 years. But Michigan went dry on May 1, 1918—almost two years earlier—allowing Ecorse plenty of time to lock everything in place before the rest of the nation turned off the spigot. So for 15 years, 7 months, 4 days, 18 hours and 55 minutes, everything went nuts in Michigan, and Ecorse went to the Mardi Gras.

In the easy come, easy go, millions of dollars changed hands. Debased and sneered at, the Eighteenth Amendment encouraged the corrupt and contaminated the clean, leaving a residue of disrespect for the law that all the BAB-O in the world couldn't scour away.

---

[5] Ibid.

Chapter 6

Saturday, October 25, 1924

Bob White was gone.

"If you want to get any information about anybody, just go to a barbershop," noted Tom Ouellette in later years. *"Well, this new barber, Bob White, was hired in February or March, when things were getting a little rough for bootleggers on the river. So some of them got together and contacted people in St. Louis. Then they had a box car pulled onto a siding and slowly loaded it with about 5,000 cases of liquor. Sat on that siding until the order was filled. On the night it was pulled out of Ecorse for St. Louis, it no more got past Wyandotte when it was stopped and pulled off into another siding. It was the FBI. Come to find out this Bob White was an FBI man acting as a barber. Cut hair for about six months. Got all his information until they got that box car loaded with liquor and they confiscated it. That was it. Never saw him in town anymore."*

George shrugged it off. "At least he only went after the big guys. I'll give him that. And you have to admit, he was a pretty good cutter." Undercover work, both state and federal, was becoming commonplace. You had to pick your confidants carefully.

By 1924, in the fourth year of the nation's Noble Experiment (Michigan's sixth), the Age of Repression was duking it out with the Age of Rebellion. Local municipalities along the river—River Rouge, Ecorse, Wyandotte, Trenton and Monroe—were fed up. Having been handed a highly unpopular law, they were told to enforce it. Since they had neither the time, nor the inclination, nor the resources, they all ignored it whenever possible. The prevailing attitude: these were federal laws, state laws. Let the feds and the state troopers implement them. Besides, this unfunded mandate caused towns to forfeit a major source of their revenues, local taxes on liquor, while fines from Prohibition violations went to the county or state.

Some blamed lax local enforcement on corruption, but it wasn't necessarily so.   There was the occasional raid in Ecorse and arrest for violations of the Prohibition Act, but local police generally were allergic to a felony charge against friends and neighbors who were trying to support their families. Cops sometimes made sure their raids were illegal, knowing that the charges would be thrown out of court.

And George? George went easier on the young. When it came to juvenile offenders and Prohibition, he rarely gave them jail time. A fine perhaps, when a point had to be made. But he vowed he'd never send a kid to the Detroit House of Correction, not for that, not over beer. A felony? Not on your life.

Legislators in Lansing were apoplectic. Toward the end of July, 1924, Ecorse was given an ultimatum: clean up its act or state and federal troopers would take control of the situation. Fine with Ecorse. With a police chief who was also the fire chief, and with a limited squad of men, Ecorse was no more capable of handling the situation than a kitchen sieve can contain water.

Governor Groesbeck ordered a Michigan State Police detachment to start patrolling Ecorse and the river on May 13, 1924. "The troopers were stationed in the Ecorse harbor on the *Aladdin*, a 40-foot gasoline cruiser, and manned five speed boats on the river, and two automobiles patrolling the shore line."[1] Within months, the state would be claiming total success. "Rum running in Ecorse has become a thing of the past," said Fred Hessler, inspector of the Wayne County detachment of the Michigan State Police. "While there are a very few blind pigs in operation, the rum running has actually ceased. The success in curbing the traffic has been due to constant surveillance and patrolling of the waterfront there."[2]

Oh, Fred, how wrong you were.

George as Justice of the Peace, using half of the barbershop for his courtroom

---

[1] "Ecorse Once Flooded Detroit with Rum, Now Wonders Where It Can Get a Drink," Detroit News, March 1, 1925.
[2] Ibid.

Saturday morning. Full house. The barber chairs were filled, the court chairs all filled. Two men waiting for a cut were slumped over the railing, splitting their focus between the haircut Paul Movinski was giving Barney Beaubien and Judge Moore's courtroom. Arthur was on his fifth shine.

"Next up: the City of Ecorse vs. Donald P. Hanson," said Judge Moore, tapping the gavel perfunctorily on his mahogany desk, his white jacket doffed, his brown suit jacket donned. The judicial bench was on a step-up platform like a small stage.

Officer Biskner, his chair tipped back against the wainscoting, returned to earth with a thud. Uncoiling his booted legs from those of the chair, he rose and approached the long wooden table which stood mid-court beneath a naked light bulb, knotted to height. Another man, in an unfortunate tie, eagerly joined him and they were sworn in.[3]

Officer Biskner opened a tall blue ledger. "Your honor, on Friday, October 17,[4] at 6:25 A.M., we received a complaint from one Edward Long of 4490 4th Street, Ecorse." Officer Biskner glanced up at Judge Moore, "That'd be midblock between State and White, sir," then returned to the ledger, ". . . that a guy going to work at Michigan Steel got the habit of driving on the sidewalk. Mr. Long said he stopped the party that morning, took his license number, M20-015, and put him off the walk. The following morning, we staked out the vicinity and, sure enough, at 6:24 one Donald P. Hanson," he pirouetted and pointed to one Donald P. Hanson, wearer of the unfortunate tie, "turned onto 4th from State Street and immediately proceeded to drive up the sidewalk."

Judge Moore was intrigued. "He just turned the corner and drove up the sidewalk?"

"Yes, your honor."

"Was he drunk?"

"No, sir."

"How do you plead, Mr. Hanson?"

Donald P. Hanson's voice boomed with righteous indignation and the after-effect of a two-week rehearsal, "Not guilty, your honor!"

"Not guilty by reason of insanity, or plain old not guilty?"

"Plain old, sir."

"I take it, by the tenor of your plea, that you don't admit to driving on the sidewalk."

"Oh, I was driving on the sidewalk, all right," allowed one Donald P. Hanson.

---

[3] George Moore was Justice of the Peace from 1922 to 1926. Most of these cases were taken from the Ecorse police ledger (1926-1928), then dramatized. But for narrative needs, all were moved to 1924. Some characters have been combined. James Stewart did handle the "wine" case, but he actually joined the force in the autumn of 1926, after a probationary period, his first entry in the police ledger being October 10, 1926.

[4] In actuality, this was March 4, 1927.

"Every morning?"

"Pretty much."

"Would it be rude to ask why?"

"Because I'm trying to save my car springs. Have you been down that street lately, sir?" asked Mr. Hanson.

"Can't say I have, can't say I haven't," said Moore. "What's wrong? Potholes?"

"I wouldn't call them potholes, your honor."

"I'll bite. What would you call them?"

"Ravines, maybe. Gulleys. When I'm feeling Spanish, arroyos."

It wasn't a thigh slapper perhaps, but amusing enough to draw a few snickers. Nothing Judge Moore couldn't plow right through. "And for that reason, you went up over the curb?"

"What curb, your honor?"

Judge Moore waited for the laughter to subside. "Road pretty bad, is it?"

"Let me put it this way, your honor," said Hanson, "we've lost three guys from my mill section to chronic concussion from smacking their noggins against their car roofs. Anyone driving that road for more 'an a year . . . well . . . not to sound disparaging of the ill and infirm, your honor, but we call 'em griddleheads."

"Why don'tcha just slow down?"

"If I went any slower, sir, I'd be on sabbatical. It ain't the amble down into the pothole that's a problem—it's scenic, doesn't take much gas—it's the drive back up. Ol' Henry didn't build his Fords to run perpendicular. Why I've known people who drove into a pothole on 4th street and . . ."

"Just disappeared?" offered Judge Moore, with a cocky grin.

"Yes, sir, and they're still looking for them two kids who set out on their bikes. Told their Ma they were going up 4th street, that's the last she's seen of 'em. Took their little dog, too."

"That so?" said the judge, over the swelling laughter. "By God, I can't wait to tell my wife, Agnes," said Moore. "I'm sure there are days she'd like to send a couple of our kids up 4th street, especially Dia."

It was obvious the defendant had been forewarned. Judge Moore prized wit. Everyone in Ecorse knew it. The way to get to the judge's heart was through a snappy riposte, rapid patter. It was a dangerous legal strategy, however; a defendant had to know when to let fly and when to go hangdog.

"Where you from?" asked Judge Moore.

Donald Hanson stood a little straighter. "Wyandotte, your honor."

"Is this a local custom in Wyandotte? Driving up sidewalks?"

"Don't have to, sir. In Wyandotte, the words street and overland trail aren't synonymous."

Judge Moore's eyes were merry. "Well, I'll be . . . . Is Wyandotte, then, without faults."

"Oh, we got potholes, your honor. But the streets are flat, in a straight line and paved."

"I didn't know that. Every one of 'em's paved?"

"Well no, sir, but the one's that aren't . . . at least the shrubbery's been removed."

The Judge leaned in toward Donald Hanson. "If you're coming from Wyandotte, why are you driving that way in the first place? Didja ever think of driving up Mill?"

"Have you seen that iron bridge on Mill, your honor?"

"Rickety is it?" asked Judge Moore, the devil in his eyes.

"Oh, I wouldn't say rickety, your honor. Rickety would be kind."

"I'll bite," said George Moore, who was known as a giving man and would volunteer a setup to anyone in need. "What would you say?"

"I'd say some kids are missing their Erector Sets."

Oh, the thigh slapping that followed!

"So you prefer 4th Street?"

"'Prefer' is a pretty strong word, sir," said Hanson. "Even your rum runners know better than to flee down 4th. Can turn a cargo of booze into a sloe gin fizz." He stopped. So had the laughter.

" *Our* rum runners?" The smile on Judge Moore's face had ambled into one of those potholes and was taking a long time ambling back out. "I'll tell you what, Mr. Hanson," he said. "All those people you pass on 4th street—the ones sitting in their kitchen window, sniffing their Maxwell House, while you drive up their sidewalk under their half-awake noses—those are the people who are paying taxes to get rid of potholes so you can have a smooth street. Now, I notice all you good citizens of Wyandotte don't mind coming to work in our town and taking all those big fat Steel Mill paychecks back to your town and paying all those hefty Wyandotte taxes so that your town fathers can fill your town potholes. So, I'll tell you what. Let's start by you giving a little money to our town so we can fix that street up nice for you." Judge Moore punctuated the tag with a bang from the gavel. "$25 fine or 30 days."

One Donald P. Hanson huffed to his chair. Like an opening act at Grossinger's, he had served up one joke too many.

"Now what?" Judge Moore shuffled through an untidy pile of papers. "City of Ecorse vs. Alex Selina on a charge of Grand Larceny."

Officer Myers, who was into his eighth reading of "The 1920 New Swimwear Fashions" in the in-house *Police Gazette*," set down the telltale pink rag, yawned, stood up, and strolled to the middle of the room, while Alex Selina, cap in hand, meandered over to the table. Right hands were raised; both swore to tell the truth.

"Your honor on Saturday, October 18,[5] at 8:45 p.m., I answered a call from

---

[5] In actuality, this was February 12, 1927.

Sam Pappas at 4678 Front St. Mr. Pappas had caught Alex Selina of 4592 Front coming out of his chicken coop with a chicken in each fist—one black monoker and one Plymouth Rock hen. There was another party with Selina, but he got away with two white hens. Selina claims he does not know the man's name or where he lives."

"Sam?" intoned Judge Moore.

Sam Pappas, who owned a Greek coffee shop near Mill, offered his statement: "It's just like Officer Myers said, your honor. I was closing up my cafe for the night and heard a ruckus outside. When I went out, I seen Selina and some other guy sneaking out of my hen house. I shined my flashlight right in Selina's eyes, but the other guy run off with my best pullets and I didn't get a good look."

"Mr. Selina. How do you plead?"

"Guilty, I guess, your honor."

Judge Moore levelled his piercing black eyes at Selina. "Sam Pappas says there was another fella."

"So they tell me," offered Alex Selina.

"Says he got away with two hens."

"So they say."

"You didn't know the other fella?"

"No, sir."

"Never seen him before?"

"Not in my lifetime."

"What'd he look like?"

"Who?"

"The other fella."

"Couldn't tell. It was dark," said Selina. Judge Moore waited; his unwavering gaze made Selina uncomfortable. "I'm trying to help, your honor, but I just didn't know the guy."

"When'd he show up?" asked the judge.

"Who?"

"The other fella. Was he there before you entered the coop, while you were in the coop, when you were leaving the coop?"

Selina hesitated. "He come in when I was there."

"Boy," muttered Judge Moore, "that hen house is more popular than Patsy Lowrie's on a Saturday night." A whoop went up, but Moore gaveled the court into silence. "He came in when you were there?"

"Yes, sir."

"But you don't know his name or where he lives?"

"No, sir."

"How'd you know you didn't know him?"

"Sir?"

"I thought it was dark?"

Selina hesitated.

"Just so I can understand this, Mr. Selina, let's recreate the event. First off, you were robbing Mr. Pappas' hen coop. Right?"

"Well, I don't know as I'd put it so stark."

"You pled guilty, didn't you? Since that was the offense you were accused of, I'm assuming that's what you were pleading guilty to."

"I guess."

"And in the darkness, some guy you'd never set eyes on walked in and joined you."

Selina hesitated. "Yes, sir."

"Tell me. When this other guy snuck into the chicken coop in that pitch-black darkness, so dark that only owls could see, did it give you pause? Did you wonder if it was the owner? Did you wonder if he had a gun? Did you say howdee, nod, share a Strohs?"

"We wasn't drinking, your honor."

"What I'm trying to ascertain, sir," said Moore, "is whether there's honor among chicken thieves? I would have thought that if another man came into your purview, he'd have the decency to leave and go find a less-congested coop." The gavel banged. "35 days in the Detroit House of Correction. Next!"

Judge Moore waited for the obligatory fowl play jokes to run their course before he proceeded. "City of Ecorse vs. G. Mach Adams[6] for violation of the traffic code."

Officer Myers had no need to leave the table. "Your Honor, I was sitting on Front Street, when a black Hudson Touring car, License #343-987, driven by a Mr. G. Mach Adams, came by at 25 miles per hour in a 15-mile speed zone on Wednesday last."

"Mr. Adams, do you have anything to say?"

A professorial type stood up. "Have you got a few days, your honor? I have a veritable mouthful of things to say."

Officer Myers muttered, "That's the same thing he said to me, your honor, when I leaned into his car. All I said was, 'What's up?' and he went ape. That's all I said, 'What's up?' You shoulda heard him."

Eyes ablaze, Mr. Adams turned on Officer Myers. "What's up was, I had been arrested for speeding! What's up was, you weren't sitting on Front Street, you were parked behind a billboard east of Front Street. What's up was, I was probably going five miles over the limit, tops!" Adams turned his fury on Judge Moore. "I cannot believe that you people don't have more important things to do. You've got a lot of crust ticketing a respectable law-abiding citizen for a trivial infraction when this town pays obsequious respect to drivers of cars sagging under the weight of rum kegs who set their own speed limits. Sitting there behind a billboard. Why don't you arrest a few of the hundreds of guys who flout the laws in Ecorse every day?"

---

[6] Incident occurred June 8, 1928.

"You wouldn't happen to be another denizen of the fair and potholeless city of Wyandotte by any chance, Mr. Adams?" asked Judge Moore.

"And proud to tell it."

"Are you the G. Mach Adams, eminent publisher of the *Wyandotte Record*?"

"In the fuming flesh."

"Well, Mr. Adams, how do you plead?"

"Not guilty."

"That's odd. I thought you said you were going at least five miles over the limit."

"I said a few other things as well."

"Mr. Adams, I'm puzzled. If you say everyone that speeds has to watch their step coming through Ecorse, why weren't you watching yours? Seems to me that if you know we're a hot bed of ticket-fining fanatics, you'd have slowed down as soon as you hit the bridge. $15 or 5 days. Next!"

If you had asked Judge Moore if he had been fair, he would have said yes. If you had asked Judge Moore if he had a bias against Wyandotte, he'd have said no. But he did; it was hard not to. Because Wyandotte had one hell of a bias against Ecorse. It didn't help that as soon as you crossed the tiny bridge over Ecorse Creek and entered Wyandotte one of the first streets to greet you was named Superior.

"City of Ecorse vs. Edward O'Hearn."

Snapping to attention, Sergeant Clark was on his feet, brusquely signaling the rookie, Officer James Stewart. Stewart took his sweet time getting up. George had taken a dislike to Stewart from the get-go; Stewart felt the same way about George. No love lost between them.

Clark addressed the judge. "Your honor, on the night of Saturday, October 11,[7] at 8:45 p.m., we got a call from Ralph Montrose of the Anti-Saloon League that some guy walks by their storefront with a jug of wine every Saturday night and taunts them. Responding to the call, we was just pulling up when Mr. Montrose appeared in the middle of the road and flagged us down. He pointed out Mr. O'Hearn having in his possession a jug of wine. When we approached, Mr. O'Hearn broke the jug on the sidewalk, but me and Officers Owens and Stewart succeeded in getting one-half ounce for evidence before we put bracelets on him and brung him in."

A French's mustard jar containing a quarter inch of Burgundian liquid was gently centered in the middle of the long table, followed by a brown paper bag whose contents tinkled for the record.

"Celebrating Christmas early, Nibbs?" asked George.

"I guess, George," said the 54-year-old with an acute case of the shakes.

"How do you plead? Guilty or not guilty?"

---

[7] In actuality, December 18, 1926. Three cases have been combined.

"Of what, your honor?"

"Hang on, I'll ask," Judge Moore turned to the officer. "What's he guilty of?"

"Violation of the state liquor law and resisting arrest," replied Stewart. He had an odd smile, a cocky smile.

Judge Moore turned to Nibbs O'Hearn. "Violation of the state liquor law and resisting arrest. How do you plead?"

"Not guilty, your honor."

"Not guilty!" Ralph Montrose shot straight out of his chair. "We caught him red-handed, your honor, and there's the evidence."

"And how was that evidence obtained?" asked George.

"Straight from the jug."

"I thought he smashed the jug."

"Yes, but we got it off the pavement," said Officer Stewart.

"How?"

"A section of the broken glass contained it."

"But how did you manage to come upon that section?"

"Pardon me?"

"Were you standing? Squatting? Bending over?" asked Judge Moore.

"We were kneeling down."

"We?"

"Yes, Officers Owens and Clark, Mr. Montrose, and myself."

"Mr. Montrose?"

"I reported it. I saw it all, your honor." Ralph Montrose approached the bench. "He has a jug every Saturday night. Walks right by the Anti-Saloon League storefront, defiant. Every Saturday night while we hold our meetings."

"Does he disrupt your meetings?"

"In a way, yes."

"How? Does he come in?"

"No."

"Does he yell?"

"No. But we're all aware he's out there, thumbing his nose."

The bell rang and Joyce timidly entered. Beckoned by her father, she walked through the gate self-consciously, then approached the bench and whispered. Officer Stewart could barely contain his annoyance.

"And what would this money be for?" asked George.

"For macaroni, tomatoes, and a nickel's worth of cheddar," recited Joyce.

To which Arthur offered, "Casserole tonight, Mr. Moore."

"Macaroni and cheese. Does life get any better?" said George as he pulled out his wallet, handed Joyce a bill, amidst a slew of bribery cracks, and watched as she left.

"Now, where were we? Ah, just let me get a clear picture," said the judge. "Mr. O'Hearn is strolling up Front Street with a jug of wine."

"Mumma never had a cent in her pocketbook, never had a penny," recalled Freda. "If she sent us to the store, she made a list and we went over to the barber- shop to get the money. The first thing on that list was 25 cents worth of apples, cause Pa loved apples. And then maybe a can of peas or green beans or corn and two pounds of round steak. Well, maybe not round steak, because round steak was about 20 cents a pound. And if you had any change you had to stop at the barber- shop and bring it back to him."

Nibbs timidly raised his hand. "Excuse me, your honor. But have we proved it was wine?"

"Sorry, Nibbs. Strolling up Front Street," sang out the judge, "with an al- leged jug of wine."

"Oh, swell, now the jug's alleged," muttered Montrose.

". . . at 8:45 in the evening. And is spotted by Mr. Montrose who calls the station and you send out three guys. Not one, but three."

"That's correct, sir, in all particulars," said Sergeant Clark.

"And three cops—not one, not two, but three cops—pull him over to the side of the curb and arrest him. Was Mr. O'Hearn armed?"

"No, sir," said Sergeant Clark.

"Possess a long record of incorrigibility, did he?"

"No, sir."

"Known to be violent?"

"No, sir."

"Drunk and disorderly?"

"Often drunk, rarely disorderly."

"I'd call breaking a jug disorderly," snapped Stewart.

Ralph Montrose was furious. "And I'd say he was more than a little drunk."

"Why would you say that, Ralph?"

"Because I followed him up two blocks."

"Was he weaving?"

"He wasn't walking in any straight line."

"Did he run into anybody, accost anybody?"

"No sir. But someone has to protect him."

"From who?"

"From himself!"

"And you're that protector?"

"Don't see nobody else doing it."

Judge Moore turned once again to Sergeant Clark. "Any reason you sent out three cops to arrest him?"

"Quiet night, your honor. And checkers goes just so far."

George Moore grinned. "I see. So the three of you are standing there, writ- ing him up, I suppose, when Mr. O'Hearn drops the jug of wine onto the pavement."

"He dropped it when we pulled up, your honor."

"Why do you think he did that?"

"To shatter the evidence, I guess," said the sergeant.

Ralph Montrose was beside himself. "What, guess? He dropped the jug to shatter the evidence! Why else would he shatter his precious jug! You stood right there that night, bald faced, and said that's why he dropped the jug!"

"I didn't say that. Officer Stewart said that."

"Because it was obvious!" Montrose glared at Sergeant Clark; Sergeant Clark glared back. Officer Stewart smirked.

Judge Moore leaned across his desk and addressed the defendant. "Was that your intention, Nibbs? Did you drop the wine to shatter the evidence?"

"I dropped the wine cause they scared the salt outta me, George. Them guys come out of nowhere, squealing brakes, banging doors, guns drawn. . ."

"Were your guns drawn, Sergeant Clark?"

Sergeant Clark laughed. "No, sir, not at all."

"Sure felt like they was, your honor."

"Sergeant Clark, if you were just ambling along, humming goodnight to Irene, and three cops jumped out of a squad car—lights flashing, doors banging, alleged guns drawn—is it possible you might drop your alleged jug of wine."

"Might drop more than my jug, your honor."

"Alleged! alleged! You call this alleged?" Ralph Montrose was at the table in one stride, grabbing the brown paper bag and turning it over. Broken pieces of glass bounced onto the table. The crowd was baffled. Judge Moore usually kept a tight rein on his seemingly informal court but, for some reason, he was letting Montrose run on. "When did we prove it wasn't wine? Did I miss something here?"

"So, just let me get a clear picture," said Judge Moore, amiably. "The alleged jug has just broken on the sidewalk, and three of Ecorse's finest are crawling around on their hands and knees to get an ounce of aging grape juice. I can't tell you how relieved I am that no one cut their finger in the line of duty."

While Officer Stewart fumed, Sergeant Clark just grinned. "We appreciate your concern, your honor. Just doing our job, I guess."

"Yeah, Sergeant, you're right. That's what makes me so sad. Thanks to those sages of the upper legislatures, your job has come to this. Used to be we'd just take the drunks home," he muttered. "Now we lock them up." Judge Moore cast his eyes downward at the shaky man in front of him. "Nibbs?"

"Yes, your honor?"

"How much time you spend looking through a haze?" Nibbs stared at the floor but did not answer. "Don't you think it'd be smart to get some help?"

"Where, your honor?"

"I dunno. See a priest or something?"

"You gonna send me to Eloise, George?"

"No, no. None of that."

"'Cause once you get in Eloise you never get out."

"Tell you what," said Moore, "Saturday night seems to be your toughest night, right?"

"Yes, sir."

"Why don't you come over here on Saturday. Lotsa fellows around. Good talk. Agnes makes popcorn. Maybe if you get through Saturday, the rest of the week won't be so bad."

"All well and good, your honor," said Ralph Montrose. "But he has broken the law. There's wine in this bottle and it's far from being alleged. And I'm an eyewitness." He took the lid off the French's mustard. "May I approach the bench?"

"You may."

Ralph Montrose thrust the French's mustard under the unwilling nose of Judge Moore. With one whiff, Moore's magisterial head reeled back as if from a blow. "Yep, that's wine all right," he said. "Though I think somebody left their socks in it."

"Then under the law, your honor," Ralph said loudly, "and under the guidelines, you are impelled to sentence him."

"Why?"

"Why? Because it goes against the 18th Amendment," said Stewart.

"No, it doesn't," said George. "The 18th Amendment only forbids manufacture, sale, and transportation within the U.S. and, importation and exportation without. It doesn't forbid the purchase or drinking of liquor. You can buy it, you just can't sell it."

"Then it's against the Volstead Act," said Stewart.

"Nope," said George. "The Volstead Act only provides for the enforcement of the 18th Amendment. And don't tell me it's against Michigan's Damon law because that only prohibits importing and blind pigs. Besides the Michigan Supreme Court found that one unconstitutional. It's not against Michigan's Wiley law prohibiting manufacture and sale cause both parts are needed. Ah, but Michigan's Lewis law. Could be against that, cause that's a dandy. The Lewis law prohibits everything to do with booze: manufacture, sale, giving away, bartering, furnishing, possessing, importing, transporting, even throwing it up. Gotta admit, I'm a judge and even I can't be sure what the law is. The menu changes every week."

"Well, one thing's sure," said Stewart. "They made it a felony."

"You're right, Officer Stewart," said George, all humor gone. "Michigan in its infinite wisdom made it a felony. It's not a felony in Ohio or New Jersey or New York or most of the 48. Just Michigan. That's so police can use their guns to shoot at suspected violators and search them without a warrant." Judge Moore pondered his position. Then, "When did you purchase that wine, Nibbs?"

"Not sure, George. A while back."

"Could it have been purchased before May 1, 1918? Before the law went into effect?"

Ralph Montrose muttered to the row of chairs next to him. "Would you call that leading the witness?"

"'Spose it coulda been purchased before the law went into effect," opined Nibbs. "I purchased a lot of wine before the law took effect."

"Would it have been for your own purposes?"

"No doubt about that, your honor."

"So it's possible that you purchased the wine for your own purpose before the law went into effect?"

"By gosh, I think I did," said Nibbs.

"This is outrageous!" roared Ralph Montrose.

"Since there's no way to prove the year of vintage. . . . Too much doubt, too many possibles. Case dismissed. Next case."

Officer Stewart returned to his seat, face of stone. George caught the black look and returned it with disgust. It wouldn't be the last time these two bumped heads.

"City of Ecorse vs. John Beausoleil for violating the traffic code and the state Prohibition law." John Beausoleil was cleaned up for the occasion. Shirt and tie and jacket; his hair slicked back.

Sergeant Clark had remained in place. "Your honor, just before daylight on Tuesday, October 21,[8] Officer Biskner and I was patrolling. . ."

"They don't patrol," muttered Adams. "They sit at the foot of the Ecorse bridge behind the Exide battery sign and eat chili dogs."

"You've had your say, Mr. Adams."

"Briefly, sir. Very briefly."

". . . and we seen a truck going south on West Jefferson which had aroused our suspicions. When we asked the driver to pull over, he took off and we gave chase."

"How fast was he going?"

"During the chase, our speedometers registered 83 miles an hour, your honor. As the truck was crossing the railroad tracks at Cicotte, a man jumped out and made his escape, but we continued to pursue the truck for three more blocks until it jumped a curb, knocked off a big pole, and came to a standstill at the northeast corner of Front and Mill."

"Was the driver hurt?"

"There was no driver, your honor."

Another whoop went up, followed by intense discussions as to how the hell.

"You were chasing a truck without a driver?"

---

[8] In actuality, composite of many cases in newspaper articles, including "POLICE MADE TWO BIG HAULS YESTERDAY AM," Wyandotte newspaper, March 16, 1923.

"It kinda startled us, too, your honor. We didn't know it at the time but the driver, Mr. Beausoleil here, was the one who had jumped out at the railroad tracks."

"What was in the truck?"

"Sixteen barrels of homemade."

"Homemade?"

"Let me put it this way, your honor. The locals call it 'strip and go naked.'"

When the laughter died down, Barney Beaubien muttered to Paul Movinski, "This guy could get 20 years."

"Not in this court," hissed G. Mach Adams, while taking copious notes on the other side of the divide. "This guy'll get 20 laughs and a croix de guerre. Wait and see."

Judge Moore turned to the driver named Beausoleil. "You jumped out, eh?"

"Yes, sir."

"What was that speed again?"

"83 miles per," boasted Beausoleil.

Judge Moore laughed. "Amazing, 83 miles per. You've got guts, Mr. Beausoleil."

"Thank you, sir."

"See what I mean," whispered Adams.

"And little else," glared the judge. "Are you aware there are kids in this town, Mr. Beausoleil?"

"Yes, sir."

"Kids that cross streets."

"It was 6 a.m., your honor," said Beausoleil.

"Kids that are out early, delivering papers."

"Yes, sir."

"And Barney Oldfield here jumps out of a truck to save his skin and lets that cannonball run 80 miles an hour through the town. Why don't you just spray our main street with a Tommie gun?" The gavel went off like a cap pistol. "$30 fine or 60 days for speeding."

"See, you're wrong about George," said Sam Pappas.

"Am I?" said Adams. "I didn't hear any fine for the cargo."

(L to R) Shay, Rowe, Joyce, and Freda

The busy porch at 4426 Monroe
(L to R) Agnes, Shay, Freda with Marce, Rowe, Joyce, Dia

Chapter 7
Monday, April 27, 1925

Every Monday—before the advent of Whirlpool dryers—women met. Not among the potted palms at the Wabeek Tearoom, and not in the stiff-chaired meeting halls of the Junior League or the DAR, but over their back fences under blue skies. Topics ranged from a White Sale at Kern's to love and death. They scrutinized, fraternized, empathized, counseled, and consoled.

Daybreak in the Moore house was customarily greeted with "Rise and Shine!" or "Morning Glory!" but Monday, ah Monday, started with the same refrain bellowed from below: "If you've got any wash, throw it down!" For Monday was washday. Before the rooster crowed, Agnes was down in the basement mixing potions like an alchemist—muriatic acid, cream of tartar, bleach, starch, Borax, benzine and Bull Dog bluing—to achieve the desired fluffiness, the correct stiffness, the perfect color, pouring in Clorox for whites, Rinso for colors, Ivory Snow for woolens.

As inmates stripped their beds, a sound could be heard—a soothing sound that in later years would bring on a spasm of nostalgia— the sound of the Maytag. The gentle rotation of the washing machine agitator created a rumbling murmur as the suds swished back and forth, lapping at the side of the inner basket. This way, that way, this way, that way, as Agnes scoured pockets, pulling change out of Murph's brown trousers. This way, that way, this way, that way, as Agnes searched for fabrics that would run, fabrics that would shrink. This way, that way, this way, that way.

Those fortunate enough to be home from school would dress hurriedly, eat hurriedly, fearful of missing *la grande finale*, Number One on the list of thrills, chills and household accidents, the gobbling, greedy washing machine wringer. One might question why a domestic appliance was more rousing than any monster from Grimm. Maybe it was the much-touted promise of danger—the newspaper reports read sternly at the breakfast table of children with mangled arms and missing parts.

With sporadic bursts of "Watch your arm! Watch your wrist!" Agnes would pluck a sopping-wet sheet from the washer's belly, follow the hem to a corner, and insert it carefully between the rubber rollers of the wringer. On the receiving end, Freda—or Rowe or Joyce or Dia when they weren't in school—would watch apprehensively as the wringer slowly ingested, digested, disgorged the sheet, extracting every drop of water. The children would guide the flattened garment or sheet from the jaws of the wringer into the laundry basket, while

Shay begged, "Can I do that, Mumma? Please!"

"I don't think so, sweetheart." Hands red from chemicals and hot water, Agnes pawed through the laundry on the floor, sorting another load: flannels and woolens in one pile, bed linens in another, colors in a third.

On this particular April day there was another child in attendance, a newcomer parked near the basement steps. Marcia Jean Moore, now five months old, was asleep in a wicker bassinet, lulled by the sound of this way, that way, this way, that way. For Agnes, it had been a painful, prolonged delivery. The women of Monroe Avenue prided themselves on their stoicism during childbirth, but with the arrival of Marce, Agnes was now known as a screamer.

A dishtowel landed on pile two, a hankie on pile one. Agnes's palm settled on the pleated lavender skirt that had recently hung from Freda and Rowe's vanity table. "Didn't I wash this last week?" She flipped the fabric into pile three. "Fine. They can iron it."

Laundry basket loaded, Agnes huffed her way up the basement steps under the weight of wet clothes. Surfacing into the light, she glanced at the sky on the lookout for dark clouds. Rain? Maybe. It was an April kind of day—warm, moist—with gusts of billowy wind left over from March. There were buds on the forsythia, buds on the lilac—nature was at the starting gate. Agnes retraced her tired steps to retrieve Marce, still asleep in the wicker bassinet, and then Shay. Though Shay was a willing worker, Agnes desperately missed Freda. But she had promised Miss Munn that Freda would improve her attendance, and she couldn't go back on it now.

Heaving her basket into the little red wagon, Agnes pitched along the makeshift sidewalk, slabs of concrete that had been laid end to end en route to the alley. Agnes was a tenderfoot; her feet would burn and swell, reaching miserable heights in summer. In deference to her age—40 and still vain—she made a conscious effort not to waddle as she pulled the wagon behind her, but rolling to the sides of her feet gave some relief.

Agnes ran a washcloth over the length of a line, wiping away the grit from Michigan Steel and D.J. Ryan's foundry. Four lines ran the length of the yard from the house to the T-pole near the alley. The Moore backyard was ringed by a semblance of fence—a wall of squat, gray wooden slats, some a few inches apart, some missing, some that had fallen and were now angled against their betters. What with children tromping, rusted toys, wagon parts and winter, the yard was a spring scrub patch. On the Hotham side of the yard stood their chicken coop.

One yard over a screen door banged. Mrs. Strassner emerged, hoisting a piled-high laundry basket in her capable arms. "Five loads," gasped Ella as she groaned her way to the line. She dropped the basket. "Can you believe it? Five loads."

"Your feet swell up in this weather?" yelled Agnes.

"No, why?" yelled Ella.

"My dogs are killin' me! Couldn't even get to church yesterday; couldn't get my shoes on!"

Ella looked over at Agnes's feet. Agnes was wearing slippers.

"What size feet you got?"

"4 1/2."

"*Tout petit!* " Ella lifted a good-sized foot. "See? You need waders like mine!" She wiped off her line and waited for a wailing train to pass. "So. Guess you know!" Her tone changed to casual, the sentence wasn't. "George took Nick out drinking again Saturday night!"

"I thought Nick took George out!"

"Not the way I heard it."

"Either way, there couldn't have been much resistance," said Agnes. "Neither one had their clothes torn!"

Another screen door banged across the alley. Mrs. Jaeger, wife of Al, grunted out, her arms taut with the weight of the basket. "Quarantine sign up near Monroe and Bourassa!" she yelled.

"What they got?" asked Agnes.

"Diphtheria!"

"Saw a scarlet fever sign over on First!" yelled Ella.

Two yards down another screen door banged. Alice Pilon emerged, dropped her basket, wiped her brow in mock melodrama.

"Don't complain!" yelled Agnes. "We could still be scrubbing on washboards!"

"Yeah, sure, you can talk," yelled Alice. "You got a Maytag!"

Pivoting from the waist, each woman bent down, retrieved a garment, shook it, and while the thumb of the left hand pinned the garment against the line, a clothespin emerged from the palm like Blackstone, clamping the small wad of fabric with its crook.

"Here comes Rowe, Mumma," said Shay

Agnes peeked above a sheet. "At ten? What's she doing home at ten?"

A swirl of dust strode towards them. Rowena Moore was marching up the alley with an envelope clutched in her fist and a face that would make Frank Buck blanch.

"She looks mad," yelled Mrs. Jaeger.

Swinging her right foot into the air, Rowe lambasted a cinder so hard it landed on top of the chicken coop, alarming Uncle Peck and Aunt Ovie who scurried out of the way with concerned clucks. "She did it again!" Rowe hit the horn before she was within 15 feet of the gate latch. "SHE DID IT AGAIN!"

"Now, don't go blowing your stack," said Agnes.

Rowe checked an impulse to punctuate her point by slamming the tired gate. "But she. Did it. AGAIN!"

"Who did what again?" asked Ella.

"Miss Prim and Proper of 1925, Miss Pom-pous!"

"Miss Munn?"

"Who else!"

"What'd she do now?" asked Ella.

Agnes glanced nervously across the alley to the rooftop of School One a block away. "Let's keep our voices down, shall we?" she cautioned. With that, the washerwomen convened at fence corners.

Rowe could hardly mouth the words that contained the offense, the outrage. "She's making me . . . miss . . . RECESS!"

The three mothers rearranged their mouths; Rowe adjusted her glasses.

"Why? What did you do?" asked Ella.

"I didn't do anything!"

"You must be doing something," said Agnes. "Or why would she make you miss recess again?"

"Precisely!" said Rowe.

"I'm confused."

Rowe sighed. "Recess is for recess, right?"

"If you say so," Agnes replied and pulled her wagon of wash to an empty line.

"And this is America, right?"

"Can't argue with that."

"And in America we're all treated equally, right?"

"Might argue with that."

"Then how come she always picks *me* to take the class money to the bank!"

"I don't know."

"What clafff money?" asked Mrs. Jaeger, puffing on a clothespin.

"We have this sixth-grade savings account to learn thrift," explained Rowe. "Once a week we all put in a nickel."

"Not a bad idea," said Mrs. Jaeger.

"But I'm the one she always asks to take it to the bank. Once a week during recess she says, 'Rowena, would you come here?' It's always Rowena, Rowena, Rowena. We've got 20 minutes for recess and I spend 20 minutes going to the bank."

"Maybe it's a compliment, maybe you're her favorite," said Mrs. Jaeger.

"That isn't why," said Rowe. "She always has patsies doing for her. She does the same thing to Freda. Doesn't she, Mumma? Sucker, Mumma calls her. Mumma calls Freda sucker."

"Once," winked Agnes. "In a weak moment."

Rowe hesitated. "Anyway, today was it."

"What do you mean, 'today was it?'"

"Today was it."

Agnes winced. "What is my third born trying to tell me, Ella?"

"I think she's trying to tell you that today was it."

"Today, I didn't want to go to the bank. I went out and played like everybody else. Then Miss Munn sent Sophie Kovach to the window. I said, 'Tell her I don't want to go to the bank.' Then she sent Frankie Suda: 'Miss Munn says for you to go to the bank.' I said, 'Tell her, I'm not gonna.' Next thing you know, another one of her stooges comes out on the playground, hands me the money and says, 'Miss Munn wants to see you.' I said, 'Ask her who was her servant last year.'"

"To Miss Munn?" asked Mrs. Jaeger. "You said that to the principal of School One?"

"No, I said it to this kid."

"That was a little sassy, don't you think?" said Agnes.

"But, Mumma, I was fed up. Just plain fed up. Pretty soon, Miss Munn comes to her office window and says, 'Rowena, come in here.' Then she really lit into me."

"In her office?"

"No, on the playground. In front of everybody."

"Did you talk back?"

"Noooo! I told her as nice as pie that I didn't want to go to the bank."

"And she said?"

"She said, I must."

"And you said?"

"Nothing. I just shook my head, turned around and came home."

"With the money?"

"I forgot I had it."

There was a sudden gust of wind. Mrs. Jaeger ran to batten down a ballooning blanket. Agnes waited for the council to reconvene, before turning back to Rowe and asking, "Without exaggeration, how often have you gone to the bank?"

"Once a week."

"For the entire term?" she asked in disbelief.

"Yes."

"During recess?"

"I've been telling you that, Mumma," said Rowe.

Ultimately fair, Agnes turned to Ella. "She has. She's been telling me that. I just didn't hear it."

Reaching into her apron, Agnes studied the middle distance; clothespins tinkled like wood chimes as they knocked together inside their lair. "Okay, take that money over to the bank, then bring me back the bankbook."

"Do I hafta, Mumma?"

"Then you'll stay home until things calm down."

Rowe was down the driveway and halfway up Monroe Street, leaving little chance for a reverse decision.

"Sure she's not just hankering for a day off?" asked Mrs. Jaeger.

"No. Rowe loves school," said Agnes. "This isn't about getting out of school."

Ella turned serious. "I wouldn't take that woman on, Ag. You got four more kids that'll have her for class."

"And don't I know it." Agnes nervously surveyed the line of housedresses. "She's trouble. I smell it. George thinks she has class. She's a phony but he doesn't see it."

Fifteen minutes later didn't Ella sidle back to the Moore fence. Ella was one of the best sidlers in Ecorse. "Here comes Miss Ranger."

Agnes looked up from the clothesline with a start. "Miss Ranger?" The first-grade schoolteacher was fluttering up the alley—hobbling over the cinders on spindly, wire legs. George had affectionately dubbed her "The Little Sparrow."

"Now what?" said Agnes.

"Bet I know," said Ella.

"That poor woman," said Agnes, shaking her head. "Now, she's got *her* doing errands."

"Gooday, Gooday," tweeted Miss Ranger, as her head performed a series of quick angular jerks. "Gooday, Mrs. Moore."

"Good day, Miss Ranger," said Agnes, picking up Marce who had begun to cry.

Obviously a reluctant messenger, Miss Ranger stopped at the Moore fence. Ella, Mrs. Jaeger, even Alice Pilon, casually moved their work to within ear-shot. On the theory that bold was best, the teacher blinked, then blurted: "Miss Munn wants Rowena to come back to school."

"She's upstairs, lying down. She's a little upset," replied Agnes. "Tell her tomorrow, maybe tomorrow. I think it'd be wise to let the dust settle."

"Now Mrs. Moore, wouldn't it be better to get the whole thing over with?"

"I'm sure. But tomorrow'll be here soon enough. Now would you mind waiting one second? I have something for you."

Excusing herself, Agnes went into the house and returned with the bank-book. "I don't want you to get caught in the middle, Miss Ranger. I know you were asked to come here. I'm sure you found it hard to refuse. But Rowena will not be going back to school today. You can tell Miss Munn that, from now on, I'd appreciate it if she let some other student take the class money to the bank. I know someone has to do it, but does that someone always have to be the same someone?"

With reluctance, Miss Ranger accepted the bankbook, warbled with forced cheer, "Gooday, Gooday," and stumbled back up the alley.

————

By early afternoon, as the clouds grew thicker and the light of day changed to a metallic gray, the women reemerged to begin the systematic deconstruction of their handiwork. As Shay entertained Marce in her bassinet and Rowe folded a sheet, Agnes plucked clothespins, filling a basket with sun-dried wash.

Just then George Moore appeared around the corner of the house, still in his barber smock, on a direct course to the wash line.

"What're you doing home?" asked Agnes.

"Heard there's been a little trouble."

"Trouble? What'd she do? Send that poor Miss Ranger over to the barbershop?"

"It wasn't Miss Ranger."

"Then who was it?"

"She came herself."

"Who?"

"Miss Munn."

Agnes let out a derisive hoot. "Oh, you must have loved that."

"She was very upset, Ag. She said she asked Rowe to go to the bank and she refused."

"There's a little more to it than. . . ," started Agnes.

He turned to Rowe. "Did you get snippy, Auntie? I'll tan your hide if you got snippy. I'm sure Miss Munn has your best interest at heart."

Agnes picked up the load of clean wash and sang cheerily, "I don't know why you don't just canonize her, George." The door cracked like buckshot as she banged into the house, then cracked again as Rowe, carrying Marce, followed.

Shay squinted up at her father as he studied the fourth slab of sidewalk. Eventually his eyes met hers—those deep, black eyes. Walking over to the coop, he lifted the bucket of chicken feed sitting outside the fence, took out a handful and stepped inside.

"But I fed 'em, Pa."

"What's that, Tee?"

"I already fed 'em."

He stood there for a moment, as if he could not comprehend what she was saying, then listlessly dropped the seed into the bucket, set the bucket outside the fence, shoved his hands in his pockets and drifted into the house. George Moore hated conflict.

George waited in the kitchen—uncomfortable, uninvited. It wasn't until Agnes rolled the fourth pair of socks into a ball that she said, "This isn't the first time, George. She asks Rowe once a week to go to the bank."

"But isn't that a compliment?"

"She never gets recess."

"Miss Munn didn't tell me that."

"Of course, she didn't. Why should she?"

"Well, right or wrong, she has to go back, Ag."

"She'll go back tomorrow."

"She has to go back today."

"Today!" yelled Rowe. "Don't make me go back, Mumma! Oh, please, not today!"

"Now pipe down, Auntie," said her father. "You're going back to apologize and you're going back today. I promised Miss Munn."

Agnes was incredulous. "You what?"

"That's right."

"Let me get this straight, George. You promised Miss Munn before you heard Rowe's side."

"He never hears my side," muttered Rowe.

"Oh c'mon, Ag, she's got to go back. What's she gonna think of us?" Agnes pulled another sock out of the basket and pawed for its mate. "Please don't make this any bigger than it is."

"Oh, I think you've already done a good job of that."

George Moore swept his arm with a flourish. "Care to join me in the consulting room?"

"Not especially." Seizing the laundry, Agnes barreled into the bedroom and heaved the laundry onto the bed. The main event started before the basket had time to bounce and her husband had time to close the bedroom door; they sparred in hushed tones. "I don't know what this is all about, George. Everything was settled."

"She has to go back, Ag."

Extracting a towel from the basket, she snapped it in the air. "School's almost done for the day. She can go back tomorrow."

"I thought Rowe loved school."

"Not this year."

He strolled to the dresser and gazed out the window. Blackbirds were holding a spring convocation in the Hotham garden. Turning round, he said reluctantly, "She has to go back, Ag."

Halving the towel, she snapped it again. "She can go back tomorrow."

"Damn it!" Two dimes leapt in terror as he slammed his palm on the dresser. "She has to go back!"

"I don't know what the hell this is about, but I can assure you it has nothing to do with Rowe! I've been bumping heads with that woman since Murph was in school. And she still has her nose out of joint because I kept Freda home to help."

"She doesn't think you take school seriously."

"And you agreed with her!"

"Of course not. And keep it down...the kids."

"You 'keep it down...the kids,'" snapped Agnes. "No one stands up to that woman. Everybody does her bidding. You know Freda hates school! You never complained before. She loves to stay home and help out and, God knows, I could use it! You're the one who wanted a big family, George."

"Now, don't start that. All I'm saying is school's important for all the kids."

"Then you *did* agree with her!"

"I didn't agree with her! It wasn't like that! And now – if you don't mind – I'd like to say something I've been holding back for a long time."

Agnes braced. "Oh, and what's that?"

"Ouch," he said.

"What?"

"Ouch." He flopped down on the bed and held his hand between his knees. Do you have any earthly idea how much that hurts?" He flexed his fingers. "And stop folding my long johns when I'm trying to make a point."

When their laughter died, they found themselves sitting side-by-side on the green-star quilt, though Agnes still didn't look at him.

"Look, Rowe will go back tomorrow and that'll be the end of it, okay?" She patted him on the leg. "Okay?"

His voice was barely audible. "She has to go back today, Ag. I promised. The woman's over there waiting. Tell Rowe, just go and make the best of it. See what's what."

Agnes turned away, picked up the folded socks, and carried them wearily to the dresser, and—with her back to him—opened the top drawer. The socks tumbled into the drawer. "Interesting," she said. "First she sends Miss Ranger, now she sends you. You're beginning to sound like another one of her stooges, George."

Rowe was sitting casually in the parlor reading, or putting up a pretty good show, when George Moore stormed out of the house. Agnes appeared in the bedroom doorway. "Better go back to school and apologize, Rowe. She's waiting for you. No lip, I don't need any more lip."

"So I went back," said Rowe years later, "and Miss Munn called me into her office. Oh, boy, did she give me hell. 'Aren't you ashamed of yourself?' and 'Weren't you wrong?' She went on and on, till she got me crying, then she says, 'You may return to your class now, but don't ev-er do that again.'"

Chapter 8

Sunday, July 19, 1925

Walter Locke stood in the middle of his houseboat diner and his blue eyes swept Ecorse Bay, from the shacks of Hogan's Alley to the north, to the long stretch of boathouses to the south known as Rum Row. Centered directly in front of the boathouses, about 500 feet offshore, was Mud Island,[1] a narrow, picturesquely named shoal. Beyond Mud was the 300-acre Grassy Island. Farther out in the bay, partially blocking the Canadian shoreline, sat the much larger Fighting Island, a long, low, amoeba-shaped bump on the horizon. Except for the famed Belle Isle, the Detroit shoreline offered a clear run across the river from Canada. But Ecorse had islands —Fighting, Mud, Grassy— that conveniently dotted the water between Canada and Ecorse's swampy shore, islands that could be used for duck and cover when the shore patrol went by.

The interior of Walter Locke's diner had an airy feel—all-whitewashed wood and windows banking three sides; a whirring fan, though barely needed, revolved. There were few customers that day. Ernie Boudreau sat dead-center at the nine-stool counter, sipping hot java from a thick white porcelain mug, reading the Sunday *Detroit Times*. A middle-aged couple were off by themselves, the lone occupiers of one of the small tables lining the three dockside windows. Ted Hoyt lounged on the end stool, his back braced against the wall, studying *Today's Specials* chalked on a small blackboard above the grill. Today's specials were also tomorrow's specials as well as next year's specials—for Walter Locke served up continuity along with beef stew (20 cents), ham and lima beans (20 cents), hamburger steak (10 cents), and sirloin beef (25 cents).

"Know what you want yet, Ted?" asked Walter, wiping his hands on his long white apron.

"Still thinkin'."

Grabbing a pan of stale bread, Walter pushed open the door and stepped out on land. When the spring-loaded screen door snapped back with a fwack, Dempsey, snoozing on a nearby patch of grass, bolted upright. Walter stepped onto the catwalk that stood near his houseboat and tossed the bread in the river. Seagulls gathered within seconds, their high-pitched cries fusing with the high-pitched shrieks of teenagers a few yards away, who were taking turns diving off the State Street dock, Freda robustly among them. She would turn 15 on Saturday and was having a terrific summer. So much so, she was even looking

---

[1] In those days, also known as Slab Island.

forward to school, though she was repeating 7th grade. Come September, both Freda and Rowe would be free of Miss Munn, as Miss Munn was about to be made principal of School Three.

A car pulled into the path and parked. A man got out and leaned against the hood, watching the divers. Walter gave him a wary eye, then set the pan on the counter of his takeout window and returned through the landside door.

"Know what you want yet, Ted?"

"Yeah, a burger."

"Want fries with that?"

"Please."

Walter swirled a ring of oil from a long-spouted tin onto the flat, grease-black grill, waited until it spit and sputtered, and tossed on a hamburger patty. Then he grabbed two heavy oval plates from beneath the counter, put on two dense slabs of meatloaf with a spatula, added two ladles of canned green beans and two scoops of mashed potatoes, which, when excavated, were filled with a lush brown gravy that overflowed their banks. He wiped the side of each plate with a dish towel and placed them before the celebratory couple who sat opposite each other at the oil-clothed table near the middle window.

George Moore pushed his empty salad bowl to the side. "Ah, Walter, you've outdone yourself."

"How many years?" asked Walter.

"Twenty-one tomorrow," said Agnes, smoothing the napkin in her lap.

Married since 1904, the Moores had entertained the idea of celebrating with a dinner at the Sunnyside in Windsor, just across the river, but both agreed they didn't have that kind of money right now. Besides, they enjoyed the informality of Walter Locke's. Agnes had doffed her hat. George was in shirtsleeves, his white linen suitcoat draped over the back of the chair beside him, his boater resting on its seat.

While George salted his salty string beans and dug in, Agnes took a slice of white bread, smeared it with a pat of butter, and took a bite. Then she gazed out the screened window. Though the southern half of the nation was suffering through a deadly heat wave that July, it was a balmy 79 on the Ecorse riverfront, with a feathery breeze that ruffled her hair and stroked her cheek.

Outside, there was endless blue sky, with an apricot haze along the horizon. Scissortail birds darted above the water; a fishing boat drifted near Fighting Island. Freda was climbing back up the wooden ladder at the side of the dock, big cheeky grin, her black wool suit sagging from the water's weight, her Dutch bob tucked under Agnes's old red bathing cap, a giant yellow daisy with eight flouncing petals pasted against its crown.

Aware her mother was watching, Freda pointed to Shay in a hand-me-down playsuit, who was planted out of harm's way on the running board of a Rickenbacker parked at the side of the path, munching a cheese sandwich, sharing her crusts with a seagull. Near her stood the Moore thermos jug, full of ice-cold lemonade. Agnes was pleased. Freda was a topnotch babysitter, especially with Shay.

"Is my ship coming in?" asked George, forking a mound of mashed potatoes as Agnes stared out the window.

"There's a coal barge coming upriver from Wyandotte," she deadpanned.

"That'll be mine," topped George. Their laughter was easy that day, not wary.

As Walter flipped and flattened the hamburger, Ernie Boudreau lowered his Sunday *Times* . "I hate to sound dumb," he said to any and all, "but what's this evolution stuff about anyways? They teach you evolution at school, Ted?"

"I'm lucky I know how to sign my name," said Ted Hoyt.

"Can't figure out what that town's so riled up about," said Ernie, brushing a fly from the edge of the counter. "Everyone in Ohio's gone nuts."

"Ohio? What're you talking about?" said Walter.

"Well, the trial's in Dayton," offered Ernie.

"Right," said Walter. "Dayton, Tennessee."

"Dayton, Tennessee? I thought it was Dayton, Ohio."

"Were you gonna run down there?" winked George.

"Almost did," laughed Ernie.

"You'da been sitting all alone in the courthouse."

Ted propped his foot on the stool next to him. "This country's getting too dang religious for me," he said, having just come from church. "All them Methodists and Baptists trying to run the show. Calling themselves soldiers of God."

"Could be worse. We could live down there," said Ted.

"Down there. Up here. What's the difference?" said George. "Wasn't it only a week ago[2] we had folks parading around in their momma's bedsheets, roasting hot dogs over a burning cross."

"Around here?" said Ted.

"Where you been, Ted? Couple of miles from here, near Lincoln Park."

"None of them KKK doofuses are from Ecorse," said Ernie.

"Think again, dear fellow," said George.

"But Catholics wouldn't be there," said Ernie. "They hate Catholics. They hate the Pope. They're trying to close parochial schools for chrissake."

"Hate to break it to you, Ernie, but Ecorse isn't all Catholic. We got those mill workers from the South."

"Wish I could spout scripture like they do," said Ted. "Wins every argument."

"Finished with the movie section, Ernie?" asked Agnes.

"All yours," replied Ernie, as he extended the paper.

Agnes shuffled to the desired page and skimmed it; George leaned in, eager. "What's at the Ecorse?"

---

[2] July 11 on West Fort Street, a mile west of Lincoln Park village.

"Ummm, *Tracked in the Snow Country* with Rin-Tin-Tin."

"What's it about?"

"A dog, I presume."

"What else you got?"

"*The Monster* 's still at the Wyandotte."

"I know the ending."

"You always know the ending, George," she said, searching the last of the listings. "I wish your stubbly patrons would quit telling you the endings.

Agnes sat up. "Oh, this looks good."

"What?"

"*Paths to Paradise*. Ray Griffith and Betty Compson."

"Where?"

"At the Wonderland."

"What's it about?"

"From the photo, cops and crooks."

"Might talk me into that one. When's the next showing?"

"Three."

"Good, we've got plenty of time," said George.

Agnes sat back. "This is pleasant," she said. She seemed her old pretty self, in her calf-length, tailored brown dress, a touch of organdy at the collar.

"I haven't seen you out of a housedress in a long time, Ag. You look nice."

"Nice?" She laughed. "I feel a little frayed."

"You look nice," he insisted, setting down his knife and fork. "And ten years younger."

Swimming in the Detroit River off Ecorse shore.
Fighting Island in background.

A cheer went up outside, a loud hurrah for Tommy Ouellette who had just done a one-and-a-half tuck. The divers were attracting a sizeable audience. Strollers parading up Front were venturing onto the street-wide path. Some congregated in clumps, some were draped against cars parked along each side of the short roadway. Others, cantilevering out over the river on the porch of a nearby boathouse, paused between forkfuls of potato salad to applaud the more daring dives, especially those of Dempsey, now in the rotation, cued with the aid of a flung stick. Egged on by the attention, the kids had taken to naming each dive, announcing it to the multitude beforehand.

With four leaps under her belt, Freda, the only girl, had become a crowd favorite. She'd already done a self-announced "Charleston," flipping her hands to the right, then left, scissoring her knees on the way down. Her "Dying Swan" had been more like a terminal lobster. Now she stood dripping near the edge of the dock, eyes red and watery, eyelashes braided, wool tunic sagging, concocting her next descent.

"What has that girl got on her head?" asked George.

"She should wear the daisy on the side, not dangling over her forehead," mused Agnes.

"Side, front, nothing's gonna help. It didn't become you either."

Ted Hoyt came to their window, mug in hand. "Maybe we'd better call a halt to this before someone gets hurt."

"We're all here watching," scoffed George.

"But what if they land on something?"

"It's at least 14 feet deep."

"You sure?"

"Of course, I'm sure, Ted. How else you gonna get ships into the dock?"

"But that current can get awfully strong."

"They'll be fine," said Agnes, cutting into her meatloaf. "Though they probably should keep their voices down. They forget it's Sunday."

That's when Freda shouted, "The *Tusca*-ninney!" and Agnes grinned. "Now what?"

With a twig for a baton, Freda stood at the edge of the wooden dock, double-tapped a dock cleat, and paused. Then she hurled herself at the sun while bellowing Beethoven's Fifth, though she'd have been hard pressed to name it. Unfortunately, she only got as far as a hurried "dadada dah, dadada dah" before meeting the surface on the downbeat. The applause, though hearty, had seriously dissipated by the time Freda finally resurfaced.

"Good, not great," said Agnes.

"Leg kind of bent," said George.

"Everything kind of bent."

But evaluations had to be cut short. Unlike Freda, Pat Dalton left little daylight between proclamation and execution. So with no ado, he called out "Reverse Frog!" did a four-step run-up, flung himself in the air backward, flayed his knees out in frog position and waved to the porch diners while plummeting out of view. He too was slow to return.

"That's the way," said George. "Brief and sassy."

"They say it can get up to eight miles," said Ted, still standing at the window.

"What?" asked George, knowing full well what.

"That current. I'd enjoy this more if they didn't stay down so long. How come they stay down so long?" asked Ted.

Agnes stared at George, unblinking; only her irises betrayed the roll.

"I hope they're not getting carried away. Are they getting carried away?"

"They'll be fine, Ted," said Agnes, with an eye on Tommy Ouellette as he approached dock center to introduce his dive. "They're strong swimmers." Then she looked to George. "What'd Tommy say?" she asked pointedly. "I missed it."

"'The Death Spiral,'" said George.

"Swell," said Ted.

Tommy took a running leap, folded his arms across his chest in mid-air, coffin-style, dangled his tongue from the corner of his mouth, and let his head loll sideways as he entered the water. Oh, the merriment. But once more the laughter had petered out by the time he reached the surface.

"How come they stay down so long?"

"Ted, you're making me a nervous wreck," said Agnes.

George tugged on her sleeve and pointed downriver. "Here comes Murph." Agnes leaned back and straddled her chair back with an elbow. A blue racing shell slid into view. The six-oared crew, their short-billed baseball caps worn backwards, their navy tank tops bisected diagonally by a yellow stripe, dipped their oars in unison, while Murph, the coxswain, faced them from the stern, urging them on by megaphone, calling out the strokes. Racing shells were a common sight along the river, with men and boys belonging to the many boat clubs—Ecorse, Wyandotte, Detroit—practicing for competitions. Murph now rowed for the high school he would be attending in the fall, Theodore Roosevelt in Wyandotte, because Ecorse was not only lacking a robust boat club but its educational system was lacking grades 11 and 12.

"Those racing shells are dangerous," said Ted returning to his corner stool. "Tippy canoe. Know what I mean? Freighter goes by, big wake. That's all it takes."

Agnes would not look at George; George could not look at Agnes, though there were one or two coughs.

With the shell nearly parallel to the State Street dock, the noggins of six oarsmen and their coxswain whipped left in unison when a roar went up on shore. It was Freda's turn once more. Solemnly, she sauntered away from the dock, trailing her faded bath towel along the dusty path—10 paces, 20 paces, slowly, slowly. Then turning, slowly, she posed—perpendicular, stiff—her fringed towel limp at her side. "The Matador!" she howled; then, still erect, she paused and winked at Shay. And when Shay stopped giggling and the spectators clammed up and the terns piped down, she raised one arm to signal "ready."

Then bravely, fearlessly, mixing her metaphor, Freda pawed the ground with each foot like an enraged bull, cocked her elbows and began to run, picking up speed, faster, elbows pumping, skinny legs ablur, stepping on a pebble, adding a limp to her lope, faster, limping out of land, soaring through the air, legs pumping, higher, arms whirling, daisy petals flogging the sky, entering the water with such a loud splat, a true bum buster, that the crowd groaned with the sting.

It was splendid. Water vacated the premises, splaying out in a great gush. Soon huge ringlets circled outward. Soon, the ringlets dissipated, then disappeared, replaced by the gentle undulations of the river. Soon, guests at the boathouse peered over the railing, searching the impenetrable blue-green expanse. Now the only sound was the shrill cry of gulls. All eyes scoured the area of entry; all eyes strained for a glimpse of the yellow daisy.

While Rum Row craned its neck, Agnes glanced nervously at George.

"You get Shay, I'll get Freda," he said, bolting from his chair, sending it clattering to the linoleum floor. But before he reached the door, an arm shot straight up out of the water, stretched high in salute, its skinny fist wrapped around victory—one cold, glistening, golden bottle of Cincinnati Cream Ale, Canada's own, its smiling-waiter cap intact. "Over here!" she yelled, in a youthful soprano. "There's crates and crates of 'em! Over here!" Freda had salvaged the long-sought first bottle of the day. Huzzahs all around!

Within seconds, the dredging began, known locally as "hauling the river." Distribution was swift, efficient. Bottle after bottle was exhumed from the sludge-bound bottom of Ecorse Bay, welcomed ashore by outstretched hands. Though money was never mentioned, most knew the going rate for a bottle of beer was 10 cents. In lieu of a till, Old Man Bourassa's ancient constable cap soon filled with bouncing nickels and dimes, then dollars with change taken. If asked what the money was for, all would have answered: the St. Francis Xavier School-Building Fund.

Ted came to the window again. "Those kids are gonna get into trouble. That's against the law."

"Kids've been diving off that dock for years," scoffed George. "You did, I did."

A yellow daisy planted itself in Walter Locke's walkup window, its petals flouncing, its voice high and outside. "Toldja there was a dump last night, Pa. Cousin Fern saw the boat from her window."

A sweet face, younger than Freda's, leaned into the window, its chin just above the counter. "It's true, Aunt Agnes. I could tell they dumped near the dock, cause I heard their engines stop. Pretty soon there's this banging and splashing."

Then Walter Locke eased over to the takeout window and talked low to Freda.

"Sure," said Freda. Withdrawing her elbow, she turned and headed toward the dock, Fern following. "Hey, Pat!" yelled Freda for the benefit of all of Wayne County. "Mr. Locke needs three beers!"

Freda was only in the rackets for a short time. Murph, Clayt, Tommy Ouellette, Barrett Lafferty, and Charlie Tank—in fact, most boys of a certain age—had been diving for almost four years. At the first sign of the Shore Patrol, bootleggers coming in for a landing would quickly jettison their cargo. If not, the Shore Patrol did it for them.

> "They'd just hit the case with an axe and throw the whole thing in," recalled Tommy Ouellette. "They had to axe wooden cases. Cause crates float." "But the jute bags are tied together at the top," noted Barrett Lafferty. "Like ears. So if you gotta dump 'em, you can come back later and dive for them and pull them up by their ears. They're not heavy 'til you get 'em to the surface, then someone in a boat can reach over and grab them and haul them in."

All along the river's shore, case after case, sack after sack, bottle after bottle, of Tecumseh Lager, Old Crow, King George whisky, Genevea gin and Gordon sherry wine would glide gently to the bottom and land on a pile of earlier arrivals.

In the future, hundreds of bottles would keep bobbing up whenever the river bed was stirred up by dredging. In the 1980s, when the owners of the Portside Inn added a boat slip next to their Wyandotte restaurant, the first scoop of the crane brought up the usual sludge and hundreds of bootlegged beer bottles. Some of those bottles now reside like trophies in the Wyandotte Historical Museum.

———————

"You know, George," said Agnes, impaling a green bean. "Ted could be right. They could get into trouble."

"With who?"

"With that guy." Agnes had caught sight of the man leaning against the hood of his car, watching. Not drinking, watching. The man had divested himself of coat jacket and tie; he had also produced a camera and was taking notes. "You know him?"

"No," said George. "But I should think the feds have more to do than pull in a bunch of kids diving."

"Never know," said Agnes.

"Freda knows the law. I made it very clear," he said, "If she finds a bottle, she can't own it, she can't sell it, she can't give it away. She can only set it on shore. If people help themselves, it has nothing to do with her, 'cause she doesn't own it, hasn't sold it, and hasn't given it away."

Agnes leaned back. "I agree the law's absurd, George, but how long do you think you can walk that line? It's pretty thin."

George didn't reply. He was too busy keeping his eye on the nameless man.

Before long, most of the Sunday promenaders had spread out along the banks of the river, some standing, some sitting, savoring their ice cold brew. Like most Americans in the 1920s, with new laws raining down on them in a steady drizzle, especially in Michigan, the citizens of Ecorse had to rewrite the moral code on the fly. Mrs. Whalen, who flaunted Prohibition with her nightly glass of sherry, would have been appalled if Seavitt's had opened on Sunday. Mrs. Seabrook, who was enjoying a refreshing swig, wouldn't be caught dead wearing white after Labor Day. Neither of them would think of flaunting societal restrictions, much less the Blue Laws. Not to say there was no loathing. Mr. and Mrs. Ralph Montrose and their daughter Ida watched the goings on with disgust.

"Felons all," muttered George, as he surveyed the waterfront, "felons all."

Agnes pointed to the takeout window. Walter grinned. The slender neck of a 12-ounce bottle was inching heavenward outside the walkup window. As it loomed, a small hand, barely clutching the bottle's mid-section, loomed with it. Carefully, the tiny hand piloted the bottle skyward until it cleared the sill. Success. One bottle of Cincinnati Cream, backlit by the sun, stood framed in Walter Locke's takeout window like an Etruscan vase.

Then the small hand went away.

Before long, another bottle snailed into view, conveyed by the same small hand, newly adroit after its brief apprenticeship.

The small hand went away.

Soon, a third bottle ascended. At labor's end, three Etruscan vases, color of mead, sat golden in the light, glistening beads of condensation trickling down their sides.

"And who do we have to thank for this?" asked Walter, folding his arms on the ledge and thrusting his upper torso through the takeout window. "Why, if it isn't Shirley Moore."

"Oops," said George.

"Oops, indeed," said Agnes, who was cocking an ear to hear what the voice outside was saying.

Walter turned to Agnes. "She said her sister Freda, umm, said ta ast Ma ta ast Pa, umm, if she could, umm, have some chips."

Agnes laughed. "Ask her if she finished her sandwich."

Walter thrust his head back out the window, pulled it back in and turned to Agnes. "She nodded."

"All right," said Agnes.

Walter reached under the counter for a small paper sack, filled it with chips from a glass jar, folded the sack to seal it, and dangled it over the ledge, "There you are, Shirley."

Half-standing, Agnes caught a glimpse of Shay as she dragged the Moore wagon, now empty except for a bag of chips, back onto the path. "Well, George," said Agnes, settling in her seat. "Guess you forgot to tell your four-year-old she can't own it, sell it, or give it away."

Walter wedged the three bottles between the fingers of one hand, "Here we go," and set them on the counter. Reaching below, he brought up four glasses and began to pour. "Ernie, George, Agnes. Sure you won't have one, Ted?"

"I still say it's against the law."

Walter glanced over at the man resting against his car as he delivered the beer. George raised his glass toward Agnes. "To 21 years," he said. "God willing and the creek don't rise, to 100 more."

Agnes returned the salute, then waited for the foam to subside before taking a sip. Both sat back, George with a satisfied "ah" while Agnes watched as the speck of Murph's shell needled through the water, passing a fishing boat as it headed toward the north end of Fighting Island. She did wonder idly why they were so far out. Generally, scullers hugged the shore.

Thwack! The screen door banged open and a wicker baby carriage reared up, preparing to pounce. Ernie Boudreau shot off his stool to hold the door, while Agnes guided the carriage in, Rowe attached to its handle. Parking the carriage near the table, Agnes set the foot brake and checked the baby beneath the gray-enameled hood. Eight-month-old Marcia Jean Moore, already seasoned by her sisters, slept peacefully within.

"You've really got to be more careful with Mrs. Strassner's carriage," said Agnes, returning to her seat.

"Mrs. Strassner's carriage?" laughed George. "What about our kid?"

Rowe flopped down next to Agnes. "I'm glad everyone's having such a good time."

"What's up, Auntie?" asked George.

"Marie Jaeger was just at our house."

"So."

"So. Marie Jaeger knows something we don't."

"And what is that?" asked Agnes.

Rowe reached into the carriage and solemnly pulled out a thin newspaper from beneath Marce's light crib blanket. "It's in this week's *Ecorse Tribune* ." After solemnly spreading it on the table, she began to read: "'School notes.'" But no one was listening. George, on his part, was staring at the counter, specifically at the bottom tier of the three-tier dessert holder. Agnes was scouring the bay for Murph's shell which, oddly enough, had suddenly disappeared, though the fishing boat still lazed near the tip of Fighting Island.

"Can you see Murph?" she asked. "His boat was there just a minute ago."

George stood up and looked out the back porch window. "Not to worry; he'll be coming back this way in short order."

"But he was so far out."

"SCHOOL NOTES," said Rowe, gazing sternly above her wire-rimmed glasses. Agnes squared her shoulders; George laced his fingers on the table in front of him. Both nodded compliantly. "'There will be a PTA meeting on September 1,'" read Rowe. "'The matter of relieving the congestion in the 10-grade system of the Ecorse schools will be discussed.'"

"I had no idea school congestion was a cause of yours, Auntie," said George.

"It isn't. This is." Rowe read very slowly. (When it came to moment milking, Rowe was the family record-holder, hands-down) "Miss Mae Munn, 2700 Richton Avenue, Detroit, 6th-grade teacher and principal at School One, has been named the new principal of School Three for the 1926-1927 term." Rowe's wire rims rose above the paper as she concentrated on her parents for the expected reaction. But they had no reaction. In fact, there was no movement of any kind, except for a slight ruffling of Agnes's hair by a breeze. Perhaps, they hadn't understood. Rowe clarified. "Miss Munn's gonna be principal of School Three next year, not this year. Miss Munn's gonna be principal of School One for another year."

Agnes pushed her plate to the center of the table. "Did you tell Freda?"

"No, I wanted to tell you first," said Rowe.

"Go tell Freda," said Agnes.

Rowe had barely cleared the threshold before George muttered, "If I never hear that woman's name again..." then trailed off. There'd been a coolness between them ever since he had ordered Rowe back to school to apologize.

"What are we going to do, George?"

"There's not much we can do."

"But if Miss Munn's still principal, she's going to be all over Freda."

"Then Freda can't miss school."

Agnes might have had a rejoinder for that if she hadn't drifted off with a "Poor Freda" as she watched her oldest daughter bound up the dock ladder, towel off, and beckon Rowe who was walking toward her. Freda seemed to be talking a mile a minute, pointing to the salvage operation, filling Rowe in. Rowe said nothing, just held out the newspaper. Puzzled, Freda took the paper and began to read.

She at long last looked up. All joy had vanished from her face. She walked trancelike to the Rickenbacker, eased herself down on the running board next to Shay, and read the news once more. Then Freda peeled off her bathing cap, ran her fingers through her blunt-cut hair, determined to stop the slight tremor in her chin. She reached down for her shoes that had been placed under the running board of the car; lingered there, head bowed, clamping each shoe on and buckling it, without bothering to brush off the soles of her feet.

Shay extended the wax-paper bag toward Freda, but Freda didn't seem to notice. Instead, she got up, tightened the lid on the thermos jug and set it in the wagon, picked up the used paper cups and set them in the wagon, then took Shay by the hand and headed for home.

"Hey, Freeds, what's up?" yelled Tommy Ouellette. But she didn't seem to hear him and kept on walking.

Meanwhile, Rowe returned to the diner to fetch the baby. Without a word, she steered the carriage out the screen door with the aid of Walter Locke and hurried to catch up to Freda. Agnes did not rise to help; she just sat there, staring at the bag of chips left on the running board of the car.

When Walter Locke arrived at their table, pitcher in hand, Agnes leaned away until he had refilled the water glasses and was out of earshot, before saying, with some hesitation, "You know, George. There might be an alternative."

"I'll take it."

"We could send Freda and Rowe to St. Francis."

George stared at her in disbelief. "I thought you said an 'alternative.'"

"That's my alternative."

"That's no alternative. What about the tuition? We're barely making it now."

"I know."

George sighed. Agnes's alternative, St. Francis Xavier School (grades 1-8), had opened its doors the previous fall. Agnes had been thinking about it for months, but knew it would be nearly impossible to convince George to go along.

"I'm not trying to be a hardhead, Agnes," said George, shaking his head, "but we can't afford that. We really can't. I'll bet it's at least 50 cents a month."

"I think it's a dollar," said Agnes.

"A month?"

"Yes."

"For each!"

"Keep your voice down."

"Be still, my heart," mumbled George. He leaned in and whispered. "That's $24 a year. Hell, Ag, I'm lying awake now trying to figure out how to pay the bills. It's Rowe's turn for shoes, where's that coming from? We've got nothing in the bank. And what about that new stove you've been talking about."

"I'll do without it."

"Then you'll want Joyce to go, I suppose. Then Dia, then Shay, then Marce. I don't know if I've brought you up to snuff lately, Aggie, but in the war between my razor and Mr. Gillette's, his little at-home blade is winning. Which means in the very near future, I won't be making more money each year, I'll be making less.

"But the shop's always full."

"Not with paying customers," George shot back. "$24 a year to avoid Miss Munn. It makes no sense."

Agnes was quiet. "I know it's asking a lot."

"A lot? Ag, you've got to help me here. I can hardly breathe as it is."

Agnes leaned in, her voice low, solemn. "I need Freda, George. There are days I really need her. I try to keep it to a minimum, but some days I'm so exhausted. . . . But if she misses school now with that woman in charge, it'll be hell on Freda and hell on me. Yes, and hell on you."

"Maybe Freda should just quit school."

"I don't want her to quit school. I thought there could be a compromise."

"There is a compromise, Ag. Just ignore the woman. Let her complain. Just ignore her."

Agnes exploded. "Did you ignore her when she came to you about Rowe?" Then she softened her tone. "Oh, George, don't you see, it's so unfair. Freda stays home to help me and gets in trouble for it. Granted, she's not a good student, but she's a solid kid—kind, reliable. It's painful to see her so belittled." George examined his middle knuckle. "You're the one that hates injustice." Silence. "Well, this is injustice." Silence. "Okay. Fine. She'll continue to use my children for her needs, while my needs don't count."

George reluctantly glanced up at her. Then: "I'm considering running for village president this fall. Whaddya think?" Agnes stared at him blankly. Then she picked up her napkin and began to refold it into a tidy triangle, running her hand along the fold to secure the crease.

"I suppose you don't think I'm good enough," he said. "I thought I did a decent job as village marshal. At least you thought so at the time." Agnes refolded her napkin into smaller and smaller triangles, running her hand along each fold. "So am I to assume you think it's a bad idea?" Agnes reopened the napkin and began to fold it once more. As she did, she glimpsed a Federal boat patrolling the shoreline; parallel to it was Murph's shell, coming back downriver. At least, one thing was going right.

"Do you think you can beat Bouchard?" she asked, ice in her tone.

"Obviously, you don't."

"I didn't say that."

"You haven't said anything."

"What do you want me to say?"

"You could say I'd make a good president."

She put down her napkin and looked him straight in the eye. "Why on earth would you want to take on all this Prohibition nonsense?"

"Don't you see, it would mean a little more money. $500 more a year to be exact." Agnes abandoned the napkin. "I'd have to win, of course, and the girls would have to start at School One, but Bouchard's getting pretty old, I might have a chance."

"But you won't know until next March," said Agnes. "What good would that do?"

"Might be good for a second-term transfer."

Vrooom! With a deafening roar and a blur of varnished mahogany, a speedboat, the length of a bus, rounded the north end of Fighting Island, streaked across the water, and thundered past.

"What the hell was that?" yelled Ted over the din.

"Clarence DeWallot," laughed Walter.

Ted cupped his ear. "What?"

"Clarence DeWallot!" yelled Walter. "He bought the *Miss America II*, Gar

Wood's racer ."

"Clayt rode in it," said Ernie. "That sucker can whip across to Canada in about one minute. Set the world speedboat record."

As the wake from the hydroplane began to reach shore, the Federal patrol boat monitoring the shoreline revved its engine and took off in lame pursuit.

Ted was incredulous. "He's using it for bootlegging?"

"What else?" said Ernie. "Clayt says he can make around $50,000 a week with that boat. It can haul 100 cases at a time."

"In broad daylight?"

"Why not, those guys can't catch him," said Ernie. "That thing can go 80 miles an hour."

While the hydroplane slipped through the chop, giving other boats wide berth as it sped toward Grassy Island, the feds bounced along, slamming against each wave. Lagging far behind, the four young men in the patrol boat steered a straight line across the bay, cutting so close to Murph & Co. that a gusher of river water rained down on the shell. While coxswain and crew hung on to the gunnels of their boat as it rocked with the wake, the men in the patrol boat continued the chase with nary a lookback.

"Hooligans," muttered George in disgust. "Punks."

His wife said nothing. Instead, she sat stock-still, waiting for Murph's swaying boat to right itself. Fortunately, Agnes was spared a closer view. She didn't know, and those ashore could not see, that the boat her son was riding in was no sleek affair, though it looked graceful, even handsome, from afar. It was a practice racer that on closer inspection was slightly chipped, slightly warped, and slightly leaky. Especially since the shell was riding even lower than usual, what with the 24-bottle sack of Old Crow stowed beneath Murph and the 12-bottle liquor sacks stowed under the legs of all six rowers.

There had been some talk of jettisoning the cargo, but the thought of losing the $35 load, at $5 a sack, was dispiriting. Besides, argued Murph, it would be hard to jettison in full view of dockside spectators, and racing shells were hard to come by. Instead, while three bailed and four manned the oars, they limped cautiously back to the tiny inlet behind the Alkali plant in Wyandotte, where they kept the scull under a clump of bushes. This was their third trip that day.

"Anyone for dessert?" interrupted Walter, arriving at the table.

George looked at Agnes; she shook her head. "Just the check, Walter," said George.

Dinner was over and they knew it. So was the movie. So was the afternoon, with not much hope for the evening.

As for the fella with the camera who had abandoned his car for a better look, Tommy Ouellette took care of him.

"Two of us quit divin' and we went over and we let all the air out of his tires. Come to find out it was a Detroit News reporter."

Chapter 9

Saturday, October 24, 1925

Saturday, October 24, 1925, was a big day for the Moores. Weeks earlier, Rowe had barreled home to tell her mother that she'd won a spelling bee. You could hear her big bazoo coming all the way up the alley. "What kind of a spelling bee," Agnes had asked, more intent on steering a straight course on the Singer then wholly listening. But it wasn't just any spelling bee. Rowe had won the *Detroit News* Metropolitan Spelling Bee with the word "quire."

> *"Oh, she got so excited; you should have heard her," said Rowe in the autumn of her years. "Mumma went out on the porch and told Mrs. Strassner: 'Rowe won the Detroit News spelling bee.' I got a tour of the News building and a whopping big Rand McNally Dictionary. Still have it in the basement; it's all unglued."*

And now, that day at four, Rowe was to be officially acknowledged at the Mother-Daughter Banquet, sponsored by the PTA, to be held at School One. And Freda, now a classmate of Rowe's, would be standing with the honorees for perfect attendance in the first quarter. Washdays had become a nightmare for Agnes, but she was pleased for Freda. It would do her good to get some praise.

Even Murph was involved. Months before, he'd promised. Now the day was at hand; he was bellyaching at breakfast, crying into his Cream of Wheat. Agnes, who was standing over the counter, forcefully mashing ripe bananas, interrupted him mid-grouse.

"Tell me again why you made that promise?"

"Because she cornered me on High Street and asked me to."

Agnes turned to him in dismay. "Can't anyone in this family say no to that woman?"

"That'd be impolite."

"You could have given her an excuse. You could have told her you were busy."

"Three months in advance?"

"But you're not even in the Ecorse School System anymore. She shouldn't have asked you."

"Try and tell *her* that," he said, as he smeared butter on his third piece of toast, then took a bite.

"Anyway, it's good of you to help," said Agnes, rinsing off the masher, sorting through her thoughts. "What time do you have to be there?"

"Not 'til seven."

Agnes twisted off the tap, her back still to him. "You know, if you're late, she'll be proved right, don't you?"

It took Murph a second to catch her drift. "Don't worry, Mum," he said. "I won't be late."

Agnes wasn't so sure. Murph, who had faithfully chronicled school doings for the *Ecorse Tribune* while at School Three ("*The P.T.A. of School No. 3 was very well attended, and the programs by the pupils of the school were enjoyed by everyone...* —Melvin Moore, *Ecorse Tribune*, April 3, 1924") had also willingly folded tables for three years running, never missed. But on this particular day it made her nervous. Because this boy sitting before her, downing a mill hand's breakfast, bore no relation to that boy. Not even the same name. That boy, who began life as George Melvin Moore and was called Melvin to avoid confusion with his father, had ambled into the house the previous autumn, announced that he was now to be known as Murphy, strolled into his bedroom and closed the door. Eventually this boy had come out, though rarely. So rarely, in fact, that George had taken to calling him "star boarder" and his bedroom the "duchy." Melvin Moore could charm the pants off a pipefitter; Murphy Moore saved his charm for his pals. Though Agnes still caught glimmers of her former son—in his humor, his smile, his less frequent pecks on her cheek—this boy was more often a prickly pear, a kid-glove kind of kid.

George was even more disheartened. "He used to like to be with us," he had said a few nights previous. "He thought we were the cat's meow."

"That's because he used to like us," summed up Agnes.

Unlike George, however, Agnes had somehow maintained a bridge across the great divide. Still, at the risk of ruining a benign moment, she whirled round to face him. "What about last night?"

"Las' nigh'?" he asked, mouth full of toast.

"Yes, last night. What time did you get in?"

"My usual time."

"And what was that?"

"'Leven," he choked.

"Try again."

He coughed to clear his pipes. "11:15?" Agnes gazed at him, arms crossed, back resting against the sink. "Would you accept 11:30?" he asked.

"Nope."

He smiled sheepishly. "Still up, were you?"

"Yep."

"How's about midnight?"

"Not yet nodding off," replied Agnes.

"I've an idea," he said, grin like a Cheshire. "Why don't you tell me what time you think it was, and I'll tell you if you're far off."

Agnes laughed and unfolded her arms. "Nice try."

"What time did Pa get to sleep?"

"Fortunately for you, about 11:15."

"So 11:15's our story, eh?"

"He wants you in the door by 11 on weekends, Murph. We both do. You know how upset he gets."

"I'll do better, Mum. Promise."

"Does that go for tonight?"

"Tonight?"

"Being there by seven, OK? That's all I ask." She stared at him, imploring. "I'm serious, Murph. This is important to me."

Murph was stunned by how vulnerable she looked, a wisp of hair that had eluded her topknot now framing her cheek. At that very moment he felt great warmth toward her, because Murph, for all his outward toughness, had the same soft center as had her former son.

"Don't worry," he said. "I won't let you down."

———————

That afternoon, as the wall clock struck three, Murph lowered his *College Humor* magazine, peered intently out the drugstore window and whispered like a gangster apprentice, "Of all the places we coulda met, why'd they hafta pick here?"

"They said they had business in the alley," murmured Clayt.

It was a slow day at Seavitt's. While Louie Seavitt filled a prescription behind a glass partition in the back and the counter girl dozed standing up, a customer was sitting alone at the marble lunch counter, crumbling an oyster cracker into her pea soup. Murph and Clayt were hanging around the magazine rack, thumbing through October issues. Louie Seavitt had long ago given them the eye.

Murph restored the magazine to its shelf, then rifled the pages of a *Saturday Evening Post*. "Yeah, but why here?" he asked a Pond's Cold Cream ad.

"For the last time, Murph, I don't know."

"Well, for Pete's sake, didn't ya even try to talk 'em out of it!" muttered Murph.

Clayt, who was squinting out the window, took a step back, apprehensive. "Here they come." Two men, serious faces, were walking up the path from Hogan's Alley. "The guy in the peacoat's Peajacket," said Clayt. "The thinner one's Bauer."

"Geez, don'tcha think I know that?" griped Murph, returning the *Post* to its slot. He gave a guilty glance toward the pharmacist, a follow-me nod to Clayt, and was nearly to the entrance when he wavered, whirled round and showered coins on the counter. "Here's 35 cents for the *Post* , Mr. Seavitt. Seeing as I read most of it."

"Don't you want the magazine?" asked Louie Seavitt from the back.

"Naw, give it to some kid." And Murph was out the door and down the steps before the drugstore bell stopped jangling.

"Everything jake?" asked Peajacket.

"Yep," replied Murph.

"Then follow us." And Peajacket set off up Front Street with Charlie Bauer, while the boys trailed in lockstep.

Murph pulled the collar up on his plaid Mackinaw and leaned in to Clayt, mumbling through locked lips, "Please tell me nobody's sitting on the barber-shop bench."

"Nope, all clear," said Clayt, after a backward glance. "But Mrs. Gregory just went into Seavitt's and gave us the once over."

"Swell," sighed Murph.

As the foursome paused in front of the Ecorse State Bank, waiting for an opening in traffic, music drifted from the waterside of Front. A door opened, a young couple exited the Polar Bear Café, and Murph flinched. It was hard on a kid to parade through a town where everyone knew his father. They also knew Joe "Peajacket" Wozniak, who was a Horatio Alger story around Ecorse. It was commonly known that the World War I vet had risen to the top of his profession; it was also commonly known what that profession was.

The block between State and Bourassa was the tag end of the business section, where trade and private homes mingled. As they passed Pilon's grocery, where Ernie Boudreau and Alex Bourassa were sitting on the stoop, deep in conversation, Murph pulled his slouch cap lower and walked on the outside, hip to hip with Clayt.

Peajacket, around 40 with a pleasant face, slowed down to let the boys catch up; Bauer, with his mid-parted, slicked-back hair, continued on ahead.

"Ever buy from LaSalle docks before?" asked Peajacket as they neared Bourassa.

"No, how's it work?" asked Murph.

"It's strictly cash and carry," explained Peajacket. "Alls you gotta do is phone Canada and place an order. It'll be waiting at the export docks."

"Who do you call?"

"Take your pick. There's Walkerville Brewery in Windsor, Calvert's in Amherstburg, Hoffer's in LaSalle."

"How do you get the phone numbers?"

Charlie Bauer whipped round and sneered, "The phone book!" Just then an old putt-putt of a Chevy with a Klaxon horn was coming up Bourassa; it *ah-oogahed* and pulled up short, idling in the middle of the side street.

"Wait here," said Peajacket. Like well-trained pups, the boys stood on the curb as Peajacket and Bauer sauntered over to the car and chatted with the driver. Something amusing must have been said because the driver gave the curbed youths a smirk before driving directly across Front Street, heading toward the water. Murph followed the car's course as it pulled into the large backyard of Ty Washell's boathouse Ty was actively engaged in the trade.

Now it was Clayt who was on high alert. The block between Bourassa and White was Riopelle country. They strolled past the home of Clayt's Uncle Charlie, then past the home of his Uncle Harry. On the other side of the street a cluster of men crowded around the first boathouse to be seen on Front. That's where Rum Row made its main-street debut, where the river met the road. It was a ragged chorus line of cottages—all shapes, all faiths, all sitting on 20-foot-wide half lots with gaps in between.

As the foursome strolled on, veering right at White, the boys kept their eyes peeled behind and ahead. Two doors down from Joe Riopelle's boathouse, just past Simmy Davis's Doll House, was Harry Riopelle's Marine Works, a low slung, dark warehouse tucked between the boathouses.

Murph could only hope that they'd be crossing over to the waterside soon, because this area was infested with his mother's relatives, all LeBlancs. They passed the home of Uncle Frank (her uncle), which sat across from the tiny boathouse owned by Uncle Syl (her brother), and were nearing the home of Uncle Peck (her other brother). Murph glanced nervously ahead to Peck's large side yard. Though there was no sign of Peck, he could see Uncle Syl sitting outside at the back of the property. Fortunately for Murph, that's where Peajacket chose to cut across the street, heading for the boathouse with the half-moon arch over the front door, and even though Syl was blind, Murph scooted across behind Peajacket, mingling in the center of the group.

"Doesn't this belong to Fred LeBlanc?" asked Murph.

"Right, I'm renting it," said Peajacket, descending the four steps, unlocking the front door. "I'll warn ya ahead; my boat's nothing to brag about." He led them into the darkened interior, across the remains of a well-trodden carpet patterned with oil stains, and through an arch to the boat well, where blades of light filtered through the wallboards.

Charlie grabbed a nearby rope and hoisted the riverside portal, letting in full light. Clayt gasped. There, lolling lazily in its berth, nose forward, was a sleek, 26-foot Chris-Craft runabout, all ping and polish, its Philippine mahogany hull varnished to a reddish glow. Its nickel-plate fittings—handles, rails, cleats and cowls—were boastful and beaming; its thin-planked decking was caulked white, exaggerating the sleekness of its seven-foot bow. And on its bow, in loving script, the name *Mamie*.

Peajacket grinned. "Just got it. Whaddya think?"

Clayt could barely swallow. "She's a beaut," he croaked. "A real beaut."

"Musta set you back a mint," said Murph, stepping backward, hands deep in pockets. "What kinda engine this got?"

"Six-cylinder Kermath," said Peajacket, freeing the port bow line and tossing it into the two-row cockpit, big enough to seat six. "225 horsepower. Cruises at 25 knots, but I can get up to 40." He clambered in and slid behind the wheel, "Grab them other lines, would ya?"

Charlie undid the starboard line, lowered himself into the front passenger seat, then grabbed the dock to steady the boat. Walking round to the other side of the well, Clayt tossed in the port stern line and climbed gingerly in the back. Murph, starboard stern line in hand, took two swift steps and flopped clumsily onto a cushion.

"All set?" asked Peajacket, turning the key in the ignition. The engine gave a perfunctory spit and sputter to clear its throat, then settled into a velvet purr. Peajacket threw the gear stick in reverse; the boat lurched. Then, hand on throttle, he swiveled round to see the river, backputted out of the well, swung about, shifted forward, and they were underway, all eyes solemn and straight ahead on a northerly course.

That's when Murph sank back into the upholstery of supple leather, rested his right elbow on the padded armrest, and with his left, gave Clayt a joyous poke in the ribs. Clayt gleefully poked back. Then Murph pointed to the wool lap robes draped over shiny rails on the back of each front seat. Then Clayt, with a slight flick of the head, directed Murph's attention forward to the ornate instrument panel, with its amperes, Fahrenheit, and oil dials, and dropped an exaggerated jaw.

Then Murph leaned over the front seat, elbows splayed. "Really is a nice boat!" he yelled. "Is this from the, ah, proceeds?"

"Could say that," replied Peajacket, wind making spaghetti of his hair.

"Who trained you?"

"Trained myself," said Peajacket, yelling into the wind. "I rowed across the first time with five bucks, got two bottles, parlayed that into a case, parlayed that into two cases; got a better boat, parlayed that. Now I've got 25 guys working for me. Didn't take long."

"How long?"

"Couple years."

Murph pressed his knee into Clayt's knee and held it there. "How much can you make in a load?" he yelled.

"Depends on the size of your wad, size of your boat," Peajacket shouted, his wrist flopped over the wheel, his right ear turned slightly toward Murph. "Decent whiskey costs $20 a case. We can double it, turn it around for $40. The Good Stuff—like Old Log Cabin—sells for $30, $35 a case; we can sell the same case for $175 to $180."

"How much can boats hold?"

"Varies. Luggers can hold 500 cases, some can hold a 1,000. Mind you, we aren't making that much," said Peajacket. "There are expenses."

"Expenses?"

"Maintenance. Salaries. Payoffs. Property loss. Rate of exchange. Right now $1,000 U.S. can only buy $850 worth of booze in Canada."

"So . . . after expenses?"

"Oh, you'd probably clear around $10,000."

Murph leaned back in shock. $10,000! If you were lucky, Ford was paying $5 a day; $1,000 a year. $10,000! With $10,000 you could buy Cincinnati. Not that you'd want it. Murph couldn't look at Clayt; Clayt couldn't look at Murph. Both were trembling with excitement. That is, until Charlie Bauer turned round and said with half-curled lip and a Texas drawl, "One question. Where you bums gonna git your bankroll?"

You'd be surprised, thought Murph. There were a number of ways for the youth of Ecorse to pick up pocket change during the 1920s. Soda jerking was common, so was clerking at Kresge's. Delivery was a popular industry. Kids delivered milk, newspapers, groceries, bribes, hush money, payoffs to Prohibition agents and warnings to bootleggers. Being a sentry paid well. So did signaling, spying, whistling and ratting. The going rate for flinging the *Ecorse Advertiser* on or near an Ecorse porch was a buck a week. The going rate for sitting atop a boathouse on the lookout for feds was $3 to $5 an hour. Most years youthful tattletales reaped nothing but enmity from their peers, but during Prohibition the right kind of snitching could reap celebrity and a five spot.

These were not youth on the fringe. There were bootlegging apprentices in civics class, Glee Club, on the debate and football teams. They sang in the choir, served as altar boys, agonized over homework, and fretted about dates. Tommy Ouellette would later boast that bootlegging put him through college.

For Murph, it had started out easy enough, at 14.

"Hey, kid, wanna make a couple bucks?"

"Sure."

"Can you whistle 'Macushla'?"

"Huh?"

"Alls ya gotta do is hang around this dock for the next half hour. If you see the law, whistle 'Macushla.'"

"For a couple of bucks?"

"Yeah."

"That's all I gotta do?"

"Yeah."

In fact, he and Clayt had been on "Macushla" duty at the State Street dock the day Ben Montie was killed.

But now the lads were looking to diversify. They were getting sick of "Macushla." As they neared the State Street dock, Peajacket swerved starboard toward Canada and gunned the throttle. Instantly, the boat reared up, and they charged across Ecorse Bay, boat bouncing, spray flying, heading toward the northern tip of Fighting Island, its red buoy swaying in the distance.

With the engine too loud for talk, they turned away from each other and stared into the wind. Murph gave one last look back at Ecorse's reedy shoreline, and the long row of boathouses that gave the town a jaunty look. He checked his watch; it was 3:12 p.m. Five minutes to cross, 15 minutes to load, 5 minutes back, 15 minutes to unload, 10 minutes for small talk, 10 minutes for horsing around. He'd be back by 4:30 easy; at the worst, 5:00. Time enough for a nap, bath, dinner and a change of clothes before dealing with Miss Munn. He sat back to enjoy the ride and Clayt felt one last poke.

A nutty aroma had just drifted out of the cracked kitchen window from the second house on Monroe Street. Mrs. Ouellette caught a whiff. "Banana nut bread," she told the passing Mrs. Gregory, who was just returning from Seavitt's, having refilled a prescription. "Agnes Moore is making banana nut bread."

"Maybe we could pop in," laughed Mrs. Gregory.

"I'd give it about ten more minutes," cautioned Mrs. Ouellette.

Agnes was thinking the same thing as she pulled open the oven door, faced away from the heat, and stuck a toothpick in a loaf; it came back with crumbs. "Not quite yet," she said to Freda who was pressing a white dress on an ironing board near the back door.

Agnes had volunteered two loaves for the banquet. Since three were almost as easy as two, and since George was fond of telling pals he'd married her for her banana nut bread, three loaves were now snugly in the oven at 330 degrees.

Agnes had spent the morning measuring, mashing and trying to shake a mood, one she had kept from Murph. Though she tried not to let on, she was stewing - had been since yesterday - ever since she'd learned that Rowe had been hauled out of class by Miss Munn to oversee chicken preparation for the banquet.

On hearing this, Agnes was livid. If daily attendance at school was so all-fired important, what was Rowe doing missing Civics to gut chickens? In the interest of education, Miss Munn had effectively stopped Freda from helping Agnes on washdays, but she'd turned Rowe into her personal handmaiden. And what was with Murph and the stacking of tables?

Agnes Moore's attitude toward education was generational. When she was growing up, school, at least high school, was a luxury. She had attended kindergarten on the same corner of High and Labadie as her children, but then it was only a small frame building, not the substantial eight-room brick built in 1912 known as School One. In the fall of 1895, when Agnes was 11 and just starting 6th, her mother became seriously ill. She would die two years later. Since Agnes had to care for her mother and three siblings, her attendance was spotty at best. Then Agnes, like most of her class, left school at the end of 8th grade. George had only gone as far as the 6th.

But Agnes's thinking regarding the value of school had evolved, and on this, the day of the Mother-Daughter Banquet, she was determined to hold her tongue, to spare her children embarrassment, to steer clear of Miss Munn.

Agnes opened the oven door, brushed back the heat, stuck a toothpick in a loaf and it came back clean. "Perfect," she murmured.

———————

It was a fairly straight shot from Ecorse to the LaSalle docks in Ontario; they pretty much faced each other. At least, it would have been a straight shot if the northern tip of Fighting Island had not insinuated itself. As it was, boaters from Ecorse had to curve around the island to get to the Canadian docks. But there was no complaint, for Fighting Island sat like a five-mile privacy fence between the two nations, providing a convenient curtain from prying U.S. binoculars.

Within one minute from the Ecorse shore, the crew of the sumptuous *Mamie* had traversed the Fighting Island Shipping Channel and the international boundary line. Once across the lesser used Canadian Shipping Channel, Peajacket slowed to a putt. It was mostly marsh ahead, a wall of feathergrass and thickets. But the marsh was misleading. All along the sleepy LaSalle shore, there were barely concealed waterways cutting through the tall grass, a labyrinth of canals, coves and creeks.

The river bottom came up abruptly, from 30 to 4 feet. Off to port they were flanked by eel grass, its ribbon-like stems straining to reach the surface, dimpling the water in shallower spots. A flotilla of black and white buffleheads, known locally as butterball ducks, rode the boat's gentle wake, plunging their heads beneath the water, causing their feathery rears to bob up.

No longer required to yell, Murph leaned forward, "Do you just pull into a slip and tell 'em your order? They ever give you a hard time?"

Charlie turned round and snapped, "Just watch; learn by doing. And keep yer mouths shut. Got that?"

"Yeah, I got that," said Murph who, caught off guard by the rebuff, clammed up.

Dead ahead, tucked in the marshes, sat the LaSalle Export Docks. "Here we go, my lovelies," said Peajacket. "Toss out the fenders."

With the motor sputtering, he eased *Mamie* past the first canal. Since it could partially be seen from the north end of Ecorse, it was not the most popular for loading. Instead, Peajacket entered the second canal, navigating between two bulkheads. On their starboard side, in front of a small customs hut built on the end of a pier, a man was casually leaning over a railing, eyeballing *Mamie* and her guests. He was all military: epaulets, chevrons, a small gold badge on his banded collar, and a triangular patch on his arm with the letters O.P.P. Murph, who well knew that O.P.P. meant Ontario Provincial Police, would ordinarily be on his second chorus of "Macushla" by now.

———————

In the first four years of Prohibition, Rum Row referred to a string of off-shore ocean vessels, bellies lined with booze, which were anchored three miles out in the Atlantic, facing the East Coast. They had positioned themselves just outside America's territorial waters, making them boarding-proof and seizure-proof. That's where Bill McCoy, one of the captains of those vessels, found fame, with his guaranteed, genuine 100% liquor, "the real McCoy." Bootleggers from Boston to New York supplied most of the nation from the ships of Rum Row, sending out fast motorboats, loading up, ferrying about 100,000 cases of contraband per month back to U.S. shores. It was only a five-minute dash each way—scoot out, scoot in—giving Coast Guard cutters little time to spot them, much less head them off. But in 1924, the Coast Guard added 20 destroyers to its fleet. Then, following hours of diplomatic negotiations, the U.S. extended the international boundary line from 3 to 12 miles, causing the liquored fleet to haul anchor and steam farther out, allowing a Coast Guard cutter plenty of time to spot a speeding motorboat and bear down on it. As a result, by the summer of 1925, East Coast's Rum Row was barely paying its way.

With Rum Row effectively shut down, the narrow-waisted Detroit River, specifically the Windsor-Detroit area, was now the major spigot for thirsty Americans. There were about 30 government-licensed export docks along a 15 mile span on the Detroit River, 50 if you were calculating the river's entire 31 mile stretch. Some were run by the Canadian government, some privately, and some by the distillery. The Windsor docks were the largest. Hiram Walker's distillery owned 1,400 feet of waterfront directly across from downtown Detroit. In LaSalle, there were the Rock Springs slip, the Carling slip, the Walkerville slip, Hoffer's slip—different slips owned by different distillers for different brews.

So in the autumn of 1925, as Mrs. Ouellette raked leaves, Agnes baked banana bread, and Murph cruised on *Mamie*, some 70% of the illicit liquor entering the United States was coming over or under that 31-mile river. By 1930, as cited in a Coast Guard Intelligence Report (RG26), it would be 80%.

Throttling down, Peajacket gave the wheel a firm turn to port and glided into a slip, while Charlie Bauer jumped onto the dock and looped the bow line around a weathered piling. An OPP officer leaned down and caught the stern line from Murph, who leapt onto the catwalk, offered Clayt a friendly hand and nearly yanked him out of the boat.

Charlie gave a sulky look round, retucked his shirt, and restraightened his tie before walking over to the boys. "Now, y'all follow me and keep yer traps shut," he said, low-voiced. "Go along with everthang I say or do. Got that?"

Murph looked away, disgusted. "Yeah, I got that." Goodtime Charlie was getting on his nerves.

It was busy on the landside promontory where a cluster of one-story warehouses with large bay doors fronted a common yard. Bauer walked toward the nearest warehouse, where a truck, filled to the top of its slatted sides with wooden cases, was being unloaded. By Murph's hasty estimate, there were about 200 cases in that truck, all stamped "Walkerville Brewery Limited, Walkerville, Ontario, Canada." Another truck turned off Laurier Road and bounced noisily into the fenced-in yard, banging over the muddy ruts from yesterday's rain, its cargo of sacks shifting and clinking. Two men, who came out of a second warehouse to meet it, slid a set of bay doors to each side, revealing the stuffed interior, where wooden cases, casks, and burlap sacks were piled to the ceiling.

Charlie opened an office door, waited sullenly for the boys to catch up, and with a humorless sweep of the arm, ushered them into a dingy, windowless room that smelled of must. A smattering of wall art adorned the darkened walls: a poster of the ubiquitous Union Jack; a water-stained photo of the king of England, handsome mustache over pointed beard, hand resting on the hilt of his sword; and a wallboard ad that recommended Canadian Club "to our American Visitors."

Murph was quick to spot the Mountie in the corner reading a newspaper, his back to the stove that was helping to ward off the outside temperature of 41° F. The Mountie had glanced up as they entered but, doubtlessly seeing nothing of import, returned to his *Windsor Star* . Charlie casually advanced toward the counter that split the room in two. Murph, feeling anything but casual, barely made it to the counter, then sprawled across it, resting his forearms on its dusty surface, partially to feign indifference, partially for support.

A clerk on the other side of the counter, sitting at a desk covered with coal suet, looked up.

"Where's Noel?" asked Bauer.

"Out sick," said the clerk.

Charlie hesitated. "Got an order for B. Fairfax?"

"B. Fairfax it is," said the clerk.

He rifled through a clump of papers pinned to a clipboard. Then he pinched the clip, pulled some forms, placed them on top and strolled to the counter. "This it?" he asked, turning the clipboard toward Charlie.

"Yeah."

"Then let's see if everything's up to snuff."

"Ah'm sure it is."

The clerk smiled. "Let's just be double sure." He put the clipboard on the counter, pulled up a stool and settled in. "Exporter," he read from the B-13 form: "Walkerville Brewery. Consignment: 200 cases of Canadian Club?"

He looked up for a response.

"Yeah," said Charlie.

"Total Value F.O.B. Point of Exit: $7,200? Currency: US?"

"Yeah."

The clerk looked up. "Vessel name: *La Esperanza?*"

"Yeah."

A dry cough came from the Mountie in the corner.

"Mode of Transportation from Point of Exit: Water? And Country of Final Destination: Havana."

"Right," said Charlie.

Havana! Murph did not move, nor did he breathe. Now frozen in his informal pose, he didn't dare look at Clayt. Instead, he squinted sideways at Charlie. Havana? Cuba? Well, one thing was sure: all the Canucks had to do was step outside, take one look at *Mamie,* alias *La Esperanza* , and know she wasn't bound for the tropics.

"So, what's the damage," said Charlie, impatiently reaching inside his jacket, hauling out a roll of bills.

But the clerk would not be hurried. "Let's see. We got $7,200." He reached for another form which was paper clipped to the B-13. "Then we got $9 per gallon excise tax for an additional $5,400. You know about the excise tax?"

"Yeah."

"Since the excise tax applies only to liquor consumed here in Canada, all you have to do is have customs in Havana sign a landing certificate, confirming that the consignment arrived in Cuba, then have your guy in Havana send it back to us. Or you can walk it in, and we'll refund the $5,400. Otherwise you forfeit it, you know, making those fellas in Ottawa very happy."

"Right. What's the total?"

"$12,600, US."

Peeling off 13 $1,000 bills, Charlie spread them on the counter.

The clerk examined the minting of the Grover Clevelands carefully before scooping the money up. Then stooping down behind the counter, he cranked open the safe below and rose with four US c-notes. "You the boat's captain?" he asked.

Charlie added the notes to his wad and tucked the roll back into his inner pocket. "No, he is," he said, giving a backward jerk of his thumb toward the end of the counter. "Need to sign off on the B-13, Mr. Fairfax," chirped Charlie on his way out the door.

Poor Murph stared uncomprehendingly at the B-13 form, its mountain of fine print, its **Export Declaration** in bold. To expedite matters, the clerk dipped his pen in the ink and turned it toward Murph. "Here," he said.

Murph just stood there. While the clerk studied him, pen poised, and Clayt memorized the floor, and H.M. George V, hand on hilt, gazed down on him, and the Mountie observed him from the corner, he just stood there, contemplating his future.

"There a problem?" asked the clerk.

"No, not at all," said Murph, cleaning his glasses, voice like castrati, "just trying to find where I sign."

Just then the door opened, the Mountie lowered his paper, and in strolled Mr. Klaxon Horn, the same guy that had given them the smirk while idling on Bourassa Street.

As Klaxon stood back to wait his turn, Murph skimmed the fine print above the signature box, the fine print that contained the Canadian government's warning: *I hereby certify that the information given is true and complete* . He took the pen and, with shaky ovals, wrote *B. Fairfax* in his best Palmer Penmanship.

The clerk gently extricated the pen from Murph's fingers, squeezed the clipboard, pulled off the two top sheets, and handed them to Murph. "Okay, load 'em up."

"That's it?" blurted Murph.

"What's it?" said the clerk. "Oh, I see. You think I'm customs. I'm not customs," said the clerk. "I'm just a sales clerk. I just take down the information as given." He bent down to close the safe, then rose once more. "After you load, you need to hand both copies of that B-13 to the customs inspector. He's the guy you'll need an okay from to clear." He leaned in toward Murph, conspiratorially. "You might want to put your thumb over the destination, though . . . when you hand that to him."

And as the door swung shut behind Murph and Clayt, they could hear the laughter from within. Then someone yelled, "Vaya con dios," and the laughter began anew.

Chapter 11

That same afternoon, 3:35 p.m.

On the kitchen table, at the ready, was a large stack of place cards secured by string. As the lone member of the Place Card Committee, Agnes had spent a morning hour with calligraphic pen point and India ink, painstakingly printing name cards. An advantage of the Place Card Committee was the opportunity to sit through the task. She needed to go easy on her feet or she'd never make it through the day.

Agnes had been going strong all morning—her tailored brown dress with the organdy collar was ironed and hanging; sashes and bows had been pressed—but she was running down. Everything seemed less formidable in the morning, even the decision making. Come afternoon and it was all uphill. And Marce, at 11 months, could be a handful. If it weren't for Freda, she mused, as she wrapped cooled loaves of banana bread in wax paper. God, if it weren't for Freda.

On leaving the office hut, Murph was hopping mad. He hauled Clayt to the side of the building. "What the hell do I do with this?" he cried, waving the export form.

"Now calm down, Murph. If I's you, I'd play along."

"Fine for you. Your name's not on it."

"Yours isn't either," cracked Clayt. "That's my point. It's Beatrice Fairfax."

"You think this is funny?" Murph started to pace. "I'll bet he's trying to set me up. Pa being judge and all." Then, slapping the form with the back of his fingers, he said, "That's it! He's trying to set me up. If anything goes wrong, I'm the fall guy."

Bauer, who was standing over a Coca-Cola tub on the dock, had Murph in his face within seconds.

"Are you trying to set me up?"

Bauer dropped a Canadian coin in a self-pay cup on the cooler and sneered. "Keep it down."

"Are you trying to set me up?" hissed Murph.

"Why'd I wanna set you up?"

"B. Fairfax?"

"So?"

"Cubahhh!"

Bauer fished in the tub and pulled a green bottle out of the icy water. "Y'all gotta fill in a destination."

"So when we shove off from the docks, we gotta pretend we're goin to Cu-bahhh?" sang Murph. "How the hell do we get to Cuba in *Mamie*?"

"Easy," drawled Bauer. "Go straight out from the docks and hang a left. When you git to Lake Erie hang another left. When you git to Buffalo hang a raht. You'll know if you missed yer turn, cause you'll go under the Falls. Any-ways, follow the Erie Canal to the Hudson River, then sit yer course south for about 1,500 miles or so. Park in Havana." He lifted the bottle, took a long swig, then swiped his mouth.

"Problem?" asked Peajacket, strolling over.

"No problem," said Bauer, quaffing a belch.

"Then let's get the boat loaded. Who's got the B-13?"

"I do," huffed Murph.

"Good. Show it to one of the guys in the warehouse." He stuffed his fists in his pea jacket and turned to walk away, but Murph blocked his path.

"I can't do that."

"Why not?"

"I'm not gonna be the fall guy."

"What are you talking about?" Peajacket turned toward a stone-faced Bau-er. "What's he talking about?"

"Got me."

"Got me!" roared Murph. "He told 'em I was captain, made me sign the B-13. False name, false destination. . . ."

Peajacket was clearly annoyed. "Geezus, Charlie." But Charlie just shrugged his shoulders and grinned.

Murph calmed down considerably, convinced he'd found a friend in Peajacket. "Look, putting phony information on that form's against the law."

"Just hand the B-13 to the guys in the warehouse," said Peajacket. "They could care less about destination."

"What about the customs inspector?"

"One hurdle at a time," said Peajacket, and he and Charlie headed toward *Mamie*.

"I don't like the smell of this," said Murph, as soon as the two were out of earshot.

"I keep telling ya, Murph, just play along," said Clayt. "They know what they're doing."

"That's what I'm afraid of."

By the time the boys returned, Bauer and Peajacket were standing by their slip with Klaxon, chewing the fat. Klaxon hadn't said much when they were introduced, and Murph hadn't caught his name, just that he was from Detroit. Fine with Murph. He just wanted to load, get the B-13 over with, and hightail it back home. He checked his watch. This was taking forever, so he was relieved to hear the roar of the Walkerville doors sliding open.

Then a man in a skycap hat and double-breasted navy suit sauntered over. He could have been the doorman at the Book-Cadillac, except for the small badge on his cap, underscored with the word *Canada*. "Greetings, gentlemen," said the customs inspector.

"He needs the B-13, Mr. Fairfax," said Charlie.

Murph fished inside his coat pocket, pulled out the Export Form and handed it over. Though the inspector thanked him politely, he didn't look at it, just held it in his hand and watched as case upon burlap case of Canadian Club was trolleyed to the wharf. Murph was concentrating so intently on the unread form that he was startled when Klaxon jumped into the flat-bottomed lugger in the next slip. Because that's when Murph noticed the name on its bow, *La Esperanza*. Nothing was adding up.

"This it?" asked the inspector.

"That's it," said the Walkerville crew boss.

The inspector scrutinized the B-13, scrutinized the load, scrutinized Murph. Murph did not move, nor did he breathe.

"What's wrong?" asked Peajacket.

"Well, by my count, his load's a case short," said the inspector.

The Walkerville crew boss took a hasty count, agreed with the inspector's tally, muttered, "Our fault, not his," and sent a boy to fetch one more case.

The inspector then folded a copy of the B-13 and shoved it into his pocket, handing the other to Murph. "Okay, Mr. Fairfax, load up." As another warehouse door roared open, he turned on his heels and headed that way. "Have a pleasant trip, gentlemen."

Murph turned to Peajacket. "What was that?"

"You have to leave here with the exact cargo that's on the B-13. Cuz unlike the rest of Canada, the province of Ontario's dry. They don't want any of this stuff leaking back in. They can manufacture booze in Ontario, sell booze in Ontario, they just can't drink booze in Ontario," said Peajacket passing a case.

Loading went fast. Bag after bag of bottles wrapped in straw were handed down to either Charlie in the stern or Klaxon in the midsection. By the time they were done, *La Esperanza*'s back end was sitting awfully low in the water, within ten inches of going under. She didn't look like she'd make it to the next slip, much less Cuba. "That guy's gonna be treading water," muttered Murph to Clayt as they boarded *Mamie* and headed out, leaving Klaxon and his low-slung lugger behind.

At the head of the marina, an O.P.P. officer, standing in front of the customs hut on their port side, gave a polite salute. Murph leaned in toward Peajacket, "But if no one's going to Cuba, no one comes back with a receipt," he said, "no one gets back their excise tax."

"That's right."

"Boy, Canada's making a fortune."

"That's right."

Murph sat back to enjoy the ride. His leisure was cut short, however, when Peajacket turned sharply to port. "We're gonna go over to Sunnyside for a cold one," he yelled. "We need to talk."

"Gotcha," yelled Murph over the lump in his throat.

Chapter 12

That same afternoon, 4:00 p.m.

Agnes was barely out the front door and down the steps before her patent-leathered feet were aching. A whistle blew at the steel mill. Time for the 4 o'clock shift. Ella Strassner came bounding out of her house with her tuna noodle casserole, gave a shout to Madeline Pilon next door, and the growing entourage, dressed too nicely to take the alley cutoff, strolled up Monroe like a royal processional. Carefully conveying one of the banana nut loaves with both hands, Freda was out front; Madeline next with offerings of radishes, carrot sticks and celery, while Rowe cradled her dictionary with one arm, striding like Cardinal Wolsey.

As they crossed Labadie, Agnes pulled her collar up to ward off the cold and gave a glance at the barbershop where George was working late. George might be right when it came to Miss Munn, she thought. Maybe she was making a mountain out of a molehill. Agnes made a vow. If she had any more dealings with Miss Munn, she'd bite her tongue.

Though it was true that drinking liquor was not allowed in Ontario, a beer could be had if you knew where to go. Peajacket knew exactly where to go.

It was just a skip from the LaSalle docks to Sunnyside. Peajacket had only to follow the Canadian shore for less than half a mile before swinging into a canal. They looped lines around posts at the canal's head and disembarked. It was Saturday at Sunnyside; the rear parking area abutting the canal was packed with cars—many with Michigan plates, some with Ohio. While the men of *Mamie* threaded their way to the rear entrance, they could hear the whistle blowing at the steel mill over in Ecorse. Time for the 4 o'clock shift. As Murph glanced skyward, a guy with binoculars backed away from a second floor window.

"He's a spotter," said Peajacket, opening the door, ushering them in. "If he gets a signal from a guy at Turkey Creek that the law is comin', he just hits a buzzer and the top half of this place folds up. Becomes a soda fountain."

Among other popular roadhouses off canals in the area, Sunnyside, just off Seven Mile Road, was a rambling wood clapboard roadhouse of many moods and many rooms. It was run by the brothers Chappus—Albemie and Alberic; another brother, Francis, a streetcar conductor by day, was also in the trade.

If Sunnyside sold anything illicit, it was not at first sight apparent to Murph. In the vast open room, the restaurant was bustling. Waiters, hoisting large oval platters heaped with perch and piled high with fries, swerved expertly between packed tables. But a few words from Peajacket to a man at the foot of the stairs allowed them access to the second floor.

As they walked along the upstairs corridor, one of its many closed doors swung open and a doorman let a fashionably dressed couple out. A din came out with them: a few notes of "Wang Wang Blues," the chatter of dealers, the clatter of spinning fruit and the clackety clack of balls ricocheting around roulette bowls. It was a room in smoky motion. Both Murph and Clayt later agreed that there were at least 100 one-armed bandits edging the room, and that its center was filled with tables—21, blackjack, craps. Both agreed they heard coins exploding into payoff returns.

But if Murph and Clayt had hoped for a tour, none was forthcoming. Instead, Peajacket led them into a side room filled with tables and a bar capable of serving cherry phosphates at the blow of a whistle. He reached inside his coat and slid out a pack of Chesterfields, then offered it around. "I gotta lotta spotters on my payroll, too," he said, once they took their seats. "Cushy job. There's a lotta different jobs."

"Like what?" asked Clayt.

Peajacket lifted a menu off a stack of four. "Like we got purchasers; we got fixers; we got drivers, warehousers, arrangers. They're the guys who arrange the shipments to speaks in Detroit, Chicago. . ."

Clayt was ecstatic. "Arrangers get to go to Chicago?"

"Think we'd send the two of you to Chi Town?" scoffed Charlie. "You'd be picked up in an hour."

"For what?" asked Clayt.

"Truancy, 'at's what."

Clayt chose to ignore the crack, though for the next few days he would howl each time Murph came out with a mocking "Chi Town," followed by an eye roll. "Chi Town," Murph would jeer. "Do you believe that jerk? He's never been further than Ferndale."

'Who does the dirty work?'" asked Murph.

"What dirty work?" asked Bauer. "Be specific."

"Specific? Okay, I'll be specific. Who does the diving? If we have to dump the cargo, who's the lucky sucker that gets to go back and do the diving?"

"We all do the divin'," said Peajacket, from behind the menu. "And, we all start out low and work up." He set his menu aside, grabbed the rest and dealt them like playing cards. "This place has the best fish fries around. Prices are good, too."

"Don't we need Canadian money?" asked Clayt.

"On me," said Peajacket. "C'mon, let's order up and talk later. I'm starvin.'"

Murph wound his watch. Well, at least he'd save time by eating now.

Chapter 13

That same afternoon, 4:30 p.m.

The Mother-Daughter Banquet sponsored by the PTA at School One was well underway. As would be reported the following week by Murph's replacement on the *Ecorse Tribune*, "The seating capacity was overtaxed to such an extent, that additional chairs had to be provided." Even so, he deemed the banquet a huge success:

> *The refreshment committee, under the direction of Mrs. Hahnke and her aids, served a delicious dinner. Following which, Mrs. A.O. Armstrong, president of the PTA, welcomed the many attendees and introduced the principal, Miss Munn, whose efficient corps of teachers had drilled the pupils, who would so excellently render a program full of thought and action. The following program was rendered:*
>
> *1. Community Singing, led by Miss Green, Music Supervisor;*
>
> *2. Tableau recital by 5th-grade girls, "The Story of a Seed";*
>
> *3. Miss Graham, the art teacher, spoke on "The Value of Art on the School";*
>
> *4. Recitation of "When the Frost is on the Pumpkin" by 6th-grade girls;*
>
> *5. All those deserving were honored, prizes were given, and Miss Rowena Moore was acknowledged by those assembled for being captain of the 7th-grade team that won the Detroit News Spelling Bee.*

As for "All those deserving" being honored, that wasn't quite true.

————————

After they'd polished off copious portions of golden brown perch, after Clayt had choked on a bone and Charlie had found it hilarious, after they'd finished their beers, Murph was beginning to loosen up.

Peajacket, who was slumped in his chair peeling the label off his Red Cap Ale, straightened up, pushed his plate aside, folded his arms on the edge of the table, and looked squarely at the boys across the red-and-white-checked divide.

"You wanna work for me? Here's the deal." He had gotten grimly serious, his blue-eyed gaze penetrating. "There's a code on the river and you gotta follow it." He waited; both boys nodded. "Like I tell all my guys, keep your nose clean, keep your word with customers, creditors, Federals. 'Cuz that's all you got is your word. Only deal in top-of-the-line booze—no cutting, no coffin varnish. Don't steal from other bootleggers, don't invade their territory, don't cross the river drunk, don't rat, and stay away from reporters and guns. I don't want any of my guys totin' guns. Got that? That's the code you gotta follow. Fair play. Always fair play. 'Nuf said?"

"Nuf said," replied Murph.

"Good." Peajacket caught the waiter's eye and twirled his forefinger. "Could we have another round?"

Murph felt a rosy glow. For some reason, he felt at ease. For some reason it was fun to talk with these guys. "That's quite a lugger your friend's got," he said.

"Bernie?" said Peajacket.

"That his name?"

"Yeah."

"How fast can that thing go?" asked Clayt.

"Couldn't beat a baby carriage," said Peajacket. "You can't outrun the Federals; gotta outthink 'em."

"Or outpay 'em," quipped Murph.

"That, too," laughed Peajacket. "That lugger can't go more'n ten miles an hour. No lugger can. They're sitting ducks if a customs boat wants to chase 'em down."

"Wouldn't take much to swamp that thing," Murph cracked. "The wake from a floating leaf, perhaps."

Peajacket sighed, chuckled twice, and sighed again. "You'll be fine on the way back," he said, stripping the label off his second bottle, "Just hike up your pant cuffs."

Murph did not move. "Pardon me?" he said.

"When you head back to Ecorse with Bernie, just roll. . . ," Peajacket paused, dismayed, and set down his bottle. "You didn't think you were going back with us, did you?"

"Course not," said Murph, vocal cords like bailing wire.

"But it wouldn't make sense. What would be the point?"

"No point at all," said Clayt.

"None whatsoever," said Murph.

Peajacket looked questioningly at Charlie, leaned back in his chair, then leaned forward again. "I mean, I thought you knew. How could you not know?"

"We knew, Peajacket. We really did," said Clayt.

But Peajacket wasn't so sure. "Let's have dessert," he said, preoccupied. "Want some dessert? Cherry cobbler's good."

Murph's spirit sank further. They weren't just having dinner and a beer. They were stalling for time. Why?

"You been out at night, right?" asked Peajacket.

Murph gazed at the sunlight streaming in the window. "Sure," he lied. "Thousands of times." Yep, they were stalling for time; they were waiting for dark. It was now 4:50 and sunset didn't arrive 'til around 5:30. "Do you always take your boats back after dark?" he asked, glumly.

"It's safer," said Peajacket. "Why?"

"A lotta guys cross in daylight."

"Lotta guys git caught, too," growled Charlie. "You 'fraid of the dark?"

"Oh, please," said Murph, with disdain.

"Wouldn't blame you if you were," said Peajacket. "Everything looks different at night. You can't see landmarks. You lose your bearings. Lotta other problems."

"Like what?" asked Clayt.

"Like engine failures in the middle of a chase for one. Coming into a dock too fast; the heavier the boat, the further she'll shoot. And when a freighter's bearing down, it's tough to tell how fast she's going." Peajacket signaled the waiter, then turned to the table. "Coffee all round?"

After they'd had dessert, after they'd had coffee, Murph was making tine dents on the tablecloth with his fork, tracing four parallel lines over and over, while Clayt chattered on to fill the void.

Peajacket watched the fork tracks for some time before inquiring. "You angry with me for something?"

Murph sat up. "No, not at all."

"'Cuz if you are. . ."

"No. Really." Murph set his fork down.

"I mean, I'd hate to get off on the wrong foot here."

"I'm fine, honest."

"Is it because we didn't spell everything out ahead? 'Cuz if it is . . ."

"Honest, I'm fine."

"You getting cold feet? 'Cuz if you are, I'd understand. Hell, I was frightened my first time across."

"There a reason y'all keep lookin' at your watch?" interrupted Charlie. "Got someone waitin' at the pier?" He turned to Peajacket. "Wanna know why I din't tell him nothin'? This is why. I don't trust him. His ol' man's a judge, for chrissake."

"You have been, you know," said Peajacket. "You've been looking at your watch since we met up."

It took a long time for Murph to find his voice. "Well, I do have kind of an appointment tonight."

"With who?" asked Charlie.

"It's not important."

"If it ain't important, why d'ya keep lookin' at your watch?" challenged Charlie.

"Let's just drop it, okay."

Peajacket sat back, baffled.

Charlie broke the silence. "Maybe ah oughta go back with 'em. And Bernie can go back with you."

"You don't mind?" asked Peajacket.

"I look forward to it."

"Well, we'd better head out," said Peajacket, reaching for the bill. "Gotta push off from the docks by sunset. Canada wants you outta there by nightfall."

Chapter 14

That same afternoon, 5:50 p.m.

The hall at School One was filled to capacity and festooned with crepe. The flaming rusts, reds and golds of autumn draped the windows and the archway, and scalloped the piano. In the center of the white damasked speakers table, multicolored Indian corn and gourds plunged out of a cornucopia onto a bed of leaves. Facing the dais was an open area which was enclosed by tables laid out in a horseshoe. 80 women and girls were in attendance, each with her own place card and mint cup.

Dinner over, chairs were pushed back. Those on the inside of the horseshoe had turned their chairs away from the table, the better to enjoy the entertainment.

Agnes had loosened the straps on her patent-leather pumps. Except for the throb from the balls of her feet, she was having a grand old time. Admittedly, the community singing had gotten off to a shaky start. As Miss Green thumped away on the piano, a few timid sopranos trilled while laggards hid behind their lyric sheets. Her fingers periodically flew from the keys to twirl commandingly in the air, and a few more voices joined in and thinly warbled of little forget-me-nots placed here and there on the kind of gown that made them walk on air. By song's end, those adept at harmonizing had sidled in, and all in the hall were soundly admitting that: till it wilt-ed they wore it, they'd al-ways a-dore it, their sweet lit-tle A-lice Blue Gown. Then Miss Green rocked the place with ragtime renditions of "Jada" and "K-K-K Katy," followed by a transportation medley that began with "Come Away with Me, Lucille," slid into "Come, Josephine, in my Flying Machine" and finished on a rouser about Johnny O'Connor who had to get out and get under, and fix up his automobile.

It was a hard act to follow. Unfortunately, what followed was the tableau recital by 5th-grade girls, "The Story of a Seed." The buzz in the room quickly dissipated and programs became fans. It was about here that Agnes noticed Rowe wasn't in her seat.

While Miss Graham began her hypnotic presentation on "The Value of Art in the School," Agnes returned to the purple type on her mimeographed program to check the order of presentation. Rowe was to be acknowledged after the 6th-grade girls' recitation, which was up next. Agnes nudged Ella, pointing to the program and the empty seat. "Should we go find her?" whispered Ella. But it was too late. The 6th-grade girls were lining up. Miss Green raised her arms maestro style and the girls began on the downbeat. "When the frost is on the punkin and the fodder's in the shock," they chimed, almost in unison.

As the girls launched into the second verse of Mr. James Whitcomb Riley's celebrated "pome," Agnes was surveying the tables anxiously.

Agnes signaled to Hollis, pointing to the empty seat next to her. Hollis smiled reassuringly and motioned toward the end of their table. There was Rowe, directly behind Margaret Montie, dictionary at the ready.

As she eased back in relief, the girls were roundly applauded. Agnes barely heard Mrs. A.O. Armstrong tell all those so designated to rise. She barely noticed one, two, three girls pop up at different tables. She barely heard Ella whispering in her ear. "Where's Freda?"

"What?"

"Where's Freda? Why didn't she stand? They just honored the girls with perfect attendance last year."

Agnes swung round and stared at Ella in disbelief.

As if in answer, the absent Freda glided through the crepe-festooned archway, fingers glued round the waist of a goldfish bowl, taking cautious steps to keep the water from sloshing, while its two startled occupants, dubbed Fanchon and Marco by Room 10, swam upstream on a slight tilt. Behind her shuffled a large landscape of a lake, with a clump of massive trees and a teeny tiny man and two teeny tiny cows along its bank.

"Here we are," chirped Mrs. A.O. Armstrong as Freda, having been quickly relieved of the bowl by Miss Munn with a mellifluous "Thank you, Freda," beamed as she walked to her seat. It was time for the highly popular and highly competitive class awards.

While Miss Munn held up the goldfish bowl, and its orange-colored residents looked out over the vast hall from a great height, Mrs. A.O. Armstrong stepped forward. "For the room having the highest percentage of mothers and daughters present in proportion to its enrollment. . . ." She paused. "The goldfish bowl and its occupants go to. . . ." She paused once more, while Fanchon and Marco sambaed round and round in lieu of a drum roll. "Room 13, the 5th grade girls, taught by Miss McKay." There was a shriek followed by a hearty burst of applause.

Then Rowe was acknowledged, and her whopping big dictionary appropriately oohed-and-ahhed over. Duly honored, she sat back down, while Freda, having applauded heartily, slid to the edge of her seat and prepared to stand.

"And now," crooned Mrs. A.O. Armstrong, as Freda sat up, ramrod straight. "And now, this beautiful picture, *The Lake* by Corot, which is awarded each month to the class with the highest enrollment of new PTA members." Freda patiently eased back in her seat as Mrs. A.O. Armstrong picked up the painting. "The prize, which will hang on the wall of the victorious class until our next meeting, goes to. . . . Room 21, the 6th-grade girls, taught by Miss Munn." The announcement was met by refined applause, since the 6th-grade girls were much too sophisticated for shrieks.

As Freda once again slid to the edge of her seat in readiness and Agnes sat silently by, Mrs. A.O. Armstrong reminded all those present of the next meeting and announced that Dr. Dixon of the Detroit Board of Health would deliver a lecture on health. Then a motion was passed expressing the appreciation of the parents for the excellent preparation by the teachers and the able rendition by the pupils of the program; chairs squealed, mothers and daughters rose, and all began to mill. Except for Freda. Except for Agnes.

Rowena Moore holding her *Detroit News* spelling bee prize,
a Rand-McNally Dictionary.

Chapter 15

That same evening, 5:50 p.m.

The air had turned chillier on the ride back to the LaSalle docks, even chillier when Peajacket and Bernie took off in Mamie, and chillier still when Murph, Clayt and Charlie Bauer boarded the lugger, and she stalled out twice. The crew of *La Esperanza* glumly rode at anchor, waiting for total dark behind the Canadian side of Fighting Island, swaying in the minor wakes caused by the silent armada filling in around them. *La Esperanza* was just one of a string of boats tucked behind the five-mile-long island, a regatta of fishing trawlers, 50-footers, luggers, motorboats, rowboats, flat tubs and putt putts.

As the sun slipped behind the trees of Fighting Island, a shady canopy slid slowly across the waiting fleet. From across the river, Murph could hear the bells of St. Francis Xavier ringing out the Angelus. It was 6:00.

Just then, a speedboat with a lone helmsman came tearing round the island; he cut the throttle and pulled up alongside *La Esperanza*. "Peajacket said to tell ya, they raided three boathouses in Rum Row not long ago. Town's crawlin' with state troopers and the press."

"Thought so," said Charlie. "Thought I heared sirens."

"Broke down all the doors. They got Federcolli and Pelafuso in the first one; had to fish 'em outta the river. Got Carlo Nebiolo in the second. But two of his guys made like Johnny Weissmuller and swam away. Then they raided Peajacket's. Lucky he wasn't there. He says to tell ya, don't go near Carlo's. Take the load to the foot of Bourassa. The truck'll be waitin' for yas there. Then dump the lugger at Washell's." The helmsman waved off.

By 6:15, the longed-for curtain of darkness had descended. The fleet was stirring. Engines were firing up, melding into one low hum of bubbles. Charlie started the engine, told Clayt to haul in the anchor, told Murph to join him at the helm, and the lugger began to lug its way along the northeastern shore of Fighting Island.

"All yours," said Charlie, pointing to the wheel.

" *Me* ?"

"Yeah. Take the helm."

"She handles like a cement mixer," complained Murph, as he steered around the tip of the island, then hugged the coast.

"See them reeds?" said Charlie, pointing south to marsh grass taller than their boat. "There's a sandy section between 'em. We'll pull in and wait for the signal."

Clayt tossed the anchor over the side, and they sat some more. A freighter slid by, not more than 30 feet away, curling waves parting at the bow as it headed upriver. Murph held on, watching closely as *La Esperanza* dipped, gunnels coming perilously close to the water line.

Murph's landmarks were vanishing. He could still make out the silhouetted tip of the St. Francis bell tower rising above the town, but Ecorse village had faded from view, replaced by unfamiliar clusters of lights.

Charlie unwound the field glasses from his neck. "You take these; I'll take the helm back."

"What am I looking for?" asked Murph, taking off his glasses.

"Boats."

"All boats?"

"Yeah."

"Why?"

"'Cuz some Prohibition boats pretend to be rum runners, rum runners pretend to be Prohibition boats, and hijackers pretend to be both," said Charlie. "Any agent tells ya to heave to, y'all make sure he's the real deal."

"How'll we know if they're hijackers?" asked Clayt.

"When they board."

"No, really. How we gonna know hijackers from Federals?"

"Easy," said Charlie. "The hijackers don't shoot first, don't bump into buoys, don't ride over rocks, don't shear the props, and they got binoculars. No one in Washington gives the Federals binoculars. Y'all believe that?" He laughed. "Ain't got no handcuffs, neither. Alls they got is a cap, a badge, a gun, and a bribe in one pocket. Don't git me started."

Murph was dumbfounded. Charlie Bauer could do more than grunt.

And Charlie Bauer was just winding up. "Y'all know 'bout signals?"

"Yeah," said Murph.

"No, you don't."

"Yeah, we do. We did 'em!"

"You just think you did 'em."

"What are you, nuts?" Murph folded his arms and leaned back against the cargo. "During the day, Mrs. Washell hangs a pink chenille bedspread on her clothesline. If the bedspread's not there, it means stay away, the feds are sniffing around. Isn't that a signal? Over in Rum Row, Mrs. Dondee's got the cleanest windows in Wayne County. If she's washing windows, it means bring the boat in. I'd call that a signal. At night, Leo Navarre uses his car beams near Hogan's Alley. Two blinks means come in. And over near Westfield, Eddie Smith and friends keep a bonfire going on the bank. They put it out when it's not safe to land. Lefty Clark pays 'em to do it. Want more?"

"Didja ever try pickin' out signals at night from this side?"

"No."

"Then ya don't know dick 'bout no signals," said Charlie. "Pan the coast. Now see that dark area? That black blotch?"

"Yeah."

"That's Hogan's Alley."

"Wow. Darker than spit," said Murph.

"It's always dark in Hogan's Alley. Git to know it. Now pan another inch. See how you go from pitch black to that clump of lights?"

"Yeah."

"Them lights is comin' from Walter Locke's diner, Robbers' Roost, Polar Bear, all them places near the State Street dock. Them lights stay on most of the night. Use that for a focal point. Got that?"

"Yeah, I got it."

"See that small dark area?"

Murph refocused. "Yeah."

"That's the embankment, the end of Bourassa. It's always black right there, 'cause there ain't a house. No streetlights neither. And Ty keeps his windows covered." Charlie rechecked his watch with the flashlight. "Wait a couple minutes, then train your peepers on the embankment. Watch for two quick blues."

"What if you get a go-ahead, then when you're almost to shore they flash a red?" asked Clayt.

"You double back. Wait for the right lights."

"You come all the way back?"

"Some nights you gotta do that three, four times."

"In this thing?" said Murph, longing to look at his watch. Instead, he trained his eyes on the blackened area at the foot of Bourassa. "There it is!" he shouted. "Two quick blues!" Murph was all charged up. "One if by land, two if by sea, eh?" he grinned.

"Huh?" asked Charlie.

"Nothin'."

They poled out of the reeds.

"We go south along the shore until we git on a diagonal to Bourassa, then shoot across," said Charlie. "Y'all gotta allow for the current. Overshoot and you'll end up in Ashtabula."

Heart pounding, deeply cold, Murph stood motionless near the helm and peered into the darkness, but his world had narrowed to within 20 feet. He could barely see the rocks in the inky water; he could barely see past the shore.

Murph was clearly on edge. It wasn't a sound that began to scare the stuffing out of him, it was the absence of sound. In fact, the specter that began to make his blood run cold made no sound at all. Because dead ahead, he could see, or thought he could see, something hidden in the tall reeds. He was sure of it. Or almost sure. He leaned forward and fixed his eyes on the portside blackness, straining to make it out.

Was that an unlit bow light? Was that a deck cleat? There was a large speed-boat anchored in the reeds; he was sure of it. Or fairly sure. He looked at Charlie; he looked at Clayt. Neither said a word but both had seen it. Even *La Esperanza* seemed to suck in her breath.

The lugger drew nearer. Now, behind the windshield sat two—no three—men. One in a fedora, two not. Probably rum runners, thought Murph. Probably harmless. But as *La Esperanza* passed tensely within four feet of the speedboat, the three men just sat there, peering back at him, grim, menacing, wordless; so still they looked dead. Until the guy on the right, the one behind the wheel, the one with the fedora, winked. Murph was sure of it. Then the apparition receded into the darkness.

"Jesus, Mary and Joseph," murmured Murph.

"Don't y'all wish," murmured Charlie. "It's either Federals or hijackers."

"How can you tell?" whispered Clayt.

"He's sittin' high in the water," said Charlie, softly. "Not carryin' cargo. At least, not yet."

An engine roared to life, an engine brazenly unmuffled, and set out with a steady hum. "Here he comes," murmured Charlie.

"But if we can't see *him*," whispered Clayt, "how can he see *us*?"

"Don't have to see us. Alls he's gotta do is follow our wake," said Charlie.

The hum did not speed up, nor did it slow down. It remained steady.

Murph leaned toward Charlie and said low in his ear, "What's he waiting for?"

"If it's the Federals," whispered Charlie, "he wants us out of Canadian waters. If it's hijackers, they're sizin' us up. They wanna be sure we're an independent shipper, that we ain't with one of them syndicates in Detroit. They'd be dead meat."

"Can't we just turn and cross? Try to lose him?"

"If you're gonna turn," murmured Clayt, "better do it now. Unless we wanna marry that freighter coming."

Until then, the contour of the shoreline had blocked a clear view of the 800-foot-wide Fighting Island channel. Now as they swung starboard to avoid a protruding bank, Murph looked downriver, toward Wyandotte, toward the head of Grassy Island. A carnival of moving lights, about the size of a two-story mountain, was coming toward them. It was the *Henry Ford II*, its low midsection about half the length of a city block.

By Murph's reckoning, the freighter was about 300 feet away. "We can make it easy if we turn now," he offered. "Maybe those guys won't follow."

Charlie didn't turn. He continued advancing toward the freighter.

Murph glanced nervously behind him. "I mean, shouldn't we try to save the cargo?" he inquired.

Charlie didn't turn.

Since there was no longer any need to whisper, Murph upped his volume and chatted breezily. "I mean, far be it from me to tell you what to do, but it would really be advisable to turn now. To have any chance at all. Wouldn't it, Clayt? This is about our last chance to do so. Turning now, that is."

Charlie didn't turn.

When the freighter was about a house lot away and the hijackers less than 30 feet behind, Murph slumped against the gunnels. Too late, he thought. Too damn pissyass late.

That's when Charlie turned the wheel lethargically to starboard.

"You're gonna cross now?" asked Murph.

"Yeah."

"Whydja wait? Why we goin' so slow?"

"Don't want them bums to know ah turned, until they know ah turned. It's about timin', kid."

With that, Charlie went full throttle, directly across the oncoming path of the *Henry Ford II*, and Clayt went bug-eyed. "What if this thing konks out again!" he yelled, but his inquiry was lost to the wind.

The freighter's slow-moving lights were deceiving. From a distance, she looked almost dead in the water; in actual fact, she was pushing along at a fairly fast clip, making 10 knots, while *La Esperanza* bobbalooed along at 7, going forward with the engine, slipping sideways with the current.

With a chill wind blowing in his face and spray dousing his glasses, Murph positioned himself for the collision. "Why don't we turn on the running lights so he can see us!"

"Wouldn't matter," yelled Charlie. "He cain't change course that fast!" Charlie just grinned and steered a straight course.

The bulk carrier was pushing water in front of her like a snow plow, kicking up a wide-curling wash two-feet high. Its 62-foot beam, twice as wide as the movie screen at the Majestic, began to block all else from view. To the crew of *La Esperanza*, it looked like the Great Wall of China was coming at them.

When the freighter was within 100 feet, Murph reached in front of Charlie and flicked on the running lights, then yanked the flashlight from Charlie's back pocket and blinked it frantically at the oncoming freighter. But the lights kept right on coming.

Suddenly, the freighter responded with five short blasts from its horn, and the wash began to drop slightly in front of the boat.

He's trying to slow down, thought Murph. But even he knew it was too late. "When do we jump!" he yelled.

Charlie held his hand to his ear, unable to hear. The sound of the freighter was deafening.

"When do we jump!" shrieked Murph, searing his lungs.

But miracles do occur. Because the freighter suddenly seemed to be turning. Two seconds later, *La Esperanza* was on the west side of the bulk carrier, and Murph watched in awe as the prow of the *Henry Ford II* slid massively by them, followed by the bridge, followed by the pilot house, followed by the loading crane, the 500-foot bed plate, the aft deckhouse, followed by the stack, fantail, stern light and flagstaff. Murph watched in awe as all 600 feet of lights, looking like a nighttime amusement ride at Bob-Lo Island, glided by.

"I don't know about you guys," yelled Clayt, over the roar of the receding freighter, "but I'm chewing on my heart here!"

"That was a miracle!" yelled Murph, overjoyed. "A goddamn miracle! I mean . . . that, *that* . . . was a miracle!"

"Warn't no miracle, Saint Edna," scoffed Charlie, cutting across the wake.

"No thanks to you!" yelled Murph. "Geezus, Charlie, you almost killed us! What the hell were you thinking?"

"We was fine," said Charlie.

"*Fine?*"

"Oh, can the dramatics, Gloria Swanson. We was fine. I know'd he'd turn to starboard, he had to."

"Whaddya mean, he had to?"

"There's a bend in the river right here. This is where the channel turns. Thought you said you know'd the river. Now shut up and go flat, if y'all wanna shake them guys. They'll be comin' across 'bout now." An engine could be heard in the distance. "See. There he is."

Cutting their own motor, they sprawled across the cargo as *La Esperanza* drifted downstream with the current.

Chapter 16

That same evening, 6:50 p.m.

It had taken about ten minutes to shake the hijackers and about five to cross. Now, the crew of *La Esperanza* drifted between the northern tip of Mud Island and the Ecorse shore, waiting for another signal near Bourassa. Intermittently, Charlie would start up the engine and return to a better position for the race in.

"Darker than spit," said Clayt, hunched at the bow, rope ready for landing.

Murph shivered and hugged himself. "Colder than spit," he said. "And where the hell's your guys?"

Even Charlie, sitting on the console, rocking with the waves, was chilled to the bone. He took off his gloves and blew on his reddened hands. "Probably got tired of signallin'."

"*They* got tired?" jeered Murph.

Lights blinked from the dark of the shore. "There it is!" whispered Clayt. "Two quick blues!"

Charlie started the engine. "The water's ten-feet deep round the embankment. But keep your eyes' peeled for the sewer dock. I'd rather not climb it. Got that?"

Charlie approached on the left, did a sharp swerve to the right, reversed the engine to brake the lugger, and pulled alongside the embankment. Above them, a welcoming committee of three, leaning over with eager hands, grabbed the lines and tied them to a nearby ladder.

"Took you long enough," carped a man dressed in black.

"Go git the goddam truck," said Charlie. "We can have tea later."

Just then, a pair of feeble headlights turned onto Bourassa from Front Street.

"Holy shit," said one of the truckers. "Keep your head down, Charlie," warned another, and all three hightailed it out of there.

Murph scrambled partway up the ladder to untie the lines, then raised his head for a better look and was mesmerized by the headlights as they wobbled toward him at an injudicious speed. Instead of turning left at Ty Washell's, they kept on coming, straight at the embankment.

"He's gonna run out of land!" yelled Murph, leaping back into the boat, lines in hand. "Duck!"

To everyone's shock, the headlights roared past the ten-foot-high embankment, sailed over the heads of the crew of *La Esperanza*, soared about 25 feet, just missing the sewer dock, then plunged into the water and were soon doused.

"Well, 'at oughta bring the law," muttered Charlie Bauer.

Then everything happened fast. For those who preferred to work in silence, it was a noisy affair. The landing of the closed-model sedan had made a resounding splash. A chorus of loud bubbles could be heard, as well as the sound of waves buffeting the car's hood. On shore, a truck revved up with a roar, squealed its tires as it turned around at Ty Washell's, then bumped and banged up Bourassa and clamored away.

For those who preferred to work in the shadows, it became a luminous affair. Lights went on in the back of Roy Livernois' house, and a window was thrown open. Lights went on at Ty's, as the sedan slowly sank, nose first. Bystanders with flashlights could be seen running from Front Street. One Samaritan, accompanied by a lantern, came from Harry Hitchcock's boathouse. All were racing to the embankment.

Charlie started the engine, "We gotta git," and quickly maneuvered *La Esperanza* back out on the river, back near Mud Island, widely avoiding the area of the listing car.

A siren could be heard. Then another. Beams from flashlights converged and lit up the auto, its back windows high and bobbing as it drifted with the current. Minutes later, an Ecorse police car arrived, training its spotlight on the river. Suddenly, the back end of the auto reared up, the car flipped over, and all four wheels shot into the air like a submissive dog. It would vanish soon after.

Murph was exhausted. "Now where do we land?"

"Westfield," said Charlie.

"Thought you said no one's dumb enough to land there at night."

"Got no choice."

"We gotta choice," said Murph. "We can hide the cargo in the attic of my Uncle Syl's boathouse. Get it later."

"What about our lugger?"

"We can tie it at his pier. Move it in the morning."

"Won't your uncle mind?"

"Toldja, he's blind. He won't even see it," said Murph, who was sure of it. Or almost sure of it. Or not sure of it at all, but much too cold and too tired to care.

The banquet was breaking up. Coats and thank yous were being doled out over the clangor, while the six members of the Clean-up Committee toted industrial-sized tubs to and from the tables. Off in the school kitchen, Mrs. Dalton sprinkled Gold Dust into the hot water streaming into the sink, then donned her apron and rolled up her sleeves.

"Where *were* you when they awarded those with perfect attendance?" asked Agnes, who had hobbled over to Freda, Ella close behind. "You didn't stand when they called your name."

Freda, still baffled by the turn of events, answered dazedly, "Getting the goldfish. She asked us to get the prizes from Room 21."

"Who asked?"

But before Freda could answer, Ella gave Agnes an elbow. Miss Munn was coming toward them.

Agnes braced.

"I had no i-*dee*-ah, Mrs. Moore," said Miss Munn from eight feet out. "If Freda had only mentioned it when she offered to get the prizes, I'd never, *ever*, have sent her. I had no i- *dee* -ah she was to be honored," said Miss Munn, drawing nigh. "Miss Leary prepared the list." Then she sincerely thanked Agnes for the place cards, asked if she'd studied calligraphy, leaned in between the two mothers and said in strictest confidence, "These affairs renew my respect for motherhood," and laughed delicately.

Then she reprised the day and all its pitfalls. And now, at the 11th hour, Mrs. Torongo had gone home sick, and the Clean-Up Committee was stretched thin, and she didn't know *what* she was going to do about the tables.

Agnes, who had draped her arm over Ella's shoulder in an effort to take a little pressure off her right foot, shot a look at the clock above the entrance. "My son's not here?"

"No. No one's seen him," said Miss Munn earnestly.

"He'll be here," said Agnes.

"I hope you're right, my dear. Because I am *absolutely* desperate. They're hard to collapse and hard to stack. They can't be cleared by children."

There it was. That's how she did it, and Agnes was determined not to bite. She looked down at her only good dress. Not on your life, she thought. Besides, she could barely make it home as it was on her swollen stubs. There was an uncomfortable silence. Ella smiled and said nothing.

After some time, Agnes felt compelled to fill the void. "I wish I could help, Miss Munn, but I have to get home. Mr. Moore doesn't close the barbershop until eight, and the only one in charge is Joyce and she's only nine. That's okay for an hour or two in the afternoon, but. ..."

"Couldn't they run on ahead?" asked Miss Munn.

"Pardon me?"

"Freda. Rowena. Couldn't they just run on ahead?"

It was over in a wink. Obviously Agnes was ill-equipped to deal with the kind of person for which *no* is only the opening bid, so she did what others do when socially caught off guard: she countered weakly. "But Rowe left with Hollis."

"Then I'm sure Freda wouldn't mind babysitting. Would you, dear?"

Freda was at a loss for words, as was Agnes. And Ella? Ella just smiled. And said nothing.

"What about tomorrow morning?" offered Agnes. "My son could take them down tomorrow morning."

Miss Munn looked down at Agnes with enormous forbearance. Tomorrow, she said, would be too late, because *to-mor-row* that very same room was to be used for basketball practice. Since she had promised *faith*-ful-ly to have the tables removed, they couldn't very well leave them up, could they?

With that, Miss Munn marched to a table, one newly naked, firmly gripped a corner with her left hand and, in one powerful jerk, flipped it over and sent it crashing to the floor, flat on its back. Miss Munn was a mite stronger than she appeared. She then proceeded to bend down and wrestle with the latch on the back legs with her left hand while bracing a leg with her thigh.

"Where do the tables go?" asked Agnes, voice flat as Kansas.

"Are you sure?" said Miss Munn, including Ella in her interrogative sweep.

"Where would you like them stacked?" said Agnes.

Soon Mrs. George A. Moore and Mrs. Nick Strassner were taking down tables at a rapid rate, though one of them was limping. For their effort, they would be recognized in next month's PTA minutes because of a motion made by Miss Munn, who had been exceedingly, grateful.

Agnes, fighting a table leg, felt so defeated that she was ready to bawl.

"I'll get that, Mum," said Murph

———

The next day's *Detroit Free Press*, Sunday edition, reported the incident:[1]

> *Jesse Millman, 42 years old, of Wyandotte, was drowned early last night when he drove his automobile into the Detroit river at the foot of Bourassa street in Ecorse. The street is not lighted in that vicinity and it is believed Millman, who was alone, did not see the danger because of poor headlights.*
>
> *The automobile, a closed model, went over a 10-foot embankment and submerged in 10 feet of water. The body was found at the wheel when the machine was brought to the surface by members of the Ecorse police department.*
>
> *A witness told authorities Millman was going 35 miles an hour at the time. He was a foreman for the Detroit Edison company.*
>
> *Millman is believed to have been returning alone from a duck hunt when drowned, as a brace of ducks was found in his car.*

The raids[2] and the sinking car were the main topics of conversation in George Moore's barbershop for weeks. Patrons waiting for a shave speculated that Millman would have known the area. Maybe his brakes gave out, said Ollie Raupp. Maybe, said Dom Dalton, but since there were only boathouses and

---

[1] "Motorist dies in River Dive," Detroit Free Press, October 25, 1925.
[2] Detroit News , October 25, 1925.

blind pigs down around there, where was he going?

"Probably thought he'd stop off for a beer at Frankie Savanna's on his way home," said George. "Probably missed the turn at Ty's. In better times, the street and a bar would have been well lighted."

———

The note that Mrs. George A. Moore sent over to Miss Mae Munn a few days after the Mother-Daughter Banquet of October 24 became family lore. That note, sent via Freda, effectively ended Freda and Rowe's schooling at School One and effectively launched their matriculation at St. Francis Xavier.

"What did she write? What did the note say," I asked my Aunt Dia many years later. Dia laughed. "It said, 'I'm sending Freda and Rowe to school to get an education, not to do your dirty work.'"

Chapter 17
Early afternoon, Sunday, March 14, 1926

It was known as the Rocking Chair Campaign. At least that's what Agnes dubbed her husband's initial bid for village president. "Never got off the porch," she told Ella. George Moore was not what one might call a physically ambitious man.

> *"Most people remember their fathers putzing around the house, doing repairs," Shay once noted, "but I don't remember him doing much of anything. He loved that rocker on the front porch. I guess he figured he had enough kids to do the work. He'd get the lawn mower out, smile and say, 'Go to it.'"*

But to give Citizen Moore credit, he worked long hours at the barbershop, had been elected councilman in 1925, continued to serve as justice of the peace, and his 1926 campaign for village president took place in one of the coldest winters in anyone's memory. George Moore had had to move campaign headquarters for the People's Party of Ecorse from his rocking chair outdoors to his Morris chair indoors, the one near the library table in the center of the living room where he enjoyed his nightly apple and popcorn.

It had snowed on election day, Monday, March 8, 1926, making walking to polling stations a slog. With state troopers stationed to preserve order, 1,336 citizens of the village of Ecorse braved the shivery 24 degrees to show up at the polls. But in a sign of things to come, 200 of them, nearly 15% of the electorate, were not allowed to vote, reported the *Detroit News*, since "their names could not be found on the registration books, or they refused to take the oath of registration at the booths."

It might have been the weather, it might have been something in the water, because the good citizens of Ecorse overturned all but one of the entire slate of village officers. To Agnes's amazement, George won by 42 votes, defeating three-time incumbent Fred Bouchard of the Citizen's Party. Since his Rocking Chair strategy proved to be successful, George would stick with it for two more campaigns: 1927 and 1928.

The following Sunday in '26, George went missing. Agnes had a good idea where he was but no idea when he'd be back. Though they were infrequent, His Honor went on benders. So on the Sunday after Election Monday, George

Moore was sitting with Nick Strassner in one of the finer blind pigs in Hogan's Alley with a schooner of beer, celebrating not only his presidency but the $500 boost in yearly income.

Ed Hartnett's houseboat and refreshment stand, sorely in need of paint, was locked in the ice off an inlet that separated Hogan's Alley from the tin mill and Beaubien's icehouse. Ed's place wasn't showy; he didn't believe in dumping dough on décor. The inside was simply furnished, with round tables, a bar serving salami wedges on saltines, and an upright piano flanking the understuffed Victorian sofa, the one with trumpeting angels carved into the mahogany backrest.

Blind pigs were lucrative during the 1920s. Tables were at a premium. Proper etiquette called for steady drinking from arrival to departure, or management would commandeer the space. But there was nothing hurried about Ed Hartnett's establishment, which is probably why George preferred it. He was having a leisurely Sunday near the wood-burning stove in the back corner. Ernie and Ollie were there. So was Ted Hoyt. So were Leo Navarre, Screech Salliotte, and George's brother Mick. By now in excellent spirits, the patrons had hoisted to George Moore's election, the bat of Harry Heilmann, the 600-volume expansion of the Ecorse Library, and the miracle at Lourdes.

The Detroit River had frozen straight across that winter of 1925-26. The temperature had dropped below freezing a few days before Christmas and had pretty much stayed that way. The few times the tugboats had come through and cut a gash in the ice, the cut healed within days. Ice fishing villages had sprung up. And the rum runners? Well, they had a new route, a 31-mile-long international ice bridge.

"There goes the Donner party," said George, as a colorful stream of humanity skated past the houseboat windows, dragging empty sleds, wagons and baby carriages, cutting across Ecorse Bay on the bias, heading toward Canada.

Nick stood up and peered out. "Looks like half of High Street."

"Who we got?" asked George.

"Couple of Drouillards, Minnie Stinson, Al Lester."

Since it was broad daylight, Ed's customers had a panoramic view of Ecorse Bay on this sunny afternoon. From the string of four ample windows on the houseboat's rear, they could see the door of Denny McGrath's fishing shanty about 100 yards out and the tip of Fighting Island. If they availed themselves of the three side windows on the right, they could see the north end of Mud Island; to their left, they could make out Beaubien's ice dock where a youthful hockey game was in progress. There was little snow on the ice; the wind had done most of the shoveling.

Within the last two hours Ed Hartnett's regulars had counted seven bands of skaters setting out from the Ecorse shore to visit "friends" in Canada, then watched as they returned with their sleds piled with jute-wrapped cargo. It was hard to discern what the lads of the limberlost relished more, the events unfolding before them or their own running commentary. Early on, when a party of six, all friends from Knox Street, had set out for Windsor hauling a sleigh large enough for 20 cases, Nick had wondered why they were all dressed up. "Probably coming directly from church," said Ernie.

Over on Monroe Street, Agnes packed off her brood with a thermos of hot chicken broth and the usual warnings, issued through a half-opened door as she blocked two-year-old Marce from venturing forth. "Now stick close to shore, come back before sunset, keep Shay buttoned up. . ."

"Fat chance," said Rowe.

". . . And duck for hockey pucks," finished Agnes. "Where's your hat?"

"In my pocket," replied Shay.

"That's a good place for it."

Shay, five-year-old foe of accessories because they cramped her style, could handle cold like an Eskimo. But she was now standing on the front porch locked in layers, confined by long johns, wool skirt, blouse, sweater, thick socks, and an unbuttoned burgundy coat. Under everyone's impatient gaze, she fumbled with the tiny buttons on the velour corduroy.

"Need help?" asked Freda.

"I can get it!" cried Shay, then clamped her mittens between her teeth and started again.

Give Freda credit. She waited a respectful interlude before gently repeating her offer. "Sure you don't need help?"

"I can gif iff!"

Shay looked back down, found her place, eased the last button into its proper slit, brushed back her bangs, hauled out her wool-knit hockey cap with tassel, the one that had belonged to Freda before it belonged to Joyce, and slid it reluctantly over her hair.

So with skates slung around necks, Freda in the lead, Rowe protecting the rear, the girls marched toward the frozen river.

Dia was the first to spot Murph, glasses and earmuffs prominent, riding shotgun in a powder-blue 1917 Reo which was coming slowly up Front, its bi-fold top down, Clayt in back, Tommy Ouellette at the wheel. Once a luxury touring car, this Reo was now a rusty jalopy, with chains on its tires, all four doors missing. They made a right turn into the Alley and slowly chinked out of sight.

"Hey, Freeds!" yelled Shay. "There's Tanks' candy store!"[1]

"You're welcome," said Freda.

---

[1] In 1926, the Tanks lived above their candy store at 4419 Front. By 1930, they were living in a small house at 4346 Front, near the railroad tracks at Cicotte.

Well, double up, fall about, roll on the floor, and slap your thigh. That's all it took. The Tanks had lived there for years, and for years all Shay had to say was, "There's Tanks' candy store," and Rowe or Joyce would reply, "You're welcome." It got Shay every time. George Moore did that, too. "Hey Pa, there's Tanks' house." "You're welcome," he'd say as they drove up Front. No one cracked a smile. "There's Tanks, Mumma." "You're welcome," said Agnes.

Not noted on municipal maps, there was an unobtrusive car launch in Hogan's Alley, a patch of land level with the frozen river. It was located near the tin mill, not too far from Ed Hartnett's houseboat. That's where a powder-blue jalopy, all four doors missing, ambled onto the ice. George Moore would have seen it crawling toward Canada had he not had his elbow on top of the piano, had he not been belting out "Only a Rose."

Admittedly, it was fairly early in the day for this type of carousing, but George had a good voice and, like Agnes, loved to sing. He and the boys were accompanied by Ernie on the upright. The harmonizers began with that boozy standby "Down by the Old Mill Stream," which led to "Down by the Riverside," which led to ♫ *That's why I wish again, that I was in Michigan, down on the farm.* While the singers huddled in soft staccato, ♫ *I want to go back . . . I want to go back . . . I want to back to the farm,* and Nick did a graceful time step, Ollie cut in with, "Wow! Look at that guy go!"

The singers fanned out in rapid response.

A sloop-rigged iceboat was rocketing up the river from the direction of Mud Island, its front side rails kicking up powder where there were thin layers of snow, its canvas sails taut, close-hauled. It was on a port tack, at a 45-degree angle to the north wind, and heading their way.

"God, ain't that a sight," said Ernie, peering over George's shoulder. "Gotta be going 60."

"Better be goin' 60," said Nick. "He's got a Border Patrol car on his ass."

"Where?" asked Ted.

"There." Nick pointed to the tail end of Mud Island where a black touring car, a ragtop, had just popped into view, clunking across the ice in tire chains in awkward pursuit. "Probably spotted him tryin' to land in Wyandotte."

"What are those idiots doing?" said George Moore in disbelief. "Chasing him for a case? How much can he hold in that skinny fuselage?"

"He's probably the only guy on the river that hasn't paid them off. He's probably the least crooked around."

George just shook his head.

The iceboat was now so near that they could clearly see the helmsman leaning out of the cockpit, guiding the rudder with one hand, trimming the sheet with the other. But the patrol car was slowly gaining. Suddenly the helmsman swung the bow of his boat into the wind, the jib luffed, the boom swung over, and the boat came about. It was an expert starboard tack. Picking up a puff of wind, he cut in front of the skidding patrol car and went soaring toward Fighting Island, earning a standing ovation from inside the pub and raised fists from his pursuers.

Within seconds, all bets were placed, the book closed, and noses were glued to the rear windows as the iceboat darted like a demented mouse, and a demented constabulary gave chase. When the iceboat passed the Fighting Island light, its sails started to luff in what looked like a failed tack, and the patrol car narrowed the gap.

But just as the feds got wise and went perpendicular to the iceboat, preparing to intercept, the helmsman did a starboard turn, his runners cutting into the ice as he came about. Then he trimmed and retrimmed his sails and scooted back toward Wyandotte on a downwind run, the wind directly at his back. The patrol car, finding it hard to brake with tire chains on ice, kept sliding toward Detroit, until it slid toward Canada.

"He'll be unloading in Wyandotte before them guys can turn around," said Ernie.

"Them guys'll be in Manitoba before they can turn around," laughed Nick.

———————

Normally, the weekend crowd would be sitting on logs three deep around the bonfire on the bank at Westfield, clamping on skates or changing into shoe skates. But on arrival, the Moore girls had sole access to the crackling fire. It was a dubious privilege, considering the great brouhaha taking place on the ice. Sitting among scattered boots, the girls threaded their skates in haste, while roars of delight swelled frequently from the river. When Shay shook off the first feeble overtures of assistance, her sisters rushed to join the crowd.

Shay, left to contemplate the downside of self-reliance, had to clamp on her skates alone in the glow of the fire, though Freda kept an eye on her from afar. And even after the Federals had skidded toward Manitoba, Shay was still fussing with the straps on her double runners, struggling to thread stiff metal tongues into unruly punch holes, while listening to whoops and squeals and hockey sticks clacking, and Dia, always Dia:

"Hey, Bunny, you got more ice on your seat than we got on the river!"

"Aw, Dia."

"Look at this! Corduroy marks all over the ice. Wide wale!"

Then Shay heard Freda call, "Sure you don't need help?"

"I can get it!" she yelled. And she finally did.

Clinging to any outcroppings, she negotiated her way to the open skating area. Near the shore, the marsh was a reedy stubble; bristles pushing up through the ice. Eight-foot-tall feathergrass lined the bank. To Shay's left, she could see the tops of the wrecks, the wooden freighters that had been partially sunk to make a synthetic reef in the bay. The wood from those freighters had been fueling Eddie Smith's bonfire for years.

Shay gouged the blunt tips of her right skate into the ice, pushed off and wobbled for almost a foot. A sequence that bore repeating. She was just getting the hang of it when along came Dempsey, overjoyed to see her. As he leapt about in ecstasy, she grabbed onto a handy piling, cased the ice for an Ouellette and spotted one playing hockey over near Beaubien's ice ramp. "Hey, Donny!" she screamed. "Would you call off your dog!"

Caught in the act of shooting, Donny hesitated, hockey stick held high, yelled from afar, "C'mere, Dempsey," then smacked the rubber heel of a shoe that was passing for a hockey puck and sent it flying. Too far. The Florsheim slid to a stop in the middle of a 16-foot strip where the men of Beaubien had been cutting ice the day before. Ed Smith used his handmade stick, more tape than wood, to reach the heel and gingerly pulled it toward him.

Though Ecorse hockey players had learned to steer clear of the area where the cutters had been the day before, they preferred to skate near the grid where the ice was smooth. Since ice freezes more slowly under snow, the company kept their vast ice field shoveled.

Flanked by Dempsey, Shay pushed off again and coasted, pushed off and coasted, movement so slight that Dempsey flopped down to watch. Shay hadn't quite learned how to stop, though she knew if she remained upright long enough she could grind to a shaky halt. This technique worked for everything but near collisions; then she just sat down. In truth, she sat down quite often. But Shay was a tough old bird. She'd just brush off her seat and lurch again. With all her compulsory garments, however, it was a struggle to get back up, giving Dempsey ample opportunity to plant a juicy smacker on her nose.

"Hey, Donny, could you call off your dog!"

The mood in the pub had taken a solemn turn until Ernie glanced outside. "Well, fellas. I see Mrs. Dondee's been washing her windows again."

Ollie stood up, incredulous. "Another convoy?"

A black jalopy could be seen creeping around the tip of Fighting Island, followed by another, then another. All told, 16 vehicles. It was a parade of junkers from an auto graveyard, cars that had seen one rut too many—some with their tops chopped off, some with their doors removed. Since black was the most common color the Detroit auto industry had to offer, the caravan resembled a trail of ants.

"That's the third cortege today," said Nick, grabbing the house binoculars, twirling them into focus.

"Do we know any of these guys?" asked George.

"Can't tell yet. Can't see their faces. Might be Clarence in the lead."

Though a few of the cars were untethered, most had cases of liquid cargo in tow: three were dragging sleds; two hauling rowboats on runners; one pulling what looked like a large raft on skids; and one was hitched to a lugger that sat a few inches off the ice, having been outfitted with steel runners from a sleigh. Bringing up the rear? An old powder-blue Reo, its bi-fold top folded down, and a fellow in glasses and earmuffs riding on the lip of the backseat, feet over boxes.

Many new highways between Michigan and its Canadian neighbors had sprung up that winter. That afternoon, four caravans had crawled across the ice from Amherstburg to Grosse Ile, some had crossed Lake St. Clair, and many had made frequent round trips from Windsor to Detroit. In February 1930, the *Detroit News* would report one convoy of 75 cars.

A lookout was standing on the running board of the lead car like a dignitary in a parade, watching for cracks and abandoned fishing holes. In the cars that followed, doors that had not been removed were kept open, so that occupants could make a swift exit at the first icy groan. On warmer days, some cars carried long planks. When rum runners encountered cracks, they'd hop out, lay the planks across the fissure like a butterfly bandage, drive across them, grab the planks and continue.

"Too dangerous for me," said Ernie.

"Aw, Clarence says it ain't so bad," noted Leo. "He says just watch for black ice, 'cuz it's thinner. If ya hear crackin', don't slow up, drive faster."

"Yeah? Well, good for Clarence, 'cuz you can't see black ice at night," replied Ernie.

"Remember that car that went through the ice near Monroe?" said Ollie. "The one that hung by its front wheels on a chunk of ice?"

"Yeah, I seen it," said Ernie.

"Gave me the creeps," said Ollie. "I heard you could see that thing driftin' for about a week before it sank."

"Aw, they're safe in a convoy, watching out for each other," said Ted. "They know what they're doing."

"Tell that to Willetts," said George.

"Willetts?"

"That kid from Monroe," replied George, "He was in a convoy. They think he got separated. Probably got scared, poor kid, 'cuz they do know he turned back. Hit thin ice."

"He go under?" asked Ted.

"Car and all," said George. "Divers found him gripping the window handle. Died trying to open the window."

"Some old lady on High Street's sure in for a shock," Ted laughed. "Come spring, Barney Beaubien'll be delivering that guy in a 200-pound block of ice." But Ted laughed alone.

"Farce to some, tragedy to others," muttered George.

———

Most of the skaters had yet to notice the convoy. Probably because Pat Dalton, who'd grown tired of hockey, had skated over toward the marsh crying, "Crack the whip!" Within seconds, a chain had been linked: boys toward the front, taller to smaller; Dia, the smallest allowable, relegated to the end. As the skaters began to snake across the ice, Shay lurched forward and snagged Dia's mittened hand.

"Better not!" warned Freda from somewhere up the line.

"I can do it!" yelled Shay.

"You're gonna be whipped around!" warned Joyce, next to Freda.

"I can do it!"

"Okay, but hold on tight!" shouted Freda. "And Dia! Don't let go!"

"I won't!" Dia grinned.

The rope gradually picked up speed, blades in the aggregate chur, chur, churring over the ice, while Shay hung on with both hands, eleven skaters pulling her along. Gaining confidence, she lifted herself from her bent position and dared the wind. It was exhilarating. It was also precarious. She retreated quickly back into a hunch.

"Hold on!" shouted Freda.

"I am!" yelled Shay as she soared across the ice, her coat, which had somehow become unbuttoned, billowing backward. Faster, faster. The tall reeds whirred by. The wrecks were a blur.

Pat Dalton dug his hockey skates into the ice, increasing the speed. Faster, faster. Joyce screamed. So did Shay. Her ankles were turning inward, her skates were turning outward, while she was going forward at a terrific clip. Heaven. She was in heaven.

Then Pat Dalton hollered, "Crack the whip!" and the boys in front of the line began to weave back and forth. The screams grew louder. Faster, faster.

Despite the speed, despite being whipped to and fro like a rabbit in a hound's jaw, Shay continued to hold on, now more from fear. But no doubt she would have been just fine if what happened next hadn't happened next. Over near Beaubien's ice dock, the hockey puck got away. One of the players broke from the game to chase it, deftly avoiding the chain of skaters as he neared. But the stinging tip of the whip, otherwise known as Shay, was uncoiling at that very moment. She came at him on a collision course, screaming "Watch out!"

The hockey player did a lateral leap, just missing her as she snapped by. Unruffled, he recovered the rubber heel, gave it a resounding slap, then skated back to the game.

Semi-gloveless, Shay was sailing across the ice, past the wrecks, through the marshy stubble, on a direct course to the wall of tall grass that lined the bank. And she had no brakes. She was running out of ice.

"Slide, Kelly, slide!" yelled Rowe.

"Use your edges!" yelled Joyce.

"What edg . . . !" That's all Shay said. That's all she had time to say as she roared up, over, and in. Hard. Into the reeds. And was out of sight.

Oooh, sweet Mama.

Freda, the first to arrive, addressed the tall grass. "You okay?"

"She okay?" asked a concerned Rowe, braking with a flourish.

"Geez, did ya see that?" laughed Pat Dalton as he reached the reeds. "She went ass over tea kettle."

Warily, Freda parted the curtain and looked in. There was Shay, flat on her face, nesting in the grass. She rolled over slowly and looked up. "I'm fine," she said. But when hauled out and propped up, she wasn't fine. Her left kneecap had wandered off. Having abandoned its socket, her peregrinating patella was now an unsightly knob, just below and beside where it should have been.

"Better get Pa," mumbled Freda.

"Better get Dr. Durocher," said Joyce.

"Better get a priest," cracked Rowe.

"I can get it! I can get it!" shrieked Shay. And she reached down, pulled the knob up, pushed it hard and popped it back into place. Then, standing unaided, she wobbled back out on the ice, and yelled, "Hey, you guys! Look! Cars!"

Dia was elated. "It's a convoy!" Then she looked to her left. "And they got compannny!"

———————

Someone in Ed Hartnett's houseboat noticed the law at about the same time as Dia. "Oh, oh," said Nick, looking toward River Rouge through his prized binoculars. "I think somebody was left off the payroll."

Heads cranked left. Three grim and humorless Packard touring cars—bull's-eyes on their sides trumpeting Michigan State Police—were heading toward the convoy.

"Here's where it really gets dangerous," George muttered.

The convoy, which by now was mid-river, slowed. Cars attached to cumbersome cargo were sitting ducks. But those rum runners, who had been holding knives in their teeth in order to cut loose from freight if the ice gave way, sliced through the ropes. Seconds later, as if on cue, black cars peeled off every which way and scurried across the ice, leaving sleds, rowboats, luggers and case after case of Canada's finest. While two of the state police cars gave chase, the third crept warily toward the powder-blue Reo, which just sat there, going nowhere, seemingly stunned.

"Why doesn't he take off?" said Ollie.

"Maybe he's a decoy; maybe he ain't hauling," said Ernie.

"Naw, looks to me like he's sitting low with a load," said Leo. "Right, Nick?"

Nick scrutinized the Reo with his field glasses. "I'd say so. That kid in the back ain't ridin' like homecoming queen for nothin'. He's planting his feet on a mountain of booze." Nick refined the focus for a better look, brought the binoculars down by his side, thought about it, put them back to his eyes, and refined the focus once more. But no matter how many times he refocused, that kid in the back with glasses, the kid busily fiddling with his shoes, was looking awfully familiar. And that other kid, the one slithering like a python over the front seat into the back, also reminded him of someone he knew. Nick turned toward George, went to say something but thought better of it.

The police car, now within ten yards of the Reo, grill to grill, stopped and idled. It was an odd standoff. Then two officers got out and walked gingerly over the ice.

"Why they walkin' so funny?" asked Ted. "Whadda they got on their feet?"

"Ice creepers, like spikes," replied the agent.

"It's like the Perils of Pauline out there," said George.

The state troopers came within four feet of the Reo when the two in the back seat scrambled out the left side of the doorless car, faster than a Red Wing coming out of the penalty box, and began to sprint toward the American shore, having donned clamp-on racing skates. As for the Reo? It sped off downriver.

"Now, them's your decoys," said Ed.

While the police car went after the Reo, the troopers slid clumsily after the skaters, shouting "Halt!" The skaters ignored them, widening the gap.

Then one of the troopers screamed "Halt!" again, and the other took out his gun and shot it into the air.

The gunshot echoed up and down the ice, to Dia's delight, as she stood, rooting on the fleeing felons. But her delight was short-lived when Freda told her to take Shay and get back to shore. One of the felons, who looked a lot like Clayton Riopelle, headed for the inlet at Hogan's Alley and quickly vanished from view, pursued by an officer. The other felon was racing directly toward them, shouting the same thing over and over.

"What's he saying?" asked Rowe.

"Sounds like, 'The cow's coming,'" replied Freda.

"No, cops, cops!" said Joyce.

"Oh, cops!" said Freda.

Eddie Smith was the one who tossed Murph the hockey stick. Pat Dalton's the one who had the players swarm round and swallow him up. Donny Pilon's the one who sent a boy about Murph's size racing for the bank, with instructions to just turn around and come back once he'd reached it. By the time the state trooper ice-crept his way to them, Murph had doffed his earmuffs and glasses, traded jackets, and was blending into a fervent, hard-fought game that included dogged scrambles for the puck and much spirited shouting—"Hey Frank, over here!" "I got it, I got it!"

The trooper stood outside the periphery for a while and studied each player closely. He asked a couple of questions of the "anybody seen" variety, but he knew he wasn't going to get any help from this crowd, seemingly all caught up in the game. He looked cold. He looked miserable. And visibly relieved when the other trooper joined him, even though the other trooper was wearing a look of disgust.

And what happened to Clayt? He could be found warming himself next to a bucket containing two circling walleyes inside Denny McGrath's fishing shanty, while Denny stood outside arguing with a very young, very baffled state trooper over whether or not the trooper needed a warrant to enter. Denny was a lawyer and knew the lingo.

And what of George? He slept over on the Victorian couch that night. On Monday he avoided both Agnes and loud noises.

Chapter 18

Saturday, May 28, 1927

Bullets were flying. The government had the irritating habit of shooting at suspects. As Prohibition continued, this habit became more problematic because the feds and state troopers began to suspect nearly everyone.

Fishing and pleasure boating were no longer safe on the river, and the danger had nothing to do with the treacherous eight-mile-an-hour current. Since the advent of the 18th Amendment, the feds had managed to kill or maim a decent number of Downriverites. Immigration officers had seriously wounded Frank DeVoss, 26, of Ecorse in July 1925 as he was out boating with friends on the River Rouge. Also in 1925, Federal agents shot at three boys boating on the Detroit River. When the three had passed the Federal cruiser, the agents signaled the boys to pull alongside. The boys thought the men were waving, so they waved back and continued. The boys had no idea that they were being pursued until the feds opened fire. When they stopped their engine and reached for the sky, the hooligans were identified. Two were sons of Charles F. "Body by Fisher" Fisher, vice president of Fisher Body. The other was the son of William M. Walker, president of Walker Bros. Catering Co. There was nothing more on board than an oil can.

Then in 1926 Federal officers shot and killed William A. Niedermeier, a South Rockwood mailman by mistake. Lawrence Campeau, 24, of River Rouge, was killed by the Immigration patrol while he and his brother John were testing a Christmas present, a new outboard motor. On February 19, 1927, a Federal agent shot 23-year-old Robert Miller at a boathouse garage at 4619 Front in Ecorse. And in May 1927, James Lee was at the wheel of his new boat, while his 11-year-old daughter Mildred sat beside him and Charles Stringari sat in the stern. According to witnesses in other boats and on shore, when the Customs cruiser came within 300 feet of the Lee boat, it swerved sharply and headed right for the Lees, traveling at 20 to 40 miles per hour, ramming it, sailing over its bow. Stringari leapt into the river, incurring five broken ribs and a broken collar bone, but Lee and his daughter were killed in the collision. Witnesses claimed that the officer and his partner were laughing as they left the scene.

1927 had been a rough winter in Ecorse. Everywhere money was tight and getting tighter. There were the usual complaints on the police blotter about boys stealing coal, though pilfering fuel was beginning to involve men: someone destroyed a section of Mr. Kernan's fence at 15 E. Charlotte to get to the coal in his yard; another broke into Mrs. Thominson's coal shed on 2nd Street; someone pried the cover off the coal chute at B.L. Sims; and two men were caught stealing a sack of coal from the National Ice Company. Then that spring, quarantine signs went up for scarlet fever at 21 Apple Grove, 41 Elton, 33 Eliza, 4412 3rd and 59 East Rockwood, while diphtheria was isolated at 24 East Woodward as well as 4435 Monroe, across the street from the Moores.

It had also been a rough winter for the Moores. George's Rocking Chair campaign for village president had been less effective in 1927. In March he'd lost his bid for reelection to his old rival Alf Bouchard by 180 votes. That extra $500 per annum was going to be sorely missed, especially since Freda and Rowe would be entering 9th grade come September. Because St. Francis stopped at 8th, their options were limited. The girls could attend School Three tuition-free where Miss Munn was now principal. Not a chance. Instead, George and Agnes planned on enrolling the girls at Our Lady of Lourdes in River Rouge.

And more bad news: the Ford Motor Plant was stopping production on the Model T to retool for the Model A. That May, 60,000 men in the metropolitan area were being laid off, with 10,000 more caught in the ripple effect. They would not return to work for almost a year. Layoffs meant that men went longer between haircuts. "Well, I can always dive for bottles," George griped to Nick.

———————

For Agnes, Saturdays in May had always been set aside for serious house cleaning. But thorough cleaning involved sending the inside outside, and this May weeks of drenching rain had put a sodden crimp in her plans. A few weekend projects had been accomplished: Freda and Rowe had re-wallpapered their bedroom once more, the upstairs bathroom had been scoured, the upstairs linen closet scrubbed and sorted. The downstairs, however, had gone untouched. To make matters worse, the Eastern poplar tree out front was having its annual seed bacchanal. White fluffs, locally known as Santa Clauses, stuck in the screens and carpeted the front yard and porch. The kids had been tracking them in for a week now.

But Agnes woke up to partial sun on that Saturday, Memorial Day weekend, and to a predicted high of 60. Perfect. By 9 o'clock, the lemonade had been made, the cold cuts prepared, and the tom-tom beat of "Cherokee" could be heard thumping from the Strassner's Victrola next door.

Though her disposition sometimes suffered from the endless repetition of day-to-day chores, a smile softened her face as she stood inside the threshold of the parlor, wearing well-worn slippers and a full apron over a faded housedress. Mrs. Moore was never in a better mood than in springtime when she was down on all fours, up to her elbows in Lysol. Agnes opted to cut a wide swath, tackling the parlor, sitting room and dining room concurrently, saving the kitchen and parental bedroom, the only other rooms on the first floor, for later.

As her ragtag crew bustled around in old dresses, bright bandannas circling their heads, Agnes infected them with her enthusiasm. The screen doors banged open; the screen doors banged shut. Out went the piano rolls and the cabinet that held them; out went the cushions from the green velvet couch. The screen doors banged open; the screen doors banged shut. Out went eight chairs and the heater from the dining room; out went the radio, the fringed lamps, the rugs. The screen doors banged open; the screen doors banged shut. Out went the drapes for Monday's washing; out came the curtain stretchers on which they'd dry.

Within the hour, the downstairs stood gutted. The front porch was crammed with furniture; rugs blanketed the clotheslines; and the kitchen, on the receiving end, had become a labyrinth where a single linoleum path snaked its way to the back door and basement.

As stark light from the overhead chandelier filled the barren rooms, Agnes shouted like an auctioneer: "Who wants the outside windows?"

"I do!" shouted Joyce.

"Great! Grab a chamois and bucket, fill it with vinegar and ammonia, and use the other ladder, the one in the garage," said Agnes, handing Joyce a fold of newspapers. "And do the parlor windows first so we can open them. Who wants to dust?"

"I do," said Freda.

"Scrub?"

"Me," said Rowe, though neither choice was surprising since dusters and scrubbers got to rearrange the furniture at will.

Dia opted for the dustpan and broom, while Shay, her six-year-old knees painted with mercurochrome, the result of a knee-first slide into third base, tugged her mother's apron. "What can I do?"

Like a conjuror, Agnes produced the carpet beater, a splendid affair. With a whoop, Shay ran across the empty dining room, bolted out the back door, wound up and gave a hearty smack to the first unsuspecting rug hanging on the line, enveloping herself in a cloud of dust.

While Agnes commended and cajoled, the hours flew by. Periodically, Joyce and Dia struggled with a bucket of dirty water, weaving like the bar car on the 20th Century as they made their way to the laundry tubs in the basement.

Around noon, Agnes was on the front porch when Ella came out onto her porch, held her mop over the side rail, and jiggled it and her bosom with vigor. Dust fluffs soared over the driveway.

"Two rooms down, three to go," said Ella.

"Good for you," sang out Agnes.

Throughout the day, Ella and Agnes kept up a running commentary—sometimes in English, sometimes in French, depending on the topic—as they talked from their front porches.

"Can you believe it's almost two," yelled Ella, as they shared another shake out.

"Beginning to run out of steam," said Agnes.

Shay thrust a dirt-streaked face out the parlor window. "Um, Freda says for me to ask you, um, don't forget Pa's fried egg sandwich."

"It's in the icebox. Think you can get to it?"

Shay nodded. And had almost withdrawn from the window when Agnes added, laughing, "Wait a minute. You can't go over to the barbershop looking like that. They'll have the Department of Child Welfare after me. At least wash your face and hands." Agnes turned to Ella. "She looks like she's been cleaning out the coal bin." She laughed, then held her side. "Whew! Think I'll sit for a minute," she said, gingerly lowering herself on to the stoop.

"Got the pains again?" asked Ella.

"Kinda wears you out."

"Been eating your prunes?"

"Yeah."

"What about Nujol," said Ella. "Mrs. Lafferty swears by it."

"By the gallon," said Agnes, brushing poplar seed Santas from her dress. "I'll be all right. Just have to work through it, I guess. But what do I know."

Around 3 o'clock in the afternoon, Agnes was crouching in the dining room, scrubbing the heat register, when she began to wonder if she could go on. She knew how to push past tired, had been doing it for years, but the sluggish feeling would not go away. Time for the Lydia Pinkham, she thought—if she could get to it. Setting down the wash bucket, she faced the maze that was the kitchen.

With difficulty, she maneuvered around the radio and sewing machine, nearly tipping over a floor lamp, then squeezed between the dining room table that had been upended and the kitchen table that had been pushed against the north wall. Leaning over the window screens propped against the sink, she unlatched a cupboard and retrieved the green bottle of Lydia E. Pinkham's Vegetable Compound that promised to be a tonic for that tired feeling, that pledged to build up her appetite, get her through the day, then induce natural sleep come night. Shifting the screens a few inches, she created a temporary space in which to inch open the silverware drawer, feel for a spoon, and guide it out. She poured the tonic into the spoon, brought it slowly to her mouth, clamped her lips over it and shuddered. It tasted of wool socks and fennel.

Agnes needed to sit. Just for a minute. She looked round for any available perch but none was at hand. The dining room chairs were on the grass in the backyard. The kitchen chairs had been overturned on top of their table, legs in the air. Even if she did bring one down, there would be no place to put it. Instead, she removed two lampshades from the brown leather seat of George's Morris chair which had been pushed against the icebox, inadvertently knocked a pile of books off the arm of the chair, thought about bending over and picking them up, left them where they had landed, and flopped. Just for a minute. That's all she'd need. She sat there waiting for a second wind.

She felt odd. Not sick, just odd. This was a tired beyond recognition. Maybe she just needed to eat, she thought. She hadn't had anything since breakfast. Marce had been fed, the kids had been nibbling all day, but she hadn't been hungry. She was never hungry. Maybe a piece of cheese. But the thought of standing up, shoving aside the Morris chair, pressing her way into the icebox, seemed insurmountable. Besides, what would she eat? Nothing sounded good.

Agnes gazed at the confusion in the kitchen, stared into the vacant dining room, thought of the unfinished register, the rugs on the line, the clutter on the front porch, thought about what was to be done next, couldn't decide what was to be done next, couldn't decide if she should get up, tried to think, tried to care...didn't care. Her stamina was somewhere in that metal wash bucket, and she'd better find the wherewithal to fish it out. There was so much more to do.

Maybe this was about lack of sleep, she thought. Maybe that was it. She and George had had another row while getting ready for bed. The hushed-and-hissy kind, so the kids couldn't hear. About money. Always about money. She'd let him have it for spending money on beer, then penny-pinching on the household. She hadn't been fair, she knew. George was careful with money, sometimes too careful, and rarely spent money on himself. He'd worn the same shapeless suit for years, so old it was wide at the knees. They'd had an ugly spat, then slipped under the covers at ten. Neither saying another word.

She was getting tougher on George, no getting around it. She felt so irritable lately. And the more she lit into him, the later he got home. The later he got home, the more she lit into him. It wasn't his fault that barbershops were struggling, though she did blame him for losing the election. She tried not to, but she did. Never got off the damn porch.

When it wasn't about money or drinking, it was about Murph. It was obvious he was in the wrong crowd. They had tried talking to him, threatening him, but it hadn't done any good. At times George wanted to set rigid hours, clip his feathers, but Agnes vehemently disagreed. That made absolutely no sense, she had told him. Murph was of age and rebellious; he'd only move out. At least this way they could keep an eye on him. But George was inconsistent; he vacillated, got lenient, then over-corrected. They'd been quarrelling over how to handle Murph for weeks.

She could hear Marce whimpering. "Would someone see to Marce!"

"I will!" yelled Freda.

Agnes winced. There was another sharp pain in her abdomen. Must be age, she thought. Things she used to handle with ease now seemed overwhelming. Her feet were in terrible shape; she had varicose veins; her constipation was getting worse. These piercing pains wouldn't go away. And she was always tired. Ever since Marce's birth. Never felt like she'd gotten up off the mat.

"What can I do now, Mumma?"

Agnes flinched. Shay was standing beside her, having returned from the barbershop. She rested her small elbow on the arm of the Morris chair and waited. Agnes stared at her blankly.

"Mumma, come help us rearrange the parlor," said Freda, heading their way. "Rowe wants to put the piano against the couch wall. But I don't think it'll work."

"It'll work," said Rowe, joining them.

"Where you gonna put the couch?" asked Freda.

"Against the porch wall, under the window."

"Porch wall?" mumbled Agnes, murmuring to herself as if the words were Greek.

Rowe hiked her glasses up the bridge of her nose and waited. "Or we could put the couch against your bedroom wall. But I think it'd look nicer on the other side."

"Then where will we move the floor lamp?"

"Next to the couch. In the corner."

"But there's no plug over there," said Freda.

"We can use an extension cord. Can't we, Mumma."

"Won't everything be all crammed up?" asked Agnes.

"Not if we move the couch against the other wall."

Which wall, thought Agnes. "Which wall is that?"

"The other wall."

"I have no idea what either of you are talking about," said Agnes.

Shay, who, fair to say, had approached her mother first and had waited about as long as a six-year-old can wait, chose this moment to exercise her rights. "Mumma."

"Where ya gonna put the chairs?" asked Freda.

"Mumma."

"Look, bear with me, okay?" said Agnes. "I'm having a little trouble thinking in the air right now."

"Mumma."

"Would everybody just back off!" shouted Agnes, flinging her arms rashly in the air to break their hold, inadvertently clipping Shay hard across the side of the head.

As the stinging slap echoed in the sudden silence, Agnes rested her right elbow on the arm of her chair and buried her face in her palm. Reaching out and feeling blindly for her second-to-youngest daughter who was fighting back tears, she rested her other palm on the crown of Shay's head and patted it soothingly, over and over. She looked up at Freda and Rowe. "Why don't we just bring in the furniture, put everything back the way it was," she said softly. "Do you mind? Just this once?"

Freda was stunned. "The way it was?"

"We could do it ourselves; we could do it quietly," said Rowe.

"I know, but not today. Okay? We've done enough."

A pall descended on the house. Faces were long, inquiries brief, instructions imparted in hushed tones. Chairs, lamps, tables were each given a desultory swipe before being borne inside by somber bearers. The screen doors creaked open; the screen doors creaked shut. When Agnes could bear the dirge-like shuffling no longer, she rose with effort and crossed into the sitting room. "Look, after we put things back, you can all walk to Annie Pie's. My treat."

"Will you go with us?" asked Shay, eagerly.

"Sure."

Agnes was sorry she'd said it as soon as she'd said it.

Chapter 19

That same afternoon

The Moores set out around 4:45 p.m. with Marce in the lead; she had put up a fuss to ride her Christmas present, a thin flat cart called an Irish Mail. Firm-

ly planted on the green-enamel seat, she took off up the sidewalk, pumping the crossbar forward and backward.

Agnes, who had not been out of the house for a couple of weeks, could hardly get over the change: "It's like a jungle out here." Because of the unremitting rain, Monroe Street was a riot of green, lush and overgrown. The Moore privet hedge had filled in. All down the block, tendrils of vines reached and grabbed. Cones of lilacs, heavy with purple flowers, begged to be cut.

Ella, banging out the door and onto her porch to retrieve a rug, stared at Agnes. "You done? You finished?"

Marcia Jean Moore with her Irish Mail cart.

"You could call it that," said Agnes.

Ella looked over at the empty Moore porch and narrowed her eyes. "You okay?"

"We're going to Annie Pie's."

"That's not what I asked."

"I'm fine," said Agnes, as she ushered the children on. "Honest."

And it was true, if her feet held out. Agnes did feel better. In fact, she felt almost chipper as they headed up Monroe. Maybe it was getting out of the house, she thought. Maybe it was the fresh air; maybe it was just the longed-for second wind. Hard to feel lousy on a day like this. Neighbors were out everywhere; children were playing in the streets.

"Your nasturtiums are going to be amazing, Alice," said Agnes.

"Can you beat it?" said Alice Pilon, down on her knees, pulling up weeds. She shifted her heavy-set frame back on her haunches. "Alls I did was toss in a handful of seeds a few years back."

"Good in salads," said Agnes.

"So they say," said Alice.

It was a short walk to Annie Pie's, about a block and a half. The girls, ambling beside their mother, were on front-pew behavior. Bickering was at a minimum; feuds were on hold. Besides, except for Marce who had to be re-strained from pumping on ahead, the girls relished the brief stopovers along the way. Neighbors were inclined to drop their guard during sidewalk-to-porch exchanges, enough so that the Moore girls could accumulate a wealth of gossip.

Across the street, Charles Lafferty bounded down his front steps with a "Hi, Mrs. Moore," grabbed the handlebars of his bike which had been leaning against the side of the house, tossed his right leg over a scuffed seat and coasted down the driveway, his front basket, full of empty bottles, clanking as he ped-aled up Monroe to State on his way to the Ecorse Bottle Exchange.

Then Russell Goodell drove down Monroe and waved, and the girls turned toward their mother, grinning, expectant. Agnes held for a few beats, knowing the longer the wait, the better the payoff, then said, "Wasn't that R U double S/ E double L/ G double O/ D E double L. Russell Goodell?" It was as good as *Tanks*.

Traffic was heavy on Front Street. Downriverites were clearing the city on this Memorial Day weekend. Though some were bound for Canada, oth-ers would wait until the following weekend. Beginning June 1, 1927, Ontario would allow consumption of liquor in its province. Though there was a law about selling to American tourists, it had loopholes.

As two clangs of a trolley could be heard, Agnes ushered her charges to the other side of State Street and crossed onto High. Agnes and her entourage were walking past Cicotte's grocery on the corner when two boys tore out of the al-ley, laughing to bust a gut. One of them, who looked a lot like a Krench, flipped over the front axle of Marce's Irish Mail and went sprawling to the pavement.

"Are you all right?" asked Agnes.

The shorter boy yanked his friend up by the arm, mumbled "Sorry," then they both took off up High, shrieking with laughter, the taller boy limping like Quasimodo. Agnes cautiously turned into the alley, and there was the entrance to Annie Pie's.

The shop, which had been there for over 40 years, was officially Torango's Candy Store. That's what the sign said, but that designation was rarely used. Freda parked the cart away from the puddle-filled tire ruts, and, Agnes in the lead, they all entered the dark shanty to the ringing of a bell.

If there ever was a better argument for not judging a book by its cover, An-nie Pie's was it. Its small interior, to be concise, was a house of JARS! And in those JARS, you had your spearmint leaves, your sour balls, your orange slices.

You had your white rock candy, your Tootsie Rolls, your Walnettos. You had your licorice babies, licorice snaps, all-day jawbreakers, root-beer barrels, B-B-Bat suckers, circus peanuts, chocolate drops, butter toffee, candy buttons, wax bottles, rainbow watermelons, red wax lips, caramels, jelly beans, candy corn, peppermint sticks, horehound drops, chocolate stogies, nonpareils and Papa Suckers, later known as Sugar Daddys.

And behind the counter, with her ample back to them, was Annie Pie, writing the names Frank Krench and Joe Kusnirzak in furious letters on the blackboard on the wall. Bearing down, she added four exclamation points. Then she broke her chalk adding another.

"Oh, dem damn kids," she said, turning to Agnes, smelling of sassafras. She was an old woman, short and round, her dress covered by an apron, her gray hair in a top knot. "Always ringing da bell. Soon as I go in da back. Soon as I get down on my knees to sort da boxes, dey open da door, ring da bell, den run like hell. Dem damn kids."

Agnes, whose son had not been immune to this temptation, nodded in commiseration. "But I thought you could turn the bell off from the counter."

Annie threw up her hands. "Den when do I know I got customers?"

Annie Pie's blackboard, which contained local listings of wayward kids of the week, was well-known. Over the years, the name *Melvin Moore* had appeared on it, along with *Clayton Riopelle*, along with *Link* and *Soxy Goodell*. Worse, Murph had once erased his name and replaced it with Pukey McVomit. He had spent a day in his bedroom for that one.

"Had enough of this weather, Mrs. Torango?" asked Agnes, clicking open her change purse.

Annie Pie rolled her eyes. "Everting's demp. And what ain't demp is demp."

Agnes smiled and planted a penny in each of the four palms that were now thrust forward. No one complained that Rowe and Freda each got a nickel. Seniority was rarely contested.

Dia headed straight for the standing gumball machine, where, if luck would have it, a prize might come with the gumballs. She liked to play the slots.

"You'll only get gumballs," warned Rowe.

Dia waved her off, slipped in her penny, turned the knob, held her bag below the door that read *Thank You*, and five uninspiring gumballs tumbled out. But Dia did what Dia always did in light of Rowe's gloating: she shrugged her shoulders and pretended not to care.

While the youthful Moores deliberated, Annie leaned over the counter and made small talk with Agnes. They had hushed words about the psychopath who had just blown up a kindergarten in Bath near Lansing, killing 45, and they marveled at Lindy's landing in Paris.

Finally, Joyce lifted the rounded tin lids of the jars below the counter, withdrew her selections and deposited them along with her penny on the oak counter, worn smooth by the oil from a thousand tiny palms.

They left the store to the sound of the bell, Marce suspending her Animal Crackers from the handlebar of her cart, Shay peeling a yellow wrapper with its tell-tale red stripe from a peanut-butter and molasses brick known as a Mary Jane, and Dia clenching a licorice pipe between her teeth, having conned Joyce into a dubious trade.

As they stood by Cicotte's grocery store waiting to cross State, traffic had suddenly picked up.

"We're gonna be here all night," sighed Freda.

Black car after black car came creeping up State, one behind the other in a steady stream. Two of the cars broke ranks and pulled up in front of Joe Salliotte's house, downshifting into an idle. The rest continued on, fanning left and right when they reached Front. Something was up.

In the distance, pedestrians hanging around the State Street dock began to disperse. Soxy Goodell, picking up his pace, crossed Front and disappeared into Pilon's grocery store. Joe Salliotte folded his newspaper, pried his creaky body from his rocking chair and went inside, screen door banging. Mrs. Tarkanyi poked her head out of her apartment window above Cicotte's grocery store, dust rag in hand. "More raids, I'll bet." Then she pointed toward the train tracks, toward Lincoln Park. "Look. They just keep coming."

The Moores followed Mrs. Tarkanyi's finger. A second convoy of black sedans was approaching, barely behind the first, its lead car hobbling over the tracks. Then car after car came toward them, some with Michigan State Police bullseyes on their sides, others unmarked.

Agnes turned to Shay. "Did any of those cars turn up Monroe?"

Shay, in the act of making a candy brick malleable and unable to comment, clutched her penny bag and nodded yes.

"How many?" asked Agnes.

Shay held up two fingers.

"C'mon," said Agnes, hoisting Marce off the cart and onto her hip. Marce let out a wail. "We'll get your cart on the way back, Marcie, I promise. We'll get it on the way back."

"Where we goin'?" asked Joyce.

"Away from this," said Agnes. "We'll go up High and wait it out at Mim and Ollie's. C'mon, hurry."

Agnes was not overreacting. It was common knowledge that the first few minutes of a raid were the most dangerous, so she hastened up High with all her children. All, that is, except Dia, who was hanging back to catch the action, angling for a better view.

"Get over here!" yelled Agnes and snatched Dia by the ear, hauling her on tiptoe up the block.

They pressed past Odettes', past Maurices' house and their large garden, past the future home of the Commires. But as they neared St. Francis Xavier Church on the corner, Agnes looked back. Three cars were turning onto High

Street at the same slow pace as the others, and Mim and Ollie's was on the other side of the street and across Bourassa, still a quarter of a block away.

Agnes was frantic. "Get in the church!"

"Aw."

"Dang it, Dia, get in the church!"

They all tripped up the three shallow steps, tugged open the heavy old doors of the main entrance, and stumbled into the foyer.

Since the windows in both the main and side entrances to the foyer had been blocked long ago, Agnes handed Marce to Freda, cracked open the main door and peeked out.

"Oh, God," moaned Agnes. "Can it get any worse?"

The same three cars that had turned up High were now pulling up in front of the church, one after the other, their occupants, at least in the first two cars, somber and jut-jawed. "Treasury agents," mumbled Agnes. And in the last car? Less somber men of the fourth estate, press passes in their hats. No doors opened; no one got out.

Agnes looked at her watch and tensed. 5:14. No one got out of the cars. Until 5:15, until sirens went off all over Ecorse, until the first car in front of the church did a jackrabbit from the curb, sailed through the intersection at Bourassa, made a screeching U turn, and came to a halt in front of the second house from the corner.

Two cars that followed pulled in behind. Doors flew open, men in fedoras piled out, pausing briefly for Detroit press photographers to stake their positions, then ran up the steps onto the deep porch of the large, white, two-story dwelling at 4515 High, the one kitty-corner from the church, the one owned by Mim and Ollie Raupp. Agnes couldn't believe her eyes.

"Open up!" yelled the agent in charge, pulling back the screen door, pounding on the inner door, while five other officers hunched forward. "Federal officers!"

No one answered.

"Open up!" yelled the senior agent, banging on the door. "Special agents with the Treasury Department!"

No one answered.

The senior agent stepped back to check for signs of life inside. Finding none, he beat on the door once more, sending the dogs inside into a frenzy. "Open up! This is your last chance!"

No one answered.

One of the men returned to a car and pulled out an axe.

Agnes tossed her change purse to Joyce, "Run to Cicotte's grocery, call your dad, then stay there," turned to Freda, "Keep everyone here," turned to Dia, "That includes you," pushed open the door, "Hear what I said?" ran down the steps and streaked across the intersection on swollen feet, feeling a little melodramatic, crying, "Wait a minute, for God's sake! There's no need for that!" But by the time she reached the curb, the agent wielding the fire axe had ascended the stairs, the *Detroit Times* photographer was poised for a nifty filler for Sunday's Rotogravure section, and the other agents had drawn their guns.

Endicott, a young officer, all of 19, caught Agnes and held her, as the agent with the axe took a hefty swing backward and a woman shrieked from behind a partially opened porch window, "Don't shoot, don't shoot! There's a child in here!"

"Shoulda thoughta that before," muttered the young officer restraining Agnes.

"Then come on out!" yelled the senior agent.

"Okay. But there's no need for guns!" came the voice from behind the damask drapes. "Please. Just put down your guns."

The men reluctantly holstered their firearms, though the young officer holding Agnes kept his close at hand. The senior agent flashed a badge, then waved a piece of paper in front of the curtains. "We've got a warrant to search these premises."

"What for?"

"Violation of the Volstead Act."

The voice went up two octaves. "You're *kidding!*"

"Just open up, Ma'am."

"But I'm here alone with my little girl and I'm not dressed," said the woman. "I was taking a bath."

"Where's your husband?" asked the senior agent.

"At his garage."

"Endicott, check in the garage," said the senior agent.

Endicott released Agnes and strutted across the lawn.

"No, *at* his garage," came the voice.

"*In . . . at.* What's the difference?" snorted Endicott with a cocky grin.

"He owns a garage on Monroe, a block away," came the voice. "He's working. Go over and see."

"Go over and see?"

"Yes."

"You want us to leave here and go over and see?" said Endicott, laughing. "Well, I'm afraid we can't do that, Ma'am. Besides, what kinda bum leaves his wife to deal with. . ."

"Can it, Endicott!" cut in the senior agent.

"Sir?"

"Would ya stop talking for a sec, so we can get in there by Christmas?"

Endicott's grin got a little stiff. "She's just stallin', sir."

"Stop!"

Jim Lowe was an honest agent, well-respected. But there was liquor inside that house and he knew it. He'd gotten a tip from a good source. He waited as Endicott sulked off, then turned to the window. "Look, Ma'am," he said. "Ya need to open the door and ya need to open it now."

Press photographers, guests of the U.S. government, scrambled for a good shot. There was a reason they'd been invited along. In 1925, after a deluge of negative publicity, the Coolidge administration needed to look tough on Prohibition. Washington had launched a new enforcement drive and set out to woo the press. When agents scored, the Treasury Department wanted cameras there to record the event; it even filmed phony raids for newsreels. U.S. officials were told to label the war against Prohibition a great success.

So, Federal agents stood impatiently outside 4515 High as the door parted slowly and Mim Raupp emerged, dripping, standing in a chenille robe, her head lathered in stale suds, her generous body blocking the curious four-year-old Butzie, as an agent held open the screen door and the press clicked away.

Lowe and three others, including Endicott, rushed past Mim and into the house, while one agent headed for the garage and another remained out front.

"I'm over here, Mim, if you need me," cried Agnes, still standing near the curb.

"Could you take Butzie?" asked Mim.

Agnes approached the officer standing near. "Is there any reason her daughter needs to be in the house while they're searching?" The officer did not look her way, nor did he respond. "My husband's Judge Moore," said Agnes, subtracting a couple of years off George's resume. "I won't run off with her. Let me take the child."

The officer walked up the steps, stuck his head around Mim, and after a minute of negotiations, brought out a wide-eyed Butzie. He led her to Agnes while Mim watched.

Then Leonard Raupp, an off-duty fireman and Ollie's older brother, came from his house across the street and tossed Mim a towel. "I'll get Ollie," he said to Agnes under his breath, then sped up the street.

He wasn't the only Raupp who showed up. Within a 200-foot radius, Butzie had four uncles, four aunts and 33 cousins, 18 of whom resided directly across the street. Needless to say, within minutes there were enough Raupps as well as friends, neighbors and kids on bikes in front of 4515 High to fill Navin Field.

Now that Butzie was safe, now that Agnes and an untold number of Raupps provided Butzie's mother the opportunity to deal with the U.S. Treasury Department unfettered, Mim, who was no pushover, could be heard inside dogging the agents' heels, commenting on their every move: "Mind cleaning while you're up there? I could hand you a cloth."

When the officers had had enough, Mim was escorted out by Endicott, who had been told to watch her. This did not sit well with Endicott, still smarting from the earlier exchange. He parked Mim on the grass in the yard, "Just stand here and pipe down," glanced over at the press, then told the outside officer, loud enough for all to hear, "That house wouldn't pass the smell test."

"What!" shrieked Mim, enraged.

"That's unconscionable!" said Mrs. Craig. Mim's neighbor.

Endicott grinned. He knew how to stifle debate. He'd learned early on that the more offensive he was, the more victorious.

"Calm down, Mim," said Herschel Raupp consolingly. "He's talking about the Pulver Bill. He's talking about using his honker to smell booze."

"And I got the best smeller in town," boasted Endicott, delighted with himself. He had, indeed, been referring to the Pulver Bill, that allowed a Michigan police officer's sense of smell to be used to justify a search warrant.

"So whadja smell?" asked a reporter, turning to a clean page in his notepad, reaching for the pencil perched behind his ear.

"Industrial alcohol," said Endicott.

"Where?"

"In the bathroom sink."

"That was Lysol!" cried Mim, watching in horror as the legman dutifully jotted down the details. "I just cleaned the sink!"

"And you oughta get a whiff of the bathtub," grinned Endicott.

"What's it smell like?" asked the reporter.

"Camay," snapped Mim.

" *Strongly* like Camay," corrected Endicott. "If you get my drift. *Strongly* like Camay."

"Would you prefer it smelled like gin?" asked Mim.

"That's my point," retorted Endicott. "Lysol. Camay. They'll use anything to cover up smells. That's what these alky-cookers do."

"*Alky-cookers!*" Mim was beside herself.

"If you're not a homebrewer, what took you so long to answer the door?" he asked.

"I told you. I was taking a bath."

"Wanna know what I think?" said Endicott to the press. "Here's what I think. She wasn't takin' a bath in the tub; she was makin' gin. She heard the sirens, pulled the plug, rinsed the tub in bubble bath, and ditched the leftover industrial alcohol down the sink. Simple as that."

The screen door swung open. An officer named Sam came down the steps carrying an open Tecumseh Lager beer bottle. He carefully stood it next to the pile of evidentiary items accumulating on the lawn—two funnels and some plastic tubing found in the garage. Photographers snapped away.

Endicott centered himself squarely in front of Mim. "Care to explain that?"

Mim shook her head sadly. Refusing to look at him, she stepped away.

He repositioned himself directly in front of her. "Well?"

"Look, it's been a long day," said Mim, eyes to the ground, trying to avoid him. "I'm tired and . . . This . . . This is just nuts."

He stared into her face. "Well?"

"Okay, I'll explain that. He got that off my ironing board."

"What was it doing on your ironing board?"

"It's my sprinkling bottle. He took the cork out of it."

"Now I've heard everything!" sneered Endicott. "Hey, Sam! Was there a sprinkling cork in that?"

"Yeah," said Sam.

"To hide the beer?"

"To plug up the water," said Sam.

Lowe, who had come out of the house and caught the tail end of the exchange, whispered to the officer next to him, "Would you tell that kid to shut the hell up."

That's when Ollie Raupp broke through the crowd, grease on his gray work shirt, his brother Leonard, out of wind, behind him. "What's going on?"

"What's it to you?" asked Endicott.

"You're in my house," said Ollie.

Jim Lowe hurried down the steps to cut off Endicott. "We've got a warrant to search it."

"What for?"

"Violation of the Volstead Act. You Charles Evans?

"No."

There was a serious pause before Endicott scoffed, "Oh, please, don't give us that one."

Lowe hesitated even longer. "Look, you can make it a lot easier on everyone, including your wife and daughter, if you just cooperate."

"I *am* cooperating."

"You own this house?" asked Lowe.

"Yep."

"Then you're Charles Evans." Lowe pulled out the warrant and pointed to it. "This says 4515 High and it says Charles Evans."

"Well, either you got the wrong address or you got the wrong name. 'Cuz I'm not Charles Evans, I'm Oliver Raupp. Charlie Evans lives next door."

Chapter 20
March 12–17, 1928

Hope springs eternal in an Irishman's breast, even when he's half French. George was running for village president again. **Vote for George A. Moore** signs went stake for stake against **Vote for Alfred C. Bouchard** signs throughout Ecorse, until a blinding storm on Friday, March 9, 1928, buried the names under a foot of snow, leaving behind empty demands of **Vote for**. By the following Monday, March 12, Election Day, customers at Moore's barbershop were well-advised to get the haircut but skip the shave, because George had the jitters. And with good reason. His family seriously needed that $500, and the smart money was on Bouchard.

Poor George. His rent had gone up, leaving his profit margins as thin as his razor. Barbershops were closing right and left, oddly enough for lack of women. Like other barbers, George had benefitted from the bobbed cut, adding just enough female clients to offset the void caused by fewer shaves, thanks to Mr. Gillette. But the Dutch bob was no longer the rage, now that most women and girls were letting their hair grow.

Then there was Agnes. He knew if he lost the election he could look forward to more rocking-chair cracks. To be fair, George was not a natural-born politician, despite the fact that he had the requisite charm. His inability to knock on doors looking for votes wasn't just about inertia, though that held some truth. He hated blowing his own horn and had brought his children up to mute the trumpet as well. If people wanted to come talk to him, ask him questions, fine. But knocking on doors, interrupting dinners, standing on doorsteps bragging about what he'd done, boasting about what he was going to do, went against his grain.

Election Day caused a slowdown at the barbershop. Well-wishers stopped in on their way to School One to vote, but few came in for cuts. Around six, as the shadows grew longer, George turned on the lights and told Arthur to go home. For the next hour, he cleaned his combs, rinsed the sinks, anything to look busy to voters walking by, looking in, waving.

He had told Agnes he'd be working late, wouldn't be home for dinner, would probably wait for the results. But he was too jumpy to hang around an empty barbershop, too on display. So just before seven he put on his scarf, slipped on his topcoat, locked up the shop and headed up Labadie, cautiously negotiating a sidewalk that was getting slick. The ridge of shoveled snow that edged the walk had melted slightly, and the runoff was now refreezing.

As he cut across the intersection at High, voters caught off guard by the plunging thermometer pulled coats tighter and hurried into School One, though Phyllis Gregory paused long enough to call out, "You got *my* vote, George!"

"You, me and Heinie Manush," shouted George.

"Did you vote yet?" yelled Paul Gregory, holding open the school door.

"Yep, this morning."

"Bet you were first in line!"

"You'd bet wrong. I was second!" yelled George, skirting a snow bank, opening the side door of the Village Hall. "Then 11th, 22nd and 81st."

For the next two hours, George could be found indulging in the warmth of the cast-iron coal heater in the main room of the firehouse, shooting the breeze with firemen Fred Pudvan and Ray Maurice and elective-hopeful Ollie Raupp. When the results came in from each polling station and the final tabulations took place in the council chamber upstairs, Ollie Raupp had been reelected trustee. But for George, though he put a good face on it, it wasn't even close. Fred Bouchard had bested him by 535 votes, 1,194 to 659, to win his eighth term. George had been the only candidate to ever defeat him.

So George was deep in thought when he walked the short distance home to tell Agnes, so deep in thought as he turned into his yard that he was almost to the back door before he noticed that the house was dark. Everyone had gone to bed. His heart sank. It wasn't even 9:30. It wasn't like Agnes not to wait up on election night, even if it was a school night.

In all honesty, he'd been looking forward to a postmortem with Agnes, sitting in the kitchen, snacking on crackers and cold cuts, talking out the loss without the need for false bravado, even if he had to eat a little crow with the salami. True, there'd be a wisecrack or two, but Agnes was usually fair. Or at least she used to be. Couldn't even count on that lately. But he knew if she saw how worried he was, she'd back off; she wouldn't rub it in. But for some reason, Agnes hadn't waited up. His only recourse was to go to bed without sorting things out. Hell, he'd be awake half the night.

Hanging his topcoat and scarf on a hook in the landing, he tiptoed up the steps into the unlit kitchen, feeling unwelcome in his own home. As he peered into the darkness, he was startled to see three humps to his right and was even more startled when each hump turned his way. Agnes, Rowe and Freda were huddled in front of the open oven, one blanket covering their shoulders, another their laps, while the pilot light flickered in the dark.

The power had gone out just past seven, right after Agnes returned from voting. She'd called over to the barbershop to see if George had heat and lights, but no one answered the phone. She'd checked with Ella, checked with others, learned they had electric, then called Detroit Edison. They promised to be out first thing in the morning. Frustrated, Agnes got out the flashlights and candles, tucked the little ones in bed upstairs to keep them warm, then called George once more to no avail. Then she sent Freda over to see if she could borrow the kerosene lamp, the one he used for emergencies, but his shop was locked up. Agnes was baffled. He had said he'd be working late, wouldn't be home for dinner, would probably wait for the results. That's when she realized he hadn't said *where*, and *where* was sure to be Hogan's Alley.

So Agnes was in a foul mood when George stood over her in the dark and told her he'd lost the election. She didn't tell him she'd been trying to reach him, didn't tell him she'd pictured him among his friends, crooning "My Wild Irish Rose," didn't tell him she was sorry he'd lost the election, which she was. She didn't say anything at all except "Not surprising."

Turning on his heels, George stumbled blindly through the darkened dining room to their bedroom, put on his pajamas in the dark, in the cold, and went to bed. He lay there for hours, stewing, and, though he was still awake when Agnes climbed in beside him, he didn't tell her he felt very much alone, didn't tell her how tired he was of her irritability, didn't tell her he was sorry that she'd had to handle the power outage alone, which he was.

The election and his loss were never mentioned again. The subject never came up. The same could not be said for "Not surprising." It stuck in his craw. He stewed over the crack for days. Tuesday, Wednesday, Thursday.

That Friday night, George went missing again. He wasn't at the barbershop on Saturday morning, either, when Agnes sent Shay over to check. Paul Movinski was covering for him.

It was St. Patrick's Day. Agnes, who had planned on cooking up a truce with George's favorites—corned beef and cabbage, blueberry pie—would have shelved the whole project for Post Toasties if it hadn't been for the kids. If it hadn't been for the pie dough. Waking up early, finding herself alone once more in bed, she had headed straight for the kitchen to prepare dinner before breakfast, pounding on the pull-out breadboard, venting her anger on a pulpy mass. Now it was just after 10 a.m.; Shay was back from the barbershop wondering what Mr. Movinski meant by "starting a day early." The dough for the crusts, enough for two pies, sat neglected in the mixing bowl, covered with a dish towel, waiting. As was Agnes. As was most everybody.

Though Agnes had the cabbage on hand and the potatoes and carrots, Rowe was waiting to go to Lafferty's for the corned beef brisket, and Freda was waiting to go to Pilon's for four cans of blueberries. The household was run by the wallet, not the purse. However, the wallet was nowhere to be seen. So, while the girls griped, Agnes took advantage of the delay to clean the oven, grease the pans, and refine her grocery list, knowing full well that some ragamuffin would arrive at their door any minute, two dollars in his mittened fist, sent by George for Saturday's expenses.

"Mumma, can I go over to Hollis's?" asked Rowe for the fifth time.

"After you go to the store."

"When's that?"

"When the money gets here."

"When's that?"

"Any minute."

As the morning slowly passed with no kid in sight, Agnes briefly considered concocting a backup menu, but she knew, beyond all doubt, that the money would arrive *any minute*, right after she threw in the towel. So she shaved the carrots, peeled the potatoes, quartered the cabbage, washed the floor, and grew uneasy about the corned beef, which by all rights should now be on the stove simmering.

Around 11, Agnes flirted with the idea of borrowing a couple of bucks from Ella and Nick, but she recalled Ella saying that they had the shorts right now. George hated to buy groceries on credit, said it looked bad, said Fred Pilon took it on the chin when people bought on credit. Besides, what with George's track record, *any minute* was becoming even more of a sure thing. For all his imperfections, George had never failed to send grocery money home. So she filled the Dutch oven with water and a bay leaf, sprinkled in pickling spices, and set the pot on low at the back of the stove, in readiness for the brisket. That done, she cleaned out the silverware drawer and tried to contain her anger over a morning spent on *any minutes*.

"Mumma, can I go over to Gen's?" asked Rowe.

"Any minute."

"But you said that an hour ago."

"Tell me about it."

But *any minute* eventually becomes 60 minutes, then 2 hours, then 4. By noon, Agnes had so much time invested in 15-minute increments that it was hard to give in and change course. But there came a point when she had to accept the fact that *any minute* would now be too late. This was so unlike George. If she hadn't been so angry, she'd have been concerned.

Decision made, she rushed down the basement stairs, past the coal bin, and threw open the door to the walk-in fruit cellar to see what she could salvage for dinner. There was plenty of macaroni but no cheese, plenty of navy beans but no time to soak, plenty of canned tomatoes and five cans of pineapple, the result of a sale at Pilon's.

"Joycie!" she yelled from the basement.

"Yes, Mumma?"

"Run over to Lafferty's. See if they've got any soup bones left."

"What kind?"

"Whatever they'll give you."

"Dia! Shay!"

"Yes, Mumma?"

"Pull up all the cushions. See if you can find any coins. Rowe!"

"Yeah, Mumma?"

"Check Murph's dresser for loose change."

By 3:30 Agnes had two pineapple pies in the oven, and a hambone, along with some macaroni and tomatoes, simmering in the Dutch oven. But Agnes had been simmering longer than the soup. Dinner might be solved, but there was still no money, and Sunday would probably arrive without George. She knew his pattern. If he wasn't home that afternoon, he wouldn't be home 'til tomorrow at the earliest, after he'd slept it off, after he'd sobered up. Or early Monday morning.

So, around five, with less than an hour to go before the sun set and the stores closed, not to reopen until Monday, Agnes took off her apron. It was time for the Kolinsky Marmot. Everyone in the house over 11 knew what that meant.

In the early years of her marriage, Agnes's annual Christmas wish list always left room for fur. Her ideal was a Hudson seal coat, though George liked to point out that at $395 it was a fancy name for dyed muskrat. Though Hudson seal was out, George enjoyed pleasing Agnes, so for Christmas 1919 he had scraped together enough for a deposit, looked up a friend who knew a friend who knew a furrier, bought last year's model in a summer sale for $148, and made payments on the coat at $9.98 a month.

The coat, black and soft and lined with sateen, was made of dyed Kolinsky Marmot. The trim, of dyed skunk, which for marketing purposes was labeled marten, had two billowing bell cuffs that reached the elbow on each striped sleeve and a shawl collar. In its infancy, Agnes saved the coat for special occasions. But familiarity when coupled with a houseful of children breeds rough usage, and the Kolinsky Marmot soon became an all-purpose pelt for cold weather.

To add to the damage, in a burst of Thanksgiving exuberance, Agnes had appended a handmade silk rose to the lapel. And there it remained, year after year, becoming one with the coat. Even so, the Kolinsky was warm, and warm was what was needed that cold, windy March in the late afternoon. So she tugged on Joycie's thick-knit hat, borrowed George's buckle boots, donned the Kolinsky over her house dress, instructed Joycie to watch the soup, enlisted the aid of Freda and Rowe, and set out to find George. Agnes, like the coffee on the stove, was on the boil.

It would not be the first time that Agnes, accompanied by Freda and Rowe, had scoured the neighborhood for her errant husband. Respectable women did not knock on the door of a bar or enter one alone, not even to fetch a husband, unless they wanted to be humiliated. Sending the firstborn to the door, the more waif-like the better, was then standard practice. Better to send a young urchin in threads, better to humiliate the one who had gone missing than the one on the hunt.

"So my mother would say, 'Come on, we're going out to look for him,'"
noted Rowe. "And we'd go all along the avenue, to each blind pig, and my moth-
er and Freda'd stand outside on the front sidewalk, and it was me that had to
walk to the door and knock and say, 'Is George Moore here?' And they'd say,
'No.'... Well, they wouldn't tell you anyhow."

Freda and Rowe, 17 and 14 respectively, knew all the blind pigs, at least within a radius of eight blocks, as they were a major source of their Humo Cigar tins. The first stop would be Ed Hartnett's houseboat. Agnes pulled her scarf across her face, nomad style, her fingertips and cheeks burning as she walked with her daughters in the ruts of Hogan's Alley. The seekers stood aside to let a truck pass. It was not lost on Agnes that she looked like a refugee from a melodrama. All she needed was a shawl; she had the graying hair.

As Agnes and Freda remained on land, Rowe stepped onto the porch of Ed Hartnett's houseboat and knocked on the door. Rowe was intrepid, she took no guff, which was why George called her "Auntie."

"Is George Moore here?" demanded Rowe.

"Better get to high ground, fellas," Ed yelled, prompting great guffaws from within.

Then he came to the door. "Sorry. Haven't seen him for ages."

"Could I come in and look?" asked Rowe.

Ed was incredulous. "Sorry, but you're a minor. That would be against the law," he said as he closed the door.

Back on Front Street, walking was treacherous, though some of the sidewalks were sprinkled with sand or salt. Agnes and her daughters walked gingerly, single file at times, avoiding the slick spots. They stopped at the Polar Bear; they stopped at Walter Locke's. Then Agnes spotted Ernie Boudreau coming out of Lafferty's and ordered the girls to stay put. Ernie spotted Agnes as well, though he didn't let on. Instead, he hurried up State with Agnes calling after him and only stopped when she caught up near Joe Salliotte's house.

"Ernie, have you seen George?"

"Who?" asked Ernie, uncoiling his earmuff away from his right ear.

"George. Have you seen him?"

Ernie tucked his hands in his coat pockets, then thoughtfully booted a lump of ice around on the sidewalk, not so much buying time as filching it. "Nope. Can't say that I have."

But his reply rang hollow, even to Ernie. So when Agnes appealed his finding with "You sure?" he thrust his hands back in his pockets, and concluded regretfully, "Nope. Haven't seen him all day." With that and a fixed smile, he replaced his muff, flicked the brim of his slouch hat in her honor, "Sorry, Ag, wish I could be of more help," then swung round and strode away.

Agnes stood motionless, leery of his willingness to take longer strides than the icy conditions called for. "What about yesterday!" she yelled.

Ernie halted. "Well, I might have seen him yesterday," he said. Then he brightened. "Come to think of it, Ag. I *did* see him yesterday. At the barber-shop."

"And last night? After work?"

"Last night? After work?"

"Yes."

"Oh, last night! After work! Matter of fact, now that you mention it, I might have. But like I says, I haven't seen him today."

Agnes latched on to his coat sleeve. "Ernie. Think. Where might you have seen him . . . if you saw him . . . last night."

"He'd have my head," he muttered.

"Was he at the White Tree Inn?"

Ernie, looked around suspiciously, waited for a Coca-Cola truck to pass, then shook his head.

"Red Front Cafe?"

He shook his head.

"Joe Rossin's?"

He shook his head.

"Hunky John's?

Ernie was silent, not a muscle moved.

"That's it? Hunky John's?"

"I didn't say that."

"That's right. You didn't. Of course, you didn't. But you might have run into him last night at . . . a certain place. On Webster, shall we say?"

"I went into a certain place last night. On Webster, we might say. To clear my throat if you get my drift," he said, flashing a guilty grin. "I wasn't there long . . . at least not as long as some of the others."

"Thanks, Ernie. I'll take it to my grave."

The sun was setting as Agnes and the girls rushed up State, using shorter steps on the slippery spots, longer strides in the clear. They pushed past Cicotte's grocery and Annie Pie's, then crossed Webster, just before the train tracks, and turned left.

Neither Agnes nor the Humo Tin Gatherers had ever been to Hunky John's, for it was fairly new on the circuit. But Agnes was pretty sure it was the first house on the block, a one-and-a-half-story brick flanked by a large, vacant double lot and run by a fellow named John Wozniak. Ella had pointed to it as they drove by one day, noting that the city politicians were beginning to hang out there. For added confirmation, there were now three cars parked out front, the driveway had been plowed, and the shades were already drawn.

Following protocol, Agnes and Freda huddled on the sidewalk while Rowe negotiated the six icy steps of the large porch, then rapped on the door. When no one answered, she banged again. Hard, with righteous gusto.

The porchlight went on. The door parted narrowly, offering a cropped view, a center fragment of a woman in a silk overblouse and a green skirt, covered by a rolled apron, while the pungent odor of cloves and cabbage went straight for Rowe's nose.

"Yes?" said the woman.

"Is George Moore here?"

"George Moore?" said the woman, clearly puzzled and clearly trying to stay warm by shrinking the gap between door and jam. "Why would George Moore be here?"

"Who's there, Bernice?" a man called from within.

Bernice turned from the door. "Some girl. Looking for George Moore."

"George Moore?" said the man, baffled. "The barber?"

"Among other things," muttered Rowe, offended. Try judge and village president, she thought.

"Why would he be here?" asked the man.

Rowe, no stranger to denials, pressed on. "Someone said. . ."

The man laughed. "Well, someone's been drinking joy juice. Tell her she's got the wrong house."

"Geez, Bernice, shut the door!" came an older woman's voice. "You're lettin' in a draft."

But Bernice inched the door open a little wider, unveiling a pleasant cheek and a strand of blonde marcelled hair. "Look, Honey," she said to Rowe, good-naturedly, "I'm afraid someone's sent you to the wrong address. Probably for a joke. Now it's St. Patrick's Day and I gotta houseful of company upstairs and we're just gettin' ready to sit down for supp . . ."

She would have continued if Rowe hadn't looked over her shoulder for help, effectively blowing what little cover Agnes had out there on the sidewalk.

"Who's that?" asked Bernice, opening the door full out. "Your mother?" She stepped onto the porch and pulled the door shut behind her, then crossed her arms to ward off the cold. "You lookin' for your husband?" she called gently. Agnes stiffened, mortified, and would have stepped back into the shadows had there been any. "Somebody musta sent you to the wrong house for a joke," offered Bernice. "He's not here. There's no George Moore here. Maybe he's up at one of the boathouses. Have you tried Charlie Dollar's?"

"Not yet."

"I know how it is," confided Bernice in fellowship. "We've all been there. But he'll turn up. They always do."

"Men!" she added as she stepped back inside. And the door was slowly and kindly shut.

Agnes returned to the corner with the girls to regroup. Now what? Simmy Davis's? Joe Rossin's? Charlie Dollar's? The streetlamp came on, bathing the threesome in a golden glow. Up the block, the clerk from Cicotte's grocery came out to roll up the awning. Time to give up and go home.

Agnes looked back at the red brick house. Lights were now visible in what was clearly the dining room. Shadows waltzed across the amber shades. The houseful would be seating themselves around the table by now. But something was gnawing at her. Beneath the dining room windows, along the bottom of the house, there were three yellow gashes, three horizontal slivers of light peeking above the icy ridge left by the plowing of the driveway.

"There are lights on in the basement," said Agnes.

"Maybe the dinner's in the basement," said Rowe.

"Maybe," said Agnes, "but she said 'upstairs.' Why would she say, "I've got a houseful of company 'upstairs'? Don't you think that's odd? Upstairs?"

"Maybe we should just go home," said Freda, growing nervous.

"Besides," said Agnes, "it wasn't just anyone that pointed that house out. It was Ella. Ella pointed right at it."

A man walked by, pulling his collar up. Agnes waited for him to pass, then studied the house once more. "How many women roll down their apron like a waitress? Especially when they're making a huge dinner? How many would tuck in their bib and not protect a pretty blouse?"

"But, Mumma, she was so nice," implored Freda.

"You can cover for someone and still be nice," replied Agnes.

Suddenly. Across the snowy, vacant double lot. Across the great divide between the house of red brick and the corner of Webster, came the muted sound of a celestial choir, a heavenly chorus singing a glorious song of old.

♫ *Ohhhhhhhhhhhhhhhhhhhhhh.*

♫ *Itttttttttttttttttttttt.*

♫ *Ain't gon-na rain no more, no more.*

♫ *It ain't gon-na rain no more.*

♫ *So how in the heck can I wash my neck*

♫ *If it ain't gon-na rain no more?*

There was a tenor in the choir of angels, one magnificent tenor leading the fold, deftly assisted by a commanding contralto and tinkling ivories, slightly out of celestial tune.

As the singing drifted over the stillness of the snow and glanced off the icy crust, Rowe broke into the devil's own grin. "Want me to go look?" And Agnes did nothing to stop her.

Rowe strolled casually to the driveway, ducked down and crept alongside the brick porch, stood up and, with her back flat against the wall, sidled along the side of the house until she hit the electric meter, darted down and crawled along the crest of snow, and elbowed her way to the first low sliver of light.

"What if someone sees her?" whined Freda.

"Who gives a damn," said Agnes.

Cautiously, while kneeling behind the snowy ridge, Rowe peered in and was met by a sea of green. Green crepe festooned the bar, green chains crisscrossed the ceiling, green tablecloths covered the many tables, green hats crowned the many heads of the Ancient Order of Hibernians and a small sampling of its Ladies Auxiliary.

♫ *How in the hell can the old folks tell*
♫ *That it ain't gonna rain no more?*

Bernice, in her green skirt, was going from table to table, serving corned beef.

It took no time for Rowe to locate her father, since she knew where to look. George, who rarely stood at the bar, could usually be found propped against the player piano, tankard resting on top. And there he was that late afternoon, exactly as described, in the far corner of Hunky John's basement.

♫ *Ohhhhhhhh, it isn't going to rain anymore, anymore*
♫ *It isn't going to rain anymore.*
♫ *The grammar's good, but what a bore.*
♫ *So we'll sing it like before.*

Rowe slid back down the ridge of snow, then rolled over and signaled Agnes.

What happened next happened very fast.

Agnes headed straight for the house, stormed up the front steps, fury for traction, and pounded on the door, which was opened shortly by Bernice. "I told John you wouldn't fall for it, Mrs. Moore," she shouted above the din. "Had bets on it."

Then the saloonière stepped back and cleared a path for Agnes. "Just cut through the dining room to the stairs in the kitchen, Hon. Just follow your ears."

♫ *Ohhhhhhh, the chick-en is a fun-ny bird*
♫ *So my teach-er says*
♫ *We eats 'em up before they're born*
♫ *And after they is dead.*

George was in the middle of a lusty "Ohhhhh" when the hem of the Kolinsky Marmot appeared at the top of the landing. Jack Farthin, who had just arrived and was not yet under anesthesia, turned to friends at his table and muttered, "Batten down the hatches."

"Agnesss!" yelled George over the singing, clearly drunk and clearly delighted to see her. "Come join uss!" Then he motioned her over with such a wild sweep of his arm that he brought a chain of crepe with it. In return, Agnes, clearly sober and clearly just as eager to see him, though her face lacked his aura of goodwill, flung her arm, emphatically imparting youcomehereinstead. George swatted the air once more, having missed the subtlety of her gesture, though he did not miss the crepe. But there was something in the force of Agnes's next gesture, something in the set of her jaw, that implied more of a summons than an invitation, a summons that took the wind out of the next "Ohhhhhhhhhhhhhhh" for most involved.

Making his way through the basement by banking off tables, George grabbed his topcoat off the coatrack, stuffed an arm in its lapel, said goodbye to all, socked his coat once more, grabbed his scarf and hat, and gave Agnes a friendly pat on the head as he passed her on the stairs.

As George, then Agnes, disappeared from view, Freda and Rowe, who had been glued to the basement window, hightailed it to the front of the house and positioned themselves beneath the well-lit porch in anticipation of their parents' appearance. They did not have long to wait.

The front door swung open and Bernice stood aside like a doorman at the Stork Club as Agnes assisted her husband out the door and onto the porch, while he continued to punch an arm through his coat. The cartoons of the day would have had Agnes grabbing George by the ear, like Maggie with Jiggs, but she didn't. Instead, she simply said, "I'll give you 'It ain't gonna rain no more, no more,'" then gave him a shove.

George, by then at the top of the stairs, took off like Lindy. His right foot flew in the air; his back foot skimmed the edges of the two top steps; his body jackknifed from the neck down, leaving his backside parallel to the ground. He would have landed on his keister or worse, if he hadn't clung to the center hand-rail on his descent, while repeating, "Ooh, ooh, watch it, Agnes."

> *"I can still hear the singing," Freda said 60 years later. "It was so cold, snowy and icy. He darn near fell down the steps. It had that doggone high step and it had the bar down the middle where you'd hang on; it's a good thing he was hanging on, 'cuz Mum gave him a shove."*

George was no piker. He had sent the money home that Saturday, but his system had broken down; he had picked the wrong kid. So, for the next few weeks, when George asked Agnes, "Are you coming to bed?" she thought about it for a while before replying, "Any minute."

(L to R) Dia, Agnes, and Joyce

George and Agnes Moore
with daughter, Marce

Chapter 21
May 18–19, 1928

On May 4, 1928, on her seventh birthday, Shirley Ann Moore, otherwise known as Shay, had officially arrived at the Age of Reason. The Age of Reason, decreed the church, began at seven, when a child could differentiate between right and wrong. Shay could differentiate all right, but she was already having glimmerings of a gray area. This Sunday to come, in celebration of her rational state, she would kneel at the altar of St. Francis Xavier for her First Holy Communion.

But before the white dress could be donned, the black soul had to be scrubbed. Thus on the Saturday before the Sunday of her First Holy Communion, Shay would undergo her First Confession. She spent the entire week boning up. Then on a Friday night sleepover, Shay, Joyce, and Dia gathered in Cousin Fern's first-floor bedroom where catechizing lessons continued. Drinking Rock & Rye and snacking on popcorn, they were superbly aided by Ida Montrose, next door neighbor and second cousin to Savonarola on her mother's side.

"What is a mortal sin?" asked Joyce, creasing a page in the gray-papered catechism.

Shay took a swig from her bottle of pop, then let fly. "A MOR-TAL SIN IS A SER-EE-US OFFENSE AGAINST THE LAW OF GOD!"

"What is a venial sin?"

"A VEEN-YUL SIN IS A MIN-OR OFFENSE AGAINST THE LAW OF GOD!"

"The thing to remember when you go to confession," said Cousin Fern, as she rocked knowingly in the only chair, "is to tell your mortal sins first. If you kick the bucket with a mortal sin on your soul, you go straight to hell and you can't be buried in the church."

"The thing to remember," corrected Dia, "is to stay away from Father Morin."

"Name some," said Fern, the oldest there, going on 12.

"What?"

"Mortal sins."

"Um, murder, treason," said Shay.

"What else?"

"Suicide, slander, sloth."

"Sloth's venial," said Dia.

"Sloth's mortal. Look it up," said Ida, a catechistical whiz kid. "What else?"

"Did Father Morin happen to mention Occasions of Sin?" asked Dia.

"OCCASIONS OF SIN!" Shay bellowed, "AN OCCASION OF SIN IS A PERSON, PLACE, OR THING THAT EAS-ILY LEADS TO SIN!" Then she added, "We gotta stay away from those."

"And what are those?" grinned Dia.

Shay hesitated. "Umm. Dirty jokes?"

"What else?"

"Dirty books."

It was obvious from Shay's performance that she had not had much occasion to ponder Occasions of Sin. But what she didn't know, Dia knew. Occasions of Sin were Dia's bailiwick. Dia launched into a recitation so thorough that even Ida was impressed. Dia was a city directory of degradation. Occasions of Sin were Rum Row, Hogan's Alley, the White Tree Inn, the Polar Bear and Patsy Lowrie's. She ripped up Mill Street and down Front Street with ease. She could list the speaks, the owners, the frequency of raids, and all manner of sinful ephemera. Minnie Stinson's was a triple occasion of sin.

The room was hushed.

"Divorce is mortal, adultery's mortal," said Ida, breaking the silence. "Not going to church is mortal."

"Not going to church is venial," said Fern.

"Is divorce really mortal?" asked Shay.

"Not going to church for more than a year is mortal because you couldn't have made your Easter duty," said Ida.

"WHAT IS AN EASTER DUTY!" announced Shay. "AN OBLIGATION TO RECEIVE HOLY COMMUNION DURING EASTER TIME UNDER PAIN OF GREE-VUS SIN! Is divorce *really* mortal?" she asked.

"And you gotta fast first," said Ida, proudly. "Going to communion without fasting is venial."

"I know someone who drank a glass of water and still went to communion," said Dia.

"What happened?"

"Nothin'."

Ida shouted, fists clenched. "Nothin! She only committed a sacrilege, that's how much nothin!"

"Mrs. Gregory is divorced," said Shay, not particularly out of nowhere. But she was sorry as soon as she said it, because Ida lit up like Rum Row on fish night.

"Is she Catholic?"

"Yes," mumbled Shay.

"Did she remarry?"

"Yes."

"Is her first husband still alive?"

"I don't know."

But Shay knew; everybody knew. "Yes," conceded Joyce.

"Then she's excommunicated and living in a state of mortal sin," said Ida. "Who's Mrs. Gregory?"

Shay winced. There was no denying it. She had casually served up a favored neighbor as so much ecclesiastical fodder. "She's a really nice woman who lives at the end of our block, on Labadie. She's really very nice."

"Doesn't matter," replied Ida. "She's still living in a state of sin."

"Maybe Mrs. Gregory got a divorce because her first husband beat her," said Shay.

"Doesn't matter," said Ida.

"What if he left her?"

"Doesn't matter."

"What *would* matter?"

"Well," Ida paused to consider. "If she found out her first husband had another wife, that would matter." The silence made Ida testy. "I didn't make the rules! We can't divorce, you know that. We can only separate and only then for good reason . . . and we sure as shootin' can't remarry."

"But if her first husband left her and she can't remarry, who supports their kids?" asked Shay.

"He does," said Ida.

"What if he doesn't?"

"She can get a job," said Ida.

"Who watches the kids?"

"She can get a babysitter."

"That's hard."

"On who?"

"The mother and the kids."

"No one said life was easy!" snapped Ida. "No one said life was fair! The thing to remember is to . . ."

But Ida could no longer remember the thing to remember and settled for a helping from the passing popcorn.

"I'll bet drinking's mortal," said Dia.

"I'd say venial," said Joyce. "What would you say, Fern?"

"Well, that's tricky," said Fern. "In the beginning, there was Prohibition in Canada but not America, so drinking was a sin for Canadians but not Americans—except if you lived in Kansas. It was a sin in Kansas. Then it became a sin in Michigan, but it wasn't a sin in Ohio. Now it's a sin for all Americans but not Canadians—except Canadians who live in Ontario. At least until last year."

"Well, alls I know is—when it comes to whiskey—it's against the law," said Ida, happy to be back on firmer ground. "And breaking the law's a mortal sin."

But the ground was not so firm as first reported. "I'd still say venial," said Joyce. "What do you think, Fern?"

"Well, that's tricky," said Fern. "In most states, getting caught with a pint of hooch is a misdemeanor. In Michigan, it's a felony. So, in most state courts, carrying a pint of hooch is a venial sin," concluded Fern. "But in Michigan courts, it's mortal."

"Is Mrs. Gregory going to hell?" asked Shay, her manner casual, her voice high and reedy.

"As long as she stays with her second husband."

"Oh," said Shay. Then she stretched, then she yawned. Then she rescued her share of the quilt and announced, "I'm going to sleep now." Then she turned her face to the wall and her back to the party and pulled the blanket up over her head. No one spoke. At least not out loud. Though Joyce and Dia gazed steadily at each other for quite some time. "I'm not sulking!" muttered Shay.

"Maybe Mrs. Gregory got an annulment," said kindly old Joyce. "Maybe she was free to marry again."

"What's that?" came the muffled query.

"When the Pope says you weren't married," replied Ida. "When he says the first wedding didn't happen."

"But if she's already married, how can the Pope say she isn't?" asked Shay from under the patchwork.

"'Cuz he's infallible," said Ida the Absolute, proudly. "He knows if the marriage didn't take place. He knows about the wedding night. He knows if they didn't do anything."

"♫ *He sees you when you're sleeping! He knows when you're awake!*"

"You're going to burn in hell, Doris!"

"Okay, Ida, if you're so smart, answer me this," said Dia. "If Mrs. Gregory is excommunicated, how come she goes to church?"

"She better be careful. Father Morin might single her out at mass. He's done it before in front of everybody," said Ida. "Besides, I'll bet she doesn't go to communion, 'cuz she can't. When everyone goes to communion, I'll bet she just sits there twiddling her thumbs. You can always tell the ones with mortal sins on their souls. Every week they just sit there twiddling. Especially at Easter."

Shay shot straight up. "She doesn't twiddle, Ida!" she hollered. "She maybe sits, but—dang it—she doesn't twiddle!" But Ida was right: Mrs. Gregory *did* just sit there—pulling in her knees and purse, picking up her kneeler for others to pass by.

"Well, all's I know is when Mrs. Gregory dies, she can't be buried in the church," said Ida.

There was a long, stunned silence. Shay's high, tinny voice: "Then where will they bury her?"

"Danged if I know," said Ida. "All's I know is unless she repents on her death bed and leaves her second husband, she can't be buried in consecrated ground."

"Even if she goes to confession?"

"How can the priest give her absolution while she's still with her second husband—you silly sappolina!" yelled Ida. "How can you be forgiven if you're still in the middle of the same sin? She's gotta leave Mr. Gregory!"

"I'm afraid Ida's right, Shay," said Fern, reluctantly. "Pa says when Big Jim Colosimo was shot in Chicago the bishop wouldn't let him be buried in the church because he was divorced."

"What about for being a gangster!" cried Shay. "What about for killing people!"

In deference to Fern's unexpected support, Ida undertook an appeal to reason. "Look," she crooned, "if you kill someone and you're sorry and you confess it, the priest'll give you absolution. You're forgiven. It's over. But if you divorce someone and remarry, all's the time you're living with your second husband, you're living in sin. Because in confession, when you tell the priest you're remarried, he'll tell you to stop living with him. Then, if you go home and still live with him, how can you be forgiven? See what I'm sayin'?"

"I guess," mumbled Shay.

"Good," said Ida.

"Will they bury Al Capone in the church?" asked Shay.

"If he goes to confession and isn't divorced, sure," said Ida, kindly.

Ida must have been reading those tea leaves—else, how did she know that some 19 years later, Al Capone, who never, ever got a divorce, would be buried in consecrated ground, having been given the last blessed sacrament by Monsignor Barry, late of the diocese of Chicago.

And what was Ida's reward for that display of reason? Zero, zilch. Because the *reasons* were not in dispute. Shay wasn't thinking about *reasons*. She was thinking about sweet, kind, pretty Mrs. Gregory. Where on earth would they bury her? Would Mr. Gregory have to haul her corpse from Protestant church to Protestant church, begging? Would they put her in a cemetery with people she didn't know, where she didn't belong? Would they bury her near the fence? Maybe Mrs. Gregory should go to the Methodist church, get to know the minister, get to know the people.

Sobs emanated from beneath the blanket while Joyce sat on the bed and patted the covered rump. And though she maintained she was just trying to help, Dia's suggestion that they put Mrs. Gregory in a Humo cigar tin and bury her in the backyard only made the wailing worse.

"I keep telling you, it's not so bad, Shirley," said Ida. "All's that woman's gotta do is leave her second husband."

"What about her kids!" came the muffled wail.

"She can take 'em with her."

"Even Katie?"

Ida was brought up short. "Who's Katie?"

"The daughter she had with her second husband," said Joyce.

Ida was beside herself. "She had another kid!"

"Yeah," said Dia, "Katie. Mr. Gregory's her father."

Ida was stumped so she came out swinging. "Mrs. Gregory shouldn't have got in this mess in the first place! Some people just mess up their lives, then they want the church to clean it up."

"She's a nice lady, Ida!" yelled Dia.

"Sooooooo! Benedict Arnold was nice, Doris! Benedict Arnold smiled at everybody!"

"So," said Dia, "what if Mrs. Gregory's first husband dies?"

"Problem solved," said Ida. "Then she can confess, be forgiven, and marry Mr. Gregory."

"So," said Dia, "what you're saying is . . . if her first husband dies, she's no longer in a state of sin and can be buried in the church."

"Absolutely," said Ida, proud of the thoroughly reasonable rules and eager to bury Mrs. Gregory with a high requiem mass.

"Problem not solved," interrupted Fern. "Not in real life. Her first husband's still up and kicking."

"Problem solved!" yelled Dia. "All's Mrs. Gregory's gotta do is bump off her first husband."

"Dang it, Dia, that's MUR-DERR!" screamed Ida, furiously threatened and not knowing why. "Then she's still in a state of mortal sin for MUR-DERR!"

"Not if she goes to confession," said Dia. "If she's sorry for killing him, the priest has gotta give her absolution and, once she's forgiven, she's home free. She can marry Mr. Gregory and who's the wiser?"

"YOU'RE MISSING THE POINT! SHE SHUN'TA LEFT HER HUSBAND IN THE FIRST PLACE! THEY COULDA TALKED THINGS OUT!" Ida was beside herself. "You don't hear 'em saying, 'In sickness or in health 'til death do us part except for extenuating circumstances,' do ya? You're not married just for the good times, when everything's hunky dory. A vow's a vow, else why have vows? Huh? HUH?"

It rained that Saturday; it was coming down hard. Over on Front Street, George Moore slumped low in a barber chair as he gazed out the window of his empty shop and subtracted the day's loss from the week's groceries. The dampness heightened the smell of bay rum. Rain was bouncing off the bench, bouncing off the sidewalk, bouncing off the barber pole. He watched impassively as steam rose above the cinders at the entrance to Hogan's Alley. The fishing shacks and houseboats were lost in a sinister mist.

Lights were on in the parlors of Ecorse. As a precious Saturday ticked away, anxious children, elbows on sills, stared out rain-streaked windows, baseballs by their sides. Lights were on in Harry Riopelle's garage as well, where windows were cracked for cross ventilation and a boat was on the hoist. Frank Lafferty, informed by WJR that this might be an all-dayer, rolled up his sleeves and scoured out his meat case. The counter stools at Seavitt's were empty. Edges of freshly made ham salad began to brown in the refrigerator.

Over on Monroe, two church-bound penitents lingered inside the front screen door. Having been instructed by Agnes to wait until it tapered off, Shay and Dia perspired freely under their tented black slickers, their eyes peeping out of visored helmets like knights of yore.

"It's never gonna let up, Mumma," said Shay, longing to stay home.

"Then go ahead. But buckle those boots!" said Agnes. "And careful crossing State."

"Don't park yourself across from the Confessional and listen in, Dia," warned Rowe.

"And stay away from Father Morin," said Freda.

"Would someone like to tell me how?" said Shay.

"Smell for Old Spice," said Freda. "Father Morin uses Old Spice. Just mosey past the confessional and get a good whiff."

Dia and Shay slipped reluctantly onto the rain-washed porch and peeked through the window. As Rowe and Joyce grinned back at them, Dia fumbled with the latch of the big black umbrella. It unfurled with a flump. Then, parasol aloft, the twosome filed tentatively down the steps. They did not, however, make a clean getaway. The parlor window rose with a swish as the conjoined couple inched along the sidewalk in lockstep. Warnings and wisecracks trailed them like a string of tin cans. Finally, after a spirited chorus of "Sing, You Sinners," the cleaning ladies closed the parlor window. The sound of their laughter lingered in the sodden air.

Arriving at the corner, the Morton Salt girls waited for a break in the oncoming traffic. A puddle the size of Lake Erie ringed the curb. Beyond that, a chain of cars crawled along, blocking their path.

Seeing a small opening in the traffic, Dia tensed her muscles and prepared for the sprint. "Ready?"

The two raced across State. The small, brick church with its square, slate steeple stood at the far corner of the block. And glory be to God, the door would always be unlocked. Dashing up the three shallow steps, Shay hauled open one of the heavy red doors and slipped inside; Dia and the black umbrella scrambled in after. As the door slowly closed, the din of the rain receded.

Shay gingerly peeled off her rain hood, then retied her triangular kerchief, making

Shirley Ann Moore (Shay),
First Holy Communion

sure her head was not uncovered in the process. To sponge up the tracked-in rainwater, someone had tossed towels on the cold marble floor of the darkened vestibule. Open umbrellas lined its corners.

Except for a few coughs, the church seemed hollow, empty. A small cluster of penitents huddled in the back near the confessionals. Muted shafts of light from the stained-glass windows streamed dimly into the side aisles. In the gloom of the vaulted shelter, the candles in their red glass holders winked and blinked.

Dia stuck her head into the sanctuary and did a cursory surveillance. The line was shorter for the confessional on the left, she whispered to Shay, but she would hesitate to recommend it. Even though Father Morin was generally on the left, he had been known to hook a right.

"So which one do we go to?" whispered Shay.

"Stay put," whispered Dia, raincoat unhinged and boots unbuckled. "I'll case the joint. Maybe we'll get lucky. Maybe there'll be a visiting priest from the missions."

Shay nodded, having been apprised of the theory of the foreign missions in evening sessions. Periodically, a priest would visit from the Congo or Outer Mongolia. The prevailing view held that the visiting missionaries had been preaching to pagans and cannibals so long it made the sins of a kid from Ecorse pale in comparison. They'd heard everything. Eating human flesh made filching a nickel off Murph's dresser look like penny ante.

While Dia swished and chinged her way down the center aisle, Shay dipped her fingers into the holy water font, made a dainty sign of the cross, and followed. Deciding to take her chances, she genuflected beside a pew on her right, glided into the empty row, opened her raincoat and turned down a kneeler.

As she faced the high white altar, with a statue of the Blessed Virgin on the left and St. Joseph on the right, the wind-driven rain pelted the stained glass windows. Dia chinged into the pew and half sat, half kneeled beside her. "Looks bad," she grunted out the side of her mouth. "What we've got here is confession roulette. Old Morin did it again. He left the names off the doors. But Bunny Strassner says there's a visiting missionary on the left. Absolution guaranteed."

"But you said Morin was usually on the left."

"Today he's on the right."

"Yah sure?"

"Would I kid you?"

Ignoring Dia, Shay stuck to her guns, and soon it was her turn. But as she closed the door on the confessional, she looked behind her one last time. There was Dia cocking her right trigger finger at her head while cutting her throat with her left.

It was dark inside the confessional. Very dark. Kneeling down, Shay faced a blank mahogany wall. As her eyes grew accustomed to the gloom, a small square grating began to take shape before her. While anxiously running over her many sins, she could hear the murmuring of the priest through the closed grate.

Then the murmuring ceased and wood slid against wood; then wood slid against wood once more as the grate on her side opened. A deep voice said, "Begin," followed by a strong whiff of Old Spice. Snake eyes!

"Begin," repeated Father Morin.

Shay rapidly patted out the sign of the cross while mumbling into the latticed divide, "Bless me, Father, for I have sinned." She could vaguely make out the silhouette of a chest.

"How many weeks since your last confession?"

"This is my first time, Father."

"You'll have to speak louder, my child."

"Sorry, Father." Then the words tumbled out just as she had memorized them. "I lied twice, coveted once, sassed four times, stole once, told a dirty joke once, committed gluttony once and sloth twice. For these sins, I am heartily sorry, especially for the sin of sloth. I have a lot of sloth, Father."

"What did you steal?"

"A nickel."

"From who?"

"My brother." She almost said Murph. She almost gave herself away. "Off his dresser. He caught me, Father."

"What was the joke?" asked the priest.

"Pardon me?"

"What was the joke?"

"The joke?"

"Yes, the dirty joke. What was it?"

"You want me to tell you the dirty joke, Father?"

"Yes."

"It wasn't very funny."

"Even so."

"I don't remember, Father."

"You don't remember?" There was a long pause. "Or you won't tell me?" A longer pause. "Might I remind you, the sin of omission is a sin, too."

Sweat trickled down the heavy rubber lining under her raincoat. How do you impart to one of God's holy emissaries a wretched joke where doo-doo is the punchline? How do you say doo-doo in church?

"He tried to pin me down," said Shay. "But I wouldn't tell him. Finally I heard 'May God grant you pardon and peace and I absolve you of your sins....'"

The rain was still pounding when they stood on the church stoop underneath their umbrella. Then Shay shoved the umbrella at Dia and took off up High Street, running, then airborne, running, then airborne, splashing through puddles. Absolution guaranteed!

Chapter 22

Prohibition was spectacularly unpopular. It was so flagrantly violated that Michigan enacted more laws, provided stricter enforcement, and stiffened the penalties. Then, in the fall of 1927, the state legislature passed the Michigan Habitual Criminal Act which required persons with three felonies to be sentenced to life prison if convicted a fourth time. It became known as Michigan's "Life for a Pint" law.

It wasn't long before the law cast wide its net and caught its first minnow. The hapless chap was a Lansing man named Fred M. Palm. Palm, who already had a pair of felonies when he was picked up for possessing two pints of liquor, was released on bail. He then did an imprudent thing: he didn't show up for his hearing, now considered his third felony. When police officers armed with a bench warrant arrived at his home to arrest him, they gained entry, inspected his house without a search warrant, and discovered a "partially-filled" bottle of gin. Back at the station, the remaining contents were meticulously measured and found to be just over 14 ounces. In the fall of 1927, Fred Palm was sentenced to life at hard labor. One of the arresting officers was Frank Eastman.

Dia was incredulous. "He's getting life for a pint of gin?"

"That wasn't his first pint, Doris," scoffed Ida. "He was arrested three times before for things. He was warned."

"But Pa says they made an illegal search."

"Doesn't matter, he knew the law," said Ida. "Oh, c'mon, Doris. Illegal or not, they found nearly a whole pint of gin in his house."

"What if he's an alcoholic and can't stop hisself?"

"Everyone can stop. They just need a little self-control. When Prohibition came in, my mom stopped drinking, so'd my dad. If they can stop, everybody can. If my father said this once, he's said it a million times. You have to be tough with these people and have the same punishment for everybody. No matter what. We can't leave it for a judge to decide. If you let judges decide, it'll be all over the place."

Down at the barbershop, Ralph Montrose was having a similar beef with George.

"But think about it, George," said Ralph. "If we let one person get away with something, we have to let everyone."

"Instead, we abuse everyone equally. King Solomon would have had a helluva time with mandatory sentencing."

———

Palm's appeal, on the grounds of unlawful search and cruel-and-unusual punishment, would be denied in January, 1929. One month before, in December, 1928, 48-year-old Etta Mae Miller, also from Lansing, went on trial for possessing two pints of moonshine. It took a jury 13 minutes to find Etta Miller guilty. Because this was her fourth moonshine offense, in the eyes of the Michigan legislature she was an "habitual criminal" with no hope of redemption. "It is the sentence of this court," said Judge Charles B. Collingwood to the recidivist Miller, "that from and after this day you shall be confined in the Detroit House of Correction for the remainder of your life." Etta, the mother of ten, was now Convict No. 1289. That same day, in the same court, a bellboy pled guilty to manslaughter, was fined $400 and freed.

"But what about Etta Miller?" said Dia.

"The law's the law, evil's evil, and there's no extenuating circumstances. Forgive her, judge, she has ten kids. What's that got to do with the price of baloney? The difference between right and wrong doesn't change. It's wrong to steal bread. Period. Says so in the Bible."

"What about not eating meat on Friday? Is that in the Bible?"

"That's tradition. We also have to follow tradition."

"The Baptist church says dancing's a sin," said Dia.

"Dancin's not a sin. No way," said Ida. "Maybe shimmyin'. Yes, I think I heard that shimmyin's a sin, but how could waltzing be a sin? Besides, why on earth would you think the Baptists are right, Dia?

At least five people in Michigan would be sentenced to life in prison for liquor violations. On April 2, 1929, despite strong protest from the Anti-Saloon League, Michigan would repeal its "Life for a Pint" law.

There would still be one new wrinkle. When Etta Miller's case was on appeal in 1930, Frank Eastman, the arresting officer in both the Palm and Miller cases, admitted during an investigation that one of his fellow officers had planted the liquor in Etta's home.

In 1930, Michigan's governor would commute the sentences of all five Prohibition violators.

Chapter 23

Thursday, July 26, 1928

Though July 26, 1928, did not fall on a Sunday, it certainly dressed like one. For an ordinary Thursday, it was putting on airs. Stores were closed, the Village Hall was shuttered, even the speaks were locked for the day. By 8:30 in the morning, hundreds were flowing toward the State Street dock, carrying babies, pushing strollers, tricked out in their church-going best, while hundreds more were already huddled around the pier or milling along Front Street, lugging baskets and blankets, bathing suits and bats. Cars were parked on both sides of Front. Others spilled into the side streets and onto donated yards, as well as Lefty Clark's parking field next to Uncle Peck's. But unlike sleepy Sundays, the air was electric, expectations high. Gloria in excelsis Deo! Or as Shay would have it, gloryoski! It was Ecorse Day in Ecorse.

For years, the parish of St. Francis Xavier had sponsored a church picnic, more often than not at Elizabeth Park, just a few miles downriver by car. Then in 1922 someone had suggested boarding a boat for Sugar Island, an excursion which met with such success that a boat left for Tashmoo Park the following year. And for the past five years, the destination had been a Canadian island in the Detroit River originally named White Woods, after its birch, beech and white-barked poplar trees.

The problem was, it was christened by the French, so White Woods was in reality Bois Blanc, a pronunciation which flowed alliteratively down their Gallic noses. Needless to say, the Americans made a quick hash of it, opting for Bo Blahnk or Bwah Blonk or dismissively Blah Blah. The corruption was completed when Blah-Blah became Bwab-Lah became Bob-Lo.

Since 8:25 Agnes had been seated on the broad fourth step of the Ecorse State Bank in yesteryear's dress—the brown one with the organdy collar and this year's hemline—hamper by her side, Dia and Marce above her, Shay and Joyce below her, waiting for the boat that would arrive at 8:45.

It was a pleasant 75°—all blue sky, with haze along the horizon and an affable breeze coming from the water. "Enjoy it now, it's supposed to get into the 80s," warned Mrs. Davies as she passed by.

"At least it'll be cool on the river," answered Agnes.

A line had formed at the dock. Freda, who had turned 18 the day before, and Rowe, nearly 15, were close to the front. They stood behind a gangplank covered by a striped canopy, ready to leap on board and hurl themselves across ten deck chairs. George, dapper in his straw hat and white summer suit, communal duffle bag by his side, stood with them, while Murph was waiting off to the side with his girlfriend Lillian.

George shared his children's excitement; he also welcomed a day off, though it meant a day's loss in income. Fred Pilon, further back in line with his family, was also feeling the pinch, as were most of the businessmen in town. With fare at 60 cents for adults, 40 cents for children, George had already shelled out $4.20 for the excursion alone, enough to buy Joycie, whose turn it was, her back-to-school shoes.

At 8:43, having asked the time so often she'd been handed Agnes's watch, Shay grew silent. Palm over eyes, she stared directly into the rising sun, training her gaze on the river, on the waters beyond Ecorse Bay, in anticipation of the white colossus that would soon drift into view above the shacks and treetops.

"Listen, dang it!" yelled Shay, hand to ear. Though faint, the music, at least from the brass section, was arriving. ♫ *By the Sea. By the sea. By the beautiful sea.*

"Dia, Joyce. Grab the hamper!" yelled Agnes. "Shay, Marce. Grab my hand!"

Near the dock a sea of hats spun left. But while the trombones increased in volume, the ship had yet to make her appearance, lending her an entrance that even Jolson would envy. Suddenly there was a long blast from a horn, and as a cheer went up and someone yelled "It's the *Columbia*!" —a majestic steamer, four-stories high and wide at the hips, loomed slowly from stage left.

Columbia bound for Bob-Lo Island (Virtual Motor City Collection, Walter P. Reuther Library, Wayne State University)

The 200-foot oval, which could hold 2566 passengers, seemed to be sitting atop the water as she slid by, seagulls circling her stern. Her long railings, one atop the other, defined her four open, gleaming white decks, and were already lined with jubilant passengers who had embarked in Detroit. But a quick glance reassured those waiting on land that many choice seats were still to be had. The pilot eased the *Columbia* alongside the State Street dock, while men tossed out lines and secured the gangplank.

As the ship towered over the crowd, Agnes cautioned her charges to stay together as they inched forward, then hauled themselves up the sloping gangway. Once on board, Agnes and the girls passed through the stained-glass doors and wove their way up the *up* side of the wide mahogany staircase to the more popular second deck, which offered a dance floor, food concession and souvenir stand.

"Over here!" yelled Freda, beckoning to her mother, while Rowe sprawled across six wooden chairs near the starboard railing and George unfolded two more. Stacked chairs were everywhere. So was the smell of popping corn. There was a departing blast from the horn, the band played "Anchors Away," then the tall feathergrass of summer and the shacks of Rum Row began to glide by in slow motion. The *Columbia* was underway.

———————

Nearly 2,500 from Ecorse would embark for the island that morning, a fourth of the population. Everyone was invited, everyone but Arthur, the "shoe-shine boy," or Arthur's children, or anyone else who lived in the colored section on Visger; they had a separate day. The Ouellettes were there; the Tanks ("You're welcome") were there; the Pilons and Strassners and Raupps were there. Even Miss Munn was there and now walking their way with a group of teachers.

George looked over toward Agnes, but Agnes barely blinked. And for good reason. Miss Munn, now principal of School Three and assistant principal at Ecorse High School, was no longer her concern. Murph had graduated; Freda had quit school; Rowe had finished 9th grade at Our Lady of Lourdes in River Rouge and would be going into 10th there that September; and the younger girls would be safely sequestered at School One.

Things couldn't have been more civilized. Agnes nodded and said hello as Miss Munn passed, and Miss Munn half-smiled and nodded back, taking in the entire family with her gaze. That was it. The war was over. In retrospect, all a little silly, really. Agnes hooked her feet in a lower rung of the diamond-weave railing, sat back and, for over an hour, enjoyed a panoramic view of Wyandotte, then the island of Grosse Ile, while Marce waved at the cars along its East River Road. Those who preferred foreign climes sat portside, as Fighting Island and the coast of Canada passed by for review.

Before docking, all the Moore girls but one capitalized on the privacy of a bathroom stall to slip on bathing suits beneath their dresses. Shay was too busy shaking her blues away on the second-deck dance floor, shimmying her seven-year-old hips. Shay was a dancing fool. Though the Ferry Company had originally banned the turkey trot and bunny hug to keep out "undesirable elements," restrictions had been eased.

So as the breeze off the river cooled her fevered feet, Shay, soon to be a 2nd grader, was taking full advantage with Dorothy Dalton, fox-trotting to "Alabamy Bound," winging it to "Runnin' Wild." Initially, the twirling twosome had little use for the waltzes, but they soon got the knack and—with heads high, arms stiff—whirled round the shiny mahogany floor, all elegance, occasionally slipping, occasionally sliding, occasionally falling with grace, to the disgust of Murph who was dancing with Lillian on the other side of the open deck.

By the time Shay sought out a stall in one of the first-deck bathrooms, it was too late. The *Columbia* was nearing the Amherstburg liquor docks, beginning its turn for a landing on the island across the way. She'd have to change in the Women's Rest Room at Bob-Lo. Instead, she rushed to join her family, who, once collected, dashed dockside, eager to get a bird's-eye view as the boat, her engines reversing, came parallel to the leafy island.

The ferry dock and covered pier loomed dead ahead. Selections began. Designated runners were chosen. There was intense debate among the younger Moores as to who was the nimblest . Joycie was finally elected.

"When you come off the covered ramp," said George, massaging her shoulder like a trainer. "You'll see the Dance Pavilion on your right, the Whip directly in front of you, and a small path to your left."

"Yeah, Pa. I remember."

"Take that cut-through to the main path and run straight across the island. You'll pass the Souvenir Stand, the Children's Playground . . ."

"And a shelter."

"That, too," laughed George. "When the path ends, when it comes to a T, just before the bathing beach, take a left. Got that?"

"Right," said Joyce.

"No, left," cracked Dia.

"Shut up, Dia," said Rowe.

"Commandeer the first two picnic tables if you can," said George. "If not . . ."

"Make sure it's shady," said Agnes. "And try to get near Mrs. Strassner and Mrs. Ouellette. Then wait for us."

"You can do this, Joycie," said George, with a mock salute. "We're countin' on ya, kid."

Joyce returned the salute with her toothy grin, then hurried down to the main deck and positioned herself near the gangway. In a matter of minutes, lines were thrown out, the gangway gate was pulled aside, and dozens of eager envoys, fleet of foot, took off like shots, flying down the ramp, fanning out every which way, Joycie among them. By the time the family caught up with her, she had found a spot among the trees, pulled two tables together, grabbed four benches, and even managed to have the Strassners to her right, and the Ouellettes and Pilons to her left.

Then everybody scrambled. George set out for one of the four baseball diamonds, having agreed to officiate the softball game between the married men and the bachelors. Joyce, Rowe and Freda tore off their dresses, revealing their bathing suits, and made a dash for the water. Agnes, with Marce by her side, began to prepare lunch.

Anxious to join her friends, Shay grabbed her bathing suit from the family duffle and raced for the Women's Rest Rooms. But she pulled up short on hearing what Dia had to say when they met on the path.

"You can't use the rest room to change," said Dia.

"Who says?"

"A sign on the door."

"What's it say?"

"It says 'Please don't use rest rooms for changing in or out of bathing suits. Use the bathhouse.'"

"But that's not fair."

"Don't blame me," said Dia, shrugging her shoulders. Then she turned and headed toward the beach, while stuffing her hair in her bathing cap.

Oh, calamitas, calamitatus! Now what? The women's bathhouse, the very public women's bathhouse, had only communal stalls with no sliding bolts.

Experts note that a child naturally starts to develop a sense of modesty around five. In the Moore household, nature got a leg up.

George Moore was immoderately modest. And since he considered inhibition a virtue, he passed it down. Little bosoms would never see the sun. This is not to say that when it came to human anatomy, the girls were inherently detached. There were other opportunities for gathering pertinent data in that upstairs bathroom. It was common knowledge that Murph hid his dirty magazines under the register on the floor. And in the hold under the eaves, along with used baby clothes, was a box of old books. One favorite, a book that had been cracked open so often its spine had come unglued, was, dare it be said, crammed with salacious pictures. It was quite large (12X15) and contained 232 double-page spreads. And on its carnal-red cover, centered luridly in an ornamental border, was its racy title: *Famous Art Reproduced*.

Joyce, Dia and Shay spent many rainy Saturdays locked in the bathroom, kneeling on the black-and-white linoleum, pouring over pawed-over pages that had each in her own way confessing in Confession the following Saturday under the sin of Lechery.

The girls would dally at Delacroix's "Sea-Gulls and Wave," where a naked woman sat on a wave, with her small, firm breasts upright. Since the size of the woman's bosom was about the same as size of those kneeling over the book, they would soon move on. The first sighting of a nude boy ("The Murmur of the Sea") generally gave pause, though his crotch, on much closer inspection, never failed to resemble a leaf.

The most favored litho, one that induced howls and a spirited slapping of the floor, was "On the Seashore," wherein five young ladies are holding hands and cavorting on a beach, while beckoning other unclad young women to join them. Rowe had long ago labeled it, "Miss Munn and her Acolytes on the Beach at Bob-Lo." But outside the immediate sisterhood, nudity was not to be borne. For Shay, having reached the Age of Reason, had also reached the Age of Mortification.

Clutching her rolled-up bathing suit under her arm, she drifted into the nearby Children's Playground to mull her fate. For a time, she slumped on the low end of a teeter-totter, resisting all overtures for a partner. Finally, she *did* manage to scale a slide, only to squeak sluggishly down the other side. Then she moped back to the picnic table, flopped down on the bench and nibbled a chip, while her mother worked around her and Marce napped on a nearby blanket.

While Shay sulked, Agnes was bustling about the table, setting out plates, setting out silver, having an animated conversation with Ella Strassner and Mabel Ouellette. Then she turned to Shay. "Why don't you put on your suit? You're missing all the fun."

"I'm gonna."

"When?"

Shay was in a pickle. It was Ecorse Day, where the chance of having to say "hi" to someone you knew, while standing there, starkers, in the women's bathhouse, was increased a thousand fold. And what if a teacher came in? Like Mrs. Judge. Oh, excruciare, excruciatus!

Unfortunately, on Shay's first attempt, the bathhouse was jammed. Stall after stall was filled. So she hotfooted it out of there fast and wandered forlornly back to Agnes.

"What's wrong with you?"

"Nothin'."

"Why don't you put on your suit?"

"In a minute."

"Well, better make it snappy," said Agnes. "We'll be having lunch soon."

On Shay's second attempt, the fleshy hordes were thinning out, so she parked herself near the door of the bathhouse and pretended to be waiting for someone, glancing periodically to the left or right. When that wore thin, she simulated the stance of the stood up, demonstrating her annoyance with an occasional sigh.

"Whatcha doin?" asked Ida from behind.

Shay jumped with a start, then regrouped. "Waitin' for someone."

"Who?"

"Joycie."

"She's swimmin'."

"I can still wait, can't I? It's a free country."

Ida, who was supremely comfortable in her own skin, waltzed into the bathhouse, while Shay retrieved an abandoned Bob-Lo pamphlet from a nearby bench and feigned absorption. She was in the act of checking her arm for suspicious moles when Ida came back out in her bathing suit, draping her clothes neatly over her forearm.

"Want me to tell Joyce you're waitin?" asked Ida.

"No," replied Shay.

"Why not?"

"'Cuz I ain't waitin' for her no more."

"Oh, I give up," huffed Ida, as she set off across the sand.

Reality was sinking in, especially when Dia yelled from the concrete barrier on the edge of the beach, "Ma wants to know what's taking so long!"

"Tell her I'm almost changed!"

"Tell her yourself! I'm goin' back swimmin'!" which was a rather grand way to say waist-high wading. Neither Dia nor Shay could swim.

Forced to concede that time was running out, that the bathhouse would never be completely empty, Shay entered timidly, found an empty stall, slipped off her Mary Janes and her knee socks, then hesitated. Removing a dress was perilous and had to be done in one Houdini-like swoop. She took a deep breath and pulled it up.

Their voices arrived first, the voices of the two women approaching, as Shay yanked her dress back down, pulled on her socks, clapped on a shoe and fumbled with the other. Entering the stall, two women set to work, casually gossiping and stripping simultaneously, while Shay fiddled with the button on her instep strap.

Removing the shoe, she upended it, checking the sole for holes, banging to rid it of any sand or stray pebbles. Then she polished a stubborn toe scuff with her thumb and considered the possibilities of reheeling the heel.

When it became apparent that these women were in no hurry, she rashly put on her shoes, marched out of the bathhouse and up the path, until Joycie yelled from the beach, "Hey, Shay! Whaddja want me for?" until Shay yelled back, "Nothin!" until Joyce yelled, "Ida said. . . ," until Shay yelled back, "Aw, tell Ida to go soak her head!" until finally the two women came out of the bathhouse.

Determination turned into frenzy. Shay sailed into a stall, tore off her Mary Janes, stripped off her knee socks. Gathering the hem on each side of her dress, she hiked the material to her waist, crossed her arms, grabbed opposite wads and pulled upward. She could feel the dress riding cooperatively up her back, could feel the front of the neck roll over her chin. With one elbow free, she urgently fished for a shoulder of cotton, then tugged skyward.

Presto!

But not, necessarily, *Chango* .

The dress was now stuck at the base of her crown, halfway over her head.

And there she stood, smothered in dress, as blind as Uncle Syl, while flashing her sateen bloomers of delicate peach. She knew it was only a matter of time before someone entered, and enter they did. And there she stood, flashing her undies, having no idea who was getting a gander and just how many there were.

"Need any help, Shirley?" came a voice.

"No. I can get it."

Shay continued to yank, tightening the noose, until the dress finally gave way.

"Hi," she said, her hair on end.

There, standing before her, was Mrs. Bettiger from her mother's Pedro Club, and all her little Bettigers.

Fed up with life, such as it was, she turned to face the wall. Then she shoved down her bloomers and blithely stepped out of them, wriggled into the navy blue bottom of her one-piece suit, ripped off her undershirt, yanked her navy blue upper up, clutched her dress and underwear to her bosom, grabbed her shoes which contained her rolled socks, bade farewell to Mrs. Bettiger, all the little Bettigers, turned and walked out of the stall, out of the bathhouse, keeping her composure, then slowly hobbled across the hot sand, wincing as she went.

After all this, did she go swimming? Absolutely not. Instead, she stashed her underwear and socks in a bag in her mother's carry all and joined her friends on the beach. Then, when it was time for lunch, she put her dress on over her picky suit with plans to wear it home.

How her sisters managed to change out of their wet suits was something of a mystery, because when they sat down at the picnic table in their dresses, four wet bathing suits were hanging on a tree limb to dry. Maybe they'd found a bush somewhere.

––––––––––––

Seated mid-bench, Shay picked at her food, rearranging her baked beans and potato salad, while her white-bread sandwich of baloney, ketchup and tired lettuce, by now pressed like trousers, had one bite out of it.

"You're going to leave all that?" asked Agnes.

"I'm not hungry."

"Tell you what, Shay. If you eat everything on your plate, maybe your father can take you and your sisters over during the games and get some ice cream."

"Wish I could," said George, reaching for a chicken leg. "But I have to run the games and hand out prizes."

"When did you sign up for that?"

"I didn't. They asked me to."

"They? Who's they?"

"Well, not *they* , actually."

"Then who?"

"Well, this oughta get your juices revved," said George, wielding the chicken leg. "Miss Munn."

"Miss Munn!"

Agnes laughed. So did Rowe. So did Freda, who knocked over the ketchup bottle. Remarks like "Gotcha, Pa" and "Now you know how it feels" were tossed his way.

"How what feels?" asked George, not willing to see the humor.

"To get suckered in," said Agnes.

"I wasn't suckered in. I was glad to help," said George, chewing on chicken. "She was desperate."

"Desperate!" roared Murph, sitting at the far end of the table with Lillian. "She's always desperate. She's desperate when she runs out of chalk!"

"When did she ask you?" said Agnes, over the laughter.

"I ran into her at the baseball game," said George.

"Or she ran into you."

"Now, Ag, be generous," said George, wiping his hands with a paper napkin. "She just asked me to run the races. Jim Bausch was a no-show. She had nowhere to turn."

"Betcha a buck she flattered you into it," said Agnes.

"Don't be silly," said George, beginning to be truly irritated. "She just asked."

"Hey, Ella!" yelled Agnes. "Guess who landed in Miss Munn's net!"

"Bet it was George!" yelled Ella.

"Was she *desperate*?" yelled Mabel.

With that, all three tables collapsed with laughter. Even George was laughing, though he wasn't. He still didn't understand what all the fuss was about.

"Sucker," said Agnes, savoring the sweet taste of vindication.

"Now, Ag. Can't very well go back on my word," he muttered.

"When were you going to tell me?" asked Agnes.

"When I was out of range."

Chapter 24
After lunch

Teamed with Joyce, minder of their ticket money, Shay headed for the three rides. Music came from the Dance Pavilion as they hurried along the mini-midway, while cheers could be heard from a nearby baseball game.

Their first stop was The Aeroplane, six planes suspended from cables. With pilot seats at a premium, ticket holders, including Shay, quickly scattered when admitted inside the wire fence. "Joycie! Joycie! Over here!" she yelled, dangling her arm over the side, Earhart-style. The plane began its slow revolve, then picked up speed, and they were soon swinging out as high as the trees, soaring over the crowd.

From The Aeroplane, it was only a short race down a tree-lined path to the airy Amusement Building. Its only occupant was a magnificent Merry-Go-Round, the frame of which had been built in 1906 by William F. Mangels at his factory at Coney Island, while his master carver, M. C. Illions, hewed two goats, two deer, two chariots, and 44 horses, no two alike. Hundreds of lights encircled the cornices of the carousel, while glass jewels and oval mirrors on its large ornamental panels transformed the hundreds of lights into thousands.

While the steam organ piped out the ricky-tick *Sidewalks of New York (♫ East Side, West Side, all around the town)* and the horses circled and pranced three abreast, Shay sat next to Joycie on a long bench, holding her ticket, waiting her turn, anxiously searching for her horse.

And soon, there he was. Good old Dan Patch: frozen in a majestic leap on the outside row, his back hocks pushing off, his front hooves curled under, more noble than the others, more certain in his jump. ♫ *Boys and girls together. Me and Mamie O'Rourke.* There Dan was again. His regal head tilting downward like an elegant chess piece, his mouth open from the bit, his nostrils flared, his teeth bared.

When her stallion came to a complete standstill on the far side, she bolted onto the platform and rushed across, only to find the horse too elevated to mount, even with the stirrup. So she placed a proprietary arm across Dan's piebald flanks, until Joycie webbed her fingers and gave her a leg up.

As she slid into his elegant saddle, his trappings of beige and blue outlined with jewels, she was surprised once more at how smooth he felt. Unlike the snorting horses who fought or strained at their bridles, he always seemed happy to see her, glad to have her on board. She handed the man her ticket and, for the next few minutes, her world passed by counterclockwise. When Joyce was high, she was low; when Joyce was low, she was high, whirring past the Aeroplane, past baseball fields, past watchers on benches and people with balloons as the pipe organ repiped ♫ *We tripped the light fantastic on the sidewalks of New York.*

When the carousel began to slow, announcing ride's end, she leaned around the gold-braided pole and whispered in Dan's ear, "I'll see you next year." It might have been a tearful goodbye had not The Whip been calling.

The Whip, like Crack the Whip, was much more foreboding, especially since one little girl from Hamtramck, just about Shay's age, had sailed out of a car only weeks before, straight into the ride's machinery, and was ground up for meatloaf. At least that's what Dia had told her. (Dia's horror stories rarely withstood close scrutiny and her victims often came from Hamtramck.) Nonetheless, bolstered by the screams coming from the riders, Shay chattered more than usual with Joycie as they waited in line.

After the Whip came to a creeping halt and riders staggered off on wobbly pins, Joyce and Shay tore across the wide bare planks and popped into the agreed-upon car. Then a bar handle came down, tucked them in, and off they went, hands clamped to the bar, fence flying past, backs thrown backward, cars thrown forward, heads snapping, lurching, jerking as they whipped out on casters on the corner turns.

Shay staggered off on rubber legs and pronounced it peachy. But three rides in twenty minutes involved an inordinate amount of revolving.

"Are you gonna throw up?" asked Joyce, pausing to look back as she hurried along the shady path toward one of the grandstands, while her sister trailed behind.

"I'm fine," said Shay.

"You sure?

"Yes."

"You look a little green."

"I'm fine."

"Then why are you so quiet?" asked Joyce.

"I just don't feel like talkin'."

Someone should have told Shay that trying to hold something down when it yearns to come up only serves to prolong the agony. Instead, as the Ecorse Day entertainment and games got underway, Shay found herself sitting on the grass, off to the side, intent on stalling the inevitable, smiling occasionally to suggest she just needed time alone.

For Ecorse Day in 1928, Don Beckmann was probably the MC, as he was for many years, and there were probably a few words from Alf Bouchard, in his thick French-Canadian accent, eulogizing "da beauty and da community spirit" of Ecorse. After a succession of fiddling, dancing, and singing, Alf would have yelled, "Let da games begin!"

George Moore stood mid-field, megaphone in hand, patiently waiting out some heckling from the grandstand, before announcing the first event, the 50-yard dash for Three-and-Under, which was almost the last, since it ate up a generous portion of the schedule. It wasn't the race that took so long; it was the ferreting out and lining up of contestants. "Here's one!" yelled Agnes, volunteering Marce.

With rhubarbs raining down, George yelled "Go!" followed by "Please!" followed by "I beg you!" and off they went, short little legs kicking, clean start by anyone's standards, the crowd urging them on. Unfortunately, about twelve yards in, Little Raymond Fantog stopped, screamed and refused to advance, victim of a bug up his nose, causing the others to lose their concentration, and the 50-yard dash became a 20-yard meander. When Mrs. Fantog suggested that they run the Three-and-Under race over, George hastily held up the megaphone to announce the Wheelbarrow Race.

Despite the delays, George was soon into it, cracking wise. As Mabel Ouellette came slowly, regally down from the stands to enter the Egg Race, "Make way for Madame Lepescu!" When Hollis and Helen Sage crossed the finish line first, ankles strapped together for the Three-Legged Race, George shot up his arms and screamed, "Tie!"

"Hey, George!" yelled Ollie Raupp from the far end of the bleachers, "How's about *you* entering a race!"

"I'm saving myself for the Over 90s!"

While George's joshing was affectionate, serving up goodwill with humor, Dia was standing on the sidelines, serving the rib without the tenderizer. Her favorite foil was Helen Brown, possibly because Miss Brown was pretty, perfect and a pushover. Dia was particularly vocal during the Potato Sack Race. As Helen stood sack bound at the start, "Get a horse!" as Helen staggered mid-race, "Get a taxi!" as Helen tumbled at the finish, "Get a hearse!"

Then word came down from the grandstand.

"Can it, Dia," hollered Freda.

And Dia did, for a while, especially after she found herself on the receiving end of a scowl from her father. Then a new opportunity presented itself and she started up again. "Hey, Helen! . . . "

But if Dia was about to lob another dazzling *bon mot*, it was lost to the ages, because that's when Agnes marched down from the bleachers and bopped Dia on the head with her hairbrush.

"Owwww! Geez! That hurt!"

"It was supposed to hurt!" barked Agnes.

Then, adding insult to injury, Agnes hauled Dia along while she sought out Shay, who was still off to the side, still feeling queasy.

"I've been watching you for the past half hour. You've barely moved," said Agnes, putting her hand on Shay's forehead. "Are you okay?"

"Uh-huh," said Shay.

"Then why are you pouting?"

"I'm not pouting."

"You sure?"

"Yes."

"But you love to race. Why aren't you racing?"

Shay shrugged her shoulders.

"'Cuz she's gonna puke," offered Dia.

"Shut up, Dia," said Shay.

"Shut up, Shay," said Dia.

"Don't start," said Agnes, who, finding no fever, climbed back up into the grandstand, Dia in tow, deposited her next to Rowe, then returned to her seat.

But if Shay didn't want to race, her mother most certainly did. "Sure could use that five bucks," she was heard to mutter before each event. And it wasn't just the first prize, though no small motivator, that had Agnes wistful. It was her athletic past. Back in the day, she could beat all comers in the Married Ladies' event. True, she had begged off for the past few years, citing worn treads, but now, for some reason, she was itching to compete. So when George announced the Race of the Married Ladies and the women began to gather on the track, Agnes impetuously stood up, smoothed down her brown dress with the organdy collar, and warned Ella to ready the Epsom Salts.

"Runner over here!" yelled Rowe.

"Well, if it isn't Paavo Nurmi!" joked George, as Agnes climbed down from the bleachers.

Once inserted into the lineup, she found herself standing next to Louella Davies, who was all of 200 pounds, which lifted her spirits considerably. Agnes leaned out and assessed the rest of the field. Of the nine women competing, most were her age or older, though Mim Raupp and Mrs. Gregory were much younger.

"Be advised, Ladies," said George. "We've got a returning winner here in our own Mrs. Moore." Then he walked to the side of the track. "Ready?"

"Ready!" they chimed.

"On your mark! Get set! . . . Go!"

Agnes got such a great start that the upper grandstand was beside itself. Oxfords pounding the dirt, arms pumping, she was well out in front halfway through the race, three women behind her in a clump to her left, Mim and Annie Pie among the stragglers to her right. But now, oxygen was in short supply, and her lungs and legs were on fire. She had no reserve for a final push. And one by one, each Married Lady ran past her, even Louella Davies, all of 200 pounds. Agnes had to push hard to run slow.

She would have come in last if she'd actually finished. As it was, she stood mid-field, bent in half to recover her breath, while George cracked, "Run out of gas, Paavo?" in the spirit of the gentle razzing that had gone before, for which she gave him quite a look, one he knew he'd be dealing with later. Then Murph came onto the track to help her off while she gasped, "I'm all right; just a stitch," though truthfully she was a little red-faced as she returned to her seat in the stands and took a long swig from Rowe's bottle of Rock & Rye, then panted, "I'll owe you one."

But Agnes wasn't all right. Because it wasn't her feet that did her in. It was her legs, her lungs. It had been a long time since she had flexed those muscles, only to learn that they were no longer there to flex.

The races

Throughout the races, Miss Munn had been assisting George, standing on the sidelines opposite the grandstand, visible to all, with her little helpmate Miss Ranger by her side. After each race, she would stroll onto the track, envelopes of prize money and ribbons pressed under her right forearm, then give them to George, one-by-one in award order. At first, Agnes just ignored the award ceremonies, treating them as a mild distraction, until she saw something that was hard to ignore. A small moment, perhaps, but telling.

As George was handing out ribbons for the Softball Scramble, and Agnes was still smarting from her dismal run, she happened to steal a look at Miss Munn while Miss Munn was stealing a look at George. It was the way she was looking at George that got Agnes thinking, something about the prolonged gaze; something about the way she averted her eyes, as if caught, when George turned toward her; something about the way she fumbled the ribbons, and about the way she pulled back when her hand grazed his while they both reached down to pick them up.

And George's quip wasn't sitting well, either.

"I've gotta get out of here," said Agnes.

"*Qu'est-ce qui ne va pas?*"(What's wrong?) asked Ella in French.
"*Allons-y!* (Let's go)," replied Agnes.

Freda was instructed to watch Marce, Bunny Strassner was instructed to watch his sister Vernamay, and their mothers were well along the path behind the grandstand, well out of hearing distance, before Agnes muttered, "That damn woman."

"Who?"

"Mademoiselle All-Airs."

"What's she done now?"

"Honestly, Ella, I don't know if it's her or me," said Agnes, trying to sort it out. "I get so jealous, lately. I don't know what comes over me. But she's got a crush on George. I just know it."

"Everybody's got a crush on George," laughed Ella. "Hell, I've got a crush on George."

"But she's after him. I'm sure of it. She's been after him for years."

"Oh, Ag."

"C'mon, Ella."

"Well," admitted Ella. "There might be something to it. She knew last week Jim Bausch wasn't comin' today, that he couldn't afford to bring his family because he lost his job. But, look, Ag, even if she is after George. What's the threat?"

"What's the threat?" laughed Agnes. "She's tall, handsome, educated, classy, dresses like a million. Other than that, no threat at all. I know George. He's smitten."

"Smitten," laughed Ella.

"Yes, smitten. I can tell when he's smitten. He's been smitten before. He genuinely likes women, likes their company, and women like him. But I always felt I could hold my own." She shook her head. "He's smitten. And he doesn't even know it."

"I don't see it."

"I'm 43, Ella. I'll be 44 in two weeks. And I'm tired and sarcastic and prematurely gray and have bad feet. She's what? Ten years younger?" Agnes pulled up near one of the many island shelters and gazed into the middle distance, on the brink of tears.

"What are you saying?" said Ella.

"I'm saying, I've got nothing to give! I'm saying, I'm so busy with the kids, he gets short shrift. And she, she looks up to him. Puts him on a pedestal. Thinks he walks on water. That's very appealing to a 44-year-old guy whose wife tends to point out his faults."

"Now, Ag. You're just working yourself into a lather for nothing."

"Am I?"

"Yes, you are," said Ella, emphatically. "There's nothing going on. Nick would have told me. Maybe not sober but in his cups."

"She's out to get him. I just know it. And it's having an effect."

"What makes you so sure?" asked Ella.

"George has a nickname for everybody," said Agnes.

"Ain't it the truth," laughed Ella.

"Yeah, well . . . He doesn't have a nickname for Miss Munn."

They were silent for a time as they ambled along—Ella at a loss for words; Agnes too angry for words. Then Agnes pulled up, doubled up, with an involuntary cry of pain.

"Damn it all to hell," she moaned. "Every time I get upset, it goes right to my gut. Hang on a minute, will ya?"

Now just before Agnes stole a look at Miss Munn who was stealing a look at her husband, Shay had drifted over to the Children's Playground with Agnes's permission and was now sitting motionless on a swing. There's no other way to say it: Shay could be moody.

"Hey!" someone said.

She glanced round for the source.

"Hey, kid!" someone repeated. "Over here!" The red-headed counterman was beckoning from the refreshment stand. "What's wrong?" he asked as she came near. "Not feeling so hot?"

"I'm okay."

"You don't look okay," he said. "You look a bit peely-wally."

"Huh?"

"Kinda pale," he said, clearing a glass, wiping off the counter. "Feelin' woozy?"

"A little."

"Then I got just the thing to fix you up."

"But I don't got no money," said Shay.

"On the house."

"I'd better not."

"How come?"

"It's charity."

"This ain't charity, kid. It's first aid." He pulled out a clear bottle from a bank of ice, popped the cap, dropped in two straws and set it on the counter. "Nectar of the Gods," he said. "You'll feel better in seconds."

She knew what it was immediately, that pale gold nectar, mellowed for four years in wood. She held it at some distance to wait out the ultra-fizzy fizz, took a sip, then another, while the roof of her mouth tingled. No one knew why the effervescent brew worked, but it did, perhaps because its excessive carbonation made you burp, perhaps because its creator was a pharmacist, perhaps because its primary ingredient was ginger root. But, over the years, as millions would attest, Vernor's Ginger Ale did the trick.

Within minutes, Shay was no longer revolving, though she could still do without the picky suit. Within minutes, she was shooting the breeze with the counterman, thrilled to be talking to a Canadian.

"I can name the provinces," she said.

"Bet ya can't."

"Bet I can. Ontario, Quebec, Nova Scotia, New Brunswick, Manitoba, British Columbia. . . " She was about to astound him with Saskatchewan when she saw her mother and Mrs. Strassner hurrying along the path. Fearful that something was amiss, she thanked the red-headed Canadian, then hurried toward them. But she stopped short when she caught up to them near the entrance to the Women's Rest Room, frightened by the look on her mother's face.

"What's wrong?"

"Nothing to worry about, clogged drain," said her mother, waving her off, though Ella, hanging back briefly as Agnes entered, whispered, "Wait out here. I might need you."

Shay dutifully stood outside the Women's Rest Room and waited. And while she waited, she had time to think. She began to feel that something was different. She looked around. The rest-room doors were still there. The small high windows on each side of the doors were still there. The sign that said "Women's Rest Room" was still there. But the sign that read "Please don't use rest rooms for changing into bathing suits" wasn't. The sign that had determined her day. The sign that had caused so much grief. The sign she now circled the stone building twice, unsuccessfully, to find. The sign that Dia had made and tacked up.

Ella opened the rest-room door. "Go get your father. Get Freda, okay?"

"What's wrong?"

"Don't worry. Everything's fine. But tell them to be quick about it."

The pains were back. Agnes had felt them coming on all day, but in a vague, discomforting way, like the rumored return of a long-forgotten foe. She had deliberately defied the stirrings in her midsection, convinced she'd be home by the time the cramps arrived, if they arrived at all.

And because the pains had returned and because they were relentless, the Moores and Strassners took the first boat back. Homeward bound, Agnes curled up in a deck chair on the first deck, the better to quickly disembark, periodically shuddering and grabbing her gut, reassuring everyone with "This too shall pass"— Freda beside her, unsure whether the sweat on her mother's brow was caused by fever or the heat of July; George huddled near, comforting the younger children, while Marce slept in Ella's lap, out for the count.

Diagnosed with obstruction of the bowels, Agnes spent five days at Delray Hospital, the first two in agony. Had she stayed home the night of their return from Bob-Lo as she wanted, her colon might have ruptured, causing sepsis, causing death. Instead, by the following Tuesday, Agnes was in her own bed, her head against her pillows, resting an exhausted colon that had gone ten rounds with Tunney.

Chapter 25

Saturday, August 4, 1928

In March 1925, the U.S. Supreme Court had ruled on a Michigan case,[1] decreeing that officers on the hunt for grog might lawfully, without warrants, search any conveyance that could roll or float. James R. Davis, federal director of Prohibition enforcement for Michigan, was pleased with the court's finding and promised that his officers would be circumspect in applying that law. Yet Davis noted that there were certain circumstances that were, by their very nature, sufficient grounds for suspicion. "For instance, the agents are instructed to search, without exception, every automobile seen driving out of Hogan's Alley, at Ecorse."[2]

It didn't take much to plug the alley. Two corks would do. The narrowest entrance, the best hidden, was a corset-like cut through between John Goodell's ex-saloon Muskrat Junction and the GAR building built for Civil War veterans of the Grand Army of the Republic who often sat outside. The GAR now contained a shoe repair on the ground floor (filled with Humo Cigar tins) and upstairs rentals, since most of the Civil War veterans had gone to that great Decoration Day parade in the sky.

But the GAR alley was fairly cramped for a liquor-laden truck. Thus, serious commerce preferred the slightly wider entrance at the end of Labadie, across from George Moore's barbershop. To the right of the opening was Tank's Candy Store. To the left, a big, white, fenced-in Victorian, known as Bahlow's old house. A cinder and dirt roadway between Tank's and Bahlow's ambled down toward the river in a fairly straight line, confined on its left by a few old houseboats and a long fence of cattails and feathergrass which fronted a sprawling fresh-water swamp. During the day, young boys played there and trapped muskrat, selling them to speaks for Friday dinners.

Along the right side of the alley, at the river's edge, rickety and rat-infested houseboats and fishing shacks huddled together, some on land with their backs in the water, some on docks, and some moored in the river a few feet off shore. Wooden boats in advanced stages of dry rot were strewn about, their owners intent on reviving them one fine day. Unlike Rum Row with its coat of many colors, the primary color of Hogan's Alley was weather-blackened pine.

So Davis's campaign proved effective: the rumrunners dispersed. Hogan's

---

[1] "Upholds Right To Search Cars," Detroit News , March 3, 1925.
[2] Davis would later become so disgusted with Prohibition that he would debunk it in 1931.

Alley had become almost prim of late. The *Detroit News* noted that the alley, once "a veritable Mecca for runners," had "fallen into disuse and quietude." But as was typical of Prohibition enforcement, once an area had been cleaned up, officials moved their limited resources to another leak in the dike, while the old leak, hastily patched, sprang anew. Long before 1928, with little fanfare, the alley was back in business.

Just past midnight, in the first hour of Saturday (August 4, 1928), while the large swamp slumbered to the buzz of horseflies, and beams from the rising moon blinked on its boggish water, elements converged.

Gentlemen of Ecorse, parched from an ongoing heat wave and desperate for relief, sought out the feeble breeze in the blind pigs that dotted the alley. Those in Ed Hartnett's houseboat, having raised many a glass to good old George who had rarely been seen since Agnes took ill, had increased the frequency of tributes as the day advanced and were now singing his saintly praises.

In Sam Grayson's boathouse, where the alleyway came to a dead end, two men listlessly fanned themselves with their cards as they played a listless game of Gin Rummy, while a third kept lookout from a window on the river, waiting to offload a large shipment that would soon be crossing from Canada, piloted by Sam himself.

Just outside, an old REO truck was parked near the reeds that edged the swamp, its tailgate facing Sam's boathouse. The two boys within, slumping woefully in spring-bound seats, were mostly silent, except for an occasional slap. When they did grumble, they grumbled over the din of the crickets and the tinkling of a far-off piano.

Denny Renaud, sitting in the passenger seat, rolled up a sodden sleeve. "Why's it so damn hot?"

The answer from the driver, a young Solomon with glasses, came swift and fast. "Because it's August."

Couldn't argue with that. So Denny just nodded solemnly, then swatted his bare arm, then rolled down his soggy sleeve and buttoned it at the wrist, then buttoned his collar. Finally, he turned toward his companion and asked, "Why's it so damn buggy?"

"Because we're sitting in a swamp."

There it was. Solomon redux. Couldn't argue with that either. So Denny just nodded mutely and swatted his cheek. Finally, when he could reflect no more, he turned to his partner and inquired, "Why the hell we sittin' in a swamp?"

"Cuz we've got the brains of an aardvark."

Indisputable.

Then the sweat-soaked seer clapped his clammy hands in the air twice before gazing at the remains of the flattened black speck. "This is such a tipoff to my pa. All these damn bites," said Murph, brushing his palms together to dispose of the corpse. "I can just hear him. 'Where you been?' he'll ask. 'Seeing a flick,' I'll say. 'What? *The Swamp Fox?*'"

"I hate bugs," said Denny, struggling to scratch the back of his shoulder. "I hate anything that flies or crawls. This is the last time I do this."

"This is the last time I put up with you sayin, 'This is the last time.'" Murph fluttered his damp shirt away from his body. "Wish it were winter," he said. "Wish it were goddam 30 below. So much easier in winter."

While Murph longed for winter, a black sedan, its lights off, entered the alley, creeping along silently, crawling over potholes visible in the moonlight. When it reached the second darkened boathouse, a long, low hut, it parked behind it on a dirt-packed verge that paralleled a slip, cut its engine, and gave the night back to the crickets and the piano. No one exited.

Three minutes later, another sedan turned into the alley. It too moved slowly and blindly, easing over the ruts, then pulled behind the first car and went silent. Soon, another car entered, eventually pulling up near Ed Hartnett's houseboat, mingling with the cars already there.

In all, five black sedans entered at intervals, each parking unobtrusively in darkened crannies amid the boathouses, each stopping short of the bend in the road that led to Sam Grayson's. Then ten federal agents slipped from the sedans and vanished into the shadows.

Up on Front Street, in the rented apartment above George Moore's barbershop, Don Ouellette had just turned off his bedside lamp, had just pulled back his curtains to let in the stagnant air, had just leaned out to savor the nearly full moon over the alley and river, when he spotted a beamless car heading toward the boathouses. His curiosity piqued, he would remain at the window for quite some time before going to his phone.

On the second floor of the large Victorian house at the entrance to the alley, Mrs. Ripton was up late, following each black ant as it crept along the roadway, pondering the predictable intervals. She pondered for a few more minutes before waking her husband.

Upstairs in a back apartment of the GAR building, a ringing phone roused Herman Buxton from a sound sleep. Even so, he warmly thanked the caller for the warning. "Thanks. I know someone bringin' in a load."

Detroit newspapers, probably cribbing from federal press handouts, would frame it as "the largest number to participate in a raid in Detroit in years," suggesting it was premeditated and well thought out, but they should have added *uncoordinated*, "the largest *uncoordinated* raid in Detroit in years." Because about 20 yards offshore, out of view of Sam Grayson's lookout, 12 Customs Border Patrol inspectors were rendezvousing in three speedboats, unaware of the Federal agents on shore. Signaling silently, they had cut their engines, thrown out lines, lashed their craft together, and were bobbing gently on the sleepy river. They'd already reeled in two men unloading whiskey off St. Clair Shores that night and were now focusing on the alley, sure there'd be a bigger catch.

Back on land, Denny Renaud pricked up his ears. "Didja hear a boat idling? That our boat?"

"No, it was over toward Joe Baumea's," replied Murph. "It's not just Clayt that's bringing in a load tonight. So's Charlie Bauer. Could be anybody." He reached for the *College Humor* magazine on the dashboard, rolled it and whacked his thigh. "Don't know why they call that Westfield area Mosquito Point. This whole damn waterfront is Mosquito Point. Do me a favor, will ya? Go inside and ask Figs for his gun."

"What're ya talkin' about?" said Denny. "Figs don't pack no heat."

"No, his Flit gun."

"Forget it, Murph. I ain't gonna get outta this truck, go into the boathouse and ask Figs if he brung his goddam Flit gun."

"Why not?"

"'Cuz he'll think I'm nuts, that's why not."

"Just a thought."

"You do it."

"Think I won't?"

"Yeah."

"Just watch me."

Defiantly, Murph swung out of the truck. But as he turned toward the boathouse, he noticed some reeds, clearly silhouetted along the river's edge, separate, then regroup. Now, as Murph well knew, the feathergrass bordering the swamp and the river was a great place to hide, especially at its August peak when it was taller than a man. Peering into the middle distance, he fixed his gaze along the edge of the road where another section of reeds now parted briefly. Turning toward the cluster of boathouses farther up the alley, he was fairly certain that the shadows contained shadows.

Murph flipped around the truck and leaned in the passenger window just as Denny was whacking the back of his neck. "Might want to slap yourself softer," muttered Murph.

"Whatcha talkin' about?"

"Somebody missed a payoff. This place is crawling with feds."

"Oh, geez."

"C'mon. Let's walk outta here. The whole damn alley's surrounded."

"Then jist how we gonna walk outta here?"

"They're not gonna tip off their stakeout for an empty truck. They got bigger fish to fry."

"You been wrong before."

"You wanna debate this for an hour, or you wanna sleep in your own bed tonight? Just come outta there, pretend you're sozzled and follow me."

"Okay, but we gotta warn Sam."

"I know."

So Denny pitched drunkenly out of the REO, using the door handle to right himself, then latched onto Murph, and the two boys staggered up the moonlit alleyway, hat brims low, arms slung around each other's necks for mutual assistance. Once they were well away from the shadows and the swaying reeds, Murph began to sing—louder than Jolson, louder than Nibbs. "♫ Ra-MONA!" he wailed. "♫ I hear the mission bells above." The bootlegging confederation had abandoned "Macushla" in recent months for the more haunting "Ramona." "♫ Ra-MONA!" he bellowed. "♫ They're ringing out our song of love." Denny was moved to join in. "♫ Ra-MONA!" they howled, "♫ We'll meet beside the waterfall!" They were still caterwauling as they entered Ed Hartnett's, where Ed, having benefited from a phone call, was now serving coffee.

Technically, there was only one spit of land that was truly Hogan's Alley. But there were two more shack-clogged spits between the alley and the State Street dock, and all three bulges were packed with Friday-night celebrants, all of them getting their dander up, all of them reeking of Dutch courage. That night all along the waterfront, in Ed Hartnett's blind pig, in Walter Locke's, the Polar Bear, the Red Door Cafe, Joe Rossin's and Charley Dollar's, the names of those who'd died by Federal gunfire were being invoked as regularly as calls for another round.

Meanwhile, on the river, Sam Grayson and three mates had shoved off from the Canadian docks in his 35-foot lugger with 4,500 bottles of beer (100 cases) and was just nearing shore when the Customs inspectors spotted his low-riding craft.

Though Sam had been flashed a warning signal to get the hell out of there, he knew it was too late to turn around. Instead, he made a dash for it. But the inspectors managed to toss off their lines, fire up their engines, and keep him in sight as he vanished into his darkened boat well. Hastily securing their boats to Sam's dock, the officers burst into his boathouse and, within seconds, had rounded up two gin players, Sam and his three-man crew. Figs Fogarty, the aforementioned owner of the Flit gun, managed to escape.

While the six men were being cuffed, two of them tried to escape, but they froze when shots were fired. That's when Sam Grayson, already in shackles, took advantage of the confusion. Sticking his head out the boathouse window, he let out a cry for help. The alley came alive. Angry men poured out of Ed Hartnett's and strode toward Sam's boathouse. Sympathizers from other venues joined in. Though the 12 men of the Border Patrol, with their backs to the water, were used to drawing a crowd when making an arrest, the size and mood of this approaching throng gave them pause. When they attempted to exit the boathouse with their six prisoners, the crowd surged forward.

Bam! A gun went off. Not from the crowd, not from the Border Patrol. Seemingly out of nowhere. Bam! Another shot. Ten heads, in quick succession, popped up above the feathergrass, while one of the heads shouted, "Federal officers! Stand back!" Then all ten federal agents who had been hunched over in the marsh, reluctant to miss their chance to make a glory-seeking bust of their own, stepped out from hiding, guns drawn, Endicott (of the infamous, wrong-address raid on Oliver Raupp's house), leading the charge. There were now three concentric half-circles: the prisoners in the boathouse surrounded by the Border Patrol, the Border Patrol surrounded by the crowd, the crowd surrounded by the feds in the reeds.

It was an uneasy standoff. Though the crowd drew back, it continued to grow, as protesters, onlookers and visiting dignitaries streamed into the alley from the houses on Front Street, from the backroom at Muskrat Junction, from the rooms over the GAR, from the speakeasies on the other promontories. Though two Detroit newspapers would report that 40 agents opposed a mob of 200, in reality there were probably only 22 opposing a mob of 200: 10 Prohibition agents and 12 Border Patrol inspectors.

Those 22 agents, borrowing from Harvard's playbook, created something of a flying wedge within which they cautiously escorted the six tariff violators, including the ever-popular Sam, through the crowd to the Federal cars, all the while advising the assemblage that it was time to go home, that there was nothing more to see, that the party was over. Some in the crowd, who seemed to agree, returned to their cars and drove off.

Once the felons were safely stowed in the back seats of the sedans, Federal and Border Patrol agents alike seemed visibly relieved to be getting out of there with their pelts intact. But as the sedans began to drive out of the alley, the crowd stood in the way of their passing.

Driving slowly through a crowd was not entirely new to the government squads. Because of the disdain for the law they were enforcing, because they were often arresting otherwise law-abiding citizens, most agents had encountered hostility. No one knows if Endicott got lippy, no one knows if someone offered a parting shot, no one knows if an officer used his car as a gentle battering ram, but something ignited the crowd.

The sedans inched forward under a barrage of shouts and taunts, under a hail of sticks and rocks, while sympathizers yanked at the doors, trying to rescue the runners and free the ever-popular Sam. "The Government cars were badly battered with rocks," reported the *Detroit News*.[3] One agent "suffered a lacerated face when a rock was thrown through the windshield of his car, scattering the glass on him," reported the *Detroit Times*.[4]

Men of the Border Patrol, who were preparing to return to their docked boats, fired more shots in the air and the mob quickly backed off. Taking advantage of the lull, the feds hit the gas pedal, intent on skedaddling up the narrow alley. But their speedometer was barely registering five mph when their head-

---

[3] "Hogan's Alley Sees a Fight," Detroit News, August 4, 1928.
[4] "40 Dry Agents Rout Wet Mob of 200," Detroit Times , August 5, 1928.

lights revealed a barrier ahead. Denizens of the alley, those who had driven off earlier, had parked helter-skelter all over the cindered path, effectively setting up a barricade. Eventually, wrote the *Detroit News* , the feds "succeeded in squeezing through with their prisoners,"[5] using their already battered cars like Dodge 'Ems, banging and butting bumpers and fenders on the way out.

———————

While 10 of the 12 men of the Border Patrol returned down the path toward their boats, dickering as to which crew would be assigned the boring task of towing the confiscated lugger to the Sibley Immigration barracks on Grosse Ile, something on the river caught their eyes.

Murph saw it, too. He was sitting at an open window at Ed Hartnett's now empty houseboat watching the river, with Denny off in the shadows guarding their truck from a distance. Murph had hoped that Clayt had *not* been given the signal to cross, unaware that Figs had done just that.

Only minutes before, Murph had watched helplessly as Charlie Bauer, coming in with 400 or 500 cases of fancy whiskey, had brazenly tried to take advantage of the commotion, attempting to pole his boat into the marsh where he could hide until the melee was over. But two of the more sharp-eyed men of the Border Patrol had caught sight of him and were now standing on shore, not four feet from Ed Hartnett's boathouse, gun pointed at Charlie, while Charlie, with one surrendering hand in the air, beached his boat.

Now other members of the Border Patrol were crowding the shoreline, binoculars raised, speculating on the course and composition of the white speck on the river. Murph knew that he couldn't flash a red light to Clayt, even if he had had a flashlight, without getting caught, without being shot at. And when the white speck began to look more like a loaded lugger, and the other inspectors broke into a trot, racing for their speedboats, Murph could only watch and wait. He stood up, trembling with adrenaline, and began to pace. Watching for his moment, waiting for his next move. Which was ... Now.

Murph crept to the player piano, slid onto the bench, checked the music roll that he had pre-loaded on the tracking bar, set the brass tempo lever at fast, set the accentuation lever at crescendo, cracked his knuckles, made the sign of the cross apprehensively and began to pump furiously. Murph and Clayt had added another song to their warning-signal repertoire, one for which they had cleaned out Kresge's music department, inserting the rolls in their long, thin boxes into all the player-piano collections in the blind pigs along the shore.

"♫ *It's three o'clock in the morrr -ning! We've danced the whole night thru!*" he howled, parroting John McCormack's flawless diction from the re-

———————

[5] "Hogan's Alley Sees a Fight," Detroit News, August 4, 1928.

cording, borrowing his affected Scottish burr, breaking the silence in such a reverberating manner he almost startled himself. "♪ *And daylight soon will be dawn -ing, Just one more waltz with yoooo.*"

Sound carries over water. Murph had no idea how near shore Clayt needed to be before he could hear the piano's golden tones. But as the hammers struck the strings and the strings vibrated and the wood of the upright resonated and the ivory keys bounced of their own volition, Murph shared his glorious tenor, commanding in its volume. "♪ *That mel-ody so entrrr-ancing, Seems to be made forrr us twooooooooo, I could just keep right on danc-ing, forrr-ever de-arrrr with yooooooo.*"

The pianist abandoned the pumps, ran to the side of the window, hugged the wall and peeked out, but Clayt's lugger was still approaching. Or was it? On closer inspection, it seemed to be backing into its own wake. Then the bow slowly turned to starboard. Saints preserve us, thought Murph. Now if only the other guys could have as much good fortune.

Figs might have, if he hadn't been caught fiddling with a gas cap. Just before the Scottish concert, about the time Murph was pacing and the inspectors were nearing Sam Grayson's dock on the trot, Figs was in the stern of one of the government speedboats, attempting to replace a gasoline cap with fumbling fingers, a cap that he had opened. As he shot his hands in the air, he inadvertently, or so he claimed, dropped a small cloth pouch over the side into the river. An inspector grabbed a pike pole and fished it out.

One look at the gray-and-gritty residue in the white cloth bag told the officers what it had held. Emery dust. Harmless enough as a filler for strawberry pincushions to keep needles sharp, it was also used on the line at Ford, where Emery wheels smoothed the steel bodies of Henry's Model A's. But it had other uses. During the labor unrest two decades before, two cents worth of emery dust was a popular additive used by saboteurs. Nothing did a better job of ruining a running engine.

With the jig up, Figs became polite, contrite and cooperative. Aware he'd have to pay damages, knowing they'd be considerable, he warned the officers against starting their engines, readily admitting he'd serviced all three. Tearfully, he begged their forgiveness, pled youthful folly, conceded that the game was over, that they had won. But Figs could afford to be magnanimous. The game was over and *he* had won. All three boats were out of commission. None of them would be leaving that dock any time soon.

In all, the riot in Hogan's Alley had lasted only 15 minutes. By the time five Wayne County deputy sheriffs came to the agents' aid, the crowd was said to be orderly, milling around like onlookers at a 4th of July parade. While Murph walked up Labadie, on his way home, others adjourned to Rum Row, specifically Joe Riopelle's boathouse, to await further developments, to await the return of Clayt.

According to Clayt years later: "Me and Gene LePriest, we took off with the boat and went over to Canada. Into Sunnyside slip. But Charlie Bauer had a boat that was caught. So the law guy put a gun on Charlie and told him to take him over there to catch me. So, anyhow, before we got in that slip over there in Canada, this law guy was standing right on the bow of Charlie's boat and he's shootin' at us. He had the nose of his boat right on the stern of ours. This Gene LePriest had a cap on, and the law guy shot a hole right through his cap. I'll tell ya, a cap fits to your head."

Clayt continued: "Anyhow, Gene, he jumped off and ran. Over in Canada. And the law guy got in my boat and took that back to Ecorse. And I got in with this Charlie Bauer. 'If you know what's good for you,' I said, 'you better take me back.'

So, when I got back, there musta been a hundred people standing on [my father's] dock. So Charlie wouldn't land. He said, "I'll go by slow and then you'll have to jump off on the dock." Which I did. And as he left, the guys were throwing stones at him, you know.

Charlie left town for a while. He thought somebody was goin' to kill him, I guess. So when he came back, as soon as he came back, I was standing in front of the White Tree Inn. Says he wanted to talk—so I told somebody—I think it was Murph—to go down and get Gene LePriest. So Gene came and the four of us went in the dining room there and we had a little talk, and he [Charlie] paid Gene $1,000 or $1,200 for his boat and he paid me, I think, $8 or $900 for the stuff I had. So we shook hands and he says, "Okay, you're back in business."

Figs was fined and given a stern reprimand. Though no one could save him from the scolding, a hat was passed in the alley. As for Murph, his record remained unblemished, his reputation enhanced. The Michigan legislature had yet to make singing in shady neighborhoods a felony.

Chapter 26
Saturday, August 4, 1928

That same Saturday Agnes had a follow-up appointment at 2:30 with Dr. Durocher. Despite the heat wave, despite being awakened in the middle of the night by an eruption of voices and the sound of breaking glass coming from Hogan's Alley, she felt much better and was looking forward to the rain which was promised for that afternoon. So, though Ella had offered to drive, she enlisted Freda to walk the five blocks with her to the corner of Front and Westfield, where a side entrance on Durocher's new large brick house led to his office. The walk, she said, even in the stifling air, would do her good.

They arrived with 15 minutes to spare, enough time for Agnes to thumb through a battered issue of *Woman's Home Companion*, a step up from the reading fare at George's barbershop, where the *Police Gazette* and other tabloids held sway and the gruesome photo of Ruth Snyder strapped in the electric chair had been filling time for waiting clientele since January.

Agnes Moore shortly before becoming bedridden with tuberculosis

"Bet Marcie'd look cute in this," said Agnes, sunk comfortably in an overstuffed armchair.

"Which one?" asked Freda, seated next to her, leaning sideways.

"This organdy pattern." Agnes lifted the oversize magazine and pointed to a Kate Greenaway-like drawing of a bonneted child. "Pale pink with baby blue trim. The material comes with the pattern. Whaddya think?"

"It's sweet."

"It is, isn't it?" said Agnes, scrutinizing the design. "But it's not cheap."

"How much?"

"$2.50. Then again, that's not bad for organdy. And it comes with this hat, too. Look. See the little vine embroidered across the brim? I could make it for Marcie's birthday. What is this, August? I'd have four months. Whaddya think?"

"You should get it."

"Don't know where we'd find $2.50, especially now with the hospital bill. But, oh, she'd look like a doll in that."

"Dr. Durocher will see you now, Agnes," sang out the nurse, Lottie Montie, coming from his office.

Agnes set the magazine on the side table, stood up and handed Freda her purse. "Get the address for me, will ya? Write it down," she said as she walked through the door.

"Don't forget to ask him about your feet, Mumma," said Freda.

Well-liked and respected, Dr. E.J. Durocher was a tall, thin man, in his late 40s, with fine features; he had a precise way of moving and speaking—precise and methodical.

"Well, Agnes," he said, standing behind his desk, motioning her to take the seat in front of him. Then sitting down himself, he adjusted the cuff beneath his white coat, shuffled papers in a folder, moved a paperclip holder that had come between them, and asked, "How are you feeling?"

"I've got enough Crisco in me to fry donuts."

The good doctor stared at her unblinking for a moment, then burst out laughing. "Oh, the hot oils."

Agnes grew serious. "But I need to apologize."

"For what?"

"For the way I acted in the hospital when you came to see me." Her voice rose. "I couldn't stop crying. Even after you'd left. I don't know what that was all about. I just couldn't stop crying."

He sat there listening, then replied, "Those procedures can be unpleasant. Demoralizing."

"Anyway, thanks for springing me."

"My pleasure," he said, smiling. "Well, now that you're safely home, how are you doing?"

"Fine. A little tired from all the fuss, you know. But fine."

"And a little naughty, I hear."

"Naughty?"

"Lottie saw you ironing yesterday. She said you had the ironing board out on the front porch."

"I had to," said Agnes, perplexed. "It was hot inside."

"But, Agnes, you just got out of a hospital."

"Oh, have a heart. I was in bed all day Wednesday, all day Thursday. On Friday, I had to get up. At least for a little while. Besides, it was just a little ironing, mostly hankies. I didn't do shirts, honest. Freda did the shirts."

"When was the last time you took a day off?"

"Bob-Lo," she laughed. "And look what that got me."

He gazed at her for a moment before smiling. Then he leaned back in his chair, thrust his elbows out and laced his fingers. "Talk to me, Agnes. . . Tell me your concerns."

"Concerns?"

"What do you worry about?"

"I don't know what you mean."

"Do you ever find yourself obsessing over things?"

"Not really," she said, though her brief with Miss Munn came to mind.

"Well, then, let me ask you this. How are you and George doing?"

Agnes looked at him, stupefied. "Doing?"

"How are you getting along?" Discomfited, Agnes shifted in her chair. "You argue?"

"On occasion," she said guardedly.

"What about?"

"What do we argue about?"

"Yes."

"Money, mostly. Discipline. George is tougher than I am. A lot tougher. Quick with the belt, you know. To be honest, when it comes to handling kids, I don't know who's right."

"To be honest, I don't either," said Durocher, gazing downward, looking as uncomfortable as Agnes with the line of questioning. After a time, he glanced back up. "What about the money?" he asked, then quickly added as he saw her hesitate, "Don't worry. I'm not trying to find out if you can pay my bill. I'm just trying to get a sense of the kind of stress you've been under."

"Oh!" said Agnes, relieved. "In that case, put your feet up."

"Tight, is it?"

"Let's just say we're definitely feeling the pinch. Used to be George worked six days a week, dawn to eight. Filled two barber chairs. Had a shoeshine boy. You know, you saw it. Now, come 3:30, 4:00, poor guy, he just sits in his chair. But he doesn't dare leave, just in case. . . . It's not his fault. Roy Livernois says it's the same for him. Except for the bootleggers, everybody in town's hurting right now. Freda's been working at Pilon's. That helps. Murph supports himself, that helps."

"How?"

"Murph?"

"This is a terrible climate for young men. Is he keeping his nose clean?"

"God, I hope so. He managed to pick up a part-time job on the assembly line after graduating in June. George isn't too happy with the company he keeps, but he's basically a sound kid."

"Any other concerns?"

"None that I can think of."

"I hear you dragged George out of Hunky John's by the ear a few months ago." He laughed. "Good for you."

Agnes reddened. "Word gets around."

"Are his benders getting any worse?"

"No, about the same."

"Once a month?"

"Sometimes. Not always."

"That must upset you."

"Doesn't make things easy."

"Takes a toll, does it?"

"Sometimes. Then, too . . . to be fair . . . some of it's me. By the time he gets home at night, I'm so dang cranky, that I don't blame him for wanting to get out."

"Cranky?"

"I get tired."

Durocher paused, then opened the folder waiting on his desk. "I have your medical history here, Agnes. But I'm missing information on your family. Can you help me fill it in?"

"I'll try," said Agnes, glad to change the subject.

He took the fountain pen out of his breast pocket and unscrewed it. "I know your brother Syl is blind."

"My sister Ovie's blind, too."

"How long's it been since your father died?"

"Ten years ago; he died at 63."

"Heart, right?"

"That's what you said at the time."

He made a note. "Any other medical problems in the family?"

"Like what?"

"Like tuberculosis, for example."

She found herself gazing at his hand through a sudden mist, her eyes pinned to the brown fountain pen he was holding, pinned to the band of green inlay near the top of the cap. The question was anything but a question. In that moment, she knew that her answer, once given, would narrow her world.

"Yes," she said.

"Who?"

"My mother."

"Kidney or pulmonary?"

"Pardon me?"

"Was it in the lungs or the kidneys?"

"Kidneys."

"Was she cured?"

"No."

He scribbled a note, then looked back up. "How old are you now?"

"43. I'll be 44 next week."

"How old was your mother when she died, Agnes?"

"Thirty-four."

"How old were you then?"

"Thirteen."

He noted her age, then looked back up. "How old were you when she was first diagnosed?"

"Five. Maybe six. She had a relapse when I was around nine."

He paused, considering his words. "You know, some children who've been around TB when they're young, who've been exposed to the bacillus, are given the gift of immunity. But some aren't."

"Do they know why?"

"Many think that stress brings it on. That stress, worry, can weaken the immune system and the bacillus can become active. And all signs say yours has."

"Signs?"

He returned to her folder. "Your tuberculin test is positive, but that's not surprising because you've been exposed. Your X-ray shows an inactive lesion in the lung, but, again, that's to be expected. Still, there are other things. You had abdominal pain in the right lower quadrant; you have mild anemia, you had fever. How often do you experience fevers?"

"Not often."

"Not often?"

"Well, I have a lot of hot flashes; I'm sure it's menopause. I just can't take the heat anymore."

"You tell me you don't have any energy. You haven't had any for quite some time."

"But that's because there's so much to do."

"You told me you were irritable."

"When?"

"Well, cranky. You said cranky."

"But that's only when I'm tired . . ."

"You told me at the hospital that going to the bathroom has become an adventure. Urgent feelings of having to go, but not going. Well, constipation is often the chief symptom of intestinal tuberculosis. And bowel obstruction comes with it." He pointed to the folder. "I have a report on another X-ray here. It shows stenosis, it shows evidence of shrinkage and thickening of the first part of your colon."

"But I feel fine."

"Do you really?"

"Well, I'm still a little tired, but isn't that to be expected? I just got out of the hospital."

"I think you're so glad to be home, it's masking symptoms. All those tears I saw in Delray, they're part of the illness, Agnes."

"And all those fights with George?"

"Probably. And one more thing. Your feet."

"My feet?"

"Yes. Your faulty plumbing's causing varicose veins, which in turn is causing the swelling in your feet."

She laughed sardonically. "There's the kicker."

He got up, went to the window and peered out. "Agnes, I'm going to tell you something you don't want to hear." She waited. "Bed rest is the only option."

"I knew that was coming."

"It's our only choice. You have to get in bed and stay there, doing absolutely nothing."

"For how long?"

"For as long as it takes to get the infection under control."

"But how long do you think?"

"I don't know," he said. "At least a few months." He hesitated. "Look, I'm sure we caught it in time. But I need you to take things day by day. If you don't listen to me, do exactly as I say, this disease'll kill you. Simple as that. It will kill you." He began to pace. "We should also talk about a sanatorium."

"Sanatoriums are for the wealthy, aren't they? Cash only."

"But I might be able to get you into a state or county . . ."

"I want to be home."

"You sure?"

"Yes."

"Well," he said, "there's a growing tendency to treat people in their homes. I'm sure you'd be happier, more contented there. All to the good. Though I must make clear, some experts disagree. They think the results may be less than satisfactory because the caregivers lack training."

"Freda's my rock. I've always been able to count on Freda."

"How old is she now?"

"18."

———

Freda was called in and he gently explained the situation. Like her mother, she remained calm, though her eyes grew wide. She barely moved while Durocher went over particulars, and Agnes, who was already being talked about in the third person, shrank into herself.

Durocher was now moving faster, as if he'd given all this great thought. Lottie Montie would come once a week, he said. Agnes would need a bland diet, low-residue. The days of overfeeding for TB were over. Expect to deal with a poor appetite, he warned Freda. But not to worry. He had plenty of booklets to give her.

"Your biggest job, besides taking care of your mother, will be to lessen the degree of contagion. Sheets will need to be washed carefully. I'd recommend you hire someone for that. Your mother's not coughing, at least not yet, so it's not an open case. But you've got to batten down the hatches. You older girls—you,

Rowe and Joyce—you'll need to take reasonable precautions, avoid undue exposure, but you'll be able to come and go in the . . ."

"Sickroom?" offered Agnes.

"Yes," said Durocher. "But let's talk about the other girls. How old are Dia and Shay?"

"Dia's nine," said Freda. "Shay's seven."

"I don't want them in her room. They can stand outside the doorway, not *in* the doorway. And I don't want them to enter."

"Ever?" said Agnes, aghast.

"Maybe briefly, for special occasions, and brief means a minute and special occasions means rare. But that's it. As for Marce. . . Marce is, what?" He looked at Freda, then Agnes. "Three? Four?"

Agnes turned cheerlessly toward Freda. "She'll be four in November."

Durocher sighed. "Sorry, Agnes." He paused once more. "She can't be anywhere near the sickroom, anywhere near you. Not even in the doorway."

"I know I won't be able to hold her, but can't I even see her?"

"I don't want her anywhere near that room."

"But she'll want to know why; she won't understand."

"If you stayed in a sanatorium, would they let her visit? Think about where you got this. You got this from your mother. Young children have to be scrupulously guarded from all contact. Back then, they didn't know that. If you don't want Marce in later years to be sitting where you're sitting, you've got to follow my instructions to the letter. The longer she's kept from exposure, the older she gets. The older she gets, the better her chances."

Agnes was fighting back tears. "But she'll be right in the house. How can we ... ?"

"There *is* an alternative."

"What?"

"Put Marce in a private home or a children's home."

Freda broke in, her voice filled with urgency. "I can take care of Marce. We all can. I'll keep her out. I promise. I'll keep her out. We'll manage."

―――――――

Around four o'clock, during his two-hour break between office hours, Ed Durocher opened the screen door of the nearly empty barbershop, overhead fans whirring, and asked George if he could speak to him alone for a minute, outside. George, who was putting the finishing touches on a college cut, fielding questions about last night's commotion in Hogan's Alley, told him he'd be right out.

They sat on the backless bench, the hot air laced with cooler puffs, a portent of the rain to come, while Durocher went over Agnes's situation in his slow, methodical way.

Stunned, George remained silent throughout, then asked in a voice low and raspy, "What happens now?"

"She goes to bed."

"For how long?"

"Until the disease becomes inactive."

"How long is that?"

Durocher paused to smooth his mustache. "When Agnes asked me that question, George, I hedged. But I won't with you. Could be a year. Could be two. Even longer. But she's not to know that. It's the fever that will tell us. Watch the fever."

He paused again, then lowered his voice. "You're going to become an ideal husband, George. No more Hunky John's, no more Hogan's Alley, no more all-nighters. Say goodbye to money problems, discipline problems. Your kids'll be star pupils; Murph'll be a candidate for the seminary. In fact, you'll have no cares or concerns, *what* soever. If you have problems, take them outside. You're going to be the soul of moderation. Not even good news, not even wonderful news. If Agnes gets excited or agitated, her temperature will rise. If her temperature rises, the disease will spread. It's as simple as that. Peace of mind is as important as bed rest and all the medicine I can give her. And if you can't do that, I'd recommend a sanatorium."

"She won't want that and we can't afford it."

"So she said."

George stared straight ahead, working up the courage to ask the first question that had come to mind, the one he dreaded. "What are her chances? Will she pull through?"

"Let's just pray we caught it in time."

"In time?" The casual wording took his breath away. George could feel his own temperature rising, but he respected Durocher and did his best to keep his voice level, to keep blame at bay. "Tell me, Ed. Is this what was wrong a year ago?"

"Yes. I'm fairly sure."

"I'm not trying to be difficult, but . . ."

"Why didn't I catch it then?"

"You. Or the doctors at Delray."

"Damn good question, George. I asked myself the same thing all night last night."

"But you knew her mother had TB."

"Frankly, George, I didn't. Agnes never mentioned it. Her mother died long before I moved here. But even if I had known, the lesions in her lung were inactive." He leaned forward, palms on knees. "TB symptoms are so vague, so general. Like Agnes's fatigue. She wasn't anemic; she hadn't lost weight. And digestive problems don't bring TB immediately to mind. So we surmised she was overworked, and I think that's true. But it's safe to say that exhaustion can ignite the bacilli in her. Inadvertently, the call for bed rest a year ago was the right call, but she didn't stay in bed."

Agnes had tuberculosis. Not the frail cough depicted in books and films, the flecks of blood on an embroidered handkerchief, the poignant death of Gentle Beth, the delicate fading away of Camille. For Agnes, the gradual consumption of her organs may have started in the lungs, but, having migrated, was now deep in the bowels. And because of that she was confined to her bed, and her world was tucked in with her.

It may not be accurate to say that George never took another drink, but the binges sure stopped.

Chapter 27
Monday, November 26, 1928

Mondays were generally quiet in Ecorse, on both sides of the law, though that would not hold true for Monday, November 26, 1928, three days before Thanksgiving. Clayt's version of what happened that day neatly dovetailed with the Detroit papers and the Ecorse police report, though Clayt did fill in some blanks.

Murph had graduated from Roosevelt High School that June, a month before he turned 21, his parents proudly in attendance. As a three-letter man, Murph had been an oarsman on one of the most successful rowing teams in Wyandotte's history, a team which won the U.S. national championship in front of 40,000 onlookers in the Trenton Channel at Elizabeth Park (August 6, 1927) and the world championship two days later. He had also been on the 1928 track team that took the state 880-yard relay and the Downriver championship.

Where he found time for his lucrative side job is something of a mystery. The only outward sign of his extracurricular antics was the bandage seen clamped across his nose in his high-school yearbook, the *Wy-Hi*. One would think he'd earned it on the football field, since it was a team photo; alas, he had come to harm taking a fast corner while on guard duty, following a truck full of churning cargo. But Murph had concocted a reasonable explanation for domestic consumption: his family were told that the accident had occurred while he and Clayt were on their way to Woodland Beach.

———

Around 9:00 a.m. of that raw November Monday, Murph and Clayt were in the dining room of the White Tree Inn, downing a hearty breakfast of eggs over easy, bacon and hash browns, toast and coffee. Neither one of them was drinking; neither one was into alcohol, except for importing, transporting and selling. The only serious tippler in the place was Nibbs O'Hearn, who was glued to a bar stool in the other room, talking an arm off a bartender filling in for Johnny Kauffman.

With a leg up from his father, Clayt had branched out. A successful organizer with his own crew of 12, he no longer crossed the waters. Instead, he paid others to cross and paid the law to look away. That morning, around 10, he had two boats coming in from Canada for which he had to coordinate the timing and the loading of trucks on Front Street.

Murph, who had offered to help, had moved up, too, though that's not the phrase Clayt would have used. Murph was now driving for Charlie Bauer, a bone of contention between the friends. Clayt still didn't have much use for Bauer, though he didn't advertise it. In their circles, it was wise to keep such feelings to yourself. Clayt was reminding Murph of that fact, however, as he sopped up yolk with his toast. "Hell, you couldn't stand him, either."

"Aw, he's okay. Once you get past the tough-guy stuff," replied Murph. "Ya gotta look tough in this business or they'll be stringing crepe."

Clayt lifted his coffee mug and warmed his hands. "Yeah, well. Some guys really are tough. That's my point. Especially guys from out of town, like Bauer." He set down his cup. "You know, Murph, I don't get it. He's like Fagin in that book we read in class. An old hound surrounded by pups. He's got Tommy Ouellette, Bones Vellmure,[1] Jack Labadie,[2] you. Seriously. What's the attraction?"

"He's not so old."

"He's in his forties, for cripes sake," said Clayt. "Think about it. Most of the older guys in Ecorse have other jobs; they're only hauling to help pay the rent. Everyone's a little short these days. And the younger ones, punks like us, we're doing it to get a car or make a pile while we can make a pile. Hell, Tommy's saving for college. But Bauer? Something smells. How long's he been here? Five years?"

"Something like that," said Murph.

"Whaddya know about him? What'd he do in Texas before he came here? Sing in the choir? Bet he's got a rap sheet a mile long. That's my point."

"Aw, you're still pissed about getting caught that night in Hogan's Alley."

There was a long silence. Clayt stared at him with disgust, then snarled softly, "We'd a gotten away."

"Okay, okay. I know, I know."

"You were there playing the piano, singing your heart out. You saw it. We'd a gotten away."

"Anyway, Charlie made good."

"He's a cowboy. Out for himself."

"Out for himself?" replied Murph. "What about that time with the barricade? When the Border Patrol had all those boats bottled up at that loading dock in Rouge? There musta been 15 Customs guys. Charlie runs up a sand pile with a pistol in each hand, stands at the top, daring the land law to take one step forward. Stood up there 'til everybody behind him loaded their cars and drove through that barricade. 18 carloads. Geezus, you shoulda been there, Clayt. Charlie jumps into our car, I take off, bullets whizzing round us. Tommy was

---

1 Later an attorney.
2 Later treasurer of Ecorse Township.

there. He saw it. If you don't believe me, ask Tommy."

"Oh, I believe you. I believe Tommy. I believe everybody that saw it," said Clayt. "Like I said, he's a cowboy. Thinks he's at the Alamo, for cripes sake. That's my point." Then he leaned across the table in earnest. "Remember when we started? We said, no risks. Remember? We were too smart for that. We'd break this one dumb law, that was all. Square guys, no guns. Remember?"

"But I'm not packing, Clayt. You know that."

"Doesn't matter. It's the company you keep."

"C'mon, be fair. It's hard to find any bunch that doesn't rely on at least one gun."

"I don't."

"Yeah, and you're gonna be sorry," said Murph. "There are some real low-lifes moving into Ecorse. Hijacking, kidnapping. Who's gonna protect us? The law?"

"And then there's Soxy," said Clayt.

"Sox?" Murph snorted. "Oh, c'mon. We've known Sox since we were little. He's all talk."

"Is that why he's out on parole?"

"He just got caught, that's all. That could happen to any of us. Doesn't make you a bad guy."

"He's doing more than bootlegging, Murph. He got three-to-ten for robbery armed."

"He said he didn't do it."

"He's a hothead, Murph. That makes him dangerous."

"Look, Clayt, the only thing dangerous about Soxy is if my dad catches me palling around with him," laughed Murph.

Clayt pushed his plate away. "Then what about Bauer? Why're you always sticking up for Bauer?"

"Aw, I don't know." Murph gave the question some thought. "Maybe because he takes good care of us. Maybe because when I tipped my car over, he dropped everything to get me to the hospital. Geezus, I was banged up."

"So?"

"So, he didn't have to. I wasn't working for him then. I was only doing a job for him. Any other guy woulda been more concerned for his load. He musta had 40 cases on that truck. Coulda lost his whole stake because of me."

"But he didn't. That's my point. Tommy Ouellette and Jack Labadie saved half that load," said Clayt. "Went over to Jack's house, got his dad's Buick, loaded about 25 cases and hid them in his dad's garage."

"Right. And Charlie paid them well for that," said Murph.

"What's your point?"

But the point had to wait, because just then Norm Smith, who'd been huddled over breakfast with a couple of cronies, dropped by their table on his way out and muttered that they should keep their eyes and ears open. He told them he'd just found out that there were at least three men working undercover on the Border Patrol, and, though it hadn't hit the papers yet, they'd put the finger on about 40 guys. Over half of them inspectors.

Smith was no sooner out the door, when Clayt and Murph began to dissect the news.

"I think I'm gonna lie low after today's boats," said Clayt. "If you're smart, you'll do the same."

"I'll check with Charlie."

"Say what?"

"I'll check with Charlie."

"But you're a helluva lot smarter than Charlie."

"Don't worry. He'll handle it right."

Clayt sighed. "See, that's my point."

"You say a lot of things, Clayt. It's hard to tell which one's your point. See, that's *my* point."

But what the point was and whether or not it was even germane, still had to wait, because about then Little Abe was allowed entry into the White Tree and walked over to their table, his cheeks pink with cold. "Hey, Sox and Charlie want to see you guys. They're down at the Red Door Cafe."

"I'm busy. What about?" asked Clayt.

"Didn't say."

"Hell, I got stuff comin' in."

"It's important."

Murph rose stiffly, grabbed his overcoat from the coat tree and fished in its outer pocket.

"I'll get it. I'm flush," cracked Clayt. "You. You're on hard times." He stood up, took out an impressive roll, peeled off a ten spot and tossed it on the table.

"That mean you're comin'?" asked Murph.

"Aw, Christ," said Clayt.

They exited by way of the bar, where Nibbs O'Hearn, having run out of funds, could be heard negotiating for another beer. "I'll pay you tomorrow, okay?" he begged, his chin a mass of bristles, his hand thrust out with his empty glass.

"You'll drink tomorrow, okay?" said the bartender, filling the sink with hot, sudsy water.

"But I'm a regular," whined Nibbs. "Johnny'll vouch for me."

The bartender turned off the spigot. "You're a regular, all right. A regular pain in the ass." He swiped the empty glass, tossed it in the water, and gave it a swirl. "Now get outta here, Bub. Sing your sad song somewhere else."

Murph stopped, then leaned casually with his back against the bar, his heel on the rail. "How ya doin', Nibbs?"

"Oh, so-so, Murph," replied Nibbs, staring at the spittoon near his feet. "You know."

"I thought you were on the wagon. That's what Pa said."

"Well, weekends, you know, they're kinda tough."

"Sure you don't wanna switch to Canada Dry? My treat."

"Starting tomorrow, okay? For sure, tomorrow."

Murph took out a five-dollar bill, set it on the bar and said to the bartender. "Give him what he wants." Then he walked to the door and turned. "And, by the way, his name's Nibbs, not Bub."

———————

Out on the street, a blast of Canadian wind swept across the river from Windsor as the threesome huddled at the corner of White and Front. It was extremely cold for November, only 24°, with traces of snow on the ground. Too cold for long speeches. So Abe just pointed a gloved finger to the row of boathouses on the next block, to the one with the red door. "You'll find 'em in the back."

"Aren'tcha comin'?" asked Murph.

"Naw, I gotta get home," replied Little Abe, pulling up his coat collar, leaning into the wind, heading west up White at a fairly vigorous clip.

Though many blind pigs closed in the wee hours and did not reopen until three or four in the afternoon, some were on tap all night, including the Red Door Cafe. Murph rapped on the door, jammed his fist deep into his overcoat pocket and shifted impatiently while he posed for the peephole, "C'mon, Joe, we're freezin' out here." The door swung open.

It was dim inside with a haze of blue smoke. Yawning massively, Joe Hughes, the bartender, returned to his bar and the spread-out sports section of the morning *Free Press*. On the mirror behind him, cryptic columns were printed in white shoe polish informing regulars that standard brand whiskey could be bought in Canada that day for $35 a case, or $45 after landing in Ecorse; champagne was $48 in Canada, $60 landed, and beer was $2.50 a case, $7.00 landed. Contraband prices fluctuated daily, depending on the efficiency of the Border Patrol.

Murph glanced around. There were a couple of stragglers in a corner; the joint's strong-arm mug was at the bar; Dutch Hessler, an off-duty cop, was off to himself at a small table; and three fellows from the graveyard shift at Michigan Steel were slumped on an overstuffed couch, chatting sleepily in Polish.

Joe yawned again, nodded at Murph, then motioned toward a large, round table far in the back. There, behind the haze and a litter of empties, looking all hooched up, sat Charlie and Soxy, along with the same dame Soxy had been with the night before. Since getting out on parole in May, Soxy was always traveling with some dame or other.

Clayt was flabbergasted. "What're they doin' drinkin', for cripes sake? We got boats comin' in."

"Not 'til noon. Ours aren't 'til noon," said Murph.

"So? They gonna sober up when they hear the noon whistle?"

But the boys put a good face on it as they approached the revelers. It was obvious even from afar that the doll was half-lit, since her right arm, which was flung across the table, cradled half her face. Soxy's condition was harder to assess. Charlie just sat there, cigarette dangling, and barely acknowledged them as he stared moodily into his beer. Charlie was still a man of few words.

"Morning all," said Murph. "What's up?"

"Geez, you guys must have pipes for guts," rasped Clayt. "I don't know how you can drink as soon as you crawl outta bed."

"What bed?" laughed Soxy.

"You mean you guys been drinking since I left you last night?" said Murph.

"Oh, did you leave?" bantered Sox, good-naturedly. "We hadn't noticed."

Soxy Goodell was well-known in Ecorse, not just because he came from prominent pioneer stock, though he did. Soxy's great-great grandfather, Elijah Goodell, fought in the Revolutionary War; his great-grandfather fought in the War of 1812 and was a captain of a company of Ecorse militia during the Black Hawk war; his grandfather fought at Gettysburg with the 5th Michigan Cavalry; and Soxy's father, John, a railroad man and village trustee, ran a tavern, Muskrat Junction, at the entrance to Hogan's Alley, where he served a complimentary muskrat lunch.

Goodells were stashed all over Ecorse, including William Goodell (Sox's uncle), who was now village president. There were upstanding Goodells, outstanding Goodells, longstanding Goodells, and those, like Sox and his brother Link, with no standing at all. Every cop on the beat knew Link and Soxy. They made frequent appearances before Judge Goodell. In November 1940, Link would be arrested for smuggling three Polish sailors across the river from Canada, for which he was provided free lodgings at the Atlanta Federal Penitentiary.

As for Sox, well, he was involved in the robbery at B.L. Sims, known as the Great Diebold safe caper. On March 18, 1925, a month before he turned 19, he was convicted of armed robbery and sentenced to 3-to-10 years at the Michigan State Reformatory.

That morning, Sox, out on parole since May, looked barely rumpled for one who'd been up all night. Having pared down to his white shirt and vest, he was still wearing his inevitable tweed cap, slouched on the side like a beret. The tomato had also retained her hat but at a more rakish angle, shading her penciled brows.

"She okay?" asked Murph.

"Oh, sure, sure," said Sox. "She's fine."

"Have you checked lately?"

Sox shook her shoulder. "Hey, Marge. Marge!"

With considerable effort, Marge raised her head. "Yeah?"

"Say, 'Hi.'"

"Hi," said Marge, greeting the Heinz ketchup. "Nice to meetcha."

"We met last night, remember?" said Murph.

"See. Whad I tell ya?" said Sox, returning Marge's head to her arm. "She's fine."

But Murph, who wasn't so sure, tilted sideways for a closer appraisal. This one was a looker, a pretty brunette, he thought, though it was safe to say she'd looked a lot better the night before. Now her face was puffy, her mascara smeared, her spit curls askew.

"See. She's fine," said Sox. "Now, pull up a chair. Take a load off." With that, he shot up to retrieve one, teetered slightly and collapsed back on himself. "Whoops," he giggled. "Got up too fast." Then, in an effort to prove he was functional, he signaled Joe with a two-finger whistle. "What'll ya have? On me."

"Thanks but no thanks," replied Murph, shaking Joe off. "Just had eggs."

"But ya know I hate drinkin' with guys who ain't drinkin'," whined Sox. "Be a sport."

"No can do."

"Cut the shit! Have a drink!" snarled Charlie.

Even Soxy flinched, though Marge barely shifted. Murph turned to see if Charlie was putting them on, but Charlie, stone-faced, gave no indication of good will. Reluctantly, the boys took off their overcoats, slung them on the backs of nearby chairs and joined the table.

"You okay?" asked Murph.

"Been better," said Charlie, still gazing into the foam. "Now, have a drink."

If Clayt was waiting for Murph to defy Charlie, and indeed he was, he was about to be disappointed. Because Murph's inclination in most instances was to keep the peace. So he rose sheepishly and turned to Clayt. "The usual?"

"Yeah," said Clayt with disgust.

"Hey, Joe!" shouted Murph, crossing to the bar. "Two Singapore Slings!" Then he folded his arms over Joe's funny papers, obscuring "The Bungle Family," and muttered, "But skip the venom, okay?"

"Even the Cointreau?" said Joe, softly, not looking at him.

"Just enough for a smell test."

"Got it," said Joe, bringing forth two highball glasses, scooping them into the crushed ice, setting them on the bar. Then he poured liberally from the gin bottle, though his finger was over the stopper, poured generously from the cherry brandy, though his finger covered the stopper, added soda, lemon, and a sprig of mint, swiped a dash of Cointreau around each rim with a toweled finger, and pushed the tall glasses across the counter.

Murph set one of the tall glasses in front of Clayt with a wink and waved the other under Soxy's flattened nose. "Strong enough for ya?" Sox took a hearty whiff, mostly of his own fumes, then sat back, mollified.

"So Sox, what's up," demanded Clayt.

Soxy grinned his bad-boy grin. "What's up is," he taunted, "we need ya."

"What for?"

The answer came through a cloud of smoke. "Bill Brewer," grumbled Charlie, his cigarette bouncing with each B.

"He's playin' both ends," said Sox. "Him and them guys at Rossin's."

Murph was astonished. "Sez who?"

"Sez us."

"But how d'ya know, Charlie?" asked Murph. "Who tipped you off?"

"O'Grady."

"O'Grady. That snot-nosed inspector?" Murph sat back. "Oh, I wouldn't be so sure of that."

"Bill Brewer's one of the best-liked guys around," chided Clayt. "He'd never squeal on anybody, even if he hated him. He and Joe Rossin are. . ."

"Bastards," spat Charlie, his cigarette recoiling in disgust.

"O'Grady said it was Brewer that snitched to the feds," said Sox.

"About what?"

"About Charlie's plant on Oakwood."

Murph turned to Charlie. "You sayin' Bill Brewer was the guy that fingered your warehouse for that raid last week?"

"At's what I'm sayin'."

"You sayin' Inspector O'Grady told you it was Brewer?"

"At's what I'm sayin'."

Murph and Clayt exchanged glances, then both leaned back and swigged their sham highballs, confident they could clear this up in short order.

"Listen, Charlie," said Murph, in slow, spell-it-out English, hoping reason could cut through the vapors. "I got news, big news. Norm Smith came over to our table at the White Tree a little while ago and gave us a heads-up. Right, Clayt?"

"Right."

"Now, listen, Charlie. Follow me here. Norm says there are three agents working undercover with the Border Patrol. Three agents assigned from Washington. Said he just got wind. And they're about to put the finger on around 40 guys. And over half . . . over *half* . . . are inspectors. It's all gonna come down soon."

"What's that gotta do with the price of potatoes?" jeered Sox.

"Don'tcha see? Don'tcha get it? If Norm Smith knows, lots of other guys know. That means the word's out. And I betcha anything O'Grady is scared shitless that he's goin' down. So he fingers your warehouse just to show he's not on the take, then puts the blame on Brewer and Rossin so you don't get wise. Don'tcha see, Charlie? O'Grady's a jerk, but he's no fool. He knows there's bad blood between you and the guys at Rossin's, so he's playin' on it. He's feedin' you a line to save his own neck. He's the one doing the double-crossing."

Murph eased back, Clarence Darrow in repose, and waited for Charlie's reaction to his closing argument, but Charlie was busy stacking sugar cubes. "Didja hear what I said, Charlie?"

Charlie dropped a cube, fumbled with another, then balanced it on the top row. "Yeah, ah heared it."

"Well. Don'tcha see? Don'tcha get it? The law's getting tough, just to prove they're not crooks," said Murph. "Hell, Charlie, I wouldn't want to be a jaywalker right now. All those agents on the take, and God knows there's hundreds of 'em, they'll be offering up guys like us, then sayin' someone else did the ratting. There'll be so many fingers pointing, they're gonna need thumbs. And O'Grady's one of 'em. Count on it."

"Norm Smith says everybody's got the jitters tryin' to find out who the undercover stoolies are,'" added Clayt. "Norm says Brewer and Rossin ain't movin' nothin' until they do."

"Norm says, Norm says," mocked Charlie. "It's all crap."

"But why would he say it?" asked Murph.

"'Cuz Norm Smith's totin' water for Rossin and Brewer. It's all crap."

"I don't get it," said Murph. "Why you guys being such hardheads?"

"'Cuz we run into Bill Brewer around 8:00 this morning," said Sox.

"Who's we?"

"Me, Charlie, Little Abe."

"Where?"

"Out front," smirked Sox. "Bones comes in and says, 'Brewer's comin' up the block.' So we run into him."

"Was Brewer alone?" asked Clayt.

"Naw. Had a couple a mugs with 'em," laughed Sox. "Boyo, ya shoulda been there. Charlie really let him have it. Told Brewer he was sick of him and his pals at Rossin's always puttin' the finger on him, tryin' to get him knocked off. Told Brewer he owed him 2,000 bucks, 'cuz that's how much he lost in the raid."

"What'd Brewer say?" asked Murph.

"Same ol' sass," drawled Charlie. "Said he din't do it. Said, 'You ain't yersef, Charlie. Come 'round when yer sober and we'll fix thangs up.'"

"*Come 'round when yer sober!*" screamed Charlie, loud enough to wake the dead, all except Marge.

"Maybe we oughta keep it down, Charlie," urged Murph, in a position to field the dirty looks being thrown from the bar.

"*Come 'round when yer sober!*" screamed Charlie, in defiance.

"Look, Charlie, I don't blame you for being pissed. Hell, I'd be pissed, too," said Murph. "But, at least Brewer's willing to meet with you. Talk it out. Maybe you guys can square this one."

"You sweet talkin' me?"

"'Course not. I'm just trying . . . you know . . . to put things in perspective."

"Pershpecsive!" shrieked Charlie, his tongue anesthetized by a case of Carling's.

"C'mon, Charlie, simmer down."

It was Sox who cut in, bailing Murph out. "Why don'tcha tell 'em the rest, Charlie?"

All eyes went to Charlie. Even Marge managed to shift her head, but Charlie had reverted to his cubes. He reckoned, barely audibly, that he'd been shoved, that that "piss ant" had shoved him.

Murph was incredulous. "Who? Bill Brewer?"

"Hard," snapped Charlie. "Knocked me down."

"Are you saying Bill Brewer shoved you so hard, he knocked you flat?"

"'At's what ah'm sayin'," mumbled Charlie. "'At's what he done." He stared at the table, little moving, then howled to the heavens, "*Come 'round when yer sober!*" and swatted the sugar cubes with the back of his hand, sending them flying.

"Wanna keep it down over there!" barked Joe from behind the bar. "That's the third time I tol' ya!"

Murph took advantage of the lull to piece together what probably had happened. Murph was beginning to suspect that Charlie, at O'Grady's urging, had spent the night building a case against the gang at Rossin's and that Sox had been egging him on. That around 8:00 that morning, when Brewer was coming up Front street, Charlie, Sox and Little Abe *accidentally* bumped into Brewer, and Charlie tore into him. That the real reason Charlie had his dander up was because he'd been tossed on his keister by Brewer in front of witnesses. Charlie couldn't afford to hear anything Murph had to say, no matter how important. Murph suspected that Charlie had been sitting in the Red Door stewing, spoiling for a fight, and Sox, who loved to set off fireworks when plastered, had been eagerly lighting the fuse. Worse, Murph had just noticed only a few seconds before that Charlie was packing a gun under his suitcoat.

"Where ah come from," said Charlie, knuckles wrapped white around his beer bottle, "when ya got a beef, ya settle it. Simple as 'at."

"What d'ya intend to do?" muttered Murph.

"Shoot up Rossin's."

"Shoot up Rossin's?" inquired Murph, politely. Give our boy credit; his reflexes were sound. He had sense enough to set down his highball before he dropped it. "You're gonna shoot up Rossin's?"

"No," corrected Sox. "*We're* gonna shoot up Rossin's."

Murph gazed at Clayt over the rim of his specs, but Clayt was staring bug-eyed at Charlie. "Are you crazy?" said Clayt. "Rossin's got protection from the Purples; they practically run the place."

"Even more reason," said Sox.

"But the Purples are dangerous; they're brutal killers," said Murph. "They'd shoot ya for usin' the wrong fork."

"Then it's time we taught 'em to have some respect."

"Have some respect?" laughed Clayt. "They'll be paying their respects to your mother."

Murph and Clayt were right, of course. The Purples weren't in Rossin's because they bought in as partners with all the legal niceties that entailed. Joe Rossin was well-liked and had built up a good-sized operation in the liquor business. He had his own bar, and behind that, his own cabaret on the water. A few of the Purples had stopped him one day and graciously offered to go in with him, strictly as a favor. Joe cordially declined.

> *"So Joe went about his business," recalled Barrett Lafferty, "and about two nights later they caught him down on Labadie Street and beat him to a pulp. He turned up at the hospital out at Eloise."*

Murph was right about another thing. The Purples were dangerous. Led by the four Bernstein brothers (Abe, Joe, Raymond and Izzy), they preyed on the underworld, ignoring every code on the river, and were hated for it. They invaded territory, cut booze, hijacked liquor loads, extorted runners, and muscled in on unions and blind pigs. All strong-arm stuff. Before they were through, they would have three massacres to their name: the Miraflores (March 1927), the St. Valentine's Day in Chicago (February 14, 1929), and the Collingwood (September 1931). Gangsters from all over the nation and parts of Sicily were moving into the Downriver area, and the Purples were thick among them.

"Anyways, this ain't about the Purples," said Charlie. "It's about Brewer."

"Listen to you," said Clayt. "One's saying, 'It's not the Purples'; the other's saying, 'Let's get the Purples.' You guys need to get your targets straight before you start blasting away."

"Look, alls we want to know is, you in or out," said Sox.

"Gee, Sox, I *sincerely* wish I could help. I sincerely do," said Clayt, standing up, checking his watch. "But I got boats coming in in about 15 minutes. I got. . . we got . . . work to do. Comin', Murph?"

"Whaddya mean, 'comin' Murph?'" said Sox. "Murph's doin' the drivin'. He's with us."

"Well—I," sputtered Murph.

"Whaddya mean, 'Well—I'? Ain't you Charlie's driver?" asked Sox.

"Murph's already spoken for. He promised he'd help my boys unload," said Clayt. "Right? Am I right, Murph?"

"Now, slow it down, all of you. Just slow it down." Murph was at a loss. If he only had time to think.

"Look, Charlie," said Clayt, sinking back into his seat. "Maybe this is how they handle things in Texas, but it's not Ecorse style."

"What's Eco'se style?"

"Have a meeting. Make sure you're going after the right guy. Then if you still have to do something, at least wait 'til dark. But don't, for god sakes, walk into a bar in broad daylight and shoot away. You'll be wearing cement shoes for

Sunday. Right, Murph?"

"C'mon, saddle up," said Charlie, twisting sideways, straining to reach his wallet. "We gotta git."

"Hold on, Charlie," said Murph. "Let's not go off half-cocked. We need time to think. Time to prepare."

"Whaddya think we been doin'?" said Sox.

"But they're gonna see you comin' a mile away. How you gonna get in?"

"We got a plan," said Sox.

"And what about Marge? Have you thought about Marge?"

"She's the plan," laughed Sox. "She'll get us in."

"Does she know that?" asked Murph.

"Sure, she knows it. She thinks it's a hoot."

"It just gets worse and worse," muttered Clayt, reaching for his scarf.

"Have you lost your ever-lovin' marbles?" said Murph. "You can't take that girl into Rossin's with you."

"I said *get us in*, not *go in*," said Sox.

The object of their concern bolted upright, slits for eyes, and stretched lazily, her arms uncoiling above her head. "Anybody else hungry?" she asked, shaking her numb arm.

"We'll eat later," said Sox.

"But I'm starvin'."

"C'mon, Marge, be a good girl," said Sox. "First, ya gotta do whatcha said ya'd do."

Marge pried off her hat, extracted a beveled mirror from her beaded bag and surveyed the damage. "Oh, brother," she grumped, licking lip rouge off her teeth, fluffing her hair with her fingers, examining the sleep lines etched on the side of her face.

"Aw, sheee-it," said Charlie, pushing himself up, nearly knocking over his chair.

"Stay outta this, Charlie," said Sox.

"Just gittin' mah coat, Sox. Just gittin' mah coat." Charlie crossed to the coat tree, put on his white silk scarf, and was soon swaddled by his black fur with its large shawl collar.

"Geez, Louise. Where's the fire? You guys been jawin' for two hours. Now you wanna go just like that," said Marge, snapping her fingers. "Well, if you want my help, you're just gonna have to wait. 'Cuz I gotta straighten my hose, fix my face."

"You sure you wanna do this, Marge?" asked Murph.

"Do what?" asked Marge.

"Go to Rossin's?" said Murph.

"Aw, don't be a wet blanket," scoffed Marge, flinging Murph the downward palm. "Nobody makes me do nothin'. And I'm goin' to the powder room whether you guys like it or not."

"Okay, okay," said Sox, "but make it snappy."

"Give me ten."

"Ya got five."

"Where's it written?" said Marge, snapping her purse shut. "You want me to getcha into Rossin's, don'tcha? How ya expect me to getcha in lookin' like this? Huh?"

"Can you stand?" asked Murph.

"Sure," said Marge.

And to his surprise, she did. Not necessarily erect. But close. And, with the help of chairs strategically located, she steered a fairly straight course to the powder room.

Chapter 28
Same day, around 10 a.m.

When Murph emerged into the cold morning air, Clayt was dogging his heels. "Are you nuts? Are you bonkers? You wanna end up in the cuckoo ward at Eloise? 'Cuz that's where you belong, Murph. That's where you belong."

"If I only had time to think."

"Take the time."

"How? How, Clayt! I can't even find time to think about how to find time to think! Aw, I gotta go warm up a car."

They parted ways: Clayt up the block to await his load, shaking his head all the way; Murph to Lefty Clark's parking lot, right next to Uncle Peck's, to warm up the getaway car.

Murph had a passion for cars, and Charlie Bauer had a car worthy of passion. A just-off-the-line Packard, a four-door sedan, dark green with beige leather interior, it was huge, over 21 feet in length, bigger than most of the cars on the road, with an electric start and roll-up windows, both uncommon. And fast? Nothing could beat that car, certainly not the law. Murph opened the trunk on the back rack, extracted a gas can, jacked up one side of the hood and filled the priming cups. Then he climbed in and turned the key in the ignition. But the Packard was not even remotely warm when Marge careened across the street, lurching through morning traffic, trailed by Charlie and Soxy.

Seconds later, Murph was doing a skillful U-turn on Front Street, gliding to the curb in front of the Ecorse Restaurant, three doors south of Rossin's, while Marge complained about the wintry temperature and begged Charlie to part with his fur coat.

Murph, grim-faced, peered up the block. All was quiet. The nondescript boathouse at 4585 was set back a little further than most of the boathouses to the north, allowing for a little more verge, a tall tree, the city sidewalk, and a short concrete walkway to the entrance. From the front, Rossin's was misleading. Behind the small house that contained a bar, a long addition extended back to a large boat well on the river, while another extension, an L-shape off the boat well, housed a sizable cabaret where Milton Riopelle often played with his six-piece band. The nightclub, with its many windows on the river, was often used as a marker for mariners.

Charlie turned round from the front seat. "Ya know what to do?"

"Yeah," said Marge, shivering in the back.

"Whatcha gonna do?" asked Sox.

"Knock on the door."

"Whatcha gonna say?"

"I'm a friend of Joe Rossin's."

"You gotta be kiddin'," complained Murph.

"Why not?" said Sox. "He's a night owl, ain't he? He ain't gonna be there to say no different." He looked at Marge. "And whatcha gonna do when the door opens?"

"Stand aside. Get out of the way," offered Marge.

"Fast," added Charlie.

"Yeah, fast."

"I'm beggin' you guys," said Murph. "Don't let her go in."

"Didn't ya just hear her say she's gonna stand aside?" asked Sox. "Can't she say it no clearer?"

"Tell ya one thing," said Marge. "You saps better shoot fast. 'Cuz I'm freezin' my patootie back here."

"Use the lap robe," said Murph.

"I'm using the damn lap robe," said Marge.

Sox was the first one out of the Packard. He skulked up the sidewalk, cut behind a tree and was lost from view, having gone to the side entrance that led to the kitchen where he was to wait outside. Then Charlie stumbled out of the car, all fur coat. He pitched up the sidewalk, then stood to the side of the boathouse, near the same tree. He beckoned Murph to pull up.

"Here goes nothing," said Murph, inching along, stopping directly in front of Rossin's, leaving the motor running. "Now remember," he said, looking at Marge through the rearview mirror. "When the door opens, stand aside. Got it?"

"I got it, I got it. How many times I gotta tell ya?" she cried, just before her transformation. Soon, she was tugging on her gloves, descending the ample running board like Marie of Rumania, imperiously bunching her wool coat at the collar for warmth while walking up the short sidewalk. Though she had a little hitch in her royal step, a little weakness in the royal ankles, a little drift in her promenade, she knocked regally on the door, then, aware she was being ogled from the other side, struck a haughty pose.

"Yeah?" came a voice from within.

"I'm a friend of Joe Rossin's."

There was a slight hesitation before the door inched open, before Charlie darted from the side of the building, sharply elbowing Marge aside, before Charlie wedged himself through the narrow passage, before he could be heard shouting "Howdee!" as the door snapped shut. Sox, hearing the pre-designated greeting, threw open the side door and dashed into the kitchen.

A petulant Marge limped back to the Packard and crawled into the back seat, favoring a rib. "Geezus, he's rough."

"You were sposed to stand aside," said Murph.

"I woulda," barked Marge. "Given half a chance."

Now they waited. While the Packard purred, heat from the floorboards above the massive engine finally began to toast Murph's feet and legs, a welcome warmth. But Marge, who was only partially benefiting from the idling engine, kept grumbling about the cold. "Wonder what's takin' so long, Why don'tcha toot the horn?"

"Give 'em time," said Murph, wondering the same thing, wishing he'd thought to muddy the license plate. He now had more than enough time to think. Too much, actually. He leaned across the seat, ready to fling open the passenger door, but no one came running.

"Do you have to keep the front windows cracked?" complained Marge.

"I need to hear," replied Murph.

"Hear what?"

"Gun shots."

"What for?"

"So I'll know when they're comin'. I'll know when to go."

"Seems to me, when they get in the car, that's a good time to go."

"Don't get smart," said Murph, annoyed.

"But it's like the Klondike back here."

"Give it a few more minutes," he said. "It's warm up front. It'll be warm back there soon." What a dumb thing to say. He knew it the minute he said it.

"Then what am I doin' back here?" she asked, sliding across the back seat, edging closer to the door.

"Look, Marge. Charlie's gonna come barreling outta there, hell bent for leather. We're not gonna have a lot of time to sort out who sits where. He's gonna land in your lap."

"But I'm freezin'," she said. Then she jumped out of the car, opened the passenger door and leapt in. "Geez, no wonder ya ain't cold. It's roasty toasty up here."

There came a resounding crack! Then its echo. "Goddamn it, Marge! Get in the back. I've been tellin' you nice, now I'm tellin' you mad. Get in the goddamn back seat. Please, I'm begging you." But Murph's entreaties went unheeded, drowned out by five more pops in quick succession.

The absurdity of it hit him with force. He'd gone along with Charlie and now all hell was breaking loose. Even worse, he was so busy dickering over seating arrangements that he had failed to notice the portly gentleman squirming out of a Rossin side window, dangling briefly before thudding to the ground; failed to see him glance anxiously at the Packard, then cut behind the shed next door; couldn't see him slinking southward, hugging the shadows, slipping into D. Mellin-Moran's garage, no doubt heading for a phone.

There were more gunshots and the sound of breaking glass. What the hell were they doing? Murph was so torn, he was immobilized. He knew he should get the hell out of there; he also knew he had to stay. With one eye on Marge's ornery puss and the other on Rossin's front door, he failed to see the Ecorse police car turn onto Front Street.

"There's a cop comin' this way," said Marge, her sharp voice lowered.

"Where?"

"Way up by White."

"Oh, swell." Murph pulled down his cap to the top of his glasses and slumped behind the wheel. "Now, don't move. No sudden moves," he warned. "Just act natural."

"What's that 'sposed to mean? Ack natural."

"Just what it says. Like we're waiting for someone. No. Like we're lost. Quick. Reach under your seat, hand me a map. Act natural."

With a put-upon sigh, Marge fished under the seat, then slid a folded map of Metropolitan Windsor across the leather upholstery.

"He's probably just making the rounds," said Murph, losing his face behind Shell's red-and-yellow fanfolds. "Remember. Just act natural."

"Will you stop with that ack-natural crap? Every time you say it, I get nervous."

"I give up. Just act like a friggin' broad who's waitin' for her friggin' sweetie who's inside shooting up the place."

"Now you're talkin'."

The patrol car slowed as it crossed LeBlanc and pulled up silently on the other side of the street. From a small rip in the royal map of Windsor, Murph recognized the tall, affable officer before he emerged from the Chevy.

"You know a cop named John Allen?" whispered Murph.

"No," said Marge.

"Good, then he doesn't know you. Now sit up straight and give me a running commentary. Tell me, without a lotta lip, what's going on. Okay?"

"Okay," she said, before pausing, before saying, "He's outta the car . . . Waitin' to cross the street . . . He's crossin' the street."

"Is he looking our way?"

"He did already."

"You think he saw me? You think he recognized me?"

"Naw. He was too busy givin' me the eye."

"What's he doing now?"

"He's going up the walk . . . Knockin' on the door . . . Standin' there, waitin', waitin'."

"Is the door opening?"

"Yeah." Marge burst out laughing.

"What's so funny?"

"Charlie just let him in."

"Our Charlie?"

"Yeah."

"Oh, Christ. Oh, Christ. Oh, Christ. Was Charlie holding a gun?"

"Not that I could see."

Murph unclenched his jaw, unhunched his shoulders, relief palpable. If Charlie opened the door, Charlie had things well in hand, because nobody in Rossin's would say a word to a cop. He sat back, lowered the map, looked straight ahead, then began to tremble. Call it premonition.

Because Bill Brewer was walking purposefully down LeBlanc, striding across Front, marching past Voisine's Fish Market. His demeanor said it all—not only had he recognized Charlie's Packard, he had seen Officer Allen enter. Even so, Murph stayed low in his seat as Brewer knocked on the door. Charlie opened it. Then Charlie stepped back into the shadows, and Brewer began to enter.

There was a loud crack! and Brewer backed out the door. Murph could hear more bullets being fired from within, then the click, click, click of an empty chamber. Murph watched in horror as Brewer crumpled to the sidewalk, drawing his gun, firing three rounds of his own. Murph gazed in disbelief as the air filled with smoke. He sat dazed, his eyes glued to the fallen Brewer as blood seeped onto the sidewalk.

Then Sox burst from the entrance, bounding over Brewer, pocketing one gun, holding another. "Get goin'!" he howled as he jumped on the running board, thrusting his fingers through the cracked window.

"Where's Charlie?" yelled Murph.

"Get goin'!"

On instinct alone, Murph pulled away from the curb and shifted into second as soon as the car was rolling. He was going 50 when he passed Flora and Sadie's, 60 when he approached Pilon's. Coming into the turn at State, the best road out of town, he took his foot off the gas. But instead of hitting the brake pedal that operated the front pads, he seized the arm brake that controlled the back pads while yanking the steering wheel with all his strength, deliberately skidding into a turn, dangerously fishtailing across the trolley tracks. Then he stepped on the gas, released the wheel, letting it spin in order to right it, and took off up State, Soxy hanging on.

Just past Third Street, Murph did a screeching right turn into the alley, came to a head-rattling halt by St. Francis Xavier cemetery and exploded out of the car, fists cocked, before Sox could climb down from the running board. "What did you do!"

"I didn't do nothin'."

"Then where's Charlie!"

"Shot, I think."

"Shot, you think!" screamed Murph. "And you just left him!"

"He was flat on the floor, for god sake!"

"You stupid sonofabitch! You stupid sonofabitch! Did you shoot Brewer?"

"Hell no, it was Charlie!"

Murph began to pace. "Now whadda we do? Will ya tell me? You stupid sonofabitch. Now whadda we do?" He kicked a stone, then kicked another, before kicking another. "I gotta go back."

"Wait a minute."

"I gotta go back. Check on Charlie."

"Anyone seen ya?" asked Soxy.

"Only Brewer."

Sox laughed. "Well, he ain't gonna be talkin'."

"You think that's funny! You stupid sonofabitch! You think that's funny!"

"Don't push it, Murph. Don't push it! I'm lettin' ya blow off steam, but I got limits."

"All right, all right, all right." Murph took out his gloves from his overcoat pocket and put them on, in a deliberate attempt to slow his heart rate. "Look, Sox, you and Marge gotta ditch the car."

"Where you gonna go?"

"Home. To get mine. To go find out about Charlie."

———————

Murph had already cut through the cemetery and was crossing the train tracks at Labadie when the sirens started. As he neared the Village Hall, police cars were spinning out of the parking area, one after another, forcing him to stand aside. Across the way, small faces appeared in the upper-windows of School One, teachers behind them, drawn by the pandemonium. Dia, who had managed to wedge her skinny frame between two large boys, spotted Murph and waved proprietorially. Ordinarily, Murph would have given her a dismissive nod, but he went out of his way to wave back. Alibis are alibis, even if they're Dia.

He glanced uneasily up Labadie toward his father's barbershop, but the coast was clear. He rushed up the alley and into the Moore back door, intent on getting his car keys, but froze halfway up the steps when he heard his mother's feeble voice coming from her sickroom, "Murph? That you?"

"Yeah, Ma," he said, backtracking down the steps, peering into her bedroom.

"What are all those sirens?" asked Agnes.

"That's what I'm gonna find out."

"Oh, there you are," said his father, coming in the front door, overcoat over his barber smock. "Just the person I want to see."

"What are you doing home?" blurted Murph.

"There's been a killing at Joe Rossin's," said George, hanging his hat on a hook.

"You're kidding."

"Ollie just called the shop. Front Street's blocked off between LeBlanc and Mill."

"Geez, Pa. I heard the sirens. . . I was just . . . I hope it wasn't Joe."

"Don't know who. Don't know how," said George, popping his head into the bedroom. "Kids are okay, Agnes. Nothing to worry about." He looked around. "Where's Freda?"

"In the basement," replied Agnes. "Stoking the furnace."

"Good," said George. Then he walked to the dining room archway, turned to Murph and said casually, "Can you come here for a second. There's something in the kitchen I want you to help me with."

"Now?"

"Yes."

"But I was going upstairs to get my car keys. Thought I'd follow the sirens. See what's up."

"Won't take long."

Reluctantly, Murph followed his father into the kitchen. George turned toward him and dropped his voice. "Not that it's any of my business, you've made that clear, but I need to know, because I'm sure to be asked, where've you been?"

"Over on Third. Over at Denny Renaud's."

"On foot?"

"No, Clayt picked me up. We had breakfast at the White Tree, then he dropped me off, said he had to get some cigarettes, said he'd be right back. But you know Clayt. So I got tired of waiting and decided to walk back. Then I heard all these sirens. Thought I'd get my car, see what's going on."

"Walked back?"

"We're talking three blocks. What's the big deal? Just cause you wouldn't."

"Thought I told you I didn't want you hangin' around Denny Renaud's. Thought I told you that his dad's getting homemade hooch from the Italians over in Wyandotte, that he's sure to be raided any day now."

"Aw, Denny's a pal. We just hang out."

"You been drinking?"

"No, not at all." But when his father looked doubtful, Murph was righteously indignant. "Aw, why d'ya even bother to ask? You never believe anything I say anyway."

"Stay away from Denny's."

"Sure, sure," said Murph, walking through the arch, turning toward the steps.

"And spend a minute with your mother before you go."

"You don't have to tell me to do that," barked Murph angrily, looking toward the bedroom, pounding up the steps, his indignation now justified. "I always do that. Or haven't you noticed."

After looking in on Agnes, Murph drove up Monroe, parked in Lefty Clark's lot, and walked to Front, measuring his pace—not so fast as to look eager, not so slow as to miss out. By his calculation, he had lost less than fifteen minutes. He caught up with Clayt in front of Johnny Cinder's place, a boathouse near the corner of Front and LeBlanc.

"What the hell happened?" asked Clayt, pointing to the next block where police cars were strewn like logs in front of Rossin's.

"Charlie's been shot. Brewer's been killed," whispered Murph. "It's a mess. A goddam mess."

"Holy shit." Clayt needed a moment to take it in. "What the hell happened?"

"Who the hell knows," replied Murph.

"You didn't go in?"

"No."

"At least that's something," said Clayt. "Anybody see you?"

"Yeah, Brewer. Poor guy." Murph shook his head. "Geezus."

"Anybody else?"

"John Allen saw the car. But I don't think he saw me."

"John Allen. The cop?"

"It's a mess. It's just a mess."

"Hole-ee shit."

"Look, Clayt. For the record. I was at Denny's. You dropped me off, forgot to come back for me."

"That your story?"

"That's *our* story, though I gotta tell Denny."

"Thought your dad told you to stay away from Denny's."

"That's what gives the alibi heft. Besides, Denny lives on Third; I was comin' from Third." Murph looked nervously over at the police cars. "Did you get your boats unloaded?"

"Yeah. About two seconds before all hell broke loose. No thanks to you."

"C'mon, let's walk down there."

They got as far as Voisine's fish market, next door to Rossin's, before they encountered police lines. An aproned Ed Voisine was watching the hubbub from his market window, while Lucile, his wife, could be seen planted in the front window upstairs. As the boys stepped inside, Murph served up his usual greeting, "Don't know what you've been up to, Ed, but it sure smells fishy in here." As always, Ed laughed, even as he continued to gaze out the window.

"What're you seeing?" asked Clayt.

"Not much," replied Ed. "They just put a guy in one of the police cars. Like a sack of potatoes. Set out for the hospital or the morgue. Not sure which."

"Anyone we know?" asked Murph.

"Couldn't say for sure. But Lucile got a good look from upstairs; said she thought it was Bill Brewer."

Then Lucile yelled from upstairs, "They're bringing out another one!" and the boys began to bob and weave, shifting for a view.

Outside, Herb Ormsby opened the rear door of his police car, parked where the Packard had been, and stood in wait. Charlie was coming out, feet first. Sharkie Montie had him by the legs, John Allen by the underarms. Though partially blocked by a sea of blue uniforms, the boys followed his fur coat as it dragged along the sidewalk. Herb reached in from the other side of the car to help maneuver the wounded man gingerly into the back seat.

"Bet they're taking him to Wyandotte Hospital," said Clayt, giving Murph the high-sign.

They bade farewell to Ed, rushed back to the lot, piled into Murph's car, drove up Monroe, turned on Mill, slowed to Front and waited for Herb's patrol car to pass, then, from a distance, followed it along Front to Wyandotte and into the parking lot behind the hospital. After attendants came out with a gurney and hauled Charlie out of the back seat, Herb parked the police car and entered the emergency-room door with John Allen and Sharkie Montie.

"So we pulled in back of the police car," said Clayt, years later. "They carried Charlie in and they left his coat in the car. So I looked at the coat and when I lifted it up, I could see the fur [where he'd been shot]. The fur from the coat was pushed in inside of the lining. I don't know how many times. More than once."

Bill Brewer must have been good with a gun. Two of his bullets struck Charlie in the chest and the third got him in the abdomen. Charlie Bauer died at 3:00 that afternoon, while Brewer, though also shot in the abdomen, was reported to be "resting comfortably."

Duke Frampton's account of what happened at Rossin's appeared in the *Detroit News* within hours. Frampton, who was Bill Brewer's roommate at 4586 High Street, had been in the blind pig at the time of the shootings. True to the code, Frampton managed to confine the narrative to the names and exploits of the deceased and wounded, a not uncommon practice. After a similar Downriver escapade, one ace reporter had noted: "A subsequent police investigation of the shooting went nowhere when every person of the group, which numbered 30, said he was in the bathroom at the time of the killing."

That night, Murph sat beside his mother's bed for longer than usual, tipping backward restlessly on a dining room chair even after Agnes had drifted off, thankful she knew nothing of his shenanigans, grateful for a second chance, cursing himself for being stupid and vowing to change. She was so proud of him, her only son, the first of her children to graduate from high school. He knew where she kept his clippings; he'd seen them in a box in the top drawer of her dresser, though she'd been too tired of late to paste them into her scrapbook.

The next morning, a more detailed account made the front page of the *Detroit News*, and, though Murph and Sox remained unidentified, they had become part of the story: "Bauer and two men and a girl drove up to Rossin's place. One man and the girl remained in the car while Bauer walked in the front door and the other man through the back."[1] But Soxy must have been on the level because, throughout the article, it was Charlie Bauer who did all the shooting. There was also an interesting tidbit as to where Charlie'd acquired his gun: the pistol had recently been owned by the Detroit Police Department.

As to what exactly had occurred inside Rossin's, Murph was as much in the dark as everyone else. Sox was lying low, probably in Canada, and Marge was nowhere to be found, so Murph and Clayt took to haunting Seavitt's before each newspaper delivery. Normally the intensity of their interest would have aroused suspicion, but the entire town was just as eager for details.

Later that Tuesday, with the lid still on the Downriver cafes and nothing much to do, the boys could be found lingering over cherry phosphates at a dinky marble table, shifting their weight repeatedly on the small wire chairs, when the *Detroit Free Press* , final edition, landed with a thud just inside the door of Seavitt's, its headlines face up: "1 KILLED, 1 WOUNDED AS RUM RUNNERS DUEL IN SALOON." As soon as Louie Seavitt's replacement cut the string on the bundle (Louie had died of pneumonia that April), Murph paid for a copy and pulled Clayt behind the magazine rack. "That's it. I'm dead," he muttered, having arrived at the second paragraph.

"What's it say?"

Murph read into Clayt's ear, dropping his voice even lower: "'Ecorse police, aided by Assistant Prosecutor John D. Watts, were combing the 'rum coast' last night in an effort to locate a pretty and vivacious brunette who, with her two male companions are sought as the principal witnesses to the affair.'"[2]

"Combing the rum coast," scoffed Clayt, though softly. "With what? A nit comb?"

"Glad you think it's funny."

"Aw, relax. If they knew it was you, they'd have picked you up by now. Betcha Frampton gave them a phony description."

"Yeah? Then what about 'vivacious brunette?' She could answer to that."

"Aw, hell. Your sisters are vivacious brunettes. Flora and Sadie are vivacious brunettes. What else it say?"

"Here. You take over," said Murph, handing Clayt the paper, pointing to the place. "I'm feeling a little queasy."

"'The fight occurred,'" whispered Clayt, "'after Bauer, accompanied by a woman and two of his gang. . .'"

"His gang," scoffed Murph under his breath. "Oh, please. I love these guys. Everybody's in a gang. You pal around with someone, you're in a gang. I worked

[1] Detroit News, Tuesday, November 27, 1928
[2] "1 Killed, 1 Wounded as Rum Runners Duel in Saloon." Detroit Free Press, final edition, Tuesday, November 17 , 1928.

for the guy; I didn't take a blood oath. Why do they do that?"

"You want me to keep reading or not?"

"Yeah, yeah," said Murph. "His gang."

"This might interest you," whispered Clayt. "'Bauer, the young woman and one man entered the saloon while the third man remained outside at the wheel of a large automobile.'"

"The young woman entered the saloon? Is that what it says? The young woman entered the saloon? She never went in the place," jeered Murph, though in muted timbre. "Now they got her enterin' the damn saloon. The *News* had it right. Why didn't they just read yesterday's *News*?"

As Clayt read on, it became apparent that Soxy had taken part in the shooting, though the *Free Press* clearly had no inkling as to his identity, repeatedly referring to him as the "tough guy." Turning to page 3, Clayt continued without interruption until he got to: "'The 'tough guy,' his male companion and the girl ran to the waiting car . . .'"

Murph was beside himself; his voice began to rise. "He just said, I was in the car. Didn't he just say, I was in the car? Not more than three paragraphs ago, I was in the car. Now he's got me running to the car. I was never in the place and he's got me running to the car."

"What's it matter?" said Clayt. "They don't know who you are. No one's squawkin."

"That's just sloppy reporting, Clayt. They oughta hang writers for that. He's messing with people's lives here."

"Keep your voice down."

"But why can't they get it right," mumbled Murph. "I mean, if you're gonna call yourself a reporter. Hell, I did a better job covering the PTA."

But it was the summary paragraph, as read by Clayt, that caused Murph to collapse onto the wooden apron in front of Seavitt's window, that caused the new pharmacist to briefly look their way. "Watts last night said that the two men and girl will be charged with assault with intent to do great bodily harm if they are arrested. The men are known, Watts said, and their arrest is momentarily expected.[3]

"That's it. I'm dead." Murph looked up at Clayt and whispered. "What do I do? Turn myself in? At least, I'd get points for being honest."

"Not so fast," said Clayt. "We gotta think. What's today?"

"Tuesday."

"Watts said that last night, right?"

"I guess."

"Anyone see you today?"

"Everyone saw me today. I wasn't hiding."

"And Marty Sage is a cop, right?

---

[3] Ibid.

"Right."

"Marty Sage lives six doors down from you, on your block, right?"

"Right."

"So, where's he looking for you? Toledo? You'd think, while he's doing all that heavy combing, maybe he'd stroll down, knock on your door."

"I passed Marty in Pilon's only an hour ago."

"And what'd he say?"

"'Hi.'"

"See, that's my point. They're bluffing, Murph. Trying to flush you out. Besides," said Clayt, "most guys in the trade know you only as Joe Murphy. They don't even know your name, unless they're from Ecorse. Just sit tight. Ya gotta sit tight."

By that night, with rain pelting his bedroom windows, Murph was tucked snuggly beneath the quilt, resting a little easier. All the major papers had weighed in and no one had ratted. Clayt was right. If the cops wanted him, he was right there.

Chapter 29

Wednesday, November 28, 1928

It was still drizzly—half rain, half snow—around mid-afternoon on Wednesday when Murph poked his head in the door of his father's barbershop, anxious to find out how much he knew. "Got time for a cut?"

"Absolutely," said George, while shaving the back of Dom Dalton's neck in an otherwise clientless room. "Got time for a cut, a shine and a box social."

"Close the door, you're letting in the cold," barked Dom.

Murph entered the gate, shed his coat and flopped down on the black leather sofa near the pot-bellied stove, listening idly to the idle chatter as he rifled through a *Police Gazette*, until he realized they were talking about the recent demise of one Charlie Bauer.

"Just the same," George was saying, "it's a shame he had to get killed."

"Well, look on the bright side," said Dom. "From what I hear, he dodged one hell of a hangover."

Soon Dom was shorn and gone, and Murph sank into the barber chair. "This a holiday?" he asked.

"Not that I know of," said George, pumping up the chair.

"Then where's your business?"

"Nice of you to notice."

"Geez, I knew it was bad, Pa, but not this bad."

"If it weren't for evenings and Saturdays, we'd be out on the street."

"Maybe you oughta raise the price. Have you thought of that?"

George sighed, wrapped a towel around his son's neck, draped a sheet over him, then rested his palms on his shoulders from behind and addressed him in the mirror. "How much you want off?"

"Short on the sides."

"And tall on top?" asked George.

"Nah, I'm through with that," said Murph.

"Don't tell me that partless, puffed-up pompadour has gone the way of the mutton chop."

"Yep."

"How come?"

"Remember my yearbook photo?"

"Hard to forget."

"That's how come."

"Well," said George, taking a comb out of his breast pocket. "Serves you right for abandoning me for Roy Livernois."

"As I recall, you and I were on the outs at the time."

"Ah, one of the many," said George amiably, as he ran a comb through his son's hair. "One of the many."

There was a momentary lull, followed by a poor transition as transitions go, made worse by Murph's labored effort to keep it light. "Have you seen the paper?"

"Which one?" asked George.

"This morning's *News*."

"Yes."

"Whadja think?" asked Murph.

"About what?"

"About Watts exonerating Brewer. Saying Brewer shot in self-defense."

"I was glad to hear it. Bill Brewer's a regular guy," replied George. "It's in the *Free Press*, too."

"Oh, is the *Free Press* out?"

"Been out."

"How long?"

"Bout half an hour. Maybe less." George stopped combing, though his hands remained above Murph's head. "Part or no part?"

"What do *you* think?"

In feigned shock, George reeled backward and clutched his chest. "You want my opinion?"

"See, this is why I go to Roy Livernois," deadpanned Murph. "Okay, I give. What's your preference?"

"Slightly off to the side."

"So be it."

George took the tip of the comb and drew a straight line through Murph's thick brown mane. "Feeling agreeable today, are we?"

"In my nature."

George used the comb together with the shears from his breast pocket and began a methodical snip, snip, snip of the hair between his fingers. Though his father often worked in silence when he concentrated on a cut, Murph grew uneasy. But he knew enough to hold his tongue until his father pocketed the scissors and stepped back for an appraisal before inquiring, "Anything new in the *Free Press*?"

"Like what?" asked George, reaching for the motorized clippers resting on the back counter, its cord dangling from a light fixture in the ceiling.

"Like. . . things that hadn't been reported."

"Loretta Young's got the flu," said George.

"That's not what I mean."

"What do you mean?"

"About Rossin's," said Murph. But the words were abruptly lost in the shrill whine of the clippers. He stared angrily at his father in the mirror, while his father, seemingly oblivious, maneuvered the screaming blades upward and outward at the back of Murph's head. "Well, is there?" yelled Murph, over the din.

"What!"

"Anything new about Rossin's?"

"Depends on what you mean by new!" shouted George, before switching off the clippers and returning them to the counter. "New to me might not be new to you." Then he worked up a foam in a cup, told Murph to lower his head and lathered the back of his neck with Williams shaving cream. "I guess you could say there are a couple of things."

Murph, finally sure that he was being toyed with, did not reply.

As the antlered buck on the wall gazed down on the silent duel, George shaved Murph's neck at a leisurely pace while Murph, with head bent at an uncomfortable angle, glowered upward. Then, after patting Murph's neck thoroughly with witch hazel and wiping his hands thoroughly on a towel, George retrieved a section of the *Free Press,* already quartered, from the side of his cash register, stood in front of the barber chair, blocking a quick exit, and faced his seated son. "Is this new to you?" he asked. "'The man with Bauer, said by police to be Edward "Soxy" Goodell. . .'"

"Oh, that's what this is all about," cried Murph. "Geezus, Pa. I didn't know Soxy was in on it. But why would he go after Brewer? It doesn't make sense. Can I see that?"

But as he tried to free a hand from under the sheet, George went right on reading: "'Goodell, who is said to be on parole on a charge of robbery armed, ran out of the place with the woman, whose name is unknown.'"[1]

"That's not what I heard," griped Murph.

"What's not what you heard?"

"I heard the woman was never in the place."

"What's the difference?"

"Well, can't they bother to get it right? I mean, if they're gonna report it. Everyone says the woman didn't go in there."

"Who's everyone?"

"Everyone, including yesterday's *News.* It said the woman was never in the place."

"*Free Press* said she was."

"Well, the *Free Press* musta got it wrong. Tell ya one thing. I'd take the *News* over the *Free Press* any day."

"You could be right," said George.

"I know I'm right."

"'Cuz this morning's *News* said that the girl and the guy in the car drove

---

[1] "Freed in Rum Feud Slaying," Detroit Free Press, Wednesday, November 28, 1928.

away while the shooting was in progress."

"Yeah, I saw that, too," said Murph. "They got it all balled up."

"But that was in your beloved *News*."

"They're both rags. Just shoddy journalism, if you ask me."

"Why you getting so riled?" asked George.

"I just want them to get their facts straight."

"But how do you know what the facts are?"

"I know a guy that was there."

"Who?"

"Just a guy."

"Did your friend tell you who the girl was?"

"I didn't say *friend*; I said *guy*."

"Did he tell you who the girl was?"

"I haven't the foggiest."

"Maybe this'll help." George returned to the paper: "'Police say she answers the description of a young woman who has taken part in several recent down-river holdups.'"[2]

"Oh, geez."

"Want to hear the rest?" asked George.

"Do I have a choice?"

"'The two got into the waiting car. . .'"

"That's just so wrong."

"This wrong, too?" asked George. "'Police say that the last name of the man at the wheel is Moore.'"[3] Murph sat there, deathlike, beheaded by the sheet. "What, no protest?"

"I'm not the only Moore around, you know," said Murph, feebly.

"How many bum around with Soxy?"

Murph had no comeback.

"I can promise you one thing," said George. "That girl you're protecting? Your moll."

"Oh, stop."

"I can promise you one thing. She'll never be identified. Your moll. Her parents'll see to that."

"Why?"

"She's 15, Murph."

"Oh, Christ."

"Fif-teen! When did you start robbing the cradle?"

"Geezus, Pa! You think I'm nuts!" yelled Murph, yanking at the sheet, freeing his arms. "I'm not dating her, I'm dating Lillian! Soxy's dating her, and he sure as hell didn't tell me she was 15."

"I don't care who's dating her. What's she doing there?"

<hr>

[2] Ibid.
[3] Ibid.

Murph gazed earnestly at his father, strangely relieved. At least, he could stop lying; at least, he could finally talk straight. "I didn't go in, Pa. No matter what the *Free Press* says. I didn't go in and I didn't let the girl go in, either."

"I know."

"You know?"

George set the newspaper back on the counter. "Yes, I know."

"How long have you known?"

"Since Monday night."

"But if *you* know, *they* know."

"That's right."

"Then why didn't . . . why haven't I been arrested?"

George stared at his son for some time, his deep, coal-black eyes tinged with sadness. Presently, he walked through the swing gate, locked the door, flipped the sign to CLOSED and returned to face Murph, resting his back against the counter, arms folded. "Because of your mother."

"Mumma?"

"Because, unlike some people I know, there are those who are concerned about your mother. Because Herb Ormsby's a good friend. Because he adores her. Because he agrees that it would kill her. Literally. And because I begged Herb to give you another chance. For your sake as well as your mother's."

"Who saw me? Who identified me?"

"Officer Allen."

"Does that mean I'm off the hook?"

"If you cooperate, they'll drop the charges."

Murph hesitated. "What do you want me to do?"

"Be a witness. Tell Herb and Watts everything you know or saw."

Since he hadn't seen much, Murph was getting off light. "Okay," he said.

"And that car of yours. It isn't leaving Monroe anytime soon."

Well, not so light. "But how will I get around?"

"Shank's mare."

"Wait a minute, Pa. I appreciate what you've done. I really do. But I need my car."

"The trolley stop's a block away."

Murph's panic turned to anger. "You can't stop me from driving my car. I'm of age. I'll just move out."

"Then I'll ask Herb to suspend your license."

"For what?"

"For driving 70 miles an hour up State Street!" yelled George. "That's for what!" He lunged forward, nose to nose. "No son of mine is gonna speed through the streets and run down kids like Nick Kirby."

"That's not fair!"

"Tell that to the five-year-old he killed. Tell that to the eight-year-old he killed."

"That's not fair! I'm not Nick!"

"Or maybe you want to end up like Channie Tripp."

Murph looked at his father as if he'd gone mad. "Who. . . in God's name. . . is Channie Tripp?"

"In all your reading these last few days, you don't recall seeing the name Channie Tripp?"

"No, Pa. I musta missed it."

"He's been caught three times in the last five years—with liquor."

"So?"

"And this July, he tossed three quarts of moonshine from his house during a raid."

"So?"

"So. Today, he was sentenced to life in prison."

"For three quarts?"

"The judge said he had no choice under Michigan's mandatory three-strikes code, even though the jury begged for mercy."

"That's just a stupid, stupid law," said Murph. "They're catching nothing but minnows with that stupid law."

"I agree," said George. "It's atrocious. But it's the law. And when they drag you off in handcuffs and lock you up for life, don't come crying to me with, 'That's not fair!' Cuz right now, smart guy, nothing's fair. Nothing's remotely fair. Welcome to the world of men. Now tilt your head forward so I can dust your neck."

There had been at least five people inside Rossin's when Charlie Bauer shoved his way in: Oscar Martin, who was tending bar; Duke Frampton and Burt Forbes, who were seated on stools before him; Nelson Olsen, the chef, who was in the kitchen; and the portly gentleman who climbed out the window, whose name never surfaced. There is reason to believe, however, by the scores of witnesses quoted in the numerous articles, that the list of bystanders compiled by the police was incomplete. To add to the confusion, during the first two days after the shootings, when no one was squealing on Soxy, all the tough-guy talk and gunslinging was attributed to Charlie Bauer, since it was safer to fink on the newly departed.

On entering Rossin's, Charlie Bauer had given a cordial "Howdee" and asked for Bill Brewer. Duke Frampton, keeping it friendly, replied that Bill had gone to their apartment but would be right back. So Charlie said he'd wait, though he remained by the door. That's when Soxy, having startled the cook, came from the kitchen with a pistol in each hand, startling everyone else, and said, "I'm one hard-boiled guy and I want to see you guys drink beer as fast as the bartender can pass it out." At least that's what he said in Tuesday's *Free*

Press.[4]

So while Charlie paced by the door, everyone in the place, including Soxy, drank "themselves into near insensibility," noted the *Free Press* . At some point, Sox complained that Duke Frampton wasn't keeping up with him. Soxy grabbed one of the pistols, stepped back and shot Duke's glass off the bar or out of his hand (versions differ). Then Sox "amused himself while waiting by shooting down rows of empty glasses."

About this time, the portly gentleman must have escaped to make his phone call, because at 10 a.m. Herb Ormsby wrote in the police ledger: "*Received call from 4585 [Front] known as Joe Rosen [sic] Cafe that there was someone [taking] off the place. Sent Officer Allen to investigate. When he got there Chas Bauer opened the door and let him in. [Allen] went to the bar to talk to the bartender when Bill Brewer came to the door. Chas Bauer went and open [sic] the door and started to shoot at Brewer and Brewer started to shoot back at Bauer.*" Patrolman Allen reported that he had to step aside to avoid being shot. Although he had drawn his police pistol, he said, he could not decide who to shoot.

Bill Brewer hadn't ratted. In the course of that week and the next, it came to light that Bauer's Oakwood plant was probably raided because of the activities of one Lawrence Fleishman, one of the few effective Border Patrol agents. Fresh off a sting in New York City, Fleishman had started undercover work in Detroit and Downriver on Sept 22, 1928, and did not fold up shop until the week before the shooting, when he got wind that Joe Rossin and others were close to unmasking him.

On Friday, November 30, four days after Bauer was killed, 13 Customs Border Patrol inspectors were arrested for accepting bribes and "conspiracy to assist liquor smuggling." On Saturday, December 1, the *Detroit News* headlined, "20 TO 30 MORE FALL INTO RUM GRAFT NET," while a subhead noted that 100 Customs men were slated to be fired. Since the entire patrol consisted of 126 men, that meant that 80% of the agents were somehow involved in collecting "more than $500,000 in graft from liquor runners operating on the Detroit River." Notice was also given that "at least 40 bootleggers and rum runners" might be indicted, further dampening activities along the river. On Monday, December 3, Ecorse police raided and closed the Red Door Cafe and arrested Joe Hughes, the bartender. The river was closed for the holidays.

So Fleishman's undercover work led to the "dismissal of most of the patrol, the arrest and indictment of 23 of its inspectors and the indictment of 18 'big shot' rum smugglers," summarized the *Detroit Free Press* in 1930,[5] "including [Norman B.] Smith and Rossin, Pete Licavoli and [Hunky] John Wozniak."

---

[4] Detroit Free Press , Tuesday, November 27, 1928.
[5] `Drank with Watkins..., Detroit Free Press , March 22, 1930.

Though Murph was a small fish in a very large and busy pond, he found it expedient for the time being to avoid Bill Brewer, Joe Rossin, the Purples, the feds, the state police, the Ecorse cops, the press and his father. Freda, Rowe and Clayt were about his only friends, and even those connections were tenuous. Murph started parking cars for customers of Lefty Clark, who had a gambling emporium above Raupp's Garage.

Clark, the man who would someday run Cuba's Tropicana, had converted the upstairs of the building that housed Raupp's Sinclair Station and Hupmobile

Raupp's Garage
(Virtual Motor City Collection, Walter P. Reuther Library, Wayne State University)

Service into an opulent parlor where the walls dripped crimson and gilt, where free lunch went from turkey on rye to elaborate spreads, where walls had slits big enough for a gun barrel and a pair of eyes, and patrons were frisked upon entry. At least that was the interior. The exterior continued to remain white and nondescript with block letters proclaiming RAUPP'S GARAGE, REPAIRING & STORAGE, RADIO & HUPMOBILE SALES, and a small, unobtrusive buzzer for DAY & NIGHT SERVICE. The swells came there. Along with Sherman Billingsley and Nick the Greek. Rumor had Billingsley buying uncut Canadian for his Stork Club in New York; and one reporter remembered the night Nick the Greek was on a lucky streak: the house had to send out for another $50,000 to cover his bets.

"After Charlie was killed, Murph went to work for the crap games, for Lefty Clark" said Clayt. *"Murph worked there, and he ran the parking lot.*

"In high school, we had four or five kids that used to drive these big Cadillacs downtown every night for Lefty," said Barrett Lafferty. *"They got $25 a night and all we did was drive down to Cadillac Square, and there was a stop and there was all our customers waiting. And they brought them out to Lefty's and then they took them back. Now we had some really highfalutin people that came out; they weren't just the dregs. High society came out there.*

Chapter 30
Sunday, June 9, 1929

As his debts mounted, George Moore took to running numbers. Mostly at night. Always on his own. He'd lie in bed next to his fitfully dozing wife, adding up the incoming, subtracting the outgoing, spending the same month's take from the barbershop—roughly $136 plus tips—80 different ways, while the luminous hands of the clock stared at him accusingly. If it weren't for the bootleggers who liked to tip big, he'd be out of business. Sadly, Arthur had left for a better location; both agreed it wasn't worth his while.

On Sunday (June 9), he was doing it again: $136 a month, running his own shop. Pathetic. And that's before business expenses, before he sliced $40 off the top for overhead—rent, heat, laundry—leaving him with $96. Couldn't do anything about that. And say goodbye to cutting hair in the evening. Come July, he'd have to start closing at 6:30 on weekdays, 9 p.m. on Saturdays, no matter what. The union was going to demand it, claiming that barbers in the area worked longer hours than other barbers. So what? Saving them from overwork wasn't the answer. Keeping them out of debtor's prison made a helluva lot more sense.

As for home expenses, he had to subtract $28.50 for deferred payments right off the bat: the refrigerator ($10), vacuum cleaner ($4), piano ($9), car, radio. Couldn't do anything about those either. Installment plans, he thought. Whose bright idea was that? Those easy little payments added up. Leaving him with what? $67.50.

And he still owed Delray Hospital. Seemed like he'd been chipping away at that $33 bill forever. And Durocher and the washerwoman and Lottie Montie and the monthly tab at Seavitt's. Another ten spot, easy. $57.50. And the 25 cents for life insurance. $57.25.

And what about the $1.80 a month for that three-piece wool worsted in layaway. What was he thinking? That leaves . . . what? $55.45. And groceries. Jesus, Mary and Joseph. Did it really take that much to feed nine? If he could only get it down to say $25 a month. Cut back on butter and meat. Buy in bulk. Stretch the rice. That would leave $30.45. No, they had to keep it under $20. That would make it, what? . . . $35.45. But how many casseroles can one family eat?

And coal. Was Freda right? Was the bin nearly empty? If so, we're down to $30.45. And ice. $27.45. And shoes. Always shoes. Shay was long overdue and cardboard went just so far. Certainly he could put a moratorium on new clothes. Then again, it soon would be time for the annual back-to-school trek to Hudson's.

What else could go?

Movies? Might as well stop kidding himself; the Sunday matinee was a weekly bill. Didn't he just plunk down $1.40 to take the kids to see Keaton in *Steamboat Bill*? But give up the flicks, the thing that made Sunday special? He'd rather eat casseroles. So where was he? Matinees: $5.60 a month . . . $21.85. And the tires on the Ford were bald, the chairs in the parlor threadbare. Even the throws could use throws. And every fly in the neighborhood knew the screens were a joke. The roof? He gazed upward, knowing just where the water stain was.

They hadn't seen a windfall since Agnes sold her hair after she caught it in the fan. How long ago was that? Five, six years?

"She sold it to Glovers after they cut it," said Rowe. "They made wigs and stuff on Fort Street in Detroit by the Hollywood Theatre. Maybe $35."

Oh, what he'd give for 35 smackaroos. He gazed down at the slumbering Agnes, her cheeks flushed, her hair short and fanned on the pillow. Salt and pepper now. Premature, really. No longer marcelled, no longer anything, just brushed by Freda daily.

If they could only talk this out, share the burden. Agnes was always good at saving money. Knew the tricks. As it was, their conversations were rote. How ya feelin', Ag? he'd say. Ok, she'd say. Good, he'd say, Flora and Sadie send their best. He'd done his job well, kept all his little crises to himself. Agnes was no longer worried about money, no longer worried about much of anything as far as he could tell. Lying there, sound asleep. He almost envied her.

If only he could mortgage the house to tide them over. But no, it was Agnes's house, Agnes's inheritance. She'd have to sign. How would he explain the need without worrying her?

Where was he? $21.85. Less than a dollar a day left to keep home and hearth. Dentist, glasses, Band-Aids. If it weren't for Murph's help from his job, if it weren't for Freda sharing her wages, they'd already be in the poorhouse. What next? The Community Chest? Agnes in a welfare ward? His family on the dole?

It was hard not to be bitter. There was so much money in Ecorse changing hands. The good guys were hurting, the bad guys were cleaning up. Isn't that always the way? He was in the wrong racket; so were the hapless dry agents who made $38 a week. The stoolies were making out, the shysters were living large. And $30, $40, $50 was the going rate to look the other way. And wasn't it just last year, when Lefty Clark was kidnapped by racketeers, that he coughed up $40,000 for his ransom? That was the rumor, that's what the papers said. 40,000 berries. How the hell?

It was 1:28 when he looked at the clock, 2:47 when he looked at the clock, 3:22 when he looked at the clock, 5:05 when he looked at the clock, 6:10 when he gave up, got up, put on coffee, and sat down heavily at the kitchen table with a pencil and a pad of paper.

———————

But it was Bugs Moran, of all people, who briefly bailed George out. Bugs Moran who paid for Shay's shoes. Because four days later (Wednesday, June 12), as George rounded Labadie on his way to work, he was astonished to see a crowd outside his shop. There were even more customers on Front Street, gathered in groups, while the ever-present ex-constable, Alex Bourassa, was crammed awkwardly among a party of four on the long bench. And for the rest of the day, for the rest of the week, those who took time off, those who were laid off, those on the nightshift and those who labored in the Canadian export trade, would line the shop, spill into the unused courtroom and fill the apron seat of the display window, obstructing the grandeur of the antediluvian ferns. But George's short reprieve had nothing to do with a financial uptick and everything to do with an urgent need to convene.

Bugs Moran was sore. A Sunday paper in northern New York, the *Syracuse Herald*, claimed that he was blaming Ecorse for the St. Valentine's Day Massacre and openly vowing revenge. Say what you will, it didn't get any better than that. Being linked to Chicago in more ways than US 112 was intoxicating; being lumped with the Massacre was heady stuff.

"The underworld's sayin' them killin's weren't Machine Gun McGurn," Root Schonscheck, an ex-saloonkeeper said, as George removed the hot towel from his face. Root swiveled his head toward the divan. "Read it, Ernie."

Ernie rose ceremoniously from his sunken seat on the backless sofa, waved the *Syracuse* newspaper in the air as evidence, and held forth: "'Despite what the police say, the underworld says seven members of Moran's gang were slain by beer runners from Ecorse.'"[1]

George waited for the cheers and whistles to die down before inquiring, "Tell me again, who made that claim?"

Ernie stared at George, perplexed, then returned to the paper and found his place, then returned to George. "The underworld."

"Nonsense," scoffed George. "Since when is Ecorse dealing with the likes of Bugs Moran?"

"Yeah," said Dom Dalton from the doorway, the front door being propped open with a brick to let in the summer air. "It'd be all over town."

———————

[1] "Lakes Echo St. Valentine Day Murders," Syracuse Herald, Sunday, June 9, 1929.

"They're sayin' Moran warned guys in Ecorse to stay outta Chicago," said Root.

"Somebody better warn Louella Davies," joked Ollie. "Wasn't she plannin' a trip to Chicago to visit her sister over the 4th?"

"Wait a minute, wait a minute!" yelled Ernie. "The Chicago beer market. Bugs told 'em to keep outta the Chicago beer market."

"Or what?" asked Dom.

"Or sell it through him."

"Sell it through Moran?"

"This is what they're sayin'," prefaced Ernie. "They're sayin' that after Moran demanded Ecorse sell through him, Ecorse struck back."

"Hogwash," barked Dom. "Does he think someone from here would machine gun seven of his guys for that? No wonder they call him Bugs."

"That's what they're sayin'."

"Makes no sense." said George, dipping his shaving brush into the cup.

"You're right," said Cletus Drouillard from the back corner, who, like Root, was a former saloonkeeper and in the know. "The way I heard it, when Moran demanded they sell through him, Ecorse guys told him to take a hike."

"Are you serious?" said George, dropping his brush back into the cup, doing his best to hide his shock. He had no idea things had gotten this out of hand. Guys in the shop were always mouthing off, talking big. He knew about the dangers; he knew about the Purple Gang; he knew Capone had been seen at the docks. He also knew they were getting hooch to the Chicago market, but he thought it was organizers, small-timers on the other end. Certainly not killers. But bad dealings with Chicago mobsters? Bad blood with Bugs Moran? Maybe Charlie Bauer's killing was not such an aberration.

"It's right here, George," said Ernie, smacking the newspaper. "Right here in black and white." He found his place, then read: "'Ecorse answered by dispatching an automobile loaded with machine gunners. An appointment, supposedly to discuss peace terms, was made for Valentine's Day. The Ecorse runners talked peace with machine guns. When their 'talk' was over, seven of 'Bugs' men were slain.'"[2]

"Could be true," said Ollie, getting up, walking toward George's counter. "We got some real lowlifes come into the garage." He set a nickel on the cash register and took the last Hershey bar. "You know. Go upstairs."

"Yeah, but they're not ours, right?" said George.

"The lowlifes?"

"Yeah."

"No, mostly from out of town."

"Where you been, George?" said Ernie.

"That's what happens when you stop hoisting with your friends," said

---

[2] Ibid. Syracuse Herald , June 9, 1929

Frank.

"What about Soxy?" offered Root, after first ascertaining with a constricted swivel of the head that the room was devoid of Goodells and offshoots.

"Nah, them killers weren't hotheads," said Duffy Renaud. "Them killers were methodical."

"I still don't buy it," said George, bending Root's nose, scraping his cheek, wiping the residue on a towel. "What about you, Joe? You ever deal with the Chicago mob?"

"All I know is what I read in the papers," said Joe Riopelle.

"Let me rephrase the question," said George. "Have you heard about any guys from Ecorse dealing with the mob?"

"Sure."

"Seriously?" asked George, startled.

"All the time," said Clayt Riopelle, who had walked in just a minute before and was now stepping around shoes to reach a corner of the sofa. "Couple guys come from Chicago just a few months ago. Right, Pop?"

"Yeah."

"At least, that's what we heard," laughed Clayt.

Clayt never ceased to amaze George. He was no longer that winsome six-year-old, playing on the swings with Murph. Though still shorter than Murph, Clayt was all grown up and sure of his craft. Both crafts. He was a crackerjack mechanic, now working for Ollie, and a prosperous moonlighter, just as well-heeled as the other importers in the barbershop, flashing a snazzy pair of ven-tilated two-tone Oxfords. But it was one thing to hear bootlegging tales from Clarence DeWallot, another to hear them from a fresh-faced kid who was often seen with Murph. So George kept on wielding his razor, with his head low and his manner light, while lending an ear.

"They wanted to buy everything," drawled Clayt, leaning forward with a tale to tell. "As fast as Ecorse guys could bring it across, they wanted to take everything. Pay cash for it. That way, the guys wouldn't have to dribble it out to customers, like 20, 30 cases at a time. Right, Pop?"

"You're tellin' it."

"When was this?" asked Ernie.

"A few months ago," said Joe.

"So they'd come with these brand new trucks," said Clayt. "Boy, they were nice. And they'd take the whole load. Pretty soon, they had everybody lined up, all along the waterfront. They come over to our boathouse one day . . . to ah . . . see a friend of mine, and they wanted to take his."

"Clayt knows a guy who knew a guy," explained Dom.

"Yeah. So my friend . . . he thought . . . What the hell do I want to sell to them for? I have so many customers now I can't handle 'em all. And I get 25 cents a case more for beer. So I . . . he . . . my friend . . . told them no. He was the only one that told them no. They never forced him or nothin'."

To a select group, including George's clientele, Clayt's livelihood was now an open secret; most everyone in the room knew that Clayt was talking about Clayt. But as far as George could figure, Clayt kept his nose clean—no strong-arm stuff, no guns, no funny business—and didn't take unnecessary chances. It would be just like Clayt to take a pass on Chicago. Just like Clayt to be unimpressed with hoodlums. He worked on his own, had his own crew, and was proud he'd made it up the ladder early, risen through the ranks.

"Well, every time them Chicago guys come," continued Clayt, "they'd say to some idiot they were buying from, 'Gee, I'm a little short this time. How's about I give ya a few thousand cash and a check for the rest.' Started out with a check for a $1,000, then it's 2, then it's 3, $4,000. And before you know it, the whole thing's all checks."

"Drawn on the National Bank of Cicero?" asked Ollie.

"Then all of a sudden them guys from Chicago disappeared," said Clayt. "There was no more business. All them Ecorse guys got caught holding bum checks."

"Our guys got stiffed?" asked Ernie.

"Yeah."

"So what happened?"

"So they were mad."

"Went after Bugs on a cold holiday in February, did they?" asked George.

"Not exactly," said Clayt.

"What exactly?"

"They drew straws. Sent three guys to Chicago to Al Capone to straighten this thing out, to get their money. They wanted Capone to entertain them."

"Who the hell'd they send?" hollered Ollie, nearly choking on his Hershey bar. "Are they still with us?"

The room erupted in laughter.

"Let's just say one of 'em runs a soda parlor," said Clayt grinning, "one of 'em passes the basket under your noses at Sunday mass, and one of 'em peddles life insurance."

"He'd need to," said Dom.

"What the hell happened?" asked Ernie.

"Capone entertained them," said Clayt. "Then sent them home."

"They get their money?" asked Ernie.

"From what I was told," said Clayt, "with all the partying, you know, with Capone being so nice, they kinda let the matter drop. They didn't feel it was the right time to bring it up."

"They're lucky they came back with their shoes," said Frank.

George turned serious. "Is all this on the level?"

"As God is my witness," said Clayt.

"Does Lefty Clark have any doings with Chicago?" asked George.

Clayt grew uncomfortable. Time to be careful; this was about allaying Old

Man Moore's fears about Murph. "Nah. Lefty's about gambling, Lefty's on his own. Besides, Ecorse is more important than Chicago."

"Oh, please," said Dom.

"You don't believe me? Then, get this," said Clayt, pausing for dramatic effect. "They just held a huge meeting of the underworld early this morning. Right here in Ecorse. Guys from all over. All the big cheeses."

"I love it," roared Root. "Don'tcha jist love it?"

"Laugh all you want, but that's what I heard," said Clayt. "Some of the biggest guys around."

"Did you go?" asked Dom.

"I wasn't invited," said Clayt.

"Where'd they meet?"

"Can't say," replied Clayt. "Though I've got my suspicions."

"Probably the church basement," cracked Ollie.

"Scoff away, fellas. Scoff away," said Clayt. "But what I'm sayin's the straight stuff."

"Aw, c'mon," said Frank Lafferty, not buying any of it. "St. Valentine's Day Massacre, gangland meetings, and Al Capone's my father. Sit around them bars long enough, you hear all kinda junk. Everybody talkin' big."

"What do you think, Nick," asked George. "Was Ecorse involved in the massacre?"

They all turned toward Dapper Nick Nebiolo, sitting off to himself in the courtroom, who had been quiet throughout. He ran his thumb and forefinger down the crease in his pants. You could hear a pin drop. "Nah. None of the locals," he said. "But I wouldn't put it past the Purples. And if any of ya quote me on that, I'll do more than call ya a liar."

Nick was right. That Syracuse newspaper might not have been far wrong. At the time, as well as in later years, many felt there was an Ecorse link by way of the Purple Gang. And since some of the top thugs in the Purple Gang had bullied their way into Ecorse and Bugs had dealt with them there rather than Detroit, he blamed Ecorse.

According to some accounts, about ten days before the Massacre, three Purples—Eddie Fletcher and brothers Harry and Phil Keywell—had taken rooms in two rooming houses in Chicago across the street from the S.M.C. Cartage Co. garage, distribution center for the Moran gang. They were serving as spotters. On St. Valentine's Day, February 14, 1929, when Bugs Moran was to enter the building, their job was to signal their confreres, the Capone-backed killers. Around 10:15 a.m., they did just that. Fifteen minutes later, five men—two dressed as cops, two in overcoats, one driver—pulled up in front of the garage in a phony police car. The "cops" and the "overcoats" entered, "arrested" seven of Bugs Moran's Northside Gang, had them line up and face the garage wall, then pulled out a pair of Thompson submachine guns and employed them with efficiency. Then the two "cops" marched the two guys in overcoats out of the building at gunpoint, shoved them in the police car and took off, gong clanging. A German Shepherd named Highball, who witnessed the killings while tied to a truck gate, howled so loudly people came running.

Although Al Capone was in Florida on the day of the massacre, he was obviously the mastermind. But the Purples had bungled their assignment. By mistake, they had fingered a member of the gang who was a Bugs lookalike. Moran, who had overslept, arrived a few minutes late of his appointed time, saw the police car out front and kept on walking.

Ecorse had little to fear from Moran. He never got up off the mat after the massacre. He left the liquor business to rob banks, and would die in prison of lung cancer on February 25, 1957, receiving the full Roman Catholic sendoff with Father O'Connor, who performed the last rites, noting, "I am sure that God in His mercy was very kind to him in judgment."

—————

That June, article after article mentioning Ecorse spilled forth from newspapers around the nation. The good folks of the town were inundated with clippings sent by long-forgotten relatives. At the Ecorse Post Office in the back of Seavitt's, Leona Genaw could barely keep up with the sorting.

George remained busy, taking in at least $15 a day. People he hadn't seen in months came in for a cut. But George was well aware this windfall would not last. He'd been a barber for 17 years, since 1912. Maybe it was time to close up shop, take a factory job, throw in the steam towel, so to speak. Still, they weren't hiring at Ford or the mill. No one was hiring. Modern Collet just opened over on Salliotte. Maybe there was work to be had there. Though he had no idea what a collet was, much less a modern one. Maybe part-time, maybe nights.

He'd already put out a feeler to Joe Riopelle during a late-afternoon cut.

"Plenty of work to be had," said Joe. "If you're not fussy."

"Fussy?"

"Yeah."

"Oh, fussy," said George, inference dawning. "Nah. I meant legit."

"Legit? Them jobs are hard to find, George. But you hate Prohibition laws. Why not take advantage of 'em? What do you care?"

"That's okay, Joe. Just thought you might know of something."

He also asked Nick Strassner during a trim.

"Too bad you gave up your Justice of the Peace job to run for village president, George. Constables are canoodling with justices in a lotta towns around here, arresting drunks so they can fine 'em and split the fees. Whole system stinks to high heaven, but you'd be a rich man by now, George. Why Nibbs alone. . ."

"Yeah, well, I'm not so sure I'd want to use Nibbs to pay for my kids' shoes," said George, reaching for the clippers. "I don't know how those guys sleep nights." Then he laughed. "Probably better than me."

"But you could go after bootleggers," said Nick. "They're loaded. You'd just be another guy skimming off the top."

"What an awful time to be living," replied George. "All this stuff could tempt Mother Cabrini."

Herb Ormsby came in that day when things had quieted down. George no sooner had Herb in the chair, than he was giving the same gentle lead-in, the same casual inquiry.

"Know of anything, Herb?" he asked, swinging a cloth in the air.

"Not really, George. Pretty bleak out there. You thinking of giving up the shop?"

"No, something extra. Nights, weekends, you know. The way things are going with Agnes, it's kinda tight."

"Well, let me think," said Herb, closing his eyes, while George went to work with shears and comb, aware that his good friend Herb, unlike some, was giving it serious thought. But, after a time, as he continued to snip, George wasn't sure whether Herb was seriously thinking or quietly napping.

He was almost finished, when Herb sat up slightly. "Boy, it's tough. I can't think of a damn thing. At least, nothing you'd want."

"So there's something?"

"Not really. Like I says, George, nothing you'd want."

"C'mon, Herb. Give."

"I don't wanna insult you, George."

"Insult away. Keeps me humble."

"Look. The only reason it's even on my mind is 'cuz it just came across my desk."

"What did?"

"An opening for truant officer at Ecorse High."

"Oh," sighed George, as the air went out of the tire.

"See what I'm sayin'."

"I need part time."

"It *is* part time," said Herb. "A truant officer's only required to be at the school when there's a case report; then he goes to the homes, deals with the kid, the parents."

"Would that have to be during the day? Those home visits? Could they be on weekends? Nights?"

"I don't see why not."

"How much does it pay?"

"Gingersnaps."

"No. Really."

"Two bucks a day."

"That's good, isn't it?"

"But that's only for days served. For days dealing with a case."

"You mean, two bucks a truant."

"Well, maybe a little more. Sometimes it takes a while to resolve a case." Herb turned round to look at him. "My God, George, we're talking truant officer here."

"How the mighty have fallen," laughed George. "Face it, Herb. Factoring for inflation, pride won't get you a Walnetto at Annie Pie's. When would I start?"

"I don't know. July. August. I can't believe you're interested. I told Miss Munn you'd never take it."

"Miss Munn?"

"Yes, she recommended you for the job. Your desk would be in her office."

Chapter 31

October 1929

Freda ran the house while Rowe was in school; Rowe took over while Freda worked at Pilon's late afternoons and weekends. Cleaning became more like work. Joyless chores were divvied up. Joyce helped with the ironing and was more than willing to do the wash, but she was not allowed near her mother's nightgowns or sweat-soaked sheets. A woman was hired to come in to do the washing, but the girls had to come home after school to do the ironing. A visiting nurse came once a day to give Agnes a "bed bath," while Lottie Montie arrived once a week to give her an enema of olive oil because she had obstructions all the time. The older girls put cloth under her heels and elbows to avoid bed sores and scrubbed the sickroom weekly with a 5% solution of carbolic acid.

Dia and Shay were warned to stay out of her room because Agnes needed rest. And as the days turned into months, they grew accustomed to the distance.

> *"We never went in the bedroom," said Dia, "even though it was on the main floor, even though the door was usually kept open. Though her bed was not directly opposite the door, more off to the side, you could briefly see her as you walked by. Seems strange now."*

Initially, Agnes tried to read. Knowing her fondness for *Cosmopolitan, True Story* and *Modern Screen*, visitors inundated her with magazines. (Rowena and Alfreda owed their names to women in *Modern Romances*.) But the periodicals soon piled up, unread, on the closet floor. Ella came often, of course. So did Agnes's sister Ovie. And Mrs. Jaeger, Alice Pilon, Mabel Ouellette, Mrs. Gregory, and Ruth LeBlanc. But a visit invariably caused Agnes's temperature to rise, as did the slightest exertion. There were days when the fever was down and the disease was at rest, and days when the fever, which often spiked in the afternoon and at night, was active. On those days, with her cheeks flushed and her eyes glistening, she was given alcohol baths. Four times a day Freda or Rowe shook down the thermometer, slipped it under Agnes's tongue, then tried to catch the flicker of silver under the overhead light.

One Sunday morning, October 6, 1929, as light edged the window shade, Agnes had been awake for all of five minutes when she once more found herself going alternate rounds with her chronic cramping and chronic remorse. She regretted so many things: her cynicism in the last few years, her short fuse, her impatience with George, her lack of firmness with Murph, her obsession with Miss Munn.

Bedbound for over a year, Agnes fought and refought long-lost battles by the hour. Slights given, slights received. Injustices, which lurked in the corners, were ready to waylay an idle mind.

"I keep having these great epiphanies," Agnes told Ella. "These great insights as to what I did and why I did it and where things went wrong. Then I forget what it was I epiphanied and have the same epiphany a week later. I just go round and round."

"Why can't you dwell on the good memories?" urged Ella.

"They only come for a visit. The bad ones move in and set up house."

That particular Sunday, as Agnes was replaying the famous Munn imbroglio from Bob-Lo Island, she thought she heard someone crying upstairs. It would not be the first time she lay there powerless while one of her children wept. Six girls in one house can induce daily squalls, but this fitful wail had all the intensity of a child in distress. By the time Agnes managed to waylay Rowe, however, the crying had stopped.

"Is someone sick?" asked Agnes.

"Everyone's fine," said Rowe, halting in the doorway.

"But someone was crying."

"Oh, that was just Marce. Dia was teasing her. Want anything to drink?"

"A glass of Vernor's would be nice."

That afternoon, Marce could be heard crying again. But when Agnes asked what was wrong, she was assured all was well, that Dia had simply struck anew.

Then, around four, soon after Freda reached in and gently closed Agnes's bedroom door, the front bell rang, followed by a flurry of hushed voices, Dr. Durocher's among them. Agnes waited for him, for anyone, to enter, but no one did. Softly she called out, but no one answered.

About thirty minutes later she heard a tap, tap, tapping. Soon after, Freda and Rowe glided in matter of factly and took up their usual positions on opposite sides of her bed—Freda to take Agnes's temperature, Rowe to retrieve her untouched tray.

"What did he want?" mumbled Agnes, weakly brushing the thermometer away.

"Who?" asked Rowe.

"Dr. Durocher."

"Oh, he just dropped some medicine off for you," said Rowe, gripping the tray tightly with both hands.

"Why didn't he come in?" asked Agnes.

"Come in?"

"Yes. Come in."

"Ah. . . He said he was in a hurry. He had another call."

"I see. Then tell me. . ." Agnes winced and grabbed her stomach. "What was that tapping?"

"Tapping?"

"Yes, Little Sir Echo," she hissed irritably. "Tapping. . . Quarantine sign go up, did it?"

Freda laughed. "You don't miss a trick, do ya, Mumma?"

"Not if I can help it." whispered Agnes. "Especially when Durocher's the health officer." She rolled on her side in an effort to blunt the dagger-like pain, then said, "Look, I know you two don't want me to worry, but this just makes me worry. Is Marce ill?"

"Well, last night she said she had a headache," said Freda. "So I gave her an aspirin. But today she seemed kinda hot."

"How hot?"

"101. Maybe just over," said Freda. "And her cheeks looked kinda puffy, so I got her to nibble on a pickle."

"Did it make her jaw hurt?"

"Yeah."

"Mumps?"

"Just a slight case," said Freda. "That's what Dr. Durocher said."

"Mild," corrected Rowe. "He said, 'mild.'"

"We put a cot for her in our room," said Freda. "'Cuz me, Rowe and Joycie's immune."

"Where's Murph?"

"Over at Clayt's. We called and told him to stay away."

"Is she in pain?" asked Agnes.

"A little," admitted Freda.

"Sore throat?"

"A little."

"How are her glands? Are they swollen?"

Rowe laughed. "She looks like Andy Gump."

"She's just sleeping a lot," said Freda. "Don't worry. We're takin' good care of her."

"I'd better get dinner started," said Rowe, escaping from the room, led by the tray.

Freda handed her mother a Kleenex and waited for the spasm to stop. This was something new, this cough, this spitting up of blood. Lottie Montie had taken to pinning paper bags to the side of her bed.

"Freda," said Agnes, hoarsely. "Where's your father? Is he out tying one on?"

"No, Mumma," said Freda, sitting down on the edge of the bed. "Honest.

He ain't done that since you got sick."

"Then where is he?"

"Promise you won't get upset."

"Promise," said Agnes, dismissively.

Freda hesitated, aware that Agnes's perfunctory pledge guaranteed her absolutely nothing.

"Well?" pressed Agnes.

"Out. Visiting parents."

"Whose parents?"

"A kid that skipped school."

"But why?"

"He's the new truant officer."

"You mean, he's closed the shop?"

"No, he's still got the shop. He does it on the side."

"But why didn't he tell me?"

"He didn't wanna upset you."

"Why would I be upset?"

"Well. . . You know. . ." Freda was walking a thin rail. "He didn't want you worryin' about money."

"That doesn't make sense. If I'd known he had a second job, I'd worry less about money."

"Well. . . He just thought. . ."

"How long's he been doing this?"

"Over a month."

"Poor guy." Agnes shielded her eyes with her forearm, signaling the need for rest. "Keep me up to date on Marce, okay? Let me know how she is."

That night, while George readied for bed, Agnes attempted to make amends. She confessed that she knew about his moonlighting, thanked him for taking firm control, and wondered why he thought it would upset her. George, who'd been warned that Agnes was in the know, was partially relieved; he hated sneaking around. But Freda had also hinted, without actually saying so, that Agnes was still in the dark about Miss Munn.

"What's it like?" asked Agnes, looking up at him from her pillow, worn out from the emotions of the day.

"Truant officer?"

"Yes."

"Busy," he said, taking off his tie, hanging it on a hook. "September seems to be national hooky month. More kids skip school in the fall." Question posed, answer given, George untucked his shirt.

"Freda said you were out seeing parents today."

"Yes."

"Who?"

"Sutherlands on 6th."

"You know them?"

"I do now."

Question posed, answer given, George unlinked his cuffs.

For Mr. and Mrs. Moore free-flowing exchanges had ceased long ago. So many topics were now off-limits, so many mine fields made each of them wary. Silence was infinitely safer. So George, who had grown unaccustomed to sharing their day, unlike the early years when they'd rehash every sneeze, silently emptied his pockets onto the dresser. But he finally realized that she was waiting for more, making an exhausted effort to connect. The least he could do was meet her halfway.

"Their thirteen-year-old daughter set out for St. Francis last Friday morning. Never made it," he said, pulling his belt through its loops. "Herb's cops spent hours looking for her. Nothing all day Friday, nothing all day Saturday. Her parents were frantic."

"Thirteen?"

"Thirteen."

"But you found her, right?"

"Not 'til today."

"Where?"

"Juvenile Detention Home in Detroit." He unbuttoned his shirt and laughed. "Instead of going to school, she hopped a trolley to Detroit. Spent a lovely day sightseeing. A patrolman found her late Friday night, wandering the streets."

"Of Detroit?"

"Yeah."

"Good lord. But why didn't he bring her home?"

"He didn't know who she was!" He sat down on his side of the bed and unlaced his shoes. "I called the Detention Home Saturday. Asked if they had a Virginia Sutherland. Nope. I called again, late last night. Asked if they had a Virginia Sutherland. Nope. Then I described her. 'Oh!' they said. 'You mean Peggy O'Neil!' She gave 'em a phony name!" he snorted, as he slid off his shoes. "All of thirteen and she gave 'em a phony name! I tell ya, Agnes. Any of ours try that, they won't sit for a week."

"Thirteen."

"That's where I was today when Durocher came," he said, removing his shirt. "Driving to Detroit, fetching sweet little Peggy O'Neil. If I'd known Marce was sick, I'd have asked Herb to do it. Sorry you had to deal with it, Ag."

He took off his pants and hung them up, then walked into the closet and partially shut the door, soon to reappear in his pajamas.

"I don't know how you can do this and still barber full time," said Agnes, forearm back over her eyes. "You must be tired."

"I don't mind the extra hours," he said, stashing his underwear in the hamper, reaching for the alarm clock. "I just hate the paperwork. Lotta forms, lotta filing. Everything typed in triplicate."

"Do you have an office?"

"I share one."

"Where?"

"At Ecorse High." He tensed, then shook his head and managed a self-conscious chuckle. "You know, Agnes. You're gonna laugh when you hear this."

"What?"

"Well, maybe not laugh."

"What?"

He paused, studying her gaunt face, until she uncovered her eyes, questioningly.

"What?"

He looked away.

"Oh, you know, silly stuff," he said, winding the clock. Then he laughed. "I ran into this kid over on High Street. Hadn't seen him around. So I got kinda pissy—I wasn't in the greatest mood—and asked him why he wasn't in school. He said he'd graduated from high school, had a year of college and was the father of two."

George had missed his chance. He knew it immediately. He was standing there, fumbling with the clock, talking nonsense, while the train pulled out of the station. Though his relationship with Miss Munn was innocent, cordial, above board, he'd just made it sneaky, turned a molehill into a mountain, all in a few dismal seconds, making it nearly impossible to tell Agnes from here on in without inflaming her worst suspicions. To go at it again over Miss Munn . . . he didn't have the heart. But one thing was certain. He'd just missed his chance.

Agnes had giggled at the father of two, as hearty a giggle as she was now capable of, though he feared it would end in a cough. Instead, she grew serious. "I've been tough on you, George," she was saying.

"There were times I deserved it."

"And times you didn't."

"Well, if I felt as punk as you, Ag, I'd. . ."

"No. Hear me out," she said, gazing at the ceiling, reflective. "Durocher says it's the illness, but that's not good enough. For some reason. I don't know why. I find it hard to give you a break."

"Well, Ag . . ."

"For some reason. For some dumb reason. Let's face it, George. I haven't been on your side for a long, long time."

George, who could be done in by kindness, lay down beside her.

Both stared upward, silent for a time.

"I've missed you, Ag," he said.

For a moment, she said nothing, then sighed. "It's been a long haul. I still don't understand why you didn't tell me. "

"About what?"

"The truant officer's job."

The following Friday, roused by the smell of coffee, Agnes woke in the dead of night and found herself alone in bed. Once again, her door was shut. Once again, there were muffled voices in the house. But this time, when she called for George, he cracked open the door. A wedge of light shot across the hardwood floor.

"It's Marce, isn't it?" she said.

"Her temperature's up a little, that's all. The kids had me call Durocher just to be on the safe side. He's here now."

"How high?"

"101."

"Please, George. I'm still her mother."

"103. But Freda brought it down with lukewarm sponge baths. She's drifting off now."

"Why'd it go up?"

"Durocher says it's like that with kids. Bounces all over. She's fine, Agnes. Just fine."

But Marce wasn't fine. Her headache was worse and her temperature had reached 106°. Marce, who would be five the following month, had meningitis, and for the past three days Durocher had been coming to the house; Joyce had been watching for him, then letting him in the back door and sneaking him up the stairs.

The doctor was visibly worried. The whole house was tense and in isolation, including George. A sign on the barbershop door directed clients to Roy Livernois. Another blow to the budget. Shots were administered all around, even to Agnes under the guise of a new mumps vaccine. Hand washing was stressed, utensils boiled, and Father Morin was on alert.

The next day Marce began asking for her mother, and Agnes, bunglingly tipped off about Marce's perilous state, was pleading to see her. George had enough Irish in him to deem it a bad omen. Sympathetic to his wife's and daughter's needs, he broached the subject as he walked the doctor to his car.

Durocher was adamant. "You hold that pathetically sick child in front of Agnes and before you know it . . ."

"She won't be in front of her, Ed, just opposite the doorway, 15 feet away."

". . . and before you know it, Agnes'll be demanding to hold her. And you won't have the heart to say no, George. You won't. I know you. " He shoved his black bag through the car's open window and onto the passenger seat. "Agnes can't be allowed to sit up."

"She won't sit up."

"Look," said Ed, "you've kept Marce away from Agnes for an entire year. And may I remind you what a nightmare that was. Marce wouldn't stop crying. Agnes was a mess. You told me so yourself. In the past few months, Marce has settled down, gotten used to it. Whatever her child's mind is telling her, it's working. And now you want to kick it all up again?"

"But what if something happened? You said yourself this is serious. Agnes would never forgive me."

Durocher paused. "I know it's cruel. I know it's brutal. But you have no idea how dangerous this is. Marce needs to be kept quiet and shielded from infection. As for Agnes, she hasn't even sat up for over a year. And you, all by your lonesome, will have everybody at risk and everybody hysterical, including yourself." Durocher opened the car door and lowered his voice. "And to be perfectly blunt, George. Agnes is far more contagious now than she was a year ago."

"When were you going to tell me that, Ed?"

———————

The next day George slouched listlessly in his rocking chair, hardly touching the fried egg sandwich on the library table, made by Joyce, put there by Shay. Upstairs Marce was still asking for Agnes, while downstairs, behind the shuttered door, Agnes was still begging to see Marce.

He'd been slumped there for more than hour when, around 2 o'clock, he bolted upright and said firmly, "Stella Dallas."

"Huh?" said Joyce, exiting the sickroom, carrying a tray.

"Is your mother awake?"

"Kinda."

He rose, walked tentatively to the bedroom door, crossed his fingers for the benefit of a baffled Joyce, then turned the knob and entered. "Agnes," he said, lowering himself heavily on his side of the bed, talking to the back of her head. "Durocher's adamant that I keep Marce away from you."

Agnes did not bother to move. "So you said. Fifteen feet," she muttered softly, so softly he could hardly hear her. "That's all I was asking."

"Just hear me out." He came around to the other side of the bed, squatted on his haunches and peered into her face. "If I could figure a way to get her within, say, a foot or two. Could you bear it?"

"Within a foot or two? How?"

"I could bring Marce to your window outside. With the window closed."

"Oh God, George, could we?"

"Well, we're not home free. There could be consequences. For one, it'd take a toll on you."

"I'll be fine."

"You couldn't reach out to her. She's a pretty sick girl, but she's been calling for you. I don't want to decide this alone. So, whaddya think?" He tried not to move while he waited for her answer.

Finally, she whispered, "Couldn't we try? Couldn't we at least try?"

"Them's my sentiments exactly." He rose, shook off the creaks and looked down on her. "But Agnes, I beg you. You'd have to stay calm. You'd have to help keep Marce calm."

"I'll try."

"That's it? That's the best you can offer?"

"That's it," she said, her eyes now closed. "I'll try."

Though George would have preferred to send the younger children over to the Ouellette's, Marce's quarantine killed that idea. So, after instructing Joyce to keep Shay and Dia entertained upstairs, he gathered the two older girls and began to reconfigure the sickroom. Quietly they lashed back the curtains, removed the oval rug, carried the bedside table into the parlor, then slid the bed sideways with Agnes in it, leaving her face, as it rested on the pillow, within inches of the only window.

Agnes, whose hollowed eyes sparkled with excitement, asked Freda to help her wash up, then asked if she could don a fresh nightgown. "I don't want her to see me this way, George." Then she wanted to put on lipstick, then she wanted a little rouge, then a comb.

"We'll start with the window open, okay?" said George. "I'll hold Marce at a distance so you can talk to her. Then we'll close the window and I'll bring her nearer. Okay, Agnes?"

"Okay," she said remotely.

"What did I just say?"

She looked at him blankly.

"Agnes, you need to listen to me."

"I'm just trying to look nice, George, for Marce's sake."

"Fine. But. You need to calm down for Marce's sake. If not your own." She stared at him and pinched her cheeks. "Hear me?"

"Hard not to."

"Agnes, you promised. Now, be forewarned. Marce has lost a little weight."

"How much weight?" she asked.

"Enough to notice. You ready?"

"Ready," she said.

As Agnes lay there waiting, her left cheek against the pillow, her hand resting on the windowsill, she gazed out the open window for the first time since she'd been ordered to bed. It was a beautiful but chilly fall day, in the high 50's, with the leaves just beginning their change—some red, some gold. From her pillowed perch, about six feet above the ground, Agnes could see over the fence into Hotham's garden where the dark green leaves of the staked tomato plants were beginning to yellow, and the corn stalks were becoming brittle. A rogue gust gently ruffled Agnes's hair.

Soon Rowe came round the side of the house and set the kitchen stool off at an angle, away from Agnes but within her line of vision. Then Agnes caught sight of George rounding the corner, Marce looking thin and sick, cradled in his arms.

"O mon Dieu," moaned Agnes. She turned away from the window for a second, gratefully snatching the tissue extended by Freda, angrily swiping each eye.

Though the girls had dressed Marce warmly, she looked like an orphan. On her head was a close-fitting, green knit hat with a wide gold stripe, which framed her fevered and swollen cheeks, and from which her combed bangs protruded.

Over her dress she had on a green coat, buttoned to her throat, with lamb-like fur trim on the cuffs and collar. Agnes recognized the coat. The fur was frizzed, the sleeves too short, and the buttonholes stretched and frayed. Agnes would never have dressed one of her daughters in that four-owner coat without taking the Singer to it. Nobody'd had the time.

George rested on the edge of the stool and placed Marce on his thigh, his arm protectively round her. There she sat, propped like a puppet, while her hands and legs hung limp. Everything about her was listless: her down-turned mouth, her vacant eyes.

Agnes, eager to keep emotions in check, smiled down on her youngest from about eight feet away. "Hello, my pet."

Marce barely stirred. But on hearing her mother's voice, her eyes wandered upward and rested on the eager face above the wooden sill. Shallow puddles formed in Marce's lower lids.

Nervously, George jumped in. "Can you say 'hello' to your Mumma, Marcie? Can you do that?"

"Hello, Mumma."

"You look so pretty," said Agnes. "Is that your new coat?"

"Huh?"

"Is that your new coat?"

"Uh-huh."

"You look so pretty. How do you feel?"

"My head hurts."

"Oh, that's the worst."

"And my neck."

"Does it still hurt?"

"Huh?"

"Your neck. Does it still hurt?"

"Uh-huh."

"Oh, I'm so sorry," said Agnes.

Agnes faltered momentarily.

"Marcie," she said, a catch in her throat. "Do you know why I can't take care of you?"

"Uh-huh."

"Why?"

"'Cuz you can catch me 'n I can catch you."

"Ohhh, see how smart you are. Because I care about you so much; I don't want you to get what I've got. Because if I come near you, I'd make you sick."

"I *am* sick."

"Sicker. I could make you sicker."

"Uh-huh."

"I can't come near Shay, either, you know. I can't come near Dia."

Marce was fading. "Okay."

"I'd better take her upstairs soon," said George.

"Yes, I think so, too," said Agnes. "Marcie, my sweet."

"Huh?"

"Can I have a kiss?"

As Rowe hastily pushed down the sash, George stood up and walked to the window, where the top of his graying head came to the bottom ledge. Marce, who was propped on his forearm, could clearly see her mother, while Agnes stared down, desperate to memorize her face. Then as Marce leaned forward, Agnes leaned forward too, and both lightly pecked the glass.

"Say goodbye to your mumma," said George. "Can you say goodbye, Marcie?"

Marce gave a timid wave. Then George carried her away.

———————

Marce survived the illness. It seemed the crisis had been averted. In reality, the crisis was delayed.

Two weeks later, after the quarantine had been lifted, after Marce was out of the woods, Ella came to visit. Agnes was buoyant, on a tubercular high. She told Ella about seeing Marce, about George's moonlighting.

"And you're not upset?" asked Ella.

"Not at all," said Agnes. "Why should I be?"

"He thought you might be upset about Miss Munn."

"Miss Munn?"

"That they're sharing an office at Ecorse High," said Ella.

Agnes stared at Ella from her pillow. Her silence was brief. Then, "Is that little stray cat still hanging around? Have you been feeding it?"

George holding a very sick Marce in front of the Moore house

Chapter 32
Sunday, March 16, 1930

They were going to The Lake. Shay, Joyce and Dia. They were going to The Lake with the Ouellettes to help open their summer cottage on Lake Erie at Pointe aux Peaux, about 20 minutes away. It had been a bitter winter. And though temperatures in the first two weeks of March had generally been in the 40s, a spring-like 70° had been forecast for Sunday. So George and Ed talked it over the Friday before, and Mrs. Ouellette offered to pack a lunch. It was a bid to get the kids out from underfoot, to give Freda and Rowe a needed break while they cared for Agnes.

Weather-wise, there was an added bonus. Throughout the colder months the same Ouellette coat attended three different masses, but that Sunday, with no need for coats, all the children—Ouellettes and Moores—would attend the same 11:30 mass, and the two-car caravan could depart around 1:15. Excitement was running high. So high that Shay found it harder than ever to concentrate on Father Morin's sermon, especially when his jumping-off point was the Transfiguration and her jumping-off point was a bucket and a pile of sand.

By 1:30 the Ford tourer, its ragtop down, was packed in the Moore driveway, while the Ouellette Buick sat curbside on Labadie, loaded with provisions. Occasionally an Ouellette would lumber out with a box of afterthoughts and add it to the stack in the backseat, while nine-year-old Eddie lounged around the car, ready to claim his favored spot—back window, right side—at the first sign of departure. Dempsey was already in the backseat, guarding the picnic hamper.

On Monroe Street, a smattering of stay-behinds had started a softball game. First base, defined by chalk, was near the Moore curb, second was street center, third near Ostrander's. It was a patchy affair. Minus the Moores and Ouellettes, each team had just enough players for an abridged infield, a utility outfielder, and a backup shagger who was positioned at the far end of the block to keep the ball from rolling onto State Street.

Bad as that, the players had to endure curbside commentary from the Moore front stoop, where Joyce, Shay and Dia were sitting on separate steps, ladder-like, with time to kill. As usual, Dia had the best pipes. "Strike 24!" she'd yell. "Ree-leeee high and ree-leeee outside!" she'd howl. But Dia saved her best barbs for Helen Brown. Why? Because Dia knew it got to her. Each time Helen came to bat, which was often, thanks to the skimpy line-up, Dia greeted her with "Everybody move in!" When Helen caught the ball, "Wow! It's Heinie Manush!"

When Helen got a hit, "Line dribble!" When Helen threw to third, "Hey, Helen, the ball'd get there faster if you walked it over!"

Though Shay was contributing her share of taunts, mostly at passing cars that held up the game, she soon noticed that Helen was getting the worst of it. Now Shay was turning into a stubbornly even-handed eight-year-old, one who was often saddled with the burden of ensuring fair play. Injustice made her blood boil. Drawn to underdogs, she championed the misfits, the outcasts, the new prey in school. How she took on unpopular causes and remained popular was anybody's guess. Perhaps because righteousness didn't enter into it. Pious didn't either. She defended her constituents with a salty tongue.

Some have speculated that Shay's emerging mores had something to do with overcompensation, with birth order, with growing up in the shadow of Dia, who championed humor above all else. For Dia, if the choice was between fair play and fair game, fair play didn't stand a chance. Nothing should get in the way of a good joke. She didn't intend to be cruel; she just meant to be funny. And often was. She generally could take it as well as dish it out and was the first to admit when she'd gone too far.

So when 11-year-old Dia began to treat 11-year-old Helen as an integral part of her play-by-play, "She swings with all her might and there's a bunt up the line," Shay had had enough.

"Aw, lay off, Dia! We don't play no better!" she yelled, a startling admission from a girl who took pride in her ballplaying.

But Dia wasn't looking so cocky around 2:15 as she shifted her benumbed derriere. "What's the hold up?" she carped, loud enough to be heard inside, not so loud that those inside would come out and respond.

"Pa's on the phone," said Joyce.

"Again?" Dia fell silent. Moments later she stood up and brushed off the seat of her dress, blocking Shay's view of the game.

"Where ya goin' now?" challenged Shay, glaring up at her, having good reason to inquire. Even though they'd been told to stay outside, Dia had been in and out of the house twice in the last ten minutes, dire thirst being her first excuse, dire bladder her second. She was determined to serve as a visual reminder to her father that they were waiting to go to The Lake. But each time she'd entered, he'd missed the hint, preoccupied as he was on the phone in the sitting room, the black cord swishing as he paced.

"I said, 'Where ya goin' now?'"

"I forgot to pack my geography book."

"Oh, please," sighed Joyce.

"But I gotta test tomorrow."

"On what?"

"On the Great Lakes."

"But you know the Great Lakes," said Joyce. "You're always braggin' about it."

"I need to refresh my expertise," said Dia to a pair of howling skeptics. "Besides, where better to study the Great Lakes, huh? Than on a Great Lake?"

"Pa told you to wait outside, Dia," said Joyce. "And that's my final word."

Dia, feigning deafness, ignored the final word. But when she tried to bypass Shay, Shay lunged across the step like Nazimova across a sofa and cut her off. "Stay outta the house, Dia. You're gonna make Pa mad."

"I'm just gonna get my geography book. What's the big deal?"

"You're just gonna ruin it for all of us," cried Shay. "That's the big deal."

Dia fell silent. You could tell she was thinking. Slowly she sidled up the side of the stairs, eluding Shay's grab for her calf, tugged open the screen door, faced her father who was still on the phone, and was about to announce her need for her geography book when he shooed her with the back of his hand with such force that she forgot her book and all the Great Lakes, including Erie. But as she backed out the door, she heard him growl into the receiver, "Where's Murph?" then snap, "Don't give me that! Put my son on the line!" Something was up and it had to do with Murph.

Dia, returning to her third-step perch, was so bloated with news that it didn't take much for Joyce to pump it out of her. "It's Murph," whispered Dia. "He's in trouble again. Big trouble."

"Oh, swell!" cried Shay. "Now we'll never get outta here!"

"What's he done now?" whispered Joyce.

"I don't know, but I'm sure as heck gonna find out."

"We coulda been playing baseball," grumbled Shay. "We coulda just gone to the show like we always do."

A few minutes later, Eddie "Junior" Ouellette came out of his house and retrieved the picnic hamper from the back seat of the Buick, dislodging Dempsey. The girls moaned. Breakfast was a distant memory and Uneeda biscuits could get you just so far. Shortly after that, Ed Ouellette emerged. But instead of going to his car, he crossed Labadie, ducked Grace Bourassa's airborne bat, and stopped behind the Moore hedge.

"Bet you guys are hungry," he said heartily.

"Starvin'," they chorused.

"Well, your dad's got some last minute stuff to do, so we thought we'd better have lunch now. C'mon. Mabel's got good chicken. All laid out."

The dining room off the Ouellette front porch was like a solarium, bright and airy, picnic perfect, with three walls of windows that had been added to the house in more prosperous times. Mrs. O. was still fussing over the long table as they entered, while four of her children were seated along the west wall like a jury, utensils ready, napkins for bibs. Bowls of coleslaw, potato salad and baked beans resided mid-table, bounded by towers of white bread, a platter of chicken, a plate of Nabiscos, an eye-catching, crumb-topped apple pie, and a jug of lemonade, its neck clogged with ice cubes. At each table end, brown bags of potato chips, darkened by oil, were ripped open, their crisp, salty offerings spilling onto the light-green oilcloth.

"Dig in," said Mabel, motioning the girls to take their seats. So while Dempsey napped in a sunny square and a reflection from a copper cap on an outside feeder danced on the ceiling, the children, as commanded, dug in with gusto. And after bellies were filled and plates stood empty, Shay and Joyce chattered cheerfully with the Ouellettes across the way, while Dia kept an ear out for any veiled references as to what was up with Murph, weighing such statements as "Watch your glass, Eddie," for possible code.

Shay was having a swell time. But when a cloud eclipsed the sun and the room darkened, she grew apprehensive. No one was making a move to leave the table; no one seemed concerned about The Lake. So she was relieved when one of the Pilon boys shouted from the street through one of the open windows, "Hey, Joyce. Shay. Your dad wants ya!"

Finally.

The girls poured out of the Ouellette house, thundered down the steps and rushed across Labadie, eager to be on their way. The baseball game had broken up. A few of the boys, including the Pilons, were still hanging around the Brown's tree lawn, some standing, some sitting, recapping the game. Then a Pilon from the middle of the pack, yelled, "Your mother's dead."

> *"You know how kids are," said Dia. "Couldn't resist. I remember it so clearly. 'Your mother's dead.' I don't ever remember being prepared for it, really."*

And where was Marce? Was she at the Ouellettes that day? No one could recall, though all agreed she must have been.

Agnes Moore died at 3 o'clock that afternoon, one day before the faithful of Ecorse would hoist a glass to St. Patrick. She was 45. When asked if the tuberculosis had been in her kidneys or lungs, Dr. Durocher told Freda, "All through her."

In the weeks preceding her death, Agnes's world had been steadily shrinking, irising out like the final frames of a Chaplin film. Because her pain required more and more sedation, she was sleeping most of the day, most of the night. She had long ago stopped reading, had little appetite, seldom said much. She no longer enjoyed visitors, no longer kept tabs on her children, no longer inquired as to the day or the hour, was unaware that she was unaware and unconcerned that she was unconcerned. Her feet were always cold, her mouth always dry. Her lips were so cracked they were feeding her ice chips, her voice so low they had to lean in to hear.

"Aw, she was thin and pitiful," said Rowe. "They used to wake us all up in the middle of the night to come downstairs that she was dying. I don't know how many nights my dad and Dr. Durocher came and woke us up, and we all went down and sat around the bed and waited and watched and, you know, she didn't die, so they said you can go back to bed now. At least two or three times they made us come downstairs."

On one of those late-night occasions, at the urging of Dr. Durocher, Father Morin had been called to administer extreme unction. Freda, prepped ahead, met him at the front door with a blessed candle, looking reasonably devout, while George and Rowe hung back in the kitchen. After escorting the priest to the bedroom, Freda closed the door and returned to the kitchen so the good father could hear Agnes's final confession, though Agnes, whose occasion for sin had been severely limited, surely had little to report. Then the kids were brought downstairs. Then the kids were sent back to bed.

But that spring-like Sunday, as they were packing the car to go to The Lake, George grew uneasy. Lottie Montie had come over around 12:45, right after church, to give Agnes her bath and change her sweat-soaked sheets. Freda told George that Agnes, who looked forward to her baths and the cool, clean sheets, had been unresponsive, even when Lottie massaged her heels and elbows with lotion. Lottie had then redone the covers and left them perfect—top sheet turned over a blue blanket, rose-patterned quilt above, Agnes's flannelled arms uppermost. Those covers, those arms, had not moved an inch.

George was torn. There had been so many premature deathbed gatherings. He didn't want to call Dr. Durocher again, didn't want to cancel the outing, didn't want to keep jumping the gun, but he was having a hard time leaving, something in his gut. He phoned over to the Ouellettes and told Ed: "Bear with me for about an hour, okay? I've just got a feeling."

Around 2:00, as George sat to the right of Agnes on a straight-backed chair and a sliver of sun edged the drawn shade in the darkened room, Agnes narrowly opened her eyes. Slowly, almost imperceptibly, Agnes extended her hand across the quilt, her wedding band sagging on her finger, and George reached over to take it.

"No," she said, pushing his hand away. "Freda."

George shot straight up. He couldn't get out of there fast enough. He almost tipped over his chair to make way for Freda, while Freda, who was standing near Rowe at the foot of the bed, hurried round to assume her father's place. Leaning awkwardly from the edge of the chair, she offered her mother her hand, and Agnes, eyes closed, squeezed it. That was it. Simple as that. Then Agnes drifted off.

George must have put a pretty good face on it, because that night, over coffee and postmortems, he turned the incident into a loving gesture. He told Freda

Freda Moore

that, on reflection, he knew why Agnes had asked for her. She was passing the baton, he said. Freda had done such a great job of taking care of her mother, she was passing the mantle. "Just as much as to say, "You take over,'" he told her. That's what she meant by the gesture, he was sure of it. So that's the explanation that stuck. No other option was entertained, at least not out loud.

That Sunday night, Freda and Rowe searched Agnes's closet for burial clothes, but there was little from which to choose: two dresses, a brown one and a black one, a bunch of housedresses, one slip, and a big black hat that no one ever saw her wear.

On Monday morning, St. Patrick's Day, Freda and Joyce disinfected the sickroom and washed the bedding while George went to see about funeral arrangements and Rowe went shopping for a burial gown. The other girls spent the day joylessly cleaning. The parlor was rearranged, the green velour couch and the player piano moved to one side. Ella pitched in, so did Mim Raupp, so did Mabel. All were determined that Agnes's house would be as spotless as Agnes had kept it.

On Tuesday morning, around 9, Frank Gallagher, the funeral director from River Rouge, knocked on the door. George knew him well. Since the advent of Prohibition, Ecorse officials had been using Frank to dispose of the misplaced bodies found in questionable resting places, such as ditches, train beds, and swampy inlets. But for years Frank had also handled those who died in their beds, and he was there to deliver Agnes.

George ordered the kids to stay upstairs while Gallagher and his staff of five, with hushed but brisk decorum, went about the business of transforming the Moore house into a mortuary. In the little-used parlor, a catafalque was set up on a slight angle in the southeast corner. The parlor shades were lowered, the drapes drawn, the fringed lamps turned on, and the gold casket shouldered in.

They hung deep red velvet curtains and a velvet drape across the archway. Black crepe was hung on the front door, wooden folding chairs were set up in the sitting room, a coat rack was installed in the dining room, the sign-in book was placed on the library table, the lid on the coffin was lifted and propped up, and the stage was set.

George, who had remained in the kitchen tinkering with a broken windup toy, something he'd been meaning to fix for months, waited until Frank and his men drove off before entering the parlor to spend time alone with Agnes. Standing by the coffin, he gazed down at her as she slept, her head resting on satin, conscious of the waxen face, the stiffly-set lips, the pasty, folded hands. Even so, she looked pretty, she looked at peace. He felt numb, dry-eyed. He stood there for some time, waiting for tears that would not come, before turning to leave, before turning back. "I'm gonna miss you, Ag. And right now, I don't dare take it in."

Returning to the sitting room, he sank heavily into his Morris chair, then heard the back door open. Murph, wearing a black armband on a dark suit, came through the kitchen and dining room. He had taken the news hard.

"Did they come?" he asked.

"In the parlor," said George.

"Thanks, Pa," said Murph, who disappeared behind the red drapes.

George went to the bottom of the stairs and called up to Freda, who had been sitting quietly on the hallway bed with her apprehensive charges, comforting them, reassuring them, attempting to brace them for the day ahead. "One at a time," he advised, a catch in his voice. So one by one his daughters walked nervously through the red-velvet arch into the parlor to say farewell to their mother. Upon exiting, eyes red-rimmed, each took a folding chair near her father, like returning communicants in church.

Shay emerged from the parlor.

"You okay, Tee?" asked George.

As if in answer, she crawled into his lap and began to cry.

> "I remember Dia sitting near," said Shay. "I sat on pa's lap and cried and cried and cried and then went back to look at mumma in the casket. All in pink, with pink satin shoes."

For the next three days, the doorbell did not stop ringing. Agnes had had many friends; George had even more. Flowers poured in. Warncke's delivery truck, bearing wreaths with satin sashes, arrived almost hourly. Soon irises and gladioluses filled the parlor, then the sitting room, then the dining room, and, by Thursday, when the weather became warm enough, they were all over the porch.

While flowers came in the front, food came through the back. The women of Monroe and Labadie cooked through their sorrow. Mrs. Strassner brought a sponge cake, Mabel, an apricot coffee braid; Ella supplied the turkey and ham sandwiches; and Mrs. Pilon sent over warm meals for the family. The kitchen and dining room tables held never-ending buffets.

During viewing hours, as official cars lined Monroe, men in uniforms filled the house. Al Jaeger paid his respects, as did the police and fire squads. Most of the Ecorse Council came. Ollie and Mim Raupp, Alf Bouchard, a string of Monties, a squad of Salliottes. Nibbs O'Hearn, somber, sober and in a suit. Miss Munn paid her respects, though she didn't stay long. The Browns, the Brazills, the Daltons, the Pilons, the Sages, the Ostranders came, as well as Screech Salliotte, sporting a helluva hangover from Hibernian festivities.

Agnes's blind sister Ovie was guided into the parlor by her daughter Violet. "How does she look?" asked Ovie, standing before the casket. Violet took her mother's hand and placed it lightly on Agnes's hair. "At peace," said Violet. "Good, she looks good," said Peck, joining them.

––––––––––

Each day, George stood at the door or sat in his chair, attending to the attendees. Each night, while the exhausted family slept, close relatives or friends kept vigil over Agnes. George's mother and his sister Hattie stayed up on Tuesday, Ella and Mabel on Wednesday, Peck and Ruth on Thursday. Each morning, the smell of percolating coffee filled the house.

An Irish wake has a distinct quirkiness, as Agnes's sendoff could attest. The bereaved entered shyly, respectfully, issuing their funereal assessments in hushed tones. "She looks so thin," whispered Mrs. Goodell. "But she looks nice. They did a good job," commented Mrs. Jaeger. "Frank Gallagher always does," said Mabel. After a time voices grew bolder, labored condolences turned to storytelling, laughter could be heard.

Even the men became less awkward, possibly fortified by the surreptitious nips out back. Soon, their concerns began to depart from the departed. At one point, Nick, Ed, Fred Pilon, Ernie, Al and Ollie had formed a small cluster, cigar smoke circling their heads as some leaned against the rear clapboard. There was a consensus building that George was a goner. It was a known fact that George couldn't rub two dimes together, that he owed Doc Durocher his shirt, his pants, and probably his liver. Wasn't much money in barbering anymore. And how much can you make as a truant officer?

Ed shook his head. "A widower with seven kids."

"I'd hate to see his tab at Seavitt's," said Ollie. "All that medicine. How the hell's he gonna pay it?"

"It gets worse," said Ed. "George told me he still hadn't paid off that two-year-old hospital bill."

"Wish I could help," said Ed.

"Yeah," said Nick.

"Must be something we could do," said Ollie.

"I been thinkin about that myself," said Nick.

"Like what?" said Ed. "I'm hangin by a thread."

"We all are," said Nick.

"I'll be lucky if I can keep my garage," said Ollie. "Rent's going up and I don't have it."

"Store's in trouble," said Fred. "No one's paying."

"Poor bastard," said Nick. "Seven kids."

Inside, the women took a different tack. "Poor motherless girls," they whispered. "Poor motherless girls."

————————

On Friday, March 21, after an 8:30 a.m. service at the house, Agnes was raised aloft by six pallbearers in homburgs, carnations in their lapels, borne out of her home at awkward angles, carried confidently across the front porch, tilted a bit going down her steps for the last time, and jostled slightly as she was guided into Frank Gallagher's hearse. Though it was a nippy 44° outside, Agnes's purple crocuses in her zinnia bed remained open for the occasion.

While the few who were not attending her funeral gazed from their porches, the hearse went slowly up Monroe, turned right onto State, turned left onto High and pulled up in front of St. Francis Xavier for a requiem mass for the repose of Agnes's soul, Father Morin officiating.

"I can just see my dad with seven of us kids trailing him down the aisle at her funeral. All in borrowed clothes," said Rowe.

But there weren't seven. There were six. That Wednesday, Shay had taken ill. George had suspected something was up when she crawled into his lap the day before. With her temperature spiking at 104°, Dr. Durocher recommended the usual rest, aspirin and plenty of fluids, and put her to bed in Agnes's room, so they could keep an eye on her during the viewing hours.

No invalid had more visitors. Those who filed past the casket filed past the sickroom and peeked in. Each time she woke, someone was in the doorway, smiling.

Once it was Mrs. Gregory.

"How are you, Shirley?"

"Fine."

Once it was Dia's lay teacher at St. Francis, the red-headed Mrs. Judge.

"How are you, Shirley?"

"Fine."

A couple of nuns looked in. So did envoys from her third-grade class at School One, two of whom waved timidly. So did Ella and Cousin Fern and Mrs. Jaeger.

On Thursday morning, her father wandered into the sickroom and leaned over her. "How you feelin', Tee?" he asked, brushing her bangs back, feeling her forehead.

"Fine," she said in a tiny voice. "But it's kinda hot in here."

"How 'bout a little fresh air? It's nice out. In the 50s." Bending over, he cracked the window a few inches, then sat next to her on the bed, his left forearm resting across her rose-quilted midsection. "Still tired?" he asked.

"Uh-huh."

"Then just lie back. Rest."

Shirley turned toward her father. And when she reached down and rested her fingers on the back of his hand, his eyes filled with tears.

Chapter 33
Early September 1930

As if things weren't bad enough, along—Oh, God—came infinity.

"All stand for Father Morin," crooned Sister Sylvester when their pastor stuck his head in the doorway. The Catechism class dutifully jack-knifed out from behind their desks and rose to their feet, Shay among them, having now transferred to St. Francis.

"Good morning, Father Morin," they chanted. As usual, Butzie Raupp was one beat behind, so the class echoed their greeting, "Good Morning, Father Morin . . . orin."

"Good morning, children," said Father Morin in his friendliest tone; his friendliest tone was one notch above stern. Sister Sylvester glided subordinately to the rear of the room and rested her black bulk against the back blackboard. The more empathic children winced. Sister Sylvester's black habit had the habit of taking on chalk. When Father Morin sat down behind the desk, the children followed suit: morning Catechism class was underway.

"Who created the world?" intoned the examiner.

"God created the world . . . orld," chorused the communicants.

"Why did God make you?"

"God made me to know him, to love him, and to serve him in every way . . . ay."

"How did God make you?"

"God made me in his image and likeness . . . sss."

And for the next 40 minutes, the catechizing could be heard up and down the corridors of St. Francis Xavier School.

"Let us close with the Confiteor," said Father.

"I . . . confess to Almighty God, to blessed Mary ever virgin, blessed Michael the Archangel, blessed John the Baptist, the holy Apostles Peter and Paul, and all the saints, that I have sinned exceedingly in thought, word, and deed." They droned on, dirgelike, abasing themselves, begging God's forgiveness for their slingshots, their peashooters, their fibs and arrows, until they arrived at the favored part, favored because they were taught to pound their breasts in remorse each time the word "fault" was intoned. Their voices swelled; their tiny fists smote their breasts in fervent contrition and hearty synchronization: "Through my fault (smite), through my fault (smite), through my most *grievous* fault (smite)," wailing out "gree-vous" as if they had been guilty of an atrocity so odious that all the angels in heaven would have to plead their case before God. The penitents pressed on, imploring, pleading, beseeching the Blessed Mary, Michael, John, Peter and Paul to pray for their shameless ways. Then they took it on home. "May the Almighty God have mercy on me, forgive me my sins and bring me into life everlasting. Amen . . . men." Butzie Raupp was amazing.

"Very good," said a preoccupied Father Morin. "Are there any questions about today's work?"

"No, Father," said Julie Charboneau who had the unfortunate habit of speaking for everyone.

But Tony Shields raised his hand. "What does 'life everlasting' mean, Father?"

"It means those who go to heaven are immortal. They will never die."

"You mean in heaven you can live to be a thousand?"

"Heaven is timeless. You don't get old. Besides, our bodies don't go to heaven, just our souls."

The class was attentive, baffled, and sincerely grateful when Tony pursued the topic. "What does timeless mean, Father?"

"It means not measurable, eternal."

Now considering that only a couple of years ago the future class of '39 was still measuring time with big hands and little hands, a month was about as long as some kids could handle. So Tony dug in. "What does eternal mean, Father?"

"It means no limits, no boundaries. It means infinity."

"What does infinity mean?"

"It means everlasting, having no beginning, no end." Over the top of his glasses, Father Morin shot his grand inquisitor a pillar-of-salt look; Tony Shields slumped behind his desk.

Ed Foley took up the slack. "Infinity just keeps going?"

"Exactly." Father Morin stood up and turned toward the blackboard.

"To your left, Father," lilted Sister Sylvester. Gliding up the aisle subordinately, she picked up a small piece of chalk from the chalk gutter, handed it to the right reverend, then glided back—chalk dust now lining the bottom of her black veil.

Using a generous portion of the front blackboard, Father drew a sideways figure 8, set the chalk down with a flourish, brushed his hands together to rid them of dust, and turned triumphantly to the class. "Can anyone tell me what this is?"

Not a sound could be heard. Only Jim Burnham's adenoidal breathing.

"This," said Father Morin, "is the symbol for infinity. Notice how the line does not break, it just keeps going." He searched the rows, eager for a small sign of comprehension.

Not a sound could be heard. Only Jim Burnham's adenoids and a momentary rude gurgle of a watery nature—like someone suctioning soda from the bottom of a Coke bottle. As Father whipped toward the source, the sound stopped abruptly, terrified.

"Boy in the third row. What are you doing?"

"Filling my ink pen, Father."

"Put your fountain pen away."

"Yes, Father."

Father Morin was in deep and he knew it. The Trinity was a tough number, but infinity was tougher. Reaching into his mental bag, he pulled out one more trick. "Does anyone know what an infinity mirror is?" He looked around. "I need two mirrors."

A wave of heads surged toward Jo Page, the class primp. Julie Charboneau lifted the top of Jo's desk, reached inside, pulled out a round mirror, and handed it to Father Morin. The class waited. Sister Sylvester waited. Julie hesitated then reluctantly offered a smaller one in a tortoise-shell frame from her own desk.

Father Morin held the large round mirror up in the air with his right hand. The class leaned in. "If you put one mirror across from another mirror," he said as he held the tortoise-shell mirror in the air opposite, "each mirror's reflection duplicates itself on and on into infinity." The luckier ones in the front row—including Shay—were allowed to file up, one at a time. Too nervous, too self-conscious to see anything, they looked in the mirrors, nodded solemnly, then returned to their seats in the same manner they used for receiving communion—reverent, serious, touched by God. Ray Livernois, Jr. came close to genuflecting when he returned to his desk, but caught himself just in time.

Father Morin set down the mirrors. "If you live a good life, an honest life, and don't commit a mortal sin—and not too many venial sins, either—you will go to heaven for life everlasting and see God."

"How many venial sins is too many, Father? Two a week, four a week?" asked Webster Stott, who had reason for concern.

Sister Sylvester coughed.

"What's heaven like?" asked Parnell DeMay.

"Perfection," said their pastor. "Glorious perfection. There's no sadness, no illness, no hunger, no floods. No one will want for anything because everyone will be rich—not in a worldly sense—but rich with joy for they will see God."

"What do they do in heaven?"

"They Rejoice. They Rejoice and Praise God."

"Will there be bugs or snakes?" asked Peggy Spaight, prompting two giggles and a poke in her back.

"Neither bugs nor snakes."

"Will Shirley Moore get to see her mother?"

Julie Charboneau had struck again. A wave of heads surged toward Shay suffused with 4th grade sympathy. Shay reddened—half pleased with the attention, half embarrassed.

"Absolutely," boomed Father Morin. "But her mother won't just be her mother, she'll be her sister, her daughter. Everyone will be related, a community of souls. We won't have our earthly need for love in heaven. God said: 'Today, thou shalt be with me in paradise.' The greatest joy for Shirley Moore won't be seeing her mother but seeing God. 'Blessed are the pure in heart, for they shall see God.'"

Shay didn't eat much dinner that night. She didn't say much either. When Joyce asked what was wrong Shay mumbled, "Nothin'," and skewered a noodle. She didn't say much when she did the dishes either. When Freda asked her what was wrong, she muttered, "Nothin'," and twisted her towel round the rim of a teacup. Nor did she lift up her voice in song that night in the parlor. Even when there was a spirited rendition of "Body and Soul."

For Shay couldn't stop thinking about infinity, that endless loop. Especially after she said her prayers, especially after she climbed into bed. Disproving all theories of innocence, it didn't take long for Dia to get to sleep. Nor Joyce. But Shay lay there, ramrod in the middle, watching the light and shadow show on the ceiling.

What did they do in heaven? If there is no sadness, no illness, no hunger? Sitting on a cloud didn't sound like a whole lot of fun. Father Morin didn't say that; Dorothy Dalton said that at lunch over egg salad sandwiches. Dorothy Dalton said that they'd sit on their own clouds and play the harp. Swell.

So what did they do all day? They rejoiced and praised God. Now God didn't strike her as the kind of guy that needed praise. Why would he need Shirley Moore to tell him he was doing a good job? What else would she say to him? "Sure like your robe." She refluffed her pillow and turned over on her stomach.

And would there be clothes in heaven? Would they wear what they were buried in? She thought about the dress her mother was wearing. It was all right, but not for infinity. Then again, Father'd said they'd just be souls. Souls didn't wear clothes. From the pictures she'd seen, souls were red kidney-like blobs. Was God the only one with an earthly body? No wonder everyone sat around waiting to see him.

But it seemed to her that seeing God would wear off in a day or two. She didn't want to be disrespectful, but if heaven was a reward, she'd rather stay on earth, thanks—hanging out with friends, chewin' the fat. The idea of seeing God for infinity was beginning to depress her.

An arm flapped across Shay's chin. She lifted it up and set it back by Dia's side.

And that was another thing. There had to be a lot of people in heaven. Crowds and crowds. How could they all get to see God? Did they see God like she saw Pa when he marched in the 4th of July parade? Maybe it was a big parade. Maybe there'd be angels walking by with big long trumpets and acolytes in red robes. Then a whole squad of priests in snazzy vestments, swinging incense, and behind them an army of nuns as far as the eye could see.

But would it be the same old parade every day? She bolted up. For infinity?

Shay tried to think of other things. But every barn she went around, every road she took led her back to the same place—an infinity path that went on and on and on for ever and ever and ever. She'd never die. Forever and ever and ever and ever.

Her nightie was limp with sweat.

Crawling over Joyce, she sneaked over to the stairwell, tiptoed downstairs, and sat huddled in her mother's chair in the parlor. Then she got up, went to the hutch, pulled her mother's shawl out of the bottom drawer, put it round her shoulders, and sat back down in the chair.

Maybe Mary would be in heaven. That was a thought. She bet Mary was the type that would take care of her if she got sick. She bet Mary'd give her a spoonful of cough syrup; she bet Mary would steam the sickroom with Vick's. And even if there was no sickness in heaven, what about when she felt blue. Shay couldn't help but think that after 1,000 years in heaven there'd come a time when she felt very blue. The sight of Mary would sure help.

As the pinks of the morning sun began to inch through the parlor window, Shay finally fell asleep in her mother's chair, dreaming that she was muffled up, skating across the ice, tracing an endless figure 8.

Chapter 34

Friday, September 19, 1930

The hot, clammy summer clung stubbornly to September. Autumn eventually arrived mid-month, energizing Ecorse with its seasonal tune-up. Everything was heightened: the air was nippier, smells spicier, shadows deeper and sounds clearer.

The morning of September 19 dawned under a dome of blue with a crisp temperature of 59°. Except for the few cars parked at the curb in front of old St. Francis Xavier Church, its owners attending morning mass, all was quiet on High Street. The only movement was an occasional leaf that, for want of wind, dropped straight down.

At 8:45, the heavy double doors beneath stained-glass tympanums boomed open and High Street came alive. From the two aging entrances, held wide by ushers, the daily devout poured out—those from the center aisle through the main door, those from the side aisle through the ancillary door—then bounded down the identical pair of pyramidal steps and hurried off, anxious to get on with their day.

After a discreet delay, the 8th-grade class of St. Francis Xavier School began to file out two abreast, the boys in front flexing their muscles, bumping into the boys ahead; the girls behind, ripping off their hats and hankies, shaking out their flattened hair. The agents of this tidy evacuation were working from within, where seven Sisters of St. Joseph and one lay teacher stood at the edge of their respective aisles, signaling with an upraised palm when it was time for their class to stand, when it was time to push in kneelers, when it was time to quit the row.

Now the 7th grade streamed out the doors, plunged down the steps, then turned up High for the seven-block walk to school, Joycie in the rear. Now the 6th, a little less sophisticated than the upper grades, a lot sillier, Dia in the thick of it, treating Mary Dalton to a dead-on impersonation of Ida walking back from Communion like St. Monica in religious rapture.

Now came the 5th, now the 4th, and out popped Shay, hugging her three-ring binder with its pack of 24 pristine sheets of lined paper, and her new protractor set (always carried but never used). The 3rd came next, then 2nd, then 1st, their foreheads glistening from wrist-deep dips in the Holy Water and speedy signs of the cross as they exited the nave.

There had been no available land near the old brick church and rectory. As a result, the school had been built on three-and-a-half acres over on Bonzano, a two-lane street which would later become the double-breasted boulevard known as Outer Drive. Thus it was a common village sight, a trail of kids as far as the eye could see, clumped in class groups, approximately 30 to a clump, marching two-by-two up High Street every weekday morning at 8:45, each clump anchored by a nun policing from behind. Wimples don't lend themselves to peripheral vision.

They paraded past the future home of the Commires, past Odette's, then paused in front of Cicotte's grocery store at the corner of State and High. There, each class waited in turn while its teacher took to the streets, bodily barricading the street against the occasional car, herding her class across like a ranch hand on a cattle drive, then falling in behind them once more with smooth efficiency. Once past State, they crossed to the east side of High to avoid merging with the children up ahead who were entering School One. Freda was coming up Labadie, escorting Marce to kindergarten.

Just after Labadie, where High Street curves, Shay looked with interest to her right as the train of children passed the home of Herb Ormsby, former chief of police, friend of her father. The lone house in that section of High was one of the prettiest in Ecorse and something of a landmark. Stark white with a white garage, it was nestled among the trees behind a white picket fence which lined the substantial bend in the road.

Just past the spur of the DT&I (a gateless crossing where slow-moving trains hauled freight to the factories and shipyards along the shore) and directly across from the marsh and the playing field (where Ben Montie had played baseball in summer and Shay now skated in winter), a stately edifice had just gone up, so new it was still being landscaped, so new it had dirt for grass.

Oh, it was grand. Unlike the old Village Hall of tired wood, this one, of handsome brick, meant business. With touches of the neoclassical, it sprawled like the White House, with two wings that angled out, the south wing containing the fire station, the north the police station. Its elegant middle entrance, like the portal of a miniature castle, could be reached by climbing nine steps to a balustraded terrace which would often be used as a staging area for public events. In lieu of columns, globed lamp posts stood at the four corners of the balustrade, while a globed sconce flanked each side of the vaulted entranceway. The only thing bland was its name, which was printed in raised letters on an entablature supported by stone brackets: MUNICIPAL BUILDING.

As the 4th grade approached the police station entrance in the north wing, Shay glanced back for permission to break ranks. The lay teacher, the very pretty, the very red-headed Mrs. Judge, nodded with a smile, and Shay scurried up the brief walkway and rapped on a windowpane to her right. The narrow sash swished open and George Moore leaned out, more handsome to her than ever, having traded his barbershop whites for a uniform of dark blue.

"Morning, Tee," he said. "What's up?"

"Pa, I forgot. I need a dime," said Shay, palms pressed against the concrete sill.

"What for?"

"They're takin' a collection for Father Morin's Feast Day."

"Oh, is that guy eating again?" laughed George, reaching into his pocket, sorting through change. He pulled out a dime and passed it down to her. "Does Dia need one?"

"No," she said, breaking into a trot. "Just our class!" She'd no sooner cut back in line when the girl from behind tapped her on the shoulder.

"I hear your dad's chief of police," she said.

"Yeah," said Shay.

"You don't act like it."

"How ya sposed to act?"

"Boy, if my dad was chief of police, I wouldn't talk to anybody."

"I thought that was so funny," recalled Shay. "Because we didn't act any different. Though I did get a kick out of driving up in his police car."

The nomads continued on, passing the old Fisher Body plant on Cicotte now owned by Schwayder Brothers, passing Benson, passing Goodell; then they turned right on Bonzano as a handbell rang them into school.

———————

Herb Ormsby was dead. A veteran of World War I, he had suffered a stroke on the 4th of July, shortly after 9 p.m. and died within 15 minutes. Husband to Marie, father to four-year-old Phyllis, friend of Agnes and George, he was 38. On July 15, 1930, George Moore was sworn in as chief of police, two days after his 46th birthday.

Looking back, Dia often wondered if it was a sympathy appointment, him a widower with seven kids, but it was a natural fit. George Moore had been involved in law enforcement since he was 20. As early as 1905, when the population of Ecorse was around 1,300, he was the street commissioner and village marshal, the town's only law-enforcement officer. By 1916, he and Agnes's brother Peck, who spent that year as his assistant, were chasing speeders along the brick pavement of Front Street on Indian motorbikes,

Town Marshall George Moore seated in front of his barbershop. Fred Bigler points finger at Ecorse's one-man police force.

Ecorse's first motorcycle policemen. (Their pay was a percentage of each ticket issued. Out of a $10 fine, the judge got $4.75, Peck or George got $3.75 and $1.50 went to the village.) George would remain village marshal for 13 years, through 1918, the year Michigan went dry.

Thanks to Prohibition, however, his hours expanded and George's need for staff exploded. It might have been this issue alone that made him hang up his badge and run successfully for Justice of the Peace. With his growing family, he could ill afford to give up his barbershop. Or it might have been the episode in the marsh. What he had been doing that night in the swamp years ago no one knows. It was likely an all-night stakeout. Whatever it was, he had lain there all night, he often told Shay, with his high-top boots full of water. As a result, by the time he became chief, he had rheumatism in his hip and walked with a slight limp.

But when George Moore was sworn in as chief in that blistering July of 1930 (Ecorse population 12,916), his timing could not have been worse. Talk of job losses and tightening credit filled the barbershops; columnists quibbled as to whether the nation was warding off a Depression, facing a Depression or already in a Depression, and all hell was breaking loose on the crime front.

Metropolitan Detroit was experiencing the worst crime wave in its history. Six years before, in November 1924, Charles Bowles, a former judge, whose primary support came from the Ku Klux Klan, had been a write-in candidate to serve out an ailing Detroit mayor's term. The KKK was anti-Catholic, anti-Semitic, anti-union, anti-foreign born and racist. Bowles's opponent was the Klan's worst nightmare, a labor sympathizer and Polish-Catholic progressive named John W. Smith, who promised to see to it that the police department hired "more colored officers." After a torched cross on Smith's lawn and the backing of the Fort Street Congregational minister's wife who admonished, "Who does not vote for Charles Bowles should be tarred and feathered," Bowles won. The result was reversed, however, on a technicality: Klan sympathizers could not spell. Smith's backers on the election commission successfully challenged 17,000 Boles, Bolls, Bowls, Bolles and Bowels votes.

Bowles tried again in November 1925, but lost to Smith by 30,000 votes. Finally, running against the incumbent, John C. Lodge, Bowles was elected mayor in January 1930. By May, with Detroit looking more and more like shoot-'em-up Chicago, recall petitions began circulating. And every night at 6:30, along with most of the Metropolitan area, the Moores would listen to WMBC's Jerry Buckley, a popular radio commentator known as "The Voice of the People" (1420 on the dial), as he lashed out against the lawlessness, the civic incompetence and the ever-expanding unemployment. The public had grown increasingly angry since the first of the year when gunmen tried unsuccessfully to assassinate Detroit Police Inspector Henry J. Garvin and in the process critically injured an 11-year-old schoolgirl.

Then came "Bloody July." On the 3rd of that month, while Buckley was broadcasting from WMBC's studio in Detroit's LaSalle Hotel on Woodward, two reputed beer runners, parked just outside the hotel's side entrance on Adelaide Street, were shot and killed in broad daylight. Jerry Buckley gave a blow-by-blow of the incident as it happened and radio listeners even heard the gunshots. In the next 12 days, eight more gangsters were slain on the streets of Detroit; photos of crowds swarming around death cars, peeking in at bullet-riddled bodies, filled the front pages. Buckley continued to hammer away at Bowles and the Detroit police department, resulting in the scheduling of a July 22 recall election. Surprisingly Buckley opposed it; he felt it undemocratic.

For some unknown reason, two nights before the polls opened, Buckley told his audience that he had changed his mind, that he supported the recall. On July 22, he monitored the results from City Hall, occasionally going on air with updates. Just after 1 a.m. on July 23, after reporting that Bowles had been recalled, Buckley took a cab back to the LaSalle Hotel, and sat in the lobby, reading the *Detroit Free Press* Election Edition, waiting to meet with a woman, name still unknown, who, his secretary would later report, had called earlier. At 1:30 a.m., three men sauntered in through the Adelaide Street entrance and pumped 11 bullets into the broadcaster. His funeral procession drew 150,000, and "Who killed Jerry Buckley?" became a Michigan tagline.

Feeling the political heat, Commissioner Thomas Wilcox did his best to turn the hero into a bum, suggesting Buckley had ties to the underworld, suggesting his death was a result of a double cross or shakedown gone sour. The public wasn't buying. A grand jury was called to find out who killed "The Voice of the People," with Wilber M. Brucker as prosecutor and a jury that included Edgar A. Guest, "The Poet of the People." No one was ever indicted.

In Ecorse, George Moore had also inherited a hornet's nest. There had been four violent deaths in July alone. On the 7th, a fellow named Cowan fired four shots into a fellow named Confer, as Confer strolled with Cowan's wife on Mill Street. Cowan then went home and took his own life with a shotgun. "Don't know why the papers are calling it a *love* killing," carped George.

He was also looking for someone who could help identify the man, believed to be Japanese, who had just washed up on a Downriver shore, as well as witnesses to the slaying of one Louis Candea, rumored to be another example of love gone wrong. Candea was shot down in a duel in the Green Lantern, later known as the Ocean View Cafe.

And Jerry Buckley's murder was having repercussions in Ecorse as well. On the hunt for the broadcaster's assassins, 15 squads of police were raiding speaks and gambling houses daily in Detroit. But the concern was that his killers and other hardcore gangsters were fleeing to the suburbs.

On Wednesday, July 30, led by the State Police, George and the suburban police chiefs of River Rouge and Wyandotte split into two parties to conduct simultaneous raids in Rouge and Wyandotte, then met in the middle to sweep out Ecorse. The goal was to find the gangsters, but in the process they took the axe to 34 of the most notorious blind pigs, disorderly houses and gambling resorts in the Downriver area, seized large quantities of liquor and beer, arrested five, all from Wyandotte, and detained thirty men and eight women who were questioned, then released.

In Ecorse, Charley Dollar's was raided; the upper floor of a barn was evacuated near Auburn; 2 State Street was invaded, along with 17 Bell, 17 Glenwood, 4571 and 4599 Front, 4131 10th, 230 and 226 Suburban, and a houseboat at the foot of State, while Walter Locke's patrons drank coffee with shaking hands just a few feet away. Doors were splintered. Walls shattered. Gambling equipment, chairs, tables were smashed. The crowds were sizeable, the entertainment free. Joyce, Dia and Cousin Fern watched from Uncle Peck's porch with raucous delight as the door of the boathouse was kicked in across the street.

No gangsters or big-time gamblers were found. Not even the well-liked Lefty Clark. His over-exposed casino above Raupp's Garage had gone dark shortly after George's appointment as chief and had remained dark through June and July, including the night of the July 30th raids.

Then on Saturday, September 13, as reported in the *Detroit News* , two State Police officers had spotted Lefty "in a reputed dice joint"[1] at 4571 Front Street, a tacky, two-story frame boathouse on the Ecorse riverfront. The officers had gone in looking for a couple of stickup men, but by the time they got past two guarded doors ("We were held up quite a while at the second door by the doorman," reported the officers[2]), there was no sign of gambling, just three dice tables and approximately 50 men chatting, including Lefty and Johnny Boyd.

If this was Lefty's new place, it was quite a comedown, but the news had State officials in a tizzy, especially since the next night, Sunday, as reported in the *Free Press*, the place was alive. Expensive cars lined that section of Front Street "and a stream of 'clients' continued to flow through its only entrance."[3]

That Monday, Attorney General Wilber Brucker, aspiring Republican nominee for governor, could barely disguise his contempt for all things Ecorse. "I shall give local authorities a reasonable time to close this place. If they don't, we will have the State Police close it. Then we will bring the matter to the attention of the grand jury and find out how it came to be operating and why it wasn't closed."[4]

George Moore, the aforementioned local authority, replied that he "knew something was going on at 4571 [Front], but didn't have enough information to take any action." He might have added "at this time," since he'd already ransacked the place in the July 30th raid. "If it's gambling going on there," he

---

[1] "Hint Gambling is on in Ecorse," Detroit News , Monday, Sept 15, 1930.
[2] Ibid.
[3] "State Will Act to End Gambling," Detroit Free Press , September 15, 1930.
[4] Ibid.

concluded, "it's being conducted very quietly. The Ecorse police stand ready to co-operate with the State Police and the sheriff's force at any time, regarding either gambling or anything else."[5]

Though to all appearances George looked oblivious and ineffectual, it must be noted that Lefty was gone a day later, having remarked on his way out that he had only re-opened to "give employment to his cappers, stickmen and other attachés, who have been unable to find work elsewhere."[6] Self-serving perhaps, but probably true.

Since Attorney General Wilber M. Brucker was lead prosecutor for that 22-man Wayne County grand jury to investigate Buckley's assassination, it didn't take a crystal ball to see that George was being goaded into raids, raids and more raids. Everyone in town braced.

On the Friday morning of September 19th, the same morning that Shay rapped on George's window and put the bite on him for Father's Feast Day, Fred Pilon was sitting outside George's office in the long, freshly painted corridor, waiting to see him. Everything was new: the signs, the chairs, the counter bell, even new toilets for the wayward in the basement cells below.

"Fred Pilon heeah to see ya, sir," said Officer Stewart, sticking his head in the door. He spoke with a noticeable Southern drawl.

"Wait a minute, Officer Stewart. Come in, close the door." Without a word, the officer complied. "I heard loud voices a while ago. What was that all about?"

Stewart looked around, playing dumb. "I didn't hear anythin', sir."

"You never do," said George, not all that thrilled at inheriting the hard-nosed Stewart who was not all that thrilled at inheriting George. "Sounded like an internal scrap."

"Oh, that. Just a slight disagreement among friends."

"Were you one of them?"

"One of the many, sir."

"So. I'll ask again. What was it all about?"

"Long forgotten, sir. Long forgotten."

"You know, Jim, sometimes I'd rather talk to a wall. These friendly disagreements have been building since I've been here. And, with or without your help, I'll get to the bottom of them."

"Yes, sir," said Stewart, flatly. "May I show in Mr. Pilon?"

"You may."

Fred, when told to go right in, thrust his head around the doorjamb and peeked into George's light-filled office, more window than wall.

"What's up, Fred?"

"Sorry to bother ya, George," he said, shyly entering the room. "Ya gotta

[5] "Hint Gambling is on in Ecorse," Detroit News, Monday, Sept 15, 1930
[6] "Police Start Gaming Drive," Detroit Free Press, September 16, 1930.

be so busy, catchin' up and all."

"Never too busy for you. Have a seat."

"No, that's okay. I won't keep ya." He paused, ill at ease.

"Forget the uniform, Fred. I'm still your neighbor. The one in pajamas getting the newspaper every morning, the one scratching his behind on the front
porch."

Fred laughed and fondled the brim of his hat, working up his nerve. Everybody liked Fred. Thin, in his late 40s, he was one of the most kind-hearted
men in town—a little more devout than George was comfortable with, but Fred
didn't demand it of others. "You mind if I close the door?"

"No, not at all," said George, puzzled.

Shutting the door, Fred returned to the exact spot he had been in. "They say
. . . I hear . . . you're gonna conduct a few raids soon."

George sat back, incredulous. "Boy, this place is leakier than a barn roof.
Where'd ya hear that? The *Ecorse Advertiser* ? 'Town Doings'?"

"Oh, people talk when they come in the store, you know," said Fred, rotating his brim. "They talk."

"Amazing." George shook his head and cocked a grin. "You worried about
your son, Billy?"

"Oh, no, no, no. Nothin' like that," said Fred." Billy's a man now. Not
much I can do."

"Know the feeling," said George with a sigh. "Well, if it's not Billy, is it your
brother-in-law? Alex?"

"Oh, no, no, no, no. Nothin' like that. Nothin' like that. It's about . . ."

"Yes?"

"It's about . . . Mrs. Stinson."

"Minnie?"

"Yes."

"But Fred. You were my moral compass!"

"Oh, no, no, no, no, no. Nothin' like that, George. Nothin' like that."

"Then like what?"

"Well, I . . ."

"Come. Sit. Take a load off."

Fred sank onto the new hardwood chair, the knobs of his bony knees scraping the new desk in front of him. "I was told," he said, inching the chair backward, "in strictest confidence, mind you . . . that you might also be raiding, ah,
disorderly houses." He rushed the last two words, making them one, then waited for George to speak, while George, poker-faced to cover his shock, waited for
Fred in return. "If that's so, I was wondering . . . were you . . . by any chance,
planning on raiding Mrs. Stinson's?"

"Now, Fred. I can't tell you that."

"I know, I know. But, well, if you are . . . "

"Yes?"

"Do you have to?"

George stared at Fred, wide-eyed. "I don't understand. You got a cousin working there or something?"

"Oh, no, no, no, no, no. Nothin' like that. Nothin' like that," said Fred, mangling his brim. "This is so difficult. You know, I've never . . . I don't condone that sort of thing, George. You know that."

"I thought I did."

"But Herb, Chief Ormsby, always left her alone, you know."

"Fred. This isn't like you at all. Why on earth would you be concerned about Minnie Stinson?"

"'Cuz she's the only one paying her bills!" he blurted. "Oh, God. I can't believe I'm doing this."

"Now, settle down, Fred. Just settle down. Talk to me. Tell me what's up."

Fred leaned forward and lowered his voice. "Everyone's runnin' up tabs, George. Everyone's comin' in, sayin', 'Charge it to my account,' but no one's payin' their bills, and I don't have the heart to say no, George. People need to eat. Then I gotta pay tax on that money, like I received it. I gotta pay tax on money I don't even have yet. Don'tcha see, George? If this keeps up, I'll lose my store. And I got seven kids still at home."

"But, Fred. How could Minnie keep you open?"

"She pays cash. She's one of the few who pays cash."

"Does she eat that much?"

"No, but she's buying for her house, ya see. For her girls, for her guests. The amount's quite substantial. It wouldn't be so bad if you hadn't shut down Lefty Clark's place over Raupp's Garage. We used to deliver $400, $500 worth of groceries a week up there. I tell ya, George. Shutting down Lefty. That was a blow."

"But, Fred you were one of the guys beggin' me to clean up the town."

"I know it. I know it," he said, shaking his head in disbelief.

"Why didn't you just warn Minnie."

"You know I wouldn't undermine you, George. It wouldn't be right. This isn't right, either. I know it. But what's right anymore? Goin' on the dole? Not supportin' my kids? It used to be a lot clearer."

"Well put," said George, though he wasn't too thrilled that the ethical dilemma had just been dropped into his lap. "One thing's certain."

"What's that?"

"We're talking your soul or mine."

> "A good friend that he brought over wanted [my father] to declare bankruptcy and then all his debts would be cancelled," said Fred's daughter, Marge Pilon, "and he said 'No, because he wasn't gonna do that and then not go to heaven.' My father was real religious." Fred lost the store in 1937 and went to work at Great Lakes Steel. "He was only there two weeks and he got pneumonia and he died," added Marge. He was 56.

Chapter 35

Saturday, September 20, 1930

The next day, around 4 p.m., George left the station in the Hupmobile patrol car, top down. The temperature was in the low 70's. "First stop: Applegrove and Front," he announced.

"Yes, sir," said Probationary Patrolman Dave Dorset, hired by George two months before.

Their destination was a deserted storefront with dingy windows bearing the name Polar Bear Club, a private offshoot of the highly popular café near State Street. A padlock was attached to the door, as was a notice: "CLOSED for VIO-LATION of the NATIONAL PROHIBITION ACT," a sign more ubiquitous in Ecorse than quarantines. Though it was true that many property owners in Ecorse were making a tidy bundle leasing their buildings and boathouses to the shadier elements, it was also true that it was a roll of the dice. With newer and tougher padlock laws, it was easier to shut down a place for peddling booze. Owners felt it when renters got pinched. A year of padlock meant a year of no rent.

No sooner had they climbed out of the car than Officer Stewart pulled up behind them in a duplicate black Hup and got out.

"What's up?" asked George.

"Lt. Sage sent me to tell ya, your hunch was right. They're out and about today," said Stewart.

"Thought so."

"Who is?" asked Dorset.

"State police," replied Stewart. "There've been raids near Eight Mile, Seven Mile and at Five Mile and Middlebelt."

"That's way out," said Dorset.

"At least for now," said George, unhooking the key ring from his belt, weighing the news. "But it sure sounds like a narrowing circle."

"Excuse me, sir," said Stewart, his eyes narrowing. "But why are you taking off that padlock?"

"Is there a problem?" muttered George.

"That restaurant was ordered locked for a year, wasn't it?" said Stewart. "By my calculations, it's got at least two months to go. I helped the feds put that padlock on myself."

"Moinet lifted it," said George.

"Moinet? The Federal judge?" asked Stewart.

"Yes."

"Was he paid off?"

"You might say that," said George, searching through the ring.

"Do you know the owner, sir?" asked Stewart.

George looked up, aware of the veiled insult, aware the rookie caught it too, and studied Stewart, wondering if this was the moment to take him on. Then he returned to his keys. "As a matter of fact, no. But whoever he is, he wised up. Took on a respectable tenant and lowered the rent."

"Even so, I don't see how he got the feds to petition to de-padlock."

"I repeat, he took on a new tenant," said George, turning the key in the lock, handing the lock to Dorset and, in his silence, declaring the subject closed.

Stewart was not about to let it rest. "New tenant or not. Still don't see why he did it."

"Moinet? His reasons were fairly clear," concluded George. "He said he was proud 'to be instrumental in letting the Salvation Army get a foothold in Ecorse.'"

"That the new tenant?" laughed Officer Dorset.

"Yep," smiled George as he checked the door lock.

"With all due respect, sir," said Stewart, with as little respect as he could get away with, "I fail to see the humor in that. It's just another black eye for Ecorse, another cheap shot from the bench. I don't know where he gets off. Half those judges are on the take."

"Oh, I don't know. Moinet seems decent enough. Trying to right the judicial ship," said George, walking back to the patrol car. "He's also lifting the padlock on that home in Hamtramck."

"Home?"

"The one where the mother and her six kids have been forced to live in an unheated barn out back because her idiot husband had a still in their basement."

"So, you don't mind that, sir?" pounced Stewart.

"Mind what?"

"That, as far as Moinet's concerned, a year is no longer a year?"

"Winter's a-cumin, James."

"They shoulda thought of that before they built a still," said Stewart.

"The father built the still," said George.

"Yeah, well, she shoulda stopped him," said Stewart.

"Were you there?" snapped George, opening the passenger door. "Look," he said, softening his tone. "I want to monitor those raids. Tell Marty, we'll hit the callboxes. But if he gets word they're headed this way, I want to know about it."

"Certainly be nice if we had police radios like Detroit," muttered Stewart.

"Certainly be nice if we had Detroit's budget," replied George. "Now, are you going back with us, Jim? Or do you want us to drive you to your car?"

Stewart walked stiffly to his patrol car. "Where'll I find you?" he asked, his hand on the door handle. "Where you goin' next?"

"Eighth and Mill," replied George.

"Minnie's?" asked Stewart.

"Mrs. Stinson to you," laughed Dave, getting in, slamming the door.

George caught the look that Stewart gave Dorset.

———————

The stop at Mrs. Stinson's was brief. George couldn't have been in the brick building more than a minute before he returned to the patrol car and instructed Dorset to drive over to 4571 Front. On their arrival, George waited in the idling car while Dorset checked the boathouse door, had a look on the waterside, then reappeared.

"Fairly sure it's deserted, sir."

"No Lefty?"

"No Lefty."

"Good."

"Now where?" asked Dorset, scooting behind the wheel.

"Turn up White," said George. "But watch out for those kids up there playing near the curb. There's sure to be a darter."

"Raupp's Garage, sir?"

"Raupp's Garage."

The rookie smiled. New York had its Chrysler Building, Arizona its Grand Canyon, Ecorse had Raupp's Garage. Mug shots of its exterior, side- and front-view had spanned four columns on Page One of the *Detroit News* the previous autumn, with a reprise this past spring.

They parked perpendicular to the large office window fronting the huge brick building, a half-block long, at 4534 Monroe. Its whitewashed visage served as a giant billboard:

RAUPP'S GARAGE
SINCLAIR GASOLINE
STOPS KNOCKS!
Radio & Hupmobile
Sales and Service
REPAIRING STORAGE
Phone Cedar 1361   Day and Night Service   Free Crankcase Service

In homage to the mild weather, its bay doors stood open, and, except for the tink, tink, tink of hammer on metal, all was quiet. The usual jumble of cars parked along the side street or across the way in the parking field next to Peck's, waiting to be serviced, was reduced to three, one of which looked as if it had had a run-in with a particularly vicious wall.

Ollie was in his office to the left of the bay doing the bills, which seemed fitting since he looked like an accountant, even in denim coveralls. Clayt Riopelle, wearing a mechanic's apron, was tink, tink, tinking under the hydraulic hoist in the far back, trying to loosen a frozen grease plug. Two cars, noticeably indisposed, dozed near the furnace behind the office, patiently waiting to be seen, their jaws propped open, their model manuals the only available reading. They were not the only shut-ins. A ragtag assemblage of ailing radios littered the long, messy workbench on the north wall. Ollie had added a sideline.

"Afternoon, Ollie," said George, before bellowing, "Afternoon, Clayt!"

"Afternoon, Mr. Moore!" Clayt bellowed back, while Ollie, in the process of tallying an invoice, mumbled something resembling "Be right with ya, George," as he carried the eight.

"No hurry," said George. "Mind if we take a look upstairs?"

"Be my guest," replied Ollie, not looking up. "It's unlocked."

Probationary Patrolman Dorset spun round and pursued George through an inner door, then found himself at the bottom of a stairwell landing. The young officer took a quick peek through the rectangular peephole of the stairwell's street door, then scrambled up the steps, where George, having briefly waited for him at the top of the landing, had opened another sturdy door and entered.

The cavernous room was empty. Autumn light from the many windows sprawled across the barren floor in wide bars. Sashes were cracked; shades were up, an unusual configuration in a room that had seen little daylight for the past two years. The crap tables were gone. The roulette wheels were gone. The slot machines, the blackjack booth, the payoff booth all gone. Nothing was left to suggest the once flourishing casino. (Though in 1948, while remodeling the second floor, workmen would accidentally uncover a sliding panel and stand in awe before a jumble of slot machines and gambling tables.)

"Well, it's official," said George. "They're out of here."

"Wish I coulda seen it in its heyday," said Dorset.

"Lotta swells," said George, leaning into the kitchen, now devoid of stove, refrigerator, tables and Chef Sam Slater who had been partially responsible for glorious free lunches.

Officer Dorset pointed to a door to the right of the stairs. "What's that?"

"Just a closet."

"Has it been checked?" asked Dorset.

"Many times."

"Want me to check it again?"

"Up to you."

Curious, the young patrolman ambled over, cracked open the closet door and reeled backwards. "Holy shit!"

"That guy still in there?" asked George.

"Hole-ee shit!" squealed Dorset. "There's a skeleton in there!"

"I know."

"But his bones rattled!"

"They always do."

The patrolman sank against a wall, hand on chest, and exhaled fully. "That's not good for your heart."

"I know."

"But why the hell would they put a skeleton in there?"

"Because every Fed, every trooper, every cop who came up here to snoop around was inclined to open that door, often to the delight of Lefty's patrons, who were holding their teacups while playing hearts," said George.

Bending down, George picked up a small blue disk from a pile of swept-up debris.

"Find something, sir?" asked Dorset, carefully shutting the closet door with an involuntary shudder.

"A $50 chip."

"Fifty bucks! Who's got fifty bucks?"

"High rollers," said George.

"Musta been a lot of high rollers."

"Yeah. And a lot of low rollers who lost their shirts."

"You gonna keep it as evidence?"

"Evidence of what?"

"That there was gambling going on up here."

"Kind of after the fact," said George, flipping it to Dorset, heading for the stairwell door. "Too bad they removed the payoff cage."

Ollie was there to greet them at the foot of the stairs. "See," he said. "All gone. That why you're here?"

"That. And I've been worried about you," said George.

Ollie glanced toward Dorset, discomfited, then turned back to George. "How's the Hup running?"

"Better since you adjusted the timer," said George, then he turned to the rookie. "Ah, Dave. Why don't you go check in at a corner call box. See what's up."

"Yes, sir," said Dorset, glancing, puzzled, at the phone in the office before heading out the bay.

"Oh, and ask Marty if Alonzo Gillette's leading the charge."

When Dorset returned, George was in the office, sitting across from Ollie on an old sofa, deep in conversation. "Gonna take a while," Ollie was saying, looking off into the middle distance.

"I'll be right out," said George to Dorset. So Dave bought a Coke, then leaned against the frame of the bay, half in, half out. He could hear their conversation. No one seemed to be interested in hiding it.

"How ya handling the lost revenues?" George was saying.

Ollie laughed. "The truth?"

"Yeah."

"It's killin' me, George. Lefty paid damn good rent, even those nights when he was out of service. Right up to June. Herb, you know, left him pretty much alone when he was upstairs."

"That was before your place got famous."

"Unfortunate but true."

"We had no choice, Ollie," said George. "We both knew it. We both agreed. Even Lefty agreed. I can't have him upstairs here, large as life, running the biggest casino for miles around. It's a black eye to the force and the town. A small game's one thing, but.... Besides, they padlock you, then what?"

"Oh, it was the right decision, George. I'm not saying it wasn't. Maybe I should have done it sooner. Maybe it was a punishment."

"Get that outta your head." George looked round and called to Dorset. "Why don'tcha check the air in that front tire. Air pump's on the side."

Ollie waited until Dorset left before continuing. "I'm just saying that if I'm feelin' the pinch, lot of others are, too. If you abruptly close up every gambling joint and speakeasy in town, you close up a lot of our commerce. All those rents on all those boathouses. That's income for half the town."

"Can't ya rent it out for something else?"

"I've been tryin'. The real-estate market's not exactly thriving. Money's so tight. When a guy needs his car fixed these days, he does it himself or stands it on its axles. Unless he needs it for work. If he's got work." Ollie paused. "I gotta ask, George, just how tough you're gonna be."

"Tough?"

"You know. On Volstead violations. On gambling. Stuff like that. I'll back ya, George. No matter what. But . . . you gonna clean up the town?"

"Wasn't that why you town council guys hired me?"

"Yeah, but everyone says that when they're hired. It doesn't mean much."

"Let me put it this way. I'm gonna try to make some sense out of this mess."

———————

George came through Raupp's bay and climbed into the patrol car. "Where are they now?"

"Lt. Sage says they've hit two places at Second Street in Wayne. Then Beverly Road near Wayne Road."

"Still pretty far out," said George, though he looked a little more concerned. "But they're making quite a wide swath. And what about Gillette?"

"Yes, sir. He's leading it."

"Who we got on the afternoon shift? You, Allen, Marty, Vintner . . . myself."

"You gonna work two shifts, sir?"

"Think I better."

"And we got four in the cars, sir. Dutch Hessler, Ted Marcotte, Charlie Tank and Stewart."

"If it gets heavy, we'll call the cars in," said George. Then he waited for Dorset to back up and pull out before asking, "There's a lot of tension in that station of ours, isn't there?"

"Tension, sir?"

"You can cut it with a knife."

"Well . . ."

"You haven't noticed? Strange. Any good cop would have noticed. What's up?"

"What's up, sir?"

"Yeah. What's up?"

"Just the usual resentments, sir. You know. You came from the outside, not from the ranks and all."

"And?"

"Well. We don't know where you stand, sir."

"On cleaning up the town?"

"Yes."

"Scheduling a lot of raids?"

"Yes, sir."

"Breaking down doors; breaking up furniture? If I wanted to run a wrecking crew, I'd change jobs. There are other ways to rein things in. But I get the feeling it's not just about me. I get the feeling there's differing opinions among the men. Nod if I'm close. Between those who want to enforce the vice laws, those who don't, and those who are on the take."

"That about sums it up, sir."

"Well, I know where Stewart stands."

"He's a hardnose, sir. Wants to come down hard on violators."

"Second cousin to Sir Anthony Absolute," George muttered. "Are honest cops getting a lot of pressure from the, shall we say, a little less than?"

"Something like that. You gonna weed those out, sir?"

"Eventually. But Herb had his way; I'll have mine. It's hard to play by the rules when the rules change daily. I'd like to give everyone a chance."

"Excuse me, sir," said Dorset. "I know I could get fired for this. But have we been cruising around the city, warning everyone about the raids?"

"Guilty on one count," said George.

"Mr. Raupp?"

"No."

Dorset was surprised. "No?"

"Personal. That conversation was personal."

"Oh," said Dorset, unconvinced.

George thought about it, then decided. "His daughter died last Sunday."

"You're kiddin?"

"His daughter Mary. Only a year and a half."

"My cousin and I took her for a walk in a buggy," said Bernice Raupp. "Suddenly, it poured rain. We ran all the way back with the buggy. She got sick; seemed like a bad cold. I can remember her laying in the big bed. We called Dr. Lewis, a pediatrician in Wyandotte. He took one look at her, wrapped her in a blanket and took her right to Wyandotte General Hospital. She died of double pneumonia. My father took it hard."

"I just wanted to make sure Lefty was out of there," said George. "Ollie doesn't need any more trouble, right now. The way I figure."

"What about Mrs. Stinson?"

"I'll have to ask you to trust me on that."

"Trust you, sir?"

"Yes. That's what I'm asking you for. Your trust. Until I give you reason not to."

"Fair enough, sir."

———————

The sun was setting by the time they parked the Hup in the precinct parking lot around six. As they entered through the front, the usual Saturday-night babble could be heard along with a ringing phone and the clacking of keys from a lone typewriter. George paused at the front desk and banged the bell on its counter. Officer Vintner appeared, yawning.

"Any messages?"

"They're on your desk, sir."

"Got a score on that Tigers' game?"

"No, but I'll lay odds the Senators won," said Vintner.

George leaned across the counter, signaling Marty Sage who was on the phone at his desk, taking notes. Marty, who looked up with a grin and a soundless "hang on a minute," returned to the phone, asked one more question, followed by "give me that address again," then held the phone tight against his white shirt. "Who's next in rotation?" he snickered.

Officer Marcotte, having watched Lt. Sage from his desk with apprehension, winced. "Just my luck. Watcha got?"

"Get over to 3957 Front," said Marty. "Ask for a Ralph Demis. He says there's a sewer stopped up and every time the people at 3955 flush, the waste flows into his back yard and stands there." Marty paused to glance at his notes. "Mr. Demis says, and I quote, 'It's about a foot deep and is stinkin' everybody out.'"

"Shit," muttered Officer Marcotte.

"Exactly," smiled Lt. Sage.

"Hold off on that, Marty," said George. "Tell Mr. Demis, we'll send someone out tomorrow. Something tells me we're gonna need all hands tonight. Any news of the wrecking crew?"

"Last report, they were in Trenton, sir," replied Marty. "They like to start in Trenton and demolish their way up."

"Get another patrol car out on the street. Though Alonzo Gillette's no hooligan—he's pretty straight up—I want those State guys to follow the law. Let's try and keep regional damage to a minimum."

"I'll get right on it."

"Did I miss anything else?"

"It's been pretty quiet, sir."

"Don't get used to it," said George, unbuckling his utility belt.

He went into his office, put his gun in a drawer, then stood in his doorway, skimming messages, half-listening with mild amusement as Officer Stewart conducted an interview in a room adjacent to his.

"Just give it to me again, Mr. Antoneo," Stewart was saying. "Slow enough so I can take it down."

Mr. Antoneo, a slight man in his fifties, was sitting to the side of Stewart's desk, in a tattered brown suit with frayed cuffs and a bandage ringing his head. He bent forward in earnest, watching Stewart write as he spoke haltingly with a thick Italian accent, strewing vowels with abandon.

"I was waitin' on da corner of Front an State when a man. . ."

"For a trolley, right?"

"For a trolley. When a man an' woman pull-up an' ask, 'How you get to Trenton?'"

"In a Nash, right?"

"Inna Nash," confirmed Mr. Antoneo, with a decided nod. "I'm-a tell 'em, 'Eesa road to Trenton.' Den dey ask if I'm-a goin' dat way. I'm-a tell 'em, 'I'm-a only goin' as far as to Wyandotte.' So dey tell me get in, dey gonna give me a ride. Which I done. Da woman, she sat in da back seat."

"Was she already in the back seat or did she get out and get in the back seat?"

"Got out and got in," said Mr. Antoneo, pleased he could verify. "When we getta to Nordline. . ."

"Northline?"

"Nordline . . . dey turn right. 'No! Eesa wrong way!' I'm-a tell 'em. Dat's when da woman in da back seat she hit me hard wid her gun. She say, 'Keep you moud shut!"

"Could you describe that woman again?"

"Brown coat wid fur collar. Brown hat."

"The man?"

"Gray coat, gray cap and leetle mustache."

"Then what?"

"Den dey drive and drive, a *tutta velocitá.*"

"How's that?"

" *Avanti.* Fast, very fast. Seema like forever. Took me way out in da sticks, took alla my money, den trow me oudda da automobile. . . Da Nash."

"Near Belleville?"

"Near Belleville."

"How much money?"

"113 dollari."

"113 dollars?" Stewart was brought up short. "Mind telling me where you got 113 bucks?"

"I'm-a earn. From work."

"You sure? Not making a leetle-a on da side?"

There was a pause. And in that pause, Mr. Antoneo, who was new to English but not stupid, grasped that the interview was veering *tutta velocitá* into interrogation. "Side-a what?"

"That's a big roll, Mr. Antoneo. Sure these weren't your partners, friends. Little larceny gone awry? Things got a little rough?"

"Whatta you sayin'?"

"I'm-a sayin', sounds like it coulda been a job gone bad. Or maybe you lost your wad at Lefty Clark's and can't tell the wife."

Mr. Antoneo rose up, donned his hat and mumbled, "*Mi scusi se la disturbo,*" then turned to leave.

"I'm jist tryin' to find out how you came by 113 bucks," reasoned Stewart loudly, so as to be understood. "Got something to hide, Mr. Antoneo?"

George crammed his messages in his jacket pocket and swiftly entered the room, blocking the immigrant's exit. "Mind if I ask a question or two, Officer Stewart?"

Stewart certainly did mind, very much. You could tell by the edge in his voice when he said, "All yours."

"*Per favore*, Signor Antoneo, sit. Officer Stewart's just doing his job," said George. "You came to register a complaint, Mr. Antoneo. Let's register that complaint." He commandeered a pack of Luckies from another desk and flicked a cigarette up. "*Fumate?*"

"No, *grazie.*"

George tossed the cigarettes, then reversed an extra interview chair, placed it directly in front of the Italian immigrant and sat on it backward, his arms entwined across the backrest. "Tell me, Mr. Antoneo. How long have you been in Ecorse?"

"Five munds," said Mr. Antoneo with distrust, though he removed his hat.

"Where do you work?"

"Meeshigan Steel."

"Last I checked," muttered Stewart, "they were barely making $17 a week over at Meeshigan Steel. If you could get the hours."

"I wonder, Mr. Antoneo," cut in George, "isn't it fair to ask . . . why you were carrying $113? That *is* a lot of money."

"Eesa fair to ask," said the Italian, "but eesa how you ask." Then he turned toward Stewart, his eyes ablaze, and responded with fury. "Eesa no safe to leave alla my money ina boarding house, an I ain't crazy enough to put ina bank deesa days! *Capisce!* "

"So you're saying it was safe to take it with you?" smirked Stewart. "*Capisce!* "

"Phooey on you, sir," said Mr. Antoneo, chest out.

"All right, all right, let's keep it civil," said George. "Now, just two more questions, *per favore* . . . Who sewed you up?"

"I already got that from Garibaldi here," said Stewart.

"I'm sure you did, Jim."

"Somma guy, he found me," said Mr. Antoneo, sinking back into his chair. "He bring me to da hospital in Wyandotte."

"Then you came right here?"

"*Si* ."

"How'd you get here, Mr. Antoneo," asked Stewart. "With no money? Hitchhike?"

"No. I no hitchadahike no more. I'm-a walk."

"Walk," laughed Stewart in disbelief. "From Wyandotte General? After getting konked on the head with a gun? That's almost three miles."

George put his hand on Mr. Antoneo's shoulder; his dark eyes filled with warmth. "Didja get a gander at that Marmon stickin' straight up outta the water while you were crossing Ecorse Creek, Mr. Antoneo? We've been laughing all day. Guy skidded right off the bridge this morning; musta had a date with Jack Daniels."

"Marmon?"

"That car, that car. That au-to. Stickin' straight up. You couldn't miss it when you looked down. Walking across the bridge on foot and all."

"Eesa no automobile in da water when I'm-a walk across."

"That's right," said George, standing up, smiling. "Where do you live, Mr. Antoneo?"

"*Settimo.* Seventh."

George called out. "Officer Mell."

"Yes, sir?"

"When's your shift over?"

"An hour ago, sir."

"Would you mind dropping Mr. Antoneo off on your way home?"

"No problem."

Mr. Antoneo stood up but grabbed the desk, a little unsteady on his feet.

"Come, sit in my office until we can drive you home. Then I'd advise you to lie down as soon as you walk in your door, Mr. Antoneo. You've had a rough day." George turned to Officer Stewart. "Get those descriptions out right away."

Stewart started to bristle, then backed off. "That's my plan," he replied.

"Marty," said George, walking into his office. "Can I see you for a minute?" He took off his blue coat jacket and hung it on a tree stand, then sat down at his desk. "What's in lockup?" he asked as Marty entered. "Anything dangerous?"

"Why?"

"They may have to double up."

Chapter 36

That evening

Around seven o'clock, while George was hunting-and-pecking a report and Dave Dorset was in the hallway at the candy machine getting his third Milky Way of the day, there was the roar of an engine, then another, so loud that everyone in the lighted rooms stopped to listen. "They're bringing in a load!" yelled Officer Allen.

"How many paddy wagons?" yelled Marty.

"Two . . . three . . . four," counted Allen, standing near a side window.

"State or federal?" asked George, stepping into the hallway.

"Looks like state."

"That'll be Gillette."

"Gonna need a shoe horn!"

"It starts," muttered George.

Captain Alonzo Gillette burst in, filling the front door. "Evening, Chief Moore. "I've got 33 lovelies outside. Got room in the inn?"

"Frisked?"

"All frisked."

"And we're booking them on . . .?"

"Mixed bag. Disorderly conduct, loitering, couple of frequenters. I'll leave my sergeant here to straighten it out, make each case."

"No gaming proprietors?"

"No gaming proprietors. Gotta hand it to ya, George," he said, with a hint of sarcasm. "Kinda quiet. No sign of Lefty."

"Do I detect disappointment?"

"A little. I'll need you to hold the evidence."

"Whatcha got?"

"One glass of rum, two slot machines, and the usual droplets from each of the places."

"How many places?"

"Looks to be around 26, so far."

"Give your swill to Marty. He'll lock it up. Any of 'em happy?"

"'Bout eight."

"How happy?"

"Very happy."

"Any women?"

"Four."

"Give me two minutes," said George.

"Two it is," said Gillette, tossing his reply over his shoulder as he thundered back out.

"Bell hop!" yelled George, banging the bell on the front counter. Vintner staggered from his desk, shaking out the cobwebs from a surreptitious snooze. "Put the women in the holding tank for now. Put the men in the cells until we can get to 'em, including the drunks, and, for God's sake, get Judge Riopelle over here pronto so we can get rid of as many as possible. I don't want to be serving 33 breakfasts in the morning, even if they are on the State."

"I'll get right on it, sir."

Escorted by State troopers, the detainees began filing through the front door like a conga line, gliding to a chorus of "Move along now. Lift them tootsies."

"Straight to the rear and down the stairs," Officer Vintner repeated in counterpoint while Marty peeled off a few and sent them into offices. "Straight to the rear and down the stairs."

"I feel like I'm in the receiving line at a wedding," said George. "How you doin', Mr. Cears? Been awhile."

"They're calling me a frequenter, George," said Mr. Cears, laughing. "I've been called many things in my life, but frequenter ain't one of 'em."

"Evening, George," said Charlie Dollar, doffing his fedora with a handcuffed hand.

"Evening, Charlie."

"Gee, Everett," said George. "They hit your place in February, we hit it in July, and now September. 17 Glenwood's getting to be the highlight of the tour."

"They're calling it a cabaret," jeered Everett. "One old couch, three dumpy chairs, and a tired wife passing around potato chips. They're calling it a cabaret."

"And where *is* Ethel?"

"Visiting an aunt in Cincinnati."

"Again?"

"You know how it is."

"Yeah," replied George. "She's got better reflexes. Bounds out those windows...."

But George's attention had drifted toward a big hulking guy in handcuffs, lumbering through the door. "Is he safe?"

"Butter wouldn't melt," said a reporter, bringing up the rear, along with two other members of the fourth estate.

"Oh, swell," griped George. "We get you newspaper guys, too."

"Compliments of the Volstead publicity bureau," cracked the reporter. "And speaking of the bureau," he side mouthed, whipping his head over his shoulder as the front door opened.

"No finer example exists," said George when Endicott strolled in.

"This guy's pie-eyed," said Endicott, who had in his possession a man's wool elbow. "I just pulled him off the street."

"Which street?" asked George.

"Right out front. High Street."

"He's walking by and you pull him in?"

"Yeah. Like I said, he's drunk."

"You drunk, Vermeel?"

"No, George."

Endicott laughed in disbelief. "You just gonna take his word?"

"Where were you going, Vermeel?" asked George.

"I weren't going, George," said Vermeel, grinning. "I was coming from."

"Where?"

"Ernie's. We went to the Tigers' game, then had burgers at his house."

"Who won?"

"Tigers. 4 to 2."

George banged on the bell. "Hear that, Officer Vintner?"

"I heard him, sir!" called out Vintner.

George turned to Endicott. "You'd be wise to release this man, unless you don't mind being sued for false arrest. He has a glass eye."

"What?"

"He has a glass eye. You guys are always picking him up."

"But . . ."

"He has . . . a glass . . . eye."

Endicott, who had been staring George down, loosened his grip on Vermeel's elbow.

"Thanks, George," said Vermeel, who put on his hat and left.

"Well now, Agent Endicott, tell me," said George, with phony bonhomie. "What brings you here?"

"To pick up that Overland truck you've been holding for us."

"Vintner!"

"Right here, sir. Never left."

"Give Agent Endicott the keys to the Overland truck."

"Yes, sir," said Vintner.

"Does it still have the evidence, those four-and-a-half barrels of beer," asked Endicott, "or did they somehow disappear?"

Ignoring Endicott, George turned to Vintner. "Did you get hold of Judge Riopelle?"

"He's on his way."

"Judge Riopelle!" roared Endicott. "Isn't he the guy that's fining speeders a pair of shoes?"

"Yep. The very guy."

"Is he nuts?"

"Why don'tcha ask the 22 shoeless kids in Ecorse who now have shoes. . . . And, yes, the truck still has the four barrels."

"Chief Moore," said Officer Allen, leaning over the counter.

"Yes?"

"You told me to report to you if there were any more calls about Nibbs. . . Well, he's loose again, sir. He's walking down Elton, holding two chickens."

"Hope to hell he's got a receipt," said George, looking round and spotting Dorset at the candy machine. "Dorset."

"Yes, sir."

"Get over to Elton. Try to find Nibbs."

"I don't know what he looks like. How will I find him, sir?"

"Follow the clucks."

"Yes, sir."

"I love Saturday nights."

When Judge Riopelle finally arrived, they set up a card table in the basement to serve as his bench, then brought the revelers out of their cells one by one. A state trooper presented each case, then a litany (How do you plead? Guilty. How do you plead? Guilty.) followed. The judge fined most $2, gaveled with a thud, then announced their release. Eventually, five would be bound over for trial.

Later that night, George asked Marty to give him a few minutes. He shut the door on his office, turned off the overhead light to ease his headache, and retreated behind his desk, comforted only by the oval glow from the green glass shades on the two-headed desk lamp. What the hell had he taken on? He was facing a moral maze and had little confidence that he could find his way out. This was a far cry from the days he patrolled the sleepy streets on his Indian motorbike.

He retrieved a folder from the bottom tier of the three-tiered wire basket, opened it and gazed at the photo of a pretty young girl. The last two months played out before him, mixed with regrets. And the biggest of these: the day Adolph "Duffy" Renaud came to see him about his burned garage. When was that? Sometime in late July. About a week after he'd been made chief, certainly before the police convention in Duluth. Did he fumble the ball? Was there anything he could have done?

"Who do you think torched it?" he had asked Duffy.

"The Purples."

"The Purples!" George had sat back in surprise. "What makes you say that?"

"'Cuz we was threatened."

"By the Purples?"

"Yeah."

"Why?"

"Well," said Duffy, sheepishly. He was a small, pleasant-faced French-Canadian, around 57. "Ain't no secret I been known to row cross da river to visit
relatives, you know, at River Canard. I mean, I was born in Canada. I got family
dere."

*"He was buying booze from a cousin there, who happened to be the priest
at the Catholic Church," said his grandson Dale Renaud."*

George smiled. "Yeah, Duffy, you've been dutiful. Your sons have been dutiful, too."

Duffy cocked a grin. "Family first, I always say. But we only brung back
refreshments, George. We ain't no crooks."

"I know that, Duffy."

"Well, word came down from on high . . . dat I should stop."

"So your garage burned down."

"Yeah."

"If I were you, Duffy, I'd heed the warning. I'm gonna tell you what I'm
telling everyone around who's got their hand in the trade, including my son . . . .
You know as well as I do, there are some dangerous guys stinking up this town.
Guys that don't belong here. Now I've got all I can do to protect law-abiding
citizens from fisticuffs, robberies, rogue bullets, speeding cars, and dog bites. I
can't protect runners from these goons, nor can I protect runners from overeager state or federal officers. When you live outside the law, even something as
seemingly harmless as smuggling hooch across the river—and I know, I know,
I've made light of it myself—the law can't shield you. In other words, if I said I
could protect you right now, while I'm getting on-the-job training, I'd be a first-
class liar."

———————

Then, George recalled, bout two weeks later, on Friday, August 8, George
had stood to greet Duffy as he was ushered into his office. George had offered a
firm handshake in an attempt to convey his sympathy, then waited for Duffy to
sit before asking, "How you holdin' up?"

"Been better."

"I don't know how you bear it. . ." George trailed off. "I see she's at Frank
Gallagher's. When's the funeral?"

"Tomorrow."

"He'll do a nice job."

"Yeah, he'll do a nice job," said Duffy. "But dey won't bury her in da church, you know. Because dere sayin' it was a suicide." Then, he pulled his chair closer to the desk, leaned in and almost whispered, "George, I'm here to tell ya . . . It weren't no suicide."

"But it's been ruled a suicide, Duffy. By the coroner. Didn't you tell him she'd been despondent? *Detroit Times* had something about her being depressed over her husband and a radio singer."

"Naw. He asked me how she was actin'," said Duffy, his voice aggrieved." "And all's I said was she'd been feelin' punk."

Puzzled, George reached for a folder in the bottom of the wire tray, opened it and found what he was looking for. "But he's got on the death certificate 'despondent over ill health. Closed case.'"

"George, I'm tellin' ya. It weren't no suicide."

"Then who do you think killed her?"

"The Purples."

"Geez, Duffy. How do you go from a burned garage to someone shooting your daughter? You got any proof?"

"Look, George. If you was gonna kill yourself, wouldja get all gussied up? Get your baby all gussied up? When we found Margaret dead in da bathroom, the baby was in da bedroom in her crib. All dressed to go out."

"What about the father?"

"She din't talk about him much. She'd only been married about a year when she come back home."

George sat back. "Okay, Duffy, let's say it wasn't suicide. Why do you assume the Purples? Why not her husband?"

"Virgil? 'Cuz we was told he's in jail."

"That can be checked."

"And 'cuz we tink he's connected with da Purples."

"Now I'm confused. Were they after you or after her?"

"I tink dey was sendin' a message to me trough her."

"If what you say is true, you're not safe either. Somebody's got their dander up."

"Yeah. I know."

"Look, Duffy, I can reopen the investigation, but chances are—if it's not suicide—this was done by a hit squad, and they're great at covering their tracks. I've got unsolved killings coming outta my ears." George reached across his desk, took a stack of stapled sheets from the top tier of the wire baskets and lifted the first page. "This is just from one undertaker—Thon's. One undertaker, out of six. They've listed three . . . five . . . nine unidentified floaters found in the river in the past few years, one more last month, all of whom are now residing in Wyandotte at Oakwood Cemetery in unmarked graves. Chances are, most weren't jumpers."

They were silent for a time. George studied Duffy while Duffy studied the floor. Finally, George said, "You thinkin' what I'm thinkin'?"

"Yeah."

"Do you have a place to go?"

"I got dat cottage up north."

"If it was me, if it was my family. . . I'd be cruising up Telegraph right now."

Late that night, Duffy packed up his family, including the baby, and left for the Upper Peninsula of Michigan, the northern sticks, not to return until years later.

> *"My grandfather was furious when the papers come out because they didn't tell his side of the story," said Duffy's grandson Dale. "He told them they thought it was murder. But they never printed it. The way the story goes is the family buried her during the night at the Xavier cemetery, packed up the kids and some belongings and headed to the UP of Michigan leaving everything behind that same night. They didn't return to Ecorse 'til the end of 1940. My grandmother and grandfather adopted the baby when they took her up north," added Dale. She was my godmother. Ruthie. She lived a full life."*

But as in the case of Jerry Buckley, no one would ever answer the questions surrounding the death of Margaret Renaud.

———————

George sat motionless in the greenish light, staring intently at Margaret's photo, wishing he could have protected the guileless girl standing behind her house in a white home sewn dress, a barrette in her short hair, her fingers self-consciously entwined before her while she smiled into the sun. He had scrutinized the picture so often that he saw it in his sleep. How do you handle the death of a daughter? How can Ollie get out of bed in the morning? He gazed across his desk at the photo of his own daughters, grouped outside the Monroe house, dressed in their Easter best. How would he handle that staggering kind of loss? One thing was sure. He'd have to be tougher on them. He couldn't let them get away from him like he had his son, though it was sure as hell harder without Agnes, especially with the long hours.

There was a knock on the door. "Sorry to bother you, sir, but Captain Gillette's returned . . . bearing 15 more guests," chuckled Vintner. "He wants to talk to you."

As the bull-necked captain boomed into the room, George stood behind his dimly lit desk. "Hit that switch over there, Alonzo . . . if you want more light on the subject."

"No need, George," said the captain, briskly. "I'll be brief."

"Got any daughters, Lon?"

Alonzo paused, thrown off stride. "Actually, George, I have four."

"How old?"

"Twelve, ten, seven and five."

"Six," said George. "I've got six."

"Six!" said Alonzo, underscored by a low whistle. "Must be hard without their mother."

"Makes my knees buckle," said George. "Any sons?"

"No," replied Alonzo, standing stiffly before him, hat under arm. "No sons."

"Lucky you," said George. "Pull up a chair, Lon, put your boots up. Want a beer?"

"You're kidding, right?"

"Yep. What's up?"

Alonzo seized the spindle chair, stuffed his muscular frame into it and palmed his knees with hands the size of garden shovels. "I have a question," he blurted.

"Shoot."

"About something you said to the press the other day."

"Ohhhkay," drawled George, sinking into his chair.

"You might find it impertinent."

"I'll be the judge."

"That's no longer technically true," said Alonzo, half-smiling. "But it *is* relevant."

"How so?"

"When you were a judge, I generally found you to be fair."

"That was my hope."

"But you also tended to . . . shall we say . . . wink at certain infractions."

"Oh, please," moaned George. "Forgive me, Lon. I don't want to get on my high horse here, but could we dispense with the word *wink* ? It's every reporter's favorite verb when it comes to local constabularies. Wink means condone. I didn't condone. If you want to accuse me of anything, you might say I overlooked certain infractions. I'll answer to that."

"Okay, for the sake of argument, how about, *played down* certain infractions?'"

"Nicely put."

"What I want to know is," asked Alonzo, "what are you gonna do now?"

"About what?"

"About liquor violations. Gambling. That sort of thing. You gonna clean up the town?"

George laughed. "You're the third person to ask me that today."

"And what was your reply?"

George studied Alonzo warily. "I didn't have a pat answer. At least, nothing on hand," he said. "What's up, Lon? You seem a little put out."

"When Prosecutor Brucker threw down the gauntlet about Lefty Clark's

new place on Front Street and it landed in your lap, you said and I quote. . . ."
He reached inside his uniform to his shirt pocket, brought forth a jagged newspaper clipping, unfolded it under the double lamp and read by its light. *"You
knew something was going on there, but didn't have enough information to take
any action. "*

"Actually, I didn't. I had just ransacked that place about a month ago . . .
with you, remember?"

"But it was the delicacy with which you chose your next words." Alonzo
returned to the clipping: *"If it's gambling going on there, it's being conducted
very quietly. "* He looked up at George. "Quiet's okay? Is that your answer?"

"No, my answer came next as I recall."

"This?" Alonzo returned to the clipping. *"The Ecorse police stand ready
to co-operate with the State Police and the sheriff's force at any time, regarding
either gambling or anything else. "*[1]

"Yeah. That."

Alonzo balled up the clipping and tossed it into the large ashtray near the
edge of George's desk. "I notice you didn't say, if there's gambling going on
there, I'll put a stop to it. You won't initiate, but you'll cooperate?"

"Is that any different from every other chief in the area?" said George, gruff-
ly.

"No."

"What are you after?"

"To be perfectly frank, George," said Alonzo, with a touch of anger. "I'm
tired. I need help. And I was kinda hoping I'd get some from you. I can't clean
up Downriver alone."

"I just said, if you ask for help, I'll gladly give it."

"C'mon, George. That's so much flapdoodle. I want to know where you
stand."

George picked up a letter opener and began to examine it, then bounced
it repeatedly off his thumb. He respected Alonzo and was fairly sure that the
respect was mutual. Even so, he was still wary. Finally he said, heavily, "How
long have we known each other?"

"Oh, I don't know. Six, seven years."

"Off the record?"

Alonzo hesitated, then placed his hat on the edge of the desk and sat back.
"Off the record."

George set down the letter opener, propped his palm against the arm of his
chair and pushed backward, twisting his body sideways. "To be honest, Lon,
I don't know what the hell I'm gonna do. Where I'm gonna draw the line. I
go round and round. But I owe it to the law-abiding of this town to draw it
somewhere. All two of 'em," he laughed. "Though how the hell I'm gonna be

---

[1] "Hint Gambling is on in Ecorse," Detroit Free Press, Monday, September 15, 1930.

consistent is anybody's guess. If I come down hard on the Prohibition laws, the gambling laws, I'd have to do it equitably. . . which leads me to the one thing I do know. I'm not gonna raid every living-room soiree or two-bit crap game."

He leaned forward into the dim light. "If I arrest everyone I know who has contraband in their house, who rows a boat across, who frequents illicit watering holes, who bets on ballgames, we'd be out at least one doctor, one butcher, a couple of judges, a caseload of lawyers, one priest, two ministers, a shitload of teachers, half the workforce at Michigan Steel, the frontline of the high school football team, most of my staff, most of the town council, not to mention my son, my brother, my brother-in-law, about 80 cousins, most of my deceased wife's uncles—trust me, she had many—and one very humble police chief. Yours truly. There isn't enough rope. All those years of loose talk in my barbershop, knowing what I know, I'd have to arrest half the town. Hell, there'd be four jail-house widows on my block alone. The only self-proclaimed saints around here. . . that I'm aware of . . . are Ralph Montrose, Officer James Stewart, and some—I stress— *some* members of the Ladies Honor Society, and I wouldn't even vouch for them."

"I understand the problem, George. But so far you've told me what you're *not* gonna do. How's about a hint on what you're gonna do."

"Clean up the town? What does that mean, Lon? Get a warrant, break down a door, blow a whistle, yell 'Raid!' and everybody dives out the window. The State, the feds, they're hauling in a hundred frequenters on misdemeanors for every felonious gambling-house operator they book. And if they do manage to haul in the proprietor, he gets a shyster lawyer and opens again the following night. Now I'm not talking about you, Lon. You've made some huge busts. Charlie Birch's alone brought in liquor worth thousands. But on the whole, these so-called cleanup campaigns are a joke. They only get the little guy, the guy who can't afford the bribes or a lawyer. They're raiding living-room speaks, finding half-pints of gin. Meanwhile, the little guy gets served up to the public as a prime catch, as a sign of the campaign's dazzling success. The whole thing's rotten to the core. The fat cats all know that, so do the cops . . . and so do you."

"Damn, it George. It's not all rotten. Some of us are really trying."

"I couldn't agree more. But I just can't agree with your methods. It's about arresting, arresting, arresting.

"So tell me again, because I think I missed it, just what are your methods?"

"With all due respect, George," said Alonzo, "I think you're missing the boat. I honestly believe that if you put a stop to the smaller crimes, the big stuff'll fall away. We need to get respect for the law back."

George sighed and threw up his arms. "Have I thought about what you've just said? Yes. Can I dispute it? No. But I think it's too late. The only thing you'll reap for cleaning up the small stuff is a Bronx cheer."

"What about the syndicates?"

"Right. Those are the guys we need to concentrate on. Period."

"So I repeat, what are you gonna do?"

"What I was sworn to do: keep the peace. These guys getting laid-off right and left will do anything to keep their families from starving. And I understand that. Even so, if I catch them filching from Fred Pilon's store, I'll arrest them. But if I catch them selling a bottle of Labatt's for profit, chances are I'll only give them a warning. And I sure as hell am not gonna hunt them down. Or, worse yet, entrap them."

"What about dope?"

"I'll put 'em out of business. Look, Lon, you know as well as I, there are bootleggers and there are thugs. And there's a huge difference between them. We're taking some of the best and brightest out of our communities and throwin' them behind bars."

"Point is, they *are* behind bars," said Alonzo, forcefully. "Want that for your son?"

"Prohibition was to protect our youth, that was one of the arguments," returned George angrily. "Prisons are far more harmful to kids than drinking."

"You're wrong, George. Just plain wrong. You let a kid disobey you, he'll soon learn he can get away with it. You say 'no' and he does it anyway, that's where the disintegration begins."

"The disintegration begins when you say 'no' unfairly," replied George. "This damn law's the devil's own."

"I agree, but it's the law. And this country's based on the rule of law.

"But it's this particular law that's doing the undermining."

"And I say, it's the lack of enforcement that's doing it."

"In the Philippines, drinking's not a vice at all. In the Philippines, our American soldiers can buy Liberty beer in the canteens, "brewed expressly for use of the U.S. Army." Says so, proudly, right on the label. I'm not going to sacrifice any Ecorse son, including my own, on the altar of this fleeting law."

"You can't just pick and choose, George. It's not up for grabs in the Michigan Police Law Manual, in the Constitution."

"We all pick and choose. No prosecutor prosecutes every crime that's been committed. He picks; he chooses." George leaned in, in earnest. "There are no ordinances against gambling on our town books. There are no ordinances against drinking on our town books. Gambling? Know of any games in my town right now that are wide open? See any lights on over Raupp's Garage?"

"I thought Lefty might be just lying low."

"And he'll stay low, if he's stays around here. My boys need to stay in the know. And the only way we can do that is to keep tabs on what's going on, monitor the games. Weed out the crooks, the fleecers. Cheating's against the law in any town."

"Well, we agree on one thing: the country's in trouble," sighed Gillette. "Remember Joe Kinsey? That sheriff in Monroe County, the one who made only seven liquor seizures in two years? Before you know it, he's being tried for soliciting campaign contributions in a gambler's furnace room. That gonna be you, George?" asked Gillette. "And what about Herb? Your predecessor? Ignorer supreme. Didn't he once appear before a Federal judge on three counts under the Prohibition Act because two collared bootleggers claimed he promised to bail 'em out?"

"Herb was set up."

"You know that for sure?"

"Positive. C'mon, Lon, be fair. The only witnesses for the prosecution were the two bootleggers. In the course of doing your job, there's a good chance you're gonna offend a bootlegger or two. The jury tossed it out."

"Maybe," said Alonzo, slyly. "But it makes you wonder, doesn't it?"

"Damn it, Lon," yelled George. "You know as well as I do that ignoring certain infractions doesn't mean you're on the take. Herb was square."

"Yeah, well, ignoring infractions can easily lead you to the take. And let's say you walk a straight path, let's say you never take a dime, ignoring infractions sure as hell can make it look like you're on the take. If you believe the press, we're all corrupt. People believe anything bad said about us. And the hoods know this; they use it to take the opposition out. Even if you aren't corrupt, you're a sitting duck for those who are. That gonna be you, George?"

"Are you saying I should haul everyone in to save my ass?"

"Depends on how fond you are of it."

Marty stuck his head in the door.

"Whatcha got?" asked George.

"A drunk old lady, says her name's Mrs. McCue. Dorset picked her up, though he couldn't find Nibbs. She can barely stand."

"Where does she live?"

"Don't know, sir. And I hesitate to put her in with the four women. Judge Riopelle ain't seen them yet."

"We got any pillows left?"

"Might."

"Put her in that repossessed Cadillac outside. It's warm enough. Let her sleep it off."

"You're not gonna arrest her?" said Alonzo.

"No," said George, "but you can."

"I think I'll pass."

"Picking and choosing, Lon?"

"I don't have an easy answer," said Alonzo.

"Neither do I," said George.

By the end of the night, George had made a number of decisions. In the ensuing weeks, his rules for his department would become clear: no drinking on the job, unless it was to their advantage undercover; avoid arresting drunks, unless they're a danger to themselves or others; no illegal raids on speaks or disorderly houses. No personal vendettas, no abuse of power, no throwing your weight around at a time when it's easy to throw your weight around. If you want to keep your job, keep your hands in your own pockets. The minute you take a bribe, they've got you in their pocket. Talk first, shoot less.

———————

About a month later, following another round of Downriver raids on October 9, Captain Alonzo Gillette noticed a dull, aching, unrelenting pain around his navel but sloughed it off. When the pain shifted and he began to experience sharp jabs in his right abdomen, he still refused to take time off. Maybe later, he said. Not when he was making some headway in his five-year drive to clean up Downriver. On Thursday, November 6, the fever rose, the pain became severe, and he collapsed at work. Taken to Grace Hospital, he was operated on for appendicitis on Friday, contracted pneumonia on Saturday, and died on Sunday, November 9. He was 34. The following Wednesday, George attended his funeral along with all the other chiefs from the cities and villages of Wayne County, as well as Caroline Gillette and her four daughters and the newly elected governor Wilber Brucker. As far as George Moore was concerned, Alonzo Gillette was one more casualty of Prohibition.

Two days after the funeral, on Friday, November 14, George was in his office when Officer Vintner stuck his head in the doorway. "Your son's just been arrested, sir."

Chapter 37

November 14, 1930

Like many young men just starting out, Murph took odd jobs, bought a car, and hired a bodyguard. (Thanks to Charlie Bauer, he'd made a few enemies.) Now 23, he was braver than he ought to be, cockier than he was entitled to be, and, to the disgust of his pals, sappier than he meant to be. For Murph had fallen oh so giddily in love, head over spats. Right down to the white-gold ring, the one with a forget-me-not crowning an aquamarine heart. The object of his affection was a blonde beauty from a working-class neighborhood in southwest Detroit who, though only 19, was giving him a run for his money. She was an Irish lass with Irish sass and a temper to back it up.

The two had only been dating a short time when Murph showed up at her door on Navy Street off Springwells one Monday in March. It was pouring rain. "Peg, that fella's outside and wants to talk to you," said her mother. "Something's wrong. He won't come in." Curious, Peg stepped onto the sheltered porch.

"I'll never forget him standing there," Peg often recalled. "Standing there, soaking wet, and he said, 'My mother died.' Then he grabbed me and started to cry. He cried for hours."

Well, that kind of sealed the deal. They married a few months later on July 19, 1930, Murph's 23rd birthday. He moved out of the Moore house, around the time that he became   maître d' at the Manhattan Club, around the time that his father's career change would cause their conflict to escalate.

––––––––––

Two pivotal events had upended Murph's business: the closing of the Canadian liquor docks and the opening of the Ambassador Bridge. Since the November 15, 1929, dedication of the two-mile-long Ambassador Bridge, the longest international suspension bridge in the world, two minutes was all that was needed to drive from Detroit to Windsor, Canada, though getting past customs with illicit bottles was close to impossible. And the Detroit-Windsor tunnel, which dipped beneath the river, was to open on November 1, 1930. Because of mounting U.S. pressure and the threat of higher tariffs against Canadian products, the Canadian government finally banned the practice of allowing liquor-laden boats bound for American shores to shove off from its wharves. Ten liquor docks, including those at LaSalle, were closed on June 1, 1930, dealing a substantial blow to the profitable Downriver liquor industry.

If their trade hadn't become so ingrained, their way of life so deeply rooted, that might have been the end of it, but many of Ecorse's youthful rum runners had been working in the industry for over 12 years now, 6 for Murph, and legitimate jobs were growing ever more scarce. Unemployment was rampant, especially in the metropolitan area. Auto production had gone from 5 million in 1929 to 3 million in 1930. When a list of places for the unemployed to register was announced in Detroit that September, over 19,000 had signed up by day's end. Within four days, 75,704. The Mayor's Commission on Unemployment, borrowing a plan from New York City, set up vendors (veterans and men with dependents), selling apples for 5 cents each. Michigan suffered more than most states during the Depression. By 1933, total unemployment reached nearly 50%.

With thin résumés, the young rum runners had to quickly regroup. Some began driving to Windsor by way of the bridge, buying allowable quantities of beer from one government store after another, then storing the accumulation in a Canadian farmhouse near the water's edge until they could return by boat to run it across the river. Some bought truckloads directly from Ontario manufacturing plants, then, instead of delivering them to government storehouses for which they were intended, diverted the shipments to luggers on Lake Erie or Lake St. Clair. Some installed stills or appropriated their own bathtubs, flooding the market with dangerous rotgut. And some, including Murph, gazed eastward, toward the province of Quebec.

In other words: *Welcome to New York!* In 1923, Governor Al Smith, who was personally affronted by the 18th Amendment, relieved the police of New York (state and local) of any obligation to enforce the Volstead Act. He, like many officials throughout the nation, felt that the responsibility for the Act's enforcement rested squarely on the shoulders of the Federal government. So, where better to smuggle from Canada than through New York. The three-day trip was certainly an onerous choice - but probably the smartest - if you wanted to avoid having your picture taken and the word *felon* stamped across your kisser.

Thus, about one Tuesday a month, starting that miserably hot June, Murph removed the back seat of an older, confiscatable car, and, with his bodyguard Johnny, set out well before dawn to fill the requests of his customers. Driving over the Ambassador Bridge, they'd cross into the province of Ontario at about 4 a.m. and cross back into the United States at Niagara Falls around noon.

Eight hours down, fourteen to go. And all fourteen would be spent on the single-lane, serpentine roads of upstate New York. They'd skirt the Adirondacks by following the Mohawk Trail from Utica, and just outside Saratoga pick up Route 9 North, known as the Rum Trail, for the 150-mile drive to Overton's Corners Border Station at Rouses Point, the only paved road within miles into Canada.

Arriving in the province of Quebec around 2 a.m. on Wednesday, bums numb, legs rubber, they'd sign into the King Edward Hotel about 14 miles from Rouses Point, sleep through the day, have a late, leisurely dinner at the Brass Knuckle, one of the loading stations near the border, and leave about 10 o'clock at night, fully stocked, with a few bottles of champagne in the running-board tool boxes; Three-Star Hennessy, Canadian Club and White Horse Scotch in the trunk; and multiple cases of Molson's or Carling's or Labatt's where the back seat should be.

In contrast to the busy Windsor-Detroit border crossing, Overton's Corners was in the middle of nowhere, surrounded by flatland and a few trees, and, except for patrols, unguarded at night. Even better, the customs house about a mile south on Principal Street in Rouses Point, where all motorists were expected to stop voluntarily and report, was closed at night, making 10 p.m. an ideal time for passing through.

And that was the last border they had to cross. Because, instead of crossing back at Niagara Falls, they'd turn south at Buffalo, follow Route 20 along the southern shore of Lake Erie into Ohio, take a right at Toledo and arrive in Ecorse around 9 p.m. on a Thursday.

The supreme irony is that after all Murph's travels, he was caught in Ecorse, one Friday night, specifically November 14, 1930, two days after the funeral of Alonzo Gillette. A stranger in a saloon approached George Cordell, owner of the Downriver Boat Works in Ecorse, and asked if he could get his hands on some good Canadian liquor. Cordell, already under indictment for bribing two Customs patrol inspectors, assured the man that he could, then offered Murph $10 to drive two cases of liquor to a designated barn in the boonies. Cordell would follow to pick up the liquor payment and provide backup in case of trouble. When they arrived and the stranger, a Federal undercover agent, was handing Cordell the agreed upon $130 in marked money, three other officers appeared. The sting was for Cordell; Murph just happened to get in the way of the barb.

The next day they pleaded not guilty before J. Stanley Hurd, U.S. Commissioner. Cordell was charged with the sale of liquor and Murph with driving the car that made the delivery. Cordell's bond was set at $5,000, two sureties, and Murph's bond at $2,000, two sureties. As one of the sureties, George put up his share of Agnes's house for the bail money and signed for him. Freda, who along with the other children, had also inherited shares in Agnes's house, used her share as collateral and signed as well.

During his preliminary hearing, Murph, with a straight face, claimed that he'd never been in trouble before, which was not exactly true. There'd been the little incident with Charlie Bauer. As for the current fiasco, he told the judge: "A man in the saloon asked who would deliver some stuff for him. He had been told by another man that I would do it. I was then offered $10 to take two packages to a barn." Their contents, he insisted, were none of his business.

Case dismissed.

Chapter 38

Sunday, November 23, 1930

Miss Munn was coming to dinner on Sunday. Freda planned to make chop suey.

George Moore and Miss Munn had, in fact, struck up something of a friendship during those many hours of office sharing at Ecorse High School. It was often said, especially by Agnes, that George loved the ladies and the ladies loved him. And admittedly George was flattered that someone so attractive, so educated, would give a 6th grade dropout the time of day. But although his continual defense of Miss Munn whenever Agnes criticized her, and Miss Munn's constant canonizing of George, provided the tinder for Agnes's suspicions, it was Agnes's disease that provided the spark. George was a lonely man in need of a kind word. Miss Munn was a soothing presence, a willing ear. Over time, she became his confidante, taking his side no matter what.

They shared an office from March until May. Miss Munn spent her summer at home in Detroit where she lived with her father and sister Ethel. Then one day in September, he'd bumped into her at Seavitt's Drug Store and joined her for lunch. They'd met once again in October for dinner in Detroit, strictly on the Q.T. Then came November and Alonzo's death and Murph's arrest, and George gave Mae a call, telling himself he just needed to talk.

George hadn't mentioned Miss Munn to his girls. Now circumstances were such that unless he wanted to sneak around, have them learn from others, he'd have to make a move. George was no fool; he knew there'd be no rejoicing. He tried to prepare them slowly.

"I ran into Miss Munn yesterday," he had said one night at dinner, apropos of nothing.

"That's nice," said Freda.

A few days later, over scalloped potatoes and ham, he broached the subject once more. "How's this for coincidence? I bumped into Miss Munn again. In Pilon's."

"I bump into her all day long at school. No cause for confetti," grumped Rowe who, wanting to take a commercial course not offered at Lourdes, had entered Ecorse High for her junior year. She was now a senior there and would graduate come June.

A few days later, during dessert:

"Guess who I saw in Seavitt's yesterday?"

"Miss Munn?" asked Rowe, wryly.

"She sure gets around," put in Freda.

Then that night, as he listened to the "R.K.O. Hour" in the sitting room, he idly mentioned her again. Rowe made another crack and he blew his top. "I will not allow you to belittle schoolteachers in my house!"

"This from a man who calls Miss Ranger the Little Sparrow," muttered Rowe.

"Damn it, Auntie! I don't know why you girls don't like her," carped George.

"It's not just us," retorted Freda. "Mumma couldn't stand her, either."

"But that's no reason!" blurted George. "Look," he said, toning it down. "I don't know any other way to say this . . . but I think your mother had a blind spot."

"A blind spot!" protested Rowe.

"Yes, a blind spot," quarreled George. "I don't think she ever really knew her."

"Oh, she knew her all right," snapped Freda with surprising force. "She knew her better than you!"

"Yes, well . . ." said George, retreating. "I just think you should give her a chance."

That weekend, George sprinkled his dinner conversation with so many Miss Munns that Freda's casseroles all tasted the same—bitter. And, on Monday last, while dining over spaghetti and meatballs, George had dropped the bomb. He hoped they didn't mind, he said, especially Freda who'd have to do all the planning, but he'd invited Miss Munn for dinner on Sunday. He thought it would make a nice change.

The reaction was surprisingly muted. Shay looked to Freda for a response. So did Dia, Rowe and Joyce. But Freda, sitting motionless, was gazing downward, intent on her fork, while Marce was splitting a meatball.

"Is that all you're going to say?" asked George, which was an odd comment since nothing had yet been said.

"What should I cook?" asked Freda.

"How about your chop suey?" sang George with false gusto. "You make a great chop suey."

"Okay."

"And perhaps a pineapple salad."

"Pineapple salad?"

"You know. A ring of pineapple on a bed of lettuce, cottage cheese on top."

"Okay."

"She specifically asked for that."

George had intentionally told them on a Monday, giving them ample time to digest the news but not enough time to change the wallpaper. As late as Saturday night, the night before the day, it was still sticking in Freda's craw. Around ten-thirty, as she and Rowe sat in the kitchen after a full day of cleaning, waiting for the potatoes to boil for their father's customary Sunday breakfast (fried potatoes, New York ham and eggs), Freda was fuming, her innate good nature parked somewhere in Ann Arbor.

"I can't believe he's bringing that woman to our house tomorrow," said Freda, attempting to fork a rock-hard potato.

"Don't worry," counseled Rowe. "Once he gets to know her, he'll run for the hills."

"But it's Mumma's house; he don't own it. She'll be sitting in Mumma's chair."

"Over my dead body," said Rowe. Then, for the umpteenth time, they redid the seating. Their father would sit at the head of the table and Freda would sit in their mother's place opposite, near the buffet and kitchen archway, the better to serve. And since Dia was always placed to the right of George, they kept her there. Dia had a tendency to spill.

> "We had a big pitcher of water that sat between Dia and my dad," said Rowe. "And invariably she'd knock her glass of water over. 'Cuz she was so nervous. And he says, 'Do that again and I'll give you a good clip,' and, cripes, then she'd knock the pitcher over."

So Dia was placed to the right of George, upwind of his clipping hand, but where to put Miss Munn? Both agreed that it would be ill-advised to seat her next to Marce who, though angelic-looking, had the capacity to surprise; both agreed that the best recourse was to cram her between Shay and Joyce; and both were floored when Shay and Joyce said it was fine by them. Truth be told, the younger girls were looking forward to the dinner, though they didn't let on. Miss Munn was pretty, had caused them no grief, and a guest for dinner meant better eats.

Rowe put pen to paper and drew up the seating arrangements. Then she repeated her soothing certainty, "Wait'll he gets to know her," as the potatoes boiled. She would have bet the house on that.

————

On Sunday morning, Freda woke before dawn to a dark and frigid room, awash in so much resentment she could barely roll over. She deeply resented having to get up early; deeply resented having to hightail it to 7:30 mass, in the cold, in the dark; and oh so deeply resented having spent her entire Saturday, her precious day off, cleaning the entire house, only to have to turn around and spend her entire Sunday serving a large meal. For that woman?

Even the weather seemed put out. The preceding week had been sunny and pleasant, in the 60s. On Saturday, the temperature had plunged, as if in pique, barely reaching 44, and Sunday promised more of the same. The overnight thermometer had dropped to freezing.

Rowe stirred, then shivered. "Geezus, it's cold. What time's the pill coming?"

"She'll be here at two."

"Geez, Freds, why didn't you wake me!" said Rowe, checking the clock. "Now, we'll never make it to early mass."

"Then go to nine and take the kids," said Freda.

"Me?"

"I'm not going."

It was the only act of rebellion afforded her.

Breakfast was on the table when the family returned from mass, but Freda made it abundantly clear there was to be no lingering. George, feeling guilty, bolted his potatoes, gulped his coffee, grabbed the Sunday paper (minus the cartoon section) and left by way of the back door, muttering something about the police station, something about making himself scarce. Then Marce (plus the cartoon section) was passed on to a willing Ella, to get her out from underfoot.

Soon cubes of pork and veal were hissing and spitting in the Dutch oven, their fatty aroma seeping through the house, while Freda, in one of her mother's housedresses, barked orders like Nelson at Trafalgar..

"Shay, get the phone!" she yelled, as she dissected a large, sweet onion. "And where's them mushrooms, Dia?"

"Be right up!" came a muffled voice from the pantry below.

"And I'll need a can of water chestnuts, that bottle of shoyu sauce and a bag of rice!"

"Cripes, Freds, I only got two hands!" came Dia's muffled reply.

"It's Mrs. Pilon for Pa!" Shay shouted from two rooms away.

"Tell her he's not here," returned Freda. "Tell her he'll call her back!"

Rowe, who was sitting at the kitchen table, chopping celery, had been grousing all morning, endlessly listing all the things they could be doing instead. "We could be going to the show like we always do." Chop, chop, chop. "We could be seeing *Hell's Angels*."

Joyce, on the other hand, ambled about the kitchen humming "Tea for Two" in a world of her own. In charge of dessert, the 14-year-old had settled on a somewhat elegant, somewhat elaborate dish, one that called for three distinct stages of preparation and required four hours to reach fruition. Though admittedly ambitious, she would not be dissuaded.

That morning, before church, she had crawled out of bed to boil a cup of water in a saucepan, then drizzled the steaming liquid directly over the contents of the mixing bowl with care, dissolving the orange powder from the two boxes of Jell-O previously poured in. She stirred, added a cup of cold water then stirred again, and apportioned the Jell-O, scrupulously and equitably by ladle, into all eight of Agnes's Pedro goblets, the ones ringed in lace. Having done all this well, she had cautiously descended the stairs, employing both hands on the tray as she went, while conveying the goblets with the orange watery mix to nature's ice-box, the unheated basement below, whereupon she set the tray delicately on the enamel counter of the old kitchen cabinet and consulted her watch, comforted in the knowledge that she had afforded the gelatin plenty of time to chill.

Now, less than two hours later, having retrieved the tray of goblets from below, having placed it on the upstairs counter, having consulted her watch once more, she was finally folding into all eight portions of the partially stiffened Jell-O, the contents from one can of Del Monte's fruit cocktail, the key ingredient that would turn an ordinary dessert into *haute cuisine*.

"Hey, Freeds!" came a voice from the next room.

"Yeah?"

"Should I use Mumma's good dishes?" hollered Shay, standing before the built-in hutch in the dining room, staring at the Blue Willow.

"Yeah!" bellowed Freda.

"We could be upstairs reading," groused Rowe. Chop, chop, chop. "We could be hangin' out with Helen and Hollis."

"Did you bring up the bamboo shoots?" asked Freda, as Dia came through the downstairs doorway, arms loaded.

"You didn't ask for bamboo shoots."

"I didn't think I needed to."

"Aw, Freeds, " groaned Dia, passing off her load, turning for the stairs. "Why don'tcha just make a list?"

"I ain't got no time for a list," muttered Freda, tossing a spoonful of sugar in with the browning meat. "And see if you can find that can of Oriental veg-etables."

"Hey, Freeds!" hollered Shay from the next room.

"Yeah?"

"Which tablecloth should I use?"

"The white one!" bellowed Freda.

Rowe sat bolt upright, aghast. "The white one! You can't use the white one, Freda. That's our everyday one."

"So?"

"So. That's been mended so often, the plates tilt."

"So."

"We can't use it, Freda," said Rowe.

"We have to. It's all we got."

"No, it isn't."

"Yes, it is."

"What about Mumma's yellow one?" asked Rowe.

"Nope."

"Whaddya mean, *nope*? We have to."

"No, we don't. No, we don't. 'Cause I'll tell you right now, Miss Priss," hissed Freda, training a wooden spoon directly on Rowe. "We ain't usin' Mumma's good tablecloth. She gave it to me for my hope chest."

"But, Freedo," broke in Joyce.

"Not for her, not for her," wailed Freda, whiplashing Joyce's way. "And I wish you'd asked before using Mumma's good goblets. I'da said no."

"Oh, that's just dandy," cried Joyce. "And just what was I sposed to put the Jell-O in?"

"Keep your voices down. Pa might come back," cautioned Rowe.

"Keep my voice down; I'll keep my voice down," said Freda, keeping her voice down within an inch of Joyce's nose. "You coulda used the Pyrex custard cups. You coulda used the juice glasses. And I hope to God you drained the juice."

"I may be many things, Rowe," Joyce finally replied, "but I'm not stupid."

"Aw c'mon, you guys, quit your squawkin'." groused Joyce. "It's my dessert, not yours."

"Okay, okay, we're using Mumma's goblets," said Freda. "But we ain't usin' her tablecloth."

"Freda, we have to," said Rowe.

"Why?" challenged Freda. "Give me one good reason."

"For Pa," said Rowe.

"Rowe's right," said Joyce, carefully picking up the Jell-O tray. "Do it for Pa." And while Freda sat down at the kitchen table, the blood draining from her face, Joyce walked gingerly toward the basement door and exited cautiously down the steps, passing Dia, arms loaded, on her way back up.

Freda had no comeback. Her look belied all 22 of her years. She appeared drawn, tired, near tears. She often said she'd do anything for her father, but never in a million years did she think it would be this. For the rest of the day, Freda had no choice but to bury her resentment, bury it deep. Miss Munn would soon be a guest in their house.

"Shay," said Freda, voice flat.

"Yeah?" returned Shay, leaning in from the dining room, silverware in hand.

"Use the yellow one."

"But I already put down the white one!"

"I know," said Freda. "But use the yellow one."

"Well, make up your mind!"

"And if you spill anything on it, Dia," said Freda. "I'll kill ya."

"What did I do!"

By noon, George was back from the police station, and if his jitters didn't tell them all they needed to know about the state of things, his short fuse should have.

"Anyone see my cuff links?" he shouted, standing in his bedroom door.

"They're where you left them!" yelled Rowe from the kitchen.

"And where is that!"

"On your dresser!"

"I looked on my dresser!"

"How hard!" brayed Rowe, who then turned to Freda and muttered, "I don't know what's worse. Getting this dinner ready. Or him."

They'd never seen anything like it.

Was this the same man who, just last Thursday, had to clean up after a particularly grisly car-train accident at the railroad crossing on Mill, who had to deal with three bodies, including a mother and her young son, then inform the daughter of the deaths when she returned home from a friend's house that night, unaware? Was this the same man who had remained outwardly calm through the whole thing, though it went right to his gut? Mr. Nerves of Steel, they called him. Now he was a basket case.

First it was his spats. He'd taken to wearing spats, six-button jobs, because Miss Munn happened to say she liked spats. Then he couldn't find his comb. There was a tall mirror on the narrow wall by the front door and he kept a comb on top of it. Then he remembered her cigarettes. He wanted to have her brand in the house, just in case, so he asked Shay to run over to Seavitt's and get a pack of Marlboros (whose ads were targeting women with such slogans as "Ivory Tips protect the lips" or "Mild as May.") Oh, and some Emeraude Perfume. Her favorite. That would be nice. Get her a bottle of Emeraude perfume. Then he wondered aloud if it was too soon for perfume. Better skip the Emeraude. Oh, and breath mints. He needed some breath mints.

"Sen-Sen?" asked Shay.

"Sen-Sen'll be fine," he said, handing her five bucks with instructions to hurry and a warning to bring back the change.

Five minutes later, realizing the time, he shifted into shrill. Where was Shay? What was taking so long? Didn't she know he had to pick up Miss Munn? Wasn't she aware he had to drive all the way to Detroit. Didn't she realize he'd never make it if he didn't leave now?

"Here she comes, Pa," said Joyce.

By Freda's calculations, they had an hour and a half at best before the "grande damn" arrived. By now, the house was so tense that the joists were strained, the lintels on edge and the doors unhinged. Freda's notions of what could go wrong were getting the upper hand, and she became evermore unglued with each clockward glance.

While thickening the chop suey, she bemoaned the fact that she hadn't made it the day before, bewailed the fact that it was always better the second day, and interlaced each spoonful of corn starch with a stream of warnings: everyone was to keep an eye on Marce; everyone was to serve Miss Munn to her left in lieu of her missing right forearm.

"And Dia?" said Freda.

"Yeah."

"If you spill your water. . ."

"Count on it," said Rowe, scraping overtoasted triangles.

"Yeah, well, fine," came back Dia. "I won't drink no water. Does that satisfy ya, Rowe? I won't drink no water, so I won't have nothin' to spill."

"We could be going to the movies," muttered Rowe. "We could be over at Ella's, reading cartoons with Marce."

"Hey, Freeds!" came a voice from the next room.

"Yeah?"

"Come look at my table!" yelled Shay.

When Freda entered the dining room to inspect Shay's handiwork, she was stunned. The table looked splendid beneath the burning chandelier; the setting was all Agnes: her yellow tablecloth with matching yellow napkins, her Blue Willow plates, her floral celery tray, her eight salt cellars, her linen centerpiece topped with her cut-glass sugar and creamer, and her 1847 Rogers Bros. silver-plated tableware, Berkshire pattern, fresh from its silk-lined box and polished the day before. And all this would eventually be joined by eight of Agnes's Pedro goblets, now sitting on the kitchen cabinet downstairs. Thickening. It was hoped.

"Whaddya think?" asked Shay.

"You done good," said Freda, trying to hide her sadness in light of Shay's eager face.

By the time Joyce retrieved Marce and took her upstairs to change and Freda had donned her best Sunday dress and a clean apron, there was still a mound of last-minute details to contend with.

"Is the shoyu sauce on the table?" asked Freda, rushing to get the folding stepladder stool.

"Yeah," said Shay.

"Is there a dish under it?"

"Yeah."

"There'd better be 'cuz that stuff stains," said Freda, banging open the ladder, giving Dia the eye. "And would somebody get the phone."

"I got it!" yelled Joyce.

Then Freda asked Joyce who that was on the phone and Joyce said Mrs. Pilon again and Freda asked what she wanted and Joyce said Pa. "And does anyone know if that dang Jell-O's jelling?" asked Freda, standing on the head step, securing her footing.

"Don't worry, it's cold enough in the basement," muttered Joyce.

"It's cold enough up here," said Shay.

"I'm too damn nervous to be cold," griped Freda, straining on tiptoe, struggling to reach the serving dish, causing the ladder to sway. Suddenly, all questioning ceased.

It would be hard to say who made it downstairs first. Dia was nearly flattened on her way up.

Freda threw open the upper furnace door and beheld—well—nothing much, just a couple of waning embers begging for oxygen. "Geezus, Rowe. Pa's gonna kill us."

"How much time we got?" asked Freda.

"Ten minutes, if we're lucky," replied Rowe.

"Then open the damper full-out!" roared Freda, crumpling last Sunday's *News* from the pile stacked near the furnace, tossing it in, tossing in wood scraps, lighting it, fanning it with her apron. "Joyce! Dia! Get some wood."

"From where?"

"Anywhere! Shay!"

"Yeah?"

"Get upstairs, light the oven and leave the door open!"

"Right," said Shay, running up the steps.

"Wood. We need wood!" yelled Freda.

Backyard twigs went in, broken pickets went in, the yardstick from Gardner's Hardware, snapped in two, went in.

"Geezus, Rowe. It's still not catching," moaned Freda.

"How about the old Jell-O tray?" offered Rowe.

"How am I gonna serve the Jell-O!" wailed Joyce.

"You won't be serving the damn Jell-O if the Jell-O doesn't set," griped Rowe. "Has it set?"

"Almost."

"Almost!" screamed Rowe. "I gotta ask, Joyce, I gotta ask. Did you drain the damn fruit cocktail?"

"Damn it, Rowe, I drained the can. All right? I drained the can."

"Wood!" yelled Freda. "We need wood!"

The doorstop went in; an old wicker basket went in; Mrs. Lyall's *A Hardy Norseman* went in; but when Rowe grabbed the long-handled scooper to add some coal, Freda bodily barred the furnace door. "There's not enough fire yet."

"Yeah, there is."

"No, Rowe. There's not," said Freda.

"Well, whether there is or isn't is neither here nor there, don't you think?" singsonged Rowe. "Seeing as how they'll be here any minute."

"Okay, smart guy, but only four lumps. And put 'em way in back or you'll smother it."

Which is exactly what happened.

"The piano was going to go in next," said Rowe, "anything to get that damn fire going again."

Chapter 39

Three minutes later

It was the first thing out of their father's mouth after he came through the front door and relieved Miss Munn of her coat.

"Did you let the fire go out?"

"Well, almost," mumbled Rowe.

He threw them a familiar look; it was easy to interpret. Then Marce whined "I'm cold" and took a punch in the small of her back, while Freda excused herself, citing the rolls, hurried into the privacy of the kitchen and leaned against the sink to calm down.

Bellies growling, hands like ice, the sisters spent the first 20 minutes in the chilly parlor, some on the couch, one on the piano bench, one sitting decorously on a hauled-in kitchen chair, working to supply the next sentence, hoping for a follow-up. Dia frequently passed the canapés (toast triangles with pimento spread), calling them as close to *can o' pee* as she dared, listening to Miss Munn rave about how nice the house looked, about the wonderful job Freda was doing. Six-year-old Marce, unobserved in the center of the couch, was observing Miss Munn, specifically the way she kept her right arm cradled in her lap while her left hand did all the work.

Though George was a bundle of nerves under his merry manner, Miss Munn was full of smiles and her *lovelies* abounded. In no time at all, each of the younger girls, those who had not had her for a teacher, found themselves questioning the legitimacy of Freda and Rowe's take on "Old Lady Munn." She seemed perfectly fine, and there was nothing "Old Lady" about her.

She was dressed to perfection in a long-sleeved, square-neck, green-print frock, probably from the Better Dresses Shop at Hudson's, certainly in the new fall style (the waist was no longer down around the hips but back where a waist used to be). She was very tall, very handsome, very pleasant, and had a light, lilting laugh, nothing like the ogre they'd heard about. It was hard to imagine her picking up a kid and throwing him down the aisle. Then again, Rowe always did exaggerate.

As she made the rounds, asking each of them about school, the schoolteacher seemed utterly intrigued by all they had to say, delighted by their every quip, and had the captivating habit of leaning in and gazing upward at the speaker, so as not to miss a single word.

Meanwhile, Rowe, who was still under Miss Munn's pedagogical thumb, excused herself often in the guise of helping Freda, while Freda, huddling near the open broiler, simmering along with the tea kettle, spent as much time in the kitchen as she could possibly get away with.

When Freda finally managed a feeble, "Supper's ready," they all adjourned to the icy dining room with enormous relief.

Joyce brought in the steaming bowl of fluffy white rice and it was passed round; then Freda brought in the rich brown chop suey, piping hot in its serving dish, and it was passed round; then Rowe circled the table, filling each cup (including Dia's) with steeping oolong tea. As a result of the cold, the room weathered as much condensation as a Trans-Siberian coffee shop.

"Would you like a sweater, Miss Munn," asked George.

"I'm fine, George," said Miss Munn.

George? No one blinked. Outwardly. But to hear Miss Munn call their father *George* instead of *Mr. Moore* was enough to set off giggles. Even George was ill at ease, aware his daughters might be uncomfortable with the maiden voyage of his Christian name.

Shay was the first to crack. Before the Parker House rolls could travel the circuit, she lunged forward to snag one, only to recall, with her hand thus thrust, Freda's many advisories about boarding-house reach. To mask her brazenness, she retrieved the entire breadbasket, then politely turned to her right, as if that were her original intent, and offered the schoolteacher first dibs.

"Would you like a Parker House roll, Miss Munn?" she asked, in a tone usually reserved for communions or confirmations.

"Thank you, dear," said Miss Munn who retrieved a hot, buttery roll and passed the basket to Joyce on her right. The rolls made their sluggish way around the entire table until they got to Marce, who didn't have the sense to pass them on, and Freda was too paralyzed to notice.

Then to everyone's alarm, Dia picked up the shoyu bottle from the saucer. Having served herself without mishap, she offered it to Miss Munn who offered to try it, "dear." So Dia put the Shoyu bottle back on the saucer while everyone quietly inhaled, picked up the saucer with much ceremony while everyone held their breath, walked round to the other side of the table with new-found decorum while everyone still held their breath, and set it before Miss Munn with measured poise while everyone exhaled. Dia then returned to her place, sat down daintily, vigorously jacked herself back and forth three times to reposition her chair, only to have Rowe subvert her effort by side mouthing, "You coulda passed it," which seemed a little unkind, coming from someone who'd once been chosen to crown the Blessed Virgin. Then Miss Munn reached for the bottle of shoyu with its dual pouring spouts, turned it sideways to pour a little and the black liquid gushed out in a stream.

All pretended not to notice.

"I'm cold," said Marce, rubbing her upper arms for circulation. "Hey! Stop kickin'!"

"Sure you don't need a sweater, Miss Munn?" said George.

"I'm fine. Truly," said Miss Munn, pinching her napkin with two fingers of her left hand, laying it over her lap.

And they all finally dug in.

Despite an occasional tableside elbow, an occasional munch with an open mouth, and intermittent cold weather updates put forth by Marce, things picked up. Indeed, everything was ambling along just fine until Dia got started. Then again, how often does a 12-year-old get to chat over chop suey with a school principal, get to demonstrate the width and breadth of her erudition? Dia was taking full advantage.

"Didja read about that woman found in the river by Slab Island, murdered? Tex Buxton found her while duck hunting. By my count, that's the sixth floater this year. One fed, three rum runners, and two ladies-in-waiting."

"Ladies-in-waiting?" said Miss Munn.

"That's what Pa calls 'em. Sure thought our bootlegging days were over once they closed the LaSalle docks. Didn't you, Miss Munn?"

"I think we all did, dear," replied Miss Munn. "Especially your father."

"Who'da thunk it. Now they're using planes," said Dia, shaking her head, marveling at the ingenuity, warming her hand over her teacup while everyone held their breath. "Forty cases of hooch. Can you beat that? Forty cases of hooch on every flight across. Right, Pa?"

"That's what they tell me," said George.

"Ever hear of Miserable Whitey and Teargas Johnny, Miss Munn?" asked Dia.

Miss Munn smiled at George. "Can't say that I have, dear."

"Bet they don't come to PTA," smiled Joyce, collegially.

"Actually, they might," said George, forking a piece of pork. "Miserable Whitey lives over on Elton and has ten kids. Other than bootlegging, he's a pretty straight-up guy."

"I see by the papers they're opening Toytown at Hudson's," interposed Joyce, in an attempt to raise the level of discourse. "Have you ever seen Toytown, Miss Munn? On the 12th floor?"

But Dia was on a roll and Hudson's would not do. She allowed Miss Munn sufficient time for a response, allowed Joyce a brief rejoinder, then relaunched.

"Ever hear of the snatch racket, Miss Munn?"

"The what, dear?"

"Where they take guys for a ride."

Rowe stared at Freda for some moments before her eyes slowly crossed behind her glasses.

"Why, they're yankin' guys off the street right and left," continued Dia, so wound up that she picked up her empty water glass, then grinned goofily as she set it down again. "Can you believe it, Miss Munn? Somebody even took Lefty Clark for a ride a couple years back. Had to pay forty grand ransom. You know

Lefty Clark, Miss Munn?"

"I know *of* him."

"Big time gambler. Really nice."

"You're on a first-name basis with Mr. Clark?" asked George.

"Heck, ya. He's always in Lafferty's butcher shop, buyin' meat, sending it to people who need it, and, if you're lucky, he'll take ya next door to C.F. Smith's and buy you a candy bar. Everybody knows he's a soft touch. He's always buyin' Mary Dalton's little sister Dorothy a Pie Face."

Rowe stared at Freda again for more moments before executing an eye roll.

The phone rang in George's bedroom and Rowe went to get it ("Pa, it's Mrs. Pilon.") and George said to tell her he'd call her back; then Dia got right back to it.

"Why, just this month, they got a bigshot bootlegger in Lincoln Park. Can you believe it, Miss Munn?"

"All right, Blackie, that's enough," said George.

"This is a lovely dinner, my dear," said Miss Munn, leaning in toward Freda, graciously smiling. "Just lovely. And the chop suey's *marvelous* . Would you write the recipe down for me, dear?"

"Sure," said Freda.

"Wonderful," said Miss Munn. "Then Rowe can bring it to my office Monday, during school." Apparently oblivious of the lag preceding Rowe's mumbled, "Sure," Miss Munn used her teacherly skills to steer the conversation in a different direction, resurrecting that old conversational saw, What do you want to be when you grow up? She had gone around the table and elicited a variety of responses: housewife from Freda; interior decorator from Joyce; actress from Rowe, who had belonged to the Dramatic Club at Our Lady of Lourdes.

Shay, née Shirley, was eagerly waiting her turn. She knew what she wanted to be, had known for years, and was exceedingly proud of her chosen profession. She was a little annoyed when Freda stood up and began clearing the dinner plates with needless clack and clatter. Worse, Rowe began to stack as well, and Freda announced that the impending dessert course was hardening in the cold of the basement and that Joyce would now go down to retrieve it. Miss Munn scored *beaucoup* points when she turned to Shay and said, "Your turn, Shirley."

"What do I want to be when I grow up?" said Shay, standing at the line, bouncing the ball, preparing to serve.

"Yes."

"Ummmm," she said, stalling, because for one thing Freeds was still banging around the kitchen and for another Marce was looking shifty, which meant there was a darn good chance there'd be interference between the toss and the serve.

Freda finally came into the dining room, wiping her hands on her apron.

"Sit, Freda, or we'll be here all night," said Rowe.

"What do I want to be when I grow up?" repeated Shay. She tossed the ball into the air and served one right down the middle. "A barber," she said.

"A barber," trilled Miss Munn. "Don't you mean a beauty operator?"

"No. A barber."

"But girls aren't barbers, dear," said Miss Munn, leaning toward Shay, smiling kindly upward. "You mean a hairdresser."

"I guess," said Shay, looking toward her father for help.

There were women barbers, of course. Though rare, they did exist. George thought about saying something, almost did, then thought better of it. Correcting a teacher in front of his children was probably not a good idea.

"And what do you want to be?" said Miss Munn, turning to Dia.

Now it might be said that Dia had also been waiting her turn in eager anticipation, but it wouldn't be true. In reality, she had been lying in wait. "A gangster's moll," she grinned, while her mole grinned with her.

"Either that or a fence," muttered Rowe.

The resulting laughter was cut short by a *Crash!*

"What the hell was that!" cried George, before begging Miss Munn's pardon.

"I'm all right!" came the shrill assurance from below.

Despite this A-1 guarantee, Rowe and Dia leapt from their chairs, tore through the kitchen, and could be heard racing down the basement steps, though their thundering hooves seemed to halt halfway.

"Wellll," elongated George, after a significant interval.

"She's all right!" confirmed Rowe from down under.

"Glad to hear it!" yelled George. "But what isn't?"

"Joyce just knocked over a jar!" yelled Dia.

"Don't worry, Pa, I'll clean it up!" yelled Joyce.

"What jar?" inquired George of those remaining at the table. All offered a collective shrug. "What jar!" yelled George.

"A pickle jar!" came Dia's belated reply.

Normally George would have demanded more in the way of details, but something told him to cut the interrogation short, hold the inquest later. Instead, he turned to Miss Munn and inquired after the well-being of her sister Ethel.

To her credit, Joyce had made it downstairs without incident. Then, positioning herself before the kitchen cabinet opposite the stairs, she had gazed down at the tray which contained the eight Pedro goblets, standing like bowling pins on their delicate stems, and squared her feet in prudent preparation. Firmly gripping the tray's side handles, she had wisely taken a deep breath, then carefully—oh, so carefully—picked up the heavy tray which held the eight goblets, waited for the orange gelatin to stop quivering and the goblets to stop rattling and with the tray carefully balanced before her, turned and tripped.

The result: a 2-3-5-7-8 split. Five pins standing, three in the gutter.

Of the five that had dug in their heels, only subtle damage had occurred.

Having glanced, one against the other, three had microscopic nicks along their rims, while two bore minor chipping on their feet. Of the three lying on their sides, one of them had a broken stem. In consequence, it was shoeless.

"Oh, lord," moaned Joyce, frozen to the tray, unable to move for fear of additional breakage. "Pa's gonna kill me."

"Freda's gonna kill you," amended Rowe, while righting two of the downed goblets and passing off the broken one for Dia to hold. "Those were Ma's glasses, you nincompoop."

"What'll we do now?" whispered Dia.

"I need to think" muttered Rowe.

"But we can't serve these," whined Joyce. "What if there's broken glass in the Jell-O?"

"We can only hope," cracked Rowe.

Upstairs, the long, discomfiting wait was testing George's patience, so he sent Shay to the landing to investigate. "Just like they said, Pa," she bellowed. "Everything's fine. They're comin' right up." Then she, too, disappeared.

Rowe was the first to emerge beneath the dining room arch, her head held high, her mouth pressed tight, the tray of stemware before her. Dia followed close behind, while Joyce, all business, hurried in and quickly took her seat. Then, as Rowe held the tray, Dia placed a goblet of orange Jell-O before Miss Munn (Oh, how lovely), then Joyce, then George, then Marce, then Freda, whose eyes visibly widened as she got a glimpse of her mother's goblet, purposefully served chip-side forward. Then Rowe placed hers before her plate, set the tray on the dining room buffet, and primly smoothed the back of her dress as she sat down, as did Dia, just as primly.

Shay entered the dining room, even more primly, carrying her own orange goblet prettily in her fist by the footless stem. She, too, took her seat at the table and, ignorant of etiquette, waiting for no one, picked up her spoon and hungrily dug in.

As Shay hatched a plan to rid herself of the footless goblet, a minor event occurred which trumped broken stemware. To everyone's relief, Marce had finally warmed up as the house warmed up, had finally shut up about her discomfort, and, with dinner winding down, had finally grown quiet. Shay, who'd been keeping an eye on her, was the only one to notice, however, that Marce was too quiet. And a little too absorbed with Miss Munn's inert arm, the one she kept on her lap.

As Shay held tight to her Jell-O stem, there was a slow and terrible dawning: Marce had never met Miss Munn, had not been told about the empty sleeve and was sitting across from her, on the bias, fuse lit. With a little luck, Dia would spill her tea.

Head erect, Shay did a slit-eyed swivel leftward to see if Freda had noticed, but Freda was playing gracious hostess. Shay looked to her father, but his attention, as it had been throughout dinner, was primarily on Miss Munn.

Then Marce slowly raised her hand. She had a question for the teacher. Desperate, Shay gave Freda the boot. Freda, whirling round, followed Shay's gaze to Marce's upraised hand, followed Marce's gaze to Miss Munn and, in that one bank shot, grasped Marce's intent, entire. Freda grabbed at any straw she could find, deflecting Marce's oncoming question superbly.

"What did you do this morning, Marcie? While you were over at Ella's?"

"Played," said Marce.

"With who? Your little friend?" asked Freda, suddenly sounding like Miss Munn but without benefit of syntactic counsel. "Marcie has a little friend. Don't you, Marcie? Tell Miss Munn about your little friend."

"What little friend?" asked Marce.

"Kenny Pilon," said Freda.

"He's not my friend."

"Oh, he is, too," scoffed Freda. "You're always playing with him."

"Not anymore."

"But you just played with him yesterday."

"Not anymore."

"Did you get in a scrap with Kenny again?" asked George, setting down his goblet. "The two of you are always scrapping."

"He started it," said Marce.

"And who finished it?" asked George.

"I did. I told him off."

"What did you tell him?"

"I told him to go fuck a dead horse."

"I see," said George. And if there'd been a cyanide capsule stashed between his back molars, he'd have bitten down hard.

"Where Marce heard that, I'll never know," said Dia, 60 years on. "She was only six. This was in 1930 and that word wasn't bandied about as it is today."

Chapter 40

June 1931

Though school was out for Shirley Anne Moore, there was no joy in Mooreville. The month of June promised to be long, wet and buggy. On the first Monday of summer vacation she sat brooding on the top step of her front porch under cloudy skies, randomly swatting at gnats, aimlessly observing the passing show. Mrs. Brown was out pruning her hedge; an aging Dempsey was over in Ouellette's side yard, snoozing; and Mrs. Gregory was going in and out of her house, shaking out rugs from her porch, music from her radio punctuated with every swing of the screen door. Shay slapped her palms together in front of her eyes, checked for bodies, but came up short. Seconds later, she was seeing spots again.

There was no sense going inside; she'd get no sympathy there. Rowe, newly graduated from Ecorse High and unhappily in charge, was the only one home. Everyone else had eagerly bolted and Freda was working at Pilon's. Besides, Shay'd twice been told to stop being pesky, to take her long face and park it.

It wasn't a case of nothing to do. There was plenty to do. She could read; she could skate; she could round up enough players to field a baseball game. It was more a case of nothing *would* do. Nothing, that is, except what Shay urgently wanted to do. Unfortunately, it involved approaching someone at the risk of being thought nuts. Over the course of the morning she'd worked up the nerve any number of times, asking herself what's the worst that could happen, only to be warned by a naysaying voice: You could be turned down flat.

Finally, just to hush the mind and shake the gnats, she stood up and brushed off the back of her dress. Then she walked down the Moore steps, cut across Monroe and Labadie, walked up Mrs. Gregory's steps, knocked on the screen door, copped a peek into the darkened interior, then turned her back on the door, the better to affect nonchalance, as she listened to Libby Holman crooning to her lover on Mrs. Gregory's radio, imploring him to give her something to remember him by, when he was far away from her, dear.

"Who is it?" came a voice from somewhere deep inside.

"Shirley," shouted Shay. "Shirley Moore."

"Just a second, Shirley."

Then Miss Holman ceased keening, Shay stiffened, and Mrs. Gregory came to the screen door, wiping her hands on her apron. "Yes?" Honest-faced and firm of jaw, she had deeply etched smile lines around her mouth like parentheses.

"Sorry to bother you, Mrs. Gregory. But I was just wondering. . . Do you need any help?"

"Help?" Mrs. Gregory looked bewildered. "Doing what?"

"Cleaning. I'm good at beating rugs, and I can wash windows, vacuum, carry buckets."

"Gee, I don't know," faltered Mrs. Gregory. "I'd have to think about it."

"That's okay. I just thought I'd ask," said Shay, swiftly spinning round, tumbling down the steps, reaching the sidewalk, turning to face her. "Just in case, you know. I had a little time on my hands, you know."

"But you were right to ask, Shirley," said Mrs. Gregory, warmly. "Who knows? If things weren't so tight right now, I might have said yes."

"Oh, not for money!"

"Then why?"

"Just for the heck of it."

"You're offering to help me clean . . . just for the heck of it?"

"Yes."

"Is it because you like to help? Or because you like to clean?"

"Both."

Mrs. Gregory stared at her, puzzled, taking it all in. Then she laughed, a light, fluty laugh. "Well," she said. "I was just about to roll back the rug. Would that interest you?"

"Sure would."

"Then, c'mon up, grab a broom," said Mrs. Gregory, holding the screen door wide open. "You don't happen to know how to get ink off a white shirt do you?"

"Boil it in cream of tartar," replied Shay, as the screen door banged shut behind them.

And that's how Shirley Anne Moore started working for that divorced trollop, Mrs. Gregory.

Then, on Tuesday, while buying a hunk of baloney in Pilon's, Shay noticed the oranges still in their box and their bin devoid of its pyramid.

"Want me to stack those for you, Mr. Pilon?"

"Naw, Shirley, I'll get to them soon," said Fred Pilon, tying her parcel with string. "They just came in."

"You sure? . . . I'm good at it."

"You are, eh?"

"Yep."

"How good?"

"Want me to show you?"

"Only if you're not expecting a paycheck," he laughed.

"No. Just for the heck of it."
"Then they're all yours."

––––––––––

On the following Monday, she helped Freda, then Ella, with the wash—just for the heck of it. On Tuesday, after the delivery trucks had come and gone, she stacked more fruit at Pilon's. On Thursday, she joined Mrs. Gregory in a good scour. And when visiting friends, she generally could be found in their kitchens, sweeping their floors. Just for the heck of it.

> *"I used to love to go into someone's house and clean it," recalled Shay. "I'd go to Brazill's. I'd do the dishes. I'd go to the store for her mother. And I always had a big feeling of accomplishment when I ironed."*

But where she really wanted to help out, where she longed to employ her own brand of elbow grease, was at a place called Bess-Ann's—though she knew it was just a pipedream. Why? Because only three weeks ago, under difficult circumstances, she'd blown her best chance.

––––––––––

Most of the businesses along Front Street were on the lower floor of no-fuss Victorian houses or no-fuss Victorian commercial buildings, typically of brick, with long flat roofs and fixed-glass storefronts. Second floors contained residential apartments or the offices of doctors, lawyers and real-estate agents. Seavitt's was no exception. Above Seavitt's drugstore,[1] the second floor was divided in two: a residential apartment overlooked Front Street (sometimes residential, sometimes a dental office), while, in back, Bess-Ann's Beauty Parlor overlooked the side of a little brick house and was just across the street from George's old barbershop. Shay glanced up at that beauty shop eighty times a day.

But, as of May, there had been three obvious obstacles: Shay had never been inside Bess-Ann's; she had never officially met Bess-Ann, though she often saw her leaning over the upstairs railing in her white smock, having a cigarette; and she had no need for Bess-Ann's services, since her father cut her hair every Friday night, and Freda or Rowe curled her hair with a curling iron every Sunday morning, just before church.

What she needed was a plan, and the Catholic Church provided. On Sunday, May 23, she was to have her forehead anointed with balm and olive oil by

––––––––––

[1] Louie Seavitt had died suddenly of pneumonia, age 44, in 1928. To lessen confusion, the building will continue to be known as Seavitt's.

no less than the bishop. She was to be strengthened in grace, to be confirmed in her faith, to be inducted as a soldier of Christ. And her Confirmation name would be Agnes.

In preparation for the day, she borrowed a dress from one of the Pilons, commandeered Joyce's old veil, 45" long, edged in lace, asked Ella to be her sponsor and begged her father for a permanent wave, specifically from Bess-Ann. Her father had agreed, and Ella had given her a small ivory missal, with a shiny rounded cover, on which a young girl, a confirmée in pink, knelt before the tabernacle. Three baby angels winged bodiless overhead.

So, on a chilly Saturday, the day before her Confirmation, armed with two dollars and an appointment, she climbed the outdoor zigzaggy staircase that led to the shop of Bess-Ann.

If she could just worm her way in—sweep, restock, clean brushes—maybe, in time, they'd let her do some shampoos or even comb outs. She knocked ("It's open, Hon") and entered.

"Well, y'all must be my two o'clock," said Bess-Ann, putting a final wave at the nape of the neck of Mrs. Genaw, forming a ridge with her comb. "Jist grab a magazine and sit yoursef down. I'll be right with ya."

The Southern drawl had been forewarned by Rowe. Due to the huge influx of people from the land of cotton seeking jobs on the assembly lines, Southern accents were a dime a dozen in the Downriver area.

After parking primly on one of the five white wooden chairs scattered about, Shay took the place in. It was a small shop, a blend of art nouveau and castoffs, with two workstations below full-moon mirrors, a pedestal washstand with a shampoo hose, three cone-like dryers, a permanent-wave machine, a large, pad-ded chair, a hotplate and a small desk which served as a counter and accommo-dated a black phone, an appointment book, and a cut-glass bowl for tips. There was a modest degree of clutter. Shay could fix that. There were towels strewn about, abandoned coffee cups; she could clear them. The magazines on a small table needed restacking; she could do that, too.

Another hairdresser, Candy Cronin, was combing out Mrs. Ralph Mon-trose's wet hair in the second chair, engaged in small talk.

"Well, she's marrying outside the church," Mrs. Montrose was saying. "Fine with me. But why would anyone think they should get a wedding present when they're marrying out of the church? I mean, they can do what they want, but don't ask me to condone it."

"Will you be going to the wedding?" asked Miss Candy.

"Not on your life," said Fanny Montrose. "I'm not alone in this. Others feel the same way."

"Afternoon, Mrs. Montrose."

"Afternoon, Shirley," said Ida's mother.

Meanwhile, having applied a net over the head of Mrs. Genaw, having put her under the dryer, Bess-Ann motioned for Shay to sit in front of the sink, then covered her with a cutting bib and clutched the hose. "Well, Hon," she said, testing the temperature of the running water on the back of her fist. "How are you today?"

"Fine," sang Shay.

"Just lean back."

Fingertips like knuckles, she gave Shay a deep shampoo, vigorously massaging her scalp, working up a billowing lather, while Shay tracked an occasional thread of water as it coursed down her neck. One rinse followed another. Then Bess-Ann rubbed Shay's head briskly with a towel, wrapped the towel around her head, sat her in the workstation chair, let the towel slip to her neck and began to comb her mane.

"Ya got a nice, thick head of hair," said Bess-Ann. Who did your cut?"

"My pa."

"Your pa?"

"Yes."

"Well, he did a good job. I thought I might have to do a little reshaping, but he did a good job."

So Bess-Ann set to work. As did Shay.

"My pa's a barber."

"He is?"

"He was. Now he's Chief of Police."

"Oh, is that your daddy?" said Bess-Ann, sectioning off Shay's locks, starting at the crown. "Wasn't that his barbershop right across the street there?"

"Uh-huh."

Bess-Ann isolated a strip of hair and combed it straight out. Then she pulled it tight away from the head, fed it through the slit of a rubber protector and pushed the protector tight to the scalp.

"He taught me how to cut hair," said Shay.

"He did?" said Bess-Ann, fastening a heavy clamp over a piece of mesh below the rubber protector.

"Yes," said Shay, head erect, as Bess-Ann brushed the isolated strand with an ammoniated solution. Then Shay bulled her way through its pungent smell. "I practice on my sister Freda all the time."

"Hand these to me, will ya, Hon," said Bess-Ann, setting a box of curlers on Shay's lap.

"And I cut Mary Lou Theisen's hair one time," said Shay, selecting a curler and holding it in the air till needed. "Did you know the Theisens?"

"Can't say as I do," said Bess-Ann.

"Theisen's candy store was right around the corner on Front," said Mrs. Montrose. "Now, it's Blais's."

"That's right," said Shay. "My sister Freda used to work there, when it was Theisen's, when they lived in back," said Shay as she held up another curler. "There was a kind of kitchenette back there. I cut her hair one time. Mary Lou

Freda working at Theisen's

Theisen's."

"How old were you?" asked Miss Candy from the next station.

"Oh, gosh, I had to be about . . . What? . . Seven."

"Seven?"

"Just about," said Shay, her eyebrows arrowing upward. "I even practice on my pa."

"What? Cutting? He lets you cut it?" said Bess-Ann.

"Well, no, he goes to Roy Livernois," said Shay. "But he lets me comb it. I stand behind his chair in the sitting room. He even lets me do spit curls and finger waves." She knew she should stop talking, but it was hard to strike a balance between bragging and submitting credentials. "My sister Freda lets me practice doing curls. You know, with the curling iron. I also practice Marcels."

"What's the difference between a Marcel and a finger wave?" asked Miss Candy.

"Well," said Shay, pitching her voice in the vicinity of Miss Candy since she couldn't move her head. "With a finger wave, I use a comb to make the waves go back and forth. For a Marcel, I use a Marcel iron. But, boy, that took forever to learn. It's hard to get a deep wave sometimes and not a round curl."

Miss Candy Cronin did not reply and was busy tapering the back of Mrs. Montrose's head. In fact, no one said anything for quite some time—Bess-Ann was focused on finishing up, Mrs. Montrose seemed annoyed, while Shay stared at four combs pickling in blue brine, listening to the sound of her own voice echoing. Was she wrong about Marcels? Had she overdone it? Did they think she was showing off? One thing was certain: it was time to cut the chatter.

Bess-Ann put in the last curler, twenty-four curlers all told. "Ready?"

"Sure."

"Then sit yoursef down over there, Hon," said Bess-Ann, pointing to a large, padded chair.

Hastily, Shay slid off her perch and took a few steps. Easier said than done. Once out of the chair, Shay was seriously top heavy. So, she walked slowly, regally to the large, padded chair, and shifted backward into her seat on alternating cheeks.

Then she felt sillier still. Because the padded chair would have been ample for Henry VIII and all five of his wives. It was hard to be nonchalant, to pretend to be comfortable, when she had to force her elbows onto the arms, then hold them there.

Meanwhile, from a far corner, Miss Bess-Ann was retrieving a metal sphere, a gigantic saucer, about 12 inches in diameter, from which dangled about thirty to forty braided strands of electrical wires, each ending with a clamp-like heater.

Grabbing the pole on which it stood, Bess-Ann rolled it across the linoleum, greeted Mrs. Ormsby who had just entered, told her to take a chair, it wouldn't be long, positioned the dangling heaters directly above Shay's dome and fiddled with the braided strands, untangling some. In brisk fashion, Bess-Ann clamped each heater onto a corresponding curler. By the time she was finished, each curler on Shay's head was covered by a heater, and each heater was connected by electrical wire to the metal sphere above. Shay looked like Medusa, she of the squirming snakes.

"Do you have to do everything here yourself?" asked Shay.

"Like what?" said Bess-Ann.

"Like sweep, clean brushes, that stuff?"

"Sure, Hon."

"Ever wish you had a sweeper?" asked Shay.

"A sweeper?"

"Someone to sweep."

"We do our own sweeping," said Bess-Ann.

But ten-year-old hints are as subtle as ten-foot-high neon and Mrs. Montrose picked up on it. "She's lookin' for a summer job," she laughed.

"No I'm not," said Shay, stung.

"How old are you, Shirley?" asked Mrs. Montrose.

"Ten."

"You're too young. Why do you think they've got child-labor laws?"

"I agree," said Miss Candy.

Bess-Ann stepped back to survey her handiwork, then bent down, plugged in the machine and threw on the switch. All systems go, she went back to her workstation and signaled Mrs. Ormsby, her three o'clock.

Eventually, Shay relaxed. It was pleasant sitting there, her chair positioned to face the window, now cracked open to rid the room of fumes. She could feel the curlers warming up.

The side of her father's old barbershop across the street took up most of the view, though the red-and-white pole had been removed. She knew as well that the Williams Shaving Soap sign in the front window was gone, the backless bench was gone, and the constable, Alex Bourassa, who for years had called it his own, was long gone. The name on the plate-glass window, in script, was now the *Ecorse Furniture Exchange*. Like many businesses that had opened lately in this shaky economic climate, it involved the word "used."

Soon Shay's attention was diverted upward as the curlers went from warm to hot, and she began to steam.

"How y'all doin' over there?" asked Bess-Ann.

"Fine."

Yep, no getting round it, those curlers were getting hot. And though she hated to admit it, her deltoids were beginning to ache, probably from holding the tips of her elbows rigid on the chair arms, faking their support.

But now the curlers were even hotter. In fact, they were a lot hotter than they were a second ago.

"They sure get hot, eh?" she said, grinning in misery.

Bess-Ann looked up, concerned. "Too hot?"

"No. Not at all."

"This your first permanent wave?"

"No," lied Shay.

"Just four more minutes," said Bess-Ann.

Uh-oh.

The major source of Shay's now considerable agony seemed to be coming from one rogue clamp, which was singling itself out just below her crown, scorching its way directly into her scalp. Something was truly wrong. Or was it?

Ow, ow, ow, ow, ow, ow, ow.

Should she speak up? Should she say something?

"How you doin', Hon?" asked Bess-Ann.

"Fine."

"Just one more minute," said Bess-Ann.

Ay yi yiyi yi.

> "It hurt like hell," recalled Shay, "but I assumed this was what it was supposed to feel like. Never spoke up, let it burn the hell out of me; didn't say a word to her." Not long after, Shay ran into Dr. Durocher at Lafferty's butcher shop. "I showed him the blister on the back of my head. He looked at it and told me it was a third-degree burn. Had a scar for years. Told Pa and he gave me a lecture about getting a free consultation in a grocery store."

Now it was mid-June, and she had given up on Bess-Ann's. But one warm day while walking up Labadie, coming back from Seavitt's, she heard someone say, "How's that permanent wave holding up, Hon?" Bess-Ann was leaning on the railing of the upper deck, flicking an ash from her cigarette over the side.

"Great," grinned Shay.

"So ya like to work with hair," said Bess-Ann.

"Yeah. A lot."

"I did, too, when I was a kid."

"You did?"

"Yeah," said Bess-Ann, tapping her forefinger on the top of her cigarette. "Was Mrs. Montrose right? Were ya lookin' for a summer job?"

"No. Not really. I was just looking to help."

"Not for money?"

"No. Really. I thought I could pick up some pointers. You know, just for the heck of it."

Bess-Ann flicked again, from habit. "Well, I been thinkin' . . . I could use a hand around here. Sweepin' and stuff. Couldn't pay ya, though. I could teach ya, hon, but I couldn't pay ya. I'm lucky if I can pay mysef. But you'd need to blend into the woodwork. Some folks don't cotton to having kids around."

"Miss Candy?"

"And others. But you can probably win 'em over. So. . . How 'bout some mornings, some afternoons.

"That would be great!"

"Saturday morning then?"

"Saturday morning! Sure."

So five days a week, Shay bounded up those zigzaggy stairs, then basked in her besmocked importance as she swept the hair-covered floor, washed out the sink, tossed out the coffee cups. Soon she was answering the phone and making appointments. Dia was incredulous. "You really belong in the looney bin at Eloise. I wouldn't even do it for money."

"But I like hairdressing."

"I hate that stuff. All them ladies gabbin'."

So Shay swept and scrubbed and dreamt of the day when she'd graduate from beauty school and have her own little shop. It would be airy, with white walls and black-and-white linoleum and a profusion of windows and mirrors. It would have comfortable chairs, three dryers, maybe more, a pneumatic chair she could pump with her foot, pictures on the wall of movie stars with different cuts, especially the blunt cut of Colleen Moore, the widow's-peak of Janet Gaynor. And she'd serve coffee, Coke or tea; give manicures and pedicures; create her own sets and waves; and turn the shrinking violets into Louise Lovelys or Evelyn Brents with the wave of her comb.

But she'd soon be left with a second scar, both permanent.

Things would have been fine if it hadn't been for Helen Morgan.

Business had slowed on the whole, but Bess-Ann's was full-up this par-ticular hot Friday in July. Mrs. Gregory was nodding off under the dryer; Mrs. Walton Jones, early for her 2:30 appointment, was slumped on a white chair, vacantly flipping through the same *Radio Stars* magazine that she'd vacantly flipped through a month before; Miss Candy was trimming Fanny Montrose's crown with the points of her shears; and Bess-Ann was assessing Mim Raupp's baby-fine locks with an inward sigh, preparing to launch a cut.

"How ya wannit, Mim?" asked Bess-Ann. "The usual?"

"Oh, I don't know," said Mim. "Can ya make it look like it hasn't just been cut?"

"Sugah," laughed Bess-Ann, "if I had a dime for every time I heard that, I'd be a rich woman."

There was a knock on the screen door, a robust knock that rattled the rick-ety frame. Bess-Ann looked up, then down again. "Get that, would you, hon."

Shay turned off the hot-water spigot, propped the can of Old Dutch on the back of the sink and went to the door, washrag in hand, wondering why she was getting the door when everyone knew to just walk in. "It's a man," she whispered.

"What's he sellin'?" asked Bess-Ann.

"Grape juice, ma'am," said the man. He was standing on the wooden porch at the top of the zigzag stairs, tipping his battered fedora from behind the patched screen.

"Sure it ain't snake oil?" drawled Bess-Ann.

"Nope. Just grape juice."

"What kinda grape juice?"

"Well, I've got several varieties: port, claret, muscatel, sherry, champagne."

"Now, you're talkin'," said Mim.

"You mean to stand there and tell me," tut-tutted Bess-Ann, "yer walkin' round town, sellin' wine door to door, big as life, while guys from the Border Patrol are sittin' in cars right over there on our riverbank" (the exact location of which was indicated by the pointed end of her rat-tail comb) "sittin' in cars for hours on end, just dyin' to catch our own good men for Volstead violations."

She shook her head. "Now, how ya expect to get away with that?"

"I'm not selling wine, ma'am. I don't sell wine."

"Well, you just said, 'port, muscatel and sherry.'"

"If I could come in and explain."

"Don't do it, don't do it, don't do it," cautioned Fanny Montrose. "You'll never get rid of him."

"Aw, let the poor guy in," said Mim.

"He does look harmless," said Mrs. Gregory.

"All right," said Bess-Ann, gently pushing Mim's head forward as she began to trim the back. "But ya be wastin' your time. And don't hold that door open for-*ev*-eh, or you'll be lettin' in more flies. We got one in here now that's drivin' me plumb loco."

The man inched his way between the screen and doorframe, then made a conscious effort to pull the screen door shut behind him. But the frame had not been on speaking terms with the warped door for years, so he wedged it in as tight as he could and left it at that. "Afternoon, ladies," he said, tipping his hat once more.

His bearing suggested he'd seen better days, same for his clothes. He wore a tired suit, shiny in spots, and carried a scuffed briefcase that matched his battered fedora. His shoes were so far down at the heel that even the added plates looked worn. Taking out a stack of business cards from an inside breast pocket, he handed one to each of them, including Shay. "The name's Charles Voelker, but you can call me Charlie."

"Hi, Charlie," said Mim, head lowered, eyes upraised.

He glanced around at the vacant chairs and waited for an invitation to sit. When none was forthcoming, he set down his briefcase, mopped the sweat off his neck with a damp handkerchief and plunged in. "I represent a grape growers' concern in sunny California."

"Sunny California?" said Mrs. Montrose, already suspicious. "Then how come this card says Fifth Avenue, Manhattan? Nothin' sunny about that."

"'Cuz that's our sales office. Don't worry. All on the up and up," he said. "I don't suppose I could have a glass of water."

"I can sell you a Coca-Cola," said Bess-Ann.

"That's kind of you, but a little water would do the trick."

Taking her cue from Bess-Ann, Shay filled a glass and handed it to him. Then she waited self-consciously as he drained it, gave a polite "you're welcome" after he handed it back with a "thank you," returned to her sink and vigorously washed it out.

"Mind if he sits, Bess-Ann?" said Mrs. Gregory. "Mr. Voelker looks a little peak-ed."

"It's just a ploy," scoffed Mrs. Montrose, head to the side to facilitate Miss Candy's shears. "You gotta watch it with these kind. They pretend they're tired, pretend they're thirsty, just so you'll buy something."

"Sit if you want," said Bess-Ann. "But you ain't movin' in. Just know that."

"Thank you," he said, sagging into a seat, setting the briefcase at his side.

"Well, get on with it."

"Right. Well." He took a deep breath to pump himself up, then leaned forward and dove in. "There's a deal to be had, ladies, and I'm here to tell it."

"Hang on to your purse, Phyllis," said Mim, while Shay turned off the water and leaned against the sink to listen.

"Now, now. None of that. None of that," sighed Charlie. "I'm an honest man, father of five, just earning a buck."

"How long you been doing this?" asked Mrs. Gregory.

"'Bout a month," said Charlie, drying the brim of his hat with his handkerchief.

"Laid off autoworker?"

"You guessed it."

"Fisher Body plant?"

"Rouge. Ten months."

"Never mind all that," snapped Mrs. Montrose. "What's the deal? And keep it short."

Mr. Voelker relaunched. "Well, ladies, with times being what they are, Herbert Hoover created a federal farm relief program, the Federal Farm Board. I'm sure you've heard of it. You look like the kind of women who follow the news."

"Oh, stop," complained Mrs. Montrose.

"How does that affect you, you ask? Well, I'll tell ya. Because of a million-dollar loan from the Federal Farm Board, grape growers had a bumper crop last November. So many, they couldn't sell 'em all. And you know what surplus means, don'tcha?"

"Too many grapes?" offered Mim.

"Too many grapes," confirmed Charlie. "And *too many grapes* means?"

"Cheap?" posited Mim.

"Cheap," confirmed Charlie.

But Phyllis Gregory was puzzled. "Wait a minute, Mr. Voelker. Why would the Farm Board give a million bucks to the grape growers to grow more grapes, when the grape growers can't sell the grapes they're already growing because of Prohibition?"

"Strange are the ways," said Charlie.

"Better yet," said Mrs. Montrose. "What do grapes have to do with sherry, muscatel and port? When it's illegal to sell sherry, muscatel and port."

"Before you answer that, Charlie, there's one thing you oughtta know," cautioned Mim with mock seriousness. "This kid's old man is chief of police."

"Your father's George Moore?"

"Uh-huh."

"Well, nice to meet ya, Miss Moore," said the man, tipping his hat. Then he laughed, unfazed. "But I've got nothing to hide, ladies. What I'm offering's all on the up and up. What I'm offering is Vino Sano, a grape concentrate. And sherry and port are just a few of our many flavors."

"Flavors!" roared Mim. "What? Like Faygo Fruit Punch, Faygo Strawberry and Faygo Muscatel?"

"Precisely."

"Vino Sano?" mused Bess-Ann. "Ain't that Eye-talian?"

"Yeah," laughed Mrs. Walton Jones. "Probably a fancy name for Dago Red."

"Not at all. Not. At. All. Vino Sano is Spanish," replied Charlie, proudly indicating a higher life form. "*Sano* 's Spanish for healthful."

"And vino?" smiled Mrs. Gregory. " *Vino* is Spanish for...?"

"*Vino* is Spanish for *Vino*," answered Charlie with a grin. "Look. Say you like the taste of Muscatel. We'll supply you with a grape-juice concentrate that tastes just like muscatel. Just tell me the flavor you want and we supply the brick."

Bess-Ann stopped cutting, her shears poised in mid-air. "The what?"

"The brick," said Charlie. "Comes in a brick."

"How big a brick?" said Mim, head still bent forward, face still serious, mouth beginning to quiver.

"'Bout the size of a pound of butter," replied Charlie. "All you gotta do is dissolve the brick in a gallon of water."

"That's it?" asked Bess-Ann.

"That's it," confirmed Charlie. "And, before you know it, you'll be rocking on your front porch, enjoying a hearty brew that tastes just like muscatel."

"Hot dog!" laughed Mim. "Kool-Aid for grown-ups."

"But I must tell you up front!" shouted Charlie, in an attempt to cut through the howls and regain the floor, "there *are* a few caveats."

"A few whats?" said Bess-Ann.

"Caveats, warnings," said Charlie. "My company requires me to say that, once you buy our grape concentrate, once you receive the grapes, there are some things you must not do."

"Like what?" asked Bess-Ann.

Charlie, late of the assembly line at Henry Ford's Rouge plant, removed a dog-eared card from his inside breast pocket and read from it, solemnly yet rapidly: "*After dissolving the brick in a gallon of water, do not place the liquid in an airtight jug or oak keg; do not add sugar; do not leave it in a cool room where the temperature hovers between 60 and 70 degrees, such as a cellar; do not keep it in a dark place, like a pantry or a cupboard; do not shake the vessel daily; and, last but not least, do not decant it after three weeks.*"

"Decant?" asked Bess-Ann.

"Let air get to it," said Charlie, as he returned to the card. "*Unless the buyer eschews these processes, fermentation will result and he'll be left with a beverage with 13% alcoholic content. And my company cannot be held responsible.*"

The laughter, which began around the time of the first caveat and rose with each caveat thereafter, had escalated to such a rollicking pitch that the pharmacist in the drugstore below lost count of his Nembutal tablets.

Oddly enough, however, despite the squeals and spirited thigh slapping, Charles Voelker remained composed, even genial, throughout his presentation, taking it all in stride, as if he'd heard it all before, as if laughter, the bust-a-gut kind, regularly accompanied his presentation.

"Is he sayin' what I think he's sayin'?" asked Bess-Ann.

"He's saying, if you ignore their warnings, in three weeks you've got swill," said Mim.

"How is this legal? Would you tell me that?" frothed Mrs. Montrose. "How is this legal?"

"It's a hundred percent legal."

"You sure?" said Mim. "'Cuz I don't want any Prohibition officer barging into my house all over again, throwing my Butzie up against a wall."

"I can assure you. One hundred percent," said Mr. Voelker. "And all because of Section 29."

There it was. Section 29. The hole in the wall, the gap in the fence, the loophole the size of Sonoma. Congress, fearful of losing the farm vote, of facing angry apple and grape growers, had muddied the waters with Section 29 of the Volstead Act, deliberately leaving the wording vague. Penalties "against manufacture of liquor without a permit," it stated, would not apply to "a person manufacturing non-intoxicating cider and fruit juices" for use in his home.

Now the content measurement for all things alcohol, as defined elsewhere in the Volstead Act, was 5%. In Section 29, however, the percentage was modified to "non-intoxicating." But how do you define "non-intoxicating?" If Aunt Alice isn't reeling after four glasses of elderberry wine with an alcoholic content of 15%, it could be argued that it was non-intoxicating. Thus Section 29 made homebrew quasi legal—if you didn't transport it past your front gate, if you didn't charge your guests by the glass.

"Isn't this just another name for that Vine-Glo they're advertising?" asked Mrs. Gregory.

"No," said Charlie. "Vine-Glo comes in a keg. The Vine-Glo company dilutes the concentrate, then comes to your home and tends it and bottles it."

"She's too young to be hearing this," said Mrs. Montrose, pointing at Shay.

"Hearing what?" asked Bess-Ann.

"This."

"You gotta be kidding, Fanny," said Mim.

Mrs. Montrose might have saved her breath. Homebrew was nothing new to Shay. In fact, she was an accessory. On certain Sundays, as George Moore and Nick Strassner took advantage of Section 29, Shay wheeled the empties, Freda cleaned the spigots, Dia and Rowe served as cappers, and Joycie shelved the finished product. There was one occasional drawback.

"We'd be sleeping," said Rowe, "and all of a sudden you'd hear pop! pop! pop! All the caps'd be flying off."

"I still don't think this is legal," grumped Mrs. Montrose, annoyed to the teeth that someone was once again smudging one of life's dogmatic edges.

"Absolutely 100% on the up and up," said Charlie. "I defy you, I defy any-one, to find an ounce of alcohol in our bricks, which, by the way, are backed by the Farm Board; which, by the way, have been approved by an ex-attorney general of these United States. Why, just last fall, members of our industry hired none other than Mrs. Mabel Walker Willebrandt as legal counsel and she ap-proved."

"Mabel Walker Willebrandt!" Bess-Ann stopped snipping and rested her scissors against her hip, outraged. "Are ya kiddin' me!"

"Who's that?" asked Mrs. Walton Jones.

"Only President Hoover's Assistant Attorney General," said Charlie, proud-ly. "For eight years, she prosecuted violators of the Volstead Act. No one knows the ins and outs better than Mrs. Mabel Walker Willebrandt.

"She's also the dame that's been houndin' Helen Morgan," said Bess-Ann.

"Who's Helen Morgan?" asked Miss Candy, looking up from her cutting.

"Who's Helen Morgan!" cried Shay.

It was a blurt. Nothing more. A gentle gibe, a warm elbow to the ribs. How could anyone not know Helen Morgan? But those three words bounced off the tin ceiling, then hung in the ammoniated air. And, as they did, Shay's inner uh-oh went off. Because the look she got from Miss Candy could have cut through steel. To Miss Candy, the echoing of her words had mockery written all over it, easily proved by the laughter that accompanied it. Everyone had joined in. But it was a blurt. Nothing more.

Then Mim, uninvited, made it worse. "Who's Helen Morgan!" she howled. "Where you been, Miss Candy!" Then she broke into song. "♫ *He's just my Bill. An or-din-ary guy.* "

"You can stop anytime," crabbed Mrs. Montrose .

"♫ *Can't help lov-in' dat man of mine* ," wailed Mim, then she laughed. "That's Helen Morgan."

Bess-Ann was still incensed: "Mabel Walker Willibrandt. Can you believe it? That dame went after Helen Morgan with every gun in her arsenal."

"Why?" asked Mrs. Walton Jones.

"She liked arresting big names," said Mrs. Gregory. "More publicity."

"Helen Morgan wasn't doin' anything more than the rest of us," said Bess-Ann. "But that dame had her hauled in time and time agin for picayune viola-tions, made her life a livin' hell." Bess-Ann turned to Mrs. Walton Jones and said in earnest, as if she were referring to the sad fate of one of her clients. "She had her nightclub smashed to bits. Illegally. That dame killed Helen Morgan's nightclub career all on her own."

"Where you gettin' all this?" asked Mrs. Walton Jones.

"These days, Honey," laughed Bess-Ann. "I gotta lotta time to put my feet up and read *Radio Stars* ."

"Well, I hate to be the one to say this, but she brought it on herself," said Mrs. Montrose. "She shouldn't have been in that nightclub in the first place. She can sing somewhere else."

"Where?"

"How about a nightclub without likker."

"Find one," said Mim.

"If she had just followed the law, that's all I'm saying," admonished Mrs. Montrose, "she wouldn't of got in trouble. All she had to do was follow the law."

"She was just singin,' for god's sakes, Fanny!" yelled Mim. "That's all she was doin'. She was just singin'! That's how she made her living!"

Though Bess-Ann was secretly pleased that Mrs. Raupp had just let Mrs. Montrose have it, she couldn't afford to lose a regular, so she turned on Charlie. "You mean to stand there and tell me that after all those years of treating regular folks like felons, Mrs. Mabel Walker Willebrandt is now on the payroll of the grape industry? Of outfits like yours?"

"One and the same," said Charlie, glad to win back his audience. "So you see, who would know better what's within the law than Mrs. Mabel Walker Willebrandt?"

"Boy, that really rots my socks," said Bess-Ann. "That really...."

"Careful," said Mrs. Montrose, nodding toward Shay.

"Intent, Ma'am," said Charlie. "It's all about intent. We are selling nonalcoholic bricks. What happens later, well, we're not responsible for that. If you leave milk out, it'll turn. Is your grocer responsible? Of course not. Nature is. If nature chooses to ferment within a given cycle and God is nature, then God is the culprit. Can't very well indict God."

"I find that kinda talk sacrilegious," said Mrs. Montrose.

"Intent, Ma'am," said Charlie. "It's all about intent."

"It's all about hypocrisy," laughed Mrs. Gregory. "That's what it's all about."

"How much is this stuff?" asked Mim.

"Two bucks a brick," said Charlie, leaning down, extracting an order book from his briefcase. "Satisfaction guaranteed."

"I won't be a part of this," said Mrs. Montrose crisply, half out of the workstation chair. "And if you're smart, Bess-Ann, you won't either. Not in your place of business."

"You hear that, Mr. Voelker?" said Bess-Ann.

"I do," said Charles Voelker, putting his order book away, snapping closed his briefcase, sighing. He got up and tipped his hat, a little more perfunctorily than on entrance.

"If you'll give me two minutes," said Mim. "I'll meet you downstairs."

"Buy one for me," said Mrs. Gregory.

True to his word, Charlie Voelker was on the up and up. The bricks would arrive, compliments of the U.S. Postal Service, and be delivered throughout town in late August 1931. And three weeks to the day, despite a few cellar explosions, Ecorse would be listing to port.

———————

A week later, Mrs. Gregory and Miss Candy were trying to decide whether to style her hair loose on the shoulders or behind the ears. Bess-Ann had stepped outside for a cigarette.

"What do you think, Shay?" asked Mrs. Gregory.

Shay, washing cups, glanced at Miss Candy for the preferred response, but if Miss Candy had one, she didn't show it. "Looks nice either way," said Shay.

"Oh, c'mon," said Miss Candy, possibly irritated. "Whaddya think?"

"Behind the ears," said Shay.

"Agreed," said Mrs. Gregory.

———————

Later that afternoon, after Bess-Ann stepped out for another smoke and Miss Candy handed a mirror to Mrs. Armstrong and asked if she wanted more off and Mrs. Armstrong said she wasn't sure, Miss Candy turned to Shay and asked, "How's the length in back?"

"Looks nice," said Shay.

"But whaddya think? Little more off?"

"Well. . ."

"Truly."

"Maybe a quarter inch," said Shay.

"That's what I thought, too."

"Fine by me," said Mrs. Armstrong.

Miss Candy asked once more that day. "Whaddya think? Shorter on the bangs?"

"I wouldn't."

"My thoughts exactly."

She did it again on Thursday, as soon as Bess-Ann stepped out.

"Whaddya think? Wave deep enough?"

"Could be deeper," said Shay.

By Thursday night, it had become routine, Miss Candy asking Shay's opinion whenever Bess-Ann's opinion wasn't handy, whenever Bess-Ann stepped out. It wasn't entirely altruistic; it served Miss Candy well. Those who were

fond of Shay, and there were many, seemed pleased that Candy was including the girl, inviting her in. In fact, it brought a little of Shay's popularity Miss
Candy's way.

"Whaddya think? Shingled high in back?"

"Well, I kinda prefer an even length all round."

"Yeah, I like that, too."

———————

They were all huddled around Miss Candy's workstation, deep in conversation, when Shay returned from an errand on Friday morning. Miss Candy and
four of her regulars. And they all clammed up. Those with their backs to Shay
glanced round for a second, as if shushed. All looked a little sheepish. And all
fanned out: Mrs. Delbo to a dryer, Mrs. Winters to a waiting chair, Mrs. Montrose into the work station chair, while Mrs. Walton Jones pulled a set of car
keys from her purse, paid her bill and left. Bess-Ann wasn't there. She'd had a
doctor's appointment but was expected back soon.

Baffled, uneasy, Shay spent the next few minutes out of view, opening a new
bottle of Lysol, continuing with her cleanup of the backroom, wondering what
was up. Mrs. Montrose had given her the cold shoulder. So had Mrs. Winters.
And she had picked the wrong day for a backroom clean out. It was hot and
sweaty work, a dusty and dirty job, and she had run out of steam halfway into
it.

Then Miss Candy leaned in and asked if she'd run down to Seavitt's and get
her a sandwich. Dutifully, Shay took a washcloth to her face and hands, hung
up her smock, then walked listlessly down the outside stairs.

Miss Munn was at the lunch counter delicately nibbling on the last triangle
of her Chicken Club sandwich. In her long-sleeved flowered frock, she seemed
oblivious to the heat and looked her usual pristine self.

Any other day Shay would have been glad to be seen on an official errand.
But not now. There'd have to be small talk and small talk took energy. What she
really needed was big talk—about what was up upstairs. A willing ear to help
her puzzle it out.

"Hello, Miss Munn," said Shay from between two empty stools, three
stools down.

"Why, hello, Shirley," said Miss Munn, setting aside her three-decker triangle, swiveling Shay's way. "How are you this *fine, fine* day?"

"Okay."

"Just okay?"

"Good. Really good."

"Your father tells me you're helping out at Bess-Ann's," Miss Munn said
pleasantly.

"Yes."

"What do you do there?"

"Oh, a little bit of everything."

"Well, isn't that *wonderful*."

Shortly after Shay's return, while Bess-Ann was concentrating on a cut for Mrs. Kovacs and Shay was carting out a box of backroom trash, Miss Candy caught Shay's eye. Pointing at Mrs. Winter's bangs, she left a quarter-inch of space between thumb and forefinger while silently mouthing the words, Whaddya think?

Shay, enormously relieved, replied, "I wouldn't go much shorter."

Bess-Ann stopped cutting and looked up.

"You wouldn't?" said Miss Candy.

"No. Because when Mrs. Winters gets home and gives 'em a wash they'll bounce up."

"I see," said Miss Candy.

"Don'tcha think so?" asked Shay.

"No, I don't think so at all," said Miss Candy with a knowing look to Mrs. Winters, then a knowing look to Mrs. Montrose who was watching from under the dryer. "There's a huge difference between fine hair and thick hair in the way they bounce up. Besides, you need to take into account the size of the face, the size of the forehead."

Bess-Ann didn't say anything, but it became obvious that she was dwelling on the exchange.

———————

That night, while closing up, Bess-Ann seemed apprehensive. She sat down behind the small desk, checking tomorrow's appointments, fiddling with a pen, while Miss Candy tidied her workstation and Shay stowed the mops and buckets, having earlier polished the linoleum floor. The room smelled of Johnson's Wax. Then Bess-Ann asked Shay to stay behind, and Miss Candy, smiling pleasantly, gave her goodnights and left. Her uh-oh system on shrill, Shay carried a chair on tiptoe across the newspapered floor, then placed it before the desk and sat down.

Bess-Ann looked tired, sad. "Hon," she said, "this isn't working out."

"It isn't?"

"Some people are complainin'. . ."

"Who?"

"That's not important," said Bess-Ann. "Look. I don't know how to put this. I'm sure it's 'cuz you're overeager but . . . you're too outspoken, too pushy."

"Pushy?"

"Putting your two cents in . . . on a cut or whatever. Offering advice. I never thought you'd do that."

"But she asks for my opinion."

"That's not what I heard. To be honest," continued Bess-Ann, "Candy came to me last night and said she's findin' it hard to work with you around. She's uncomfortable, feels inhibited, like you're her boss."

"Her boss?"

"She says you're always offerin' your opinion, especially when I'm not around, that you take over. She said others feel the same way, especially Mrs. Montrose."

"But she does. She asks for my opinion."

"That's not what she told me. Besides," continued Bess-Ann. "Why would she? She's been cutting hair for years, see what I'm sayin'. Then today. . ."

"Today?"

"Well, I gotta say, I stuck up for you last night. She thinks you're braggy. I said she's not braggy, she's just proud of what she knows. But she said there's nothing worse than a kid who doesn't know her place, who mocks her elders. I told her you weren't like that, that you were a thoughtful kid, that I'd never seen you do that. But she said, 'Watch her.' And today, for no reason at all, just like she said, you just up and criticized her work."

"But she asked what I thought," cried Shay.

"I didn't hear her ask."

"She nodded her head."

"Shay, Hon, listen to me," said Bess-Ann. "It's just not working out. And there's Mrs. Montrose. She's adamant about your age. She thinks a ten-year-old has no business being here in the first place. I can't afford to lose a regular, Hon. I appreciate all you've done, but it's just not workin' out."

"But why didn't Miss Candy just say something to me if she was upset?" asked Shay, fighting back tears. "She never complained to me. She never said a word."

"She said she did."

———

The next morning, Saturday, Shay was sitting on the top step of her front porch, fending off gnats. She hadn't told anyone yet about Bess-Ann's, not even Freda; she was too ashamed. Maybe she'd been a pest; maybe Bess-Ann just wanted to get rid of her. Whatever the reason, she'd lost the respect of someone whose respect she prized.

Just then her father pulled into the driveway in the family Ford. "Just the person I wanted to see," he said, slinging his uniform jacket over his shoulder as he got out. "I hear you ran into Miss Munn yesterday," he said, climbing the steps, standing over her.

"Yes, at Seavitt's. I was getting a sandwich for Miss Candy."

"She said you had a dirty neck."

"Who?"

"Miss Munn. She said you had a ring around your neck. Streaks. Beads of dirt."

"But I was . . ."

"I don't care what you was, Tee! Don't you ever go out like that again."

"He gave me holy hell for that," recalled Shay.

Injustice is the bird pecking at your liver until you die.

Chapter 42
Wednesday, August 26, 1931

Initially, Dia's doghouse days were caused by the occasional spill and other related foul-ups. But her unintentional mishaps were now becoming intentional. Sometimes when she stayed home alone, too "infirm" to attend school, she made phone calls. She called a Moving & Carting company in Detroit, said she was Mrs. Brown and needed to move two floors of furniture. On the appointed day, the Moving & Carting Co. backed their van up over Helen Brown's tree lawn, while Dia rocked back and forth on the Moore glider.

"Cripes, I sat on that porch and watched the van back over their grass right up to their front porch," recalled Dia. "I watched them put the back down, walk up to the door and Mrs. Brown standing there, shaking her head."

Dia sent long-stemmed roses to Mrs. Bouchard, "To Mother from her Evelyn." She sent the Ouellette's a sewing machine. She sent everything to everyone. C.O.D. Frank Lafferty, the butcher, was a favorite target. She'd ask for a wedge of baloney; he'd go into his meat locker to get it and she'd hip the door shut. Since there was no door latch inside, Frank would be in the frosted window motioning her to open it. He never seemed to catch on.

––––––––––

Then came Wednesday, August 26, 1931. For years, it was known as "The Longine-Wittnauer Hour," or the day Helen Brown cleaned Dia's clock.

The front porch of the second house on Monroe Street was more than a porch. Standing above five wide steps, it was a citadel, a bastion. If, by some remote chance, a Moore girl blundered innocently into a fight, she could hightail it to the porch, secure in the knowledge that no one dared follow, for behind the screen door were fresh Mooreville recruits—sisters who, despite a proclivity for annihilating each other, reserved this privilege for the immediate family.

The porch was a perfect size. With the glider, a wide-planked railing and George Moore's rocker, it sat six comfortably, eight raucously. When the front windows were open, porch regulars could converse with insiders or listen to the player piano exhorting them to do do do what they done done done before,

Baby. From this vantage, they could divine the comings and goings of Monroe, Labadie, State, even Front Street when winter dropped its curtain of leaves.

For George Moore, it was the bleacher section, where he sat and rocked on a summer's eve, watching the neighborhood baseball game—hollering, hectoring—greeting Junior Ouellette as he rounded second base: "Pull up your pants, Junior!"

For Dia—ah, for Dia—it was a box seat at the Roman Coliseum. And she was Nero.

But there came a time that Dia did one thumbs down too many. It was a balmy afternoon in summer—no school, no rain, no one in authority within shouting distance—and Dia and Shay were passing the time of day. Sitting on an old bedspread that covered the glider, their bare feet pushed against the wooden railing like pistons, pumping the swinging couch back and forth. "Wish we'd have a tornado or something," said Dia. "Or a typhoon." As they chewed their wads of gum in cadence, the glider's underparts groaned with each glide, hoarsely pleading for a teaspoon of oil. "I'd even settle for high winds." The flag fluttered on its pole near the catalpas, then changed its course. "Maybe a tidal wave from Canada. Roll right down Lake St. Clair."

Dia sat up abruptly. The glider eased to a halt. "Oh, boy." A pinpoint was coming up Monroe Street, a pinpoint of green walking just so easy—like a lamb to the slaughter.

"Leave her alone, Dia," warned Shay.

Helen Brown was nectar to Dia's bee. Possibly because Helen Brown had made the unfortunate blunder, five years before, of moving into the big white house that sat kitty-corner from the Moore's at the intersection of Monroe and Labadie. That's all Shay could figure. That's all any of them could figure. So as Shay burrowed into the fold of the glider, Dia followed Helen Brown's approach like a cat with a thrashing tail. Only the pupils of her eyes were moving. Behind slits.

"I mean it, Dia," muttered Shay. "Leave that poor girl alone."

Dia waited for Helen's head to float across their privet hedge before she broke the silence. "Hey, Helen, your mother's been lookin' all over town for ya!"

Helen looked up with a start, puzzled. She was dressed very nicely—her short-sleeved dress well-pressed, her white collar starched. "My mother knew where I was."

"She said you shoulda been back a long time ago," said Dia.

"But I've only been gone about an hour." Helen's voice was soft, high, feminine. It threatened every tomboy on the block.

"An hour to go to Pilon's?" Dia was incredulous. "They don't even have an hour's worth of Nabiscos."

"I wasn't at Pilon's. I was at Virginia Brazill's."

Blowing a sphere of pink, Dia held the bubble by its knobby tail, admired the size, popped it back in her mouth, bit on it, and felt the air explode inside. "Your mother came to our porch and said, 'Doris. Have you seen my Helen?'" Dia did a great imitation of Mrs. Brown. Dia could mimic just about everybody, lending luster to her whoppers. "I said, 'I saw her go down the block about two hours ago, Mrs. Brown.' Your mom said: 'If I find that girl, I'll lick her three shades to Monday.'"

"But I told her where I was going," whined Helen. "All she had to do was call."

"She tried to call, but the line was busy. Didn't she, Shay?"

A sudden gust of wind whipped the flag, causing it to crack loudly. It was clear that Dia had landed one, because Helen's face turned the color of Ivory. Helen and Virginia were probably on the phone the whole time.

"You're making this up, Doris Moore."

"Now why would I make this up? If I was makin' it up, you'd go home and ask your mother and she'd tell you I was makin' it up. Why would I bother, Helen?"

Helen turned and cut across the street. Dia jabbed a laughing elbow into Shay's side, but Shay was not amused. "You're gonna rot in hell for that, lame brain."

"For what?"

"For embarrassing that girl, embarrassing me."

They pushed off once again. As the sun began to set and their gum began to taste like melted asphalt, Marce came out and sat on the stoop. Then Mrs. Ostrander emerged from her house and rested on her cane. "Would you girls like some rhubarb!"

Dia was across the street in no time. "Would we ever!"

"Tell Freda there's more than enough for two pies," said Mrs. Ostrander, pointing to a large brown bag inside the door that overflowed with large stalks. Then she pointed to another. "And there's some tomatoes, some green peppers and green beans." Hiking up a slipping bag, Dia started back across the street as Mrs. Ostrander closed her front door.

The whack! was the first thing they heard. When questioned that night over the dinner table, all three of them agreed that the whack! was the first thing. Because the screen door of the white house on the corner of Labadie flew open, and Helen Brown marched out of her house like high noon.

"You're going to fight, Doris Moore!"

Shay slowed the glider to a standstill while Marce took cover behind the screen door. Dia, however, barely moved at all. Over the top of the tipping bags, she could see Helen Brown standing four-square on her stoop, nostrils flaring. "I mean it, Doris Moore. You've picked on me long enough."

To this day, there is conjecture as to what possessed Dia to push it. She wasn't in the best of positions—encumbered by those two very large, very unfortunate bags of Michigan produce—but she pushed it. "Oh, kiss my patootie," she said.

Helen Brown let out a high-pitched shriek and was off her front porch with a bound.

"Run!" screamed Shay.

Seconds later, Helen Brown was pelting Dia with five years of pent-up rage. Rapid jabs to the chin, a kick to the knee, a right to the arm, a left to the rhubarb. Half the blows landed; half the blows fanned the air. But as Helen Brown darted and wove, Dia just stood there with her eyes closed, holding tight to the bags.

"Drop the bags! Run!" yelled Shay.

Helen danced around her intended, dukes up, Jack Johnson style, the great-whitehope for Monroe and beyond, slugging and slashing and butting and biting, affably opining that Miss Moore had been requesting this for years too numerous to calculate, frequently inquiring as to whether Miss Moore had had enough, calmly suggesting that if Miss Moore did not forswear certain behavioral tendencies that the terminal part of Miss Brown's forelimb would meet somewhere in the area of Miss Moore's proboscis.

The bags began to scissor. When Dia lunged blindly for the rhubarb, green beans dribbled onto the street. When Dia lurched for the green beans, rhubarb spilled forth. Followed by two tomatoes. Followed by a lone green pepper that rolled toward the curb.

"Run, you dodo!" But Shay's exhortations only served to goad Helen on. And Dia just stood there, her eyes sealed shut.

Then Shay and Marce howled so hard their veins popped out on their necks: "DROP THE DANG BAGS!!"

Dia must have heard them, something must have snapped because, at long last, she dropped the bags and raised her arms. One of those arms went to protect Dia's face, the other went to protect her body. Dia wasn't fighting back, she was warding off the blows. Her right knee came up to protect her tender areas. Then her left knee, then her right knee; she was sidestepping Helen's flailing arms like a Mexican jumping bean. To no avail. Because Dia still had her eyes clenched tight.

Then Helen gave a good swift kick to Dia's privates and Dia fell to the ground. Could things get worse? They sure could. For out of the corner of her eye, Shay saw the screen door of Helen Brown's house slowly open and out stepped Mrs. Brown.

What happened next was celebrated by some, deplored by others, and dissected at that night's dinner table for close to an hour. At first, Mrs. Brown just stood there while Dia crawled to her feet. Then, with her hands balled into fists, Mrs. Brown let loose a cry of delight. "Give it to her, Helen! For every time she gave it to you! Give it to her good!"

Shay, who always rooted for the underdog, even when it was Dia, blubbered convulsively. "Oh god, oh god, oh god."

"You're all mouth, Doris Moore!" yelled Mrs. Brown. "You can't whip a turnip! You're all mouth!"

"I'll call my dad!" Shay was hysterical. Tears streamed down her face. "He's the chief of police. I'll call my dad!"

"That's it, Helen!" encouraged Mrs. Brown.

With that, Helen grabbed onto a wad of Dia's brown hair and yanked.

"Ow!" bellowed Dia.

To Shay's relief, at that precise moment, a touring car turned onto Monroe from State Street. Now they'd have to halt the action, now the gladiators—well, the gladiator and the less-than gladiator—would have to evacuate the area and Dia could make a break for it. Shay stepped out onto the porch steps and announced between quivering sobs, "Ff-ff-ff car!"

Everyone looked up.

"You'll hafta get out of the ff-ff-ff street. Ff-ff-ff car!"

So that's what Helen did. Locking onto Dia's scalp, she dragged Dia out of that street, over the curb, right up to the Brown's front yard. Dia had no choice but to follow with little short steps saying, "ow ow ow ow ow." Mrs. Brown leaned over the porch railing. "You hear me, Doris Moore! You're all mouth!"

Chapter 43

Friday, November 6, 1931

When a 1924 article appeared in *Literary Digest* on "How to Shoot a Boot-legger—With a Camera" and mentioned Wyandotte, the town took to its bed with smelling salts. A.G. Gibson, secretary of the Wyandotte Board of Commerce, shot back an indignant letter to the editor: "If there is a more law-abiding community as a whole than Wyandotte, Michigan, in this state or for that matter, in the country, we would like to know about it. We object strenuously to being in any way classed with Ecorse, especially when such an impression is circulated in a publication as important and influential as *Literary Digest*."

Over in George Moore's barbershop, Ernie Boudreau struck a pose and mocked as he read: "If there is a more law-abiding community as a whole than Wyandotte, Michigan, blah, blah, blah."

"Oh, I love it!" yelled Frenchie Navarre, amid groans and whistles.

Ernie shushed them and continued, flaunting his forefinger in mid-air: "We object strenuously, *strenuously*," he repeated, "to being in any way classed with," he paused and surveyed the room to great effect, "*Ecorse*." Good old Ernie, he dragged out "*Eeee-corse*" longer than it took the 20th-Century Limited to make it from Chicago to Flagstaff. "Especially, especially," he repeated once more, finger wagging, "when such an impression is circulated in a publication as important and in-flu-en-tial as *Literary Digest*."

Despite its protestations, Wyandotte found itself continually linked to its dishonorable neighbor. And it didn't help that Ecorse had a population that included "coloreds." Wyandotte did not sell to black folk; it was in the deed of every house. But that's another story.

———

Joe Rivett, 47, a former shipworker, operated a series of speaks in Wyandotte over the years, including one at 3032 First Street, right behind City Hall, which was largely patronized by businessmen and professionals until it was padlocked. He reputedly ran "clean places" and offered only the "good stuff." He also had an underground brewery on Plum Street, then opened a saloon at 128 Oak Street. On Thursday, October 15, 1931, Joe Evola, 32, a local fruit wholesaler and unlisted brewer, had gone there to collect on a bill. Some say he was also there to muscle in, demanding that Rivett carry only his brand of beer.

An argument ensued. When Evola made a menacing move toward Rivett, Rivett grabbed a gun from beneath the bar and shot him. Evola died two days later at Wyandotte General. He was given a gangland funeral, Sicilian style. Following morning services at St. Patrick's Church, "there were several hundred men on foot, a brass band, and a long line of automobiles, many of them Lincolns," reported the *Wyandotte Herald.*[1]

Rivett, a widower with a son and three daughters, claimed self-defense and was released by the Wyandotte police. Concerned for his health, he closed his saloon and made plans to go to Florida where his son was living.

Shortly after dark on Friday, November 6, 1931, about 8 o'clock, a driver pulled up to Charley Tear's Cozy Inn at 3331 Biddle and kept the engine running. Three men in light-colored overcoats and tan caps, toting two shotguns and a submachine gun, got out of the brown sedan. They walked into the bar and opened fire, spraying the room with bullets and piercing the cast-iron stove, then nonchalantly turned, walked outside and drove away.

Since Tear's speakeasy between Eureka and Orange was a block from the heart of Wyandotte's business district and two blocks from the Wyandotte police station, a number of witnesses on the busy thoroughfare, including a 12-year-old newsboy and the owner of the Studebaker garage located next door, saw them leave. Many of them ran immediately into the speak, then staggered backward, shocked by the carnage. Inside, only two were left alive: the relief bartender, Sam Messer, who had dropped down behind the bar and was saved by two half-barrels of alley beer; and a small, frightened cat with an arched back that hissed and spat when police opened the backroom door.

Three men had been riddled with bullets: Charley Tear, 34, a former Wyandotte police officer; John Pelletier (also known as Peltier or Pelkey), a former shipworker and the porter at Tear's saloon; and Joe Rivett, there to have a farewell drink before departing for Florida.

———————

"'It is unfortunate that one of the most outlandish, horrible and fiendish massacres in modern gang warfare had to be committed in Wyandotte—and that this city had to receive the publicity resulting from it,' says the editor for *The Gateway Chronicle.*[2] 'Why didn't the killers just stay in Ecorse, where all such killings belong?'" finished Walter Locke, amid laughter, as he read the paper aloud to those lunching in his diner. "Whaddya think, George?" he said, refilling Chief Moore's cup.

"There but for the grace of God," muttered George.

"Yeah, maybe you're right. But I get pretty sick of . . . 'if it happens in

———————

[1] Compilation of two articles in Wyandotte Herald: November 13, 1931 and October 23, 1931.
[2] The Gateway Chronicle, November 12, 1931.

Wyandotte, it's an aberration,'" said Walter. "'If it happens in Ecorse, it's to be expected.'"

Ignoring convention, the inquiry into the Cozy Inn killings was held in the Edinger apartment building at 114 Oak, where reluctant witnesses and carping suspects, most with surnames ending in a vowel, were ushered through a rear entrance via the attached garage in an attempt to keep identities secret. Authorities even questioned Minnie Stinson, though it seems that Minnie had a standing invitation to any and all inquiries.

The triple homicide resulted in a massive crackdown throughout the Downriver area, including Ecorse. State police began nightly patrols. Blind pigs were closed, basement breweries were destroyed, and "To Rent" signs began to appear on former saloons.

Raiders found a veritable arsenal behind shelves of canned fruit in a building at 704 Ash Street. While investigating "Black Ben" Sciacca's home at 256 Felice, state troopers turned their attention to a small, fenced-in dog pen abutting Ben's garage, now occupied by a lone chicken. Lifting the protesting hen, scraping back the straw on the floor, they uncovered a trapdoor which, in turn, led to an underground brewery beneath the garage, "one of the most elaborate ever unearthed," noted the *Gateway Chronicle*.[3] Accompanied by a warning buzzer, a pipeline from the 5,000-gallon brewery led to Joe Tocco's yard, two doors over at 238 Felice.

Giovanni "Joe" Tocco, father of four, was a prime suspect in the Cozy Inn killings. Said to be the brains behind Wyandotte's bootlegging business, he was also linked to Joe Evola and to the arsenal. But Joe Tocco had an alibi for the night of what was fast becoming known as the Wyandotte Massacre: two ticket stubs to a Detroit boxing match. To put the squeeze on, Wyandotte police arrested him for tax evasion and for operating the underground brewery with Sciacca and his brother Sam Tocco.

Eventually the police arrested eight additional men in conjunction with the slayings, part of a Sicilian bootlegging gang subpoenaed to appear before the Kefauver Senate Crime Committee. But the nine witnesses, blinded by terror, failed to identify any of them, and all eight men were released. The charges against Joe Tocco were dropped.

Three months later, Sunday, February 21, 1932, Joe Tocco's two-story brick home on Felice Street was rocked by several explosions. Bricks reportedly flew in all directions, and four windows and two doors were blown out of the home of a neighbor, though no one was home in either house. The perpetrators were never found.

Seven years later (Monday, May 2, 1938), at 9:30 p.m., Joe Tocco, then operating the chic Kit Kat Club in Detroit, took six slugs in the back as he was being chased into a neighbor's front door at 275 Antoine Street. Though he

---

[3] Gateway Chronicle, November 19, 1931.

was conscious for several hours, he refused to name his assailants or admit to any knowledge of the Cozy Inn killings of Rivett, *et al.* He died on Tuesday, May 3, after which he was laid out in his living room where a nun tended his body every day during the visitation (he gave often to the church and was never, ever divorced). Buried from St. Elizabeth's Church on Saturday, May 7, he was interred in Mt. Carmel Cemetery in a copper coffin "secured by a combination lock." Eleven cars were needed to ferry the floral tributes.

For over 70 years, Wyandotte, fat with stills, car chases, shootouts, rum-running in broad daylight, and the unsolved killing of Immigration Officer Franklin Wood, whose boat was rammed near Michigan Alkali while he was pursuing rum runners, would not own up to its part in the Prohibition follies, despite the blood stains on the ceiling of Charley Tear's ex-saloon during its subsequent ten-year run as a used-furniture store.

Edwina M. DeWindt was extremely thorough when she wrote the history of Wyandotte. Published in 1955, it seemed to cover everything in its 522 pages: Wyandott Indians, first settlers, city achievements, business, schools, undertakers, Civilian Defense during World War II. She titled it *Proudly We Record*, possibly boxing herself in, for how to proudly record the doings in Wyandotte in the 1920s and 30s? So she didn't. She skipped that era entirely. It wasn't until 2004 that a supplement came out to fill the gap, George Gouth's *Booze, Boats & Bad Times: Recalling Wyandotte's Dark Days of Prohibition.*

Chapter 44

Tuesday, May 24, 1932

The merrymaking had been muted on May 4, 1932, the day Shirley Ann Moore turned 11. It was becoming increasingly clear that, come June, come report cards, both she and Dia would be repeating their respective grades, Shay (5th) for lack of concentration, Dia (7th) for horsing around. Shay had been in hot water for the entire month of May, having foolishly hinted about the impending calamity, intent on softening the blow. She should have known better; she wouldn't get off any easier: her father would never allow for time served.

Then on a warm Tuesday in spring, Marce only added to Shay's misery. Having hurried home from school and changed into an old dress, having slung her roller skates over her shoulder and her skate key round her neck, Shay nearly made it out the door when Freda came from the kitchen and snagged her.

"Where you goin'?"

"Betty Navarre's."

"Did you do your homework?"

"Some, I'll do the rest later."

"All right. But no radio."

"There's nothin' on anyway," replied Shay, backing out the screen door.

"Why don'tcha take Marce with you," offered Freda, "so she can play with Midge."

"Awwww, Freds."

"Would it kill ya?"

"But what if she gets in a fight?"

"Why would she get in a fight?"

"Why would she get in a fight!" cried Shay. "She's always getting in fights. And Midge won't take no guff."

"Nothing's gonna happen if you keep a close eye on her," countered Freda.

"Awww, Freds."

So Shay was soon skating in a tight circle on the sidewalk while Marce sat on the bottom step, clamping on her skates.

"Don't go far, dinner's at six!" reminded Freda as they roared off.

The girls soared up Monroe, steel wheels spinning. Once across State, they sailed up the sidewalk, rumbled across Bourassa and past the two huge shade trees of the old Raupp homestead. Ahead, just past a house set way back, stood the Navarre home, a long, narrow, two-story bungalow with gently sloping gables.

Betty was at the door, clearly looking for a break. "Thought it was just us," she mumbled.

"Thought so too," tight-lipped Shay.

"Midge!" yelled Betty.

Eventually the foursome pushed off, Shay and Betty out front, beefing about younger sisters, backtracking past the Raupp homestead and its two huge shade trees, Shay periodically glancing uneasily over her shoulder to check on Marce who seemed to be chatting affably with Midge, a feisty towhead, as they rolled along, no fights in sight.

They turned west on Bourassa and skated past the alley, maneuvering over the rough bits; took a left onto High; waved at Nettie Raupp, who was down on her knees preparing her garden beds; cruised around Charlie Evans' Hupmobile, which was partially blocking his sidewalk; gave a shout out to Butzie Raupp, Betty's cousin, reading on her front porch; then picked up speed when they hit a long patch of smooth surface.

Throughout, Shay kept one eye glued over her shoulder. But Marce and Midge seemed deep in talk; so deep, in fact, they were lagging behind.

"You getting tired?" she yelled.

"No!" unisoned the younger girls.

"Then keep up, okay?" yelled Shay, reaching the intersection, swerving left onto White, glancing warily over her shoulder until Marce and Midge, all love and harmony, rounded the corner as well.

They glided past the half-block of darkened windows that lined the side of Raupp's Garage, gave a Hi! to its mechanic who was bent over the fender of a broken-down Buick. Then they rounded the corner onto Monroe once more and rolled past the front of the garage, exchanging waves with Nibbs O'Hearn who was seated on a green bench beneath the plate-glass window, rolled past its double-bay doors, rolled by its upstairs entry door, former home of Lefty Clark.

Shay decelerated for about half a block, craning her neck until the younger girls appeared at the corner. Then she caught up with Betty. But when she glanced back seconds later, Marce and Midge had disappeared.

"Aw, dang it," whined Shay, coming to a halt.

"What?"

"They gave us the slip."

"Maybe they just doubled back," offered Betty.

"Nawww, Marce is up to something."

"Why Marce? Midge is no angel."

"Trust me. She's up to something." With that, Shay grabbed her key, fell to one knee and tightened a clamp. "I'll kill her."

They hit the pavement hard, retracing their route. Arms pumping, they zoomed past Nibbs O'Hearn, sitting on his green bench; plunged up White; streaked past the mechanic leaning over the Buick; swerved onto High, hail-ing Butzie; whipped round the Hupmobile still partially blocking the sidewalk; waved at Nettie Raupp, down on her knees; screeched to a halt at the corner of Bourassa. Nothing. Then, whirling round, they shot back up High, streaking past Nettie, whipping round Charlie's Hup, using his bumper for propulsion, lurching onto White, shooting past the grassy side lot and the mechanic adding water to the battery, then careened round the corner and found themselves back in front of the plate-glass window of Raupp's Garage, bent over double, feebly attempting to force air into their lungs.

"What are we gonna do?" wheezed Betty.

"Don't know," gasped Shay, hands on hips, lungs burning. "Don't know."

"Maybe they crossed White Street."

"Naw," wheezed Shay. "It's dirt," she gasped. "They woulda. Hadda. Cross slow," she croaked. Then the clock through Raupp's front window caught her eye. 6:00. Dinner. "I'm dead meat."

Nibbs O'Hearn, all grin, motioned the girls closer. "They're in there," he whispered from his green perch.

"Pardon?" said Shay.

"They're in there."

"In where?"

"In there," he said, pointing to the open garage and its blackened interior. "Barreled right by me. Fwoosh. Right in."

"But didn't they come back out?" asked Shay.

"Nope."

"You sure?"

"I'm old but not that old."

"Don't worry," said Betty, voice low. "Uncle Ollie never let kids play in there. Red won't either. "

"Red's not in there," confided Nibbs.

"Then who's in charge?" asked Betty.

Nibbs crimped his nose in disgust. "The guy fixin' the battery on the car round the corner. None too friendly, either."

That said, the guy fixing the battery on the car came round the corner, watering can in hand, muttered, "You kids still here?" and ambled through the wide doors of the front bay.

Shay rolled down Raupp's wide driveway into the paved street, motioning Betty to follow. They settled on the grass of the treeless lot across the street and unclamped their skates. Then they waited, certain that their charges would soon come flying out on their ears or rears, whichever landed first.

"My pa's gonna kill her," said Betty.

"My pa's gonna kill *me*," moaned Shay.

Well, speak of the devil.

A police car was coming slowly up Monroe. Shay silently followed its progress as the black car pulled to the curb across the way. George Moore, still in uniform, leaned out the driver-side window and beckoned with an almost imperceptible flick of an index finger. Shay was halfway to the car, Betty in tow, when he asked affably. "What time's dinner?"

"Six o'clock," said Shay.

"What time is it now?"

"See, Pa," said Shay. "This is why I need a watch."

"Try again," he said, pointing to the clock in Raupp's window.

"Quarter after six."

"Exactly," said George. "And what's Freda like when her dinner gets cold?"

"Mad."

"Precisely. And what's my reaction when I'm sent to fetch you?"

"Not good."

"Bingo. Now get Marce and get in the car."

Shay hesitated. Then she climbed on the running board, leaned in the back window, set her skates on the seat and returned to the ground.

Betty filled the lull. "Marce and my sister are in Raupp's Garage, Mr. Moore."

"Marce and Midge?" said George.

"Yes."

"What for?"

"Wish we knew," said Shay.

"But you were told to keep an eye on her."

"I *was* keepin' an eye on her, Pa. One minute, they're skatin' behind us. The next minute, they're gone."

"But what makes you think they're in Raupp's Garage?"

"Mr. O'Hearn saw 'em go in."

"Nibbs?" said George, glancing through his windshield, locating Nibbs parked on his perch. "How long ago?"

"I'd say about nine-a-half minutes."

"Nine-and-a-half minutes?" said George, amazingly straight-faced.

"Pretty much."

"Tee, why didn't you just go in and get 'em?"

"Cuz I figured she'd come out. Cuz the guy in charge doesn't look too happy as it is."

"Do me a favor."

"Sure."

"Just go in and get 'em."

"But, Paaaaa."

"Thank you."

George idled impatiently, along with his engine, while the girls entered the yawning bay. They soon returned and slumped against the driver-side door.

"What a grouch," whispered Shay.

"Who? Red?" asked George.

"No. That mechanic."

"Whad he say?"

"They're not there."

"Then where are they?" asked George, growing uneasy.

"They gotta be in there, Pa," said Shay. "We been watching the door."

"Honest, Mr. Moore," said Betty. "They never came out."

"They must have."

"They didn't, George," murmured Nibbs, who had moseyed over. "I been right here the whole time. They skated in but they didn't skate out."

"Then they probably went out the back door and up the alley," said George, getting out of the car, slamming the door. "Can't be far." He walked up the driveway, strolled into the garage, scanned the darkened interior, peeked past the furnace and finally spotted the mechanic underneath a 1928 Ford. "How ya doin'?" he asked a pair of legs.

"Busy as hell," replied the legs. "And I'm closing."

"Red here?"

"No, he took the week off."

"Sick?"

"Gone fly fishin' up north. Thunder Bay."

"And you are?"

"What's up?" asked the mechanic, sliding out from under the Ford, wrench in hand, annoyed, revealing by the flicker of an eye that he wasn't particularly fond of men in blue.

"George Moore," said George, extending a hand.

"Hank," said the mechanic, ignoring it.

"Hank?"

"Just Hank."

"Have you seen two little girls. 'Bout eight?"

"I already told them kids just a minute ago. Ain't no girls in here."

"Look, two girls are missing and one of 'em's mine."

"That so?" said the mechanic, still seated on the dolly. "Well, they ain't in here."

"But Nibbs saw them come in about ten minutes ago."

"What for?"

"Don't know."

"Look. For the last time. They ain't in here," the mechanic replied, jut-jawed.

"What about the back entrance?" asked George. "Can anyone get out that way?"

"Nope, it's locked. And Red's got the key."

"And the door upstairs, the one to the fire escape?"

"Chained."

"Mind if I check?"

"Not at all," said the mechanic, wiping his hands on his bibbed overall. "If ya got a warrant."

"Look," said George. "I'm just looking for my daughter. If you won't let me check upstairs, I'd consider it a great favor if you'd do the honors."

The mechanic dropped his wrench with an aggrieved clank and rose stiffly from the dolly. Then he strolled past the furnace, opened the upstairs door and could be heard doggedly climbing the stairs. He soon returned.

"Nobody up there."

"Didja check the kitchen?"

"Look. Sir. I got a car to fix—three to be exact—and we're closing."

"Can't I at least look in the cars you've got sitting around, waiting for servicing?"

"Be my guest," said the mechanic, who then shadowed George as he opened and shut each door.

"Satisfied?" asked Hank.

"Not really," replied George.

"Anytime," returned the mechanic.

———————

"Any sign of 'em?" asked Nibbs, as George came through the bay doors.

"No."

"They go out the back?" asked Nibbs.

"He says its locked and Red's got the key," replied George. "You sure they didn't give you the go-by?"

"Positive."

"Would you guys mind standing over there," said Hank, coming to the edge of the bay, shooing the group away from the doors. "Like I says, I'm closing." With that, the double-bay doors swung shut.

"Oh, Pa!" wailed Shay.

"Now, calm down. They're around here somewhere," soothed George, his stomach tightening. "Betty," he said.

"Yes, Mr. Moore?"

"I want you to go home and tell your mother. Now, don't alarm her. Nothing to be alarmed about. Just ask Hattie if she'd mind looking for 'em on foot. Tell her, I'll be cruising the area in my car. Okay?"

"Okay."

"Nibbs."

"Yah, George?"

"Stay here and keep an eye on this exit. If they do come out . . . if that jerk finds 'em and tosses 'em out, I want you to take 'em down to Hattie's. Okay?"

"Sure, George."

"Shay."

"Yah, Pa?
"Get in the damn car."

———————

George eased the police car away from the curb and turned right on White. After driving around the block, he turned right on White once more, then cruised up the alley behind Raupp's Garage, while Shay sat rigid in the front seat, peering anxiously out the open window. "I thought you were told to keep an eye on her," he said more than once.

As he came out of the alley, he took a right on Bourassa, a right on Monroe, took a left on LeBlanc, then another left and headed slowly back up Front Street.

"Marce knows better than to go on Front," Shay offered timidly.

"And you knew better than to take your eye off her," he said, approaching White.

"Freda's gonna kill us."

"Freda's the least of it," muttered George, as he slowed the car and stretched out his arm to signal a left-hand turn.

"Pa, wait!" screamed Shay, so shrill and with such urgency, he slammed on the brakes. "I think I just saw Marce!"

"Where?"

"By the riverbank!"

"But what would she be doing on the bank?" he said, steering the patrol car over to the curb near Joe Riopelle's boathouse.

"Back up! Back up!" barked Shay.

"Okay! Okay!" yelled George, shifting into reverse, backing up slowly in the parking lane.

"There!" shouted Shay, pointing to nothing. "Stop here!"

He leaned in toward Shay, and the two of them stared through the open window, scrutinizing the bank where a gap offered views of the river. Two shallow waterfront lots, just dirt and rocks and green shoots of spring feathergrass, now separated Joe Riopelle's boathouse and Harry Riopelle's Marine Works. Simmy Davis's Doll House, at 4535, had sat vacant most of 1931, until it was torn down. Ecorse boathouses were falling faster than ducks in duck season, thanks to the closing of the Canadian docks.

"Pa, I swear I saw her."

"But how on earth could she get way over here when you claim you were keeping an eye on her?"

"But I was," said Shay, near tears, her eyes trained on the bank.

"Well, Tee," he said, snapping off the engine. "You did a lousy job." Then he froze, spellbound. A crown of brown hair was rising above the ridge of the bank. When its owner got a gander at the police car sitting within eight yards of it, it ducked back down.

"My daughter, Houdini," muttered George. And they both jumped out of the car, front doors slamming, ran to the bank and peered over.

"Hi, Pa," said Marce, as she and Midge gazed up at him from about four-feet below. They were standing on a lower shelf of the bank, the lip on which the entrance to Simmy Davis' boathouse had been resting, their dresses, faces and hands streaked with dirt.

"Hi, Pa?" said George. "That's it? Hi, Pa? Gol darn it, Marce! If I've told you once, I've told you a hundred times. Never. Ever. Cross Front Street."

"We didn't cross Front Street."

"Don't lie to me."

"I'm not."

"Then how'd you get here?"

"Hard to say."

"You'd better say, sweetums, or you won't be able to sit for a week."

Marce glanced at Midge. Midge considered her options. "Follow me, Mr. Moore," she said. With that, the twosome scrambled down the gently sloping rocks that held the bank, heading toward the water's edge.

"Oh, for cryin' out loud," muttered George.

He descended delicately, one boulder at a time, booting an old dock board, stepping over a rusty oil can, often checking on Shay who was right behind him. "Now that's far enough! That's far enough!" he yelled to the youthful duo. "Those rocks close to the water are slippery! Don't go any lower! Hear me! I'm not in the mood for swimming!"

"But it's here!" bellowed Marce, slipping between a cluster of large boulders.

"Good! Now just stay there! Don't move! Okay? Don't . . . ow!" he said, nicking his knee on a particularly brutal rock. And when he finally caught up with Marce, he found himself on a rocky plateau, gawking at a rabbit hole for a very large rabbit, about four-feet high, which clearly could not be seen from the water and certainly could not be seen from the bank above. "Where's Midge?"

"In here," said Marce, scooting inside.

"Oh, for the love of God," said George. He removed his officer's hat and handed it to Shay. Then he unbuttoned his brass-buttoned coat, extracted his service flashlight from the holder on his gun belt, thumbed the switch and, with a long sigh, sank down on his hands and knees and crawled into the rabbit hole. Shay ducked to follow, her father's hat teetering on her head.

Once inside, still on all fours, George swept the beam over the dirt walls until his eyes grew accustomed to the damp, musty dark. Then he went slack-jawed. The tunnel had ballooned in size. Its shaft, crisscrossed with snipped roots and makeshift supports, was tall enough for a short man and wide enough for two fat ones. Further on he could make out a wider area, probably to accommodate wooden cases. No doubt about it, they were in a bootlegger's burrow, dusty from disuse.

Twin beacons of light shot back at him, indicating that the tunnel sloped downward. George headed down the modest incline with Shay in hand until the path straightened out, until Marce and Midge could be seen about fifteen yards ahead, two squat shadows behind their flashlight beams.

"Isn't this neat?" echoed Marce.

"Where'd you get the flashlights?" asked George.

"C'mon, we'll show ya," said Marce as the beams turned abruptly and illumined the path ahead.

Then the tunnel began to rumble overhead. Then it began to quake.

"What's that!" wailed Shay, hands over head, as the rumble became more thunderous and the tremble more distinct.

"Street noise!" yelled George, as the booming began to abate. "We must be walking under Front Street. Probably a trolley passing overhead."

The occasional rumbling grew softer as they padded along the well-tamped path, penetrating the darkness, following footprints and wagon tracks and old cigarette butts.

Why hadn't he noticed this tunnel before? he asked himself. Because, fool, its entrance had been hidden under Simmy Davis's boathouse. Except for its oddball architecture, Simmy's didn't call attention to itself. Most of the boathouses along the river lived up to their names; they actually looked like houses. Not Simmy's. Simmy's resembled a railroad car, with a row of eight windows high up on each side.

"Marce, Midge, you okay?" he whispered, having tightened the distance between them, keeping them always within view.

"Sure, Pa."

"Boy, Pa," said Shay. "If this keeps up, we'll be under High Street."

"If this keeps up, we'll be under Des Moines."

Finally, his flashlight beam locked onto a dirt barrier in the distance. Tunnel's end. His best guess: they'd marched for about 300 feet, about as long as a city block. George and Shay made a sharp right turn where the path began to rise. The girls were standing beside a ladder dead ahead, looking somewhat dirty, somewhat angelic beneath a faint beam of light.

"From here on, not a word," whispered George as he joined them. "I mean it, Marcie. Not a giggle."

He stood under the dim ray and gazed upward. The opening above was large enough for one man, or one man bearing a case of Scotch, though too small for a keg. "I'll go first," he said. "All of you stay right here, until I call you. I mean it, right here." Then he cautiously climbed the eight-rung wooden ladder which rested against the opening's lip and stepped off the final rung onto a concrete floor.

"Geezus," he muttered. "Where the hell am I?"

Wherever he was, he had come to a circular dead end. Still unable to rise to full height and barely able to stretch out his arms, he was trapped inside a corrugated cave, about 48 inches in diameter, big enough for three men standing, empty but for a box of flashlights from Gardner's Hardware, barren but for a jumble of roller skates.

Then he began to grin. If he didn't know better, he'd say he was in the gutted belly of a warm-air furnace. No firebox, no ash pit, no cast-iron radiator. No innards of any kind. Above him: a squat tin ceiling, tin exhaust ducts and a dangling low-watt bulb. Before him: a heavy, cast-iron loading door. At his feet: a small cast-iron draft door centered within a larger cast-iron ash-pit door. Surrounding him: the outer shell of a Hercules steel furnace with octopus ducts. And all those tentacles were just for show. And all those doors were closed. And all those latches were on the other side.

Uncertain as to who or what he'd find outside this combustion chamber, he leaned over the opening, gave the girls the shush sign and signaled for them to come up.

"Tell me this isn't a furnace," he whispered, as Midge stepped onto the concrete.

"Yah, it is," tight-lipped Midge.

"Did you turn on this light?" he whispered, pointing to the pull chain.

Yes, she nodded.

"But how'd you get in?"

"I'll show ya," said Midge, softly.

"Okay, but just show me," side mouthed George.

Midge nodded vigorously, squatted down in front of the heavy ash-pit door, took aim, then thrust her arms abruptly through the awning-like draft door, the door within a door. George cringed. Now, using her forearms, Midge boosted the entire door about a half-inch, then nudged it. The heavy, cast-iron ash door creaked narrowly open.

With little room to maneuver, George lifted Midge and set her aside, then got down on his knees. Warily, he pushed open the heavy ash door, stuck his head out, turned back to give the all-clear, then crawled out through the furnace like Alice in Wonderland. But unlike Alice, George's girth made it a little more difficult, and he knocked over the poker which was resting against the side of the furnace with a resounding clang.

"What the hell!" roared Hank, about ten feet away, as he slid out from under the Ford.

"Hello, Hank," said George, rising with effort.

"Son of a bitch. Son of a bitch!" cried Hank, hand on heart. "Where the hell did you come from?"

Hank's query was quickly met as he greeted Midge ("Son of a bitch"), then Marce ("Son of a bitch"), then Shay with skates ("Son of a bitch"), while they came crawling out of the Hercules. "No wonder Red told me that furnace was out of order."

George dusted off his uniform and looked around. No wonder, indeed. No wonder there was no shortage of aperitifs at Lefty Clark's. No wonder no one had ever been caught. They had just been in one of the two furnaces at Raupp's Garage. And what a perfect place for transport. The gas-tight joints were light-tight. Sounds were muffled by galvanized steel, asbestos and corrugated tin linings. And cases could be handed out sideways through the feed-door opening. What a perfect place for loading a truck late at night.

Another thing was certain. Those two furnaces had been there as far back as George could remember. That tunnel had probably been in operation for many lucrative years, even while Ollie and his brother-in-law Leo spent a year in service during World War I.

Now it can't be said that the mild-mannered, mild-looking Ollie was bootlegging. Nor can it be hinted that Ollie's brother-in-law, the fun-loving Leo, father of Betty and Midge, might have been in on it, though Leo did prominently list "bootlegger for Charlie Evans" on his resume in later years, along with Marine, foundry worker, beer-store owner and nightman/taxi driver for Raupp's Garage. And it is true that Ollie was mechanically inclined and could build anything. And that furnaces in 1916 came in parts and were touted as easily installable with the help of a booklet from Sears. And it is worth asking how each of them knew not to throw coal or light a fire in the foremost furnace.

> *"I was in that tunnel once," said Pat Dalton. "It was on the other side of Front, but I can't remember exactly where. And I don't know how we discovered it. The thing was at the same level as the river. I remember just going down and right back up. I was scared.*

> *"And it is true that Midge 'got her ass whipped,' said Mike Mitchell, Midge's son. "She told me that story more than once. 'We went down in that tunnel,' she said, 'and walked to the river. Walked to where the opening was at the water.' And when her father found out, she got her bum warmed."*

In 1937, the old brick pavement of Front Street was torn up, the street widened, the shacks and boat wells of Rum Row having already been removed. In their place was a park along the river, running from Ecorse Creek to half a mile east. But each and every spring the Wayne County Road Commission was called upon to repair a section of Front where the road sagged.

> *"They had to come out and fix the road by White Street," said Fern LeBlanc. "Because I can remember we'd be in bed at night and we'd hear boom boom as the cars would go by, 'cause the road had sunk down."*

Spring after spring. Until engineers filled in the tunnel in 1955. But fill settles. As of 2010, a large crack can still be seen crossing Front Street (West Jefferson), from the park to the corner of White.

July-September, 1933

On Saturday, July 29, 1933, with guests sweltering in the oppressive heat, Freda Moore married Lloyd LaBeau, cousin of Clayt. She had been dating Lloydie for close to five years, since she began work at Theisen's. Though the wedding at St. Francis Xavier and the reception at home went off smoothly, the prenuptials and postnuptials were another matter.

When Miss Munn arrived an hour before the wedding, she was appalled by the length of Shay's dress, a dotted Swiss number in mint green. Shay, who owed her fashion sense to the pages of *Modern Screen*, begged to differ. No words were exchanged; Miss Munn just told George that any frock below the knee was much, *much* too adult for a child of twelve, then offered to shorten it. Shay, in silent rebuttal, hid the light-green thread, then looked everywhere for it, even asking Joycie to help. Nope, couldn't find it.

Half an hour later, shortly after George had lifted an empty jar of mustard from the trash while passing through the kitchen and chided, "There's enough mustard here for a sandwich," and Rowe, who was facing a mountain of unpeeled eggs, had snarled, "Fine, I'll get you two slices of bread." Joyce realized there was a shortage of same for the afternoon reception. She told Dia to bum a buck from her father, then run over to Pilon's. Dia, being Dia, went up to George in the parlor and silently scratched his left palm, her usual waggish take on one of his many adages: an itchy right palm means money coming in; an itchy left means money going out. This was a little too cocky for George's taste, especially in front of Miss Munn. So he betook himself and herself, voile dress and all, to the kitchen where he kept the paddle by the breadbox, gave Dia a licking for being, in one account, a wiseacre, in another, a smart ass. The bride came downstairs to *oohs* and *aahs* and *ows!* and *owwws!*

As to the postnuptials:

The honeymoon was to be brief, the happy couple too poor for time off. Lloyd had managed to get a job at Great Lakes Steel, where he would work as a turner in the rolls shop for 30 years. Since the groom had to punch in on Monday, the honeymoon consisted of a single Saturday night at the newly opened Commodore Perry Hotel in that lush Eldorado, Toledo, just across the Ohio border. For Sunday's return, the newlyweds had leased a second-floor apartment on Westfield, near St. Francis Xavier School.

As the guests encircled the wedding car and Lloyd sat behind the wheel with a sheepish grin, relieved the festivities were over, anxious to be off, Freda, all smiles, went from celebrant to celebrant in the stifling heat, extending a wide embrace. She leaned down to hug Marce, and Marce burst into tears and would not let go. Briefly it was thought endearing and drew tender sighs from the on-lookers. For her part, Freda continued to hold Marce while soothing her, making promises she knew she could not keep. She tried to break away once more, but Marce held her even tighter and wailed, "Nooo!!!"

"Freda's not going away forever, Marcie," said George, hunkering down to comfort her. "She's coming right back."

"Not to here!" screamed Marce, her arms wired around Freda's waist.

"But you can visit her," said Joyce.

"Noooo!!!" screamed Marce.

Everyone grew uncomfortable, standing there with forced smiles for what seemed like hours. Murph and Peg tried to placate her, so did Ollie, so did Mim, but every attempt only served to intensify the length and volume of each horrid "Nooooo!!!"

"Just go, Freda," advised Rowe. "She won't stop until you go."

So while Rowe and Joyce held onto Marce, and Freda disentangled herself, Marce became even more hysterical, sobbing, shrieking, "Noooooo!!!"

Miss Munn had had enough. "We don't do that!" she said sternly, as she leaned down and grabbed Marce's arm, intent on putting an end to it. "We don't do that!"

"She's only a little girl, for God's sake," muttered Peg, as Murph fumed and George looked helpless and Shay stood off to the side, alone, fighting her own panic over the loss of Freda. But all held their smiles and waved as the wedding car lurched down Monroe and took a right onto State.

Marce was eight when she lost a mother for the second time.

Now it was Rowe's turn to rule the roost. But Dia wasn't about to take orders from her, and George gave too little support. Rowe was fed up with double duty. During her senior year at Ecorse High, she had worked at the township clerk's office on Front Street, typing up tax rolls. When Rowe finally did put Ecorse High behind her, two weeks later she clocked in at Modern Collet, which manufactured tools and parts for automatic screw machines. She also wrote for the *Ecorse-Advertiser* as their social reporter.

As for Freda and Lloyd, they were struggling. Lloydie was only making 34 cents an hour at the mill. During the week they charged their groceries. By the time Lloyd got his check and paid the rent, $25 a month, and the grocery bill, well, hell, they'd take the cushions off the couch to see if they could find a nickel so he could go get a beer. Since May of that year, 3.2 beer was legal.

Because they were struggling and Rowe was miserable, the newlyweds proposed that Rowe, now 19, take a room in their apartment, share in the room and board. And George, aware that ruling the roost was not Rowe's strong suit, went along.

With Rowe gone, the Monroe house kicked off its shoes and stretched out. Joyce and Dia moved into Rowe and Freda's old room, Shay moved into Murph's, Marce had the daybed in the alcove all to herself, and conflict was somewhat reduced, especially with easy-going Joycie, soon to be a 10th grader, in charge.

———————

Meanwhile, George had put a lid on the town. Ecorse could no longer be counted on to fill the front pages. Now it was Wyandotte. Which is not to say that the seven vices had packed their bags and shuffled off to Buffalo. They had just heeded George's counsel and become more demure. Most of his staff had come around. Now regarded as an able leader, he was considered to be firm but fair.

And repeal was in the air. On February 20, 1933, Congress had proposed the repeal of Prohibition, sending it to state conventions for ratification. Michigan couldn't endorse it fast enough. The first state to vote for repeal, Michigan ratified the 21st Amendment on April 10. Although it was up to the other states to ratify and only a matter of time, for some it would be too late. People were dying.

Many looked on the closing of the Canadian docks as a resounding success. George didn't. Ecorse bootleggers had always been proud of their smuggled product. The Canadians manufactured safe, high-quality beer and bonded whiskey. Americans were manufacturing poison.

Since alcohol was used in thousands of industries for dyes, paints, photography, textiles, anesthetics, the U.S. Prohibition Bureau stepped up the practice of "denaturing" it, making it unfit to drink by adding toxins, chiefly wood alcohol. Thus, millions of gallons of denatured, industrial alcohol worked their way into the bootleggers' distribution system, where they were inadequately redistilled. The government's proposed response was to double the amount of wood alcohol, making it twice as deadly. Editorials everywhere cried foul, noting the ensuing manslaughter of American citizens by its own government, perpetrated in the name of morality.

And although enforcement by death horrified many, there were those who saw it as a reasonable deterrent, a way to rid the county of lawbreakers. If, as the Prohibitionists claimed, liquor was detrimental to your health, a goodly number of them didn't seem all that concerned over the deaths of thousands from poisoned liquor. So what if they died, fulminated the fundamentalists; they shouldn't have been drinking in the first place. This was lost on several bereaved mothers in Chicago who had given their children a spoonful of whiskey to cure their colds.

Close to 12,000 Americans died in 1927 alone. Paralysis and blindness were also common. Over a four-month period in 1930, there were 15,000 cases of "Jake Foot," a paralysis of the foot for which there was no cure.[1] "Stumble-bums," sufferers on canes or crutches, dragged their feet in the unemployment lines or into the front door of poor houses. With the closing of the Canadian docks, Downriver communities, including Ecorse and Wyandotte, had even more household stills operating in many neighborhoods to fill the void. Basements, attics and bathtubs processed gallons.

George had seen death by rotgut. A call had come over his car radio on a Monday, at 7:30 a.m., when he was heading to work, a call from Officer Genaw to get over to 4303 8th Street. On his arrival, he was led downstairs to the basement, a converted rumpus room with tables and old furniture, obviously a basement speak, though all evidence had been removed. A woman who had been covered with a throw was lying on an old divan. By the look of her, she must have had a long, hard night. Witnesses said she'd been drinking for four hours, passed out at a table, then was moved to the couch and left there to sleep it off. The proprietors had discovered her body on waking.

"I gotta tell ya," said George. "It's hard raising girls these days."

———————

Sure enough.

The call came at around 6:45 a.m. on Sunday, September 24, 1933, and woke up the entire Monroe house. It was Freda phoning from her apartment on Westfield to say that Rowe was sick, very sick. Yes, she had called Dr. Durocher. Yes, he was on his way. "But he wants you to meet him here. He says it sounds like alcohol poisoning."

"What happened?" asked George when Freda, sleepy-eyed but fully dressed, answered her door. Lloyd gave a solemn wave from the kitchen archway, while the smell of perking coffee filled the rooms.

"Oh, Pa, I'm so sorry."

"About what?" said George in alarm.

"Getting you up this early on a Sunday."

"Good God, Freda, that's the least of it. What happened?"

"She was over at Duke Underill's on a double date. She was with Frank Butler, Duke's brother-in-law. He's living at Duke's now."

"Was Duke there?"

"No, him and his wife had gone out. But Duke told 'em they could stay and use the rumpus room, fix themselves whatever they wanted to drink. Rowe says

———————

[1] Alcohol laced with a tincture of Jamaica Ginger Extract, known as Jake, would partially paralyze at least 50,000. [pg. 309 in Ardent Spirits by Reynolds Price]

they just sat around playing cards. That they had a nice time."

"They?"

"Rowe and Frank, Hollis Sage and Richard Perry."

"What time'd she get in?"

"She says around two," replied Freda. "Then she woke us up around three and said she had a headache, that she felt dizzy, nauseous, had the chills. I says, 'Rowe, have you been drinking?' She says, 'Not that much.' I says, 'Did you throw up?' She says, 'I'm tryin' to hold it down.' I told her to go back to bed and sleep it off. We thought she was drunk. Then she woke us again around six-thirty, said she had cramps, that things looked blurry, said she wanted me to call Dr. Durocher. I says, 'Can't you wait 'til later in the morning?' She says, 'I may not make it 'til later in the morning.'"

Rowe's bedroom door was open, so George hurried in, acknowledged Durocher who was examining her pupil with his eye scope, then bent over his daughter from the opposite side of the bed. She looked pale blue and very small. Her glasses were on the bedtable, her pupils dilated, her hair and nightgown wet from sweat.

"How you feeling?"

"Not whistling Dixie," muttered Rowe, then she let out a moan and curled into herself. "Oh, Pa, I feel so woozy. My head's pounding and this pain in my gut . . ." She shuddered. "It just keeps hitting . . . in huge waves."

"How's your eyesight?"

"Everything's blurry."

With his usual precision, Durocher returned his ophthalmoscope to his bag on the dresser, gave a nod to George, and they adjourned to the living room.

"She says it was gin," said Durocher in a low voice. "She says Frank Butler mixed it with Vernor's. That it was a fancy drink with a cherry in it."

"How many'd she have?" asked George.

"She says two. If that's true, she had about two shots. Can I trust that?"

"If Rowe says two, it was two," said George. "Is it Jake?"

"Doesn't look like it," replied Durocher. "I need you to get over to Duke's right now. Find out what she drank, when, and how much. Oh, and . . ."

"Bring back the bottle," cut in George, halfway out the door.

While church bells chimed on a cloudless autumn morning and families walked hand in hand to 7:30 services, George pulled up in front of the Underill house. He'd have preferred this quest ended anywhere else. Duke was a big wheel in Ecorse, the town greeter, an unfailingly pleasant glad-hander, and a firm believer in Section 29. Politically, he was also a member of the loyal opposition, though he played both sides of the aisle. George had no idea if he'd cooperate or run defense, for fear of a lawsuit.

He rang the bell, pounded on the door, then cursed the wait, then pounded again. Finally, Duke appeared at the door in pajamas and dressing gown, purposely rubbing his eyes, obviously put out. Once apprised, however, he didn't hesitate; he hauled Frank out of bed, and all three of them tumbled down to the bar in the rumpus room.

When Frank dug into a wastebasket and recovered the empty, labelless pint in question, Duke turned white. "Damn it, Frank! That was raw alcohol. 90 percent."

"I thought it was gin! I thought I'd finish it up for ya!"

Reaching behind a string of bottles, Duke grabbed a labeled quart bottle. "What's it say?"

"Gin."

"Damn right it's gin. I mixed it myself. It's water and glycerin and oil of juniper. With a few drops— *a few drops* —of raw alcohol for a base. You served Rowe undiluted, 90% alcohol. Jesus, Frank."

Frank fell all over himself apologizing, so did Duke—both seemed genuinely concerned—but George cut them short. "Did *you* drink it?"

"No. I had beer," said Frank.

"What about Hollis and Richard?"

"Hollis had wine, Richard had beer. Rowe's the only one that had this."

"I'm sure it's pure, George," said Duke. "It's not craw rot. I get the best."

"Geez, Mr. Moore, will she be okay?" said Frank.

"How many drinks did she have?" asked George.

"Two," replied Frank. "Both with Vernor's."

"You sure."

"Absolutely. She nursed 'em. I mixed the first around 9, the second around 10 or 10:30, which finished the bottle. I offered to make her another one around 11:30 when I saw her glass was empty, but she just waved me off. Said she felt happy enough."

"Did you use a shot glass?" asked George.

"Yes."

"One shot per drink?"

"Yes."

"Generous? Moderate?"

"Moderate. I didn't want to act grand with Duke's booze. I knew there was only enough for two drinks, that I'd have to open something else."

"Where'd ya get it, Duke?" asked George. "Who's your source?"

"I can give you a name, George, but it's not gonna mean much."

"C'mon, Duke, where'd ya get it?"

"I'm serious. It's a dead-end. I got it in Hamtramck, from a guy who knew a guy who knew a guy. But I'll see what I can find out."

"Right away?"

"Right away, promise."

"And I'll need this bottle," said George.

"For evidence?" blurted Duke.

"Let's pray—for all our sakes—it doesn't come to that," said George. "See what you can find out." But he knew even as he said it that it was fruitless, that any name uncovered by Duke wouldn't tell him what he needed to know.

———————

Back at Westfield, George looked in on Rowe, who was finally sleeping, before they all gathered round the kitchen table, now blanketed with coffee cups, a half-filled plate of powdered donuts and sections of Sunday's *Detroit News*.

"*Pure* raw alcohol," said Durocher, shaking his head, holding the empty bottle. "That's what Duke thinks?"

"That's what he says," replied George.

"Then he's naive. You know it and I know it. I'll lay you ten to one he's been sold industrial alcohol, carelessly redistilled, that they probably sifted through old newspapers. There's no such thing as *pure* raw alcohol these days. Unless you live in Canada, unless you have a prescription. Ninety-percent alcohol's bad enough, but if this bottle contained wood alcohol, Rowe might as well have ingested anti-freeze or embalming fluid. Hell, arsenic's less deadly."

"But if it *is* wood alcohol," said Lloyd. "Wouldn't someone over at Duke's be blind or dead by now?"

"Not necessarily," replied Durocher. "He says he's only using a few drops. By cutting it with water and extracts for gin or lacing it with burnt sugar and fruit syrup for whiskey, he's diluting the hell out of it. Then he serves it in mixed drinks, diluting it further. Rowe got hers almost straight."

"Couldn't ya just make her throw up?" asked Freda, circling the table, clearing the clutter.

"That's the worst thing we could do," replied Durocher.

"But she's getting better, isn't she," said Freda. "The pain must be gone 'cuz she's finally sleeping. Wouldn't that prove it was grain alcohol? Isn't the worst of it over?"

"Well," sighed Durocher, with a look to George, "we'll know soon enough."

"Know what?" said Freda, catching the look.

"If it *is* wood alcohol, she can't just pee it away."

"That's what does the damage, Freda," added Durocher. "It stays in the body for days while it degrades into formic acid and formaldehyde. If it *is* wood alcohol, and if Frank Butler's timeframe is accurate, these symptoms are going to reappear with a vengeance—probably late tonight."

"What are her odds?" asked Lloyd.

"For recovery?" replied Durocher. "I haven't a clue. Responses to wood alcohol poisoning vary enormously . . . if it *was* wood alcohol. Depends on how generous Frank was with that damn shot glass."

"Well, all I know is, this isn't fair to the newlyweds," said George, standing up, passing his cup to Freda. "This isn't their responsibility. Would it be okay if I took her home, Ed? So I can keep an eye on her?"

"Fine, if you keep her warm," said Durocher, rising, straightening his vest. "Meantime, I'll go home, get some breakfast, then meet you there. But she needs to keep drinking water, as much as possible. Got any castor oil at home?"

George turned to Freda. "Do I?"

"There might be some in the upstairs linen closet," replied Freda.

"I'll bring some," said Durocher, thrusting an arm into his suitcoat. "Oh, and George . . . if she does need to throw up . . . hold her and lean her forward. We don't want that coffin varnish getting into her lungs."

Shay held open the front screen door of the Monroe house as Rowe, hair short and tousled, shuffled past in her robe and slippers, George steering from behind.

"How's she doin', Pa?"

"Just don't light a match."

"I changed the sheets," said Joyce. Then Joyce and George inched Rowe up the uncarpeted stairs while Dia stood below, barely concealing a grin.

"Dang it, Dia. This isn't funny," whispered Shay, while Marce giggled near the dining room arch.

"Aw, she'll be fine," said Dia. "She always exaggerates."

Freda must have called ahead because Rowe's old room was welcoming: the sheets were pulled back, the shades drawn, the quilt folded at the end of the bed, and a bottle of castor oil, as well as the kitchen water pitcher and a glass, stood on a bedside table.

While George monitored Rowe, Joyce herded the younger ones to 9 o'clock mass, then, on her return, checked movie listings, got them to agree on "Gold Diggers of 1933," fixed lunch, then popped popcorn, the smell of which caused periodic gagging in the upstairs sickroom. At 11:55, George dropped Shay, Marce and Dia off at the Majestic in Wyandotte, brown bags in hand, and thanked God for double features, comedy shorts, cartoons, serials and Movietone News.

"What time's it get out?" he said from the car window as they got in line for tickets.

Shay studied the times posted, dime sweatily in hand. "4:15," she yelled.

"I'll pick you up at 4:15, out in front," yelled George. "You hear me, Dia? Out in front."

"Don't worry, Pa," said Shay. "We'll be here."

Freda arrived around one, bearing her sister's overnight case, and briefly looked in on a frightened Rowe. Freda was scared to death too, but what really galled her was that it had happened on her watch. She *did* feel responsible, but she was also furious with Rowe. Rowe had known that her living with Freda and Lloyd was a trial, and she should have been on her best behavior. Besides, Rowe wasn't the only one dealing with nausea. Freda had been throwing up regularly every morning for a week. She wasn't feeling so hot herself.

Rowe slept fitfully most of the day. She couldn't eat. Nothing stayed down, not even broth. George, returning home after picking up the younger girls, sat in a bedside chair watching the clock, watching his daughter, longing for Agnes. He brought the radio upstairs, and they listened to Father Coughlin who was now linking the Depression to international financiers (read Jews) and the ideas of "Karl Marx, a Hebrew." Rowe dozed through most of it.

After dinner, while Joyce sat beside Rowe's bed, periodically blubbering, and Dia sat in the kitchen with Mary Dalton, periodically speculating on the state of Rowe's teeth ("Think they're black yet? Bet the enamel's gone."), George rocked on the front porch and enjoyed a couple of innings of the evening baseball game, a welcome diversion. Then around nine that night, George buttoned his pajamas, climbed the stairs with a *Liberty* magazine under his arm, and entered Rowe's room.

"Time for your castor oil!"

"God!"

"If you weren't so old, I'd take you over my knee," he said, pouring the oil into a tablespoon. "But this oughta make you think twice next time."

"There won't be a next time," muttered Rowe, before opening her mouth obediently.

"Good. Now drink some more water."

"I just did!"

"Have another," he said as he poured a glass and handed it to her. "One for the road."

Rowe elbowed herself up and forced the water down. "Why don't you just screw my mouth to the faucet?"

"Not a bad idea," he said, coming round to the other side. "Now move over."

"You sleeping here?"

"Yep," he said, crawling in beside her, springs creaking in protest in the old, wrought-iron bed.

"Why?"

"Keep an eye on you."

"You don't have to, you know. I feel a little better."

"Good," he said without moving.

"This isn't fair, you know," whined Rowe. "I know people who practically drink from the vat, who knock down case after case of Old Joe. How come I get sick and they don't?"

"Perhaps you have more to atone for," said George.

"Thanks, Pa."

"My pleasure."

"I'm never gonna hear the end of this, am I?"

"Not if I can help it."

"And Miss Munn?"

"What about her?"

"Does she need to know?"

"Not unless she's invited to the funeral," he said.

"Seriously."

"She already knows."

"Couldn't you have told her flu or something."

"Could have. Didn't."

"Well, just don't bury me in that damn Kolinsky Marmot," said Rowe, handing him the glass, turning off her table lamp, rolling over.

"Sleep tight, Auntie," said George, tilting his bedside lampshade, opening his magazine.

He positioned his pillow and settled in, but was immediately unsettled by the opening-page editorial. *Liberty*'s exceedingly wealthy publisher was railing against those who rail at the rich, calling it "un-American to the last degree." If a way could be found to measure the happiness of people, argued Bernie Mac-Fadden, it would show that "those who live on what they earn week by week and who feel reasonably secure in their employment are far more happy than those who are rolling in wealth." Oh, please, groaned George. Show me a man who's reasonably secure in his employment these days, and I'll show you a relief worker.

George soon realized that he'd picked the wrong magazine. He gazed down at his sleeping daughter. Rowe looked so vulnerable without her glasses; they were such an integral part of her face. All he could do was wait and pray. If it was pure grain alcohol, she'd be sick, but maybe not that sick. All he could see was the woman lying dead in that dingy 8th Street basement.

Around 11, he woke with a start, his table lamp still on, Bernie MacFadden tented across his stomach. After quickly checking on Rowe, who was still sleeping peacefully, he turned off his lamp, eased out of bed and crossed to the window, where, for a time, he gazed at the stars and the sliver of a moon above Mrs. Ostrander's. But he was sound asleep again when, around midnight, as timely as the ringing of the Angelus, Rowe let out a cry, grabbed her abdomen and began rolling from side to side in agony.

George was on his feet in an instant, taking half the bedclothes with him. He woke Joyce, called Durocher and got dressed.

For the next several hours, as Rowe, bathed in perspiration, drifted in and out of consciousness and repeatedly recoiled from cramps, amber light streamed from the windows of the kitchen and upstairs bedroom of the Moore house, illuminating the slumbering street. At times, she complained of nausea. At times, her breathing was labored. Much of the time she felt cold and clammy to the touch, her lips and fingernails blue.

Around 6 a.m., Durocher pointed downward, signaling George across the sickbed. They tiptoed past the alcove of sleeping children, crept down the steps, and huddled in the dining room.

"I've injected her with bicarbonate solution and will again, George," said Durocher. "I've done all that's in my arsenal to cleanse her intestinal tract, but as far as I can see, she's not responding."

"Are you throwing in the towel?"

"No, George, not at all. But . . . I know it's expensive. I know it, I know it. . . . But I'm advising you to call in a specialist. And right now would be as good a time as any."

The doctor from Harper Hospital arrived around eight and was immediately shown upstairs to examine her, the kids having already left for school in the rain. Half an hour later, in a kitchen consultation over a cup of coffee, the specialist didn't offer George or Durocher much hope.

"Wood alcohol. No question in my mind," he said matter-of-factly. "I'll have to report this to the Health Department." He took a sip, then returned the cup to its saucer. "In layman's terms, she's wreaked havoc on her stomach. Even now, it's burning the lining. And it still could attack the optic nerve."

"So what do we do now?" asked George, desperately.

"Good question," he replied. "You need to slow down the production of formic acid and formaldehyde in her system."

"But how? Are you saying there's not a blessed thing you can do?" said George.

"I can understand your frustration, Mr. Moore. But as far as I can see, Dr. Durocher here is following correct protocol. All you can do is wait it out."

"Are you saying there's no other antidote?" said George.

The specialist hesitated; then he pursed his lips and shook his head. "None that I know of," he said. But as he took another sip, George had the distinct impression that behind that cup rim he was holding something back.

"What if she were your daughter?" said George. "Then what would you do?"

The specialist from Harper paused once more, only this time he seemed to be giving the question serious consideration. Then he drained his cup and set it down on the table. "There is one thing I might try. . . if she were my daughter," he said. "But it's not been proven and it could be dangerous. Actually, it *would* be dangerous. No *could be* about it."

"What?"

"Well, in my experience. . . . Mind you, I'm not recommending this. If anything happens, you're on your own."

"We hear you," said Durocher.

"Well, you might try giving her a shot of good, bonded whiskey every hour or so. If she can keep it down. But it has to be pure, it has to be the real thing, right off the boat. The wrong kind—any denaturants, adulterants—would surely kill her."

George looked at him in amazement. "Whiskey?"

"Yes. Ethanol, grain alcohol. To get in there and mix it up with the Methanol, the wood alcohol. It might slow down the production of poisons." The specialist turned to Durocher. "She'd need careful monitoring to protect her airways, you understand. But if she can drink it safely, without aspirating, you might try inducing and maintaining a slightly intoxicated state."

"You mean, get her drunk?" said George in dismay.

"Precisely."

Since doctors could not issue more than one hundred prescriptions for whiskey within a 90-day period and most doctors saw it as a beneficial curative agent, Durocher and the specialist began to discuss who was nearer his limit. The specialist proved to be the better candidate. "But I must warn you," he said, taking out his prescription pad. "Even medical liquor can be tainted these days, which is one more reason to think twice about this."

"He's right, George," said Durocher.

"Then hold up on that prescription. No sense taking a chance," said George. "And no sense waiting for Seavitt's to open, either. I know where to get the real thing."

————————

Within fifteen minutes, George returned with the antidote, a prized bottle of Canadian Club with its Ottawa revenue stamp intact and Hunky John's sleepy assurance that he had purchased it himself from a government warehouse in Windsor.

Eyedropper by eyedropper, George managed to get an ounce down a somnolent Rowe. And though she was out of it for most of the day, her attendants administered the antidote regularly until the danger of aspiration had passed, until they could exchange the dropper for a shot glass.

For the next two days, with Rowe happily looped, visitor after visitor traipsed upstairs from the front porch waiting room to pay homage, while Rowe entertained. She was a veritable one-woman show, sitting up half-lit when she wasn't nodding off, planting an affectionate arm around each sister ("You know, Dia, I've always loved you. Deep down."), singing old camp songs, hoisting her bottle of castor oil, toashting to better daysh. Not for her the anxious sickroom guest, sitting in mindful reverence near the bed. Whoops and howls came from the room.

No doubt about it, she was out of the woods, but she still wasn't eating. Her stomach was still a mess. Though the Underills were sending over the choicest of edibles, nothing would stay down. On the third day, around three in the afternoon, a guilt-ridden Frank Butler sat bedside and begged, "Can't I bring you something? Anything?"

"How 'bout a new stomach lining? Something in plaid."

She was out of circulation for weeks. "Rowena Moore is home sick in bed," was how they put it in the society pages of the *Ecorse-Advertiser* (a clipping of which was brought over by Cousin Fern). Murph dropped by often. Ella rubbed her back daily to fend off bedsores. And Dia repeatedly stuck her head in the door and inquired solicitously as to the state of her teeth.

Chapter 46

Saturday, October 21, 1933

After the Hothams moved away, a woman rented the house on the corner of Monroe Street—a pretty woman, in her 20s, name of Molly Zelman. Soon a stream of suitors could be seen going in and out of Molly's house. All the boys were gaga. When windows stayed open on hot, muggy nights, the Moore girls were treated to endless spinnings of Libby Holman moanin' low. ("♫ *Moanin' Looowww, my sweet man is gonna go. If he goes, oh lor-dee. . . . He's the kinda man, needs a kinda woo-man. Like me.*") Rowe remembers sitting out on the porch one evening, gagging to "Moanin' Low," when Mike Pilon sauntered by and timidly knocked on Molly's door. Not long after, Fred Pilon, father of same, strolled by. Rowe barely had time to crouch down and muster Freda before Mr. Pilon was seen escorting his son home—arm in arm. That Saturday, George Moore was heard telling Nick Strassner that Miss Zelman might be a woman of "easy virtue," and the Moore girls latched onto the phrase with glee.

It was long after dinner, the last half of a warm October day, a brief reprise before Canada puffed its cheeks and sent down a northern blast. Rowe, Tommy Ouellette, and Pracky Price were playing gin rummy at the kitchen table. The windows were thrown open. Erratic, high-pitched screams underscored the Monroe Street twilight tripleheader. Shay could be heard chattering from the third-base curb: "Put it in there, Virginia. No batter, no batter, no batter."

"What say we go get a chocolate shake," said Pracky.

"Can't," said Rowe. "Gotta take care of the kids."

"That's all you do," said Tommy.

"Tell me about it." She banged the deck on the table hard, then proceeded with a four-way cut. "That . . . damn . . . Dia."

Pracky laughed.

"Sure, laugh, but she's getting worse," she said, chopping her words with an overhand shuffle. "I punish her, she resents it. Freda says, 'Why do you have to punish them? I don't punish them.' 'Yeah,' I says, 'Easy for you. They listen to you.' Freda makes it sound so simple. She likes playing mama. I'm not cut out for it."

As she flicked a card toward Tommy, there was a sharp rap on the front screen door. "It's open!" sang Rowe, and Molly exploded into the house, crossing the sitting room, entering the kitchen. Rowe peered above her rimless rims. It looked as if Molly had just gotten out of bed – swaddled as she was in a wrapper of huge red flowers while her usually well-coiffed locks haloed her head in pre-Raphaelite friz. She looks frightened, thought Rowe. Either that, or annoyed. There was ample reason for the confusion. Molly had drawn her eyebrows on in such haste that two dark-pencilled hyphens floated above her eyes in a state of Maybelline surprise.

"Do you know where your sisters are?" she demanded.

"Outside playing," said Rowe. "They don't have to be in 'til the streetlight comes on. Why?"

"Come with me," said Molly.

"Where?"

"Come with me and you'll find out."

"Want us to come, too?" asked Tommy.

Rowe tossed the deck on the table. "Might as well."

Rowe and Tommy Ouellette and Pracky Price followed Molly out the door and down the steps, marched up the sidewalk, sidestepped Bunny Strassner's grounder to right, stumbled across the bumpy ridge rows in the neglected Hotham garden, and entered Molly's garage—a series of weathered boards still standing from memory. With a sudden signal to hush, Molly tiptoed to the rear and squirmed between the front end of her roadster and the wall. Rowe followed. Outside in the alley they could hear a familiar voice jabbering in rapid gun bursts. Molly pointed to a tiny window, floating head high. Rowe stood on tiptoe and peeked out.

Just a few feet away, a touring car was idling in the alley—a large, gleaming four-door sedan, all chrome and two-tone tan. Two men were sitting in front with their windows rolled down. The one hanging out the window was nice looking in a pretty-boy way. The driver—who resembled Eduardo Ciannelli of movie villain fame—was not. And there were Joyce and Cousin Fern, stooped over, rumps out, lolling against the front fender. Since their mouths were closed, it was obvious *they* were not the source of the familiar jabber.

"Hear about the killing last month?" Dia was saying.

Pretty Face laughed, "In this town? Which one?"

"The one in Snyder's Place. That blind pig," said Dia. "Made all the papers."

* * *

Rowe backed away from the window in disgust. "I can't see her."

"Who?" whispered Tommy.

"Who else, and two guys."

"What guys?"

"Older guys. Italian guys."

Mistress Zelman quietly inched an orange crate forward. Rowe stood on it and gazed down. There was Dia, sitting on the ridge of the running board, chewing her gum, talking tough, her small mole bouncing up and down her cheek.

* * *

"Din'tcha read about it. This guy, Snyder, was corked by his barmaid. I know the barmaid, Sonya Dean. *Son-yaaaa Dean,* " she groaned. "More like Sonya Demkowski. My sister goes to school with her brother. Say, I like your hat."

Pretty Face leaned out the window and plopped his brown fedora on Dia's head. Fern stepped back for a look-see. "Suits you, Dia."

"Think so?" Shooting straight up the passenger door, Dia maneuvered for a reflection in the side-view mirror. "This a present? Can I keep it?" In lieu of reply, she groaned, "*Son-yaa Dean,*" and slid back down to the running board. "She even lied to get her job. Told Snyder she was twenty-two. Heck, she's only two years older than me. Heck, she's the same age as Joyce."

Pretty Face cocked a smile at Joyce. "How old is Joyce?"

"Seventeen."

Joyce smoothed her hair.

"*Son-yaaa Dean.* Can you believe it? Then again, if I were Sonya Demkowski, I'd change it, too. Heck, if I were Dia Demkowski, I'd move to Hamtramck." Fern laughed. So did Dia. Then, she craned her neck for a reaction, but Pretty Face was still eyeballing Joyce. And Joyce? Well, Joyce was examining the silver-winged swan sprouting from the car radiator. Pretty Face had eyes that did the Fox Trot.

Dia worked her gum until she made it crack. "You guys from Wyandotte?"

"How come everybody thinks we're from Wyandotte?" grumbled Eduardo, the driver.

"All Italian guys come from Wyandotte."

"Yeah?" he sneered. "So, how'd you know we was Italian?"

* * *

Four feet away, behind the tiny pane, an apprehensive Tommy leaned in toward Rowe. "Better get 'em outta there," he whispered. "Them guys work for Joe Tocco."

"So?"

"So. If she says 'Dago,' she's dead."

"Let her dig her own grave," said Rowe.

"Whaddya think they're doin' here in the first place?" muttered Pracky.

"Most likely waiting for a truck from Hogan's Alley, most likely waiting for a load," whispered Tommy.

Then Rowe returned to the window, possibly to look, possibly to avoid Molly, who was standing beside her with a fist slammed against her hip of red hibiscus.

* * *

"Why'd she kill 'em?" asked Pretty Face.

"Who?" asked Dia.

"Son-yaa Dean."

"'Cuz she was late for work."

"'Cuz she was late for work?"

"Yeah."

"In that case, he shoulda killed *her* !" said Pretty Face, grinning at Joyce, giving a wink; his eyes did the Samba.

But Eduardo had a bee in his bonnet. "How'd you know we was Italian."

"Just did," said Dia.

"C'mon, give, why'd she kill 'em?" asked Pretty Face.

"Who?"

"Son-yaa."

"I just tol' ya. 'Cuz she was late for work. Snyder was bawling her out."

"Hey, kid. I ain't askin' again," Eduardo leaned in. "How'd you know we was Italian?"

Dia looked at Pretty Face. "Your friend's gotta broken record."

"I'd answer him if I were you."

Dia turned to Eduardo. "How could I tell you was Italian?"

"Yeah."

"Easy."

"How so?"

"The way you talk to women," said Dia.

"What way?"

"Like you're interested."

"You think of yourself as a woman?" sneered Eduardo.

"I ain't no cheese grater."

"How'd she kill 'em?" interrupted Pretty Face.

"Who?" said Dia.

"*Son-yaaaaaaa!*" snarled Eduardo.

"With a gun," said Dia.

"What gun! Whose gun?"

As the streetlights began to flicker, Dia inched up the brim of the hat with her trigger finger. There it stayed, casually resting on the back of her crown. "They kept a gun behind the bar."

"And Snyder's bawling her out," sang Pretty Face.

"Yeah, and Snyder's bawling her out. So Sonya was really mad. So she goes behind the bar like she's gonna put on her apron. Then Snyder turns away and Sonya picks up the gun and blam, right in the back. Know how they caught her?"

"How?"

"The bartender grabbed the spittoon and beaned her with it. Swear on a stack." Dia let out a hoot. Fern hooted with her. "My old man smokes cigars," piped Dia.

"What's that gotta do with the price of potatoes?" asked Eduardo.

"Hell, I don't know." Dia pulled the brim of the hat low over her eyes. "I know you're just dying to give this to me."

Pretty Face extracted a pack of Luckies, tapped it against his fist, and two cigarettes sprang up smartly. Dia leapt up and snagged one.

"Rowe's gonna kill ya, Dia," said Fern.

"Who's Rowe?" asked Pretty Face.

"My sister, Ol' Muttpuss."

Squeaking backwards down the length of the door panel, Dia settled on the running board, stretched out her gangly legs, rested her elbow on the spare tire, and took a deep puff of the blackened and barely lit cigarette. "You know how I could tell you were Eyetalian?"

"No, how?"

"Process of p-tu elimination," said Dia, dispersing flakes of tobacco from her lower lip. "First off—correct me if I'm wrong—but first off, I figure you ain't Chinks."

Fern and Joyce shifted position for the run home.

"You got a smart mouth," growled Eduardo. "You know that?"

"You're not Pollacks, 'cuz you're not blond and you don't say 'dese, dem and dose.' You're not Hunkies, 'cuz you gotta sense of humor. Canucks and Micks I'd know in a minute 'cuz we're canucks and micks. Since all we got around here are Canucks, Micks, Hunkies, Pollacks, and an occasional Chink, then you guys must be . . ." Dia stood up and propped her elbow on the ledge of the car window. "Bet you thought I was gonna say 'Dago'."

Pretty Face was now smiling through a mouth of clenched teeth. "It had crossed my mind."

"Or ginney or spic or paisano or wop."

The two men did not move.

"But I didn't, did I?"

"Time to go home, Dia," said Joyce.

Dia shinnied back down the passenger door. "Sure you don't want this hat? Why don'tcha take us for a ride?"

Pretty Face's eyes were barely dancing. In fact, Pretty Face's eyes were sitting this one out.

"Where you wanna go?" rasped Pretty Face.

"The Gaiety," said Dia.

"The Gaiety? In Detroit?" said Eduardo. "That's a burl-e-cue. Like to see naked girls?"

"Like to hear dirty jokes," corrected Dia.

Pretty Face cracked the door open. "Okay," he growled, "hop in."

Joyce wasn't sure if Dia had noticed the tone change. Joyce wasn't sure if Dia ever noticed tone changes or just chose to ignore them, but the tone change was raising eyebrows in that garage.

* * *

"We can't let her get in that car," hissed Pracky.

"She won't get in. She's talking tough," said Rowe.

"You sure?"

"I'm telling you. She won't get in."

Pracky looked doubtful. He also looked around for a weapon. Because Pretty Face was pushing that car door open, wider and wider.

* * *

Eduardo leaned in closer. "How old are you?"

"Eighteen," answered Dia.

"Eighteen-year-old girls don't chew gum like that," snapped Eduardo. "They don't beg for no hat, neither."

"She's *fif-teen!* " said Joyce, stuffing both syllables with the Mann Act, the Lindbergh law and the Napoleonic code. "Three weeks ago she was *four-teen* ."

Pretty Face's whisper was deadly. "I'll take my hat now, if you don't mind."

"I thought you gave it to me."

"Well, you thought wrong."

"Give 'em his hat, kid," rasped Eduardo, "or you're gonna be laid out for viewing."

> *Years later, over a six-pack of Schlitz, the sisters would speculate as to why one of their number, the one with the mole, always went one step too far. While ordinary souls backed away from a detonator, Agnes's fifth born would add lighter fluid. Though some held with the theory that she just liked to "stir things up," others argued that it was her way of reducing tension. Throughout the discourse, Dia would hold her ground, steadfastly maintaining that the reason was much simpler. "Hell, I was so busy delighting myself with my own wit, I never saw the fuse."*

Because Dia then rose to Pretty Face's level, looked straight into his eyes and said, "You pack a gat?"

Pretty Face stared straight back. "Yeah, I pack a gat."

"What kind?"

"Colt .25, automatic."

"Show me."

Reaching under the seat, Pretty Face pulled out a small, hammerless, snubbed-nose automatic about the size of his fist.

"Is it loaded?" asked Dia.

"Yeah."

"Can I touch it?"

Pretty Face glanced up the alley. Then, palming the gun, he placed the snubbed-nose automatic on top of his right elbow as it rested on the open window. "Well?" he said.

Dia brushed her forefinger lightly across the square-gripped pearl handle. Then, she brushed it across the Colt medallion. Then, she walked two fingers toward the half-moon trigger.

Bam!!!

Everyone jumped. Because suddenly a garage door slammed and Dia's ear became a straphandle. "Time to get home, Doris Moore."

"Keep your damn hands off of me, Pracky Price!"

Then Ol' Muttpuss came tearing around that garage corner, yelling her head off.

Shay was in the kitchen frying a hunk of baloney when she heard the commotion. Count of one, the screen door banged open and in ran Dia. Count of two, the screen door banged open and in ran Fern, followed by Joyce. Howling with laughter, they disappeared round the corner and thundered up the steps. Count of five, the bathroom door slammed shut. Count of three, the screen door banged open and in ran Rowe. "I'm gonna tell your mother, Fern LeBlanc! I'm gonna tell your dad!" Then she disappeared round the corner and rumbled up the steps.

Shay adjusted the fire under the skillet. Count of five, the screen door parted an inch. Then Tommy Ouellette and Pracky Price sauntered in—casual—like they'd been away. Tommy breathed deep, taking in the salty aroma of the sizzling baloney, but it was hard to ignore the banging that was going on upstairs.

"Open this door!" yelled Rowe.

"You think we're crazy?"

"OPEN THIS DOOR!"

As Pracky leaned his elbow on the kitchen counter, a light breeze billowed the curtains over the sink.

"Hi, Shay. Whatcha doin'?"

"Fryin' baloney." The thick slab hissed and spit in joyous concordance.

"OPEN THIS DOOR! I'm not going to spend the rest of my life chasing you down the alley, Dia!"

"So stop chasin'!" Peels of muffled laughter slid under the bathroom door and cascaded down the steps.

"Want some baloney?" Shay asked Pracky.

"No thanks. Just ate."

"All I could hear was your big mouth, Dia! Talking tough, popping off!"

"Oh, come off it! We were just havin a little fun!"

"Fun? Would you take me to the Gaa-yaa-tee?'"

"I didn't say it like that!"

"What say we adjourn to Walter Locke's?" said Tommy.

"Nice idea," said Pracky.

With a "tell Rowe" and "see ya later," the boys were out the door like two burglars ahead of a Doberman.

"Open this door! OPEN THIS DOOR!"

The door on the upstairs bathroom was quaking from the assault. And there was Fern, sitting backwards on the bathtub's end, legs dangling, mouth clamped, holding down a roar that one small giggle from an unexpected source could easily detonate. And there was Joyce, a potential source, jackknifed in the bottom of the bathtub. And there was Dia, leaning against the door with a towel draped over her head.

> *"Boy, was she mad when we locked her out," said Dia. "And she's holler-ing, 'I'm gonna tell your Dad, Fern LeBlanc. Wait'll you go home. I'm gonna tell your Dad.' And Fern and I were all laughing."*

With that, a delirious Fern keeled backwards into the tub, smothering Joyce who let out a loud snort.

"That's right, make Fern laugh. Make Joyce laugh. You're always leading them around."

"I'm 17, Rowe," yelled Joyce. "I can think for myself!"

"Coulda fooled me, Joyce! How'd you feel if you had to take care of a pas-sel of brats!"

Dia whipped the towel off her head. "You take care of us! You don't know how to take care of us! Freda knew how to take care of us!"

"Well, if I'm so lousy, then Pa can take care of you when he gets home! He's gonna tan your hide, Dia!"

As usual, Dia chose not to stay angry. "My old man smokes cigars," mocked Dia.

As Rowe's tirade continued, Dia began moanin' very low and very loud. "♫ *Don't know any reason why she treats me so poor-ly, what have I gone and done? Makes my trouble double with her worries when shore-ly, I ain't deservin' of none.*"

Down in the kitchen, Shay cut into the sizzling baloney with its blackened edges, then shimmied her way to the ice box and reached for the ketchup, "♫ *Moanin' Looowww, my sweet man is gonna go. If he goes, oh lor-dee.*"

Outside on Monroe Street, as Bunny Strassner rounded the third base curb in the failing light, he could hear four lilting sopranos taking it on home. "♫ *He's the kind of man, needs a kind of woo-man. Like meeeeeeee.*" Then, the quartet slid into raspy, phlegm-clearing baritones: "♫ *H'ya tat ta, h'yat tat tata-tata,*" and the house began to sway like Steamboat Pete. "♫ *H'ya tat-ta, ta-ta ta.*"

While Rowe stood alone outside the door.

Chapter 47

Saturday, August 4, 1934

Dia was the first to hear. She and Mary Dalton had been sharing the back end of the ice wagon one damp and drizzly day in spring when Mary gave her the needle.

"I hear your dad's gonna marry Old Lady Munn."

"Naw," said Dia.

"That's what my mother said. Your Dad's gonna marry Old Lady Munn."

Dia hadn't guessed. To minimize dissent the girls had been told on a need-to-know basis. Dreading an uprising, George wisely split the ranks. Freda and Rowe had been told first. Freda, summoned from Westfield, Rowe, from upstairs, found themselves sitting opposite their father at the dining room table.

"And he says to me, 'Mae and I are going to get married. Where are you going to live?' recalled Rowe. "And Freda said, 'Don't worry. She'll come and live with Lloyd and me.'"

Each younger daughter heard it in her own way, and each in her own way wondered what he was thinking.

"What do you think he sees in her, Joycie?" asked Dia.

"Ya got me."

"It's all your fault, Dia," said Rowe. "You and your damn pranks. He thinks you need a mother."

"I think he's marrying her 'cuz she's a schoolteacher," offered Freda. "He's impressed. He thinks she's smart."

"Well, she *is* a teacher, isn't she?" said Dia. "So she *is* smart."

"She teaches 6th grade, for god's sake," said Rowe. "You don't have to be Isaac Newton to teach 6th grade."

"Who's Isaac Newton?" asked Dia.

There's no denying the fact that George was susceptible to flattery. Miss Munn's devotion fanned a mid-life ego. But Rowe was partly right. George was, indeed, looking for a mother for his children.

Agnes had done a good job with the older girls. Freda had turned out to be kind, thoughtful and reliable. Rowe could be caustic, but she'd done very well in school and was pretty much on her own. Joyce was easy-going, sensible, a decent student, and would be starting 11th grade at Ecorse High under the watchful eye of his intended. Marce seemed to be doing okay, except for her noticeable short fuse.

But George was more than a little apprehensive about Dia and Shay. They were not exactly scholars, and Dia was out of control. He knew the path they were on; he could recite it chapter and verse. As chief of police he saw girls their age often. The lost girls, the ones in trouble, had all started out this way: failure in school, lack of discipline, lack of parenting. So, for the sake of his children, he'd marry. And what better bride than a schoolteacher, a principal at that?

———————

"Old Lady" Munn was 39 when she married "Old Man" Moore on that cloudy day in August. He had just turned 50. They wed at her neighborhood basilica, the cavernous Visitation Church on Detroit's west side, wedding banns having been posted for three successive Sundays. A flood of teachers and Mae's three sisters were in attendance. As for George, all of his off-duty police officers showed up. A small reception followed.

> *"Peg and Murph were there, Rowe and her new beau John, Freda and Lloyd. We kids weren't invited," Dia recalled.*

The previous spring, while designing her invitations, Mae had mentioned to George that she was sure, *ab-so-lutely* positive, that the younger girls would rather stay home and play baseball. Since George would have preferred to stay home and watch, he had no comeback. Besides, weddings were not for children, Mae added, before returning to her invitations. "Joyce can take charge. She won't mind."

So on August 4, 1934, while the younger girls stayed home, the bride walked solemnly up the long, majestic aisle to an overture by Handel. She was a handsome woman. She got "all dolled up," reported Shay to Virginia Brazill the following day. Yep, she was a handsome woman, who, in the vernacular of her day, was about to go from an old-maid school teacher to a wife and mother of seven in the time it took to say *I do* .

Though "what was he thinking" had been on many lips for three months now, only Mae's sisters had bothered to ask what *she* was thinking.

"You sure you want to take this on, Mae?" broached Ethel on first hearing the news, even though Ethel truly liked the girls. "I mean four full-blooded girls. Talk about a handful."

"Handful!" laughed Gert. "Try wardful!"

But Mae Munn blithely disregarded the problems inherent in raising stepchildren. All easily resolved if approached correctly. After all, she'd grown up with three sisters, hadn't she? And hadn't she been shepherding children for over fifteen years now, eight as principal? She knew how to discipline.

And, even though she hated to speak ill of the dead, she would teach them grammar and manners, something their mother had failed to do. She would give them proper guidance; there was more to mothering than coddling. Yes, it was true, she had her work cut out for her, but she was sure she could turn Agnes's feral and begrimed brood into refined, resourceful, well-scrubbed members of society, as befitting the daughters of the Chief of Police. She would learn to love them as her own, and they would learn to love her. If not love, at least respect. Yes, she relished the challenge.

George had assumed that, once married, Miss Munn would simply move into the Monroe house, share the parenting. During their dating days, she gave him no reason to think otherwise. Once engaged, however, she reluctantly admitted that, in giving his *dar-ling* house serious thought, she couldn't help but conclude that a few changes might be required. A new coat of paint perhaps, inside and out? (Good idea.) And a new bedroom set? (That goes without saying.) Then there was the parlor. (The parlor?) Lord knows, she didn't wish to denigrate Agnes's taste, but Agnes's taste was not her taste and, really, dear, she chided affectionately, wasn't that green velvet couch a little the worse for wear? (Well, yes.) And the wallpaper? They could hardly entertain their friends in there, especially with his position in Ecorse society. (Entertain?) And didn't he think the bathroom needed remodeling? (I suppose. Anything else?) No, that was pretty much it, though she hoped she could find a full-time maid willing to work in such cramped quarters.

"A maid?"

"Oh, my goodness, George, I just assumed."

"And rightly, rightly," he quickly cut in, then censured himself for being such a dolt.

She'd always had a maid. At least, since she had been teaching. And, well, with her arm.

"But my girls could. . ."

"The girls are still in school and, forgive me for saying so, they need to spend more time on their studies."

"But shouldn't they have chores?"

"Yes, of course, but they could never keep the house the way a house should be kept. And shouldn't be expected to."

"But they've kept up the Monroe house."

"Let's just say, they've tried," she laughed lovingly.

"Tried?"

"Men don't notice."

"Notice what?"

"Little things."

"Like what?"

"Like scuff marks on table legs. Smudges on the molding. Fingerprints on the doorknobs. When was the last time they changed the curtains, added new furniture? How often do they change the sheets? "See," she laughed good-naturedly, "you don't even know."

Here's where he almost got angry. Here's where he almost said, my kids keep a clean house. Here's where he almost said, we haven't had the money to change the curtains, add new furniture, although Agnes and the kids have been begging me. But then he thought, maybe she was right; maybe he just didn't notice these things. Besides, it had been a long, tiring day. It would only provoke. And he, for one, didn't need the hassle.

So George began to see the house through her eyes and through her discerning peepers it did look fairly shabby. But where on earth was he going to get all that money? It was impossible.

One Saturday night, as he sat in her parlor on Richton Street, he waded in, determined to deal with the problem head on, make her face reality. "But, Mae, all those changes will cost a small fortune. Hell . . . Heck, a guy could build a new house for less."

"That's been my thought too, dear."

He paused. "What thought?"

"That it would be cheaper to build a new house."

It was over in a blink. His main argument for cutting back had become her argument for going forward. George, who had always been in charge of the wallet, doling out nickels for years, was so stunned that he just sat there.

During that August there was significant transferring within the Moore family. Rowe was the only one who stayed put. On Tuesday, August 1, four days before the wedding, Freda and Lloyd moved back into the family house, hauling the crib for Beverly, soon to be known as Day, their month-old baby. Their one-year lease had just expired on Westfield.

That same day, while his children remained with Freda, George and Mae moved temporarily into Alden Park Manor in Detroit. They were to spend August at Alden Park while Mae readied the High Street apartment.

George was more than happy to let Mae handle all the domestic arrangements. His attention was elsewhere. Politically, Ecorse, was in turmoil. All hell was breaking loose and he wasn't sure why.

That August of 1934, George's daughters remained under Freda's joyful and ample wing. While George commuted to work and tried to distance himself from a brewing political firestorm, Mae set out to clean and furnish their High Street flat.

With the help of Edna, the newly hired maid, and Hula, 20-year-old son of the owner, Mrs. Moore set about to decontaminate the apartment. She had them sterilize steps, Lysol counters, disinfect the bathroom and moth-ball closets. "I used to be married to Harriet Craig. Now I've married her sister," George told Ernie, jovially. "You could eat off our floors . . . if you were so inclined. We'll be renting out the dining room for occasional surgery."

Once the flat was purged to her satisfaction, Mrs. Moore shopped for lamps, picked out curtains, and found the perfect couch at Himmelhoch's. Except for a few choice items from her house or his, everything was new. Most of the Monroe furniture was left behind for Freda, including the sewing machine and the old player piano with all its sheet music.

> "Then Mae came over and took everything of my mother's out of the buffet," said Freda. "She went in there and she took the big white tablecloth and napkins. She wanted the little yellow one, but it was in the wash. She said, 'Well, I'll get it when it's laundered.' And I never gave it to her."

Mae went to great pains to give her four daughters *lovely* rooms, ordering bedspreads, shopping for curtains, buying rugs. Joyce and Dia, who at times accompanied her on Detroit excursions, found themselves caught up in her excitement. "A girl's room must be comfortable, a haven," Mae told George. "Something they look forward to coming home to. Not like their doorless room on Monroe Street. They're getting too old for that."

When George, who, some said, still had his first nickel, opined that a radio in each bedroom might be unnecessary since they could all listen together in the living room, she stared at him, then playfully tapped his hand. "You don't know yet, do you, dear? Nothing so blind as a man with all girls. Children of this age love to be off on their own, *need* to be off on their own. They're growing up."

In truth, George was charmed by it all, his fears laid to rest. To have her spend so many hours, so much thought, on his daughters' rooms boded well. She was going out of her way, above and beyond, "knocking herself out to get things just right for them," he told Ernie. "Wants things just so."

Chapter 48
Tuesday, August 28, 1934

On a cool summer evening in 1934, about 30 moviegoers arrived for the 7:30 showing of *The Black Cat* at the Majestic in Wyandotte. At the Rialto down the block a similar number were queuing for *Of Human Bondage*. But at the Ecorse Theater, few had turned out for *Tarzan and His Mate*. Business was also hard hit at Hunky John's and Snyder's Tavern, though Snyder's bartender was expecting a crush just after 9. Over on High Street, however, close to 300 people were lining up in front of the Municipal Building, on hand for the Ecorse Village Council meeting of Tuesday, August 28. The hottest ticket in town.

When the streetlamps blinked on, along with the sconces on the balustrade, Chief Moore strolled out of the police station in the north wing. Accompanied by two sergeants from the state police and eight of his squad, including a rookie, Bob McWhirter, he walked the ten or so feet to the main entrance of City Hall. By now, the line snaked back and forth on the terrace, down the steps, then extended north for a block and a half, with a break between curbs to allow for passing cars at Cicotte.

Once some of his men were positioned inside and some were placed along the queue's route, Chief Moore signaled for the recessed doors to be opened and endured some good-natured ribbing for allowing the fedora'd fraternity, bearing press cards and cameras, to file in first. Then he stood aside and ushered in the crowd, sprinkling pleasantries in with his advisories: "Evening, Burt. One at a time now. No pushing. Evening, Ernie, Frank."

"Evenin', Chief," said Charlie Dollar, who was out on bail, scheduled for trial for operating a disorderly house at 4262 7th. "Fine night for a scrap, don't you think?"

"I don't know what to think," said George. "Evening, Ollie."

"Evening, George," said Ollie, who, having lost the 1934 election as a trustee, was there as a civilian.

"This better be good, George," said Mim. "I'm missing *True Story*."

"I'm missing my honeymoon," laughed George.

Two men were already slouching in prime seats when the crowd began entering the small council chamber. The unfamiliar faces belonged to "Toy's boys," members of Harry S. Toy's prosecutor's office for Wayne County. Their presence reinforced the rumor that something splendid was pending.

Half the room filled up rapidly, split in two as it was by a solid mahogany railing. On the visitors' side, about 200 spectators managed to grab the coveted mahogany chairs, while about 60 others, including six of the ten policemen and George, stood crammed, double thick, along the sides and at the back. Others huddled in the doorway. The overflow filled the outside corridor, blocking the doors of the Ecorse Library and the American Red Cross, then continued down the stairs on which some sat two abreast, leaning aside for anyone passing.

In the still vacant governing arena on the opposite side of the rail, ten chairs had been spaced around a long table. When the regulator clock on the back wall struck 7:30, city officials filed in from another door at the back of the inner chamber, spiking their hats on the antlers of two coat racks, then took their seats at the long table with much jovial finger-pointing to friends in the crowd and many silent nods of recognition.

There appeared to be some subtle jockeying among the six trustees as to who sat next to whom, with Town Attorney Kenneth C. Weber motioning Paul Movinski into a specific chair. But most eyes were on the village president, Bill Voisine, who entered last. Looking dapper in a dark suit, white handkerchief casually fluted in his breast pocket, black onyx ring on his left hand, he took his seat mid-table in front of the official gavel—Don Beckmann, village clerk, to his right, Paul Movinski to his left, Kenneth Weber, Village Attorney, further down.

Assistant Wayne County Prosecutor Bill Buckingham turned to a staff reporter from the *Detroit Free Press* and commented, "We're not here officially. Just came out to watch the fireworks." Everyone in that room expected something to happen, though only a few knew what that something was. One or two of them, without offering details, had promised his nearest and dearest that there would be hijinks, and word had spread. Who tipped off the press would be the subject of much speculation in the near future.

Then, because he was seated closest, Frank Morris wound up the portable phonograph residing on a small table against the wall, placed the needle, and the first tinny strains of John Philip Sousa's "Stars and Stripes Forever," tuba-ed the start of the alternating Tuesday meeting of the Ecorse Village Council, Bill Voisine presiding.

Stormy meetings were the rule. Throughout Ecorse's political history, stubborn men contested issues: some loudly articulate, some profanely inarticulate. In 1922, when Fred Bouchard defeated Paul Vollmar and became village president, the issue was wasteful extravagance. Over his many years as president, Bouchard fought for better transportation and paved roads, and sometimes paid village employees out of his own pocket. He had died of apoplexy on an alternate Tuesday (1928) in the council clerk's office, following a fervent discussion over the merits of a new municipal building, the one they were sitting in this very night.

Now Bill Voisine gaveled the meeting to order, as Fred Bouchard smiled down from his wooden 12x14 frame. Then everyone rose to face the flag, partially obscured in the corner between the two hat-packed coat racks, and pledged their allegiance to it.

Onlookers were respectfully silent as minutes were read and approved from the August 14th meeting. Next, various reports were presented and accepted along with a resolution from the Safety Commission that instructed Police Chief Moore "to keep all slot machines and machines of chance from being in any public place in the village of Ecorse."

Then Voisine waded into controversial waters by having an opinion read into the minutes from an assistant in the State Attorney General's office in Lansing in regard to the *loyalty* (Voisine stressed the word) of the Village Council. In past years the naming of the town's Justice of the Peace had been left to the discretion of the village president. But at the previous meeting, after Attorney Weber asserted that it was within their right, the Council had usurped that power. Though Voisine preferred Albert J. Montie, the Board had blindsided him, rapidly moving, seconding and installing James Clark as judge. Voisine now proposed to countermand that move and return Al Montie. Those nodding off in the back of the room sat up. Maybe this was where sparks were supposed to fly.

This was by no means the only time the Council had trumped Voisine of late. Voisine had appointed Al's brother, Earl Montie, to the post of village attorney. The trustees, however, had denied that appointment too and designated Kenneth Weber, now seated to Voisine's left, whose opinions in his four weeks as village attorney inevitably favored the Council. Since most of the Council seemed to be in lockstep, Voisine was being regularly outflanked. But the Village President was a known scrapper. He was now refusing to sign any pay vouchers for Weber, claiming that Weber was acting illegally as village attorney.

But one-upmanship has no limit. The board now asked Attorney Weber his opinion of the Lansing opinion, and Weber opined that they could disregard the Lansing opinion until he could investigate it and give his opinion on Lansing's opinion. A resolution for same was made and carried. In the meantime, cases would continue to be heard by Judge Clark.

But sparks did not fly. The moment passed, the clock ticked on. There was approval for solicitation of bids for road work, a defeat for an amendment to a building code, funds set aside for the repair of a railroad crossing. By 9 o'clock, after the board had moved and seconded, approved and amended their way through the printed agenda, photographers were packing up, the crowd was plainly disappointed, and Voisine was feigning equanimity.

"I can't believe it," he said, picking up his gavel with a mischievous grin, preparing for adjournment. "We just might get outta here on time. Any new business? No? Good. Then, if there is no objection. . . ." But he was toying with his board. Obviously, Bill had known something was up when he arrived at City Hall, else why the crowd, why the cameras, why his request for extra police, why Toy's boys? A Judas in this bunch was about to pull a fast one. Which malcontent would raise his hand? Born, Movinski, Pettijohn, King?

———————

"Mr. Chairman."

Ah, King.

"Chair recognizes Trustee King," baritoned Voisine, looking to his right, to the man at the far end of the table who was rising slowly.

Charlie King, 37, owned a gas station at the corner of Front and Union. His tie was always a little off center, his shirt collar often curled, and he spoke with a western drawl, a little bit Okie, a little bit Kansas.

No one messed with Charlie, possibly because he'd stare you down. Legs splayed, hands on hips, which caused the parting of his suit jacket and the baring of his vest, he gazed down at a typed document on the table. "I move," he said, addressing the chair without looking at the chair. Then he licked his thin lips and began. "I move the adoption of the following resolution . . . that President William W. Voisine be removed from the office of Village President."

It would be hard to argue which came first, the gasp from the crowd or the flashing bulbs. George was caught off guard, and Trustees Ranson, 24, and Morris, 39, gazed at each other dumbfounded.

Oddly enough, the remaining trustees and the village clerk seemed unaffected. Clerk Beckmann, expressionless, logged the resolution into the minutes, Paul Movinski doodled, Jesse Pettijohn, 30, studied the agenda, barely hiding a nervous grin, and Bill Born, the old man of the group at 52, sat back confidently in his chair—suitcoat unbuttoned, one hand dangling over the backrest.

As the shock wore off and the smell of burning magnesium from the flashbulbs lingered, there came a smattering of applause, which was quickly drowned out by loud booing. To add to the cacophony, one man could be heard laughing. It was Bill Voisine. He continued to laugh until the boos petered out. He then rapped the crowd into silence with a drum tattoo from the gavel.

With the room hushed, King began again, relishing his opening salvo, "be removed from the office of President, " slowing down for the new stuff, "for official misconduct and improper performance of the duties of his office; that he be suspended immediately. . . THAT HE BE SUSPENDED IMMEDIATELY!" he yelled over the rising boos, "PENDING A HEARING TO BE HELD NEXT TUESDAY EVENING AT WHICH THE SIX VILLAGE TRUSTEES WILL ACT AS THE JURY. . ."

"What's going on?" asked a stupefied Trustee Morris, his head swinging back and forth between Ranson and Movinski.

"And that Paul Movinski," continued King, "AND THAT PAUL MOVINSKI! PRESIDENT PRO-TEM! BECOME ACTING PRESIDENT DURING SAID SUSPENSION FOR THE FOLLOWING 15 CHARGES: . . ."

"Point of Information!" hollered Ranson.

"Order! Order!" yelled Voisine, pounding the gavel, waiting for silence. "Chair recognizes Trustee Ranson."

"Does Trustee King have the charges written down?" asked Ranson.

"All mimeographed and stapled, Mr. Chairman," said King.

"Then don't be shy, Mr. King," said Voisine. "Haul 'em out."

As Paul Movinski continued to doodle and Jesse Pettijohn renewed his battle with a stubborn grin, Charlie King slid his hand in his open briefcase at the side of his chair, extracted a pile of papers and passed them around the table. Voisine, meanwhile, addressed the crowd. "Everybody be warned. According to village code, persons disturbing a meeting will be asked to leave. Chief Moore is here to see to that. Right, Chief?"

George, standing near the doorway somewhat puzzled, nodded. "Absolutely, Mr. Chairman."

The booing had ceased; the muttering hadn't.

"Whereas, President Voisine: *One,* acted as a dictator on village affairs, assuming the powers of the trustees."

"Oh, how I wish," muttered Voisine.

"*Two,* encouraged traffic violations by fixing tickets; *three,* used and encouraged others to use village-owned gasoline for private purposes; *four,* unlawfully employed a team of horses owned jointly by himself and Floyd Moshier on city work."

"*Five,* used village trucks to move stone and coal to his own home and to the home of Police Lieutenant William Montie."

"Way to go, Sharkie!" yelled Ernie.

Chief Moore looked over at his lieutenant, Sharkie Montie, who was stationed on the opposite side of the room, while Sharkie smiled sheepishly in return and mouthed, "Tell ya later."

"*Six,*" continued King, sonorously, "provided a village truck to move the household goods of Fred LeBlanc to a summer cottage . . . "

"*Seven,* encouraged the wrongful taking of village sewer crocks for use of private individuals, particularly Edward Ouellette."

The following charges (*Eight, Nine, Ten* and *Eleven*) concerned a nightclub called the Show Boat Promise, the repetition of which caused laughter.

Kenneth Weber's points, as read by Charlie King, were increasingly serious.

"*Twelve,* threatened to do violence to the properties of opposing trustees; *thirteen,* neglected and refused to enforce the laws and ordinances of the Village with reference to bawdy houses and unlicensed places selling liquor; *fourteen,* solicited, or caused to be solicited, $30 from one Charles Dollar, alleged operator of a disorderly house, as a condition upon which said bawdy house would be permitted to operate."

"Bullshit," muttered Charlie Dollar.

King droned on. "*Fifteen,* encouraged the violation of the State Liquor Law, declaring some places could not afford to pay the license fee required and "should be allowed to cheat a little." Then King brusquely sat down, the document clutched in his hand.

"That's it?" asked Voisine. "You through?"

King nodded, poker-faced.

"Sure you don't want to divide that baby up, Trustee King?" asked Voisine. "That motion's got more attachments than my Hoover. You seem to be proposing my ouster, my trial and my jury all in one go. Stop me if I get this wrong, but I believe there's a motion on the floor. Is there a second?"

"I second it," said Trustee Born.

"It has been moved and seconded that I be removed from office," said Voisine, "for . . . What was that again? . . . Oh, yeah, malfeasance."

"Point of order, Mr. Chairman," said Pettijohn. "Needs to be exact words."

"Then why don't we have our village clerk read it?" said Voisine. "I'm sure he knows the exact words. Am I right, Mr. Beckmann?"

As Fred Bouchard looked down in amazement from his wooden frame, Beckmann read from the memo. "It has been moved and seconded that William Voisine be removed from the office of President for official misconduct and improper performance of the duties of his office . . . that he be suspended immediately pending a hearing to be held next Tuesday evening at which the six village trustees will act as the jury. And that Paul Movinski, President Pro-tem, become acting president during said suspension for the following 15 charges: . . ."

"How about the abridged version, Mr. Beckmann?" asked Voisine. "Do we really have to listen to all that goop again?"

"How about this," said Born. "'Which are included in the *resolution* submitted *in writing* by Trustee King.'"

"That should do it," said Beckmann.

"Everyone through?" said Voisine, sitting back in his chair, observing the interplay. "Can I, as dictator, continue now?"

"By all means," said King.

"Then the floor is open to debate," said Voisine, looking around for hands. Not a single eye met his.

"No debate?" asked Voisine. Voisine knew the rough and tumble of politics; he was able to disagree with someone and still call him a friend. But it was doubtful that he had ever met up with such animosity. Though Voisine was playing it tough, those who knew him well could see that he was hurt. Certainly George could.

Weber gave Pettijohn a nudge. "I call the question," said Pettijohn.

"Since there is no further debate," smiled Voisine, "then we're ready to vote on the motion. So. All those in favor of suspending me raise your hand."

"I think something of this magnitude is beyond a show of hands," counseled Weber. "It needs a voice vote, Mr. Chairman."

"Voice vote it is," said Voisine. "Trustee Born, how say you?"

"Yes."

"Trustee Movinski?"

"Yes."

"Trustee Morris?"

Trustee Morris did not answer. Instead, he looked around the table in wonderment. "I have no idea what's going on here. I pass."

"Just mark him 'abstained,'" said Weber.

"Trustee Pettijohn?"

"Yes."

"Trustee King."

"Yes."

"Trustee Ranson?"

Ranson, still looking confused, voted a muted Yes.

"Five yeas, one abstention," laughed Voisine. "The yeas have it. The resolution is carried and I am suspended. Now what?"

"Now you surrender your gavel," said Weber, "and the president pro-tem takes over."

Voisine slid the gavel like a puck toward Paul Movinski amid loud boos. Movinski, 46, called the roll to make things official and continued with the meeting, while Voisine sat back, hands folded in front of him.

On the other side of the railing, one Salliotte turned to another Salliotte and whispered, "Can they do that?"

"They just did."

"I know that. But can they do it?"

As the boos grew louder and the crowd angrier, George signaled his patrolmen to be on the alert.

Then Movinski adjusted his rimless specs, recognized Trustee King, who proposed that a representative from Toy's office sit in at the hearing to be held next week. The motion was quickly seconded and quickly approved, while Toy's boys duly nodded.

"Chief Moore," said Movinski. "Are you satisfied with the handling of the ordinance cases by Judge Clark?"

"Yes, I think so."

"Then you're instructed to continue to send all ordinance cases to Justice Clark," said Movinski. Then in rapid succession, King moved to adjourn, Pettijohn provided the second, Movinski polled the group and banged the gavel. "This meeting is adjourned."

Voisine, no longer muzzled by Robert and his Rules, shot up out of his chair. "It's all politics and it's all bunk!"

"The vote has been taken and this meeting has been adjourned!" shouted Movinski.

"Weber's behind this!" shouted Voisine. "Because I protested his appointment and because I refuse to sign his pay vouchers! Weber drew up these charges!"

"This meeting has been adjourned!" hollered Movinski. Then, with a sweep of his arms, he bellowed, "Chief Moore! Clear the room!"

George didn't know what to make of it. He knew Bill had enemies. You couldn't be involved in Ecorse politics and not make enemies, but there was something very odd about all this. The whole thing seemed elaborately rehearsed.

So who do you listen to? The village president? Or the president pro-tem, who has just pulled off a coup? And how do you avoid choosing sides? Well, if this was a trap, George had no choice but to go along, and fast. He signaled his men to clear the room, then came through the gate and up to Voisine.

"Sorry, Bill," he said. "Legally, this meeting's been adjourned."

"Legally?" snorted Voisine.

"Well, let's sort out the legalities later," replied George. "This could get even uglier."

"I'll be on hand to testify for you, Bill," yelled Charlie Dollar, leaning over the railing.

"Thanks, Charlie," replied Voisine.

The next day, Voisine showed up for work, ambling up the steps of the Municipal Building at his usual hour, 10 a.m., affably working his way through a shaft of reporters while promising plenty of face time, singing out his usual cheery "good mornings" to City Hall staff, as he swept through his outer office where Anna McMurdo, his secretary, handed him a sheaf of vouchers for the semi-monthly payroll which needed to be signed, and Mary, an assistant he sometimes shared with Chief Moore, poured his coffee. After attending to the vouchers and other business, the suspended president spent the rest of the morning doing interviews with the men of the press, intent on making the afternoon and evening editions.

"The village board has no power to remove me from office," Voisine told them while leaning back in his chair, fingers laced behind his head. "I was elected by the overwhelming vote of the people of the village, two-to-one, and only their vote or the governor can remove me."

"What about the charges?"

"Charges?" he grinned. "Oh, is that what you're calling them? All trumped up. It's laughable. They all wanna be president. King, Born, Movinski. They've all run against me at one time or another. Last year I had almost 1,500 votes, Born had 178, King 290. Naturally, they're sore. Along with Pettijohn, these guys sit around snacking on peanuts at Snyder's Tavern, holding secret meetings, making policy among themselves. They even vote at these little soirees, then railroad their pet measures through regular meetings. Now they've trumped up some charges and say they're gonna try me. You really think I'd get a fair trial? It's laughable. All the charges made against me by the council are either utterly false or greatly distorted."

"What about the vice situation?"

"There is less vice in Ecorse now than there has been in years. Every one of the known establishments operating illegally in Ecorse has been raided time and again by the police department. It's Weber who's behind this.

By Thursday the town was at a standstill. Early that morning, the Voisine-signed vouchers crossed the hall at City Hall and landed on the desk of the tall and lanky Village Treasurer, Paul Vollmar. Vollmar balked at issuing the $4,500 in payroll checks, saying he didn't know who the Village President was. He called the office of Kenneth Weber, city attorney. "It's simple," advised Weber. "Make new ones and have Movinski, as acting president, sign them." Vollmar did and Movinski did.

But then Paul Vollmar lost his nerve. And because of that, he now had two sets of signed vouchers, one set of unsigned checks and a migraine. He was still uncertain which set of vouchers to draw the checks against. If this was not cleared up immediately, city employees would get stiffed on the morrow.

Mid-morning, at Vollmar's request, he, Don Beckmann and Charlie King piled into a city car for the two-hour drive up US 16 to the state capital at Lansing, intent on getting a ruling from the Michigan State Attorney General as to which set of vouchers was legal. Lansing's answer took many by surprise. The Deputy Attorney General ruled that same afternoon: "No provision of the Michigan statutes gives the council the specific right to remove or suspend the village president."

On hearing this, Weber was unperturbed, calling it just a curbstone opinion, since no authorities were cited. "We will pay no attention to this because it's wrong. The power to remove its officials is inherent in municipal corporations. That's the law."

But Effie Vollmar, acting as her husband's deputy, made one thing clear to the *Free Press*. "'Employees will be paid Friday in accordance with the Attorney General's decision.'"

———————

By Friday, it seemed to be going Voisine's way. Young Emmet Ranson was having second thoughts. They began, he said, about two minutes after he voted *yes* to suspend the mayor. "I was in kind of a daze. It came up suddenly and I just voted with the rest of the boys." Calling the charges a "frame-up," he filed a notice of reconsideration to force a new vote at the regular council meeting on September 11, though it only needed four for removal and young Emmet was the fifth vote.

But September 4th came before September 11th. And the "trial" was set for September 4th. Steering through this turmoil was going to require all the skill that George had at his command.

Chapter 49
Monday, September 3, 1934

On Saturday, September 1, Labor Day weekend, the newlyweds moved into the High Street flat. The girls joined them on Monday, one day before Voisine's "trial." But that was George's problem. Ecorse politics barely made a ripple in their lives.

Fittingly, it had been raining or threatening to rain for the past three days, making the move even gloomier. Everyone worried about an explosive scene from Marce, but Marce seemed resigned. Like her sisters, she was tired of living in limbo and wanted, was even eager, to get on with it. So on a gray day, soon after lunch, they bade farewell to Freda and Rowe and the house they'd grown up in, and Lloyd drove them over to their new home on High Street, 12 blocks away. Suitcases in hand, they trudged up the stairs and were shown to their rooms. Dia was to share with Joyce. Shay was in with Marce.

Though the girls were encouraged to take pride in and decorate their *lovely* rooms, they were also told to use hangers and hooks provided, refrain from handling the curtains, put unsightly slippers in the closet in the morning, close bureau drawers, shut closet doors, keep schoolbooks neatly stacked and magazines neatly bunched.

> *"Mae would discipline like a schoolteacher," said Dia. "She'd hide our stuff. If we left our slippers under the bed, if we didn't put them in the closet, they weren't there when we came home at night. So we couldn't get them for three or four days."*

"Don't worry about the beds. Edna will make your beds," said Mrs. Moore, as she stood in the corridor, addressing both bedrooms. "All I ask is that you strip them every Monday morning. All bedding and linen will be sent to the laundry weekly."

"Can we have some cellophane?" asked Marce.

"It's *may* , dear," said Mrs. Moore. "*May* we have some cellophane."

"*May* we have some cellophane?"

"For what, dear?"

"To hang our pitchers."

"It's *pic-tures*, dear," smiled Mae. "*Pitch-ers* hold liquids. *Pic-tures* are graphics. Of whom, dear?"

"Shirley Temple. Shay's got some, too."

"I'd rather you wouldn't put tape on the freshly painted walls. Pennants are for football games and movie-star photos should remain in the magazines."

So the *Modern Screen* clippings from a Monroe Street wall were relegated to a drawer in Shay's bedside table, and her bat, ball, and mitt were stowed. No matter. High Street wasn't the type of thoroughfare you played softball on anyway. Too much traffic.

Once unpacked, once beds were tested, once squabbling had concluded and dressers had been divvied and filled, the girls gathered in Joyce and Dia's room, door closed, sizing things up in low voices. They lay around, lounged around, sprawled around, waiting for orders, waiting for guidance, waiting for what to do next.

It was two o'clock. Dinner was not until six.

The door swooped open and Miss Munn swooped in. "Here are your towels, dears," she said. "Edna forgot to hang them." Two nickel-plated towel bars had been installed near the bureaus in the girls' bedrooms, the single exception to the bare-wall policy. "Do you know how to fold and hang a towel? No? Well, you have much to learn and this is a good time to start."

They rose quickly and huddled round as Mae spread an open towel on the bed. "Now, there's a right way and a wrong way to fold a towel. The wrong way's like this." With deliberate indifference, she briskly folded the towel in half with her lone hand, then quartered it, leaving a top square with three edges showing beneath. "Now, tell me, is there anything attractive about that?"

"No, it looks crummy," said Marce.

Mrs. Moore smiled indulgently. "*Dreadful* would have sufficed, dear. *Crummy* should be confined to sentences involving baked goods." Then she addressed them all. "Any house that stacks towels looking like this tells you a great deal about its mistress."

"But that's how Freda does it," said Shay, with a glance at Joyce.

"Sometimes, not always," replied Joyce. "But she always has us iron 'em and fold 'em neatly."

"That's okay, then, right?" asked Shay, turning back to Mae.

"Freda's been a *won-der-ful* caretaker," purred Mae, affably. "She's done her best to raise you properly, and I know you love her very much, but you must not assume that Freda's way is necessarily the best way."

"Now, let's get back to business, shall we?" she sang. "The right way to fold a towel is the hotel way and calls for folding it into thirds. Joyce, will you be my folder?"

Now Joyce, at 17 (18 in December), was nearly old enough to vote, almost old enough to marry and, for her father's sake, mature enough to play along. Which is why Joyce, who now felt like a four-year-old, said, "Sure."

"Watch closely," said Mae. "First, take an open towel and hold it lengthwise before you." Joyce draped it under her chin. "Good. Now fold its right outer-edge inward, a third of the way. That's right. Now fold its left outer-edge over that. See how they meet? Now fold the towel almost in half . . . about an inch from the edge. Good. Now fold once again. There. See how beautifully that stacks?" she said, taking the towel from Joyce and unfolding it.

"Now *you* try it, Shirley."

"Like this?"

"That's right. That's right. Excellent. Now instead of folding it for stacking, straddle it over that bar on the wall near its midsection. Leave it slightly longer in front. *Per-fect.* Have you washed yet, Shirley? Frankly, dear, you look a little dusky."

Joyce's jaw dropped, though she quickly recouped. "But Shay took a bath this morning. We all did."

"Even so," Mae answered as she exited the room and headed for the kitchen. "I'm sure you will *all* want to bathe before dinner."

Now Mae Munn Moore was very, very pale. All of her sisters were very pale. Her ancestors, who were decidedly English, were whiter than the cliffs at Dover. Fortunately, George, in his Irishness, also had a light complexion. So there was only one conclusion to be drawn from the fact that Shay spent most of the year looking like an Indian. Poor hygiene.

But there was another explanation for Shay, who, by summer's end, took on the bronze hue of a Pottawatomie. She *was* a Pottawatomie. At least partially. Agnes's great-great-grandfather, François LeBlanc, was a well-known French-Canadian fur trader, who married Josette Jourdain, a Métis, the granddaughter of Symphorose Ouaouaboukoue, said to be the daughter of a Pottawatomie chief.

Miss Munn had long been convinced that one or two of Agnes's younger girls rarely washed, but, for the record, they took a bath on Saturdays like everyone else, took sponge baths daily like everyone else. Still, Mae couldn't seem to shake her suspicion that Shay, in particular, hadn't washed since the death of Harding. And that dirty neck in the summer of 1931 had sealed it.

"I think there's enough hot water for four baths if they stagger them, don't you, Edna?" they heard Mae call to the maid, who was well-scrubbed and pale enough to get the job.

———————

The girls drew straws to determine sequence and Joyce went first, while the others lounged on the bed in her room, waiting. Severe lethargy was setting in.

"God, I'm tired," yawned Dia, her head hanging off the side of the bed.

"From what?" asked Shay.

"From sitting around."

"Yeah," yawned Marce, with a yawn so wide that her eyes disappeared. "This is so dumb. We already took baths. Why don't we just not do it?"

"Cuz we gotta," said Shay.

"Why?"

"To keep the peace, Marce," said Shay.

"Why?"

"For Pa," said Dia, invoking the mantra.

Then a berobed Joyce came into the room, towel draped over her arm. "You're next, Shay."

"Swell."

"Just one thing," said Joyce, hanging her folded towel neatly over its rack, leaving it slightly longer in front.

"What's that?"

"No lock on the door."

"Are you kidding me," whispered Shay. "Six people, one bathroom, no lock."

So throughout the day there would be a lot of polite knocking on the closed door and a lot of "Anyone in there?" and a respectful wait and another light knock and another "Anyone in there?" followed by a slow opening of the door and a careful peek before entering.

The bathroom was still cloaked in steam when Shay entered, nearly fully dressed, her towel, washcloth and robe over her arm. Standing on tiptoe, she wiped the moisture off the mirror with her washcloth, then set it on the side of the white porcelain tub, at the ready. Unlike the free-standing, claw-footed tub on Monroe Street, this modern behemoth was built-in, wide-rimmed and footless, nesting tightly beneath the window at the end of the room.

She knelt on the oval rug before the tub, studied the overflow trap, and turned the China-handled lever to plug the drain. After carefully examining the HOT and COLD wall controls, she turned on the HOT and let it run until it lived up to its name and inched on some COLD.

As the tub filled slowly, she killed time by sniffing from afar the delicate bottles and flowery tins, many French imports, on an open shelf. There was the ever-present Emeraude perfume. There was a jar of Pacquin's hand cream, Manon Lescant talcum powder, Mum deodorant, a box of English Peach face powder from Yardley's of London, and Mennen's for her father. But the most marvelous smell of all emanated from the English Lavender Bath Salts stationed on the right-hand corner of the tub. She unscrewed the cap, poured salts into the flowing water and watched as they swirled round and bubbles began to form.

Finally, with the water level well above half, with bubbles about an inch thick, she kicked off her slippers, wriggled out of her skirt and hung it on a hook on the back of the bathroom door, shrugged out of her blouse and draped it on top of her skirt, then paused. Keeping one eye on the unlocked door, prepared to shove her 88-pound body against it, she whipped off her slip, dropped her panties and slowly lowered herself into the steaming tub.

Now fully submerged, with lavender vapors rising, covered almost to her shoulders by a sudsy blanket, she could feel her muscles relaxing, muscles that had been taut most of the day. When the water was almost to the top of the tub, she leaned forward and turned off both taps. Ahhhhh! This was living.

Enervated by the heat, pores wide open, she retrieved the Lux bar from the glass tray on the wall, lathered her washcloth, sat up and scrubbed her face, her neck, her ears, her shoulders, her back. Then she took the small scrub brush in the glass tray on the wall, soaped it and scrubbed her nails. She momentarily rested her head against the back of the tub and stretched herself out beneath the suds, keeping the sudsy blanket pulled high, letting the warmth caress her. Without changing position, she felt for the washcloth, wrung it out, and laid it over her face like a hot towel. Ahhhhhhhhhhh!

BAM! The door burst open and Mrs. Moore sailed in, along with a cold blast of air. "How are we doing, dear?"

Ripping off the facecloth, Shay shot upright, threw her arms firmly across her chest, covering what little there was to be covered, and peeped, "Fine," which could barely be heard above all the wave action, as a wall of water within the tub angrily surged forward. When the water ebbed, Shay shivered in the draft and waited to see what it was that Mrs. Moore had come in for—possibly the Pacquin's, possibly the Emeraude—resolved to ride this out with composure until the woman left.

But Miss Munn continued to advance toward her, plopped down sidesaddle on the generous rim of the tub and said, "Hand me your washcloth, dear. I'll scrub your back."

Speechless?

Totally.

Mortified?

Need you ask?

With one arm remaining tight across her chest, Shay felt under the water with her other arm, careful not to disturb the suds, and handed the dripping washcloth to Mrs. Moore.

"Wring it out for me, dear."

Shay, now far more disadvantaged than Miss Munn when it came to available hands, pulled the washcloth to her right side and without moving her upper arms, especially the one snug across her chest, wrung it and wrung it and wrung it, then handed it to Mrs. Moore while limply averring, "But I washed already."

"I'm sure, dear," said Mrs. Moore, resoaping the washcloth. "But your efforts leave something to be desired." Then, protected by an apron, she began to scrub.

"But I done that already."

"Did, dear."

Eyes downcast, Shay sat there, being bumped and jarred, while her stepmother scrubbed and scrubbed in her vain attempt to scrub the Pottawatomie right out of her. But the dirt wasn't coming off. Skin perhaps, but not dirt. "Are you looking forward to school starting, dear?"

"Yes," gasped Shay as her shoulders bounced.

Mrs. Moore plunged the washcloth into the water, wrung it out with her strong left fist, added more soap and returned to Shay's back.

"It happened with me and with Shay," said Dia, "and certainly Marce. She didn't dare wash Joyce."

Once they were all washed, once they had toweled off and changed back into the same clothes, the girls sprawled on the bed, Shay, Marce and Dia up against the pillows, Joyce at the foot of the bed, getting more sluggish by the minute.

Joyce rolled on her back and stared at the ceiling. "Maybe we should be out there helping."

"Want me to go ask?" said Dia.

"Naw, I'll go," said Joyce.

But Joyce slipped back into the room within one minute.

"What news from the rialto," asked Dia.

"I offered to help cook," reported Joyce, "but she says, 'Everything's under control.'"

"Who says?"

"That woman that married our Pa." Then, like falling timber, Joyce landed face down on the bed. "She says, 'Just relax and enjoy your *love-ly* rooms.'"

"Who?" said Marce.

"You know who."

"Don't," whimpered Shay.

Then Marce paused for a wickedly long time, long enough to build comedic tension, before striking the M word like a gong. "Mum-mmm?"

"Please, Marce, don't," said Joyce, thrusting her top lip over her bottom lip.

"Mum-mmm?" repeated Marce, as the word reverberated throughout the room.

"All right. That's enough," said Shay, firmly. "I'm serious. That's enough. She's gonna hear ya."

Hours had been spent naming this woman. Dia was once asked, "You called Agnes 'Mumma' and Mae 'Mum,' right?" "Among other things," deadpanned Dia. "We didn't feel like calling her Mae, and we certainly couldn't call her mother. I don't know who decided on 'Mum.'"

Once they got a whiff of the sizzling meat emanating from the kitchen and realized with relief that it was 5:55, the girls exited the bedroom, then sat around the living room, low-voiced, like guests at the Grand Hotel, waiting for dinner.

Joyce yawned; Shay was almost comatose.

Just to shake things up, Dia lifted her voice in order to be heard, "Dinner smells *won-der-ful!* " then walked to the dining room and peeped in. "The table looks *won-der-ful* , too," she said.

"Why, thank you, Doris," said Mrs. Moore from the kitchen.

"Do you want me to set the plates?"

"They're fine as they are, dear."

"What's that *won-der-ful* China pattern?"

"Dresden Rose."

"And the silverware?"

"Derry goldware. But don't touch it until you're at your place and it's time to use it."

"I've never seen such an attractive setting," said Dia. "Have you, Joycie?"

Joyce cocked an eyebrow, none too thrilled to be included in Dia's unctuous flattery.

"The centerpiece looks *won-derful* ," Dia said again, as she rejoined her sisters in the living room. "Mums are just the right touch for a rainy day!"

"Butter wouldn't melt," muttered Joyce under her breath.

"If you can't beat 'em, join 'em," grinned Dia, her mole on the rise.

————————

Finally, George arrived home, heavily preoccupied, and went straight to their room to change out of his uniform. It was six o'clock.

"Where do you want us?" asked Joyce, as the girls entered the dining room and stood awkwardly around the table.

"Well, dear," replied Mae. "I'll be seated on this end, closest to the kitchen; your father opposite, near the window. And, Doris, he wants you next to him, to his right. Other than that, it's up to you." Dia was once more positioned to the right of her father's backhand, though no one was sure if a clip was appropriate when using the crystal.

They all sat stiff-backed—grins frozen—waiting for rolls, if there were to be rolls; waiting for grace, if they were to say grace (bets had been placed); waiting for what to do next. George, too, when he finally joined them, seemed a little stiff, possibly because he was seated behind a stack of six plates. Then Mrs. Moore, formerly Miss Munn, picked up a silver bell to her right and shook it vigorously. Even George flinched.

With the tinkle still resounding, Edna appeared in the dining room archway in her all-white uniform.

"You can begin serving, Edna."

"Yes, Mrs. Moore."

Edna reappeared with a large platter, bearing a veritable butte of a rump roast, surrounded by blackened carrots, halved potatoes, scorched onions, and set it before George. She then vanished once more, only to rematerialize with the Dresden Rose gravy boat, a wedding gift.

All eyes were on their father to see what came next. George rose, picked up the carving knife, flicked it with a flourish against its sharpener, then began to carve. And it wasn't even Thanksgiving. And that wasn't even turkey.

Slicing a thin slat of beef from the blackened rump roast, revealing its pink, juicy side, he positioned it on a Dresden Rose plate edged with gold, sliced another thin layer of moist, pink beef and laid it atop the other, then with a silver serving spoon, added two potato halves, one whole onion, and three quartered carrots. But before he could pass the plate to Dia, who stood ready to pass it to Marce, Mrs. Moore cleared her throat and said gently, "You forgot the *aux jus*, dear."

"The what?"

"The *aux jus*, dear."

"Ah, yes, the *ohh joo*!" sang George, slightly Fieldsian, to his daughters' relief, glad to see the old twinkle still there. Then he picked up the Dresden Rose gravy boat, poured the *jus* over the *bœuf* and sent the steaming plate by way of Dia, by way of Marce, to Mrs. Moore.

That done, he sliced off another slat of beef, placed it on a plate, added potatoes, onions, carrots, and passed it to Dia who passed it to Marce. Next he sliced off more beef, put it on a plate, added the essentials and passed it to Dia, who happily placed it before herself while muttering, "*Merci* buckets," which earned her a look best described as "You're within range." George sliced off another piece, placed it on a plate, added potato, onion, carrots and passed it to Shay who passed it to Joyce.

Aware that the next plate would probably be hers, Shay watched with some apprehension as George, in the act of slicing off another piece of beef, ran into gristle, struggled mightily, grew impatient, hacked off a voluminous piece, plopped it on a plate, added only one potato and three hated carrots while his attention was diverted by Dia's, "Need a cleaver, Pa?" and set it before Shay, who stared down at the rubber-veined chunk and wanted to cry. Then George cut a slice for himself.

Mae tinkled her little bell and Edna re-materialized to remove the platter, which meant that the second helping of savory beef, roast potatoes, sweet onions and charred carrots receded into the kitchen and could be heard being scraped into bowls for tomorrow's leftovers.

And, as they would soon learn, this was not just for special occasions. Every morsel that went on their plates would now be selected, cut or spooned by George. The days of family-style dining, picking and choosing, were over. The dreaded threat of boarding-house reach had been nicely eradicated. There was no longer the threat of unseemly reaching, because there was nothing to reach for.

"Bless us, Oh Lord, and these thy gifts," started Mrs. Moore, and the girls lowered their heads, butted elbows, and mumbled in unison.

Then George said, "Dig in," the only recognizable Monroe Street tradition left, and they did, most of them gratefully.

Shay was miserable. She hated "chewy meat." On those rare occasions when roast beef was on the Monroe menu, George would give her a nickel to go over to Lafferty's for a hunk of baloney. But she was well aware that her baloney days were over, so she sawed the beef into small pieces, forked each politely into her mouth, bypassed the chewing and swallowed the lump as best she could.

Dia was just as miserable. This was the kind of cut glass formality she'd been put on earth to shatter. But she had other concerns. Specifically, the cut glass goblet to her right. Confronting the problem head on, she picked up her goblet with both hands, little caring that she looked like a toddler, drained it, then set it out of the way.

Dining discourse was infrequent, except for the occasional lessons on grammar and etiquette. "Elbows off the table," or "Close your mouth when you chew, dear." "Marce, you're slouching, dear. Please sit up straight. And why aren't you eating your carrots?"

"I have a bellyache."

"Stomach ache, dear," corrected Mae. "Bellies are for babies."

> *Looking back, Dia said: "Mae's sisters used to correct her once in awhile, when she'd get after us for something. Gert used to say, 'Now Mae, she's just a young girl.' I do give Mae credit. I think I learned a lot as far as manners and socializing and etiquette and grammar."*

After dessert they adjourned to the living room. Long and narrow, it went the length of the front of the house. George had his own chair in one corner (not his Morris chair which had been deemed inadequate and left on Monroe Street); Mae had her own chair in another corner. Thus, the girls knew that the uncomfortable couch with unforgiving arms was meant for at least three of them; while its companion chair was reserved for one other.

"Can I get you anything, George?" asked Mae. "A glass of sherry?"

"Sounds good." said George.

"Joyce, would you get your father a glass of sherry?"

"Sure."

A tilted frame had been set up near Mae's chair where she liked to hook rugs in the evening. George picked up the *Evening News* and Mae hooked her rug, and the children sat there waiting for orders, wondering what would come next. It was only seven o'clock, early evening. The day had a long way to go.

"Would it help if I cut the loops for you, Mum?" asked Dia, her *Mum* hanging playfully in the air.

"Well, how thoughtful, Doris."

"That's a beautiful run pattern." Dia's game plan was becoming obvious to her siblings. Clearly fascinated by Mrs. Moore and clearly trying to impress her, she set out to outflatter a gifted flatterer. She was already taking on the inflections of her new stepmother. Besides, like Joyce, she'd never had Miss Munn in school, had no reason for long-held grievance, and was admittedly impressed with her positions as assistant principal of Ecorse High and principal at School Three. Dia sure knew how to turn on the charm. Within an hour of her arrival, she even had Edna singing her praises.

"Can we turn on the radio?" asked Marce.

"May we," replied Mrs. Moore.

"May we?"

"Your father's reading, dear."

Finally, Shay rose and gravitated to the front window. But it was now dark, except for the streetlamp on the corner. There was nothing to be seen.

"Please don't touch the curtains, Shirley," said Mae. "They're hanging just right."

"Sorry."

"You look through sheer curtains, dear. You don't lift them." Mae hooked, then sighed. "I'll bet you girls are tired after a long day. Why don't you all go to your lovely rooms? I'm sure you'd be more comfortable."

No need for a second invitation, and before they made it to the hallway, Mae was up plumping the down-filled cushions.

Chapter 50

Tuesday, September 4, 1934

On the following overcast Tuesday in the inner chamber of the Municipal Building, four of the six trustees of the Ecorse Village Council took their seats as the Village Trial Board, Paul Movinski presiding. The other two trustees, Frank Morris and Emmet Ranson, both opposed to Voisine's suspension, were crammed in with the curious on the opposite side of the railing, refusing to take part. William W. Voisine was nowhere in sight. Friends said he had gone to Detroit to see a movie since this was not a regular session, nor, according to Lansing, was it legal.

It was a stormy session, claimed *The Detroit Times*, with "500 persons" jamming "the council chambers."[1] Which was a little off the mark considering the room's capacity. But those counting heads *did* say that the size of the house had swollen considerably from the week before, leaving one to assume that the stairs, corridors and outside terrace were full to bursting, and that the family of Andy Bzovi, owner of the Ecorse Theater, would soon be on relief. George had also elevated his numbers. A solemn police presence was evident outside. Inside, he and seven of his men had ringed the room.

At 7:30 on the dot, Paul Movinski, acting president, opened the meeting with a crisp bang of his gavel, sped through the Pledge of Allegiance without benefit of Sousa, then, on a point of clarification, immediately called on Kenneth C. Weber, village attorney, who rose to declare, in grave, senatorial tones, that: (1) This court was completely legal, the opinion of the Deputy Attorney General in Lansing notwithstanding; and (2) Voisine's presence was not required.

To give the proceedings legitimacy, an empty chair had been placed in the middle of the governing area to suggest a witness box. The trustees, along with their table, had been moved off to the side to suggest a jury box; and Paul Movinski, sitting dead center within the jury, had been instructed to use his gavel only when he was acting as president, never when he was acting as juror, so as not to confuse. The flag, the only constant, remained in place.

For the next 90 minutes, while Bill Born, Jesse Pettijohn, Charles King and Paul Movinski sat stone-faced at the jury table in solemn judgment, and George Moore stood stone-faced in the back of the room in nagging pain (the threat of rain having aggravated his rheumatic hip), Village Attorney Weber, now serv-

---

[1] "Voisine Ousted by Ecorse Trustees," Detroit Times, September 5, 1934.

ing as acting prosecutor, called on a parade of witnesses, who swore to tell the truth, all of it, and nothing but all of it, the oath being administered by Don Beckmann, village clerk acting as village clerk.

The most damaging testimony was served up almost straightaway by James J. Stewart, formerly of the Ecorse police department. George had managed to get Stewart discharged in 1931 for being "overactive politically." He had been causing no end of trouble. Then, in 1933, Stewart had managed Voisine's campaign for mayor. In exchange, Voisine had not only promised to get Stewart back on the force but to promote him to a position with far more power. On April 11, about two weeks after the election, Voisine recommended to the Safety Commission that Stewart be appointed officer *in full charge* of the Detective Bureau. The Safety Commission, seeing a hot potato, tabled the recommendation until they could confer with George.

George, not surprisingly, blew his top.

On May 2, the Safety Commission hedged, appointing Stewart to his old job as detective sergeant but adding that he had "to work under the supervision of the chief *and* the Safety Commission." In essence, he was on probation. But George couldn't even stomach that. So he went to Voisine and urged him to pull the appointment, telling him that Stewart was a detriment to the force, a highly unpopular troublemaker who had many destructive traits, one of which was an inability to keep his naysaying mouth shut. Voisine, who was already experiencing some of what George was claiming about Stewart, backed down. And that was the end of that. Or so everyone thought.

As Stewart sat, elbows out in the witness chair, looking very rumpled, George stood behind the seated crowd and studied him with interest. Stewart, with his thin comb-over, managed to avoid his gaze.

After a few friendly and innocuous questions, Weber went to the heart of the matter. "In April 1933, you were Mayor Voisine's campaign manager, were you not?"

"I was."

"And were you involved with his fundraising?"

"Certainly."

"Tell me *Detective Sergeant* Stewart. . ."

"Oh, please," muttered George.

". . . Were you ever asked to do more than raise funds?"

"Meaning?"

"Were you ever asked to solicit a bribe for the mayor?"

"Yes."

Ordinarily the defense would have leapt out of its seat to contest the word *bribe* but, since there was no defense, nor a seat for same, no one involved with the trial objected. Some in the crowd, however, who found the use of the word less than complimentary, made their feelings known, while others latched onto the word and called for Voisine's head.

"Order! Order!" yelled Movinski, now acting as president, to temper the grumbling coming from both sides.

Weber, unmoved, continued. "From who?"

"What?" asked the crafty Stewart, intent on setting up the question once more for full effect.

"From who?"

Well, if Weber didn't get it, Stewart would help him out. "Are you asking me who, specifically, Voisine asked me to put the squeeze on?"

"Yes."

"Charlie Dollar for one."

"When was that?"

"April 1933."

"For the record. . . ." Weber looked over to Don Beckmann who, now acting as court recorder, was scribbling furiously, then waited for Beckmann to catch up before saying, "For the record . . . Mr. Dollar is now on trial in Circuit Court on a charge of operating a disorderly house in Ecorse." He paused, giving Beckmann a little more time, then continued. "Detective Sergeant Stewart." George winced. "Tell the court about the circumstances involved with this *bribe*."

As an ex-cop, Stewart knew just how to testify, so he leaned forward in his chair in order to address the audience and dove in. "In April 1933, Voisine told me to see Charlie Dollar and Minnie Stinson."

"Mrs. Anderson?"

"Yes."

"For the record," said Weber, "Mrs. Anderson, formerly Mrs. Stinson, is awaiting sentencing for running a disorderly house in Ecorse." The room fell silent as Beckmann scratched out the words. Finally, he said, "Got it," and Weber turned back to Stewart. "Continue."

Stewart shifted in his chair, curled his lip, unveiling his eye tooth, then shouldered on. "Voisine told me to see Charlie Dollar and Minnie Stinson and get $25 from each. He said he was losing his furniture and had to have money. Dollar told me he didn't have that kind of money on him, that he'd see Voisine that night, then warned me not to go to Minnie. 'That woman will squawk and blow the lid off the town,' he said. The next day Voisine gave me a check for $30 signed by Dollar and told me to get it cashed. So I cashed it with my wife present and gave him the money."

"Told ya he was a crook!" yelled Ed Doughty, whose words, though they hung in the air, were oddly not gaveled down.

Weber called Ethel Stewart (wife of James) to the stand, to confirm the cashing of the check. Then he called on Thomas Fesko, who rose from his chair and walked to the gate amidst growing discontent. If the trustees were indeed sitting as a "trial board," something was missing. Cross-examination perhaps?

George stood aghast and exchanged a look with Ollie standing beside him. Both were dumbfounded. Guilty or not, hadn't anyone been delegated to defend

Voisine? Stewart had just testified that Voisine was a crook and that was supposed to be that? Stewart who, in George's estimation, lied through his teeth, was now Voisine's Lord High Executioner? Whatever happened to fair play?

But the trustees *had* addressed the issue. On Friday last, in a special session at Snyder's Tavern (as members of the Wolverine Republican League), the four trustees and Don Beckmann had agreed unanimously that if Voisine had no interest in defending himself, even better. It was not their problem. And Weber, their legal counsel, had hoisted a now-legal brew and assured them that they were in the right. Justice would still be served, he said, since justice, in this case, meant finding Voisine guilty.

The crowd, still stunned but respectful of Fesko, watched silently as he was sworn in and took his seat, listened carefully as he acknowledged that he, too, had once managed Voisine's campaign, then split their sympathies as he testified that the mayor ordered him to deliver a truckload of coal from the railroad tracks to his home. "The railroad detectives said the coal was lying on the tracks and might as well be given to the needy," said Fesko, "so I suppose Voisine figured he was as needy as anybody."

That drew a laugh, but mostly from those in the crowd who disdained Voisine and were rooting for the trustees.

Lack of cross examination or not, George knew Tom Fesko, father of seven who worked at the steel mill, to be a fairly decent guy, which lent credence to what he was saying. But George was saddened to see him enjoying his moment of fame.

"The court calls Trustee King to the stand," boomed Weber, village attorney now acting as prosecutor.

Charlie King left his position as juror or trustee, whichever he was feeling at that moment, and was sworn in by Don Beckmann, now village clerk, to take up the position of witness, though King had already been sworn in as juror.

"Trustee King," said Weber, in his most resonant voice as he walked round the witness chair like Clarence Darrow. "Did the Ecorse Village Council reject an application from a nightclub called the Show Boat?"

"Yes, I believe it did," said King. "It should be in the minutes."

"I know this is unorthodox," said Weber, which for some reason released a pent-up howl from the other side of the gate, "BUT JUST TO SAVE TIME! the court asks the village clerk to find the resolution in the minutes.

"Order! Order!" yelled Paul Movinski, no longer a juror, now a president, then sat back, again a juror, to listen.

"Mr. Beckmann," said Weber, ignoring the laughter. "Can you find that resolution?"

Don Beckmann, village clerk, now acting as a quasi-witness, just happened to be at the desired page in which the said minute was evident. "Yes, sir," he said, then he read the section pertaining to the rejected application.

"Thank you, Mr. Beckmann," said Weber, before turning his attention back to the witness. "Trustee King. Did the mayor then cause a restaurant license to be issued to said Show Boat after the council had rejected the application?"

"Yes, he did."

"And how do you know this?"

"Because Emmet and me. . ."

"Emmet? You mean Trustee Ranson?"

"Yes. Me and Emmet went to visit the Show Boat and asked to see their license and they showed it to us. Then we went to see the mayor and told him he must halt the operation."

"And how did he respond?"

"He said that if we continued to make a big fuss over it, he'd throw us off the decks of the Show Boat."

"So what you are saying is," summarized Weber over the laughter, "that he threatened to do violence to you and to Emmet Ranson."

"Yes . . . . Well, legally I can only speak for myself, I know. But he did threaten Emmet, too. In my hearing."

"It's all bunk!" yelled Emmet from across the rail.

"Order! Order!" yelled Paul Movinski, now a president, no longer a juror.

Told he could stand down, Trustee King then left the witness box, strutted to the table and sat back down to listen.

Next, Richard C. Penny, Jr., 29, a town fireman, took the stand and testified that the mayor had the fire department sprinkle the lawn in front of the Show Boat.

"So what you're saying is," summarized Weber, "that the mayor illegally loaned fire department equipment to a nightclub."

"Yes. That's correct."

His father Richard C. Penny, Sr., 59, street commissioner, testified that Voisine allowed the operators of the Show Boat to use a city grader.

"So, what you're saying is," summarized Weber, "that the mayor allowed the operators of the Show Boat to use city highway equipment for private purposes."

"Yes. That's correct."

In a surprising move, Acting Prosecutor Weber called himself to the stand. And in a series of swift maneuvers, he was sworn in by Don Beckmann, and sat down dramatically in the witness box, while Paul Movinski stood up majestically and walked toward him.

The crowd dropped its collective jaw. The sequence, done with such precision and grace, made it stunningly clear that Weber, no longer a prosecutor, was now a witness, and that Movinski, no longer a president, no longer a juror, or even a barber for that matter, was now a prosecutor.

(*This really happened.*)

"Is it true," started Paul Movinski in deep voice, "that you told the council that Mayor Voisine conspired with Floyd Moshier, his brother-in-law, to buy a team of horses to rent to the village for street work?"

"Yes," replied Weber.

"How do you know this?"

"I overheard a conversation between Moshier and Voisine. They agreed to share the profits."

"Did you dust off your knees when you got up from the keyhole!" yelled Ernie.

"Order! Order!" gaveled Jesse Pettijohn, no longer trustee, no longer juror, but acting president because he was sitting nearest the gavel.

"Was the team hired?" asked Movinski, above the roar.

"Yes."

"And you informed other members of the council about this. Did you not?"

"Yes, specifically trustees King, Born, Pettijohn and you."

"And then what happened?"

"It's a matter of record. The council ordered the team of horses fired."

Movinski brushed aside the laughter. "When did the council order the team fired?"

"Three weeks ago. At the meeting of August 14th."

"And what was Voisine's response?"

"He became angry."

"Angry? You say he was angry?" repeated Movinski, the better to make the coming point.

"Yes."

"How angry?"

"Very angry."

"And then what?"

"And that night," said Weber, "windows in the business establishments of three trustees were broken."

"Mwah," muttered George. "This from a lawyer."

Paul Movinski ceased being acting prosecutor by virtue of crossing back to the table, and Kenneth C. Weber ceased being a witness by virtue of rising from his chair. With breathtaking skill, Weber swirled round and faced the crowd as acting prosecutor. "I call to the stand the chief of police, George Moore."

George sighed, took a subtle elbow from Ollie, then walked down the narrow aisle and through the gate with his police cap under his arm, consciously striving to limit his limp. Sworn in by Beckmann, he took his seat, resting his hat on his lap, glad to be off his feet.

"Chief Moore."

"Mr. Weber."

"Did President Voisine ever command you to *lay off* saloons that had not obtained liquor licenses?"[2]

---

[2] With Prohibition over, the state saw a chance to make money with license fees.

George was stunned. "Command?" he said, shaking his head. "No."

"Instruct?"

"No."

"Let me rephrase that," said Weber, strutting around him like a litigious peacock. "Did you and the mayor ever discuss unlicensed saloons?"

George was puzzled. Where did that come from? Was there another trouble-maker on his police staff? Was it the new guy? McWhirter? Else why would Weber even know about a conversation about unlicensed saloons. "Yes, as I recall, we did chat about it once."

"When was that?"

"I think late June. After the Safety Commission instructed me to close all public places operating without a license."

"And in that . . . *chat* ," sniffed Weber, "did Mr. Voisine order you to lay off saloons that had not obtained a liquor license?"

"Order?"

"Request, demand, ask."

"No, none of the above," said George. "I can tell you exactly what was said."

"Then do."

"We, the police department, had spread the word to all the blind pigs in town, telling them, 'If they didn't close within 24 hours, they would be raided.' When the mayor heard about this, he mentioned to me . . . 'If you do that, all of them will be on welfare.'"

"What else did he say?"

"That's all. He didn't tell me to raid them, and he didn't tell me not to."

"Didn't he also say that those owners who could not afford to pay the license fee required by the State, and I quote, 'should be permitted to cheat a little.'"

"Not to me."

"So what you're saying is," summated Weber, "he hinted strongly that you should *lay off* saloons that did not obtain liquor licenses."

"What I'm saying is," replied George, "he didn't tell me to do anything, one way or the other."

"Isn't it *also* true, Chief Moore," cut in Weber over the laughter. "That the mayor fixed traffic tickets."

George solemnly nodded. "Yes, that's true."

As the crowd leaned in, Jurors Pettijohn and King broke out in broad grins, while Fred Bouchard, up on the wall, smiled down.

"How would you quantify the frequency?" asked Weber. "Would you say a couple of times, a few times, many times?"

"I'd say many."

"Many?" said Weber, pausing for effect, letting the word *many* rattle around the chamber, the better to sink in. "So you would say *many*. Is that correct?"

"Yes," replied George. "I'd say, over the past year, that many tickets have been fixed by the mayor . . . and by the trustees."

"Order! Order!" gaveled Movinski, now president, over the hearty laughter and resounding applause.

"Show me a politician who hasn't fixed tickets and I'll show you a politician who hasn't been reelected!" shouted Ernie.

As reported the next day in the *Detroit News*, Weber hurried through the rest of his questioning, told George he could step down, and summed up his case to the jury.

The Village Tribunal then left the council chambers and spent a half hour in secret deliberations. On their return, Chairman King, declaring that failure of some witnesses to appear prevented the board from proving to their satisfaction all charges, pronounced Voisine guilty of 9 of the 15 counts of misconduct, having delicately dropped the charge of fixing tickets, which might explain the need for the 30-minute delay.

King then declared the president's chair vacant, and announced that Paul Movinski would act as president until next spring, "when an election of three trustees is scheduled."

The following day, the *Detroit News* reported the proceedings as a farce worthy of Feydeau, suggesting it be titled, "Ousted from Office, or Is He?," sprinkling ironic quotation marks freely throughout (the "counts," the "trial," the "jury"), underscoring the laughter.[3] Hearst's *Detroit Times*, however, covered the story as if Voisine had been tried before Chief Justice Charles Evans Hughes. The carnival atmosphere was never mentioned, nor were tactics, procedure, or lack thereof. There was no indication that Lansing had said it was illegal, no indication that Voisine did not face his accuser. Its headline, "VOISINE OUSTED BY ECORSE TRUSTEES: Village Board Finds President Guilty on 9 of 15 Counts of Misconduct," said it all: the verdict was in; Voisine was ousted; the evidence was damning.[4] And that same assessment was repeated time after time in subsequent editions of the *Times*, a turn of events that made George's next move even more difficult.

That Wednesday, Voisine arrived for work at his usual hour, merrily bounding up the steps of the Municipal Building two at a time, working his way through a mountain of reporters hunkered in his outer office, telling them that he wasn't ousted, that no one except Governor Comstock could remove him. He also promised to be on hand to chair the next *regular* session of the Council on Tuesday, September 11. "And anyone who tries to take the gavel away from me

---

[3] "Voisine Ousted in Ecorse Trial, Detroit News, September 5, 1934.

[4] "Voisine Ousted by Ecorse Trustees," Detroit Times, September 5, 1934

is likely to get hit on the head with it."

Trading shots in print, Weber countered in the *Times* : "If he tries it he will be forcibly ejected by the police. And if the police do not obey orders to eject him, the council will fire the police." This includes, he told the press, keeping Voisine from even entering his office.

Countered Voisine in the *Free Press*: "I'm anxious to see what means Police Chief George A. Moore will use Thursday (September 6) to try to keep me out."

The growing journalistic herd migrated to George's office to uncover the means. "We have no orders from anybody to keep Mayor Voisine out of his office," said George warily. But even as he spoke, orders were being drafted. Reported the *News* : "Kenneth C. Weber, village attorney, dictated a letter to Chief Moore, Wednesday afternoon, at a special council meeting, instructing Moore to 'use the resources at your command' to enforce compliance with the removal order."[5] Trouble was, there was only one key to the president's office, Voisine had it, and, by the time the letter reached George, the mayor had left for the day.

Voisine, on hearing of the letter, told the press: "Well, you can tell them that I've got that key and I'm going to use it to enter my office tomorrow morning. I'll be down there as usual at 10 a.m."

---

[5] "Ouster Notice Given," Detroit News, September 6, 1934.

Chapter 51

September 5–25, 1934

That Wednesday night, deep in slumber, Shay was at Ouellette's cottage at Pointe aux Peaux, elbows dangling over an inner tube, floating in the cooling waters of Lake Erie. Sun above, azure sky. Then the cool lake, with the caprice of dreams, became a warm stream. Shay lunged out of bed and switched on the table lamp. "Marce, Marce, get up," she said in an urgent whisper, shaking her. But before Marce could even groan in protest, Shay was stripping the bed of its blanket and top sheet, flinging them to the floor. "Get up! Quick! You wet the bed again. Don't let it get to the mattress!"

Marce vaulted out of bed with practiced agility, only to reveal a darkened blotch on the white bottom sheet which, when ripped off by Shay, pillows flying, revealed a petite facsimile on the white mattress cover.

"Aww, Marce," moaned Shay, running her hand over the spot on the mattress cover, feeling for dampness. Then she pinched it away from the mattress, tenting it.

"Can we take the cover off?" whispered Marce.

"In the middle of the night? We'd wake up the whole house," said Shay, rolling the wet bottom sheet into a ball, setting it aside.

"Not if we're careful," said Marce, blowing on the spot, fanning it.

"Look. Do me a favor," whispered Shay, noiselessly sliding open a dresser drawer, pulling out a blue nightie, pulling out peach undies, tossing them at Marce. "Go wash up. But be quiet, for god's sake."

While waiting anxiously for Marce's return, Shay donned a clean nightie, then untied two ties of the mattress cover's opening at the foot of the bed, grabbed one of the new Turkish towels from its rack, slipped it between the cover and the naked mattress and began to inch it upward toward the spot, making every effort to keep the towel flat. But the towel crumpled like an accordion. She slumped down at the foot of the bed and waited for Marce.

Marce slipped back into the room and closed the door softly, wincing with each squeak, then tendered her wadded nightie. "Where do I put this? In the hamper?" she asked, shame-faced.

"Geez, no."

"Then where?"

"I don't know," said Shay, casting about. "Stick it in the back of the closet for now. Help me get this towel into position." Kneeling opposite each other on the bed, they maneuvered it upward until it rested between the bare mattress and the damp spot. Shay climbed down off the bed and picked up the balled bottom sheet. "We gotta get the smell out before it sets or we'll never get it out. She'll smell it when she does the sheets."

"But she don't do the sheets," said Marce. "Edna sends 'em out, remember?"

"Then Edna'll smell it when she sends 'em out."

"Maybe not."

"I'm tellin ya, Marce. We got no choice. I gotta wash it out now," said Shay, listening at the bedroom door. The only sound was the ticking of the clock. She cracked open the door and let out a yelp. Mrs. Moore, also known as Mum-mm, was looming over her in her nightgown, hair disheveled. "Is something wrong, Shirley?"

Shay was a pathetic liar. It wasn't a question of heightened morality, holier-than-thou stuff. She was just lousy at it. She couldn't get her mouth to cooperate, to wrap around the fib. Even so, in desperation, she plunged in. "There's been an accident."

"What kind of accident?"

"Ah . . . we spilled . . . ah . . ." a little apple juice. But don't worry, I'll wash it out."

"We?"

"Me and Marce."

"Marce and I."

"Marce and I," parroted Shay, only too willing to apologize for poor grammar.

"At 4 a.m.?" asked Miss Munn. "Tell me, Shirley. And I want you to be honest, dear. Did you wet your bed?"

" *Me!* "

"Not so loud, dear. You'll wake your father."

"*I* did," said Marce, with a hint of defiance.

Mrs. Moore's face remained unchanged. "Stay right here and don't move," she said, exiting the room.

"Think she's mad?" whispered Marce.

"What do you think?"

"I dunno," said Marce. "I can never tell with her."

"You can leave the mattress cover on for now. I'll have Edna take it off in the morning," said Mrs. Moore on her return. The girls nodded as they backed deeper in the corner, intent on staying out of her way. "In the meantime, use these to make the bed." She handed clean sheets to Shay. "Have you wet the bed before, Marcia? Does this happen often?"

"Not a whole lot," offered Shay.

"Well, it's time she grew out of it. Fourth-grade girls do not wet the bed. And where is your nightgown?" Silently, Marce opened the closet, bent over, picked up her balled nightie and handed it to her. "Put it in your hamper, dear. In future, if this happens again, and it won't . . . Will it, Marcia?"

"No, Mum," said Marce, holding the count one sarcastic beat too long, one beat shy of obvious.

"In the future, get clean sheets out of the linen closet, put the wet sheets in the hamper, then tell me in the morning. Now go back to sleep, both of you. It's almost five o'clock. I don't know how I'm going to get up for school."

She left the room and closed the door.

Marce crawled under the unwelcoming sheets and turned her face silently toward the closet. Shay crept in, turned her back to Marce and stared at the curtains. After a while, she could no longer bear it. She got up, put on her chenille robe, stole into the living room and sat stiffly on the couch facing the large window. And as she watched the glow from the rising sun slowly turn the sheer curtains to amber, she wondered if Freda was waking on Monroe Street.

Uh-oh.

A hallway door opened. A floorboard creaked. Then the overhead light was switched on in the kitchen and spilled wanly into the hallway, into the living room, vaguely illuminating the curtains. She could hear a cupboard door being opened, then shut, hear running water filling a glass. Now another floorboard groaned, now a shadow grazed the curtains.

"You all right, Tee?" said her father, gazing down on her, shadows for eyes. He was clad in his blue pajamas with the gold crest on the pocket, a Father's Day present from Mae.

"I'm fine."

"You sure?" he asked, sitting down beside her, squatting on the edge of the couch, setting his glass on a coaster.

"Marce wet the bed again."

"Oh, God, that's all we need," he said.

"Don't worry, she already knows. She gave us clean sheets."

"Oy," said George. "What a way to start the day. Was she angry?"

"Hard to tell."

"Did she yell at you?"

"No, not really."

"Marce okay?"

"Yeah."

"Then if you already changed the sheets, why are you out here?"

"Couldn't sleep."

"That makes two of us. I've got one lollapalooza of a headache. Just took two aspirin. That your problem? Headache?"

"No."

"Bellyache?" he smiled.

"It's stomachache, Pa."

They both grinned.

He shivered and longed for his bed, but she looked so miserable, trying not to look miserable. "Got a lot on your mind, do ya?" he asked. She nodded. "Me too," he said.

"Like what?"

"Just a little trouble at work."

"What kind of trouble?"

"People trouble. Always seems worse at night, somehow. Ever notice that? Always looks better in the sunshine. Finding all this kinda hard, are ya, Tee?" he said soothingly.

"Oh, Pa," she wanted to say, but she knew she'd only worry him. Nothing he could do about it now, nothing he could fix. She wanted to tell him that this was not a pouty thing. For some reason, she just felt sad. Nothing he could do about that either, so she said nothing.

"Missing Monroe Street?" he said. "I'm gonna miss that, too, you know. Sittin' on the porch, watchin' the baseball games. But you're popular. You'll make new friends in the neighborhood. Before you know it, you'll be batting with the best of them."

"But where'll you watch from? There's no porch."

"I'll set a chair out on the sidewalk."

"It's not the same."

"Yeah, you're right," he said. "It's not the same. But we can go down to Freda's once in a while. You can play, I can watch. How's that?"

She nodded, then gave him a weak smile. "I'm ok, Pa, honest. But you'd better get back to bed. We're gonna get in trouble."

"She's a good woman, Tee. You'll see. She's trying very hard. Not a mean bone in her body. She wants to do right by us. Give us a nice home. Can you see that? And you have your own room, almost. With a door," he laughed. "She'll take good care of us. It'll be fine."

"Pa?"

"Yeah?"

"Does this mean we can't sing 'Hello, Central' anymore?"

"Does what mean?"

"Living here."

"Miss your Mumma?"

Shay nodded, then looked up and away, making room for a rising tide.

"Of course, it doesn't. We can sing 'Hello, Central' anytime we want."

"Now?"

"Yes."

It was an old song, the kind that Shay and Dia delighted in poking fun at, a source of scorn for daughters of the jazz age, for the ♫ "Jada-jada-jing-jing-jing" set. He had sung it to her many times in the weeks following Agnes's death. Then he had stopped, possibly because he feared she would cry, possibly because he feared his own tears. Now he rarely mentioned their mother, rarely said her name.

"We never talked about her, like they do today," said Dia. *As she spoke 60 years later, she began to cry softly.*

So George began to sing. "♫ *Hello, Central/ give me heaven/ for my mother's there."* He sang it faintly so as not to wake the house; he sang it softly, for her ears only, the lilting tenor that graced so many bars now serving him well.

"♫ *You will find her/ with the angels/ on the golden stair.*
I will speak to/ her and tell her/ that she should come home.
You just listen/ while I call her/ on the telephone."

"Oh, Pa," Shay sighed, burying her face in his gold pocket crest.

"Now just what are you two *naugh-ty* conspirators up to?"

Father and daughter shot guiltily to attention as Mae sank down on the couch, tight against George, slung her arm around his shoulder in playful affection. "What's wrong now, Shirley? I can't believe you're still up after all that other commotion. It's after five."

"Oh, we were just greeting the dawn," murmured George, mourning the loss of the moment as much as Shay.

"Talking about old times, I'll bet," winked Mae.

"And new," said George. "And new."

"Yes, and new," said Shay.

"Well, your father needs his sleep, dear. With all that's going on at City Hall, he really *must* get his sleep."

"I'm fine, Mae. We'll be right in," said George.

But it was apparent to him as well as to Shay that Mrs. Moore wasn't going anywhere. There'd be no more singing now. So he rose and headed for the kitchen to return his glass, and Shay rose and headed for the hallway.

———————

Later that Thursday morning, the worse for wear, George called Sharkie Montie into his office. "Tell me again about this coal."

Sharkie sighed. "Someone stole some coal from the railroad yards, then ditched it. It was strewn all over the tracks. Voisine complained to the railroad yard, but they showed no interest in cleaning it up. So he asked me if I'd mind taking care of it; we could split it. Then right after that, the authorities over at the rail yard musta had another meeting about whose responsibility it was to clean it up. Somebody probably raised their hand with a swell idea, why not give it to the poor of the village, have them clean it up. The poor bit came after I took it. I cringed when I heard it."

"Why'd they drop your name from the charges during that so-called trial? Why'd they only mention Voisine?"

"Probably because the guy weaseling on me got cold feet."

"Any idea who that was?"

"Yep. Because there was only one other guy I mentioned this to. And he was a cop."

"Which cop?"

"I'd just as soon you wouldn't ask me that, Chief. You know. Hard feelings in the department and all."

"The new guy? McWhirter?"

"Like I says, I think my informant was not about to sit in a witness chair and accuse me of stealing coal. Have you noticed the size of my neck lately?"

George drove the short distance to the home of William W. Voisine, letter in hand instructing George to remove Voisine from office.

For the last four years George had managed to remain above the fray. Now he was smack dab in the middle, getting it from all sides. There was a ruthlessness to this that he'd never seen before. This group was determined. It was hard to separate those who were honestly opposed to Voisine's brand of politics from those who were opposed to his very existence, but George knew one thing: most of the charges were petty.

George sat on the sofa in Bill's study. "I gotta ask, What's all this about that nightclub, the Show Boat?"

"Poor bastard came to me for help," said Voisine, swiveling in his desk chair. "He couldn't pay his fees. He was going under. So I told him to skip the fee until he got on his feet. Went under anyway."

"And the fire department watering the 'poor bastard's' lawn?" asked George.

"I said, 'When are you guys gonna test your equipment again?' They said, 'Tuesday.' I said, 'Well, instead of pouring it in the river, would ya mind doing your test on the Show Boat lawn? There's a fire hydrant right there.'"

"What'd they say?"

"They said, 'Sure.'"

"And the grader?"

"I rented the village grader to the Show Boat for $1.50 an hour, but the village hasn't collected yet."

"That's not like you, Bill. Since when, in the history of Ecorse, has a president charged a voter for the use of city equipment?" George shifted position and massaged his dicey hip. "What about the horses?"

"The guys said they needed a team of horses for street work. I said, 'I know where you can get a team of horses.'"

"And lending that truck to Fred LeBlanc?"

"Fred asked me if he could borrow a truck to move some of his stuff to his cottage. Hell, I hate saying no to anyone.

"Did you break those windows?" asked George.

"Please," said Bill. "Have you ever known me to be that stupid? Or that vindictive?"

"No."

"And I never received a check from Charlie Dollar," said Voisine. "This whole damn thing started over Earl Montie. King, Born, Movinski, all three of 'em were urging me to reappoint Earl. Made sense to me. Earl's been village attorney for years. No one had any beefs."

"Earl's been fine."

"So I come to the meeting three weeks ago saying, 'Earl it is,' and they do a 180. Out of the blue comes this guy Weber. Who the hell's Weber? He doesn't even live in Ecorse. He lives in Lincoln Park."

"Didn't you even know him?"

"Never heard of him until that night. But I warn ya, George. That guy's got so much up his sleeve, he can hardly lift his arm. And I'll tell you something else."

"What?"

"It's none of the old families, none of the old timers, causing all this fracas. I began to wonder, so I asked Anna to check. Beckmann and Ranson grew up in Nebraska; King was born in Oklahoma, grew up in Kansas; Pettijohn and both Pennys grew up in Missouri; Weber grew up in Ohio; Born came from Bohemia; Movinski's the only one of the loyal opposition grew up in Michigan."

"Meaning?"

"That's what I'd like to know."

———————

Though Bill Voisine had only been in office for 18 months, he was immensely popular. Residents soon learned that if you went to him, he'd fix what ailed you. Pothole in your driveway? No problem. The road crew can take care of that when they're in the vicinity. Alley needs cleaning up? No problem. It has been said that, over the years, he found jobs for 400 men. Few questioned his methods.

When he died in 1959, the *Ecourse Advertiser* printed his obituary: "From the beginning of his public life, no one who came to him for a job, a hand-out or help with a personal problem, was ever turned away. Seated behind his huge mahogany desk he would welcome as many as 50 persons in a day, most of them asking for some kind of assistance," wrote the *Advertiser*.[1] . . . "When

_____

[1] Voisine obituary in Ecorse Advertiser, July 1, 1959.

money became scarcer during the final days of the depression, he and Judge John Riopelle set up a food distribution center in Riopelle's combined court and legal offices, where every Friday fish was made available to needy families. . . . He took hold of the public works and staggered the work so that everybody had work and not a favored few."

Voisine used anything he had at hand to help people out, even if it was a town truck. He listened to complaints, then solved them; no one had to ask twice. Many had a story to tell, and gladly told it, about the time they went to his office in City Hall and asked for a favor and got it. And many could verify that he often dipped into his own pocket "when money was sorely needed for medical expenses or a loan of coal or clothing for youngsters."[2]

> *"Bill was tremendous," said Joe Younts. "I'm going to tell you the truth. When I come out of the service, I didn't have a lot of money. I'm not the most educated. But I was in Carter's Restaurant one day. Bill was in there every morning; he'd get coffee to take to City Hall. And I was down in the dumps and he dropped down in the booth and says, "What's the trouble, Joe?' and I says, 'I got a chance to buy a business, I don't have enough money.' He says, 'Well, how much do you need?' I says, '$1,500. I gotta have it by 2 o'clock this afternoon or I'll lose the deal.' It was for a big cleaning company [for coal-fired furnaces]—and Bill says, 'Come up to City Hall about ten o'clock.' I went to City Hall at 10 o'clock and the secretary there says, 'Bill's waiting for ya.' So I went in the office and he says, 'Close the door.' I close the door and he says, 'You need $1,500?' and I says, 'Yah.' He counted out 1,500 in one-hundred dollar bills. I said, 'How much interest is on this?' He said, 'Nothing.' I said, 'What do you want me to sign?' He says, 'Nothing.' He says, 'If your word is like your dad's, I'll take it. If somebody's word is no good, I have no use for 'em.' I left and bought the business. Well, hell, I've been in business 35 years, so you can see."*

Yes, Bill Voisine was a glad-hander. But with a difference. He genuinely liked people and liked helping them. He wasn't selective. You didn't have to campaign or vote for him.

There's no getting around the fact that Bill Voisine cut corners. While bureaucracy moved at a snail's pace, all Bill had to do was snap his fingers. People, he said, couldn't eat red tape. The city worked. He would eventually give his constituents a pumping system to prevent basement flooding, black-topped alleys, three public wading pools, municipal facilities, free ambulance service, excellent street lighting, a huge 4th of July parade replete with fireworks on the river, fine service clubs, and reliable garbage pickup. But this cutting of corners would lead to a perjury conviction in 1950 and time spent in Federal prison. Following his release, he was again elected mayor of Ecorse in 1953 and 1955.

---

[2] Ibid.

In the end, George halved the hot potato. He told the trustees that he didn't think he had the authority to evict Voisine forcibly and advised them to get a court order. "I recognize the [Village Council] up to a certain point. But I do not intend to use force to remove Voisine, until they get a court order to that effect. I don't know what the legal status of this thing is."[3]

By the morning of September 11, an alternating Tuesday, Voisine was granted a temporary restraining order from Circuit Court to stop village officials from ousting him. By the next alternating Tuesday (September 25), Circuit Court Judge, Clyde I. Webster, ruled that "the Board of Trustees of Ecorse had no authority to order the removal of Voisine."[4]

The war was over. Or so it seemed.

---

[3] "Ouster Notice Given," Detroit News , September 6, 1934
[4] "Voisine Wins Battle for Job," Detroit Free Press, September 26, 1934.

Chapter 52

February 16, 1935

On Monday, February 19, 1934, three weeks before Ecorse's annual electoral slugfest, George Moore and Al Jaeger had been standing in front of the rubble of a small cottage at 3859 17th, near Hyacinthe, under a quarter moon, while their men investigated the suspicious incendiary fire in which James E. Bailey, 28, had died. His wife had been away at the time.

Jim Bailey had been a black activist. He had come north from Alabama around 1928 to escape the indignities and restraints that came with segregation. He had found a job as a janitor in an apartment house, married, had a daughter, and been politically involved. In the months preceding his death, he had been stumping for Bill Voisine.

For George, the tragedy proved puzzling. Bailey, who had been to a political meeting that night, preparing for the Ecorse primary election the following day, had gone home about 9 p.m. Ninety minutes later, the Ecorse fire department was battling flames shooting out of his house. His body was later found, badly burned. Ostensibly, Bailey had made no effort to get out of bed.

Nearly a year later, on the night of Saturday, February 16, 1935, three days before the anniversary of the suspicious death of James Bailey, and three weeks before Ecorse's March election, three white men were driving around Ecorse in an old sedan, intent on finding Clarence Oliver, working with tips on his probable whereabouts.

Oliver, a prominent black progressive, then 32, was active in the 1935 campaign of Bill Voisine. One of seven children of an illiterate millworker in Arkansas, Oliver had arrived in Detroit with his wife around 1925, fathered a son Clarence, moved to Ecorse around 1930, then divorced and remarried. During those early days of the Depression, when blacks were the first to be laid off, Oliver had formed an Unemployment Council in Ecorse. He was also a dedicated labor organizer, more commonly referred to by factory owners as a "labor agitator." Having started as a janitor at Ford Motor in Dearborn, he had worked his way up to machine operator within a few years.

That Saturday, with the temperature just below freezing, the three men in the sedan drove by Oliver's house at 3829 10th St., canvassed his haunts, and came up empty. Finally, they parked within sight of his darkened house around 11 and waited. He had to come home sometime.

In the cold, in the dark, the threesome sat there for over an hour—a thick-set man in the passenger seat, a surly type in the back, and the driver. The man in the back grew impatient. Eventually, it was later reported, he ordered the driver to "drive around and find a negro," though chances are he didn't put it that delicately. "Anyone," said the man, "as long as he's black."

Under the silvery glow of a full moon, the three men cruised the sleepy, de-serted streets of the "mixed-neighborhoods" of Ecorse for some time before they saw a black man walking down Salliotte, lunch bucket in gloved hand, returning from work. They turned their auto around slowly and followed.

> *Ethel Stevenson, a black community worker who recalled the incident and knew Edward Armour, was about 20 at the time: "Edward Armour worked at Ford in Dearborn. Afternoons. Took the streetcar to Shaefer. Would come home at night on the streetcar—it stopped at Outer Drive and Electric—and would walk down Salliotte to his home."*

When Armour turned left onto the east side of 17th, walking north for the final two blocks, the aging sedan turned the corner with him. That area of Ecorse, not yet built up, consisted mostly of field and meadow. There was only one house between Salliotte and Hyacinthe. Since it was now around 1 a.m., all its lights were out. No help to be had there.

The man with the surly face rolled down the back window and called out, keeping his voice light, jovial, friendly. "Hey, fella, come here a sec," he said. "We wanna ask you something."

Hearing that Kentucky accent and sensing a redneck attitude, thinly dis-guised, must have sent a chill down the spine of the auto worker. Officially des-ignated by census as a mulatto, Edward Armour, then 33, had grown up in New Orleans before coming north in the 1920s, and he surely had the ability to detect the hidden agenda in dulcet white tones. Armour ignored the man and kept on walking, though he shoved the lunchbox under his arm, removed his gloves and stuffed them into his overcoat pocket.

As the driver guided the auto up the west side of the street, paralleling Ar-mour, the man called out once again. "We just wanna talk to you. Just wanna ask you a question." Armour only increased his pace, briskly crossing the inter-section at Hyacinthe, fearing they would make an abrupt turn and cut him off.

All pretense was gone when the man in the back called out again. "Better do as I say, *boy*."

Staring straight ahead as he kept on walking, his house about 100 yards away, Armour reached nonchalantly into his pocket and palmed his door key. There were only two other houses between Hyacinthe and Francis—one of them, also darkened, he had just passed; the other, across the street from his own, was a burned-out hulk where his neighbor, Jim Bailey, had perished the year before.

The car came to a halt. The man in the back seat and the stocky man in the passenger seat jumped out, guns pointed. Edward Armour dropped his lunch bucket and took off running. He was on his porch, at his door, when the surly man took aim and fired. Then he yelled, "Let's get the hell outta here," and the two men jumped back in the auto and took off.

Armour, shot in the back, was seriously wounded. The bullet lodged in his spine, and he spent several months recovering at Henry Ford Hospital. When questioned, he said he had no idea why he was attacked.

Chapter 53

May 1935

If, in later years, the Moore girls had to sum up their days under the aegis of the school principal formerly known as Miss Munn, they would reply in unison, "Why don't you go to your *love-ly* room."

To give due credit, the second Mrs. Moore had gone out of her way to furnish chambers for them, to provide clean, well-appointed nests. So could anyone tell her why, after all her hard work, after all that money spent, the girls insisted on congregating in the living room after dinner, slumped on the sofa, barely concealing their middle-school miseries, their adolescent angst? That was no place to do homework, that was no place to put their feet up, which they would certainly have done if she hadn't asked them nicely not to.

The girls soon caught on that if they wanted to remain in the living room, talking or listening to the radio together, squabbling was out. Muttering, too. And cracks had better be funny. But even on best behavior, it didn't take much. One yawn would invite: "You're plainly exhausted, dear. Why don't you relax in your lovely room?" One fidget would warrant: "Is your back bothering you, dear? Perhaps, you'd be more comfortable in your lovely room."

They'd sit in the living room after supper, tense, on edge, waiting. Even absolute silence backfired, since silence can be interpreted as sulking and sulking provoked: "Wouldn't you be happier in your lovely rooms?" So the four of them would rise as one, fluff up the cushions, offer a polite goodnight and head for their rooms around seven. Soon, Mae began to suggest it the minute they came in the door. Why not go straight to their rooms to do their homework? Before long, for all practical purposes, the living room was considered off-limits, even when she wasn't home. Saturdays, Sundays: all spent in their rooms.

For most girls of a certain age, their room is a sanctuary, their first line of defense. But since Mrs. Moore continued to enter unannounced, the rooms did not serve to shut anyone out, only to shut them in. It also separated them from their father. Though they felt the loss keenly, he didn't seem to notice, probably because his mind was on other things. He was rarely home. And when he was, he seemed preoccupied.

———————

Then on a dismal Sunday in May of 1935, nine months after their fateful move, it had reached the point where going to their lovely rooms wasn't quite far enough.

It had been raining all morning, a steady, unrelenting patter. Mrs. Moore was sitting in the darkened living room, wading through the bloated Sunday edition of the *Detroit News* under the glow of the table lamp, still vexed over a sassy encounter with Marce on the ride back from church, over Marce's "stubborn need" to make those piglet sounds, over Marce's claim that it "wasn't on purpose," over Mae's certainty that it was. Now, long after a strained lunch, George, who had not attended mass as promised, was still not home. Marce was in her room sulking, Dia was in her room listening to her radio at low volume while dining on a jagged corner of a fingernail, Joyce was at Freda's, and Shay was off in the kitchen, ironing. Banging, really. Because every time iron met fabric (Mrs. Moore would later complain to Mr. Moore), there'd come a bang. Every single time.

Mae turned to the Society pages with an audible sigh. Her dreams of family life had not included the thousand annoyances that crop up in close (bang) quarters. It was going to be a long (bang) day.

But while the combination of rain and ironing made for jangled nerves in the living room, it was having a salutary effect in the kitchen. With the window cracked open providing a slight breeze, with the rain drumming on the driveway below and the gutter above, and with a cardinal in the nearby pine tree trilling to beat the band, Shay was content.

She liked the rain; she was a true mudder. She also loved to iron; it was a good time to get away. Not for her a stroll on a beach or a snoozy boat ride on a sleepy lagoon. Give her a Westinghouse Adjust-O-Matic, a basket of dampened clothes, the promise of instant results and, well, God's in his heaven. And on this cozy Sunday, her many results were folded in neat piles on the kitchen table or lined up on hangers in the doorway.

Reaching for a yellow shaft from a pyramid of rolled clothes, she unfurled a damp apron, spread half of it lengthwise on the board, and as she pressed the point of the iron between each ruffle, she was back home in the Monroe kitchen, playing grocery store with Dia, the ironing board balanced between the table and a chair like a counter, canned goods from the cupboards piled in pyramids on top. "I'll have a pound of this and one of those," she could hear Dia saying. She could see herself writing down the price, putting the pound of this and one of those in a bag, hear her mother laugh, "You'll never make a living at those prices."

"I wish you would stop that banging," came a plea from the living room.

"What?" yelled Shay, nosing into a ruffle.

"I wish you would stop that banging."

"What banging?"

"That banging."

"Oh. Okay."

What banging, thought Shay, as she swooped down on the apron's pocket and heard what might be defined in some circles as a bang. "Sorry."

She folded the apron and added it to the finished pile. Then she picked up one of her stepmother's sheer hankies, set the heat control to low, waited before moistening her finger and touching the iron's bottom to check its temperature, knowing that both the living room and kitchen would benefit from the silence. Then, as she softly pressed the beveled plate down and steam came from the double M monogram, back she sailed to Monroe.

She was rounding the corner from Labadie in her mind's eye, coming home from a game at the Municipal Field, tossing and catching a softball. She could see it so clearly. There was her mother straight ahead, ironing on the front porch. When was that? It was hot, so it had to be summer, because Agnes had set up the ironing board outside in a bid to cool off. The laundry basket on the swing was sky high with dampened rolls. "Can I help, Mumma?" she had asked, coming up the steps. "Great," Agnes had replied. "Pull up a board." So she borrowed a board and iron from Ella, set it across two chairs, and they ironed side by side. The two of them. Side by side.

"Please stop that banging, Shirley. It really is too much."

"Sorry."

"I know you don't mean to, dear, but you're banging the iron down on the board too hard. There's no need for that. Set it down easy."

"Guess it just takes some getting used to," said Shay, pitching her words toward the archway in an effort to be heard. "Ours had legs. It didn't come out of the wall. It's kinda hard to keep this one from bouncing."

"Even so, Edna doesn't make that much racket. It's uncalled for."

Mae turned the page and idly skimmed the Home section. School would be out soon, then what? She would be home all day; her stepdaughters would be home all day; Marce would be home all day. Lord, hear my prayer. And the Lord, in His infinite mercy, must have been sitting over there on the sofa because just then her eye tripped over a bordered box at the bottom-right quadrant of the Home page. The *Detroit News* was offering its annual summer camp programs at Island Lake near Brighton for girls from 8 to 15, provided they could pass a physical. Just fill out the application provided, include preferred dates, and send it and a check to the *News* business office, Second and Lafayette, Detroit. Hurry, it warned, openings are filling up.

Two weeks. Two *entire* weeks. True, Joyce was too old, almost a senior in high school. Then again, Joyce was no problem. And Marce? George would say she was too young, too immature. Pity. But the girl now banging away in the kitchen was just the right age, having turned 14 only (bang) last week.

"Shirley!"

"Did I do it again?"

"Yesssss!"

"Sorry," said Shay, digging out a rolled shirt from the dwindling pile. Now the rain was just rain and the bird was long gone.

Mrs. Moore had that application filled out within the hour and Joyce's promise to post it by noon the next day. Before the month was out, she sat Shay and Dia down in the living room with *won-der-ful* news. She had signed them up for two *entire* weeks at summer camp and weren't they thrilled. You'll *love* it, she bubbled. Nestled in the piney woods of Michigan on a *beau-ti-ful* lake. Nothing but fresh air, friendship and congenial counselors.

"Does Pa want us to go?" asked Shay.

As a matter of fact, replied Mae, their father had graciously agreed to pay the $7 for each of them for the first week, which included transportation to and from camp by bus, and the $6 each for the additional week. "As I told your father, and he agreed, there's nothing around here for kids in summer, except typhus and infantile paralysis."

"But we don't swim in the river," protested Shay. "Not anymore."

"Because you can't. At Brighton, you can swim to your heart's content. I know how bored you get in summer. Nothing to do."

"We don't get bored. We never said we were bored," said Shay, concerned that this false claim had been used to pry open their father's wallet, fearful that he'd based his largesse on a lie. "Besides, I don't even have a bathing suit."

"No matter. You can borrow one," said Mrs. Moore. "Look," she said, pointing to the brochure in Dia's hand. "Nature study, woodcraft, baseball, dancing. Why, I thought you'd be thrilled."

"Dancing?" asked Shay.

"Yes."

"Baseball?"

"Yes."

"What about Marce?" asked Dia.

"Your father thinks she's too young," replied Mae.

"And I'm too old," said Dia.

"I know, dear, but . . ."

"Wait a minute," said Shay. "Wait a doggone minute. If I go, you go."

"Sorry, pal," said Dia, grinning as she waved the brochure, her mole riding along. "This says 8 to 15. I'm already 16. I've been 16 for so long now, I'll be 17 in October."

"True, dear, but I did a little fudging," said Mrs. Moore.

Dia laughed in disbelief. "You lied on the application? You told them I was 15?"

"I didn't have to lie. I just told them you were going into 9th grade," said Mae. "Face it, dear. You might not be the right age, but you are *cer-tainly* in the right grade. And, by June, you'll be two grades behind."

"But what if I pass?"

"I don't think we have to worry about that, dear. Do you? Trust me, Doris. You'll thank me later. A lovely cabin in the woods, the breeze off the lake, away from the stifling heat."

"But they'll *know* ," groaned Dia.

"Who'll know?"

"Everybody."

"What does it matter?" asked Mae. "Who would it hurt?"

"Me!"

"How?"

"*I'll* know."

"Now, you're just being silly." Mae reached over and pulled Dia's hand away from her mouth. "Please stop biting your nails, dear. They're nothing but bloody stumps. You're too old for that."

In almost every domain but one, that one being school, Dia was a whiz kid. Often the phrase "doesn't miss a trick" was invoked on her behalf, though you wouldn't know it by her grades. Dia had finished 9th grade at St. Francis. Well, she was finished with St. Francis; she wasn't quite done with 9th grade. Last autumn, she started 9th grade anew at Ecorse High School where an embarrassed Mae could keep an eye on her. Four eyes to be precise. Hers and those of her good friend, Minerva Hunter, Dean of Girls. It hadn't helped.

> "I had three years of high school," recalled Dia. "They were all in the ninth grade. One year at St. Francis, two at Ecorse High. Too much time entertaining the class. And they'd all pass and go on to the next grade, and I'd wait for the next class to come in. New kids, new audience. If I had stayed at St. Francis any longer, Shay would have caught up with me."

Chapter 54
July 1935

On July 14, a Sunday afternoon, the girls remained in their best dresses after church, then were driven, moping all the way, to a designated suburban parking lot where, blankets flung over their arms, suitcases at their sides, faces longer than Arthur Treacher's, they stood with their father and stepmother on hot asphalt while waiting for their names to be called. It was 84°, breezeless and sticky.

"See," said George, trying to make the best of it. "You'll soon be in the cool woods, while we go back to a house that's sweltering."

"Yeah, but we're gonna miss the pennant race," groused Dia.

"I'm sure they've heard of radios up there," replied George.

"We'll be lucky if they've heard of the Tigers," quipped Dia, as 200 campers began to hand over their tagged luggage and board one of six Greyhound buses, each supervised by two congenial counselors, clipboards in hands. "Sure, laugh. You don't care," she said, which, of course, made him laugh even harder.

"Aren't you going to kiss your father goodbye?" chirped Mrs. Moore.

He looked at them. They looked at him. All were dumbfounded. And, since this custom was so rare in their realm that it might have been Mayan, they inwardly reddened and awkwardly pecked.

By 1:15, buses packed, Shay was sitting near a window on Bus Four, a little frightened, a little ticked at her father for sending her away, ignoring him as he stood outside. George was concerned.

"She'll be fine, dear," reassured Mae.

"Famous last words," said George.

At around 3:00, about 50 miles west of Detroit, having endured "She's a Grand Old Flag" and many bottles of beer on the wall, the bus driver turned onto a dirt road, and as the campers began to exaggerate the depth of the potholes by the height of their bounce, the road got narrower and dustier and the arrow signs grew larger.

When Bus Four came up over a rise, Shay, half-standing, could see a cluster of white cabins and the sparkling blue lake directly below. They pulled into a roundabout, parked behind the other buses, and the girls debussed, then waited in the sun while the drivers and counselors set bedding, baggage and duffle bags in long rows on the grass.

"Say, where you guys been?" Ida Montrose was smashing through the assemblage, bedroll strapped across her chest like Teddy Roosevelt at San Juan Hill. "Did your stepmother tell ya I was coming?"

"Odd," said Dia. "She forgot to mention it."

The Moore suitcases were easy to spot. Most of the other campers were burdened with full-size luggage or large duffels which they could barely budge. A few even had trunks. But the Moore girls were traveling light, bearing overnight cases left over from Freda's wedding. Dia had Freda's brown bag with the moire lining; Shay had her brother-in-law's black leather Gladstone bag, like Dr. Durocher's. So Dia and Shay reclaimed their cases with ease, while Ida went to hunt hers down.

"Boy, you two sure know how to pack," said an older girl in seersucker slacks to their left, two girls glued to her side.

"That's us all over," laughed Dia, wary. She knew something was coming. Girls can be dangerous in packs.

"How'd you get everything in those dinky suitcases?"

"It wasn't so hard," smiled Shay.

"Even your sheets?"

"Sheets?"

"You're supposed to bring a blanket and two sets of sheets. They were on the list."

"The list?"

"The list of what to bring," said one of the other girls. "You don't have sheets?"

"Don't worry about it," snapped Dia.

Then the clipboards returned and names were called out. Shay and Ida were assigned to Sycamore, Dia to Birch.

———————

Sycamore, like all the small cabins, was the very definition of rustic. Squatting on short legs with a two-step entrance to a screened-in porch, it had an unadorned bunkroom with exposed rafters, while its walls—unpainted plank boards darkened by the years—were adorned with inspirational messages from those who had gone before: *Gladys couldn't get to sleep here. Careful where you polka.* The windows had no glass, only screens, which were covered by wooden awnings that opened and closed with a rope.

Shay hastily surveyed her lodgings. There were ten cots to the room, five on each side. That was it. Accommodations for sequestered disrobing were nonexistent. Forget about a changing room. There wasn't a curtain, a closet, a shadowy area or even an indentation. But she had a bigger fish to fry: the mattress and pillow on each metal cot were stripped to their blue ticking essentials.

"All right, ladies," said the counselor in yellow polo shirt who had just introduced herself as Miss Dee. "Make your beds, stow your luggage under them. I'll be back in a few minutes to see how you're doing."

Shay, second cot on the right hand side, was standing between her second cousin Ida and another first-timer, a frightened girl, smaller than the others, with saucers for eyes. They all turned to the task at hand. Taking the Canadian blanket of bold stripes from under her arm, Shay unfolded it to half and carefully covered her cot with it. She could wedge herself in like a letter in an envelope; she could sleep in between, though wool made her itch.

"Didja forget to bring sheets?" asked Ida.

"It's not important," mumbled Shay, smoothing her blanket.

"What're you gonna do for a pillow case?"

"Frankly, I rarely use a pillow," said Shay, stiltedly. "Hurts my neck."

"What's wrong?" asked the girl across the way.

"She forgot to bring sheets," announced Ida.

Soon all of Sycamore was in on it. To a squad of 12-to-14 year olds, this was of great consequence.

"How we doing, ladies?" said Miss Dee, appearing in the open doorway.

"She doesn't have any sheets," said Ida.

"But you were told to bring sheets," said Miss Dee. "Two sets of cotton sheets and one woolen blanket."

"This is fine," said Shay. "This is the way I like it."

"Dottie!" yelled Miss Dee, leaning backward into the screened-in porch . "Run to the office and ask Mrs. Thomas for a set of sheets."

"Can I get another set for my sister?" asked Shay.

"She doesn't have sheets either?"

"No."

"What cabin's she in?"

"Birch."

"Get two sets, Dottie!"

Miss Dee turned back to Shay. "Do you have a pillow case?"

"No."

"Dottie!"

About an hour before dinner, while the campers were given time to read, write or rest, Shay found Dia behind Birch, as prearranged, sitting on a towel to protect her dress from grass stains, feasting on a fingernail.

"Pull up a corner," said Dia, donating half the towel.

So, knees pulled up, dresses pulled down, they sat in the shadow of the cabin, facing a stand of trees.

"Lousy start, eh?" said Dia.

"Yeah."

"Anyway, thanks for sending over the sheets."

"You think Mae knew we had to bring 'em?"

"Count on it," said Dia, voice rising. "They musta sent her a list. Everybody else got one. She forgot, and I'll bet she knew we'd get separated because of age, too."

"What are your inmates like?" asked Dia.

"Snooty," said Shay. "Yours?"

"Same," said Dia. "She sent us to a rich girl's camp."

"I'll say," said Shay. "They all went shopping for *camp wear.* They all went to Hudson's and loaded up. Playsuits, even flannel bathrobes."

The Moore girls, who were more familiar with layaway and Hudson's basement and who had only recently stopped inserting cardboard in their shoes to cover holes in soles, were definitely on the low end of the totem pole.

They were silent for a while, reflective, Shay yawning decisively.

"I sent Pa a postcard," said Dia.

"Where'd you get it?"

"They sell 'em in the office."

"Whadja say?"

"Having a rotten time, wish you were here."

"Did you really?"

"No. But I wanted to."

———————

Day Two (July 15) dawned with a jolt, the blasting of reveille at 7:15. Flag raising followed. 200 groggy campers, hands over hearts, pledged allegiance to one nation indivisible, which, when shouted by one earnest eight-year-old as one nation *invisible*, caused snorting down the line. Though the sky was overcast and produced periodic sprinkles, the temperature was a pleasant 79°, while a breeze, as promised, came from the lake.

At 8:00, breakfast, cafeteria-style, was served from large steamers: scrambled eggs, bacon or sausage, toast (make your own in one of twenty toasters). Milk, cereal, bananas. Along with the constant chatter came a stream of announcements.

Shay and Ida and the little girl with saucers for eyes filled their trays, then joined Dia who had found an empty picnic table.

"Do you believe that?" grumbled Dia, unfolding her napkin. "Last night, this morning."

"Believe what?" asked Shay.

"The checking before we can enter the cafeteria. 'Palms up, palms down, ladies.' Geez. Every time one of those camp *leaders* looks at my hands, I get a comment about my fingernails. Every damn time."

"Aw, they just wanna make sure we washed our hands," said Ida, setting her tray down, awkwardly climbing into the bench connected to the table. "No big deal."

"No big deal to you, maybe, but it's a big deal to me. They're treating us like we're five? That doesn't bother you?"

"Naw," said Ida. "Being blown out of bed at 7:15 bothered me. But palms up, palms down? Nothing to it."

"At least we get to serve ourselves," said Shay, spreading her napkin onto her lap, gazing at her scrambled eggs. "At least we can have all we want. Unlike our *lovely* home. Wonder what's for dinner."

At 8:45 there was clean-up followed by bunk inspection. After arts at 9:30 and crafts at 10:15, it was time for the 11:00 dip, which necessitated the first outright undressing. So as the girls of Sycamore changed into their mostly one-piece muted wool suits, Shay fussed with the lock on Freda's suitcase, waiting for the bunkroom to clear.

Ida, however, remained to the last. "How come you're always in a dress?" she asked, seated on her cot in her bathing suit, hands clasped around one knee. "How come you never wear shorts?"

"Pa doesn't like shorts on older girls. I bought a pair once with my babysitting money," returned Shay. "Pa made me watch while he burned them in the furnace."

"Well, you're gonna die if it gets any hotter," said Ida.

"Let's go, ladies," said Miss Dee, poking her head in the door. "You're holding up the parade."

"Be right there," sang out Shay. Then she picked up her bathing suit and turned to Ida. "I gotta go to the bathroom first. Tell Miss Dee I'm on my way." Shay changed quickly in the privacy of a bathroom cubicle, but her difficulties were far from over.

> "Most of the other girls had been there before, so they knew what was going on," recalled Shay. "All had fancy suits. Ours were pitiful. I had borrowed mine from Hollis. It was orange. Then, thinking I was clever, a fashion delight, I had made a large purple bow out of yarn, like the stuff you make potholders out of, and sewn it on the back. To top it off, the bathing suit was wool. I can't wear wool, never could."

She did, however, thank God that she'd declined Freda's offer of Agnes's old bathing cap, the one with the yellow daisy. Instead, she donned a plain white cap, then rushed down to the dock and ran into the icy lake, to stop the itching, to avoid the gawking.

Shay trudged to an area just inside the boundary buoys, far from the splashing and whooping of 200 girls. Standing waist high in the lake, she bent her legs when anyone came near, dipping her purple bow below the surface. She stood alone, except for Miss Seersucker and friends who were sprawled like seals on a large, flat, half-submerged rock nearby, sunning themselves, secure in their comradery, finding everything "heavenly" or "keen." Shay kept her front to them. Three bigshots, with nothing to do, getting a gander at her purple bow could do considerable damage.

She was unaware of the black inner tube floating her way. "What's that on the back of your bathing suit!" yelled Ida. "Should I kill it!"

"Would ya shoot me. Would ya just shoot me," groaned Shay, joining Dia at the same table for lunch. "And while you're at it," she added, "would ya tell me why you let me sew on that stupid bow. Why you stood there and said it looked nice."

"It *did* look nice." replied Dia, chomping on her third digit, left paw.

"Not anymore."

"That's because we're out of our league."

Shay picked up a triangle of ham sandwich with both hands, studying the thin line of butter between the white bread and the ham. "How come you never wait for us? How come you're always ahead of us in line?"

"No reason," said Dia, gnawing at the nail.

"You ever gonna go in swimming?"

"Can't swim," said Dia.

"Well, neither can I."

"How many more days?" asked Dia, taking a half-hearted bite of pickle.

"Counting today?"

"Yeah."

"Thirteen," said Shay. "Wonder what's for dinner."

"There you are!" said Ida, setting down her tray, making a show of her palms. "Passed with flying colors. Both hands."

Ticked, Dia climbed out of the table and hoisted her tray. "Well, I gotta get back to my *lovely* cabin."

"Aren't you gonna finish your sandwich?" asked Shay.

"Nope. Don't feel so hot."

"What's wrong?"

"Bellyache."

"Stomachache," corrected Shay.

"That, too!" yelled Dia, from halfway across the room.

After lunch and mail call, after "Selected Activities," Dia was sitting on her towel behind Birch, dining on her second digit, when Shay rounded the corner, enraged. "Shoot me. Would ya just shoot me! Whoever heard of dancing in your bare feet!"

"I warned ya it wasn't up your alley," said Dia. "You can thank Isadora Duncan for that."

"Yeah. Well. Where's Ruby Keeler when you need her?" said Shay, bending down, scooping up a stone. "That ain't dancing, that's skipping. And what's with the dumb scarves?"

"Veils," said Dia.

"'Fly, girls, fly,'" jeered Shay. "'Form a circle and fly. Like birds of the air, fluttering your wings.' That ain't dancin', that's ballet. If I'da known they were gonna shove dumb-old ballet down my throat, I'da never signed up for it. Ballet," she sneered. "Who they tryin' to kid? Just give me the good old soft shoe any day."

"Can't wait to get back there, eh?" said Dia.

"I felt so silly," said Shay, winding up, pitching the pebble, bouncing it off an oak. "'Flutter 'em, flutter 'em.' Boy, would I like to show 'em real dancing. I'd knock their socks off. And you shoulda seen Ida. She loved it. 'Flutter 'em, flutter 'em.'" She paused to scratch an ankle. "Bare feet. How can you tap in bare feet? You go to Red Cross?"

"Yeah."

"Whadja learn?"

"Schaeffer's Re-sus-ci-ta-tion," elongated Dia.

"What's that?" asked Shay.

"Not what it's cracked-up to be. All you do is sit on each other's backs and push on each other's lungs. '*Out* goes the bad air, *in* comes the good air. *Out* goes the bad air, *in* comes the good air.'"

"I don't know why you signed up for lifesaving when you can't even swim. What if someone's drowning?"

"I'll toss them Ida," said Dia.

Tuesday brought a break in the weather, a pleasant 78° under clear skies. It was around 4:30 when Shay came around the corner and joined Dia behind Birch. "Shoot me," moaned Shay. "Would ya just shoot me."

"What's wrong now?" asked Dia, dining on her middle finger.

"Softball for starters."

"What about it?"

"We're put on teams, right?"

"If you say so."

"And this stuck-up girl asks me, 'Did you bring a mitt?' I says, 'Huh?' She says, 'Did you bring a mitt?' I says, 'I don't need a mitt.' That's it. That's all I said. 'I don't need a mitt.' And Ida cracks, 'Well, get *her*.' Like I was showing off. And everybody got all quiet. So I says, 'What I meant was, I never use a mitt because I never owned a mitt.' But that only made it worse, because Ida went, 'Awwwww.' So I says, 'You know what? I don't feel like playing baseball.'"

"So?"

"So I sat out the game."

"You sat out the game?" asked Dia in disbelief.

"Who needs it? Anyway, they play like girls.

Shay dropped down next to Dia and rested her elbows on her knees. "So. How's *your* day been?"

"Sent Pa another postcard."

"What'd ya write?"

"Is *eve* -REE-body *hap*-py?"

Hearing something in her sister's voice, Shay asked: "Dia, what's wrong?"

"It's the damn hand check," said Dia, tears forming in her eyes.

"But why would you let something that stupid ruin everything? It's not like you."

"I'm trying to get over it," said Dia, "but I can't. They say, 'Do you bite your nails?' 'Yes.' 'What an awful thing to do with someone who has such beautiful nails.' Breakfast, lunch, dinner. Always a different counselor, always a damn comment. And now there's the Sultan of Swat, the one built like Babe Ruth. She lays a zinger on me every time. 'What a waste. Grown girl like you. I'll bet if you stop, you'd have beautiful nails by Christmas.' How the hell does she know?"

"And how would you feel?" she continued. All those junior debs standing behind me, giving each other the elbow. Today it got worse. I couldn't stop shaking. They made me so damn nervous. Both hands, shaking like a leaf. They just stared at me. Like I had palsy. Cripes, I had the shakes so bad, I couldn't sign the log-in sheet. I'm so damned embarrassed. I swear, that's my last meal."

"You can't not eat," said Shay.

"I'll live off my nails," said Dia, tears streaming down her cheeks. "And I can't stop weeping, for god's sake. Look at me. I'm older than everybody here," she sneered, "and all I do is cry."

The brass dinner bell began to clang, loud and insistent.

"Look at this. Look at this," said Dia, thrusting out her hands. "See what I mean? The minute that bell starts to ring, I start shaking like an old Ford."

By Wednesday, Day Four, Shay had the old striptease down pat. Getting into pajamas at night was a cinch, since she could retain her bloomers. In the morning, a trip to the restroom solved the out of, and into, problem, though the communal showers almost did her in. But she learned to shower last, quick in, fast scrub, quick out. Yes, there'd be moments of frontal flashing, but they would be mercifully brief.

By now, Shay had made a few friends—a barber's daughter from Northville, a tomboy from Dearborn, a straight-talker from Highland Park—and she had taken the little girl with saucers for eyes under her wing. All in all, things were looking up, though it was getting hot again, a high of 85°, and hard to cool off while confined to wading.

When she joined Dia behind Birch during the afternoon rest period, Dia was clearly miserable. "I wanna write Pa a letter," said Dia. "To tell him I want to come home. Okay with you?"

"He won't get it for three or four days."

"Okay if I write it anyway?"

"That bad?" said Shay.

"Aw. . . nothing's going right. I'm so damn homesick," said Dia. "And on top of that I started."

"Started what?"

"My period."

Shay scanned the treetops to be sure the leaves hadn't heard, then leaned in. "You mean the curse?"

"I got to thinking . . . Maybe it's the reason for some of this tension, for all this silly weeping.

"Didn't you see it coming?"

"No."

"How come?" whispered Shay. "To hear Butzie tell it, you kinda know."

"Hell, I'm never on time. I skip months," said Dia. " Joycie says it's always like that when you first start. It's irregular. I only started last November."

"Last November?"

"Yeah."

"Wait a minute, you stinker!" said Shay. "Aren't you the guy who's always tellin' the nuns you got cramps, just to get out of school? You've been singing that song for the past three years."

"Works like a charm." said Dia with some of her old twinkle. "I'm always telling sister, 'I have cramps; can I go home.' Tell her that about two times a month. Nuns don't keep tabs. Anyway, I had to go to the office and buy some pads. They sell them there," said Dia.

"Oh, there you are!" announced Ida, as she whipped round the corner of Birch. Then she plopped down next to them on the grass, leaned back against the cabin wall and cradled the back of her head. "Ah, this is the life. Ain't it. Peel me a grape. . . . What time is it now?"

"How the hell should we know?" said Dia. "You're the one with the watch."

"God, you're cranky," said Ida. "If I didn't know better, I'd say you had the curse."

"How'd you guess?"

"Saw you coming out of the office. Bag in hand," said Ida. "No wonder you're crying all the time. When my ma's got the curse, she cries all day long. We have to use a rowboat to get between rooms."

By Thursday, the mercury was soaring, the humidity was merciless. It was 93° by the time Shay and Ida stood in line with their plates, waiting to enter the cabin for lunch. All week there had been a long wait to get inside for eats. Generally, there were no complaints; the girls could chatter in line as well as at table. But today Shay stood hatless in the noonday sun, beads of sweat on her upper lip, beads darkening the underarms of her short-sleeved blouse, beads rolling slowly down her spine.

"God, it's hot," said Shay, fanning herself with her white dinner plate, the sun directly overhead. "What's the holdup?"

"You wouldn't be so impatient if you were wearing a hat," said Ida, shielded by a sailor hat, brim pulled down.

"You sure Dia's not already inside?"

"Not when I looked."

"Wonder where she is?"

"Probably making a run for it," said Ida. "Boy, I tell ya. I never thought Dia'd be the first one to crack."

Suddenly Shay spied Dia in the distance, walking slowly up the path.

"Say! Where ya goin!" yelled Ida.

"Meet you inside!" cried Shay, running across the grass. "What's up?" she asked, converging with Dia. "Where ya been?"

"I had to go to the office."

"What for?"

"To ask if I could use their phone."

"Why?"

"I wanted to call Pa. To ask if I could come home."

"Because of the heat?"

"BECAUSE I'M MISERABLE!"

"Sorry. Sorry," winced Shay. "What'd they say?"

"They talked to me, you know: 'Oh, now, you don't want to do that. You've only been here a few days. Why don't you give it a chance?'" Dia looked away, fighting the tears. "I said I would."

"Geez, Dia. I've never seen you like this. Ever."

"I ain't so tough." Dia picked up her white plate off the dish table. "Where's Ida?"

"Probably inside."

"Good," said Dia as they joined the back of the line. "'Cuz she's the last thing I need right now." Then she froze. "So's that."

Puzzled, Shay followed the trajectory of Dia's gaze. It fell on the Sultan of Swat who was guarding the screened entrance, demanding the show of hands. And as the sun beat down on their hatless heads and the line moved slowly but inescapably forward, Dia went perilously quiet. It was obvious that she was about to erupt. One callous comment about her fingers and she would either blow her top, dissolve in tears or worse. This would not end well.

Dia was staring straight ahead, watching each girl dutifully proffer her sweaty palms, flipping them on request, while the impenetrable Sultan, on the lookout for dirt or anything else she might begrudge, was now within earshot. "Palms up, palms down, ladies."

Tucking her quivering plate under her arm to minimize the tremors, Dia remained silent, preoccupied. The line was disappearing fast now. They were only two girls shy of the door.

"Palms up, palms down, ladies."

"God, it's hot," said Shay. "Feels like an oven. There's no air."

"You gonna throw up?" asked Dia.

"Palms up, palms down, ladies."

"God, it's hot. Feel a little giddy. I'm seeing spots."

"Are ya?" asked Dia. "Are you gonna throw up?"

"Palms up, palms down."

Tremors forgotten, swiftly taking charge, Dia flashed her paws at the Sultan, "Yep, you're right," she said, wiggling all ten digits under the woman's nose. "Nothing but bloody stumps. Bitten down to the quick, damn near. And, yep, you're right again. If I let them grow, they'd be *bee-oo-tee-ful*." Having rendered the Babe speechless, Dia then rushed Shay to the closest unoccupied bench and thrust Shay's head between her knees.

For the record, Shay did not throw up. But Dia soon did. Having bolted down her sandwich, Dia turned in her tray and took to the woods where she puked. For the rest of her life, she blamed it on being homesick. Maybe it was homesickness. Maybe it was heat exhaustion. Maybe it was a little of both.

Dia threw up on Friday too. Just after lunch.

It was hissing hot, 94° in the sun, 104° if you factored in the humidity. Shay, baking behind Birch, was waiting for Dia, , fanning herself with the day's schedule.

"You okay?" she asked as Dia came shimmering out of the woods, folding her handkerchief. "It's hot enough to roast a duck."

"Let me see that," said Dia, tucking her hankie in the pocket of her skirt, grabbing the program. She sat down on the towel to look it over. "Just what I thought."

"What?"

"Campfire," said Dia. "Are they out of their ever-loving minds. Campfire? In this heat?" She handed the schedule back to Shay in disgust. "Where's Ida?"

"I gave her the slip."

"Good," said Dia. "Because I wanna call Pa."

"They won't let you."

"Well, they didn't say I couldn't," said Dia. "They just keep talking me out of it."

"Well Pa must have really wanted to get rid of us. I mean, for him to shell out 26 bucks."

"Mae paid. Bet ya anything," said Dia. "Bet it came out of her savings. Can't you just hear her telling her sisters—'I *know* the girls will *love* it. And it was well worth the sacrifice, my dears. Worth *evv-ry* penny.'" Dia flattened a hapless mosquito. "I wanna go home."

"It's only a few more days."

"Try nine."

"Pa'll kill us," said Shay.

"Better dead than here."

"Better here than there. Why would ya wanna get back to Mae? Stuck in our lovely rooms all summer."

"I'll tell him it's just me."

"No," said Shay, reluctantly. "If you go, I go. Anyway, he'll probably tell you to stick it out. You really gonna call him?"

"Yeah."

"When?" said Shay, eager to go in search of shade.

"Now!" With Shay right behind her, Dia walked around Birch Cabin with long, purposeful strides, climbed the squat office steps, opened the ill-fitting screen door and let it bang shut behind her.

Shay located the nearest shade, a solitary tree by the roundabout, which was within sight of the office door. Under the tree's canopy, where sunlight laced the ground, she perched herself on the top of a warm picnic table, her feet on the bench, and kept one eye on the office door and one eye out for Ida.

"Over here!" shouted Shay, waving, as Dia finally came out of the office and down the steps, wiping her cheekbone with a bent knuckle. She had been crying again. And, in direct contrast to her recently determined gait, she moseyed across the grass.

"There was a new woman on duty. She was alone," said Dia as she climbed the picnic table and sat next to Shay, wrapping her skirt around her legs. Her eyes were red-rimmed. "I asked her if I could call Pa."

"And?"

Dia took a moment to fight back more tears. "And she asked me if this was the first time I'd ever been away from home. I said, 'Yes. First time for both. My sister's here, too.' She said, 'How's your sister doing?' I said, 'Better than me.'"

"You told her that?"

"She said, 'Couldn't you just write your father?' I said, 'I've written him every day.' She said, 'That bad, eh?' I said, 'I can't stop crying, I can't stop shaking, I can't stop throwing up.' So finally she said, 'If you talked to your Dad, would it make you feel better?'"

"Wow! What'd *you* say?"

"I wanted to say, 'Geez, let me at that phone.' Instead I goes, 'Yeah, probably.' So she said, 'Okay, come behind the counter. What's the number? So she gave the number to the operator, then handed me the phone. Somebody answered, 'Ecorse Police Department.' I said, 'Chief Moore in?' He said, 'Yes, I'll put him on,' and, geez, all I heard was 'Hello' and I start blubbering, bawling like a baby. 'Pa! I wanna come home!'"

"What'd he say?"

"'I'll be right there.'"

Chapter 55

Thursday, July 18, 1935

By 2:00 Shay and Dia were sitting on the verge at the top of the hill, sun overhead, luggage by their side, waiting.

"You're sure this is where we're supposed to be?" worried Shay, wiping the sweat from her forehead.

"For the last time, yes."

"Hope he's got a map," said Shay. "He'll be mad if he gets lost."

"He might be mad anyway."

"Wait a minute, Dia. You never said nothin' about him sounding mad."

"He said four words, 'I'll be right there,'" said Dia. "How can I tell from, 'I'll be right there.'"

"Oh, God. Bet he's mad."

"Could be."

"And he ain't gonna be happy about losing 26 bucks, neither," said Shay. "Might be a long ride home."

"Oh, there you are!" Ida was wending her way up the hill, apple in hand. "What you guys doin'? Waitin' for a streetcar?"

"Pa's coming to pick us up," said Shay.

"How come?"

"It's not for us," said Dia.

"What's not for you? Swimming, hot dogs, lazing in the sunshine?"

"Like I said."

"You do know it'll be even hotter back home," said Ida, who then took a bite of her apple. "You do know everybody in Ecorse will be blowing town for all parts north, and there you'll be, driving back in."

"It's not the heat."

"If not the heat, then what?" Ida's eyes widened, then she reared back theatrically, apple clutched in her claw. "Please tell me this isn't about "paws up, paws down," Dia. Are you out of your mind? Why don't ya just wear mittens?"

"Oh, bottle it, Ida," muttered Dia.

Shay jumped up. "There's a car!"

"Where?"

"Squint! You'll see it! Is it a Ford?"

Dia was silent, intent, as the car rumbled slowly toward them along the dirt road, kicking up dust. "Yeah. Latest model, too."

"Is it blue?" asked Shay. "Is there a siren on the side?"

"Looks like it," said Dia.

The navy blue police car with the Ecorse Village insignia on its front doors slowed, then came to a halt next to them. George was a little misty eyed himself as he hobbled out of the car in his shirtsleeves, legs stiff from the long drive. He swiped his neck with his handkerchief, put on his brass-buttoned coat jacket, donned his hat, then walked around the back of the car.

"Afternoon, Chief," said Ida, offering her wrists for cuffing. "I knew it was just a matter of time."

"Well, if it isn't Kid Lavigne," laughed George as he opened the small door at the top of the trunk and began to lower in their luggage. "You going with us?"

"No, thank you. I think I'll stick around this dump mooching marshmallows." She took a bite of the apple. "Got another hot card game tonight, and I've been making out like a bandit."

George laughed again, then turned to his daughters and said simply, "Get in."

Even Ida knew it was time to leave. "So long, suckers!" she said as she started back down the hill.

Shay took the front seat, Dia sat in back, both slumping silently and sheepishly into the white leather, while George climbed in and started the car. But instead of turning it around, he continued down the dirt road into the camp, then parked in the roundabout. "I have to go to the office. I have to let them know I'm taking you."

He got out of the car, opened the swollen screen door and let it slam almost shut behind him. While he was gone, Dia remained silent in back, off in her own world, while Shay sat proudly in front, feeling like a big shot, hoping against hope that her father wasn't mad and that Seersucker and Co. would wander by and get a gander. Finally locating them off to her left, standing under a tree, she looked sharply to her right, fairly sure she hadn't been caught.

"Don't look now but there's Seersucker," said Shay, lips pursed like a ventriloquist.

Dia hunched over the front seat. "Where?"

"Geezus, Dia, sit back," said Shay. "Don't let 'em catch ya lookin'."

Dia sank backward. "So. Where are they?"

"Over there, to your left," replied Shay. "Bet they're in shock."

"About what?"

"That our pa's chief of police. Now who's got the last laugh, eh?"

Dia snickered. "Certainly not you!"

"How come?"

"Have you been drinking? Here we are. The two of us. Sitting in a police car, while the chief of police gets out of the car, slams the door and goes into the camp office."

"So?"

"So. How do they know he's our father? Why wouldn't they think we're under arrest?"

"Damn."

"Why's he taking so long?" asked Dia, staring at the partially shut screen door.

"Trying to get a refund, I'll bet. You think he's mad?"

"Can't tell."

"It feels like he is."

"Yeah."

"Damn."

The arresting officer limped out of the office, took off his coat jacket, got in the car and drove slowly round the roundabout, then up the rise, kicking up dust, onto Grand River, then Kensington. As they turned onto US 16, he finally spoke. He was mad all right, but it wasn't about a refund.

"Goddam it," he said, pounding the steering wheel with the palm of his hand as the girls sank deeper into the leather. "I knew you weren't going to like it up here. I told her you wouldn't like it. I told her and told her. Anything I hate is to see kids homesick." Then he gave the steering wheel another slam. "Goddam it!"

―――――――――

The girls rode in silence, staring out the open windows, passing farm after farm along the rural road, while row upon row of corn, head-high, sailed by. The colorful roadside stands, shimmering in the heat, offered green beans, tomatoes, sweet corn, cucumbers, leaf lettuce and rhubarb for a fraction of their city cost. The wind that blasted their faces, whipped their hair and ruffled their collars was hot, dry and filled with grit.

George was in another world. A world of intimidation, threats, and death. James E. Bailey dead; Edward Armour seriously wounded. Both incidents still unsolved. Was there a connection? New reports of bodies found in ditches or washing up along the river bank.

Now, another George, George R. Fink, who founded two steel mills in Ecorse, Michigan Steel and Great Lakes Steel, and merged them with two other firms to form and become president of National Steel, was receiving death threats. Fink, who employed 8,000 workers, had heard grumblings to the effect that some of his executives were hiring only Southerners and out-of-state workers in both Ecorse plants. Local, highly experienced workers couldn't get hired; foreigners need not apply. When Fink began asking questions, the threats began. The police now had him under heavy protection, not only at his home in Grosse Pointe Farms but when he was on site in Ecorse.

Who was after Fink? George had tried to make sense of it, all the way to

Brighton. Finally, to his passengers' relief, he deigned to speak. "Dia, would you please get your mitts out of your mouth."

"Sorry, Pa."

"If you chew your nails any faster, you'll perforate your spleen before we get home." But he seemed to be in no hurry to get there, because then he said, "How 'bout some sweet corn tonight? I passed two little girls running a small stand around here somewhere. Farmers are struggling. Think they could use our dime. Keep your eyes peeled left."

For the next few minutes, Shay had her palm on the window frame, concentrating on the left side of the road, but Dia saw it first. "That it, Pa?"

"Yep," said George, slowing the car, pulling to the side of the road near a ditch.

Most stands were better stocked, but few were as clean, with produce washed and trimmed. This one, not far from the screened-in porch of the old farmhouse, was comprised of three boards strung across two sawhorses with appended signs ("Tomatoes. Three pounds for ten cents. Corn. Dime a dozen)" and had for its meager offerings about five boxes of vegetables and a large bucket of corn. Sitting behind the produce were two towheads wearing large straw hats, the small-flower pattern on their dresses bleached nearly white by the sun. One girl, with a mass of freckles, was a little younger than Shay. The other, around six, with more gaps in her mouth than a picket fence, was sitting on an old kitchen chair under a large umbrella that had been jerry-rigged for shade.

"Wanna buy thum corn? Wanna buy thum beanth?" sang the gap-toothed, six-year-old (whom George in the later telling would refer to as Thum Corn). But the older girl took one look at George's car and uniform and shushed her.

"Afternoon, ladies," he said as he limped across the road. "Don't worry," he hastened to add, "You're in the clear."

"You on the lookout for Karpis?" asked the older girl.

"Actually, I'm on the lookout for sweet corn."

Then, as Dia and Shay crossed the road, George held up a husk. "Just picked?"

"Ma done picked it this morning," replied the older girl.

He stripped back a section of entwined layers of green sheath, splitting the cover, revealing the inner silk and the cool yellow kernels, beaded with dew. "Ah, God's bounty," he said. "We'll take a dozen."

The older girl opened a used Kroger bag, putting it in Dia's outstretched hand. "You run a nice, clean stand," said George, sorting through his change, handing the older girl a dime. "Tell your ma I said so. You run a nice, clean stand."

Suddenly a gust of wind lifted the umbrella and sent it flying. As the umbrella tumbled spoke upon spoke across the lawn, Shay gave chase. But the comedy was cut short by another gust.

"Breezing up," said George, startled by the dark and ominous clouds gathering in the west, suddenly aware of a precipitous drop in temperature. "You might want to get your ma. Tell her I think there's a storm coming."

The older girl grabbed a box and gave a nod to Thum Corn, who took off running. There was another gust—stronger, longer.

"Here, let us help," said George, stacking two boxes. "Just show us where they go."

So George and his daughters and the older girl grabbed the boxes and buckets and were hauling them to the screened-in porch of the farmhouse when the mother came running from the fields, Thum Corn in hand, concern distorting her face as she focused on the clouds.

Shay had never seen anything like the inside of that sagging porch with its tufts of cotton batten poking through the holes in the screen to keep the flies out. It was filled with detritus: an old, sagging sofa, chipped enamel pans, springs, car parts, an old breadbox. There was nothing but worn linoleum on their floor, even in the living room.

Then George, with some urgency, hurried Dia, Shay and the corn into the car, intent on outrunning the storm. All Shay could think of, on the long ride home, was that linoleum floor and that mother running from the field, her face lined with concern, her arm slung firmly around her daughter.

———————

At noon, the temperature had been 94°. At 2:00, it had dipped to 91°. But, at 3:00, as George and the girls neared Telegraph Road and hastily rolled up the windows, it had plunged to 64°. The lightning, which had followed them most of the way, was now hot on their tail, splitting the sky incessantly like flickering neon. Then the storm caught up. As the gale shook and swayed and rattled the car and the lone windshield wiper fanned back and forth, barely keeping up with the hail and driving rain, George was torn as to which was more prudent: pressing on, or stopping to find shelter. They were in the thick of an electrical storm. The shrinking intervals between the unrelenting lightning and booming thunder made the decision for him. Abruptly, he pulled over to the side of the road to wait it out. "Keep your hands and feet away from the door handles. Don't touch anything metal," he warned. "But we're safer in here than outside."

Skies were clear by the time they pulled up to the house on High Street where the trees were dripping and puddles abounded. Though there were some clogged sewers, some damaged property and a downed line, the town had escaped the worst of it. But three people had been electrocuted in the Metropolitan area, including one 15-year-old ballplayer who, before the rain started, was struck by a bolt of lightning while on the mound, pitching; five other players had been knocked to the ground.

"Go on upstairs while I get your cases," said George. "But, by all that's holy, take your shoes off and leave them on the landing. Don't track in any mud."

Dia was the first one in. Mae saw her from the kitchen. "What are you doing home?" Then, looking at Shay: "You too? The maid just finished cleaning
in here!"

George, the last up the stairs, was entering the kitchen, depositing the bag of
corn on the table, about to say a rehearsed "Boy, that was some storm," about
to express his relief at making it home, about to launch into "I would have called
but ... ," when he caught the tone of "*The maid just finished cleaning in here.*"

So George said, "Where's Marce?" And Mae said, "Over at Stockton's."

*"That was all he said to her," said Dia. "Then he picked up the corn, turned
to us and said, 'Come on, put on your shoes. We'll go down to Freda's where
we're wanted.'"*

In the Ecorse election of March 1935, Jesse Pettijohn, one of Voisine's political foes, had been reelected trustee on the Reform Party ticket. Pettijohn's confederate, Charlie King, had not. Bill Born, Paul Movinski and Frank Morris were also reelected, while James Hardage was newly elected and Ollie Raupp was returned to the Council.

Unfortunately Pettijohn had few alliances, because memories of the attempt to oust Voisine had left a bad taste. His fellow trustees, except for the newly elected Hardage, kept their distance. Even Born, even Movinski. As for Voisine, more often than not he went out of his way to treat Pettijohn with extreme politeness.

It was common knowledge that Pettijohn was unhappy about his status on the town council. He often sat in Snyder's Tavern brooding, telling cohorts that he was sick of being "pushed around." When the votes had gone his way, he had basked in the fruits of democracy. When the votes did not, he resented those in authority. To be on the losing side was to be bullied. To be told what to do, even if by a majority, was dictatorial.

Pettijohn decided to borrow a page from the Anti-Saloon League, one that had been used handily to secure Prohibition. Think local, they said. Infiltrate. Get like-minded people on the schoolboards and town councils. That was the way to get things done. Use local press to question the motives and patriotism of the opposition. Muddy the waters: insinuate, accuse, discredit the enemy.

Thus on a rainy, humid Tuesday, July 23, a perfect day for fishing, Jesse Pettijohn marched up the steps of City Hall in the late afternoon, twirling his fedora, on his way to see Bill Voisine. And, after sham felicitations from both sides, the trustee took a seat in front of the village president's huge mahogany desk, baited his hook with a crawler and threw out his line.

"I hear there's a gambling house running at 4420 Front," said Pettijohn with his faint Missouri twang.

Bill leaned back. "That so? Where's that?"

"Next door to Seavitt's," replied Pettijohn. "Those three little one-story buildings joined to make one—4420, 4422, and 4424. Where B.L. Sims used to be. Since Sims moved out, it went private, like a club."

"Well, I don't know anything about it," said Voisine. "And don't wanna know anything about it."

"There's a gambling house running there and I wanna cut," insisted Pettijohn.

Voisine stared at him, bewildered. "You want a cut?"

"Yeah."

"Why come to me?"

"Because all you boys are gettin' a cut outta that joint and I want mine," said Pettijohn. "Either that or I'll tip it over."

Voisine laughed heartily. "All us boys? What the hell does that mean?"

"All you boys on the Village Council."

"But *you're* on the Village Council. When did it become 'all us boys' and you? I don't know who's been feeding you this load of pap, but if you wanna get money in that way, trundle on over to—where was it? 4420?—and get it yourself." Then Voisine stood. "Can I help you with anything else, Trustee Pettijohn? Extra tickets for the Policeman's Ball? A seat on a float in next year's parade?"

To say Jesse Pettijohn was seething when he pounded down the steps of City Hall is to understate the steam pouring from his ears. At the very least, he had hoped to land a muskie large enough to meet the size requirement. Instead, he had been sent packing with an empty creel. Little did he know, having left his hook dangling, that he was about to bag a splendid rainbow trout—with a limp.

———————————

On Wednesday morning, with radio forecasters promising another brutal day in the 90s and no letup from the humidity, Mary Gulley, acting as Voisine's secretary, rang up George, her alternate boss at the Police Station, and told him Voisine wanted to see him.

"Tell him I'll wring myself out and be right over," said George.

Since "be right over" meant going through a couple of doors, George appeared straightaway.

"Another day in the tropics," said Bill, right hand outstretched, hanky in the other.

"It's the damn humidity," said George.

"Shift that fan. Point it at your chair," said Bill. "And feel free to strip to your shirtsleeves. This might take a minute."

It actually took three minutes for Voisine to fill George in, while George sat slack-jawed. "I can't believe it. Pettijohn? This guy ran on the Reform Ticket, swaggering around like Fiorello La Guardia."

"Tell me about it," returned Voisine. "I wanted to say, 'Aren't you the clown who tried to oust me a year ago. Aren't you the guy who accused me of taking bribes, fixing tickets, ignoring vice laws?"

"Why didn't you?"

"Because I wanted to see where the hell he was going."

"So did you?"

"No such luck," laughed Voisine. "And God knows where he gets the idea that the Village Council is one big, merry band of extortionists? It's preposterous. We can't even agree on where to put traffic lights."

"You could always lodge a complaint that he demanded a bribe," said George.

"He'd deny it. Then it'd just be my word against his," returned Bill. "And the press would have a field day, branding it Ecorse politics as usual, accusing me of sour grapes. That's just the kind of publicity Ecorse doesn't need."

George sat back in his chair and sighed. "Well, if he knows about the place, he must know my son's employed there as a dealer. It's such small potatoes."

"I know," said Voisine, who then straightened his desk set, then squared off his desk pad. "George, can't you talk your son into getting a legit job?"

"Know of any in this market? With no skills?"

"Has he looked?"

"Yes, Bill. He really has."

"Then have him see Paul Pulliam, village employment manager. We hired him to get our young folk jobs in the factories. I'll put in a word."

"Thanks."

"And I'd humbly suggest you have your boys raid the place."

"We already raided it," replied George. "Couple months ago."

"Might be smart to raid it again," said Voisine. "Up to you. But I don't trust that goon. He's likely to claim that he alerted us and we didn't do anything about it."

"No sooner said," replied George. "But I've never been tough on a card game at this level, and I'm not gonna start now."

"I couldn't agree more."

"What a waste of time. Bunch of guys sitting around smoking stogies, playing cards, and I'll have out half the force to quell them. Meanwhile I've got unsolved shootings, death threats on Fink, and Karpis running around the area, loose."

"I just wish I knew what the bastard was up to."

"Who?"

"Pettijohn."

"Maybe he's desperate. Maybe he really needs the funding," said George, rolling up his dampened shirt sleeves. "Maybe the Depression's taking its toll. Maybe—like Fred Pilon—he's losing his store because customers are buying on credit and not paying him back."

"George, you're too generous," laughed Voisine. "Can you honestly see that son of a bitch offering his customers credit? I'll bet the only thing he offers is free advice: 'Whaddya mean you can't feed your family? Just work, like I do. Get off the dole.'"

"But it's gotta be about money or what's he doing?"

"If you want my opinion," said Voisine, "I think he's having a first-class tantrum."

"Tantrum?"

"Yeah. Somebody at Snyder's sold him a bill of goods, and he's got his nose outta joint. I think he really does believe that we're all in this together, raking in the dough. That everybody's getting cupcakes but him."

———————

Now to put things in pershpecshive, as Charlie Bauer might say, jurisdiction was up for grabs when it came to gambling.

In 1930, Governor Green claimed that the enforcement of the *state*'s gambling laws was the duty of the *county* sheriff. Green said he would not interfere "unless it was shown that the sheriff wasn't doin' his duty."[1] Now the Wayne County sheriff, Ira Wilson, passed that one along saying that the enforcement of the state's gambling laws in the villages of Wayne County was the duty of the *village* police. Sheriff Wilson also said that he wouldn't interfere unless it were shown that the village authorities were not doing their duty.

The *Detroit News* reported: "The village authorities, having no one to whom they could pass the buck, have said bluntly that they would not interfere with the joints so long as they were conducted in an orderly fashion. They said that with their limited manpower they had all they could do to handle crime."[2]

In the Ecorse police ledger for 1926 to 1927, there was not one record of a gambling raid solely by Ecorse police. They sometimes entered the dives to keep the peace and would confiscate liquor, but they usually ignored gambling.

And that's exactly where George Moore stood on the issue. He would willingly accompany state or county officials on raids, as much to protect his citizens as to arrest them, to keep an eye on abuse of power by state and county authorities, to keep things on the up and up. But he would not, as he told the press during the attempt to oust Voisine, be "Harry Toy's lap dog. Jumping up and raiding every time the Wayne County prosecutor yells raid."

But looking away did not mean he was on the take. Like many in authority, George had been offered bribes. He'd just laugh them off and move on; no one ever caught him accepting one. Cakes perhaps. Free coffee refills. A bottle of whiskey here and there, especially during the holiday season. But he saw those only as gifts of appreciation—not meant to influence his decision-making, because it didn't.

———————

Then, on a humid Thursday (July 25), the day Freda turned 25, Murph's

---

[1] "Bolt from the Blue," Detroit News, February 21, 1930.
[2] Ibid. "Bolt from the Blue," Detroit News, February 21, 1930.

workplace at 4420 was raided, occasioned by the same old pounding on the doors, the same old "Open Up, Police!," the same old non-responsive silence, except for the nasal drone of the soapy radio saga "Just Plain Bill" in lieu of the fourth game of the Tiger-Yankee series which had been rained out.

"Open the door, Whitey!" yelled George, as he glimpsed Miserable Whitey peeking out from the side of a shade near the back door.

"I know this is serious, George," said Sharkey Montie, poised to take down the back door with an axe. "But sometimes ya just gotta laugh."

"Be funnier if my son wasn't in there," sighed George, swiping his neck with a handkerchief. "Let 'er rip."

It took all of four strokes to splinter a panel, to reach inside and unlock the door. Once in, the place was empty, though five men were caught trying to exit simultaneously, having pretty much wedged themselves in the front door. All would post bond which they would subsequently forfeit, since none would appear at trial. But there were no members of the staff among the arrestees. No Whitey. No Murph. No Chinese cook. No Peck, who was employed to do the parking.

After some searching, Sharkie found the hidden door that led to the hidden stairs that led to the opening on to the flat one-story roof, but when he stuck his head and shoulders above the roof line and did a 360, there was no one in sight.

"Nobody there, Chief," he said, returning.

"How'd they get away?" said a baffled George. "I had men in back, men in front. They would have seen them jumping from the roof."

After the catch was loaded into the Black Maria and carted off, after his men left, George stood alone in the room, stubbing out a cigarette which was still smoldering in an ash tray. A Regents, Murph's smoke of choice. Then he gazed at the uneven stacks of chips, piled on the green felt table, before idly turning over each poker hand. He whistled softly. Some poor bastard had been holding three queens and was now surely cursing the darkness. If life was fair, they'd reduce his fine.

He listened for a creaking board, for a cough, for even a misplaced snicker, but the only sound was that of the purring radio and the whirring fans.

"You can come out now," sang George. But no one came.

Now Murph was something of an escape artist, which George well knew. More scrupulous than the fire department when it came to emergency exits, Murph always made sure he had at least three: one for cops streaming in, one for clients streaming out, and one for himself and his fellow employees. Not for him a window overlooking the river and a quick dunk. The emergency door on one of the places where he dealt led to the balcony of a movie theater. When it was raided, Murph would send bettors through the door. Everyone just took a seat.

Finally, George came out and closed the splintered back door. But as he was cutting across the grass behind Seavitt's on his way to his parked car on Labadie, he heard a familiar voice.

"Hi, Pa."

George swirled round, saw nothing, then backed away from the building and looked up. There, directly above him, sat Murph, peering over the back-porch railing of the now-vacant apartment, formerly known as Bess Ann's. But Bess Ann had left a few things, like the old rocking chair that Murph was sitting on, his one leg crossed, his foot jiggling. Another seasoned chair contained Sammy Li, his cook.

"How'd you get up there?" asked George.

"Shank's mare," replied Murph, not about to tell his father that Bess Ann's side railing, though not visible from the street, bordered a section of the roof next door. "Sammy's been regaling me with his heathen life in old Changchow." Sammy laughed.

Murph with son, Richie Moore,
in front of the Moore house

"You left a place setting for ten next door," said George.

"I have no idea what you're talking about," replied Murph.

"You never do," said George. "You got a key to Bess Ann's?"

"I'm its caretaker." Murph turned round and yelled into the screened doorway. "Well, guys, thanks for coming. Gotta lock up now."

"'Bout time. We're missing 'Just Plain Bill!'" yelled someone in return.

A column of men began to exit Bess Ann's, zigzagging down the rickety wooden steps, tipping their hats as they passed George, who stood on the grass bemused.

"Morning, Chief."

"Morning, Chief."

"Morning, George," said Peck.

"Morning, Peck," replied George. "How's Ruth?"

"She misses your kids."

"They miss her, too," said George.

"Morning, Chief."

"Morning, Whitey," said George. "Coulda swore you were next door just a few minutes ago."

"There's a guy running around town looks just like me," said Whitey. "Dead ringer."

"He kinda sounds like you, too," said George.

"See. What'd I say," said Whitey to Peck as they zigged down the last zag together. "That bastard's gonna get me in deep trouble one of these days."

There were ten of them in all (five gamblers, one bartender, two employees, one bodyguard, one Chinese cook), most of whom George knew, most of whom George liked.

"You coming down or am I coming up?" asked George, staring up at his son.

"Depends on your mood," said Murph.

"Get your sorry ass down here," said George.

"Now, talk nice."

"Goddang it, Murph. If I have to come up there," warned George.

"Oh, please!" roared Murph. "I didn't even fall for that when I was a kid. I knew you were too damned lazy to come up those stairs."

"Had I known what was at stake," said George, grabbing the railing, mounting the zigzag steps. What the hell am I gonna do with you?" asked George, taking off his jacket and settling in for a talk. "Still looking for work?"

"What do *you* think?"

"I'm asking you."

"Still looking for work," replied Murph, taking off his suitcoat, following his father's lead.

"Sure you didn't just get used to the quick buck?"

"This from a man who spent a year as truant officer. You've got a short memory when it comes to job hunting. No one's hiring. You know that. Unemployment in Detroit's at 50%."

"I'm told they're hiring at Great Lakes Steel," said George.

Murph burst out laughing. "Yah, Southern guys."

"That's nonsense."

"I'm tellin ya, Pa, it's true. Ya gotta know someone from Tennessee or Missouri or Ohio or Kentucky. Ask around. Nobody I know's getting hired. You need a cornpone accent."

"Oh, c'mon, Murph. That's the kind of stupid rumor that guys use to avoid looking."

"Not this guy."

"Bill says to see a man named Paul Pulliam. Maybe he can get you in."

"Thank Bill for the tip. I'll get right on it. But don't get your hopes up."

"What the hell am I gonna do with you?"

"You could try writing my name on Annie Pie's blackboard."

"Well, things aren't as funny as they seem, smart guy," said George, loosening his tie. "Unless you're planning on moving to old Changchow."

"How so?"

"You're hot stuff." Then after glancing downward through the railing to check for passersby, and after waving to Mrs. Mallette, sitting outside her Furniture Exchange across the street, George proceeded to recap the whole sorry mess with Pettijohn, finishing with, "I gotta ask. Is there anyone on the council in on this? Anyone on the council getting a cut?"

"A cut of what?" asked Murph. "We hardly make enough to pay the guys and pay the rent. No one's fixed. I told you that before."

"Then someone's gotta get through to Pettijohn that this is small game," said George. "Penny-ante stuff. No fix, no money changing hands. Someone's gotta nip this in the bud. Do you know Pettijohn?"

"Barely. But I'll do it if you want."

"No," said George reluctantly. "He'd never believe you. And it might just give him more ammunition. If this is political—and I think it is—I don't want you getting caught in the crossfire. No, I'll have to do it. Hate it, hate it, hate it, but I don't think I have much choice. I'll try to reason with him."

"Thanks, Pa," said Murph. "But if he talks money, don't negotiate. Keep yourself clean."

"Well, I've always been straight up with these guys," said George. "They know that. My word might still be worth something." He stood up. "C'mon. Let's go downstairs to Seavitt's, get Freda a birthday card, some perfume. I'll go halves. Poor Freda, she's gotta be miserable. Can you imagine being pregnant in this heat?"

———

It was clear and pleasant on Monday afternoon (July 29) when George drove over to Pettijohn's Market on Front St. and asked him to step outside. They sat in George's police car on the side street exchanging pleasantries, Pettijohn still in his white apron having been caught off guard, George reluctant to launch. Finally, he took the plunge. "Bill tells me the two of you had a talk."

"We've had many talks," said Pettijohn, bewildered and a little nervous. Why was the chief now in on this?

"Don't worry. This is a friendly visit," said George, nodding to Mrs. DeMay passing by. "I just want you to know straight away, that place you're talking about? Trust me. It's a small game. One table. No fix. None. No money to be had."

"That so?"

"Truly. I wouldn't even be here if it weren't for Murphy."

"Murphy?"

"My son."

"Your son?" It took a minute for Pettijohn to connect the dots, since Murphy Moore's involvement was news to him. When he did, he could barely hide his glee. "Oh yeah, right."

"So what say we just drop it, eh?" said George. "Before things get out of hand."

"What say we don't," said Pettijohn. "I think I should get something out of it."

George was mystified. "Like what?"

"What everybody else is getting."

"Who's everybody else?"

"The whole damn Village Council and probably the County prosecutor's office," said Pettijohn. "They're all getting a cut. I know that for a fact."

"It's not true, Jesse. I'm telling you. It's not true."

"I got my sources."

"On my father's grave, it's not true," said George. "There's no money changing hands; you're not being left out. Whoever's telling you different is feeding you a load of bull."

"Why should I believe you?"

"Have you ever caught me in a lie?"

"No."

"Then why should I lie now?"

"If you're so on the up and up," sneered Pettijohn, "why're you here?"

"I told you. My son," said George. "One table, come on. How much you think the take is on one table? You think one table can support house employees, the Wayne County prosecutor's office and the Village Council? Cut that many ways, one table won't buy you a box of Jujubes. So I'm asking you to drop this, Jesse. Whaddya say?"

"What do I say? I say, $25 a month."

They were silent, George in the driver's seat, staring through the windshield, completely bowled over; Pettijohn sitting grim-mouthed, staring out the side window, stifling his delight. George turned toward him.

"Look, Jesse. I'll level with you. I've got a son and I love him dearly. He's a decent man, a good man, with an enormous heart. But he got off to a rocky start like so many other kids around here because of Prohibition, and because, well, I obviously failed him. You've got kids; you know how it is. Now he's got a terrific wife and terrific children—one four, one three—and that one table that we're talking about is putting bread on their table. Not only his but the tables of some other unemployed guys: a cook, a landlord, a parking attendant (Yes, my brother-in-law), couple of boys who do the cleaning."

George looked directly at Pettijohn to gauge the response, but Pettijohn sat poker-faced. "C'mon, Jesse. You know as well as I, he's never gonna get a job in this climate. Even if he had experience, no one's hiring. And I don't want to see my son go on the dole. It's a one-way street. I got a brother who went on the dole. He's now in the poor house at Eloise. If you got a beef with me or Bill, fine. But don't take it out on my kid. I'm begging you. Leave this alone. Whaddya say?"

"What do I say? Have them throw in back pay."

"Back pay?" That's about as much as George could eke out. The man's in-difference took his breath away. He began to appreciate just who he was dealing with, just what he was up against. If Voisine was right and this was a tantrum, it was backed by sheer, unadulterated hate.

"Yeah, back pay," said Pettijohn. "I want what everybody else has been get-ting since the place opened three months ago."

"I told you, Jesse. No one's getting a damn thing. What's it gonna take to get through to you?"

"25 bucks a month. For me and Hardage."

"Hardage?"

"Yeah. He and I are the only ones frozen out of this. $25 bucks or I squawk to the state prosecutor and I squawk to the papers and put your son and the whole damn council out of business. And maybe get him some jail time to boot. I'm sick of being treated like crap."

"All right, all right," cautioned George. "Let's just step back from the brink here, shall we? I'm not here to negotiate; I didn't come to negotiate. But I'm will-ing to talk to people to see if I can straighten this out."

"Like who?"

"Hardage for one."

"You'll be wasting your breath with Hardage. He feels the same way I do."

"Even so, I want to talk to him. Then I'll need to talk to my son and he'll need to talk to his boss. So it's all gonna take a little time."

"How much time?"

"At least the week. Probably the weekend."

Pettijohn reached inside the bib of his apron and pulled out a small appoint-ment book from his breast pocket. He checked its calendar. "So you'll let me know Monday."

"Yeah, I'll get back to you on Monday," said George, starting up his car. "Wait. No. Damn. I'm gonna be out of town this coming week. From Sunday to Wednesday."

"Where you goin'?"

"A convention."

"What convention?"

George winced, aware of the absurdity. "A chief's convention. Can we shelve this 'til I get back?"

"You stalling?"

"No."

Pettijohn conferred with the calendar. "You'll be gone from August 4th to the 7th?"

"Yeah."

"Well, okay," he said, penciling the days with a circle, making it official.

"Even if you are stalling, it's no skin off my nose. Back pay will just mount up."

———————

But there is no rest for the weary. When George returned to the station, he was informed that Toledo detectives had been within seconds of capturing Alvin Karpis, who had replaced Dillinger as Public Enemy #1 on Hoover's Top-Ten list. Karpis, a bank robber and kidnapper, creepily known as Old Creepy, was one half of the now defunct Karpis-Barker gang, the other half—Ma Barker and her son Fred—being dead, and the FBI thought he might be hiding in one of the Ecorse haunts on the river. So a search was on from late Monday night into Tuesday morning, enough to keep George awake half the night, the heat and humidity doing its job for the other half. But they came up empty.

So it wasn't until Wednesday afternoon (July 31) that George asked James Hardage to come to his office. He'd always gotten along with Hardage. No bad blood.

"Jim, I need your help," said George, motioning toward a chair.

"With what?" said Hardage, setting his white felt hat with rolled-up brim on George's desk. He was a good-looking man with white, white hair, though his round, black-rimmed glasses leant him more wisdom than he actually had. Born in Alabama, he had been living in Ecorse, running a restaurant since 1926.

"With your friend Pettijohn."

"About what?"

"I suspect you know what. 4420. I'll give you anything if you'd get him to lay off. It's just a small-time game. No money changing hands, no fix. I'm telling you true."

"Gee, George. I don't know."

"I told Jesse, I'll tell you. I wouldn't be doing this if it wasn't for my son. Someday he's gonna stop all this. Someday, when the job market opens up, he's gonna go legit. If I can just keep him safe until he wises up. No rap sheet, you know. You've got a son about his age. You know how it is. Too old for the wood shed. But I don't want him getting caught up in petty politics. He hasn't crossed anybody. He keeps it clean."

"Well, I don't know," drawled Hardage, avoiding George's gaze. "It's the principle of the thing."

"Wait a minute," said George. "Weren't you the guy who complained to me when we raided McBroom's? Weren't you the one who came to me and said, 'Why was this place closed? If you close this one, you're gonna have to close everyone in town.' That you didn't approve of big time gambling, but what was the harm of a few slot machines.'"

"That was different," countered Hardage.

"How so?"

"Because Jesse and I are being played for patsies. Jesse says everyone's in on the cut but us. Like I said, it's the principle of the thing. We're just asking for our share."

George slammed the palm of his hand down on his desk. "There is no cut! There is no fix!"

"Well, I'm sorry, George, but that's not what I hear."

———————

On Friday (August 2), having been asked by George to stop by, Murph arrived at the Ecorse police station with four-year-old Richie in tow. Richie, who was used to this routine, sat down on a chair outside the chief's office in his white sailor suit, grasping the nickel given to him by his grandfather for the candy machine down the hall. Desk Sergeant Vintner had offered to keep an eye on him.

Every cop passing by had a comment.

"Hi, Richie. You get busted again?"

"Aw, he's only here to renew his driver's license," said Officer Vintner, hanging over the counter, winking at him. "What are you drivin' these days? A Chrysler."

"A Buick," grinned Richie.

Meanwhile, Richie's father was slouched in a chair inside the chief's office, door closed, getting more miserable by the minute as George furnished the latest from the other side of the desk.

"And now Hardage's in on it?" asked Murph.

"Yep."

"And they want 25 bucks a month?"

"Yep."

"And back pay?"

"Yep."

"What is this? The Grand Illusion?" said Murph.

"Like I said, the guy's playing hardball."

"But we're not making that kind of money," griped Murph. "So what am I supposed to do? Ask Jack Dawson to put in another table so these two pelicans can make money? One table's a game, two tables make a den of vice."

"Now, I'm not suggesting that."

"Well, how else? Look, Pa, it's just small game, one table, and the county prosecutor's office told Dawson that if we kept it small, they'd leave us alone. They told me the same thing."

George was brought up short. "Are you talking about a fix?"

"No! Christ no. I just felt them out."

"Who out?"

"I got friends downtown. You know that. I'm a likeable guy."

"In the prosecutor's office?"

"Yeah," said Murph. "They said, 'Keep it small.' They said, 'If you get more tables, the newspapers get on our backs, and we have to raid.' Geez, Pa, you know that. You say the same thing."

"Well, all I know is, if you want to keep open, and I damn well wish you'd shut down, you have no choice but to cough up $25 a month."

"I can't make that decision," said Murph. "I just run the table there. Let me talk to Dawson, one of the bosses. He pays the rent, the overhead. Maybe he can get creative, maybe he can find the funds. And say he does. Do I approach Pettijohn?"

George sighed. "No," he said reluctantly. "Pettijohn's a hardnose. He's also thin-skinned. And, from what I can see, very, very angry. Since it *is* political—and I'm sure of it—he's gotta be handled with kid gloves."

"What about Hardage?"

"As Pettijohn goes, so goes Hardage." George leaned forward. "I hate this. I hate this. I hate this, but I'm already in up to my neck. Let me handle it."

"So you'll stall him off? Give us time to figure this out?"

"I'm already stalling him off. I leave for Manistique on Sunday."

"Sunday? I thought Sunday was your first wedding anniversary."

"It is."

"In the doghouse?"

"No, Mae's okay about it. I'll be back late Tuesday. If you're smart, you'll have an answer by then." George stood up. "This is the last time, Murph. I know I sound like a broken record, but after this, you're on your own."

"Just keep my name out of the papers, wouldja? They always use Melvin."

Chapter 57

August 6, 1935

Eighteen days after the camp debacle, Shay asked to spend the night at Agatha Roody's on Knox Avenue. George wasn't home, hadn't been home since Sunday. Because he was in the Upper Peninsula, at least ten hours away, attending a Michigan Association of Police Chiefs convention at Blaney Park near Manistique, she asked Mae, who readily agreed. This was the upside of living with the new Mrs. Moore: requests for eating out, overnights and long visits at houses of friends got quick approval. Fine with Shay, who couldn't wait to skedaddle. It was Tuesday, August 6, 1935. Everybody involved would remember that night in vivid detail.

Shay liked Agatha, a hustling outfielder. The girls had been friends for two years, about the time that Agatha entered 6th grade at St. Francis. An only child, called Gaytha by her parents, she was an expatriate from Elyria, Ohio. Her father, a foreman in an Ohio steel mill before the Depression, had brought his family to Ecorse around 1933, where he managed to get a similar job at Great Lakes Steel.

That afternoon around five, under an overcast sky, Shay walked the three short blocks from the High Street house to Knox to keep Agatha company; her mother was out of town, and her father had the night shift. Thunderstorms were predicted. The impending rain could be felt in the air.

Shay and Agatha cooked dinner for her father. By the time John Roody punched in over at the mill, they had done the dishes, swept the kitchen floor, cleaned the kitchen counters and mended a basket of socks. Then they sat on the porch in the early evening, rocking side by side, watching contentedly all the comings and goings.

Agatha's house at 19 Knox was a tiny bungalow tucked snugly between its slightly larger neighbors. To the girls' right, at 17, lived the Spaights in a wood-frame dwelling with an ample porch. To their left, at 21 Knox, lived the Voisines in a substantial, one-and-a-half story brick. Since Bill Voisine was still village president, his residence gave Knox some cachet. So did the fact that Burt Loveland, pharmacist and Commissioner for Public Safety, resided across the street and slightly kitty-corner, at 26, and that Ray Mell, one of George's patrolmen, lived at 35.

The girls sat and rocked and chatted about absent friends and impending school where they would be entering 8th grade in a few weeks. They waved to the Voisines as they got in their car and drove off, then waved to the Lovelands when they drove off as well, and gabbed with Peggy Spaight when she came out on her porch to retrieve the evening paper. Soon after, a brief thunderstorm with a heavy downpour sent them inside, where they spent the rest of the evening listening to the radio while Shay styled Agatha's dark brown locks. Drunk with freedom and Orange Crush, they didn't retire until 11:30.

Since Agatha's bedroom was on the small side, cramped by a dresser and a bedside table, the ivory-enameled headboard on the full-sized steel bed was pushed up tight against the open sash window. To take advantage of the cooler night air brought by the storm, Agatha had to reach behind the tubular headboard to roll up the shade. Then she switched off the bedside lamp, and both girls settled in beneath the summer sheet.

Shay had just about tripped into sleep when she sensed a glow seeping through her shuttered peepers. A quick glance upward set her heart pumping. A beam of light, most likely from a flashlight, was wandering freely across the darkened ceiling, uncovering its peelings, baring its cracks. As she watched, riveted, the beam slid over the overhead light, then plied a corner, then searched a wall.

Frozen, she listened intently, acutely aware that the window was open, that the shade was up, that someone had to be standing on the narrow path between the houses, that the only thing separating the back of her head from a perilous universe was a skinny pillow, the surrounding darkness, and a flimsy screen too old to thwart mosquitoes. Did the pillow or the headboard block his view?

And who could help? It was a weeknight, a work night, so Knox Avenue had already turned in. Quietly she put her hand over Agatha's mouth and pointed straight up. Eyes wide, eyebrows rising, Agatha caught her drift. Warily, she groped for her glasses on the bedside table and slipped them on. Then, paralyzed, the two watched, helpless, shrinking under the sheet, as the roving light crept about the blackened room, seemingly on the hunt for something, probing the closet door, rummaging around the dresser, lighting on the St. Francis Parish Festival pennant on the south wall.

"Did you lock the front door?" whispered Shay, her mouth pressed against Agatha's ear.

"Think so."

"Hope so."

Had he heard her? Had she tipped him off? Because the ray of light seemed emboldened now. Moving with purpose, it strolled down the wallpapered wall, rolled past the dresser, unearthed the tubular rail of the bed and rapidly explored its length. But just as it lit on the sheet, the light vanished...possibly because an old sedan with three men inside slowed down out front and eased to a stop. Seconds went by, accruing into minutes. Eventually, the car accelerated, driving east, and was gone. But the girls did not move or speak. They waited, ears cocked, to be sure that the light's ominous wielder was gone too.

Finally, flipping over like a pinned-down doughboy, Shay peered through the bedposts. It was pitch black out, with a waning moon behind a leaden sky and no street lamp near. Her eyes, however, were accustomed to the dark. Even so, except for a lone firefly which alternately made its whereabouts known, the path was empty. There was no one there.

"Gone," she said, flipping back over, sinking her head into the pillow. "Whoever it was hotfooted it outta here because of that car."

"Maybe it was Mr. McDowell coming home from the steel mill," offered Agatha. "He lives in the garage behind Voisine's."

" Why would he shine a light in your window?"

"Got me."

With that, the light shot on again, reappearing on the closet door.

"Dang," groaned Shay.

But instead of creeping, it went wild. It zipped across the ceiling, raced around the wall, swooped and swiveled, dodged and darted, then landed on the mirror of Agatha's dresser and began to dance in its own reflection.

"Bobby Voisine," muttered Agatha.

"Ya think?"

"Gotta be," said Agatha. "That's his bedroom window right next door, about four feet away."

"All right, scrap the flashlight, Bobby!" cried Shay, rolling over, bravado back in force. "We know it's you!"

The light went out. It also giggled, followed by a snort, followed by a disembodied voice in the darkness, which did not sound at all like Bobby Voisine. "We were just trying to see your toes."

Another snort.

Then the sunken eyes and cavernous face of Jack Spaight appeared in the screened-in window directly opposite, half lit by the flashlight beneath his chin. "Welcome to Transylvania," he said with a wretched Hungarian accent. "My what lovely necks you have." Then he bayed, howled actually, before shoving the torch below Bobby Voisine's chins. As luck would have it, Jack was staying over with Bobby.

> "I used to sleep over there a lot when his parents went out," said Jack, "'cuz Mr. Voisine was village president, and they did a lot of going out, you know. And they'd always call over and ask if I could stay."

"Love your pajamas," laughed Shay.

"Now, none of that dirty talk," said Jack, flicking the flashlight on and off.

"Shhh!" shushed Bobby. "Is that a car? Is that a Buick? My folks could be home any minute."

The same old sedan, coming east on Knox, slowed down, seemed to pause out front, then drove on. Jack followed its course until it picked up speed.

"Gone," he said.

Before long, the girls were lying side by side in the dark, hunched on their pillows, whispering through the ivory bars of Agatha's headboard, conversing through the screen. For their part, the boys, also in the dark, were sprawled diagonally across Jack's twin bed, legs bending in the air.

Jack Spaight had been the talk of the summer. At 15 and a grade ahead of the other three, he was leaving St. Francis to enter the seminary, a startling revelation from someone who seemed so easygoing, so devil-may-care. It was also a great loss for St. Francis Xavier girls, since Jack, by consensus, was exceedingly popular and good-looking.

"When do you leave?" asked Shay, her forehead pressed against the bed grates, her hushed voice barely spanning the narrow path between the houses.

"Couple weeks," replied Jack.

"You gonna be a priest?"

"Thought I might."

"How come?"

"Great way to attract girls."

"Where ya gettin' the moola?" asked Agatha.

"Got a scholarship from the Passionist Monastery in Detroit."

"What's Passionist?" asked Agatha.

"They're missionaries, mainly to China," said Jack. "Hunan, China. You know, they wear sandals on their feet, can't have watches, sleep on a bed of straw."

"Hunan?"

"Hunan."

And so the next few minutes were dedicated to such witticisms as: Who Nan? Who knows? Who she? Who he? Who nun.

"Car!" interrupted Agatha, as an old sedan with three men inside slowed out front.

"Ours?" asked Bobby.

"No, it's passing," said Agatha, as it continued slowly east on Knox.

"I just had an awful thought," whispered Shay. "What if I get you for confession?"

"I'll go easy."

Jack flicked his eyebrows upward and smiled seductively.

It was around midnight when Agatha leaned into the screen. "Car pulling up. Not just slowing. Parking."

Bobby went on high alert. "In front of my house?"

"Looks like it," said Agatha. "They just turned off their lights."

"Anybody getting out?"

A car door slammed. There was a recognizable cough.

"Night alllll," sang Bobby in a droll lilt.

"After we quit talking," said Shay, "Agatha and I decided we better get some sleep, so we shut the window and, for some reason or other, instead of staying at the head of the bed, we threw the pillows to the foot and slept reverse. No telling what the boys might do next."

It was an un-alternate Tuesday. No council meeting. Instead, the Voisines and the Lovelands had been out playing bridge. Since Bill Voisine had promised to put in an appearance at the American Legion Carnival over on Tecumseh Road, and Helen Voisine preferred bridge to the midway, he left his wife with the Lovelands around 11. Bill was the first to arrive home; Helen and the Lovelands arrived ten minutes later, about 12:10. Then Bobby, having said goodnight to his parents, joined Jack and called it a day.

Helen Voisine went into the bathroom, preparing to retire. Bill Voisine, still wound up from the festival and still dressed in his summer whites, took off his jacket and tie, pulled down the shade, and settled into his chair in the front room to read the evening edition of the *Detroit Free Press*. He was skimming the front page when he heard what he later described as an "old auto" roar down the street and suddenly stop. But he didn't think anything of it, nor did he think anything was wrong when he heard muffled footsteps on the sidewalk. Bob McDowell was probably coming home from work.

Shay heard the footsteps, so did Jack and Bobby.

Then the footsteps stopped and the engine of the car started and Voisine began to wonder if something was up. But there was only silence, so he returned to his paper, possibly checking the weather, possibly reading about the two Wyandotte boys who had drowned because of the strong current the day before.

As Bill turned the page, there was an almighty roar. The house shook violently, the door and windows blew in, the porch floor cracked, stone chips flew like shrapnel, and he was thrown out of his chair.

"It knocked me right out of the bed," said Jack, "right on the floor. Mrs. Voisine was near hysteria. She came running out of the bathroom and Mr. Voisine says, 'What the hell happened?' and she says, 'I don't know. There's been an explosion.' Then Bill checked on us; then he looked at the door; then he went and got on the phone, and he says, 'Send the police over here. This is Mr. Voisine,' you know. And they said, 'There's no police here. They're all over at Tecumseh Road.' 'Well then,' he says, 'send the fire department. Send somebody. They just bombed the front of my house.'"

Windows were blown out within a two-block radius. Clocks and statuary flew off mantels, sleepers were thrown from their beds, landing on floors littered with glass. Shards, the size of a "man's hand," had sailed like daggers and stuck in walls opposite. The Lovelands had their windows blown in and their four children—ages 3 to 14—"shaken" from their beds. The fact that no one was seriously injured or killed was considered fortunate by all but the bombers.

Lights went on in the bedrooms of Knox, Elton, High and Ridge. The curious poured out of Snyder's Tavern on the corner of Knox and Front. "The entire neighborhood was in panic," reported the *Free Press*. Sirens could be heard in the distance, setting dogs baying.

Patrolman Ray Mell was first on the scene, since he lived about six doors up. Next the fire trucks arrived. Mell managed to get hold of Detective Sergeant Charles Miller. Then he called George, who had arrived home from Manistique not more than ten minutes before.

Unnerved, George put down the telephone and addressed a shaken Mae. "Isn't Agatha Roody on Knox?"

"Yes, right next to Bill's."

"Jesus. Call over there, will ya, while I get dressed. See if the kids are okay."

By the time George drove the three blocks to Knox, the streets were clogged with people. Rather than try to wade through the crowd with his car, he parked on High Street near the Ecorse Cabinet Company and half-ran, half-limped down Knox, avoiding puddles. Neighbors were out sweeping the glass off their porches as he hurried by. Some were taping cardboard over their windows.

The Roody porchlight, turned on at the behest of the police, offered George instant relief. Shay and Agatha were sitting on the side railing in their robes.

"You kids okay?" he asked, as he cut across the path on the side of Voisine's house.

"Yeah, Pa," said Shay. "But, jeesh, was it ever loud. My ears are still ringing."

"Do they hurt?"

"No."

"Let me see your ears," said George. As Shay bent forward, he took his flashlight from his belt and trained it on each ear. "Agatha. You, too." Agatha bent over and proffered her ears, first one, then the other. "Where were you when it went off?" he asked.

Shay leaned over the railing and pointed around the side of the house. "In Agatha's room."

"That back window?" asked George as he stepped out on the path and trained his flashlight between the houses. He shuddered. "The one that's blown out?"

"Yes."

"And you're not cut?"

"We were sleeping in reverse."

Catching sight of Detective Sergeant Miller strolling toward him, he hastened to add, "Stay on the porch, okay, or go inside. Didja call your dad, Agatha?"

"He's on his way."

"Good," then he turned to Miller, "Whatcha got?"

"A crater, sir. On the front porch, near the door. An 18-inch crater, the size of a barrel."

"How deep?"

"Through to the cellar," replied Miller. "Basement windows are all shattered. Fortunately, most of the blast went downward. If it hadn't, I'd hate to think."

"Any idea what they used?" asked George.

"Our vote is dynamite. Had to be at least four sticks. They weren't kidding around."

"Was it hurled?"

"No, sir," said Miller. "Had to be a fuse bomb. There was a three-to-four-minute delay the way Bill tells it. Come on, I'll show you."

George walked gingerly up the six concrete steps, using the wrought-iron railing, for there was broken glass and rubble everywhere. The roofless porch on which they stood went the length of the house which had two front gables. The crater was in front of the lesser peak, where a screen door was hanging by one hinge, its wire screen in tatters, its frame partially ripped away from the portal. The front door was blown inward.

"Anarchists," said Ray Mell, coming up the walk toward George. "Betcha anything."

"Why the hell would anarchists want to kill Bill Voisine? It isn't logical."

"Ever hear of a logical anarchist?"

George leaned into the doorless doorway. "Bill?"

"Yeah" came a voice from inside.

"Could you come out here for a second?"

Voisine appeared in rolled up sleeves, handkerchief in hand, and stared down into the sink hole.

"You okay?" asked George.

"A little rattled but fine."

"How's Helen?"

"Still shaking."

"Bobby?"

"Bobby and Jack," corrected Bill.

"Spaight?"

"Yeah, he was staying over."

"You think it's political?" asked George. "You think it's got anything to do with your ouster?"

"Nah," said Bill. "What politician's gonna bomb a guy over that nonsense?"

George turned to Miller, "Have you reset the scene?"

"We were just about to do that, sir."

"Do me a favor, Bill," said George. "Go in and sit where you were sitting when the bomb went off."

"What? Now?"

"Yes, while we've got the same lighting. Set the scene the way it was for the whole house. If the lights were on, turn them on. Off, turn them off. All of them, just as they were. If shades were drawn, draw them. Curtains closed, close them. And turn the porchlight off."

"What about the screen door?"

"Have to let that hang, I guess."

As Moore and Miller watched, Voisine turned off all the lights, turned on the table lamp, pulled down the shade, sat in his chair and picked up the paper. As he moved, his shadow could vaguely be discerned from the street.

"Think they waited for him?" said Miller.

"That's my guess," said George.

"To scare him or kill him?"

"Not sure," said George. "But when you speak to the press, tone it down. Tell 'em we don't believe this is a murder attempt. Tell 'em we believe someone for some reason wanted to frighten the Voisines, perhaps in revenge for some slight. A 14-year-old boy doesn't need to know that someone's gunning for his father. Neither does Helen, for that matter."

"Racketeers," said James Hardage who agreed to meet with the press. "Gambling syndicates. They're to blame."

"Racketeers," echoed Ex-Trustee King.

"Racketeers," echoed ex-policeman James Stewart.

Pettijohn, who had just returned from Lansing, agreed. "Racketeers," he said. And they all hinted that Voisine had brought this on himself.

––––––––––

Pettijohn wanted far more than $25 a month . . . and back pay. He wanted scalps. The morning before the bombing had found him at the state capitol in Lansing, where he had met with an old acquaintance, Harry S. Toy, formerly Wayne County prosecutor during the unsuccessful bid to oust Voisine. Toy was now Attorney General for the state of Michigan.

Pettijohn had poured out his frustration, telling Toy that it was the same old story, that nothing had changed since he and Kenneth Weber and Charlie King had filled Toy in the year before. He said that Ecorse was still a den of vice. He and James Hardage were the only men on the Council on the up and up. Gamblers rode around town in police cars, using them like taxicabs. He reported that at a meeting of the village trustees he had told Voisine: 'You had better close some of those gambling houses,' but Voisine had just smiled and shrugged his shoulders. Now two large gambling syndicates vied over who could dominate the town. One, run by the son of the chief of police, was established in Ecorse.

Another was trying to gain a foothold. Village officials acted as fronts for disorderly houses and gambling places. Jobs in gambling houses were offered for political patronage. Corruption, included payoffs to the Wayne County prosecutor's office, might go as high up as the new prosecutor, Duncan McCrea himself.

Could he prove it? You bet he could prove it. Because this time the chief of police was involved. In fact, Pettijohn told Toy, the Ecorse chief was so far down in the trough, he couldn't see out for the muck. George Moore had offered him $25 a month to let that gambling house run, the one where his son was a dealer. Only a week ago, on Monday, July 29, Moore had driven over to his corner store, had him come out and get in his car, said, 'You boys on the Council should get something for getting all these beefs on gambling houses,' then laid down an envelope on the front seat of his automobile. "He said there was $25 in it," said Pettijohn. "I didn't take it, of course, I wanted to see you first."

But Toy knew that Pettijohn's tale of the proffered envelope would never hold up in court. They needed actual proof.

"Can you make Moore?" Toy had asked.

Damn right, he could make him, replied Pettijohn. Because his dealings with Moore weren't over. If they wanted, he could get Moore to repeat the offer within their hearing, get him to say that the fix was in, not only with the Ecorse Village Council and its president, but, he'd be willing to bet, with the Wayne County prosecutor's office. With a little help, he could get Moore to sing like a canary and, with that one stroke, open the can of worms and finally rid Ecorse of Voisine and all his cronies. "I can set up Oliver Raupp, too. He's also dirty. They're all in on this."

Obviously, by the end of the session, Toy was intrigued. Bust this wide open and he would not have just one feather in his political cap; there'd be an eagle flying around completely bald. So he brought in William C. Buckingham and had Pettijohn repeat the story. Buckingham, who had followed Toy from the Wayne County prosecutor's office to the office of state attorney general, was tapped to run the sting.

"Stall Moore," Buckingham told Pettijohn, "Give us time to set up the plant."

Chapter 58
August 8–20, 1935

Two days after the bombing, George could no longer delay the inevitable. But when he called Pettijohn to set up a meeting, he was asked to wait. Pettijohn would call him some time the following week. Since both were stalling, anxious for a delay, both got off the phone relieved.

One week later, George was wading through his in-basket when Pettijohn phoned to say he was sick in bed with a nasty cold. Couldn't seem to shake it. But let's get this business over with, eh? Could George stop by his house after work?

"Sure. How about 6?"

"Fine."

"Where?"

"My place, 4272 Beach."

The fact that it was August 15, Agnes's birthday, was not lost on Chief Moore as he walked to the parking lot around 5:55. What the hell was he doing? Simple. He was doing what he'd been doing for years now, protecting his son. Why couldn't he just let the chips fall? Let Murph take responsibility for his behavior, take his lumps? If only he'd put his foot down consistently. If he had it to do over again, what would he do differently? Maybe not laugh at Prohibition in the first place. Oh, sure, the whole damn thing was laughable, but there was nothing funny about the results. The whole town was changed. It was no longer the drowsy little village that he'd known when he was young. Then again, the steel mill had as much to do with the changes as anything wrought by Prohibition.

But he hadn't arrested other boys for being juvenile idiots, so why arrest Murph? An arrest wouldn't salve George's moral conscience because his moral conscience saw nothing wrong with a poker game. Even so, he had to face it. His theory that Murph would grow out of it, get a decent job, was blowing up in his face.

It was a short trip. The address on Beach that Jesse had given him was almost directly parallel to the Municipal Building on High. But it was on the other side of the NYCRR tracks, without a direct route. Two minutes later, three at most, George drove slowly up Beach, straining to see the addresses as they went up. Some houses were clearly marked, some not at all. How the hell did the emergency services know? There it was, 4272, at the foot of Bondie, isolated between two vacant lots. He pulled up behind Pettijohn's car out front. It was a two-family house, similar to the one the Moores were renting on High Street. From what he'd been told on the phone, Pettijohn and his family lived on the first floor.

Stiffly, reluctantly, he got out of the car, straightening his uniform coat, putting his cap under his arm. Grace Pettijohn answered the door, greeting him with the same Missouri twang as that of her husband. The children were away, she said, having dinner at their friends, so it was nice and quiet. They wouldn't be disturbed. She didn't know where Jesse picked up the cold, she added, as she escorted him down a long hallway and into one of two bedrooms at its end, but it was hanging on and hanging on. "Jesse. Here's Chief Moore."

The room smelled of Vicks and had all the trappings of a week-long confinement. Kleenex and medicine on the bedside table, magazines piled by its side. Jesse was sitting up in bed in his pajamas, a robe lying across the foot, his closely cropped hair ruffled and uncombed. The small lamp on the bedroom table was on, though not needed, since the room was suffused with a rosy glow. The shades were up, the curtains open and the late-afternoon sun was pouring in.

George was urged to take the chair which had been placed by the side of the bed. Mrs. Pettijohn left the room, shutting the door behind her.

"How you feeling?" asked George.

"Not much better," replied Pettijohn. He didn't usually take to his bed with a cold, he said, but this one had taken the wind out of his sails for some reason. He sniffed; he certainly sounded clogged. So George did his best to keep his hands on his lap, not wanting to carry the bug back home to High Street.

"Let's get down to it, shall we?" said Pettijohn.[1]

George took a breath and leaned forward. "I can arrange to have the proprietors pay $25 a month to keep you quiet," said George, his voice low and hesitant.

"How about the back pay?" asked Pettijohn.

"Some of the fellows are squawking about having to pay too much, and the fix being too big," said George. "They only have one table. If they put in two tables, the newspapers might find out about the joint and be after them."

"Is that what Prosecutor McCrea said?" asked Pettijohn, referring to the Wayne County prosecutor.

"*Somebody* in that office," replied George. "All I know is what Murphy tells me. That everything is all right with the State and County prosecutors. Murph doesn't take care of that. But the man who takes care of the financing said, if they kept the game small, the prosecutors wouldn't bother them. So can we just agree on the $25?"

Agreed.

---

[1] The following dialogue is taken from the transcript of Mrs. Ottilie Stanczak of the Michigan Attorney General's office.

Good, thought George, end of "back pay," because no one was going to agree to that.

"I wonder if the Village Council's all set?" added Pettijohn. "I don't want to get this money for just one month and then have the place knocked over and not get any more."

George was nonplussed. What the hell was this guy talking about? What did the Village Council have to do with it? Was he still convinced that the entire Village Council was on the take? Well, don't get into it with him. Paranoids aren't easily convinced.

"You can rest assured," he said, "just as long as the place is there and Murphy has any connection with it, you'll get the money." He stood up, eager to end the parley. "In fact, I wouldn't monkey with this stuff at all if it wasn't for my kid. That's the only reason I'm messing in this. For my son. So, I guess you're all set as long as there's only one table."

"On account of the prosecutor?"

Again, George was taken aback. Why another question about McCrea? "I understand so. The prosecutor said if the joint ran in a small way they wouldn't bother them."

"What about back pay?"

"No back pay. *No back pay*," insisted George. "Look. If the prosecutor would give the go sign on another table, it would be different. I'm doing this for my boy, and I agreed to take care of you and Hardage."

"From what I hear all the rest of the boys are taken care of," said Pettijohn, "but Voisine put me and Hardage on the dead list."

Geezus, what a hard head. Why all this repetition? George wondered. Every voice in his head said, Stick to the subject at hand and get the hell out of there—placate, placate, placate.

"Bill's a funny fellow," George said, standing up. "He'll be with you one day and against you the next. I don't have too much to say to him. I treat him with respect, but I don't get too personal with him."

George walked to the door and opened it. "So if that's it, I'll be on my way. Take care of that cold."

George was so relieved when he was finally outside that he took great gulps of fresh air. It never occurred to him that he might have been set up. You'd think someone who had been in law enforcement since he was 20 wouldn't be so naive. But it takes a conniver to smell a conniver.

George had no idea that two state troopers were in the adjoining children's bedroom, listening amidst stuffed teddy bears. He also hadn't noticed the chink of light defining the bottom of the closet door in Pettijohn's bedroom. He had no idea that Mrs. Ottilie Stanczak, crack stenographer and employee of Harry Toy's attorney general's office, was seated stiffly on a kitchen chair in that stuffy closet, steno pad in hand, taking down every word that had been said, including "Take care of that cold."

If George had known about the sting, he'd have thought twice about his next move. Instead of going directly home where dinner would be waiting, he stopped at Loveland's Drugstore on Front and purchased a fifth of Four Roses whiskey, nicely boxed. Then he pulled into the precinct parking lot, hailed Patrolman Jack Cicotte who was heading out on patrol, and handed him the box, along with the same slip of paper that held the Beach Street address. "Take this over to Pettijohn's," said George. "Tell him I said, 'This might help his cold.'"

The mad scramble that ensued when Jack Cicotte's police car pulled up to the curb at 4272 Beach about ten minutes after George left can only be imagined. It must have thrown those who had poured out of bedrooms, come out of closets, gotten out of bed and tossed a Kleenex, into a tizzy. What is certain is that they scurried back to their stations. Coughs began anew before Jack Cicotte was led into the sickroom and presented Pettijohn with that bottle of whiskey with the chief's compliments, then left. Was there dancing that followed?

That Saturday (August 17), a day of intermittent showers, Rowena Moore married John Mascow at St. Francis Xavier on High Street, having borrowed her stepmother's wedding gown. Walking his daughter up the aisle, something clicked with the father of the bride, the family protector. Maybe it was the gathering of his family, maybe it was the abrupt changing of priorities, maybe it was all that liturgical pomp. During that long walk, George continued to mull things over. Could it be that the family protector was protecting one of his own at the expense of *all* of his own?

As the reception at the Monroe house was winding down, George went looking for his son. Peg was in the kitchen, along with Freda and Rowe.

"Where's Murph?"

"Outside drying his car."

"You're kidding."

"You don't understand, Pa," laughed Peg. "It's a mess. There are raindrops all over it."

Murph was in his shirt sleeves, happy as a clam, when George came out the front door. With a family of four, Murph had grown out of coupes and was now the proud owner of a used Buick, 4-door sedan, which he had pulled into the driveway. Rag in hand, he had done the top, done the sides, done one fender and was scrubbing away at the hood. George leaned against the opposite fender.

"What's up, Pa? You've got that look."

"Nothing in particular."

"Something in particular, or you wouldn't be leaning across my hood. Is it Pettijohn?"

"Yes."

"I thought you said it went well with him. That everything was hunky dory."

"That's how I felt Thursday night. Yesterday, I was having second thoughts. Today, I'm on my 97th."

"But you told him the place wasn't fixed, right? Didn't he believe you?"

"I got the distinct impression he didn't want to believe me. That what he's really after is Voisine, the Council, even the Wayne County Prosecutor's office. That this has nothing to do with you or Dawson or that place. That we're being used for bait. And he seemed . . ."

"What?"

"Stilted. Half his comebacks had nothing to do with what I was saying. And there I'm sitting, a nervous wreck, chattering away like Billie Burke to make every little point.

George walked around the front of the car and stood next to him, leaning against the hood, their upper arms touching. "I'm telling ya, Murph, if you have any respect for me, close it down. For good. If you're going to gamble, if you're going to continue in your chosen career, don't do it in Ecorse. Makes both of us easy marks. If I give that bastard one single penny, I'm in his hands. I vowed I'd never put myself in someone else's hands. I'd be out on my ass in no time. I told my officers the same thing. Close it down. Now."

"Now?"

"Now. Get everything out by tomorrow. I've got so many alarm bells going off in my head, I wanna jump on a firetruck."

"But, Pa, it's not my call. It's Dawson's."

"It *is* your call. He'll listen to you. Tell him there's serious trouble brewing. And we don't know enough about it to fend it off."

"Geezus."

"I know."

"How'm I gonna feed my family?"

"I'll give you a loan 'til you find something else."

"I hate to do that, Pa."

"You'll pay me back. I have no doubt."

Murph was silent. With a palmed rag, he continued to massage the hood of his car.

On Monday morning (August 19), Jack Dawson left town. That afternoon, his gambling establishment was raided by the State Police. No one was there. Even the radio was gone; the Tigers had to play elsewhere. On orders from Toy, the troopers chopped up the place.

That October, two months after the closing of the gambling joint at 4420 Front, Murph would bid farewell to Ecorse and take a job dealing Blackjack and 21 for Lefty Clark in a gambling emporium on Van Dyke in Warren, out in the sticks. After Lefty moved on to Las Vegas, for a time Murph ran the gambling concession at the luxurious Blossom Heath roadhouse in St. Clair Shores. Then, in 1941, Peg put her foot down, handing her husband an ultimatum: "That job, or me and the kids. Can't have both." So Murph threw in his hand. But he had no skills. At one point, he was loading bags of cement into railroad cars. He would finally get a job at Modern Collet, starting in nuts and bolts, eventually becoming a machinist. He worked as a machinist until he retired.

On Tuesday (August 20), an aide for Bernard A. Boggio, chief assistant prosecutor for Duncan McCrea, called George and asked him to come to their office in the Wayne County Court House in Detroit. Nothing important, he said; they just wanted to talk. Normally a short drive, the trip up Fort Street to downtown Detroit was very long indeed.

In his statement to Boggio and Assistant Prosecutor Garfield A. Nichols, George answered candidly about the Pettijohn matter. He told them that Murph had been offered a job at 4420 and had asked him if he should take it.

"I counselled against it," said George. "I told him if any complaints were made, I would have to raid the place whether he worked there or not."

"And did you raid it?"

"Yes. Complaints were made and my men raided it twice. On May 15, two men were arrested, posted bond, and forfeited that bond when they didn't appear for trial. On July 25, five men were arrested."

Midway through George's statement, Boggio picked up a paper and read aloud: "'Just as long as the place is there and Murphy has any connection with it, you'll get the money.'" He looked up at George: "You remember stating this?"

"I can't . . . " George fumbled for words, finally aware of what was happening. "That is, of course, that part was discussed. I just don't know whether that is the exact statement made."

"Maybe you remember stating this." Boggio returned to the paper and read. "'So, I guess you're all set as long as there's only one table.'"

George sat humiliated while Boggio continued reading from the transcript, periodically asking George to confirm. Finally, Boggio said, "Why don't we bring in someone who can corroborate these statements. Mind, Chief?"

"Course not."

"Send in Mr. Pettijohn."

Three men walked in, including Jesse Pettijohn.

"Chief," said Boggio. "This is Sgt. Philip Hutson and Trooper Joseph Pristas. The troopers were in an adjoining room when you were having your conversation with Trustee Pettijohn."

"I see," said George.

"There was one other person there," said Boggio. "Mrs. Ottilie Stanczak, stenographer and employee of the State Attorney General's office. We're using her notes."

"She was taking notes?" said George, his voice noncommittal.

"Yes."

"Next room?"

"Closet."

"I see," said George. "Look, I don't know what he's been telling you, but I never approached anyone else about taking a bribe from the gambling house. He," George said, nodding toward Pettijohn, "called me over to his house and I was acting in good faith. He was a Trustee."

"You actually intended to pay Trustee Pettijohn?" asked Boggio, startled at the frank admission.

"I was going to see my boy," replied George.

"See if your boy could pay it?"

"Yes."

They then turned to Pettijohn.

"What was your occasion for calling Mr. Toy?" asked Nichols.

"What was the occasion?" repeated Pettijohn, now on the defensive, and secretly furious that Harry Toy had handed the case over to Duncan McCrea. "I thought he was the logical man to call."

"You knew we had a prosecutor in Wayne County?" said Nichols.

"Yes."

"Did you ever tell Buckingham that you thought the Wayne County prosecutor's office was fixed and also the sheriff's office?"

"Chief Moore told me that himself," said Pettijohn.

George, who had been sitting slumped in his chair, could hardly believe what he was hearing. He reared up. "I never did."

"Of course, you did," argued Pettijohn. "You did repeatedly. It's in the transcript."

"You're imagining it. I said no such a thing."

"Okay, hold it, hold it," said Nichols. Then he turned to George. "Chief Moore did you tell Pettijohn that the Wayne County Prosecutor's office was fixed?"

"I did not," replied George firmly. "The statement I made was: that I understood that as long as the newspapers didn't make a kick, the prosecutor's office and the sheriff's office wouldn't take any action. I never said they were fixed."

"Yes," agreed Nichols. "That *is* what you said."

"How many times do I need to say it?" said George. "I was led to believe that there was not a fix as long as the newspapers didn't kick, that is, that the prosecutor's and the sheriff's office wouldn't bother. It was small stuff."

But George wasn't out from under. He had approached Pettijohn, offered him a bribe and it had been duly recorded and transcribed. Simple as that.

After George returned home from the County Court House in Detroit, he spent the evening on the phone in his bedroom, sitting on the edge of the bed, apprising key people of the situation, while Mae brought him a roast beef sandwich and more than one hot coffee. First he called Bill Voisine, then Burt Loveland, head of the Safety Commission. Finally he called Murph, and they talked for about an hour. It would be hard to ascertain who was bucking up whom, since Murph felt wholly responsible for his father's plight and kept repeating, "I'll do anything, Pa," often followed by, "That son of a bitch." He concluded with: "If it comes to a hearing, disown me on the stand, Pa. Don't worry about me. I'll take care of me." George even gave a heads-up to Freda and Rowe, telling them not to worry; it was only Ecorse politics at its best. As for his other daughters, Dia and Joyce stayed out of his way, aware that something was very wrong. Shay was spending the night at Virginia Brazill's, oblivious. Marce, who was being punished for teasing a playmate, was alone in her bedroom.

Yes, George was in serious trouble. In Michigan, the promise of a bribe to a public official was a felony, punishable by a jail term of one to four years. Everything he'd worked for—job, home, reputation for fair play—was about to go up in smoke. But his wife's response confirmed his choice. Mae Munn Moore may not have been the perfect fit for his girls, but throughout the long, miserable night, she was comforting, solicitous and trusting. His word was never questioned, though he did have to caution her from putting all the blame on Murph.

The following morning, Wednesday (August 21), Ollie Raupp called the precinct and entreated George to drive over to his radio shop as soon as possible.

"Could we make it later?"

"Now would be better," said Ollie, though he sidestepped the why.

George, up to his ears in neglected paperwork, reluctantly agreed.

Under a light drizzle, with little traffic on Front Street, he had no difficulty parking in front of Raupp's Radio Sales & Service on the northeast corner of Josephine, though he could barely get out of the car. His level of energy was down around his ankles, his depression palpable. But the thought of Ollie, and everything Ollie had been through, put things in perspective.

Six months before, in March, four-and-a-half-year-old Sonny Raupp had been hit by a car and died the same day at Wyandotte General. George could barely retain his lunch when a report was called in to the station about a small boy having been hit in front of 4515 High Street.

"He had a new tricycle," said Bernice Raupp of her brother. "He was riding up and down the sidewalk. My cousins were playing ball in the yard across the street, and when the ball went into the street, they heard him yell, 'I get it! I get it!' He was hit so hard his high-top shoes were knocked off his feet."

Oliver Raupp had lost his daughter, his son, his garage and was about to lose this store. He'd had such high hopes for it, but the economic climate just kept on bludgeoning hard-working people. Ollie's shop window was filled with the kind of signs that smacked of desperation. Half off this. Half off that. Used this. Used that. Terms available. When plug-in refrigerators began to usurp iceboxes, Ollie had even gone to Frigidaire school for a crash course in Freon, then added *Refrigerators: New, Used and Repaired* to the signs in his window. Each new sign made it look more down-at-the-heel.

Ollie had the same problem as Fred Pilon. People bought on credit, then didn't—couldn't—pay up. One of the town's leading citizens owed Ollie dearly, then fell on hard times himself. But most shop owners were in accord: it was better to offer credit and bear the risk, than risk losing the sale in the first place. All three of Mim's brothers were out of work and living with him, and Ollie was doing his best to support them. He had also been co-owner with his sister Hattie of the steel mill property from West Jefferson to the mill, but they couldn't pay the taxes. They lost it. They didn't sell it; they lost it.

Ollie, 41, who was at his happiest tinkering with anything mechanical, was a different man. But he never complained, just marshaled on and was no less friendly. So George was not surprised to see a smiling and welcoming Ollie when he opened the door and stepped onto the wood floor of the showroom to the tinkle of the bell.

"Have you had your coffee yet?" asked Ollie, dressed like a salesman in tie and white shirt with rolled-up sleeves. He had come through the archway from the back room.

George laughed. "First you add refrigerators to your showroom. Now you're hawking coffee?"

"I fix electric percolators," smiled Ollie. "Come on back. I've got a pot on."

"What about your customers?" asked George.

Ollie gave a derisive snort. "No problem there."

George laughed ruefully . "What's up?"

Along with the rich smell of roasted coffee, the back room which served as Ollie's repair shop was jam-packed. Every working surface was filled with gutted electronics, tools and parts. In the room's center there were two partially-opened boxes, their stuffing hanging out; two Atwater-Kent floor-model radios, their veneers covered in dust; two Frigidaire refrigerators, their insides outside; and two men sitting on kitchen chairs, their grins obvious.

"Morning, George," said Burt Loveland, 39, as he reached down by his side to pick up the cup of steaming coffee at his feet.

"Morning, George," said Bill Voisine, who, at 37, was the youngest man there. He stood up and offered his seat. "Age before beauty."

George shook off the offer and laughed. "What's this? A meeting of a secret society?"

"Wait. I've got another chair up front," said Ollie. "Marie's old kitchen set." He returned within seconds, handed the chair to George, then poured him some coffee. "Cream and sugar?"

"Please," said George, still puzzled. "But I didn't see your cars. Where you parked?"

"In back," said Bill.

"Walked over," said Burt.

"Ollie's got something to tell you," said Voisine.

Ollie, like a cat with a mouse, took his time. After handing George his cup and a spoon, he cleared a section of the workbench, hoisted himself up, then bent forward, his palms clutching the edge: "Pettijohn came over here about two weeks ago," he said. "August 8th to be exact."

George froze mid-stir. "And?"

"And . . . I'm sitting behind a display case, working on a Philco, when he leaned over and whispered with that twang of his, 'I want a cut in that gambling joint you fellas are operating.'"

"I can't believe this," said George. "Why didn't he just give it to Walter Winchell?" He looked at Voisine, then at Loveland, then back at Ollie. "What the Sam Hill did you say?"

"I told him I didn't know what he was talking about. Which was true," replied Ollie. "So I said 'what gambling joint?' He said, 'The one at 4420.' I said, 'Where's that? Seavitt's?' He says, 'No. Next to Seavitt's.' I said, 'Never heard of it.' Which, of course, was not true. Then he said, 'I understand all you boys are getting a cut and I want mine.' I said, 'All you boys?' He said, 'Yeah.' I said, 'What the hell are you talking about, Jesse? Who's *all you boys*?' He said, 'You know.' I said, "Trust me, I don't.' He went on and on, goading."

"How'd you leave it?" asked George.

"I told him I couldn't give him a cut because I didn't have a cut to give, but I could give him a good price on the Philco I was working on."

"So he left pissed?"

"He left *very* pissed."

"Oy. Why did you wait until now to tell me?"

"Sorry, George," said Ollie, peeling off his wire-rimmed glasses, wiping them with a handkerchief. "I figured it was none of my business. As for *all the guys* being in on it—and I assumed he meant the Village Council—I knew that was a crock. Pettijohn's always paranoid, always thinking the Council's out to get him. Probably because he's out to get the Council."

George took a sip of coffee, then sighed. "He's convinced we're all on the take."

"Is he?" asked Voisine, one eyebrow raised. "Or is he just trying to set us up?"

"And what about Hardage?" asked Loveland.

There was some muttering about hillbillies sticking together before Burt asked, "What exactly did you tell Boggio?"

"The assistant prosecutor?" said George.

"Yes."

George sighed, then plunged in. As he gave a blow-by-blow of his statement to Boggio, along with the doings of Mrs. Stanczak and Pettijohn, the groans emanating from the back room of that radio repair shop might have been heard in the produce section of the A&P across the street.

"It's all politics, George," concluded Loveland. "He wants to be village president and doesn't care how he gets there. The bastard set you up."

"Well, I can only blame myself," replied George. "I handed him the handcuffs."

"Aren't you being a little hard on yourself?" said Burt. "You were only trying to help your son."

"Everyone in this room knows how it feels," said Bill. "We've all got sons." There was an awkward pause before Burt cleared his throat and Bill blushed red. "Geezus, Ollie, I'm sorry."

"No. You're right," said Ollie. "We all know how it feels to have a son."

Burt Loveland set his coffee mug down on the floor, put his palms on his knees and addressed George. "You've got to go back," he said.

"Where?" asked George.

"To the prosecutor's office. You've got to go back. Make another statement."

"But I have nothing to add to the first statement. What I told them was the truth."

"And the truth will get you one-to-four in Jackson," said Burt. "You've got to make another statement."

"But they'd still have that first statement," said George. "And it's damaging."

"George, the bastard set you up," said Burt. "Are you going to let him get away with it?"

"Time to play hardball, my friend," said Ollie.

"You're gonna go back and tell them that Pettijohn approached you *first*. To solicit the bribe," Burt continued.

"Blatantly lie?"

"You bet," laughed Bill. "The more blatant the lie; the more people believe it."

"But he didn't approach me," said George. "I approached him—like an idiot."

"To solicit a bribe?" asked Burt.

"No," said George. "To see what he wanted."

"Exactly," said Ollie.

"Pettijohn's the one who started it all. He's the one who did the soliciting," prodded Burt. "First, he solicited Bill, then he solicited Ollie. We're not talking about Little Lord Fauntleroy here."

"I'm uncomfortable with this," said George.

"Listen to me. Listen to me," said Burt, leaning toward George with urgency. "You're going to tell them that Pettijohn approached you and that you only went along to get enough rope to hang him."

"Oh, Christ."

"Listen to Burt, George," said Ollie. "He knows what he's doing."

"This is what you're gonna tell Boggio," said Burt. "This is what you're gonna say: 'I was told by Burt Loveland, president of the Safety Commission, that anyone approaching me with bribery in view should be encouraged to commit himself, and a report made to the commission afterward. The next meeting of the commission is on the first Tuesday in September. I would have presented the evidence against Pettijohn at that time. I went to see Pettijohn to trap him.'"

"I can't tell them that," said George, his voice rising.

"But it's true!" bellowed Loveland. "I did tell you that! Don't you remember?"

"Yes, but that was ages ago. In casual conversation!" cried George. "You're splitting hairs!"

"No! You're splitting hairs!" said Burt.

"George, George," said Bill. "Listen to us. It's the end of your career. It's a stay in Jackson prison. You'll be selling apples when you get out."

"Were you personally taking a bribe?" asked Ollie.

"No," said George.

"Did you stand to make a penny?"

"No."

"This guy was spreading manure all over town," said Bill. "The only thing you did wrong was step in it."

"Pettijohn, Hardage, the newspapers," said Ollie, "they're gonna make you out to be just one more corrupt Downriver sleazeball, just another chief on the take."

"Ollie's right," said Bill. "Since Prohibition tainted local administrations, everyone's willing, even delighted, to believe the worst about Ecorse officials, though the same doesn't seem to hold for Wyandotte, despite the body count."

"This will reflect on your wife, a school principal, for god's sake, and your daughters," said Ollie. "And how you gonna earn a living? We've already got four barbers in this town, and they're not living off the fat of the land. And for what? For some guy who's out to get you. Out to get Bill. Out to get me. Out to get who-the-hell-knows-who- else. You gonna let that sucker win?"

"Look, George, this is not some wild, hare-brained scheme," said Burt. "Ollie can testify about Pettijohn asking for a bribe 'cause it's the truth. Bill can testify that Pettijohn came to him for a bribe 'cause it's the truth. I can testify that I told you to go along and gather the evidence, 'cause it's the truth. We can all honestly corroborate what you will be saying."

"He's charging you, you charge him," said Bill. "It's that simple."

"But there's still that first statement," said George.

"Let us worry about the first statement," said Bill.

"What do you mean?" asked George.

"Just what I said."

"For god's sake, Bill," said George, "don't offer to pay anybody anything."

"We won't need to," said Bill. "The boys in the County prosecutor's office are sympathetic. Don't forget. Pettijohn went after them, too."

George toyed with pursuing the line of thought further, then thought better of it. "Well, friends," he said, "thanks for the powwow." He eased out of his chair, walked to the sink in the backroom bathroom, washed out the cup and spoon, set them by the percolator, then stopped in the archway and looked back. "Damn, I hate to lie."

"Oh, c'mon, George," groaned Bill. "Give up the cherry tree."

"No, you don't understand," said George. "I'm not a saint. I'm just a lousy liar." Then he turned to go, muttering, "Well, if you're born to be shot, you'll never hang."

George set up an appointment with the prosecutor's office for the next day, Thursday, and gave a second statement to Garfield Nichols in which he said: "I was told by Burt Loveland that, if any bribe offers were made by gamblers, I was to gather the evidence and present it to the next meeting of the Public Safety Commission. The next meeting of the commission is on the first Tuesday in September. I would have presented the evidence against Mr. Pettijohn at that time."

On Friday, the whole sorry business, with charges and countercharges, hit the papers. That Sunday, Judge Charles Rubiner was appointed to take over the one-man grand jury regarding Ecorse.

Over that same weekend, Oliver Raupp, Burt Loveland, Bill Voisine, James Hardage and Melvin Moore were all called to make statements.

In his statement, Voisine corroborated Moore.

In his statement, Loveland corroborated Moore.

In his statement, Raupp corroborated Moore.
In his statement, Moore corroborated Moore.
In his statement, Hardage corroborated Pettijohn.
The sides were set.

The next Thursday (August 29), the first day of testimony in front of Rubiner in Common Pleas Court, those subpoenaed were William Voisine, Burt Loveland, and all four trustees: William Born, Oliver Raupp, Frank Morris and Paul Movinski.

Born, Morris and Movinski all said they knew nothing about the gambling place, though Movinski said he'd heard that a place was being run by a Jack Dawson. Voisine, Loveland and Raupp gave testimony as planned, though Voisine added one more dollop, saying that Pettijohn had also asked for a cut out of a public-works contract.

There was no mention of George's first statement.

On Tuesday (September 3), when the Common Pleas Court inquiry continued, George was the first to take the stand. He admitted he had offered Pettijohn $25, but had done so on orders of his superiors to determine whether Pettijohn would accept a bribe. Questioned about Murph, he said: "He's 27 years old and he won't listen to my advice. He's been mixed up with that sort of stuff for several years and there's nothing I can do about it. I can't control him."

Next Hardage took the oath and tarred Ecorse with his usual den-of-vice brush. He emerged to tell the press: "I like Moore, but I don't see why he and Voisine have to take orders from racketeers and front for them all the time." The following day (Wednesday, September 4), he added: "I know that one gambling syndicate was established in Ecorse and that another was unsuccessfully trying to gain a foothold. Three days after the bombing of Voisine's home, the second gambling syndicate came into town and set up shop."

Then Charles P. Steffes, Ecorse building inspector, backed Voisine's accusation, testifying that "Pettijohn demanded and received $20 to approve a voucher for $100 which I had presented for work done for the village as a private contractor." Asked about his testimony by the press when he came out of the grand jury room, Pettijohn sputtered that he was "framed" by Voisine, Moore and Steffes. "I don't remember the voucher and I wouldn't, because approving vouchers is routine. The whole thing is a frame-up by Voisine and Moore to discredit my testimony."

"You never mentioned Steffes and the DPW to me," said Loveland to Voisine as they sat outside the jury room.

"Oh, I just tossed that in to get the bastard," said Voisine.

But George had only temporarily dodged a bullet. His first statement had not been entered as evidence. Just over a week later, on September 6, it all came crashing down in Rubiner's courtroom.

First Buckingham testified, then Mrs. Stanczak, then Murph, who, while repeating his testimony to reporters, was quoted as saying that he knew nothing about any payoffs, that it was a small gambling house, that his Uncle Peck did the parking, and it gave them employment. Otherwise, they'd all be on welfare.

Then came the bombshell. While Sgt. Philip Hutson, one of the state troopers who'd been hiding in Pettijohn's house, was testifying, he casually mentioned the existence of George Moore's incriminating statement to Wayne County Assistant Prosecutor Boggio. He also introduced the humiliating news about George sending over whiskey for Pettijohn's cold.

While prosecuting the case in county court, Boggio had suppressed that first statement. For whatever reason—maybe he smelled a rat, maybe he was sympathetic to George, or maybe he was just put out that Pettijohn was also trying to implicate the Wayne County prosecutor's office—Boggio was in big trouble. Judge Rubiner was furious. Boggio now had no choice; he turned the first statement over to Rubiner.

That Saturday (September 7), while George was dealing with more tragic matters—Thelma DeVoy, 16, and Virginia Merrow, 10, on their way to play baseball, had just been killed by an MCRR passenger train as they crossed the tracks near Cicotte within yards of the Ecorse police station—two investigators arrived at the station to arrest him. Arraigned before Judge Rubiner in Common Pleas Court, George pleaded "Not Guilty" and, after some family scrambling, was released on a $2,000 personal bond. Bill Voisine and Earl Montie, village attorney, drove him home.

Ten days later, on Tuesday (September 17), a special meeting of the Safety Commission was called to deal with the charges preferred against George A. Moore. Judge Rubiner had written the commission, asserting that there was reason to believe that Moore was "guilty of misfeasance and malfeasance of office and willful neglect of duty and attempt to bribe a public official (namely one Jesse Pettijohn, Village Trustee)."

Burt Loveland had no choice. He moved, and it was seconded by Charles Heide, that the commission institute removal proceedings to be held at a time designated by the commission. But before a vote was taken, Commissioner James Compton made the following amendment: that George be suspended until trial could be held and decision could be rendered. On the amendment, Loveland and

Heide voted no; and Compton, Wilson Koch, and Chris Raupp voted yes. On the original resolution, all voted yes.

––––––––––

Eleven days later, on Saturday (September 28), the Ecorse Public Safety Commission, sitting as a trial board, met to decide George's fate. Witnesses included Hardage, Pettijohn, Voisine, Raupp, Mrs. Ottilie Stanczak and Murph. When Pettijohn took the stand, he testified that he had approached several Ecorse officials, that he had complained to Moore, as police chief, "several times" about 4420 and gambling, and Moore had offered the bribe as a result. Earlier however, Boggio had helped George's cause by saying that "no evidence had been presented indicating Pettijohn ever had complained of the gambling house to the council or Ecorse police."

George continued his claim that he was "just trying to lead him on." So it was a draw. Except it wasn't. The recorded offer of George's bribe to Pettijohn seemed certain to bring him down.

Chapter 60
October 5, 1935

A seemingly unrelated event unfolded on October 5, 1935, one of those crisp, autumn Saturdays in Michigan when "Hail to the Victors" can be heard throughout Washtenaw County as the helmeted U of M Wolverines take to the field. That evening there was to be a meeting of 300 to 400 different Wolverines in another field, this one in Oakland County.

On that day two men, Fred Gulley, 25, (husband of Mary Gulley, secretary to William Voisine and George Moore), and Earl L. Angstadt, 34, both of Ecorse, both members of the Wolverine Republican League, were sitting in a Wyandotte restaurant at around 3:30 p.m., sipping coffee, listening to Game 4 of the World Series (Tigers 1, Chicago Cubs 1, in the 4th), when Sgt. Clarence A. Petraska of the Wyandotte Police Department strolled in. He had been tipped off by a nervous patron that the men were carrying concealed weapons. When the officer frisked them, only one gun was found and that on the person of Gulley, though Angstadt claimed it was his. The trigger, he said, needed repairing; they were taking it to a shop. Sgt. Petraska let them go.

But a repair shop was not their destination. Angstadt, Gulley and a third man, Thomas F. Cox, had been ordered by Harold Lawrence, senior captain of the Wolverine Republican League, to bring a man named Robert Penland to Saturday night's meeting. By force, if necessary.

"I ain't so sure of these mugs," groused Angstadt. An Ohio-born ex-seaman and veteran of World War I, he was also an ex-con who been convicted of auto theft in 1923 and, following his release, had moved to Michigan to look for work.

"Yeah," replied Gulley. "They've had the bases loaded twice, but they can't bring 'em in."

"Not the Tigers, dimwit," said Angstadt. "These other mugs in Michigan. I mean they're not like the Black Knights in Ohio."

"Maybe it's because they aren't the Black Knights in Ohio," offered Gulley.

"Aw, you know what I mean," said Angstadt. "You're from Ohio. Better class of people."

Angstadt leaned in and kept his voice low, confidential. "In Ohio we worked *with* law enforcement. My father and my grandfather were Black Knights. When I turned 21, my Pa told me all about the Knights and the rituals. It's somethin' to aspire to. Here, it's different. I asked about it once, but they told me they were young, that when got it well-organized, membership would be handed down in the family from father to son."

Gulley hailed the waiter for a coffee refill, watched while he poured, waited for him to clear the area, then leaned in toward Angstadt. "Having second thoughts about this?"

"Naw, naw, it ain't that," said Angstadt. "Penland's missing meetings. If you're AWOL, you gotta be disciplined. Besides, we're under orders. What choice we got?"

While others in the restaurant were singing the praises of Detroit's pitcher, General Crowder, the two men huddled to discuss ways of getting Penland out of his house without arousing suspicion. They did pause briefly during the sixth when Flea Clifton scored for the Tigers. The restaurant erupted. Tigers were up by one.

Around 4:45 p.m., with the game over and the Tigers now leading the series three games to one, Cox sauntered into the restaurant, walked to the counter and ordered coffee, then joined them. A good-looking man of 30, he had helped recruit Angstadt into the Wolverines. Cox, who lived on Bell in Ecorse with his wife and five-year-old daughter, had spent his life chasing work in the mills. Born in West Virginia, by 1930 the family was in Wyandotte, with father and son working at Ecorse's Michigan Steel. Like Angstadt and Gulley and even Penland, he now worked at Great Lakes Steel.

At around 5:20 p.m., the three men pulled into King's gas station on Front Street, where James J. Stewart, ex-detective of the Ecorse Police Department, was now employed pumping gas for Charlie King. Stewart had gone from a police uniform to the shirt and tie of a detective, to the shirt and bow-tie of a station attendant. When they asked for Penland's address, Stewart went inside the station, came back out and pointed north.

"'Bout six blocks up," he said. "65 East Auburn. Take a right, go all the way down, not far from the tracks."

It was 5:30 p.m. when the men pulled to the curb in front of the Penland home. Gulley, the only one of the three who knew Penland, got out and rang the doorbell while Cox remained in the passenger seat and Angstadt, the driver, kept the engine running.

Penland, 30, a small, unassuming man, was eating dinner with his wife and their six-year-old daughter. He put down his napkin and came to the door.

"Sorry to interrupt your dinner, Bob," said Gulley, "but your foreman wants to see ya." He pointed to the idling car. "Wants to talk to you about mill relief." Penland came out on the porch and walked with Gulley to the car, but when he glanced in the windows, he didn't see his boss, only two men he'd never met. "I know what you want," he said. "If you'll just let me finish my dinner, I'll go with you to the meeting."

Gulley reached into his pocket and shoved a gun into Penland's back. "Get inside," he said.

As they drove off, his wife thought nothing of it. Penland, a crane repairman and operator, was often called at night to do emergency fixes. She just put his dinner away for reheating.

During the long drive, the three men were nothing if not gracious. As the oncoming night lowered the temperature, Penland, who was sitting in back with Gulley, began to shiver in his shirt sleeves, so Angstadt turned on the car's heater and Gulley loaned him his overcoat. Because Penland had come away without his cigarettes, they passed him their own. Because he had not finished his dinner, they offered him some grapes. Meetings of the Wolverine Republican League were on the long side.

Born in Alabama, the youngest of six, Penland had, at the beginning of the Depression, moved to Warren, Michigan, where he found a job as an electrician in an auto parts factory. By 1933 he was in Ecorse, working at the steel mill. Like other initiates of the League, Penland had been approached by another worker and asked if he'd like to join a good American organization, one that could secure and protect his job. Trust me, he had been told. But it had been hard to remain trusting when he found himself kneeling down, taking a rather mirthless oath. Not so sure? Too late now. You're a member, bud. Attendance is required. Once a member, always a member.

"Where we goin'?" he asked.

"Ask Angstadt," said Cox. "Only the drivers ever know."

"You'll see when we get there," said Angstadt.

"How do you like them Tigers, eh?" asked Gulley.

Cox turned around from the front seat. "They got Crowder to thank."

"Or Greenberg," said Gulley.

"Whaddya mean, or Greenberg?" growled Angstadt.

"Papers are saying it was Hank Greenberg's two-run homer in Game 2 that gave them this momentum," said Gulley.

"Bullshit," scoffed Angstadt. "I for one cheered this week when Hymie Greenberg fractured his wrist. And I ain't alone."

"Why's that?"

"Simple. If the Tigers win the World Series, no one can say it was because of some kike. He won't even play on Yom Kipper."

"But you have to admit he's their best," said Gulley.

"Propaganda," said Angstadt. "Jews own the papers, Jews build him up."

"How can you say that?" complained Gulley. "He led the league in home runs and RBIs. They can't make that up."

"I think we got ourselves a Jew lover in this car, Tom," laughed Angstadt.

"Aw, cut the shit," groused Gulley. "Not even close."

"Bet he even roots for Joe Louis," ribbed Cox.

As the men cruised north up Outer Drive, a parade of cars was streaming off Lahser Road onto White Boulevard, a narrow, rutted dirt road in Oakland County, then pulling in and parking in a huge meadow. Eventually, there would be about 150 cars in all. The field, completely isolated, with only an old farm-house half a mile away, was between 8 Mile and 9 Mile Roads. It had been used for open-air meetings of the Wolverine Republican League on several occasions.

The sun had set, the half-moon was rising, and the meeting was well under-way when the car containing the four men turned right off Lahser onto White and bounced along the furrowed road. When they reached the field and flashed their headlights three times, it was about 6:40.

"Sit tight. It'll be awhile," said Angstadt. He got out of the car, kicked the kinks out of his legs, then strolled away. Cox and Gulley and a nervous Penland sat in the car and waited.

Meetings of the Wolverine Republican League were often held in concentric circles. The largest circle that night, the Outer Guard, was made up of about 300 armed men, mostly privates in street clothes standing sentry.

Around 8 p.m., League officers robed in black approached the car and hus-tled a terrified Penland out. Silently, they marched him through the ankle-high grass into an inner circle, known as the Inner Guard, where he was put on trial for disobedience.

"Major of No. 12 Regiment," ordered the Major General, resplendent in the white robe reserved for high officials. "Step forward!"

The Major of No. 12 Regiment, an officer in a black robe, stepped smartly out of line and saluted. On his head was a cockade hat, similar to the one worn by Napoleon, though this one prominently displayed a skull and crossbones. He, like most of the others, was not wearing a mask that night.

Then the Major General singled out the man, shivering in his shirt sleeves. "Is he the man?"

"Yes, Major General," replied the Major of No. 12 Regiment.

"Private Penland!" barked the Major General. "Step forward!"

Penland, legs like spaghetti, did just that.

"Private Penland!" barked the Major General. "You are in bad standing!"

Then the Major of No. 12 Regiment and Senior Captain Harold Lawrence grilled Penland: why wasn't he attending meetings?

With his eyes downcast, his voice low, Penland said there had been illness in the family, but that he'd try to do better.

"Were you not told that once a member, always a member!" roared the Major of No. 12 Regiment, striding before him, the half-moon low in the sky his only light.

"Yes."

"Yes, what!"

"Yes, Major."

"Were you not warned that if you resign or abandon this organization, your only escape from punishment would be suicide or leaving the country?"

"Yes, Major."

Threats and intimidation continued until the Major General in white, a

Department of Steel Railways (DSR) worker from Highland Park named Wilbur Robinson, bellowed, "Officers of Regiment 12, what is your verdict? Guilty? Or not guilty!"

"Guilty!" yelled the Major of the 12th Regiment and the Senior Captain.

"Penland!" shouted Robinson. "You are charged with violating the meeting attendance rule and have been found guilty! Your punishment will be 16 lashes!"

Stripped of his shirt, his suspenders dangling, Mr. Penland was placed, face first, against a large maple tree, one of the very few in the meadow, and ordered to embrace the trunk. His hands, barely meeting on the opposite side, were bound. He waited apprehensively but nothing happened. Then he heard several cars start up and flinched when their headlights flooded the stage, exposing his thin, pallid back.

Those in the outer circle looked on with renewed interest. While all 300 men watched, an anonymous man in black robe, black hat and black mask came forward. He was holding a cat-o'-nine-tails, a leather affair about two feet in length, with a leather hilt and nine knotted strands, commonly called blades. Mustering force with an upraised arm, he lashed Penland over and over while the chimes of Dunscotus Friary at Nine Mile and Evergreen rang out, calling the seminarians to Holy Hour.

Chapter 61
October 7–12, 1935

The Detroit Tigers won their first World Series on Monday, October 7, 1935, beating the favored Chicago Cubs 4—3. That same Monday, while Michigan danced in the streets, four of the five men of the Safety Commission bitterly wrangled behind closed doors for five hours about whether or not to reinstate George Moore as Chief of Police. Finally, with tempers frayed, they agreed to table the matter until their next scheduled meeting, Monday, October 21. Then they went out, grabbed their tin horns and joined in the pandemonium.

Meanwhile, the tension at the Moore house was palpable. On suspension, out of work, with the prospect of reinstatement looking less and less likely, George had nothing to do but sit around all day, listening to the radio, reading the paper. Up until that Monday, he at least had the Series to look forward to. Now Mae and the girls would hurry off to school, Joyce would hurry off to work, and George would spend the long hours in no hurry whatsoever, fiddling with the radio dial, longing to escape Mussolini, trying to stay out of Edna's way, withdrawing his feet while she vacuumed.

Ordinarily when George made the papers, his wife bought extra copies. These days one copy sufficed. As corrupt Wayne County law-enforcement officials paraded in handcuffs across the front pages of Michigan dailies, George was lumped in. In the minds of those who did not know him, he was just one among many.

Mrs. Moore handled the cracks and snickers in the school hallways with her usual assurance, but her husband, his reputation shredded, was demoralized. It was just as well that invitations dwindled. He hated going out, having to pretend that he was insensible to the strained smiles, forced grins and stiff handshakes, oblivious to the sudden clamming up of huddled colleagues as he entered a room.

"How ya doin'?"

"Can't kick."

Some of his men—men he had great respect for—had lost theirs for him. Even McWhirter, on the few occasions when they crossed paths, was obviously uncomfortable in his presence. Maybe it would be better to lose his job. With all respect gone, how the hell would he lead his men?

He told everyone he was fine. Probably thought he was. True, his gums were a bloody mess, but prolonged stress will do that. Hadn't this whole sorry saga been going on since the end of July? But he wasn't fine, not by a long shot. He got his first glimpse of how far from fine on Saturday, October 12, 1935, Columbus Day, the day Dia turned 17.

———————

On that cold, gray Saturday morning, with the thermometer below freezing, Dia kicked off her covers and leapt out of bed, eager to put on her uniform. Though still in 9th grade, she had landed a part-time job at Affholter Bros. Creamery in River Rouge. Ellen Barbour worked there with her.

> *"Ellen had a tandem bicycle," recalled Dia. "I'd walk to her house on Charlotte, then with me on the bike we'd take off down Front and pedal to work. Everybody waving and tooting."*

Thanks to Mrs. Moore, Dia was not new to waiting tables. The same girl who sent flowers to Mrs. Bouchard "from her loving daughter Evelyn" had been serving at Mrs. Moore's Poodle-Dog Teas—at least that's what George called them—for some time now. Since Mae often held weekend teas, inviting fellow teachers or women from her Woman's Club, she purchased a frilly maid's apron for Dia, taught her to serve from the left, retrieve from the right, and Dia spent many a contented afternoon relishing the chatter, attending to the ladies as they swooned over *Goodbye, Mr. Chips.*

> *"It served two purposes," explained Dia. "I liked doing it, and she liked putting on the ritz." Rowe was less generous: "Mae had more crust than a pie factory. She just loved to be waited on. Thought she was high society. She'd call me to come over the night before to fix the meal and [then] let on that she cooked it."*

On her cloudy autumn birthday, Dia worked a full shift at Affholter's, raked in a munificent 65 cents in tips, then, come 6 p.m., she and Ellen pedaled furiously back to Ecorse on the tandem—cars tooting, guys waving—and Dia ran the two short blocks to the house on High, hurriedly changed out of her uniform, managed a sponge bath, bolted a sandwich, telling Mae not to worry, she wouldn't be late, that they were going to the early show at the Lancaster in River Rouge and she thought it let out about 10:15.

She had purchased a coat for the occasion on time payments—now that she had a job, now that she could get credit—a tweed coat with wide lapels lined with fur for $9.98—$1.50 down, $1.58 per month, for the next six months.

"Your prince has arrived," said Marce, bursting into the bedroom where Dia was applying lipstick in front of the dresser mirror.

"How do you know?"

"I peeked through the living-room curtains."

"With Mae in the room?" laughed Shay, sprawled across the bed.

"Yeah."

"What'd she say?"

"Three guesses."

"And what'd *you* say?" asked Joyce, sitting sideways in the overstuffed chair, legs dangling over the overstuffed arm, buffing her nails.

"I ain't ruffling no curtains."

"Geez, Marce. After all her correcting," moaned Joyce. "You know better than 'I ain't.'"

"Yeah, but it gets her goat."

"Yeah, but it doesn't help things, riling her like that," warned Joyce. "Then Pa gets it, then we get it."

"Aw, Pa's not even here."

"Rest assured, he'll hear about it."

Shay yawned. "Sposed to warm up tonight," she said, apropos of nothing. "Go from 40 to 80."

Dia, who had just dropped her lipstick into her purse and snapped it shut, looked up, alarmed. "What time tonight?"

"What's it matter?"

"She wants to wear her new winter coat," explained Joyce.

"Got that right," said Dia.

So with the tweed coat fashionably over her shoulders, the one-feather brown beret slanted sideways on her head, purse at her side, gloves in hand, it was off to the movies with Murray McQueen.

———————

That evening, about 10:15, Shay, Marce and Joyce were off in their lovely rooms awaiting Dia's return, knowing they'd be asked to make a brief appearance. Mr. and Mrs. Moore sat in the living room in their robes and nightclothes, anticipating the birthday girl. Gifts and cards were laid out artfully on the dining-room table, the vanilla ice cream was in the freezing compartment, and the two-layer cake was on the kitchen counter, its 17 candles waiting to be lit.

George was growing resigned to his daughters' tendency to hide in their rooms. He knew that children changed as they grew older, that he mustn't take it personally, that, like Murph who once buried himself in his bedroom, his daughters preferred to keep to themselves, always heading straight for their rooms whenever they entered the house. Admittedly, his initial inclination had been to force them to come out, fearing his bride would be hurt, until he realized that Mae, with all her experience as an educator, didn't take it personally either. That she accepted their need to be alone.

But lateness was another story. Around 10:30, Mrs. Moore set down her rug hook with annoyance. "She said about 10:15."

"She said, 'It let out about 10:15,' countered George, lowering the volume on the radio, tempering the latest news on Mussolini. "Isn't that what she told you? Let out? They'd still have to drive home. Say goodnight."

At 11, Mae let out a distinct sigh, then reached down by her side to pointedly check the newspaper for curtain times, while George pointedly ignored her.

About 11:15, Mae went into the kitchen, put the cake in the cake box, then stuck her head through the archway. "Sorry, George. But I'm really out of the party mood."

"We can celebrate tomorrow. Dia won't mind," replied George. "Did she know about the cake?"

"No. I thought we'd surprise her."

"Well, if she didn't know . . . ," he drifted off.

"Even so, you don't need this," said Mae softly, returning to her living-room chair. "With all you're going through. She knows you can't sleep until she gets home, but she just does as she pleases. They all do. It's thoughtless. Shay's the same way."

"Shay? What's Shay got to do with it?"

"Please keep your voice down, dear. I'm only saying. . ."

"I know you're only saying, but I don't get it," he whispered. "Why are you always on Shay? What's she doing that keeps ticking you off?"

"I'm not *always* on Shay."

"You are, Mae. You are."

"If I am, there's good reason."

"What reason?"

"You don't notice it," said Mae. "You can't see it."

"Okay, then tell me. I'm all ears."

"Attitude.

"Attitude?"

"Yes, attitude. She's filled with resentment."

"About what?"

"About me. About her teachers. About everything. She's hostile. An angry young woman. She doesn't say much. But I can feel it."

"Shay?"

"Yes, Shay. Your beloved Shay."

"You sure you've got the right *woman*?" he laughed. "Last I looked, she was still a little girl."

"You know what I mean."

"Well, I don't see it."

"Of course, you don't, dear. She's not like that with you. But she's jealous of our relationship. Always has been. She just *refuses* to share you. And I, for one, am getting tired of it."

"Well, I'm sorry if she's giving you grief. I truly am," he said, standing up, belting his robe. "Coming to bed?"

"Aren't you going to wait until Doris gets in?"

"We'll leave the table lamp on in the living room. She'll be along soon."

While George removed and folded the bedcover, then crawled into bed, Mae opened each door of the adjoining bedrooms, informing the girls that the party was called off, that they'd better get some sleep if they wanted to be bright-eyed for mass in the morning. Then she entered the master bedroom without a word, shook her pillow to plump it, and crawled in beside George, who, without a word, was lying on his side, his back to her. Then, without a word, she slid Clarence Day's *Life with Father* off the bedside table and rested the book against her blue-blanketed knee, turning to her bookmarked page.

"Going to read, eh?" offered George, his back to the light.

"You know I can't sleep, dear, not until Doris gets in. For all you know she's sitting outside in a car, doing Lord knows what."

"She's not," he laughed. "I looked." Then he turned over and pointed to her book in a bid to make amends. "Has that guy been baptized yet?"

"Who?"

"Clarence Day's father. Has he been baptized yet? You said, he was upsetting the whole family because he hadn't been baptized."

"I'm sure he will be, dear, at the end."

"Undoubtedly," said George.

Mrs. Moore barely managed four pages of the sputtering Mr. Day before marking her place with her thumb. "You're too easy on them, George."

"Now, don't start."

"You are, dear."

"Some have said the opposite."

"You're too kind, and they take advantage. They pull the wool over your eyes. Look at Murph."

"Oh, here we go again."

"I know, dear. But facts are facts. He took advantage, did as he pleased, and guess who's paying for it? It makes my blood boil. What he's done to you. He's ruined your career."

"I did it to myself."

"See."

"My father was tough."

"I know, dear."

"So tough, I was out on my ear at 15," said George. "I vowed I wouldn't do that to my son."

"Maybe you overcorrected."

"Maybe I did."

"And what about Rowe almost killing herself on bad gin?"

"Is this going to be another litany of my kids' shortcomings?"

"I *a-dore* your children, George. You know that. But good parenting means putting your foot down. They need to know who's boss."

"I don't know where you get the idea that I'm a pantywaist, that they walk all over me. Now can we just leave this? Save it for another day? I haven't had a decent night's sleep in a coon's age."

"Don't blame me. I'm not the one who might be out in a car somewhere."

"Let's just leave it."

And leave it she did, for three more pages.

"I'll bet they didn't even go to the movies," she said, fanning the flame.

"What was that?" asked George, having nearly drifted off.

"I'll bet they didn't even go to the movies," repeated Mae, closing her book, returning it to the bedside table. "Girls that age can't be trusted. I deal with them every day of the week, George. So do you, the ones who get into trouble. Like her friend Jean."

"We've been over that."

"Taking Dia to the Gaiety in Detroit to see a burlesque show, buying her a box of Sanders chocolates."

"Mixed assortment, I heard."

"I'm surprised you think it's funny."

"You're right. You're right."

"There are bad girls and there are bad men. And Dia gravitates toward rough trade."

"Wait a minute," said George, turning her way. "Are you trying to tell me something?"

"About what?"

"About this guy? This Murray."

"Not specifically."

"What do we know about him, specifically?"

"Joyce says he's a carpenter," replied Mae. "From Ohio. Moved here with his family a couple of years ago."

"A carpenter? I thought he went to Ecorse High."

"From what I hear, he's out of school."

George bolted upright. "How old is he?"

"Joyce said he turned 23 yesterday, that he practically shares Dia's birthday."

"23!"

"Now George."

"23!"

"Now, darling."

"Did you know he was 23?"

"No," said Mae. "Joyce just told me." Which was not exactly true; Joyce had told her weeks before.

———

By now, it was eight minutes past her midnight curfew, and Dia was proving him wrong. George rolled out of bed, put on his robe, then made a show of opening the closet door and retrieving his black cowhide belt from his hangered pants.

"Will this suit you?" he asked, dangling the belt.

"Up to you, dear," replied Mae, reaching for her book.

He went to the kitchen, folded the belt in half and placed it on the table, then sat down on the hard, uncomfortable kitchen chair, hungry for sleep. He didn't bother to turn on the lights, just sat there in the half dark, light spilling through the archway from the table lamp in the living room.

Finally, four minutes later, George heard a car pull up out front, heard a car door slam, heard the street door open, heard high heels quietly but rapidly clicking on the stairs, watched calmly as Dia tiptoed in.

"Geez, Pa, my heart," she said, startled.

"How was the show?"

"Quelle stinkaroo," replied Dia, setting her purse and gloves on the kitchen table. "The second feature topped the first by a mile."

"Yeah?"

"Yeah. Big, fat bomb. They shoulda just dropped it on Mussolini," she laughed. "Sorry I'm a little late but . . ."

"Where'd you go?" he cut in, smiling.

"Lancaster in Rouge."

"Yeah? What'd you see?"

"*Woman Wanted.*"

"Yeah? Who was in it?"

"One of your favorites, Edgar Kennedy," replied Dia, nervously taking off her beret, fluffing her hair, now aware she was being played, now aware of the belt on the table. There was a hint of malice in his friendly questions, a hint of sarcasm. "Shoulda gone to see Dick Powell and Marion Davies in *Page Miss Glory.*"

"What was the second feature?"

"*Smart Girl,*" replied Dia.

"Yeah?"

"Boy, am I in trouble. You're gonna pass that title up without a crack, eh?" she laughed, though her mole was a little shaky. "Not a good sign. But the only reason I'm late is . . ."

"Who was in it?" he interrupted.

"Ida Lupino. I love Ida Lupino," laughed Dia. "Tougher than most of your cops."

He laughed with her, sort of, then said, "You sure you went to the show?"

"Huh?"

"You sure you went to the show?"

"What are you talking about? Of course, I went to the show. We couldn't get a seat. The place was packed. So we went over to the drug store and had a shake and waited for the start of the second feature, then sat through the first. Got out at half past 11."

"And now it's past midnight."

"Well, cripes, we had to walk to the car, drive home. I had to say goodnight for Pete's sake. C'mon, Pa. My weekend curfew's at midnight. I'm only a couple minutes late. Be fair."

"You told your mother you'd be home around 10:15."

"I said, It *let out* around 10:15."

"Same thing."

"Not quite," said Dia, heading for the hallway. "But I'll bet I know who's been egging you on. And happy birthday to me."

He was out of his chair in an instant, grabbing her by the sleeve of her coat, hauling her back into the kitchen, the sound of the rip lost to the sound of their raised voices. He was a man possessed, flailing away at her backside with his belt, the buckle landing smartly with each snap.

"Don't use that tone on me! I'm still your father!"

"Hey! Ow!"

"You think because you turn 17 you're legally free! You no longer have to listen!"

"Ow. Ow!"

"Well, think again!"

"Ow!"

"You gonna dance for me, Blackie!"

"Pa, I didn't do anything!"

"You gonna dance?"

"Pa, stop!"

"I'll make you dance for me, Blackie!

The scuffle could be heard in every room in that apartment and in the Kovac apartment below. George's other daughters were lying in the dark, crying softly in their lovely rooms.

Dia always made light of it, bragging that she let out great howls but didn't feel anything because she was wearing her new winter coat. But there were variations in the telling.

> *"Now my dad was sound asleep,"* said Rowe. *"He would never have known Dia was late, but Mae woke him up to let him know. And he came in, in the kitchen, and slapped Dia around and tore her new coat that wasn't even paid for, and she peed all over the kitchen."*
>
> *"We all got our lickings,"* said Shay. *"What the hell? In those days, people beat their kids if they didn't behave. And I'm sure we misbehaved."*
>
> *"Everybody got clipped a little bit,"* said Rowe. *"More than a little bit. He wasn't ornery. He was just strict. We all were afraid of him. But I think Dia was more afraid of him than anybody."*

George's remorse was immediate. He knew the difference between a spanking and a beating. Presumably he never spanked again. And he bent over backwards to make it up to Dia.

> *The next day, Sunday, "he brought the cake and ice cream down to my house," said Freda, "and we had the party on Monroe Street. He loved his kids, but ... he was in between two fires."*

He was, however, still oblivious to the fact that his children were miserable. Outside his house, he was extremely observant. He was a blind man at home.

———————

Finally, on Monday, October 21, 1935, the Safety Commission met again. That night, they lifted George's suspension, cleared him of all charges, and voted to reinstate him as Chief of Police "to take effect immediately." The Wayne County prosecutor's office, however, did not follow suit. Pettijohn, determined to clean up the town, was still pressing criminal charges. And once a reputation is smudged, no matter by whom, erasers are useless. George Moore's reputation was in tatters.

Chapter 62
January-March 1936

Now there were a myriad of stars in the galaxy, mostly hoofers, all vying to be Shay's all-time favorite. Colleen Moore had been usurped, even if she had Moore for a last name and came from Port Huron. Sue Carol had also been demoted, as well as Nancy Carroll. It mainly depended on which musical Shay had seen the week before. And no one danced better than Eleanor Powell. So every Saturday, sometimes Sunday, it was off to the movies with Mae's blessing. The only thing ruining those magical trips was Marce.

Marce blew bubbles in the movie house. She'd sink down in her seat, dip a wand and blow bubbles. When Gentle Beth was dying and all her sisters were gathered round, all these bubbles welled up from the seat next to Shay. And Marce always laughed at the wrong time. When King Kong clutched Fay Wray in his fist, she laughed. When Dracula plunged his fangs into some lovely's neck, she laughed.

> *"She laughed to get my goat," said Shay. "I suppose it could have been because of her illness. I don't know. I used to warn her I wouldn't take her again. 'Oh, Shay, I won't laugh, honest.' And she'd do it every time. God, I was embarrassed. I'd get up and move and she'd follow. Sometimes I left in the middle of the picture."*

Sometimes angelic, the best-looking of the bunch, Marce would turn 12 that November. She was also spinning out of control. Unlike her sisters who put up with their stepmother's ways for the sake of their father, Marce was fiercely honest in her assessments. Stripped of artifice, she said what she thought as soon as she thought it, and her emotions were quick to surface: anger, sadness, exuberance. She could be bossy. She could be loud. She could be querulous, disruptive, angry.

"But she was good," said Dia. "A good person...generous to a fault. If you said her dress was nice, she'd take it off and give it to you. I don't think I saw signs when Marce was growing up that something was wrong. But I think that Mae did. Cause Marce would get in the landing there on High Street and start cussing. Oh, God, Mae hated to hear that. Marce'd be mad about something that happened outside—quite often she was mad about something. When Marce would let out an expletive such as 'damn,' Mae would counter with 'My Jesus mercy.' She'd say, 'shit,' and Mae would make the sign of the cross. I can still see and hear them arguing in the bedroom, and Mae grabbing Marce by the neck with her only hand and shaking her and saying, 'You're going to behave yourself,' and Marce saying, 'Take your damn hand off of me! You're not my mother!'"

As for Joyce, who was about to graduate from Ecorse High that June, love was in the air. On that miserable day when the girls moved into the house on High Street, Julius Kovacs (known as Hula), whose mother owned the building, was on his hands and knees with a pail of water, scrubbing the staircase to the upstairs. Joyce muttered to Dia, "That guy's for me." And she meant it, too. They would marry on May 6, 1939 and move into the top floor apartment at Mim and Ollie Raupp's.

The Moore girls at Joyce's wedding. (Back L to R) Freda, Shay, Dia, Rowe, Joyce; (Front, L to R) Judy (Rowe's daughter), Marce, John Boy

As for Dia, it was obvious that she was failing 9th grade again. To alleviate any further embarrassment, Mae threw in one of her well-folded towels and encouraged Dia to quit school and enroll that April in Glover's Beauty School, upstairs over the old Hollywood in Detroit. She would graduate with her license from the Michigan State Board of Cosmetology on September 1, 1936. In 1937 Dia would meet her husband-to-be at the Happy Hour, where Murph's gambling parlor had become a legit bar with a three-piece combo for dancing. In April of 1938, Dia would marry Gus Szeles and move out of the house on High Street.

As for Shay, her future was secure. She was going to be a hairdresser or Eleanor Powell, whichever came first. After all, she had been doing the soft shoe since she was in booties. Dancing was Shay's escape, her opiate.

At first, she had made do with the metal plates appended to her shoes to correct runover heels. They made a nice click. Then Christmas of 1934, Shay and Marce had been given tap-dancing shoes, black patent Mary Janes with black bows. From then on, they sang and tapped together at holiday parties, often doing "challenge" dancing like the Four Stepbrothers, each trying to top the other.

> *"We used to put corn meal on the cement floor in the basement," said Rowe, "and we'd turn on the record player and dance. A little 'Tea for Two.'"*

It never occurred to Shay to attend dancing school, though she didn't mind copping a routine from those who did. Picking up steps like a linguist picks up languages, she danced to school, danced to Virginia's, danced to C.F. Smith's, repeated her steps up High and down Knox. She'd exit the latest musical with a new step (kick ball change step step), practice under the theater marquee and have it down pat by the time George pulled up to drive her home.

On New Year's Day (Wednesday, January 1, 1936), she and Agatha were dancing up Front Street, returning home from the Ecorse Show under a near full moon, having seen the latest Gold Diggers or Broadway Melodies. Shortly after they had turned up Knox, not far from Agatha's house, they stopped to practice a time step under the circle of a streetlamp. An old sedan containing three men approached from the east. The man on the passenger side—with his cavernous face—gave Shay the eye and the creeps as they passed by. She was home and tucked in bed next to Marce before she began to wonder where she had seen that car before.

Later in January, 1936, rehearsals began for a minstrel show, "Hit It Up," to be presented at Ecorse High School Auditorium. Sponsored by the Ecorse

Post of the American Legion, anyone could audition, young and old. Rehearsals were at the high school, after school and weekends. Leo Navarre was in it, so were Paul Movinski, Duke Underill, Frank Butler, and Murray McQueen. So was Bill Voisine, as one of the Gasoline Buggy Boys. Butzie Raupp was in a skit called Playtime. Jeannie Faulder danced.

Minstrel shows, where performers performed in blackface, were all the rage. A variety show with skits and songs, tambourines and corny jokes, its lead comic performers were always named Mr. Tambo and Mr. Bones and its master of ceremonies was known as Mr. Interlocutor.

Interlocutor: "Mr. Bones! Mr. Bones!"

Mr. Bones: "Mr. Interlocutor?"

Interlocutor: "Let me take your order."

Mr. Bones: "I wanna order a bowl of chicken soup."

Interlocutor yells to the cook in the kitchen: "Bowl of chicken soup!"

Mr. Bones: "Mr. Interlocutor."

Interlocutor: "Yeah, Mr. Bones?"

Mr. Bones: "I's gwine to change dat order. Instead of da chicken soup, give me da pea soup."

Interlocutor yells to the cook in the kitchen: "Hold da chicken, make it pea."

What the black citizens over on Visger thought of the local minstrel shows has not been recorded.

––––––––––

One shivery Saturday night (February 8) under a gorgeous full moon, George picked Shay up from rehearsal in his police car. His attention had been diverted by three men in a passing sedan, one he'd passed just a few minutes before. What they were up to was anybody's guess.

Most of the neighborhood was still covered with snow, having endured four inches of the white stuff a few days before.

> *"We're driving down Salliotte, kicking up slush," recalled Shay, "and he asked if I was having a good time. I said I was having a great time, that I loved rehearsing. Then I asked him what jailbait meant."*

George glanced her way and nonchalantly inquired, "Jailbait?"

"Yeah, Pa," said Shay, "we were kiddin' around with these older guys, and I heard one of 'em say, 'Careful, George Moore's daughter's jailbait.'" (Now Shay, at 14, was growing up. She had dark skin and green eyes and a softly hooked nose ala Barbara Stanwyck. In fact, she looked a lot like Barbara Stanwyck.)

"That right?" asked George breezily, slowing for the left-hand turn onto

High Street. "What else did they say?"

"Nothin' much. They were just sitting around telling jokes, like the ones in the show."

"That right?" he said again, casually. "Like what?"

"The Interlocutor says, 'Mr. Bones, Mr. Bones. Where ya'll been?' And Mr. Bones says, 'Oh, I been layin' linoleum.' And the Interlocutor says, 'Who's linoleum?'"

George, who just happened to be slowing down for a left-hand turn into their driveway, slammed on the brakes, pitching them forward like the Whip at Bob-Lo. Then after a short period of reflection, he executed the turn, caught a portion of the curb, upended his side of the cruiser at a 20° angle, parked in front of the garage, turned off the engine and said, "That's the last time you're goin' there."

And it was.

True, the name *Shirley Moore* can be found on the old playbill for "Hit It Up," but Shirley Moore did *not* dance in that show.

———

That same night, February 8, George was called out once more. A bullet had shattered the front window at the home of black activist Clarence Oliver, bringing back memories of the bullet that had entered the spine of Edward Armour a year before and the fire that had killed James Bailey a year before that. February, election season, was a dangerous month for blacks in Ecorse.

Ecorse police were dispatched to a large, white quadraplex at 3839 10th, on the northeast corner of Francis, in a section of Ecorse then known as a "mixed neighborhood." Someone had fired a bullet through the living room window of the first-floor apartment where Clarence Oliver and his wife Zana were sitting, narrowly missing Clarence.

The incident drew a crowd which, when not complaining about the cold, began to speculate. There were those who latched on to the stray bullet theory (some idiot was probably drunk and let fly with no intent to harm), and a few who wondered if it had anything to do with Oliver's year-old skirmish with the Ecorse School Board or his recent political activity.

No denying it; there had been quite a fracas a few years back. Though blacks were still fully integrated in Ecorse High School, black children were taught in basement classrooms in Schools One and Three, classrooms that were known to be damp and poorly heated. An epidemic of bronchial and respiratory ailments among these children had the community's black physician, Dr. Samuel "Milt" Milton, urging parents to complain to the school board.

Clarence Oliver and Roland Gaston were chosen to lead a delegation. But when they showed up at a regular school board session, the board immediately adjourned. Gaston and the articulate Oliver demanded to be heard. Instead they were ushered from the premises with the aid of a fire hose. Seeing the dignified

Clarence Oliver suffer such an indignity had repercussions for the board.[1]

Oliver, who had been actively campaigning for Bill Voisine for the coming election, had made a speech in the black section of Ecorse earlier the day the bullet went through his window, and was heard lambasting "those Alabama crackers who are trying to run the town."

But for all the speculation as to how a bullet happened to be on a straight trajectory through the Oliver's window, there was only one lead: a possible description of a car that might have been involved. So the officers in charge ignored the incident, left the bullet in the wall, and the crime went unsolved. It would be another four months, acting on new information, before Patrolman Robert McWhirter and Detective-Lieutenant Dave Genaw would pry the bullet from the wall to be used in a ballistics test against newly seized guns.

That March came the Winter Revue of 1936 at St. Francis Xavier High School. Two years before, Shay had seen a little nugget called *Gold Diggers of 1935* . It wasn't the sappy love story between Dick Powell and Gloria Stuart that forced her to sit through two showings one Saturday afternoon, then return on Sunday for two more. Nor was it the lightweight laugh of Frank McHugh (ha ha ha), which, to Shay's mortification, made Marce howl beyond measure, earning unwanted attention and snarling remarks from five rows back.

"Dang it, Marce."

"Okay, okay. I won't do it again."

What really gave shivers, what really sent chills, was the "Lullaby of Broadway" number, the seven socko minutes of song and dance.[2] She'd never seen anything like it. If the Expressionistic set was lost on her, the accelerated hoofing wasn't. It gave her goosebumps. At all four showings.

The sequence starts with the face of a woman, a small white oval in a screen of black. As she sings, her visage swells:

♫ *Come on along and listen to*
The lullaby of Broadway.
The hip-hooray and ballyhoo,
The lullaby of Broadway.
The rumble of the subway train,
The rattle of the taxis.
The daffodils who entertain
At Angelo and Maxie's.

---

[1] Dr. Milton, who would found a community hospital in the neighborhood three years hence, threatened a lawsuit in the interest of the children's health, an approach that caught the attention of the school board. As they politely listened to how Milton proposed to solve the problem, he proposed the building of a school for black children to be taught by black teachers. Claude J. Miller School would open in 1939. (In 1949, Milton would be elected Wayne County coroner, the first black coroner in the state of Michigan.)

[2] Lullaby of Broadway: Harry Warren composer, Al Dubin, lyricist

Then, at song's end, after many verses, her face transmutes into the skyline of Manhattan, setting off a somewhat sinister narrative montage: she's a party girl coming home in the wee small hours, pouring cream for a kitten outside her door, going to bed, rising again at 6:45 in the evening for another night on the town. Cut to her seated with Dick Powell at a table in a massive nightclub, gazing down at the dance floor. Two ballroom dancers, cushioned in the bubble of a follow spot, gently turn and twist on a series of expansive platforms and stairs, swaying to the sound of the lullaby, her gown flowing while he executes gentle lifts. Dance done, they run off.

And then. *And then!*

From both sides of the vast stage, a horde of dancers sashay in—men in light bolero jackets from stage left, arms pumping Fascist style; bare-midriffed women in black dresses from stage right, hips undulating Berkeley style.

For five throbbing minutes, they dance in unison in rotating geometrical patterns. Step! Step! Stepstepdoublestep. Hitting the boards aggressively, kicking back, kicking out. Break! Break! Fivesixseveneight! Makes you want to swallow your soul.

Unfortunately, Shay was too caught up in the dance to notice that the party girl, because of her dissolute ways, ends the evening plunging several stories to her death, while the kitten outside the door waits for the cream. Otherwise, she might have thought twice about reprising the song and its dance when it came time for the Winter Revue of 1936 at St. Francis Xavier High School.

Every night for two weeks, Shay and Parnell DeMay stayed after school to nail down a routine. On the great day, as Shay peeked from the side of the roll-down curtain, class after class, guided by nun after nun, funneled through the three double-wide doors at the back of the auditorium, which also served as a gym, and flowed down the aisle in orderly fashion. Grade schoolers to high schoolers, emitting a low buzz, picked up their playbills from their folding chairs and took their seats, while other dignitaries filled a row of chairs on the narrow mezzanine, where Tony Shields stood ready to operate the follow spot.

Houselights dimmed, footlights brightened, the audience hushed, the curtain went up, and the master of ceremonies commandeered the stage, introducing each act with a "yowsa yowsa yowsa." There were comedy skits, chorus numbers, soloists. Ruth Movinski danced to a recording of "Begin the Beguine." Gertie Gee did a turn. But the first showstopper had little to do with talent and a lot to do with cornball humor, as the SFX football team strolled across the stage in fright wigs and ill-fitting gowns while a chorus sang "Lovely to Look At."

Butzie Raupp stage managed with aplomb, expertly sending each act out. Then someone lip-synched to "Isn't this a Lovely Day (to be caught in the rain)," then two boys sang "The Peanut Vendor Song," convulsing the audience each time they yelled "Peanuts!" Finally came DeMay & Moore, there to close the show.

The lights faded to black, the follow spot wobbled stage right, and Parnell entered from the wings in a borrowed tuxedo, white silk scarf and shiny top hat. Well, the audience was beside itself. Clearly egged on, Parnell took his sweet-old time placing his sheet music on the upright, ad-libbed a bow, then sat with much ceremony, milking the moment. Parnell could have twitched his nose and laid them in the aisles. That's how popular he was.

Then the spotlight strayed from Parnell to center stage, only to reveal Shay, leaning on a cane, all aglitter, having spent countless hours running up a spangly number on Agnes's old sewing machine under Freda's guidance. Another roar. And when she repositioned herself, capitalizing on the click of her metal shoe plates on the hardwood floor (a sign of things to come), she brought down the house. That's how popular she was.

Then someone in the auditorium, a 6th-grade heckler, yelled: "Get the hook!"

Then someone, a nun more than likely, responded, "That'll be enough of that, Marcia Moore!"

Then Shay gave an upstage nod to Parnell (laughter), then Parnell nodded back (laughter), then he began to play and she began to croon:

♫ *Come on along and listen to/ The lullaby of Broadway* (hands on cane, knees bobbing)

♫ *The hip-hooray and ballyhoo/ The lullaby of Broadway* (circular strut)

♫ *The rumble of the subway train/ The rattle of the taxis.* (reverse circular strut)

♫ *The daffodils who entertain/ At Angelo and Maxie's* (bob knees, cane extended).

♫ *When a Broadway baby says, "Good night"/ it's early in the morning.* (circular strut)

♫ *Manhattan babies don't sleep tight/ until the dawn:* (reverse circular strut)

Except for the stage lights spilling into the first two smiling rows, Shay sang into a darkened void, gauging response by the silence—no coughs, no shifting bottoms, no inappropriate laughter. But silence is not always an accurate indicator. At least not on this occasion. It failed to warn Shay of the rash of horror creeping up the face of each and every bewimpled nun. Slowly, their tapping black oxfords, their smiles of appreciation, their musical nods tapered off. The Sisters of St. Joseph couldn't quite believe what they were hearing.

♫ *Hush-a-bye, 'I'll buy you this and that,'*
You hear a daddy sayin'.
And baby goes home to her flat
To sleep all day:

Then Parnell took a solo turn on the piano (*Good night, Baby*), slowing down the melody to a soothing lullaby, intent on giving maximum contrast to Shay's impending dance turn, the better to heighten her take off. And take off she did. She tossed her cane to Butzie in the wings, then dug in her steel-plated heels and let fly.

"Sell it, Shirley!"

Truth to tell, things got a little out of control toward the finish. Shay's style, which might be called tomboy eclectic, consisted of whatever step she had managed to filch and master. But to an undiscerning eye, she was out-Nicholasing the Nicholas Brothers. She might have been flailing but she was flailing to the beat. Her energy and exuberance had most of the audience enthralled, at least those who had not donned a habit.

DeMay & Moore stopped the show cold. There was a standing ovation; there was hooting and howling; there were shouts of *Encore!* from the 6th-grade heckler and all manner of carrying on. Parnell was delighted. The audience was ecstatic. Shay was overjoyed. She had no way of knowing that the only reason she had not gotten the ecclesiastical hook was because the nuns, sitting in the dark in a state of shock, were as frozen as Niobe.

Her first clue came about an hour after the show.

> *"I was coming down the stairs and a nun coming up the stairs gave me a dirty look," said Shay. "I asked her what was the matter and she said, 'What do you think is the matter? What did you think you were doing up there?'"*

Uh-oh.

———————

Mae knew about the debacle before Shay even walked in the door, though she took her sweet time before addressing it. "Stay on the newspapers, Edna just washed the floor," she shouted from the living room where she was hooking a rug. "Then come into the living room, dear. We need to talk."

Is there anything worse than "We need to talk?"

"Something wrong?" asked Shay, coming though the archway in her stockinged feet.

"Aren't you a little late getting home."

"I was over at Virginia's."

"I thought her brother had chicken pox."

"Over a month ago."

"Still, did you wash your hands? No? Well, go and wash them, then come back in here. I want a word with you."

Is there anything worse than "I want a word with you?"

Shay did a bitter about-face and returned to the kitchen, jumping from newspaper island to newspaper island. Then she lathered up, let the hot water run over her hands, scalding all germs, came back to the living room, took a seat on the sofa's edge to avoid denting a pillow, and braced herself for whatever was to come. Instead, Mae continued to hook her rug in silence.

"Dia home yet?" Shay asked, munching on a fingernail, having joined Dia in the ritual.

"She came and went," replied Mae, not looking up.

"Marce?"

"At Compton's."

"Joyce?"

"Still at work, but you know that." Pushing back her rug frame, setting down her hook, Mae picked up a pack of Marlboro's from the end table and lit up.

"My dear," she said, softly inhaling. "What *on earth* (exhale) were you thinking?"

"When?"

"This afternoon. In that assembly. Singing that *dread-ful* song."

"*Lullaby of Broadway*?"

"Where was your head?"

"But what's wrong with it?"

"Don't plead ignorance, young lady."

"I'm not pleading ignorance. I wasn't pleading ignorance. I just don't understand what's wrong with it."

"You honestly don't know?"

"No."

"Well, you should. You really should."

"But I don't. I really don't'," said Shay. "What's all the fuss? It's just a song."

"Just a song? Really, Shirley. You don't think. You never think." She took a puff on her cigarette. "That song isn't remotely appropriate for a Catholic school performance."

"But why?"

"Do I have to spell it out for you?"

"I wish you would. I sure wish somebody would."

Mae leaned in and gazed directly into her eyes. "'*When a Broadway baby says good night, it's early in the morning.*' You don't see that?"

"See what?"

"That? You don't see what's wrong with that?"

"No."

'*Hush-a-bye, I'll buy you this and that, You hear a daddy saying.*' You don't see that?"

"See what?"

"That. You don't see anything wrong with that, either?"

"No. Honest."

"Then what *on earth* would possess you to sing a song when you haven't the faintest idea what it's about?"

"But I *do* know what it's about," whined Shay. "It's about Broadway. It's about the Great White Way."

"It's about showgirls and sugar daddies."

"Aw, c'mon!"

"Now you just stop! Just stop that right now! I've had enough of your belligerence!"

Mae took a minute to regroup. But regroup she did. "I've always had your best interest at heart, my dear," she said, and she believed it. "I've always tried to be meticulously fair." She believed that, too. "And I'd just like a little thanks, a little recognition, a little cooperation on your part. I know I'm not your mother, but I'm trying here. And I'd like you to meet me half way."

Now Shay had not studied the lyrics. And even if she had looked closely, as the nuns had, as Mae was now doing, she would have missed the implications. Those seamy lyrics that were causing so much consternation had gone right over her head, along with the linoleum. She knew all the words for "Love for Sale," too, but didn't have a clue to the goods being marketed or the name of the retailer.

"And you know as well as I, it wasn't just the song" continued Mae. "From what I hear, you were practically doing the hoochie-coochie."

Shay reared back, humiliated, outraged, scornful. "The hoochie-coochie! No one does the hoochie-coochie anymore, that went out with Clara Bow."

"They said you were shimmying and shaking your hips during the whole sordid affair."

"It's called dancing!" said Shay, near tears.

"It's called begging for attention. It's called showing off. It's called disgracing your father, over and over. That's what it's called."

Shay shot back, "I don't go around disgracing Pa."

"Yes, you do."

"When. Tell me when."

"You're always embarrassing him with your behavior. You're always letting him down."

"Does Pa say that?"

"All the time," sniped Mae, who then thought better of the lie. "Besides, he doesn't have to say it. I can see it in his eyes. You don't care how he feels. And he knows it."

> *"Sometimes, as a kid, I couldn't wait to be alone," said Shay, "to daydream or replay special moments."*

That evening, Shay went to bed thoroughly humiliated. Shame seeped into the marrow of her bones.

Early in the morning, while Ecorse slept, there was another thunderous boom that shattered windows for blocks around, sending shards of glass across Front Street. Something had exploded in the basement of Snyder's Tavern on the corner of Knox and Front, not far from the homes of Agatha Roody and Bill Voisine. Once the hangout of Voisine's loyal opposition, Snyder's had changed hands. The new owners had named it The Whip Cafe.

That morning, with bribery charges against George still pending in State court, he was rousted out of bed by a ringing phone and soon assaulted by a number of theories as to what had happened. By mid-afternoon, some were speculating that a defective ice machine had caused the blast, but George's best investigators held that someone had planted another bomb.

The heat was on. Not on the perpetrators, just on George, because of an outcry from Snyder's former patrons—King, Hardage, Pettijohn, Eugene Penny—that The Whip Cafe was now a book run by racketeers, had probably been bombed by opposing racketeers, and should be shuttered.

Racketeers? What racketeers, thought George. Who were these faceless, nameless racketeers? Two bombs in the last nine months and these self-styled reformers were again standing in front of reporters with their racketeers routine before investigators could even sift through the rubble. Unless they knew something he didn't, Ecorse was hardly a hotbed of racketeers. Why were they always so willing to blacken the town's eye?

George scanned the afternoon's police bulletin for anything that might help, but it only served to discourage him further. Another unidentified body had been found in a ditch; this one on Gulley Road in Dearborn Township. By nightfall, the evening papers announced that the police had identified the body as a man named Poole. Charles Poole. Quick work, thought George.

———

The following afternoon the Ecorse police were still investigating The Whip bomb when Officer Vintner wrapped his upper frame around the chief's door. "Sir."

"Yes?" said George, looking up from his writing.

"They found another body."

"So what else is new?"

"This one's within our purview."

"Geezus." George screwed the cap back on his fountain pen and set it down. "I thought when we bid adieu to Prohibition, things would settle down. Where now?"

"In that watchman's building on Fighting Island. That tall brick shed across from Michigan Alkaline Works in Wyandotte. They own it. He was hanging from a beam, wearing only his shorts, piece of cable knotted hangman-style round his neck."

"Have they identified him?"

"Just came in. Guy's name was Pidcock. Roy Pidcock. Worked here in Ecorse at Michigan Steel but lived in Wyandotte."

"He from Wyandotte?"

"No. Kentucky."

"Who found him?"

"An employee at Michigan Alkali."

"When?"

"Ten o'clock this morning. Coroner said he'd been dead for seven or eight hours."

"That would mean he died . . ."

"Maybe two, three," cut in Vintner, "Wednesday morning."

"Same morning The Whip was bombed."

"That was my thinking."

"Busy night."

"Yeah."

"Who's got the case?" asked George. "Wyandotte?"

"No," said Vintner. "Since Fighting Island's on the Canadian side of the international line, they handed it over to Ontario Provincials. But seeing as Pidcock worked in Ecorse, they're asking for any information we have on him. You know, run-ins at work, union stuff, that sort of thing."

"What's the thinking?"

"Ontario's calling it—and I quote—'a clear case of suicide.'"

"No inquest?"

"No inquest."

"Let me see that."

Vintner crossed to the desk and handed the bulletin to George, then stepped behind his boss and read along.

"Doesn't add up," muttered George, glancing up at Vintner. "Have Mac and Dave Genaw come in here."

"Yes, sir."

George was still studying the bulletin when Vintner returned with the officers. "Take a look at this," said George, standing and extending the dispatch toward them. "Tell me what you think."

The two men stood side by side reading. Then Genaw relinquished the dispatch to McWhirter. "Doesn't add up."

"My thoughts exactly," said George. "Take a seat. Let's kick it around."

Genaw pulled up a chair, while McWhirter, still reading, sank slowly into another one. Vintner leaned against the door and crossed his arms.

"At the time they discovered this guy," said George, "not one boat was found beached, tied or anchored near the island or among the rocks. Not a boat around. On the entire island. He'd have to be one helluva swimmer with that current."

"Unless there *was* a boat and it broke its mooring," said Genaw. "Or he didn't tie it up."

"It says they looked for a loose boat all along the Canadian and American shores," said George. "And his clothes, what little he had on, weren't wet, and they hadn't dried on his body. Then it says his feet were dangling ten feet off the floor, but there was nothing, no ladder, no support beneath him that he could have kicked out of the way."

"Best of all," continued George, "according to the bulletin, the floor of the shed was littered with coal ashes, yet the bottom of his feet were clean. What do you think, Mac?"

McWhirter looked up as if from a trance. "What do I think?" he said with a trace of anger. "I think someone carried him into the place and hung him from the rafter. Plain and simple."

"One?"

"More than one. Had to be."

"I agree," said Dave. "And one of 'em probably worked at Michigan Alkali; one of 'em knew about that building or why would they make it their destination? If you're gonna haul a dead body across the Detroit River in the middle of the night, you'd wanna know where you're going."

"Any of you know him?" asked George. "Or know someone who knew him?"

Somberly, McWhirter slid the paper onto George's desk. "Might."

"Might what?" asked George.

"Might have some thoughts. Let me and Dave check around."

Three days later (on Sunday, May 17), Bill Voisine phoned George at home. "I hate like hell to interrupt your Sunday, George, but Fred Gulley's been in my study all afternoon, telling me some hair-raising stories."

"Fred Gulley. Mary's husband?"

"Yes. He's finally willing to talk to you, after some urging on my part."

"About what?"

"About the bombing of The Whip, among other things. You're not gonna believe what you hear."

"Aw, Bill, couldn't it wait 'til tomorrow morning? Couldn't I see him in my office? We'll be sitting down to dinner here in about an hour, hour and a half. I've got a wife who's four months pregnant and won't take kindly to my absence."

"He won't come within a thousand feet of your police department."

"Then let me send one of my detectives."

"He says you and you alone."

So, George drove the two blocks over to Knox on that warm spring day, muttering all the way, and Bill came out of his house to greet him.

"Where's his car?" asked George.

"Parked in back. I'm telling you, George, there's a reason for the hush hush. I'm not being dramatic. Also . . . you need to know . . . I made a deal with him."

"Not in my name, I hope."

"No, no, no," said Bill. "I wouldn't do that. I told him, if he tells you what he's told me, I'll say he was working for me undercover."

"Undercover for what?"

"To spy, you know."

"Shades of Pettijohn," said George. "You've gotta come up with new material, Bill."

"He's terrified. Someone's gotta be on his side. If what he's saying is true, and I don't think you can make this stuff up, the thugs he's dealing with are ruthless."

"Fine," said George. "But I'm not in a position to make any deals, especially when he won't talk at the station in front of others. Does he know that?"

"Yes, he knows that. Though I think he's hoping you'll eventually give him immunity."

"Immunity from what?"

"Fred's a good guy. Got in over his head."

"Look, Bill, I'd be lying if I said I was comfortable with this...no statement, no stenographer. If he gives us anything of importance, he could deny it in an hour."

"At least we'll be in the know."

———————

George followed Bill up the steps where bomb damage could be traced by new bricks and entered by way of the new screen door as Bill held it open.

Fred Gulley was seated uncomfortably on a sofa in his buttoned vest when Bill ushered George into his study. Gulley jumped up. "Afternoon, Chief Moore."

"Fred," said George.

"Sit here," said Bill, offering George his desk chair.

Few words were spoken as Bill retreated and returned with a chair from the kitchen. When all were seated, Voisine broke the silence: "Relax, Fred. You're among friends."

"I don't know where to start."

"Same place you started with me."

Gulley leaned forward and plunged: "I think I know who bombed The Whip. And it wasn't racketeers, like they're saying."

"Then who?" asked George.

"I can't give names," said Fred, looking nervously at Bill. "Didja tell him? I can't go that far, but . . . I was told by a fellow in a beer garden that this outfit that I belonged to was going to bomb The Whip."

"Outfit?"

"He'll get to that," said Bill.

"Did he tell you why?" asked George.

"Because it was a gambling joint operated by Jews."

George looked at Gulley as if he had four heads. "Jews?"

"Yeah."

"They bombed The Whip because it was operated by Jews?" George turned to Voisine in disbelief, then laughed. "What? They gonna take out Sims next?"

"It's serious," muttered Fred.

"He knows whereof he speaks, George," said Bill.

"Okay, okay. Let me backtrack," said George. "Did they bomb it because it was a gambling place? Or because it was operated by Jews?"

"Both."

"So you're saying it wasn't racketeers. Not a racket thing. Not someone muscling in."

"No."

"Where was the gambling going on?" asked George. "In the basement?"

"That's what this guy said."

"Big-time gambling?"

"One table. Neighborhood card game."

"They bombed the place because someone was holding a neighborhood card game in the basement?"

"And because it was run by Jews," added Fred.

"Who's the fella who told you this?" jeered George.

"Like I said, no names," said Fred, squirming on the sofa.

"Who's the fella?"

Gulley looked nervously at Voisine. "I'd rather not."

"Who's the fella?" said George.

"They'll kill me."

"You've come this far, Fred."

"Eugene Penny."

"Richard Penny's kid?"

"Yeah."

"And just why would Eugene Penny be bragging about that to you?"

"Because I belonged to the same outfit, though I don't go to meetings any-more. As far as I'm concerned, I'm no longer a member. As far as they're con-cerned, I still am. They don't let you quit." He paused, reflective. "Anyway, I'm fairly sure that Penny was in on the bombing, though I can't prove it. And there was at least one other guy . . . but I really can't tell you his name."

"Really can't or really won't?"

"Both."

"Why not?"

"Because he's too big in the outfit, too important. And because he'd kill me."

"I'm telling ya, Fred. I'm getting a little cross here," said George. "Member of what outfit?"

"If you knew how hard this was. . ."

"Well, all you're giving me is vague . . . I need names. If you want us to help you, make it safe for you, we'll need to know who, what and where. What is this outfit? What's its name?"

"I'm a dead man. If they find out I talked, I'm a dead man. No one's ever ratted on these guys and lived to tell about it. They always brag that the only ex-members are six feet under."

"Oh, please. You're getting carried away. They sound like schoolyard bul-lies."

"Not even close."

"Then what's their name?"

"I can't tell you."

"This is all so much goulash." George eased himself out of his chair.

"The United Brotherhood of America," snapped Fred.

"That anti-union outfit?"

"Also known as the Wolverine Republican League. Also known as The Black Legion."

"The Black Legion?" scoffed George. "Any relation to the Green Hornet?"

"I'll tell you right now, right up front, I won't testify against these guys," said Gulley, having gone much further than he'd intended. "I've got a wife and a new baby at home. But I'll tell ya what I can, what I know."

George sat back down and looked at his watch. "I've got one hour before pot roast. After that, my life won't be worth living either. Shoot."

"Well," started Gulley. "A couple of years ago..."

"Try and be specific," cut in George. "When's that? '34? Spring, Fall?"

"Spring's about right," replied Gulley. "I was invited to a barbecue."

"Who invited you?"

Couple of friends of mine. They'd been after me for two or three weeks to go on a barbecue with 'em. So I told 'em the first chance I got I'd go. One Satur-day night, I went out in their car to a place off Lahser Road. I smelled a rat when I got there, because I knew it wasn't any ordinary stag party. That's how I come to join. I didn't want to, but there was nothing I could do about it."

"Forgive me, Fred," said George. "You're a grown man. How can they make you join?"

"With a gun."

In the course of that hour, Fred told them that the Legion was formed to oppose Communism, fight for clean politics and defend the Constitution. There to promote, protect and preserve Protestantism, create and guard the welfare of the Protestant people, socially and politically.

"Membership requirements similar to those of the Grosse Pointe Yacht Club?" asked George. "No Jews, no blacks, no Catholics, no foreign-born?"

"You could say that."

"You just said that," said George. "Is there anybody these fellas like besides themselves?"

Gulley was getting into it now. He told them that, unlike the Klan, the Legion worked in the shadows, adhering to a strict hierarchy, with only the highest officials privy to what was going on.

"How many of you are there?" asked George.

Gulley explained that they had five brigades in the state, each with a brigadier general. That each brigade was divided into regiments which in turn were divided into battalions and companies. That names were not used in addressing each other, only rank. Often, he didn't know the names of the higher-ups.

"And who did each brigadier general answer to?" asked George. "God, I suppose."

"No," said Gulley. "Some guy in Ohio."

"Swell, so what happened when they got you to the meeting?" prodded George.

"OK, first they had me fill out an Accident Insurance Prospect Card so they had my signature. Then the Legionnaires got into a circle around me while they made me kneel down to answer some questions."

"What kind of questions?"

"They wanted to know where I was born, did I believe in God, what church I belonged to, was I a family man, where I worked. Oh, and was I against letting foreigners immigrate. Would I fight against Catholics getting into elective office. Did I believe that white, Protestant people should rule and would I lie to defend and protect any member of the organization."

"Then a Lieutenant Colonel spoke and said I might have to perform some higher service that would require a blood pact. Was I willing to sign my name in my own blood? Also, did I have a gun or could I get one as soon as possible. Then the chaplain stepped forward."

"The chaplain?" asked George, incredulous.

"The chaplain," said Gulley. "He said a few words, then I was forced to take an oath."

"How forced?"

"With two men on each side of me, .38 caliber pistols in their hands pointed at my heart."

"I don't believe it."

"You should believe it. 'Cause what I'm sayin's true. They said if I wavered on one word while repeating the oath, they'd shoot me." Gulley reached into his breast pocket. "I had to read it from a piece of paper, then burn it in the campfire, but I have another copy here. There are copies floating around. Wanna hear some of it?"

"Can't wait."

In the name of God and the Devil, one to reward and the other to punish, and by the powers of light and darkness, good and evil, here under the black arch of heaven's avenging symbol, I pledge and consecrate my heart, my brain, my body and my limbs, and swear by all the powers of Heaven and Hell, to devote my life to the obedience of my superiors; that I will exert every possible means in my power for the extermination of the anarchist, Communist, Roman hierarchy and their abettors."

"Somebody's been listening to too much radio," muttered George.

"*I further pledge my heart, my brain, my body and my limbs,*" continued Gulley, "*never to betray a comrade; and that I will submit to all the tortures mankind can inflict, and suffer the most horrible death, rather than reveal a single word of this, my oath.*"

"Yep," said George. "Green Hornet."

"*Before violating a single clause or implied pledge of this, my obligation, I will pray to an avenging God and an unmerciful Devil to tear my heart out and roast it over the flames of Sulphur; that my head be split open and my brains scattered over the earth, that my body be ripped up, my bowels be torn out and fed to carrion birds; that each of my limbs be broken with stones and then cut off by inches that they may be food for the foulest birds of the air; and lastly, may my soul be given unto torment; that my body be submerged in molten metal and stifled in the flames of Hell; and that this punishment may be meted out to me through all eternity. In the name of God, our Creator, Amen. Arise.*"

"Arise?" said George.

"Yeah."

"a-RISE?"

"Yeah."

"And did you a-RISE?"

"Yeah."

"Amazing," said George. "And when they had you saying, 'May my head be split open and my brains scattered all over hell and gone,' didn't it occur to you that you weren't joining the 4-H Club, that maybe these weren't such nice fellows? What the hell were you thinking?"

"Well, what would you do sandwiched between two men with guns pointed at your heart?" said Fred. "Besides, I just thought it was so much mumbo jumbo to make us think twice before spilling the beans. To me, it was always about jobs. I mean, it works," said Fred. "Every Legionnaire I knew eventually got a job and kept it. No foreigners barging in, taking the few jobs available. Now they're the enemy."

"I notice they don't mind taking jobs away from Michiganders," said George. "People who lived here all their lives. That's okay, right?"

"You can forget about locals getting jobs over at the mills," replied Fred. "The Legion's got that all tied up. They run the personnel department, give jobs to Legionnaires."

"That's why I hired Paul Pulliam," said Voisine, "to get jobs for locals. But I had to fire him about six weeks ago. The bastard was hiring my opponents."

"That's cause he's a Legionnaire, sir."

"Paul Pulliam," said Voisine in surprise. "What state's he from?"

"Alabama."

"No wonder Murph couldn't get a job at the plant," said George. "Born in Ecorse, Catholic to boot."

"These guys are tough," said Fred. "They're not afraid of anyone."

"Except each other," said George. "Look at you. You're quaking in your boots."

"Not always," said Gulley. "I pissed them off last February. I made the mistake of saying out loud that I wouldn't vote for Newt Hawkins when he was running against Bill here. They came around to my house in two cars, but I stuck a gun on my hip and went out and told them they'd better be going or I'd shoot holes in their tires. They left. I went to one meeting after that. They were sore, but I got right with them by promising to vote for Newt."

"What do they have against me?" asked Bill.

"Well, for one thing, you're Catholic," explained Gulley, as if that were enough. "For another, you hire colored campaign workers. Then last February, when you recommended two colored officers for the police force and Chief Moore recommended them to the Safety Commission, some Legionnaires were furious."

"Why? It didn't pass," said George. "The Village Council voted it down by one vote. Hardage's wasn't it?"

"Doesn't matter," said Fred. "You both proposed it."

"With these guys, George, it's the thought that counts," quipped Bill.

"Why'd you quit?" asked George.

"As far as I was concerned," said Fred, "we were crossing too many lines."

"When?"

"Well, October, last year, they had us do something I wasn't proud of. I can't say what, but I stopped goin' to meetings, period. When they threatened me again, I pulled a gun again."

"What other lines," asked George.

"Well . . . "

"What other lines?"

Bill cut in. "These are the guys that bombed my house, George."

"Son of a bitch," said George. Then again, "Son of a bitch, does he have proof?"

"Nothing written down," replied Gulley.

"Tell him," Bill urged.

So Fred told them that on Tuesday, July 23, of last year, he had driven to an open-air meeting.

"Open air?"

"Big meadow. Out in the woods," he began.

The meeting was led by Harvey T. Davis, formerly of Kentucky, an electrician for the Department of Public Lighting in Detroit. A colonel in the regiment, very tall, imposing, Davis was a handsome man in a sullen, clean-shaven way, with a long, Lincolnesque face. It was said, more than once, that he resembled Raymond Massey. And when he stood on a rise and spoke, his followers listened.

That day's main rant was about Roosevelt being surrounded by Jews. "All his UN-OH-FISH-AL advisors are Jews! You know that, don't ya?" yelled Davis. "They're dictating policy, including that socialistic, communistic New Deal. Listen to who Roosevelt's listenin' to: Felix Frankfurter, foreign-born and Karl Marx professor at Harvard, Louis Brandeis on the Supreme Court, Henry Morgenthau, Sr., Bernard Baruch, Frances Perkins, Roosevelt's Secretary of Labor, all Jews!"

Obviously, someone that day had had a local beef and shared it with Davis beforehand, because Davis then used his skills to further lather up the crowd— not too difficult since most members were there to be lathered.

He continued: "And now, my brothers, let's turn to one William W. Voisine, who, along with certain other members of the Ecorse Board of Trustees—we all know who they are—is so corrupt, he defiles anything he touches. Bill Voisine. Who's up to his ears in bribes. Bill Voisine. Who treats the town like his own little fiefdom."

The assemblage, comprised mostly of fine tinder and kindling, was soon ablaze. Boos rent the air.

"Dictator!" someone shouted.

"Bill Voisine . . . who's got only three allegiances: himself, dirty money, and the Pope! What are we gonna do about him?"

"Turn him out of office!" yelled one.

"Take him for a ride!" proposed a family man and strict Methodist in the back row.

Suddenly somebody shouted, "Bomb his house. Bomb him!"

George had barely moved throughout Gulley's bombing account. He had never heard anything like it. No wonder they couldn't solve the bombing. Could Fred be believed?

"And another thing," said Gulley. "I think some of these guys might be connected to that Pidcock case. There's a lot of Legionnaires at that Alkali plant in Wyandotte."

"How'd you know the identity of Pidcock?" asked George. "The papers haven't released it yet."

"Mary saw the police bulletin," said Gulley. "We talk, you know, like any married couple."

"Why do you think this . . . Legion . . . was involved?" asked George.

"'Cause Pidcock was a member," replied Gulley. "I knew him."

"Why wouldn't you give me this information at police headquarters?" asked George.

"Bob McWhirter."

"Bob McWhirter? *My* Bob McWhirter?"

"Yeah. He's a member, too."

The following morning, Monday, May 18, was overcast when George crawled out of bed with dread. Confrontation cost him plenty. Bob McWhirter wasn't perfect; admittedly he was a little rough around the edges, but he had been a good cop, served him faithfully, or so he thought. And just how the hell do you accuse someone without accusing? Without divulging your source? Since he couldn't reveal his talk with Gulley until he was sure of McWhirter, how would he even start?

But George hadn't been in his office more than five minutes when Vintner brought in his coffee and the news that Officer McWhirter wanted to see him. McWhirter, who stood directly behind Vintner, saying, "I need to talk to you, sir," then shut the door on the vanishing Vintner and pulled up a chair within inches of George's desk. He spoke in a near whisper. "I can't say I know the perpetrators for sure, but I now have reason to believe that the same bunch of guys might be responsible for the bombing of The Whip, the killing of Pidcock, that guy on Fighting Island, and even . . . possibly . . . the bombing at Bill Voisine's."

"And what outfit is that?"

"A secret society, sir."

"Does it have a name?"

"It does." McWhirter paused, looked down, rotated his wedding ring . "They call themselves the Black Legion."

"And how would you know that?"

"Because I was once a member." He leaned forward, his elbows braced on the arms of his chair. "Got a minute?"

"Got all day." George leaned back and nodded at McWhirter. "Go ahead. I'm all ears."

"Two years ago, sir—as you know—I left the steel mill to become Voisine's campaign manager, with an eye to getting on the force. There were promises. You know."

"I figured."

"That was early in '34," said McWhirter. "Anyway, sometime between April and May of that year, while I was waiting for my probationary appointment as patrolman, a trustee told me that if I wanted the sympathy of the Village Council, I'd better join."

"Join what?" asked George.

"The Black Legion."

George jackknifed forward. "Wait a minute, a trustee said, if you wanted the sympathy of the Village Council, you'd better join the Black Legion?"

"Yes."

"Sympathy?"

"If I wanted the vote."

"Which trustee was that?"

"I'll get to that, sir."

"But you came highly recommended from Bill," said George. "And after I interviewed you, I recommended you just as highly to the Safety Commission. I couldn't have been more positive."

"Don't forget. I still needed the okay from the Council."

"But that's a matter of form," said George. "They rarely turn down my recommendations. They tend to let department heads run their departments."

"If you recall, sir, that was the summer when they tried to oust Mr. Voisine. It was a fractious time. Voisine wasn't running the Council; the Council was running him. If you recall, sir, a few of these guys had a lot of power and turned down your recommendation for two black patrolmen."

"Are you saying that was all the Black Legion?"

"Also known as The Wolverine Republican League."

"Yeah, sure. Half the guys that hung out at Snyder's belonged to something called the Wolverine Republican League. You're gonna sit there and tell me. . ."

"I am, sir."

"Are you saying this trustee was speaking for the entire Village Council?"

"A hefty share. And they'd bamboozled others into voting with them."

"Well, if you disdain them, why did you join?"

"I wanted this job so bad. I thought it was a harmless club, what could it hurt to join? I went through this weird ceremony at a house in Detroit led by a man named Harvey Davis, a colonel in the Black Legion."

"Bunch of little boys playing army."

"Bunch of little boys with .45 caliber *revolvers* playing army," replied Mc-Whirter. "Anyway, I soon figured out that they hated me for supporting Voisine and wanted me in their pocket. And, like an idiot, I had jumped right in. That's how it works. They get their hooks in you and don't let go. They get something on you, like being a member, then they own you."

"But how?"

"Threatening, stalking, menacing. If you don't go to meetings, they take you out into the woods and beat the tar out of you. I despise these assholes with all my heart, but I didn't dare tell you. I wanted to keep my job. Frankly, I wanted to stay alive. I stuck around through that summer, but by fall I stopped going to meetings; I'd had enough. So they took me for a ride beyond Ypsilanti and threatened me with a whipping. I promised to go to meetings but never did. I went armed after that."

"Even off duty."

"Especially off duty."

"How do you know they bombed Voisine's?" asked George.

"I suspect it," said McWhirter. "I don't have proof."

"Who's the trustee that got you to join?"

"My life won't be worth a plug nickel."

"You've gone this far. Who?"

"Charlie King."

"I might have known."

"King's a major in the 12th regiment, the Downriver Regiment."

"Others?"

"James Stewart."

"James Stewart? My James Stewart? James Stewart, the cop?"

"Yeah."

"Well, that explains a multitude."

So McWhirter named names. Charlie King, born in Oklahoma, grew up in Kansas, formerly Ecorse town trustee who had run for justice of the peace in early 1936 and lost; James J. Stewart, born in Kentucky, formerly with the Ecorse police department; Don Beckmann, born in Nebraska, still village clerk; James Hardage, born in Alabama, now Ecorse town trustee; Lawrence Madden, steelworker, whose wife was the village nurse; Richard C. Penny, Sr. with his son Eugene, both born in Missouri; Kenneth C. Weber, formerly Ecorse town attorney.

"Kenneth Weber? The guy that used to be our town lawyer? The guy that practically took over the council?"

"Yeah, they forced him on Voisine, remember? That's what they do. They get their men into city government, then take over."

"Movinski? Born?"

"No, they were the ones bamboozled."

"Who else?"

"Jesse Pettijohn."

George banged his fist on his desk. "That toad! That malicious toad! When I think of all the misery he . . . That mud-dwelling, oily toad!"

The next day, Tuesday, May 19, George had mixed emotions. If he used his men to investigate, one of his officers was tainted. Better to get the Wayne County prosecutor, better to get outside help. So he tried in vain to get in touch with someone high up at Duncan McCrea's office but was repeatedly told: "Everybody's out. Can they get back to you? We got our hands full here." Something was going down.

On Friday morning, May 22, George was stirring his coffee when Vintner stuck in his head. "You've got a call, Sir. Prosecutor's office."

"Who?"

"Harry Colburn, Duncan McCrea's chief investigator."

"Finally," said George, picking up the phone, thanking Colburn for returning his call.

"I'm not returning your call, Chief," said Colburn. "I'm placing one. We've been up most of the night here, so if I sound a little woozy, you'll understand."

"What's up?"

"Ever hear of the Black Legion?"

"Oh, no. Not you, too," said George. "For the past couple days, nothing but."

"I got a blabbermouth over here," said Colburn. "The guy's telling tales that'll make your hair curl."

"I already bear a startling resemblance to Shirley Temple," laughed George. "Whatcha got?"

"I need to come see you. We need to coordinate. Ecorse is infested with these guys."

"Got names?"

"Some," said Colburn. "We'd better move fast. 'Cause this is gonna explode. Can't keep the dailies at bay forever. And for God's sake, don't say a word to anyone until I see you, not even your Village Council, not even your staff."

"I won't. But if you're worried about Robert McWhirter, don't be. He'll tell you everything he knows."

That night, as the evening papers landed on porches throughout the Metropolitan area, they bore headlines and photographs worthy of Warner Bros., launching a bizarre, international story that would unravel like a Saturday cliffhanger for the next eight to nine months, shaking up police and sheriff's departments, town councils, auto plants, steel mills, city halls, and many a marriage.

Chapter 64

Friday, May 22, 1936

Harry Colburn, McCrea's chief investigator, had quite a story to tell concerning the death of a man named Poole. His source was Dayton Dean, triggerman and central figure in all that came next. As Colburn filled George in that Friday morning, his version would be incomplete, limited by Dean's unwillingness to cough up details. Dean had a tendency to name names only after names had been named. But the surprisingly quick resolution of the slaying of Charles Poole would uncover a vast nest of vipers infiltrating Michigan municipalities. The story would send shivers up spines from Lansing to London and add a starring role to the budding career of Humphrey Bogart. The nation's paranoids would scribble incoherent notes to J. Edgar Hoover en masse. America, they said, was under attack.

According to Dean, and as reported by Colburn, the morning of May 13, at 6:45 a.m., Mrs. Frances Horvat went out to milk her cow and discovered a bullet-riddled body in a ditch on Gulley Road, a country lane in Dearborn Township that fronted her pasture. Fingerprints were sent by AP wire photo to the FBI lab in Washington D.C. that afternoon; they belonged to Charles Poole, an unemployed auto worker and part-time organizer for the Works Progress Administration (WPA), who had been arrested for vagrancy in 1926.

Initially, gossip was thought to have been the cause of Poole's death. Harvey Davis, a colonel in the Black Legion, overheard someone say that Poole had been abusing his wife. "A man that would do his wife like that," said Davis, "ought to be took out and whipped or beat up." Davis called for a business meeting of the Wolverine Republican League for Tuesday, May 12. "It'll be a necktie party for Poole," Davis told Dean and Ervin Lee. "We'll take him out and hang him and let the other fellows get their feet wet. Whether we use the rope or not, it'll be a one-way ride. And we need to get John Mitchell out on one of the jobs," said Davis, "so we have something on him if he's elected to the office he's running for."

It was to be a busy night. Around 8:30 p.m., 50 to 60 members and nonmembers began to gather dutifully at Findlater Temple on West Lafayette Boulevard and Waterman Avenue in Detroit. They all piled into a cramped room.

Robeless, Davis disposed of general business, then took up a collection to pay for the rent of the small basement room run by the Masonic Temple Association. Several speakers covered the coming elections, among them John Mitchell who was petitioning to be a candidate for State Representative on the Republican ticket. Then the guest speaker, a self-styled "White Russian," who had supported the czar, bolstered the crowd's concerns about the menace of Communism.

After the non-members left, a smaller coterie of at least 24 locked the doors and continued the meeting. Davis retook the floor and in heated terms denounced Charles Poole before the fellowship. "A woman is in Herman Kiefer hospital," he said. "A young woman named Rebecca Poole, only 21. She's there because her husband Charlie kicked her over and over and over, breaking her ribs, blackening her eye. He beat her so badly when she was pregnant that the baby's not expected to live! What do you think of a man who beats his wife when she is to have a child!" he shouted.

"Tyrant! Villain!" returned the group.

As Davis continued to roar, fists were raised. When the meeting turned into bedlam, hanging was proposed. Davis took a voice vote, and the shrillest voices won. Then he ordered Ervin Lee and Dayton Dean to pick Poole up and called for volunteers to accompany them. Urban Lipps, 32, formerly of Mississippi, and Paul R. Edwards, 31, formerly of Georgia, stepped forward.

But the ruse for picking up Poole had already been arranged. Earlier that day, Harvey Davis had gone to Poole's home, introduced himself as a man who worked at Timken Axle, and asked Poole, an avid sandlot baseball player, if he wanted to go to a Timken team organizational party where he'd be measured for a uniform because they wanted him on the team; obviously, this would also give him a leg up for a position in the plant. Except for WPA work two days a week, Poole, one among many, was having trouble finding full-time work.

That evening, after a few unsuccessful attempts to locate Poole, the men had finally found him with a couple of his friends at Joe's Pavilion on Livernois near the Ternstedt plant. Urban Lipps went inside and asked Gene Sherman, a friend of Poole's: "Are you Poole?"

"No," said Sherman. "This is Poole."

"Well, ya ready to go to the baseball party?"

"Sure, where's it gonna be?" asked Poole.

"Out on the West Side. Come on, let's get goin'."

"Why don't we all go," volunteered Ralph Hyatt, another of Poole's friends.

"Sorry, car's full. Got room for only one."

Poole went along eagerly, still talking of the baseball party as they drove back to the Findlater Temple, then remained in the back seat of the car with Dean while Lipps, Lee and Edwards went inside. It was nearly 11 when Davis adjourned the meeting, announcing to attendees: "We have Poole. Get in your cars and follow mine. Time for a straightening-out party."

There were six carloads of men driving up West Fort, with Lee's car in the lead, while his cargo, Poole, sandwiched between Lipps and Dean in the back seat, affably talked more baseball, completely unaware. Davis's car, being driven by Edgar Baldwin, 28, formerly of Missouri, shot past them. It contained Baldwin, Davis, George C. Johnson, 72, and Paul Edwards.

After the first two cars crossed the Rouge River, the drawbridge suddenly rose, leaving the last four cars stranded. The two lead cars continued down West Fort. Eventually, the trappings of civilization began to recede: houses were replaced by fields, roads became rougher, ill-lit. Said Lipps later: "Poole din't say nothing 'cept to ask where was the baseball party." They drove for another 20 minutes or so up a rutted road. When they neared a small bridge which spanned the west branch of the River Rouge, the lead car pulled up by the side of a pasture. Lee parked about 30 feet behind Davis, turned off his lights, then waited for Davis to make the first move.

"All out, everybody," said Davis, stepping from the lead car into the road, followed by Baldwin and Edwards. "Let's have a drink first." The aging Johnson, a retired railroad engineer with a tricky ticker, remained in their car and would later maintain that it was his first Legion meeting and that Baldwin, his neighbor, dragged him along.

Climbing out of the second car, Ervin Lee and Dayton Dean walked toward Davis, while Lipps remained behind with Poole. As hip flasks were uncorked and Luckies were lit, they waited and waited for a car driven by fellow Legionnaire John Bannerman. Scattered cigarette butts found at the scene would attest to how long.

Mostly they were waiting for the rope. "It was going to be a necktie party with the robes, hoods and everything," recalled Dean. "We thought it would be more impressive that way."

Finally, Davis corked his flask, muttered something about "The others musta got lost," then said to Dean: "Get Poole. Bring him over here."

Dean pulled out two guns—a .38 caliber and a .45 caliber—walked back to the second car and pointed them at Poole, telling him to get out.

"Okay," said Poole, who willingly obliged.

"Poole," said Davis, addressing the 32-year-old sandlot player, who was now standing alone on the opposite side of the narrow gravel road, facing his trial board. "You've beaten your wife for the last time."

Poole was taken aback. "You've got me all wrong. I never beat my wife. There must be some mistake!"

Davis continued to accuse Poole, while Poole continued to deny the accusations. Then there was an awkward pause.

Without warning a jittery Dayton Dean fired five bullets from the .45 and three bullets from the .38 directly at Poole from about eight feet away. Ervin Lee also fired two or three shots, but later denied aiming at Poole, saying he fired into the air. "I was supposed to do something."

Nothing had gone as planned. Instead of quickly picking up Poole, they had wandered the streets looking for him. Instead of six cars, there had been two. Instead of 24 men, there had been eight, counting Poole. Instead of intimidating black robes, they were standing around in street clothes. Instead of imposing cockade hats with skulls and crossbones, they had on cloth caps or fedoras. And, instead of a necktie party, well, it's hard to hang a man without the rope, which was in Bannerman's car. Months later the real reasons for Poole's death, as planned by leaders Harvey Davis and Ervin Lee, would be confirmed: 1. Charlie Poole was Catholic.   2. Poole had been overheard poking fun of the rites and rituals of the Black Legion.

At least 24 men, Pettijohn, King and Lawrence among them, knew who had killed Charlie Poole when they read about the unidentified body found on Gulley Road in the late editions the following evening, Wednesday, May 13. Some of those 24 also knew who had put the bomb in the basement of The Whip, and some knew who was responsible for the body found in the deserted brick shed on Fighting Island.

That Thursday they also saw photos of the blonde-haired Becky Poole and her newborn baby which filled the front pages. And they learned that the single reason Becky Poole was in Herman Kiefer Hospital was that she had had a daughter, Nancy, on May 8th. When the Black Legion was later exposed and members accused her husband of beating her, she strongly denied it: "It's a lie! Charles never laid a hand on me in the three years we were married. He was always good to me."

The break in the case came quickly. On Tuesday, May 19, Poole's friend, Gene Sherman, saw a man walking down Fort Street, whom he recognized as having picked up Poole the night of the murder. Sherman called a cop, had the man arrested and later identified him. Others involved in the Black Legion soon came to light. Dean, who was shocked to learn that Poole had not been beating his wife, quickly confessed to shooting him.

The preliminary hearing began on Tuesday, June 2, and took place in the impressive supervisor's room on the fourth floor of the County Building. "Detroit's greatest judicial spectacle," as Common Pleas Judge Ralph W. Liddy had referred to the case, drew national and international attention. The entire production involved special telegraphers in an adjoining room who clicked the story throughout the country. From New York City, the Atlantic cable relayed it to London, Paris, and Berlin.

On the second day, Dean stunned everyone in the courtroom, including his own lawyer, by saying that he wished to make a statement. His fellow defendants stared at him in anger and disbelief. Judge Liddy looked over at Dean, shackled among the accused. "You're at liberty to take the witness stand if you wish, but you're under no compulsion. Is that clear?"

Dean, manacled to John Bannerman, nodded and said it was. He was unshackled and brought to the stand. Prosecutor McCrea stood and launched the pro-forma questions: name, occupation, age. Then: "Did you know Charles

Poole?"

"No."

"When did you first hear of him?"

"Three or four days before his death."

"From whom did you hear of him?"

"From Harvey Davis."

Dean talked and talked, heaping damaging detail upon damaging detail, while his mother, Mrs. Clarence Nacker, listened with head bowed and his fellow defendants glared at him through narrowed eyes. It was the first time in anyone's judicial memory that a triggerman was giving an eyewitness account, a blow-by-blow of a one-way ride, in open court.

At the end of the day, 12 fellow defendants walked out on shaky legs, while Dean strutted out like a bantam cock. "I told the truth," he said. By the end of that day, Dayton Dean had destroyed the Black Legion. One of its own had broken every oath in their playbook. Dean had been a "good soldier" for Davis; now, switching allegiances, he became a "good soldier" for law enforcement officials. And he couldn't talk fast enough. Since Dean had been in on most of the killings, successful or aborted, he was the man of the hour.

Eleven of the twelve men tried for murdering Charles Poole would be convicted, nine by jury on September 29, 1936, and two in a bench trial. Mandatory life sentences (Michigan did not have the death penalty) for first degree murder were handed down to Harvey Davis, Ervin Lee, Urban Lipps, Paul Edwards, Edgar Baldwin, Lowell Rushing, and John Bannerman. Albert Stevens, John S. Vincent, Thomas R. Craig and Virgil Morrow, who were convicted of 2nd degree murder, got 3½ to 20 years. Herschel Gill was the only man acquitted.

Dean, who pled guilty and was also sentenced to life imprisonment, continued to testify in later trials in 1936 and 1937, leading to 46 convictions in four separate cases, including the murders of Poole and a black man named Silas Coleman, and the attempted murder of William Voisine.

Seven members of the Black Legion accused of the murder of Charles Poole.
(Rear L to R) Dayton Dean, Urban Lipps, Harvey Davis; (Front L to R) Ervin Lee, Lowell
Rushing, Hershel Gill, John Vincent. (Virtual Motor City Collection, Walter P. Reuther
Library, Wayne State University)

On Saturday, May 23, a working day for most of the precinct, Vintner strolled into George's office with a sly grin and handed George the *Detroit Times*. "Turn to page 3, Chief. You might see something of interest."

"Well, I'll be," said George, folding over the first page.

The *Times* was reporting that four of the 16 Black Legionnaires held in Poole's murder appeared on the letterhead of the Wolverine Republican League as officers: John Bannerman as a director; Roy L. Lorance and Ervin D. Lee as heads of the membership committee; and Harvey Davis as head of the entertainment committee. Other names on that letterhead included those of three prominent attorneys, as well as Arthur F. Moore, ex-president of Melvindale, and Leslie L. Black, clerk in the Court of Common Pleas for Judge L. Eugene Sharp. Yes, and Jesse J. Pettijohn, Ecorse Township clerk. According to the *Free Press*, "Pettijohn, a Republican, said that he was not a member of the organization, but had heard of it several times, and had been invited to join."[1]

"We got him now, Sir."

"Don't get your hopes up," said George. "The guy's slick. He'll come out of this smellin' like a rose."

On his arrival that morning, George had glimpsed Mary Gulley, face white as a sheet, sitting in the corridor next to her husband. Now, what with news of the Legion unraveling, Fred Gulley was there to talk, this time for the record. With the information Gulley supplied that Saturday, Moore and Colburn decided they needed to move fast. With Sunday intervening, there would be no time for warrants.

On Monday night, May 25, and continuing well into Tuesday morning, raiders were in and out of the Ecorse police station, accumulating an arsenal on a cleared-off table in the evidence room. Led by Colburn in plainclothes and white straw boater and McWhirter in plainclothes and a white panama, a dozen investigators for the Wayne County prosecutor's office and eight Ecorse policemen raided one garage and four homes in Ecorse.

The first raid on the list was King Electric & Brake Service at 3824 Front St. (West Jefferson). Next stop, 17 West Glenwood, where Charlie King graciously allowed them to search his home. In both cases guns and ammunition were confiscated and taken back to the station to see if they were registered and to check

[1] "Court Clerk is League Chief; Asserts Murder Stuns Him," Detroit Free Press, May 23, 1936, p 6.

against bullets found in various and sundry bodies.

"No robes, no hoods?" inquired George.

"No robes, no hoods," said Dave Genaw. "Just some chain letters, sir, in Charlie King's office files."

"Chain letters?"

"They say Negroes shouldn't have the same rights as whites in the public schools. Claim it's a known fact that many Negro kids are criminally attacking white children in grammar schools."

"Funny," said George, "I would have thought it was the other way around."

"He seemed kinda proud of his arsenal," said Genaw. "You know, like someone showing you their stamp collection. But he didn't seem so proud of the chain letters. I'm standing there reading this crap, and I look over at Charlie and he says he never saw 'em before. 'Maybe somebody put 'em there.'"

"Are you thinking what I'm thinking?" said George.

"Clarence Oliver, Edward Armour, James Bailey."

"Time to reopen some unsolved cases."

Raids were also conducted that day at the homes of Edgar Lawrence (73 Broadway) and George E. Lee (31 East Auburn) yielding one unregistered .45 caliber pistol.

"No robes, no hoods?"

"No robes, no hoods."

"You saving the best for last? You know who I'm waitin' for, don'tcha?"

McWhirter glanced at his notes. "If you're referring to Jesse J. Pettijohn, I kinda figured that."

"Find anything at his abode?"

McWhirter returned to his notes. "Two automatic pistols (.25 and .45 caliber) and a shotgun and ammunition. All registered."

"No robes, no hoods?"

"No robes, no hoods."

"Dang," said George. "And I was so looking forward to trying his on."

McWhirter laughed. "Just suits and dresses, Sir. He's still claiming he never heard of the Black Legion. We couldn't bring him in for questioning. We've got nothing on him."

"Actually, I'm surprised he even let you in," said George.

"So were we," said Genaw. "But we think we know why."

"Sir," said McWhirter. "We think there's a reason we were allowed into all those houses without a warrant. We got the feeling they'd been tipped off. That all signs of the Legion had been stowed."

"Think the leak came from here?"

"No," said McWhirter. "If there was anybody else in the Legion on this staff, I'd know about it. I think there might be Legionnaires in McCrea's office."

"Colburn?"

"No."

"McCrea?"

"Doubt it."

That evening, the *Detroit Times* accused Duncan C. McCrea of joining the Black Legion on July 21, 1934. It was never proved, one way or the other, that he belonged. But Legionnaires had a habit of implicating anyone who implicated them, and McCrea certainly prosecuted Legionnaires with a vengeance. In any case, the waters had been muddied beyond belief.

On Saturday, May 30, while George marched with his police force, Fred Gulley drove Bill Voisine in the Ecorse Memorial Day parade. Three days later Robert Penland was brought into McCrea's office for questioning. According to McCrea, Penland appeared to be "scared to death" and refused to talk, possibly intimidated into keeping quiet. He reluctantly acknowledged that he had been taken from his home at gun point, but would not say by whom, and refused to say he had been flogged. Implicated in the abduction, Earl Angstadt, Fred Gulley and Thomas Cox were taken into custody that same day.

At their arraignment on Thursday, June 4, the three men pleaded guilty to the kidnapping of Robert Penland. Gulley, dumbfounded over his arrest, continued to maintain that Penland was whipped, while Angstadt claimed Penland argued his way out of the flogging, and Cox maintained he was standing so far back that night he saw nothing. When Charles Rubiner of Common Pleas Court warned them that this was a serious charge, they asked for an attorney. Rubiner then changed the record to read that they stood mute and entered a plea of not guilty for them. They were held on bond of $50,000 each.

That night McWhirter and Genaw also arrested Charles King, James Stewart, Harold Lawrence, Ed Wineinger, Harry Clawson and Jesse Pettijohn on charges related to Penland. Wilbur Robinson of Highland Park was also apprehended. After spending the night in the Wayne County jail, the men were confronted with the statements of Angstadt, Cox and Gulley. When six men were indicted for kidnapping and flogging Penland (King, Lawrence, Robinson, Angstadt, Cox and Gulley), James Stewart and Jesse Pettijohn were not among them. Stewart also claimed that he had been standing too far back to see anything, and Pettijohn, tight-lipped when giving his statement, claimed that he had proof that he had not attended that flogging.

"That guy dodges more bullets than Harry Carey," complained George.

Gulley's courage was transitory, possibly because someone had promised him immunity and had not followed through, probably because somebody got to him before the trial. At the eleventh hour, while on the stand, he changed his story and perjured himself. There had been no flogging, he said. Consequently, with no proof of a whipping, King, Lawrence and Robinson went free. However, Gulley, Cox and Anstadt were found guilty of abduction and given three years.

But members of the Legion were not about to roll over. McWhirter told George that he had been threatened anew with a beating by Black Legion members when he was leading prosecutor's officers on raids. Then Bill Born said he too had been menaced by the Legion. "My wife and I have been threatened numerous times the past two years by phone calls and other means. We were told, 'You're going for a ride.'"[2]

Early Saturday evening, June 6, Voisine answered his home phone. The voice on the other end was gruff, the message succinct. "You'd better lay off this investigation, or you'll get a one-way ride."[3] Voisine hung up and immediately called George.

"You need protection. Can you get out of town tomorrow?" asked George. "I need time to set things up."

"Okay," laughed Bill. "But I can't get it through my head that someone would want to kill such a swell guy like me."

Just after breakfast, on Sunday, June 7, the Voisine family packed their car and drove to Bay City to visit Helen's parents and get in a little fishing. They didn't return until late that night. From then on, George had two policemen guarding Bill's home day and night and two plainclothes men accompanying Bill at all times. Voisine applied for a gun permit. Ira, his partner in Labadie-Voisine Auto Sales, also took out a permit and became a kind of personal bodyguard.

(Front L to R) Harold Lawrence, Earl Angstadt, Wilbur Robinson, Charles King; (Rear L to R) Thomas Cox, Fred Gulley (*Detroit News*)

---

[2] "Deny Legion, Ecorse Orders All Employees," Detroit Times, June 7, 1936, p 13.
[3] "Voisine Goes on the Stand, Detroit News, June 17, 1936.

Chapter 66

Wednesday, June 17, 1936

Though Fred Gulley had been saying that the Black Legion was behind the bombing of Voisine's home the previous August, he had not been a witness to the actual bombing. But on Thursday, June 11, Dayton Dean dropped his own bomb. He admitted that he had driven around Ecorse a number of times in an attempt to kill Voisine, and he implicated Harvey Davis, John Bannerman and Ervin Lee, all facing trial for the killing of Charlie Poole.

On June 17, following Dean's testimony, the three men, Davis, Bannerman and Lee, were also to face a preliminary hearing before Judge John P. Scallen of Recorder's Court on charges of conspiring to kill Bill Voisine. Scallan had tacked the case onto the end of a hearing over a Black Legion plot involving eleven defendants charged with attempting to kill Arthur L. Kingsley, a Highland Park editor and newspaper publisher whose articles in the weekly *Highland Parker* opposed the election of Legionnaire N. Ray Markland for mayor. Dean was the star witness, and he clearly enjoyed the notoriety.

Bill Voisine was in the courtroom, loaded for bear, a revolver in his belt, armed bodyguards on either side of him. No one thought it unnecessary. He looked on from the back of the courtroom and listened as Aldrich W. Baxter, attorney for two of the eleven defendants, cross-examined Dean as he slouched in the witness chair, relaxed and nonchalant, even through the most blood-curdling testimony.

A short recess was declared. Dean, excused from the witness stand, took a seat on a table near the watercooler in the courtroom and lit a cigarette. Voisine sauntered over. Now the same charm that got Bill Voisine elected over and over again in the town of Ecorse was at play in that courtroom. Bill perched himself on the corner of the table next to Dean, his left leg dangling off the front, his right foot on the floor, and schmoozed.

"See you got your soldier's bonus bonds yesterday," said Bill.

"Yeah, can you believe that postman?" replied Dean. "Coming all the way over here to hand deliver it. Guy oughta get a couple of bucks for that."

"I'd heard you served in the war," said Bill. "Navy, wasn't it?"

"Yeah. Had 512 bucks coming."

"All there?"

"Yep," replied Dean. "Ten $50 bonds and a check for 12 bucks. I'll give it to my ma or my kids."

"I'm Bill Voisine, by the way."

Dean laughed. "Yeah, I know. I wantcha to know, it was nothin' personal."

"I appreciate that. In fact, I wanna thank you."

"What for?"

"Testifying in front of some pretty angry guys," said Bill. "I'll give it to you. Ya got guts. I've got one slight problem, though."

"What's that?"

"Well, you're in jail. Harvey Davis is in jail. John Bannerman's in jail. Ervin Lee's in jail. But somebody who's not in jail is still out to get me. I've been shadowed for the past two weeks. You wouldn't happen to know who's involved in that, would you?"

"Tell ya one thing," said Dean. "The guys that are shadowing you ain't the guys that want you killed. The guys that want you killed don't have the guts to do it themselves. Get the guys that want you killed, and the guys in the shadows will go out with the sun."

"Is it King?"

"Who?"

"Charlie King?"

Dean took a puff but said nothing.

"What about Jesse Pettijohn? Stewart? James Stewart?"

"I don't like to implicate the unimplicated. If you know what I mean."

"Yeah, I know," said Bill. "But they'll probably be implicated after I'm dead. Then, knowing what I know about you, as a stand-up kinda guy, you'll step up to the plate and be testifying against 'em anyway." Bill laughed. "Maybe we could skip the part where I go down in a hail of bullets. I've got a swell son, you see. I'd kinda like to stick around."

"Yeah, I got a 14-year-old daughter and 12-year-old son. He visited me in jail Sunday. He won't be seeing me much."

As the clerk signaled the end of recess, Dean took a deep puff, dropped his cigarette on the marble floor and crushed it with his shoe. "Stick around," he said.

Once testimony was concluded regarding Kingsley, McCrea set out to present his case against Harvey Davis, John Bannerman and Erwin Lee in the murder-conspiracy hearing involving Bill Voisine. First, McCrea had Voisine take the stand and tell of renewed threats

Then Dean was called. He began to testify eagerly: "Sometime in the fall of 1935, Harvey Davis met me in the restroom of the Findlater Temple in Detroit. He asked if I wanted to make some easy money, from $100 to $200. I said, 'Sure. How?' He said, 'We need to take out the mayor of Ecorse, a guy by the name of William Voisine.'"

"Did you ask him why?"

"Yeah."

"What'd he say?"

"He said Voisine was in the way," answered Dean. "That we couldn't make any headway in Ecorse 'til we got rid of him. About a week later, we went to a beer garden in Ecorse."

"Who's we?"

"Me and Harvey Davis, Ervin Lee, John Bannerman."

"What was the name of the beer garden?"

"Snyder's, I think. Yeah, Snyder's. Anyways, the guys from Ecorse we were supposed to meet were down in the basement. They had tables down there. Little more private, you know."

"You were meeting some guys from Ecorse?"

"Yeah."

It was news to McCrea, who was obviously thrown. McCrea had been led to believe that Davis, Bannerman and Lee were the only names that Dean would volunteer. It was also news to Bill Voisine, who gently leaned in.

Dayton Dean loved to eke this stuff out, dropping pearls about once a week; he knew how to keep the headlines squarely on himself. "So we meet these guys and Harvey tells 'em that I'm the guy that's gonna do the job. Kinda brags me up. That I can be relied on, you know."

"Let me get this straight, just for the record. You were meeting men from Ecorse who knew what you were hired to do?"

"Yeah."

"That you were there to kill William Voisine?"

"Yeah."

"That they . . . the men from Ecorse . . . were the ones that wanted it done?"

"Yeah."

"How many men?"

"Two."

McCrea: "Did they tell you, either one of them, why they wanted to get rid of Mr. Voisine?"

"Why, yes."

"Who told you?"

Dean shifted in his seat, scratched his head before responding. "Jesse Pettijohn."

"Jesse Pettijohn?"

The gallery gasped.

"Yeah, Jesse Pettijohn. He's a councilman over in Ecorse. Also runs a store. Well, he said that Voisine was in their way out there, and on account of him being Catholic, and him bothering them. Well, I don't know, they seemed to have a political fight out there, the way he explained it. That Voisine was a menace to the organization out there."

Prosecutor: "Pettijohn said this?"

Dean: "Yes."

"They got the bastard!" thought Bill Voisine to himself, leaning back, grinning, and wondering how fast he could get home to tell George. "They got the bastard! Thank you, Dayton Dean."

Jesse Pettijohn was arrested that Thursday, the 18th. The next day, Dean divulged the other man's name. He was Lawrence Madden, a steelworker, whose wife Kay Madden, the Ecorse Village nurse, had been supplying the Legion with information on the whereabouts of Voisine.

On April 4, 1937, Pettijohn and Madden would be found guilty of "entering into a conspiracy to kill William Voisine..."[4]

Bill Voisine (L), candidate for Mayor of Ecorse, with Dayton Dean, 1936 (Virtual Motor City Collection, Walter P. Reuther Library, Wayne State University)

---

[4] "2 Vigilantes Sent to Cells," *Detroit News*, April 25, 1937.

With George so preoccupied, the girls were on their own. And two of them were floundering. Shay had never really gotten over the humiliation of her "Lullaby of Broadway" debacle, and her grades kept going south. Now she hated home and hated school. She knew her stepmother couldn't abide her. Mae couldn't abide Marce either, mainly because Marce continued to challenge her. There were periodic explosions when George wasn't around.

Then came the day that Shay began to cry. She'd been dashing down the hall, fearful of being late for history class, when Sister Ansgar gave her a sidelong look while standing in the corridor and then shut the door, even though the bell was still ringing. Shay stared at the stained-glass barrier, wondering what to do—go in, stay out, go home—then she broke down. Just started weeping. Sister Thoma came strolling down the otherwise empty corridor, beads clicking, and asked what was wrong.

"Nothing."

"Must be something. Why aren't you in class?"

A week later Shay was out in the hallway, blubbering again. This time, she'd been on time for class, just couldn't bring herself to walk through the door.

She became a veritable weeping willow when alone, crying on her way to school, crying in the girls' lav, crying while roller skating to River Rouge to apply unsuccessfully for a dime store job. She didn't know why she was crying, but the girl who prided herself on an ability to hide her feelings couldn't turn off the waterworks.

Finally it was Sister Clarita who, having caught Shay crying behind a potted palm, sent her to Mother Superior's office on the second floor and made her sit outside on the penal bench until she was called for.

"What's wrong, my dear?" asked Mother Norine.

"Nothing, Mother."

"From what I hear, seems like more than nothing. Problems at school?"

"No."

"Home?"

Shay hesitated. "Kinda," then blurted, "I wanna go live with my sister Freeds." The tears gushed forth.

"But that's impossible. She's married. With her own family."

"I know."

"It's time to accept things as they are, Shirley. You have a new mother now," said Mother Norine, handing Shay a tissue. "One who, by all accounts, loves you deeply. I know Mrs. Moore. A more charming, kind, devout woman you couldn't ask for."

As usual, Mae knew all about the tête-a-tête with Mother Norine before Shay came through the kitchen door. "Are you feeling ill, dear?" she asked, purring as she poured herself a cup of tea. Then she ushered Shay into the living room, set the teacup on her side table and hid her anger behind that same low, soothing voice.

"No," replied Shay, sitting on the edge of the couch.

"Did you have a fight with one of your friends?"

"No."

"Then what's wrong now?"

"Nothing," said Shay, head down as she worked at a particularly stubborn cuticle. Following in Dia's footsteps, Shay had become a nail-biter extraordinaire.

Mae reached for her pack of Marlboro's, shook one out, and struck a match. "Well, it must be something. Or why would the nuns find you constantly sobbing in hallways?"

"I'm not constantly sobbing in hallways."

"No? Then how would you describe it?" asked Mae, as Shay continued to work her cuticle. "You are the moodiest girl I've ever met."

"Sometimes I just feel sad."

"Sad?" Mae scoffed. "My dear, all of us feel sad from time to time. We learn to contain our emotions. Or is it just a bid for attention? If so, it *really* must stop. What kind of message does it send? About me, about your father."

"But I can't control it," said Shay. "I just start crying."

"Nonsense," said Mae, tapping an ash against the side of a nearby ashtray.

"Wish I could live with Freeds," muttered Shay.

"Oh, don't be so childish," said Mae in disgust.

"That's not childish."

"It's childish. Time to grow up and take responsibility. You just turned 15. Freda's married now, with two children of her own. Why *on earth* would she want you horning in on her household? No, dear, your place is with your father." Mae sat back in disgust. "And please remove your hand from your mouth, Shirley. You look ridiculous."

————————

What an awful year it had been—Lullaby, weeping, slipping grades. School had gotten off to a horrendous start the previous autumn. In September, the two Ecorse girls, Thelma Devoy and Virginia Merrow, had been killed by an MCRR passenger train.

The students at St. Francis had been truly rattled. Shay even more so, since the column about the girls' deaths on the front page of the *Detroit Free Press* abutted a column headlined, CHIEF OF ECORSE POLICE IN COURT ON BRIBE COUNT, along with a headshot of her sheepish father gazing into an invasive camera.

Then in 8th-grade history class, someone had asked Sister Ansgar about the dead girls, and Sister Ansgar, newly arrived at St. Francis, muttered in disgust, "Shouldn't have been on the tracks in the first place."

Connie Motok, 13, who had just swiveled round to pass back assignment sheets, exchanged glances with Shay, next row over.

The fact that Thelma DeVoy had gone to confession just one hour before her death was a comfort to her classmates. But on hearing Sister Ansgar's disdain, the fate of her soul was once more in question.

"If Thelma was doing wrong, disobeying by crossing the tracks, can she still go to heaven?" asked Peggy Spaight.

"Since she was Catholic and disobeying is only a venial sin, probably," said Sister Ansgar.

"What if Virginia wasn't?" asked Shay, raising her hand.

'Wasn't what?"

"Catholic."

"She was," said Ida.

"I know, but what if she wasn't. Would Thelma go to heaven and Virginia not?"

"That's correct," replied the nun, matter-of-factly. "Outside the church, there's no salvation."

"But say she was very, very good," returned Shay. "Better than all of us here. Say she went to the Presbyterian Church just up the block every Sunday."

"Listen to yourself. Listen to what you're saying. How can you honor God in a so-called church, a house that has no God in it? There is only one true church."

It was a teaching moment and Sister Ansgar seized it. She reached for a piece of chalk in the narrow tray beneath the blackboard, rolled back her black sleeve and drew a crude box with a steeple. "That's why we study history, children. Christ founded the church and it lasted hundreds of years intact until someone . . . Can anyone tell me who?"

"Martin Luther," sang out Ida.

"That's correct," said Sister Ansgar, drawing a slash through a third of the church and writing *Martin Luther* in sprawly letters across the board. "Martin Luther, a heretic, broke away from the church, and a number of Catholics chose to follow. As a result, the world has many false churches and many fallen-away Catholics." She set down the chalk. "I am *not* unkind. I will pray for Virginia. You must all pray for Virginia and her immortal soul."

Shay set down her pen, crossed her arms and slumped. "But Virginia's fine.

Virginia *was* Catholic," said Shay, deflated. "I was just saying 'what if.'"

"Oh, well, in that case, problem solved," laughed Sister Ansgar. "And that's why you should also pray fervently for all your non-Catholic friends, for their conversion, so they might be saved. Anyone can convert. It's not a closed shop."

Now that kind of thinking was beginning to set Shay's teeth on edge. To Shay, it had never made a whole lot of sense. Just because she was baptized Catholic, she had a leg up when it came to heaven? But Leonard Duckett, the Presbyterian pastor's son, could attend their service every day of his life, but it wouldn't do him much good. In fact, it was a serious poke in the eye of God to hear Father Morin tell it. Meanwhile, all some gangster had to do was confess his sins, and there he'd be, cavorting around heaven. About the only section of the missal Shay had down cold was the manner of baptizing babies and non-Catholics in case of an emergency. She viewed baptism as ecclesiastical CPR.

That day after school, Shay and Connie Motok walked up rain-soaked High Street, passing Thelma DeVoy's house, gravitating to the scene of Saturday's tragedy. They stood in respectful silence, imagining the event, the hurling of Virginia, the dragging of Thelma, the terror of Virginia's little sister, 7-year-old Theresa, who told the police that she ran faster than her sister "and got out of the train's way."

"Think I'll go home by way of State," said Connie, shuddering. "Cross under the viaduct."

"I'll walk ya," said Shay.

"But it's way out of your way."

"Better than going home."

"Then I'll walk you back," said Connie. "Same reason."

Connie Motok was a true underdog. She entered 7th grade as a transfer in the autumn of 1934 and had incontestable credentials as an outsider. An "A" student with the kind of good looks that could brand you as stuck up, she was first-generation American — in essence, a foreigner. The kids called her the "Rumanian." She lived with her aunt and uncle on the other side of the tracks in a house that heard little English. That much was known. There was much that was not. It was thought that her parents were dead, and, even though siblings were hinted at, they too were unaccounted for. Indeed, Connie Motok was something of a mystery.

It was only a matter of time before Shay and Connie became friends, once they got past "Hi" in the hallway. Connie would later tell Shay how her father, a Rumanian immigrant, had fallen apart after his wife died in March 1934 and was sent to Eloise Asylum; how Father Morin had stepped in to get her three sisters and one brother placed. Her kid sisters were sent to St. Vincent's orphanage, and her brother was placed in St. Francis de Sales Home for Boys in Detroit. She ended with: "I was the lucky one," said bitterly.

"Connie swore when she got older she'd get her siblings together." said
Shay. *"And she did too."*

Connie had backbone, serious backbone, which was brought to light in
Sister Ansgar's 8th-grade history class.

Sister Ansgar thought Adolf Hitler was the cat's meow. The daughter of a
German immigrant, Sister Ansgar viewed the Führer as Germany's savior, Fred-
erick the Great incarnate. And she, along with Father Coughlin, whom she frequently quoted, couldn't get enough of Benito Mussolini. For her effort, Sister
Ansgar was known in some circles as "The Kraut."

And every time Sister Ansgar praised these men, Connie Motok would mutter something impenetrable under her breath.

"What's that, Miss Motok?" the nun would ask.

"Nothing, Sister."

One day that spring Sister Ansgar sang the praises of Adolf Hitler once too
often, something to do with the upcoming Summer Olympics and the glories of
its host city, Berlin.

Connie raised her hand. "Sister Ansgar," she said, "My uncle says that the
Nazis are funding the Iron Guard in Rumania."

Shay leaned forward, hearing something in Connie's voice.

"The Iron what?" snapped The Kraut.

"The Iron Guard. They're marching through Bucharest, killing people. They
hate Communists. They hate Jews."

"With good reason."

"Pardon me?"

"With good reason," repeated Sister Ansgar. "The Jews are what's wrong
with this world. They run the banks, the film industry, the press. They control
the air waves."

"They killed Christ," supplied Ida.

"They killed Christ," agreed Sister Ansgar. "They're parasites, a people
apart. They never assimilate into the nation they live in; they only enjoy the
benefits, giving nothing in return.

"So it's okay that the Iron Guard's killing people? That it's not safe in the
streets of Bucharest anymore?"

Oooooh! Careful, Connie. The children sat stiffly at their desks, loath to
move, fearful of coming into the crosshairs of Sister Ansgar's sights. You didn't
talk to a nun like that, not if you wanted to see another sunrise. Sister Ansgar, it
was commonly thought, cast no reflection in a mirror.

"Frankly, Miss Motok, I smell dinner-table patter," smirked Sister Ansgar.
"Aren't you showing off, just a little? If anything, these marchers are making the
streets safer. All across Europe, good people are marching. They've had enough
of Bolsheviks, Jews and traitors. It's an exciting time in which to live."

"But they're hooligans."

"They're not hooligans."

The higher Connie Motok's voice rose, the lower all 19 jaws dropped in Room 21. Severe rictus had set in. Agatha Roody slid beneath her desk; even Butzie had a frozen grin. No one had ever seen anything like this.

But to Sister Ansgar it was another teaching moment. She grabbed a second piece of chalk from the narrow tray beneath the blackboard and wrote in bold, proud script, *Il Duce*. "Since Mussolini took over Italy, the streets are cleaner; they hose them down. The cities are quieter; drivers can't honk their horns. There are no rowdies, no troublemakers, no beggars in the streets."

"Okay, but where did *they* go?" challenged Connie.

"Watch your tone, Miss Motok. Watch your tone. I repeat, there are no beggars in the streets. So there's no crime, no lawlessness, no corruption. Everything's under control."

"But they assassinated the leader of my country," said Connie. "Is that right?"

Bless me, gentle Jesus. Tony Shield, holding onto both sides of his desk, swallowed and braced for impact. A memorial service for Connie Motok would be held tomorrow morning at 9 a.m.

"I'm not privy to Rumanian history, nor, do I think, are you. Germany needs stabilizing!" shouted Sister Ansgar. "Germany was in economic ruins, thanks to England, thanks to France, and needs a strong hand! You don't have any idea what you're talking about! Hitler's doing great things."

"Oh, baloney!"

Now no one in their right mind had said, "Oh, baloney," to a woman in a black veil, equipped with beads and chalk, in the history of Western civilization. The news spread like wildfire. Quiet Connie Motok had taken on Sister Ansgar and her beloved Hitler. Connie was a hero, even though no one in that class had a clue what either of them was talking about.

Shay was truly inspired.

One day, the following June, just before school let out for summer vacation, Shay, Dorothy Dalton and Virginia Brazill were sitting on a bench out in front of Ma Genaw's soda fountain near St. Francis, leaning against her front window while polishing off purchases. They had just approached Father Morin, asking if they could start a girls' basketball team next term, asking if they could wear culottes or something besides skirts. His reply, "Absolutely not!"

"So what do we do now?" asked Virginia, sucking on a jawbreaker.

"Scratch it," replied Shay.

"Scratch basketball?"

"I'm not gonna play basketball in a skirt," said Shay.

"We play baseball in skirts."

"That's different."

"How so?"

"Just is," said Shay. "Burns me up."

Now directly across the street from Ma Genaw's was one of Sister Ansgar's "so-called" churches, Christ Presbyterian. Built in 1910 of stately red brick, it was imposing but not ornate, boasting only two large stained-glass windows in front. On the left, beneath a battlemented bell tower, ten steps led to a small peaked roof over the entrance.

While munching on her Milky Way, Shay watched two women with platters of food enter its front door. "Bet they have mother-daughter banquets there, same as us," she said, as two more misguided women entered. "But what do I know. Wonder what heathens serve at a potluck supper."

"Probably other heathens," cracked Dorothy.

"Infidels on toast," laughed Virginia.

Shay didn't laugh. "When a friend of Mae's got married out of the church, Mae wouldn't go in there. She was invited to the wedding, but she wouldn't go in there. Ever wonder what would happen if we went into that church?" asked Shay.

"What, are you crazy, Kemo Sabe?" cried Dorothy. "In broad daylight? With a junkload of nuns half a block away."

Shay neatly folded her empty candy wrapper and handed it to Virginia. "Hold this for me, will ya?" She waited for a lull in the traffic and crossed the street.

Then after tucking in her blouse and straightening her skirt, she strolled up those ten steps, opened the heavy door, and stepped into the vestibule. After a couple of minutes, she emerged and walked sedately down the steps and crossed Front Street.

"How'd it feel?" asked Dorothy.

"Good," said Shay. "It felt good."

———————

The afternoon of Friday, June 19, George left work early, eager to give Mae the news about Pettijohn's arrest and the upcoming arraignment. George also knew that Ecorse trustees had asked Wayne County prosecutor Duncan McCrea to drop all of Pettijohn's charges of bribery against him in light of the recent revelations. "The charges against Chief Moore apparently are spite work on the part of the Legion," said Voisine. McCrea would eventually comply.

Walking up the steps, George heard raised voices in the dining room. Marce and Mae were locking horns again. There was a tone—one he never had to endure. Spying her father through the archway, Marce bolted for her room.

"What goes on here?" asked George.

"Marcia got in a fight again today," said Mae, "with the Compton girl. Always trying to stir things up."

"Give her time. She's only 12," said George. "Most of my kids went through a rocky stage."

"Time? George, dear, you have no idea," said Mae as she headed for the kitchen. "Have you eaten? Let me fix you a sandwich."

"I'm fine."

"Then how about a cup of tea?"

"Sit. Put your feet up," said George. "I'll make *you* a cup."

Mae was five months' pregnant.

> *"When Mumma was pregnant, he'd wake her up in the morning to get him breakfast," said Freda. But Mae, he'd get her breakfast.... We used to say, 'Boy, Mumma never got that.'"*

"Wait'll you hear what happened today," said George, from the kitchen, pouring boiling water into the teapot.

But Mae, in the living room, couldn't hear him over the sound of her own voice. "Two weeks into summer and the house is already at sixes and sevens. This is no place to raise a baby. One of them won't listen to a word I say; the other one's spent the year moping around school corridors, crying at the drop of a hat. She's still doing it, whimpering half the day away."

"Who?" asked George, carrying a tray into the living room, setting it on the coffee table.

"Your beloved Shay," said Mae. "I've already had one go-around with her today. She stormed out of here, a bucket of tears, 'I wanna go live with Freda.' If I dare look at her, 'I wanna go live with Freda. I wanna go live with Freda.' That's all I hear. Day in, day out. 'I wanna go live with Freda.'"

"But she can't live with Freda," said George. "That's impossible. Freda's got her own life now."

"Try and tell her that."

"I *will* tell her that. And nip it in the bud. I don't know where she got that idea. It's certainly not fair to Freda." He set her teacup on a doily on the table. "How long's this been going on?"

"About two months."

"Two months? Why didn't you tell me?"

"You've been so busy, dear, so worried about important matters. Besides, it was just her way to get your attention. I wasn't about to give her the satisfaction."

"That's not the kind of attention she'd want. Crying at school. There must be a reason. She needs understanding."

"She needs a good wallop. She's driving me up the wall. I can't stand her moods. Frankly, George, I wish she *would* go."

"Pardon me?"

"I wish she *would* go. Not to Freda's, but perhaps a boarding school. I've been looking into some in the area. There's St. Mary's in Windsor or St. Mary's in Monroe. Both fine, *fine* schools. You know her grades aren't the best. Marce could join her. You have to admit, what with our own baby coming, there's no room, and the new house on Salliotte won't be ready. Dia and Joyce will probably marry soon. Don't you see, dear, we could get a *lovely* fresh start, with our own family. If Shay's so miserable here, let her go elsewhere. She'll soon learn that . . ."

George stood up. Mae had been so busy pouring tea that she hadn't noticed his face.

"Where are you going?" she asked.

"Out."

"When will you be back?"

"Don't know."

"But, George, dear, if I've said anything . . ."

"Mae," he said, softly. "You knew I had these kids when you married me."

He went down the steps, then slammed the outer door.

———

That same day, around 5:45 p.m., Shay was sitting on the State Street dock, looking toward Canada with her back to the fading sun. A car pulled up on the rutted gravel path, a police car. George got out and strolled toward her.

"What brings you down here?" he said, struggling with difficulty to sit down next to her. "You *do* know I'll need a crane to haul me back up."

She laughed briefly, then said, "Oh, pa. I'm so down in the dumps."

"From what I hear, you and Mae are at loggerheads again. Why can't you two stay out of each other's way? Help keep the peace?"

"She's mad at me as soon as I walk in the door."

"Now that's not fair. And I'm sure it's not true. She's a kind, loving woman or I wouldn't have married her."

"Kind to you, maybe."

Both sat silently as they watched the water for some moments. Then George strained to get up. "C'mon, Tee."

"Where we goin'?"

"Home."

"Do I have to?"

"Well, you can't stay here all night."

Reluctantly, she stood, dusted off her skirt, and climbed into the police car. He drove up Front, turned left at Seavitt's, past his old barbershop, but instead of going up Labadie to High Street, he turned left on Monroe, parting the softball game in progress.

"Pa."

"Yes?"

"How come only Catholics get to heaven?"

"Let me put it this way," said George. "Did you hear the one about the Protestant, the Muslim and the Jew going to heaven."

"Again."

"Yes, again," laughed George. "When they got to the pearly gates, they noticed a group of people off to the side. They asked Peter: 'Who are those people over there?' 'Sh!' whispered Peter. 'Those are the Catholics. They think they're the only ones here.' He looked her way. "Is that what you were arguing about?"

"Among other things."

"What other things?"

"Nothing. I keep my mouth shut most of the time."

"You mean, swallow it?" He grew serious. "Are you that miserable, Tee?"

"Oh, Pa," she said, as he put his arm around her shoulder and she brushed back a tear.

"Things that bad?"

"Can't get much worse."

As they pulled into the driveway, Freda was out on the front-porch glider, Baby George on her lap, chatting with Ella across the way.

"Like I was just tellin' Freda," yelled Ella from her porch. "I've got some extra rhubarb and leaf lettuce in our garden. Interested?"

George waved. "Thanks, Ella, but I gotta run. Mae's got dinner waiting.

George got out of the car and opened Shay's door on the passenger side. "Well, I'd better get along on my get along."

"Where you going, Pa?"

"Home."

"Without me?"

"You're already home, Tee," he said, his voice cracking. "We'll get your belongings later."

> *"Pa had already gone over to Monroe and asked Freda if I could move in with her," Shay recalled.. "I guess he knew Freda kind of worried about me. She said, 'Sure.' I was tickled to death, cause Pa was always over to Freda's anyway, so I saw as much of him over there as I would have living with Mae."*

Within minutes, Shay had joined the undermanned team at shortstop. They were delighted to have her. Who wouldn't be? Wasn't this the girl who hit a homerun with the bases loaded when St. Francis played St. Henry's in Lincoln Park just last spring?

Later Freda yelled: "Shirlee! Time to set the table."

"Yeah, yeah, I'll be in."

"Shay!"

"In a minute!"

"This is the second time I'm calling."

"Ah, Freeds, just one more inning!"

Epilogue

Marce

By the summer of 1938, while Shay was still living with Freda, the rest of the Moores, including John Munn Moore (known as John Boy), born October 13, 1936, had moved into the newly built Georgian colonial house, designed by Mae, at 60 Salliotte Street, just around the corner from the house on High Street. After Shay moved out, Marce's other allies left one after the other. Dia was married in April, 1938; Joyce would marry one year later in May, 1939.

Marce was bright and her grades at school were good, but she was a hot-head. Little things would lead to bigger things, and she seemed to get into fights with everybody. Left behind in a beautiful new home with a full-time maid and two cars in the garage, she seemed to delight in stirring things up between Mae and George.

So, in the summer of the move to the new house, Mae, still an advocate for the leafy benefits of camp, sent Marce, now 13, to a camp in the Irish Hills. Predictably, Marce's stay was cut short. The director called one memorable night and demanded that someone come pick her up immediately; she had been in fights with everyone. There were many charges, but she finally got kicked out because she made fun of a girl with a birthmark on her face. George was at a police convention, so Rowe and her husband John packed up daughter Judy in the car at nine o'clock at night and drove out to Irish Hills to bring Marce home.

Marce's problems at school were far more serious than Shay's and Dia's had been. She first boarded at St. Mary's Academy in Monroe, one of Mae's many solutions. However, after a few months the nuns refused to allow her to return. They reported that she was incorrigible, disrupting the entire dormitory, that several parents were up in arms and had threatened to remove their daughters from the school. A stay at St. Mary's in Windsor, Ontario, in 1940, had similar results. Marce, again disruptive and explosive, was expelled. This time, Shay went with her father to pick her sister up. "Here we go again," George said.

Weekends Mae and George went visiting, but they didn't take Marce with them. With quarters and half dollars from George, Marce spent much of the summer parked on a stool at the Coney Island Diner on Front Street. Alone, she'd often go to the movies - and frequently get kicked out - or roam the streets. She knew she wasn't wanted at home and was a pushover for anybody who showed her some attention.

> Very good looking, "She was an easy mark," said Rowe. "Guys would come along and she'd take off with 'em."

For some time Marce lived on her own in a series of rooms or apartments which George rented for her, but she never stayed anywhere very long. There was a time when Marce, at 15, stayed at Rowe's for a week, Freda's for a week, Dia's for a week. Peg, Murph's wife, also had her for a while.

> *Marce stayed here a couple of times when Pa and Ma would go on one of their trips for a few days," said Shay. "Argue, that's all we did. She'd take off all the time. I didn't know where she was." Dia remembered that Marce often said, "wherever I hang my hat is home sweet home."*

By the time she was 18, Marce was pregnant with the first of three children in as many years. Her daughter, born in August 1943, at Providence, the Catholic hospital, was named Mary Faith by the nuns. Even at Providence Marce got into trouble, this time for threatening another girl with a meat cleaver. Mary Faith's father was from Ecorse, but when Marce went to his house with the infant in her arms, his mother claimed, "That's not his baby!" and shut the door in her face. Marce's second child, a son, born at the Florence Crittenton Home for Wayward Girls, was taken from her for adoption. Her third baby, another boy, born in April 1945, at the Trenton Maternity Home on Third & Elm, was also taken from her and adopted. Marce had married the father, Tommy Haggerty, the previous fall, but she threw him out of their apartment, and his parents eventually had the marriage annulled by a priest.

Marce was uncontrollable. George continued to find places for her and Mary Faith to live, but she either started trouble or left. Often described by her sisters as "good-hearted" and "generous to a fault," they also said, in different moments, that she was angry or mean. At one point, when Marce and her daughter were living alone in Lincoln Park in an upper flat—her father again paying the rent—neighbors called George, fearful for Mary Faith.

> "They told Pa that Marce was up all night crying, and that the baby was crying and they were afraid she was going to hurt it," explained Dia.

George put his foot down: Marce was forced to give up Mary Faith when the child was 18 months old. Marce had lost her mother in early childhood, her second mother when Freda married, and now she had lost her own child.

Dr. Knox, a general practitioner in Ecorse, was the first to suggest to George and Mae that something was seriously wrong with Marce. In the summer of 1945 George reluctantly signed papers committing Marce to Eloise Asylum, making her a ward of the state.

To those in Michigan of a certain age, the name Eloise evoked dread. Or grim humor. Eloise Mental Hospital, which was founded as the Wayne County Poor House and later also became a center for tuberculosis patients, was known as "the crazy hospital" when it began to house mentally disturbed patients as well. The facility sat on 902 acres and at one time housed more than 10,000 patients in over 75 buildings. Once considered a forerunner in such "modern" medical treatments as electroshock and insulin drug therapy, the hospital was closed in 1981; most records have been destroyed or lost, but over 7,000 numbered graves remain.

Marce was never diagnosed with anything specific; she was just having too much trouble "out in the world." Nearly every week, usually on Thursday, George picked up one or two of the sisters to go with him to see Marce. When they visited, she was often in restraints, both hands in a muff, strapped to a straight-back chair at the shoulders and ankles. When the family protested, the staff explained that the restraints were at her own request. Marce was released several times, on leave, for home visits, and in early 1948 on furlough, but she always wanted to go back in. She said she felt safer there.

> *"She was happy," said Dia. "She never cried when we left; I'd come home and cry."*

Marce wrote notebooks full of poetry and frequent letters home.

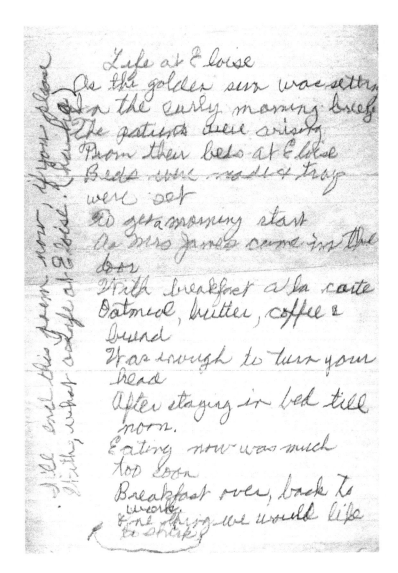

On the morning of September 12, 1949, Marcia Moore Haggerty, then 24, was found dead in her bed. Marce, who had been teasing another patient for being fat, had told one of her sisters that she was now afraid of the woman. Officially the cause of death was listed as acute congestive heart failure. One of the doctors, however, privately suggested that someone in the family investigate further: he had a suspicion that Marce had been smothered. She had been found with a pillow over her face. The girls never told their father. They reasoned that George had had enough grief with Marce; nothing they could do would bring her back.

Marce was laid out near the fireplace in the Salliotte house. Thomas Haggerty signed the register that day, but Mae wouldn't let him come in for the visitation. One welcomed guest was Bill Voisine; people were grateful that he'd come. Mary Faith's adoptive mother brought Mary Faith, who, when she saw the body, said: "I know this lady. She used to come over to play with me."

Funerals

Saturday, May 24, 1997

In the downstairs bedroom in the middle house on 23rd Street, Shirley Shedd, formerly known as Shay Moore, rose slowly, ate little, then faced a meager closet. At 76, she had another funeral to go to, another sister, the fourth Moore girl to die. The fifth was staying home, rooted to her chair, an invalid. Shay donned her comparative best, dreading the throng, the visibility, the vulnerability, then cursed herself for dwelling on her own concerns. There's Dad, with all he's been through, out in the garden alone, she thought, wondering and worrying about what he was going to wear; none of his pants fit, not since his illness. She opened the screen door, walked to a row of young plants, and told him he need not go; everyone would understand. He demurred. She said it again. "Maybe I won't, then," he said, resting on one knee.

She pulled out of the driveway early for the 15-minute trip. The funeral mass was at 9:00; she left at 8:20. One less anxiety to deal with. She steered carefully up Oak, making a mental note to water the flowers when she got home, to fill the birdbath. Then, too, she should thin the large primroses. Sneaky buggers. If you looked away for two seconds they'd take over. Can't handle a garden that size much longer, she told herself. Time for Dad to cut back on his vegetable garden too.

She thanked God she'd remembered a hat. Except for Freda's funeral, she hadn't set foot in a Catholic church in years. That's all I need, she thought, Kleenex on my head. There'd be people there she hadn't seen in years. She no longer had much to offer, she thought, this wizened old woman, this woeful imitation of a spirited girl once known as Shay Moore, one of the more promising shortstops of her day, her distinctive green eyes now hidden behind glasses and sagging lids. Her face, once pleasant, often tan, now as white as her hair. Would they notice how tired she was? How small, how unimportant she felt? But the others would be changed too, she thought. Small comfort. Then again, did it matter what they thought? She almost wished it did. Nothing much mattered anymore. Dad, maybe; the kids.

She stopped for the light on 12th. The car idle, set too high, vibrated with its distinct quiver, putt and ping. They'd need a new car soon, she thought, though this one might go the distance. Then again, she didn't plan on hanging around much longer. Of that, she'd warned everyone. She'd been accused of having one foot out the door for years. Too true. The light changed; a horn startled her. Oh, give it a rest, she thought. Brake released, the car lurched forward.

She thought about her last sister, still sitting at home, avoiding the funeral home, avoiding the funeral, claiming she didn't want to upstage Rowe. Dia hated the attention her wheelchair brought her. Or maybe she didn't want to feel like a hypocrite. Dia's relationship with Rowe had soured over the years, though they still made each other laugh on those infrequent family occasions that brought them together. Or maybe, just maybe, Dia also wanted them to re-member her as she had been—full of hell. Hard to be full of hell in a wheelchair, one hand limp and lifeless.

Shay smiled. That damn Dia. Everyone called her that. Uncle Peck used to say, "Here comes Freda, Rowe, Joyce, Shay, Marce, and that damn Dia." Then it took on a life of its own. It was said in one word: Thatdamndia. Sometimes two: Thatdamndia Moore. But no one made her laugh as much as Dia. Even in the midst of pain, even when Dia had her stroke. She could remember that phone call so clearly: "Can you come over? I think I'm having a stroke." Racing out the door, running across the street, yanking the storm door off its hook, call-ing 911, shaking until the ambulance arrived. The aides questioning Dia as she sat stunned on the floor, trying to discern how alert she was.

"What's your name?"

"Doris Lucille Moore."

"Who is the president?"

"George Bush and his lovely wife, Barbara."

You had to laugh.

She turned onto Superior, a comforting, tree-lined street, one of Wyandotte's two boulevards. Ahead she could see the distinctive square spire of St. Patrick's Church. There were only two cars in the church lot as she drove in, easy maneu-vering, plenty of parking room. She looked at the dashboard, 8:35, rolled down the windows to let in the spring air, and rested her head against the headrest.

When she died, she wanted to go fast, like Joyce, she thought, though not quite so visibly. Poor Joyce, the first of the older girls to go, dying at Freda's 50th wedding anniversary party. When was that? Definitely July 29, probably 1983. Freda and Lloyd were married on July 29, 1933. What was the name of that place? Pennsalt Club, one of those large, warehouse-like halls inside with two tones of paint, sort of a poor man's wainscoting. Prettier outside at night. Not so pretty in harsh daylight.

Rowe had made a crack under her breath as soon as she walked in. "I like Simac's better."

Dia had countered. "Simac's costs an arm and a leg."

"$9.95 tops," said Rowe.

"What can you get at Simac's you can't get at Penn-Salt for a lot less?"

"Tablecloths," said Rowe.

Joyce had said she wasn't feeling well, that she almost hadn't come but knew she should. She looked thin, almost ethereal, but the party energized her.

She seemed happier that night, happier than she had seemed in a long time, seeing her sisters and so many old friends. They were all sitting at one of the many round tables, sans tablecloth: she with Dad, Joyce with Hula, Dia with Gus. They'd just had dinner. Rowe had come over to join them. She'd been sitting at the head table with Freda.

"Did you notice we all married husbands who never laugh at our jokes?" Joyce was saying. "I just want to go on a cruise or something before I die. Just us sisters. Leave the men home."

"Freda and Lloyd are going to Niagara Falls in August," Rowe dodged. "Why don't you join them?"

Joyce had laughed. "Freda and Lloyd go to Niagara Falls every August. How much can it change?"

Dia'd grown serious; she'd been worried about Freda. "With all her problems at home, I think she dreads coming back. She told me her heart constricts every time she returns from Canada, every time she comes across the Ambassador Bridge."

"Why doesn't she take the tunnel?" deadpanned Joyce.

There was a guffaw over that one.

Seems we only laugh hard when we're together, thought Shay. Or when they did one of those dumb refrains, the kind that drove their husbands nuts. They had gotten into one that night. She remembered it clearly.

"You know, Joyce, you're right. We oughta take a cruise," Rowe was saying.

Dia turned to the heavens. "I think I'm hearing my voices again."

"We oughta take a cruise," said Rowe.

"There it is again. Hear it?"

"Look, Joan of Arc, if you'd stop horsing around, you'd appreciate what I'm saying," said Rowe.

"What are you saying?" asked Dia.

"I'm saying, I'd forgotten how much I enjoyed you idiots."

"All for one and one for all," said Dia, ala D'Artagnan.

"I liked you better as Joan of Lorraine," said Rowe.

"Ingrid Bergman did Joan of Lorraine," said Joyce.

"Ingrid Bergman did Joan of Arc."

"Julie Harris did Joan of Arc."

They were off to the races.

Then the band started playing, and she and Dad got up to dance. "Here comes Miss America," Freda'd said, as they danced by the head table.

She had laughed. "Cripes, Freda, I'm almost 65. When you gonna stop saying, 'Here comes Miss America?'"

Freda was radiant, more beautiful than she'd ever looked, dressed in light blue, her hair carefully coiffed, a white rose corsage pinned to her shoulder, her eyes sparkling behind her glasses, laughing, chatting. One of the biggest nights of her life, her kids renting the hall. But before that first dance was over, people were gathering around Joyce. At the table, they'd been laughing about an old fur coat someone had given Dia. She'd walked home in 90-degree weather in that damn fur coat. Dia said she looked at Joyce for a response, but Joyce was resting her head against Hula's shoulder, while Hula talked to someone else. Then Gus made a slight nod to Dia toward Joyce. Something was wrong. Dia got up, stood behind Joyce, and raised her head. Blood was coming from her nose. She knew that instant that she was gone, Dia said.

It had been sprinkling when they arrived at the hall; it was pouring when they came out. Boy, did it come down. She was surprised to hear she couldn't ride in the ambulance. No one was allowed, they said. Why hadn't she put her foot down? That was her biggest regret, that she hadn't gone to the hospital with Joyce. Instead, she hustled Hula into their car and took him with them to Wyandotte General. He just sat there in the back—wet, dazed. Rowe drove to the hospital too. Thunder and lightning all the way.

Six years later, Freda was dead. Day before Thanksgiving, 1989. They should have known she was sick; all she wanted to do was stay in bed, didn't want to get up. That wasn't like her. Pancreatic cancer. The diagnosis came too late.

She remembered the look Freda gave her just before she died. "My little girl," she'd said. There I was, Shay thought, all of 68, "my little girl." But it had meant a great deal to her. After their mother died, she'd always been Freda's little girl. She could never get her memories straight. She'd start telling a child-hood story and Freda would cut in, "that wasn't me, that was Mumma" or "that wasn't Mumma, that was me." She missed Freda terribly. She'd gone over for coffee in the morning, went there all the time. She'd call and say, "You got any coffee left?" Freda'd say, "Sure, c'mon over." She didn't realize until much later that Freda had begun to make extra coffee.

After Freda's funeral, she'd called Rowe. "We'll have to stick together," Rowe had told her. "We'll probably be the last to go." Dia was irate when she heard that line. "Tell that horse's ass if she thinks she's gonna outlive me, she's crazy." "She'll outlive us all," Shay had said. Wrong again, she thought. No Cassandra, she.

She sat in the parking lot and looked at her watch, then looked again. It was close to 9:00, but there was not another mourner to be seen, no cars had turned into the lot. Uh-oh, something's wrong. Rowe might have been contentious, but not enough to have an empty house for her funeral. She could just hear her: "Oh, swell. My last hurrah and all I get is a Bronx cheer." As the minutes ticked off, she grew more anxious. What if she was at the wrong church? What if the service was at the funeral home?

Suddenly one side of the massive front door of the church opened, and an old man came out. She snatched her scarf, purse, keys, shouldered open the weighty car door, and hurried to him. Not an easy crossing on aching legs, tired feet .

"Is there a funeral service today?" she asked.

"Yes," he said. "10 o'clock."

"Oh, 10!" she laughed, relieved. "Oh, thank God, I thought it was 9! I'm an hour early."

"You can go in and wait if you want." He held the door for her.

As she entered the vestry, the bulky door rumbled shut behind her, its latch bar bouncing. Routinely, she dipped two fingers in the font of Holy Water and made the Sign of the Cross. Never lose it, she thought, never goes away, once a Catholic, always a Catholic. Then she froze, startled. The double doors that led to the nave became a proscenium arch, a framed tableau. Natural light from the towering stained-glass windows lining each side of the church threw a lambent carpet up the long aisle. Down front, beyond row after row of empty pews, stood Rowe's open casket, flowers from friends and relatives surrounding it, tall brass candles flickering on each side like honor guards. She hadn't expected Rowe to be there, alone, unattended.

She hesitated, then walked down the wide marble aisle, a gimpy procession of one. She approached the casket and peered down. There was Rowe, wearing her ever-present glasses, dressed in a pink negligee, swaddled in silk. She looks pretty, she thought—thin, but pretty, and less tired than when she saw her last.

She stayed there for some time, her elbows resting on the cushioned casket, then walked to the first row and took a seat. For the rest of that hour she silently conversed with her sister, remembering things, remembering the house on Monroe Street, the town of their youth, the promise, the pain, the laughter—mostly the laughter—remembering it all.

"Oh, Rowe." she whispered. "It went so fast."

Shirley Anne (Moore) Shedd (1921-2007)

In May, 2006, at age 85, my mother, Shay, told me that she had been dancing to "Lullaby of Broadway" in the living room, shaking it up, amused that her
only concern now was not to fall.

"But it's a great way to go out," I said.

"You're just looking for a perfect ending for your book," she said. "That's
all you're looking for."

Anne Commire

Anne Commire, author and playwright (1939-2012)

A Note from the Editor

Anne Commire and I met and became friends in college. Once we had both graduated and were teaching English at Michigan high schools, we got together often to talk about teaching, favorite writers, favorite books. In 1966 I traveled to Germany to study; Anne began working at Meadowbrook Theater and went off on a long stay in England with theater friends.

Our friendship continued when both of us were back in the States. Anne had gone to New York to become a playwright; I had met and married Bob while in Germany, and we had returned to Virginia. Anne and Bob hit it off immediately, a lucky thing for all of us. She was in NYC and we were living in Northern Virginia when Anne and I first began collaborating on *Put Them All Together*, a future O'Neill Award winner (#2).

On visits to Alexandria, Anne, who wrote every morning, began giving me her previous day's draft. Then she either disappeared to begin working on another scene, or she and Bob would walk down to the Waffle Shop on King Street while I read and scribbled notes on her copy. Afternoons and evenings we talked for hours over each scene. Anne always wrote what I thought was a bit too much, and, although we usually argued about my suggestions and cuts, she accepted many of them, and we both liked the result. That was the beginning of our working relationship.

When Bob and I moved to Vermont in 1976 with daughters Sarah, 3, and Emily, an infant, and Anne moved nearly full-time to Connecticut, she continued to give me things to work on: sketches from her encyclopedias, her good friend Mariette Hartley's *Breaking the Silence*, her last play, *Starting Monday*, (O'Neill #4), and "Women in World History," her 17-volume encyclopedia of women that won the ALA Dartmouth Medal for best reference work of the year. For over 30 years she and we traveled back and forth. She came to us with a succession of dogs: Duffy, Dulcie, and Toby; our girls thought her book-stuffed home on the Nyantic River was heaven.

On one of her '80s trips to Vermont, Anne learned that she had breast cancer; she had surgery while staying with us. When she visited, we often worked on early chapters of *Mooreville*. And every summer she also went home to Wyandotte and Ecorse to see her mother and her aunts. She became a regular at the libraries, especially the Wayne State University Library, where she researched many of the events in this book. And every summer she gathered aunts and their neighbors to talk about life in the Downriver area in earlier days, tape-recording the conversations and the laughter. She mined those tapes for the highlighted quotations throughout the book.

Anne had wanted to write this story for many years but had been busy earning a living with her research projects. She even thought she had enough material for two or three volumes. Unhappily, in about 2010 or 11, she learned that her cancer had returned. I lived with her in her last months. Bob visited often, treasured neighbors Kenny and Eileen ran errands, close friend Mariette Hartley visited from California, and kind hospice nurses came regularly. Every day Anne fought her way to her keyboard and wrote scenes I had never seen before, then revised her own work from the previous day.

Over the years I had heard tales about her Moore family, but always with the idea that "someday" she would write the story. At her death I inherited folders full of chapters nearly finished, folders of chapters just drafted, folders with notes, a huge collection with a modest outline. And, I had promised to finish her work. This book, which I have been calling a "true novel," is the result. Bob has been an invaluable help along the way. All of the good material belongs to Anne. (I can just hear her complaining, "Geez, Schermer, you're cutting all my good lines!") All of the boring stuff that attempts to connect the events is my own.

Anne is the child of Shay's early marriage to Robert Commire. "Dad" is her stepfather and father of her brother Ron Shedd and stepsister Judy Trupiano. All of the events in the book are true. The dialog and the characterizations, of course, are Anne's.

Anne is now buried in the Jericho Center Cemetery, next to the Schermer plot. We miss her every day.

Gail Lawrence Schermer

Many thanks to our early readers :

Mary Jane Dickerson
Kenny O'Pasek
Linda Rodd
Marion Rose
Miles Wolff

Special thanks to Shirley Knight

Love and gratitude to Bob Schermer

CPSIA information can be obtained
at www.ICGtesting.com
Printed in the USA
LVHW080306021120
670435LV00015B/1306